Egypt

Lonely Planet books provide independent advice. Accredited Lonely Planet writers do not accept discounts or payment in exchange for positive coverage.

كـتـب "لـونـلي بلـيـنـت" تـزود الـقـارئ بـالمعلومـات والآراء المسـتـقلة. والكتـاب المفـوضـون مـن قـبـل "لونلي بلـيـنـت" لايقـبـلون مكافـآت مـاليـة أو تخفيـضـات لإعطاء صورة إيجابيـة عن أية مؤسـسـة أو جهة ما.

ISBN 0 - 86442 - 395 - 0

9 780864 423955

Australia	$24.95 RRP
USA	$17.95
UK	£11.99
Canada	$25.50
France	140,00 FF

4th Edition

Egypt

a Lonely Planet travel survival kit

**Leanne Logan
Geert Cole
Damien Simonis
Scott Wayne**

Egypt

4th edition

Published by
Lonely Planet Publications
Head Office: PO Box 617, Hawthorn, Vic 3122, Australia
Branches: 155 Filbert St, Suite 251, Oakland, CA 94607, USA
               10 Barley Mow Passage, Chiswick, London W4 4PH, UK
               71 bis rue du Cardinal Lemoine, 75005 Paris, France

Printed by
Pac-Rim Kwartanusa Printing
Printed in Indonesia

Photographs by

Chris Barton	Geert Cole	Geoff Stringer
Chris Beall	Greg Elms	Rob van Driesum
Glenn Beanland	Leanne Logan	Scott Wayne
Kristie Burns	Damien Simonis	Tony Wheeler
Bethune Carmichael	Paul Steel	

Front cover: Ninth Pylon, Temple of Amun, Karnak (Bethune Carmichael)

First Published
February 1977

This Edition
November 1996
Reprinted with March 1997 Update supplement.

National Library of Australia Cataloguing in Publication Data

Cole, Geert.
    Egypt

    4th ed.
    Includes index.
    ISBN 0 86442 395 0

    1. Egypt – Guidebooks. I. Wayne, Scott. Egypt & the Sudan.
    II. Logan, Leanne, 1964- . III. Title. IV. Title: Egypt & the Sudan.
    (Series: Lonely Planet travel survival kit)

916.2

text & maps © Lonely Planet 1996
photos © photographers as indicated 1996
climate charts compiled from information supplied by Patrick J Tyson, © Patrick J Tyson, 1996

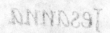

Leanne Logan

Bitten by the travel bug before even reaching her teens, Leanne has long been lured by travel. She explored parts of her homeland as a reporter for several newspapers and Australian Associated Press after completing a journalism degree at the Queensland University of Technology. In 1987 she set off through Asia and the Middle East to London where, as deputy editor of a travel magazine, her wanderlust was temporarily fed but not sated. Eventually she bought a one-way ticket to Africa and, like many others, fell in love with this amazing continent.

Leanne joined Lonely Planet in 1991 and, while conducting research into Belgium's 350-odd beers, she met a local connoisseur, Geert Cole. The pair have been a team ever since and have worked together on several Lonely Planet travel guides, including *France, New Caledonia, Western Europe on a shoestring, India* and *Africa on a shoestring*. Two of their most recent projects were *Egypt travel atlas* and *Middle East on a shoestring*.

Geert Cole

Born in Antwerp in Belgium, Geert swapped university and art studies in the 1970s to discover broader horizons and other cultures. With each trip an extra diary was put on the shelf and another job experience added to life's list.

In more recent times, when not running his stained-glass studio, Geert has been found sailing the Pacific, sorting Aussie sheep and, among other challenges, trekking through Alaska and diving tropical reefs.

Damien Simonis

Damien is a London-based journalist. With a degree in modern languages and several years' newspaper experience on, among others, the *Australian* and the *Age*, he left Australia in 1989. He has worked and travelled widely in Europe, the Middle East and North Africa, and put in several years' hard labour on such London papers as the *Guardian* and the *Independent*. In addition to updating the 3rd edition of this guide, he has worked on travel survival kits for *Morocco, North Africa, Italy* and *Jordan & Syria*. Damien is now co-writing Lonely Planet's forthcoming guidebook to Spain.

Scott Wayne

Scott Wayne, the original author of this book, is an American who has lived, studied and travelled in the Middle East, Africa and Europe. He graduated from Georgetown University's School of Foreign Service with a degree in International Relations. He also completed graduate studies at the Royal Institute of International Affairs in London and the University of Southern California. His studies at Georgetown included a long stint at the American University in Cairo and many adventures up and down the Nile. Scott has also worked on Lonely Planet's *Egyptian Arabic phrasebook, Baja California,* and *Mexico*.

From Leanne & Geert
Many people helped us to produce this book – either by providing information or simply by sharing our zest for Egypt. Full credit and appreciation is given to them at the back of this book.

Dedication We would like to dedicate our share of this book to Dorothy Logan (Owen), who assisted us in many ways on previous books, and whose enthusiasm, not only for our work but for life as a whole, was a constant inspiration. We know you can hear our thanks, Dee, and we send your spirit our love.

This Book

Scott Wayne researched and wrote the first two editions of *Egypt & the Sudan*, and Damien Simonis researched the third edition. Leanne Logan and Geert Cole researched this, the fourth edition of *Egypt*.

From the Publisher

This edition of *Egypt* was edited by Rachel Scully with assistance from Miriam Cannell and Diana Saad. Rachel, Miriam, Diana, Helen Castle and Susan Noonan were responsible for proofing. Cartography and design were coordinated by Geoff Stringer with mapping assistance from Michael Signal, Rachael Scott, Chris Klep, Adam McCrow and Daryl Cheney. The illustrations were drawn by Geoff, Indra Kilfoyle and Verity Campbell.

Thanks to Michelle Glynn and Christine Niven for writing material for Pharaonic Egypt, and to Piers Crocker of the Australian Institute of Archaeology for his recommendations in this section. Thanks also to David Kemp for the cover design and Adam McCrow for back-cover cartography; Janet Austin for advice regarding the literature section; Kerrie Williams for indexing; Dan Levin for the soft fonts; Chris Love for the climate charts; Leonie Mugavin for her assistance in research; the readers' letters team for all their assistance; and to Sam Carew and Greg Herriman for their advice and support. Thanks also to Peter Ward of Peter Ward Book Exports for his help with the bookshop sections.

And finally, thanks to Lonely Planet authors Andrew Humphreys, Gordon Robison and Damien Simonis for their good-humoured assistance with some last-minute research.

Thanks

Thanks to the travellers who wrote to us about their experiences in Egypt. Your names appear at the end of this book.

Warning & Request

Things change – prices go up, schedules change, good places go bad and bad places go bankrupt – nothing stays the same. So if you find things better or worse, recently opened or long since closed, please write and tell us and help make the next edition better.

Your letters will be used to help update future editions and, where possible, important changes will also be included in an Update section in reprints.

We greatly appreciate all information that is sent to us by travellers. Back at Lonely Planet we employ a hard-working readers' letters team to sort through the many letters we receive. The best ones will be rewarded with a free copy of the next edition or another Lonely Planet guide if you prefer. We give away lots of books, but, unfortunately, not every letter/postcard receives one.

Contents

INTRODUCTION 9

FACTS ABOUT THE COUNTRY 11

History 11
Geography 24
Climate 24
Ecology & Environment 25
Flora & Fauna 27

Government & Politics 30
Economy 31
Population 32
People 32
Education 33

Arts 33
Society & Conduct.................37
Religion..............................39
Language............................42

PHARAONIC EGYPT 49

Tomb & Temple
Architecture........................50

Gods & Goddesses in
Tomb & Temple Art 61

FACTS FOR THE VISITOR 68

Planning............................ 68
Suggested Itineraries 69
Highlights 70
Tourist Offices 71
Visas & Documents 72
Embassies 75
Customs 78
Money............................... 78
Post & Communications 82
Books 84
On-Line Services 88
Newspapers & Magazines........ 88
Radio & TV 89

Photography & Video 89
Time 90
Electricity...........................90
Weights & Measures...............90
Laundry.............................91
Health...............................91
Toilets...............................91
Women Travellers..................91
Gay & Lesbian Travellers 93
Disabled Travellers................93
Senior Travellers...................93
Travel with Children...............93
Dangers & Annoyances............ 94

Legal Matters 95
Business Hours 96
Public Holidays & Special
Events...............................96
Activities............................97
Courses..............................99
Work................................100
Accommodation...................101
Food................................103
Drinks..............................106
Entertainment.....................107
Spectator Sport....................108
Things to Buy......................108

GETTING THERE & AWAY 113

Air.................................. 113
Land................................ 119

Sea..................................122
Departure Taxes 124

Organised Tours 124

GETTING AROUND..126

Air.................................. 126
Bus................................. 127
Train................................ 127
Taxi................................. 128

Car & Motorcycle................. 129
Bicycle 130
Hitching 130
Camel...............................130

Donkey & Horse 131
Boat.................................131
Local Transport 132
Organised Tours 133

CAIRO...135

History 135
Orientation......................... 136
Information......................... 137
Central Cairo 149
Western Cairo 153
Heliopolis 157
Islamic Cairo 159
Roda Island 176

Old Cairo 177
Giza.................................180
Language Courses 187
Felucca Rides......................188
Dive Clubs 188
Horse Riding.......................188
Hammams..........................188
Swimming..........................188

Organised Tours 188
Special Events......................189
Places to Stay 189
Places to Eat.......................195
Entertainment......................203
Things to Buy......................206
Getting There & Away 206
Getting Around 212

AROUND CAIRO 218

Memphis 218
Saqqara 220
Dahshur............................ 227

Helwan 227
Al-Faiyum Oasis...................228
Pyramid of Meidum...............233

Birqash Camel Market........... 233
Wadi Natrun.......................234
The Nile Delta......................236

THE NILE VALLEY – BENI SUEF TO QUS 240

Beni Suef 241	Tuna al-Gebel 247	Sohag............................255
Gebel at-Teir & Frazer Tombs 242	Tell al-Amarna 249	Al-Balyana 258
Al-Minya 243	Dairut 250	Qena 261
Beni Hasan 246	Al-Qusiya.......................251	Qift 264
Mallawi.......................... 247	Asyut 252	Qus 265
Hermopolis 247	Around Asyut.................255	

THE NILE VALLEY – LUXOR 266

History 267	Activities....................... 299	Entertainment................307
Orientation.................... 267	Organised Tours 300	Things to Buy.................307
Information.................... 267	Special Events............... 300	Getting There & Away 307
East Bank...................... 270	Places to Stay............... 300	Getting Around 309
West Bank 278	Places to Eat................. 306	Around Luxor 310

THE NILE VALLEY – ESNA TO ABU SIMBEL... 311

Esna 311	Daraw 319	Temple of Philae 335
Al-Kab & Kom al-Ahmar 313	**Aswan** **319**	High Dam.......................337
Edfu 313	**Around Aswan** **334**	Kalabsha, Beit al-Wali &
Silsileh 316	The Aswan Dam 334	Kertassi.........................338
Kom Ombo 316	Sehel Island.................. 334	**Abu Simbel**.................**339**

THE WESTERN OASES 342

Kharga Oasis 343	Dakhla Oasis................. 347	Bahariyya Oasis 354
Around Kharga 346	Farafra Oasis 352	Siwa Oasis.....................357

ALEXANDRIA & THE MEDITERRANEAN COAST 365

Alexandria **365**	**The Mediterranean Coast 389**	Marsa Matruh.................392
Around Alexandria.......... **388**	El Alamein 390	Sidi Barani 397
Abu Mina...................... 388	Sidi Abdel Rahman........ 392	Sallum 398
Rosetta (Rashid) 388	Ras al-Hikma................. 392	

THE SUEZ CANAL & THE RED SEA COAST 399

The Suez Canal **399**	'Ain Sukhna................... 418	Port Safaga....................435
History 399	Zafarana........................ 418	El Hamarawein 437
Port Said 401	Monasteries of St Anthony	Al-Quseir.......................437
Qantara 408	& St Paul....................... 419	Around Al-Quseir 438
Ismailia 408	Ras Gharib 420	Marsa Alam 439
Suez 413	Hurghada (Al-Ghardaka). 420	Berenice 440
The Red Sea Coast **417**	Around Hurghada 435	Bir Shalatayn..................440

SINAI 441

Oyun Musa 446	Sharm el-Sheikh & Na'ama	Taba 468
Ras al-Sudr................... 446	Bay 448	St Catherine's Monastery........469
Qalat al-gindi & Nakhl 447	Shark Bay...................... 456	Wadi Feran 472
Hammam Fara'un.................. 447	Dahab 457	Rafah.............................475
From Abu Zenima to El-Tor... 447	Nuweiba 463	
Ras Mohammed National Park 448	Nuweiba to Taba............ 467	

HEALTH APPENDIX 477

GLOSSARY 492

INDEX 495

Maps 495	Boxed Stories................ 495	Text 496

Map Legend

BOUNDARIES

International Boundary

Regional Boundary

ROUTES

Freeway

Highway

Major Road

Unsealed Road or Track

City Road

City Street

Railway

Underground Railway

Tram

Walking Track

Walking Tour

Ferry Route

Cable Car or Chairlift

AREA FEATURES

Parks

Built-Up Area

Pedestrian Mall

Market

Cemetery

Non-Christian Cemetery

Reef

Beach or Desert

Oasis

HYDROGRAPHIC FEATURES

Coastline

River, Creek

Intermittent River or Creek

Rapids, Waterfalls

Lake, Intermittent Lake

Canal

SYMBOLS

✪ **CAPITAL**	National Capital	
◉ **Capital**	Regional Capital	
⬤ **CITY**	Major City	
● **City**	City	
● **Town**	Town	
● Village	Village	

■ ▼	Place to Stay, Place to Eat	
☕ 🍺	Cafe, Pub or Bar	
✉ ☎	Post Office, Telephone	
❶ ⑤	Tourist Information, Bank	
⊖ ⓜ	Transport, Metro Station	
🏛 ⌂	Museum, Youth Hostel	
🚐 ⚘	Caravan Park, Camping Ground	
✝ ✚	Church, Cathedral	
☪ ✡	Mosque, Synagogue	
🏛 ⊠	Temple, Pyramid	
✚ ★	Hospital, Police Station	

○ ⛽	Embassy, Petrol Station	
✈ ✚	Airport, Airfield	
▭ ✿	Swimming Pool, Gardens	
❖ 🐘	Shopping Centre, Zoo	
⚘ ▱	Winery or Vineyard, Picnic Site	
← A25	One Way Street, Route Number	
🏛 ⚐	Stately Home, Monument	
☖ ▣	Castle, Tomb or Mausoleum	
⌒ ⌂	Cave, Hut or Chalet	
▲ ✳	Mountain or Hill, Lookout	
🗼 ⚓	Lighthouse, Shipwreck	
)(◎	Pass, Spring	
🏊 ⛵	Beach, Surf Beach	
∴	Archaeological Site or Ruins	
	Ancient or City Wall	
	Cliff or Escarpment, Tunnel	
	Railway Station	

Note: not all symbols displayed above appear in this book

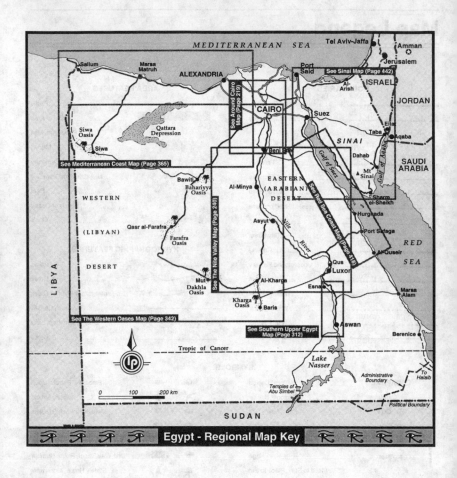

Introduction

Ever since Herodotus, the ancient Greek historian and traveller, first described Egypt as 'the gift of the Nile', the country has been capturing the imagination of all who visit.

The awe-inspiring monuments, left by the Pharaohs, Greeks and Romans as well as by early Christians and Muslims, attract thousands of visitors every year – but the pyramids, temples, tombs, monasteries and mosques are just part of this country's fascination.

Modern Egypt – where mud-brick villages stand beside Pharaonic ruins surrounded by towering steel, stone and glass buildings – is at the cultural crossroads of east and west, ancient and modern. While TV antennae decorate rooftops everywhere, from the crowded apartment blocks of Cairo to the mud-brick homes of farming villages and the goatskin tents of the Bedouins, the fellahin (farmers) throughout the Nile's fertile valley still tend their fields with the archaic tools of their ancestors.

In the gargantuan city of Cairo the sound of the muezzin summoning the faithful to prayer or the mesmerising voice of Om Kolthum, the 'Mother of Egypt', compete with the pop music of ghetto blasters and the screech of car horns. And everywhere there are people: swathed in long flowing robes or western-style clothes, hanging from buses, weaving through an obstacle course of animals and exhaust-spewing traffic or spilling from hive-like buildings.

Spectacular edifices aside, the attraction of this country, which is officially known as the Arab Republic of Egypt, lies in its incredible natural beauty and in the overwhelming hospitality of the Egyptian people.

Through everything the Nile River flows serene and majestic, the lifeblood of Egypt as it has been since the beginning of history.

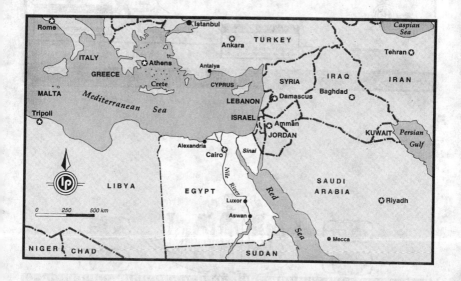

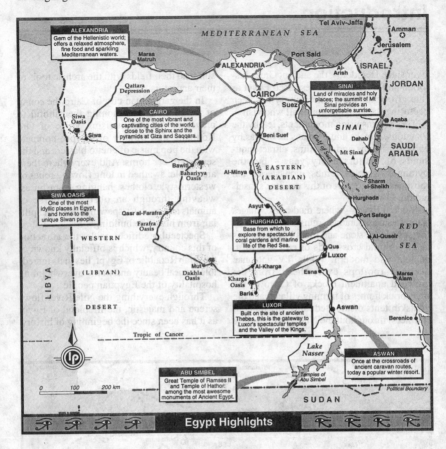

ALEXANDRIA
Gem of the Hellenistic world; offers a relaxed atmosphere, fine food and sparkling Mediterranean waters.

CAIRO
One of the most vibrant and captivating cities of the world, close to the Sphinx and the pyramids at Giza and Saqqara.

SIWA OASIS
One of the most idyllic places in Egypt, and home to the unique Siwan people.

SINAI
Land of miracles and holy places; the summit of Mt Sinai provides an unforgettable sunrise.

HURGHADA
Base from which to explore the spectacular coral gardens and marine life of the Red Sea.

LUXOR
Built on the site of ancient Thebes, this is the gateway to Luxor's spectacular temples and the Valley of the Kings.

ASWAN
Once at the crossroads of ancient caravan routes, today a popular winter resort.

ABU SIMBEL
Great Temple of Ramses II and Temple of Hathor; among the most awesome monuments of Ancient Egypt.

Egypt Highlights

Facts about the Country

HISTORY

About 5000 years ago an Egyptian king named Menes unified Upper and Lower Egypt for the first time. No-one is quite sure how he did this, but it is known that his action gave rise to Egypt's first relatively stable dynasty of kings. Menes' powerful and civilised reign suggests that civilisation must have been developing in the Nile Valley for many centuries before this time.

The history of Egypt is inextricably linked to the Nile. Ever since the earliest known communities settled the Nile Valley, the river has inspired and controlled the religious, economic, social and political life of Egyptians. For many centuries the narrow, elongated layout of the country's fertile lands hampered the fusion of those early settlements, which held fast to their local independence. But once again it was the river, this time as a common highway, which broke the barriers by providing an avenue for commercial traffic and communication. The small kingdoms eventually developed into two important states, one covering the valley as far as the Delta, the other consisting of the Delta itself. The unification of these two states, by Menes in about 3000 BC, set the scene for the greatest era of ancient Egyptian civilisation. More than 30 dynasties, 50 rulers and 2700 years of indigenous – and occasionally foreign – rule passed before Alexander the Great ushered in a long, unbroken period of foreign rule.

Fifty centuries of history! Obviously, it is not within the scope of this book to cover it in great detail. To give some idea of the major events in Egypt's history, the last 5000 years, from the time of Menes, can be divided roughly into seven periods:

Pharaonic times	(3000-341 BC)
Greek rule	(332-30 BC)
Roman & Byzantine rule	(30 BC-638 AD)
The Arab conquest & the Mamluks	(640-1517)
Turkish rule	(1517-1882)
British occupation	(1882-1952)
Independent Egypt	(1952 onwards)

Pharaonic Times (3000-341 BC)

Little is known of the immediate successors of Menes except that, attributed with divine ancestry, they promoted the development of a highly stratified society, patronised the arts and built many temples and public works.

As you travel through Egypt, it is easy to be overwhelmed by the many names and dates of Pharaonic rule. Some of the books listed in the Facts for the Visitor chapter offer a detailed account of the long period encompassing the Old, Middle and New kingdoms.

In the 27th century BC, the construction of Egypt's pyramids began. King Zoser and his chief architect, Imhotep, built what may have been the first, the Step Pyramid at Saqqara. Zoser ruled from the nearby capital of Memphis. Until his reign, most of the royal tombs had been built of sun-dried bricks. The construction of Zoser's massive stone mausoleum, therefore, was not only a striking testimony to his power and the prosperity of the period but the start of a whole new trend. It was also during the period of Zoser's rule that the sun-god Ra became the most important of the deities worshipped by Egyptians.

For the next three dynasties and 500 years – a period called the Old Kingdom – the power of Egypt's Pharaohs and the size of their pyramids and temples greatly increased. The size of such buildings symbolised the Pharaoh's importance and power over his people. The pyramid also gave the Pharaoh steps to the heavens, and the ceremonial wooden boats, known as solar barques, buried with him provided him with symbolic vehicles to the next life.

Not long after Zoser's Step Pyramid was completed, 4th dynasty Pharaohs built several more in the relatively short period between 2650 and 2500 BC.

Pharaoh Sneferu built the Pyramid of

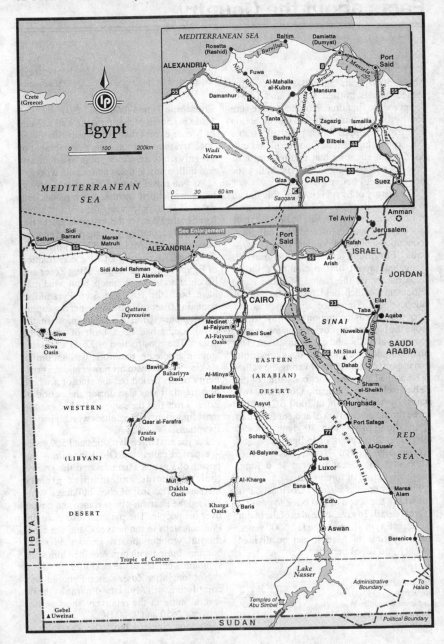

Meidum in Al-Faiyum and the Red Pyramid of Dahshur near Saqqara, and took royal power and the accompanying artistic and commercial development of Egypt to even greater heights. During his time, trading vessels nearly six metres long began plying the waters of the Nile. He brought back thousands of prisoners from successful campaigns against the Nubians in the south, and defeated all enemies who threatened the country.

The last three Pharaohs of the 4th dynasty, Cheops, Chephren and Mycerinus, built the three Great Pyramids of Giza. Cheops took the throne when the Pharaonic era was reaching the apex of its prosperity and culture, and if his colossal pyramid is any indication he must have been one of the greatest of all the Pharaohs. Its sheer size and mathematical precision is not only a monument to the extraordinary development of Egyptian architecture; it also suggests, as many Egyptologists believe, that the era of Cheops saw the emergence, for the first time in human history, of an organisational principle. Under his rule, and through the enormous labour and discipline involved in the construction of the pyramid, Egypt became a highly organised state.

As the centuries passed and the 5th dynasty (about 2490 to 2330 BC) began, there were changes in the power and rule of the Pharaohs. One of the first indications of this was the comparatively small pyramids built at Abu Sir, 12 km south of Giza. The Pharaohs had begun to share power with various high officials and nobles in the vast bureaucracies they had created, so unlike their predecessors they were no longer absolute monarchs and did not have the same resources for the construction of immense funerary monuments.

As control became even more diffused during the 6th and 7th dynasties (about 2330 to 2170 BC), a number of small local principalities popped up around the country, and a second capital was established at Heracleopolis (near present-day Beni Suef) during the 9th and 10th dynasties. The princes of these small dynasties ruled Egypt for many years,

but their constant feudal struggles prevented any possibility of economic or artistic development. With the collapse of the Old Kingdom a state of disunity succeeded the unparalleled grandeur of the early Pharaonic dynasties.

Civil war at the beginning of the 11th dynasty finally put an end to the squabbling. An enterprising member of the Intef family rallied all the principalities of the south against the weakness of Heracleopolis, and established an independent kingdom with Thebes (present-day Luxor) as its capital. Under Mentuhotep II the north and south were again united under the leadership of a single Pharaoh. The princes of Thebes became rulers of all Egypt, and the Middle Kingdom period began.

With political order came economic stability and social and artistic development. Thebes prospered for about 250 years. Tombs and temples were built throughout Egypt; their remains can be seen today in almost every Egyptian town. The Pharaohs Mentuhotep, Amenemhet and Sesostris built monuments at Lisht, Dahshur, Hawara and Lahun – all of which are near Al-Faiyum and Saqqara. Their building frenzy diminished as the governors and nobles of the nomes (provinces) once again began squabbling among themselves and demanding more control (around 1780 to 1660 BC). Royal power was weakened by this lack of unity; the empire was divided and ripe for conquest by an outside power.

These invaders came from the north-east. The Egyptians called them the Hyksos (Princes of the Foreign Lands). They ruled Egypt for more than a century, but are remembered for little more than having introduced the horse-drawn chariot to Egypt. By about 1550 BC the Egyptians had routed the Hyksos and expelled them from power. A new kingdom, with its capital first at Thebes and thereafter at Memphis, was established and Egypt truly entered the ranks of the great powers.

The New Kingdom represented a blossoming of culture and empire in Pharaonic Egypt. For 400 years, from the 18th to 20th

The Preparation for Life Eternal

It was death, of course, that prompted the construction of the Egyptian pyramids but the incredible amount of resources, effort and time that went into them was indicative of many aspects of life in those days. The tombs served a variety of purposes, not the least of which was to provide the final resting places of the owners and repositories for their worldly possessions.

The size and grandeur of the tombs were designed to enhance the owners' greatness in the eyes of their people during the owners' lifetimes, but their tombs also became places of worship for their subjects after the owners' deaths.

The pyramids were also a symbol of life and death, of life over death and of life after death, serving to preserve the Pharaohs in the memory of their people and to ensure the Pharaohs' continued existence in the afterlife. It was not a fear of death, or even an obsession with it, that guided the ancient Egyptians; rather it was a belief in life eternal and the desire to be one with the gods and their universe that inspired such extremes.

The pyramids were seen as an indestructible sanctum for the preservation of the Pharaohs' kas. These spirits, or life forces emanating from the gods, were the 'doubles' of living people but gained their own identities with the deaths of those people. The Pharaohs' kas would either continue to exist in their tombs – hence the need for all their worldly belongings – or would journey off to join the gods. The survival of the ka, however, depended on the continued existence of the body, so the process of mummification developed alongside the technology of tomb building.

Prior to dynastic times the dead were simply buried in shallow graves on the edge of the desert and covered with sand. Because of the dry atmosphere and hot sand this practice often caused the bodies to dehydrate before the tissues decomposed and this natural method of preservation did not go unnoticed. As the ancient Egyptians changed their burial rituals and introduced coffins, the technique of mummification was developed to artificially preserve the dead bodies of those who could afford the process, as well as to preserve an incredible number of sacred birds, reptiles and other animals.

For humans the mummification process took about 70 days. The most important aspect was the removal of the vital organs and the drying of the body using a dehydrating agent called natron (a mineral of hydrated sodium carbonate). The actual wrapping of the body in bandages played no role in the preservation of the corpse.

The treatment took place in six main stages:

- The brain was extracted by being broken up and removed through the nose.
- The viscera (except for the heart and kidneys) were removed through an incision in the lower left abdomen. The intestines, stomach, liver and lungs were dehydrated with natron, treated with resin and stored separately in containers known as Canopic jars.
- The body was sterilised and the internal cavities were temporarily packed with natron and fragrant resins.
- The body then underwent the main preservative treatment of being covered with natron for about 35 days.
- The temporary packing was then removed; the limbs were packed, under the skin, with clay; and the body cavities were permanently packed with linen soaked in resin, bags of cinnamon and myrrh, and sawdust.
- The body was then anointed with fragrant oils and ointments, the abdominal incision was covered with an amulet of the Eye of Horus, and the skin was treated with molten resin.
- Finally the body was wrapped up, with pieces of jewellery and protective amulets placed among the bandages.

dynasties (1550 to 1150 BC), Egypt was a great power in north-east Africa and the eastern Med. Renowned kings and queens ruled an expanding empire from Memphis, and built monuments which even today are unique in their immensity and beauty.

The temple complex of Karnak at Thebes became an important symbolic power centre for the empire. The temple seemed to grow as the empire expanded. Each successive Pharaoh of the 18th and 19th dynasties added a room, hall or pylon, with intricately carved hieroglyphic inscriptions on every wall and pillar. Some of what is known about Egyptian life during this time comes from the stories told by these inscriptions.

Significant expansion of the empire began with the reign of Tuthmosis I in 1528 BC. He grabbed Upper Nubia, and became the first Pharaoh to be entombed in the Valley of the Kings on the west bank across from Thebes. His daughter, Hatshepsut, became one of Egypt's few female rulers. A spectacular mortuary temple was built for her at Deir al-Bahri on the west bank.

Tuthmosis III, Hatshepsut's nephew, was next in line; he became Egypt's greatest conqueror. He expanded the empire past Syria and into western Asia. He built and contributed to temples at Thebes, Buhen, Amada and other locales throughout Egypt.

Empire expansion and temple/tomb building continued under the following three Pharaohs – Amenophis II, Tuthmosis IV and Amenophis III – and reached its peak in 1417 BC under Amenophis III. He built the Luxor Temple and a massive mortuary temple, of which the only remains are the Colossi of Memnon on the west bank at Luxor. During this period the country was relatively prosperous and stable.

Amenophis IV quarrelled with the priesthood of the god Amun, the leading god of Thebes, and took the name Akhenaten in honour of Aten, the disc of the rising sun. Akhenaten and his wife, Nefertiti, were so devoted to the worship of Aten that they established a new capital, called Akhetaten, devoted solely to the worship of the new god. Some historians believe that this worship represented the first organised form of monotheism. Today, the scant remains of Akhenaten's capital can be seen at Tell al-Amarna, near the town of Al-Minya.

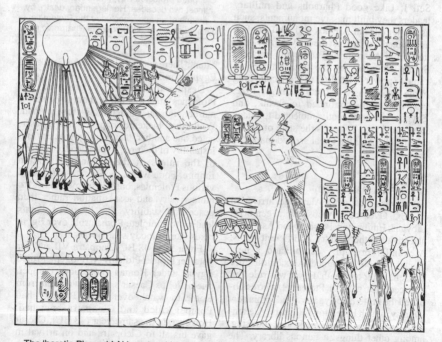

The 'heretic Pharaoh' Akhenaten, his wife Nefertiti and their children make offerings to Aten, an aspect of the sun-god Ra. Their devotion to Aten is said to represent the first organised form of monotheism, however, the cult of Aten did did not endure after Akhenaten's death.

After Akhenaten's death, the priests of Thebes went on a rampage and destroyed any signs of his rule and his monotheism. This included the Temple of the Sun at Karnak. (An American archaeological team photographed the hieroglyphic inscriptions on more than 35,000 stone blocks from the temple which had been scattered around the world. From the photographs, the archaeologists were able to reconstruct the temple and learn more about the lives of Akhenaten and Nefertiti.)

Akhenaten's son-in-law, Tutankhamun, ruled for about nine years and died just before reaching manhood. His tomb was discovered in 1922 with almost all its treasures untouched.

For the next few centuries, Egypt was ruled by generals: Ramses I, II and III, and Seti I. Like good Pharaohs and military leaders they built massive monuments, such as the temples at Abydos and Abu Simbel, and waged war against the Libyans and Hittites (from Anatolia in Turkey and northern Syria). However, by the time Ramses III came to power (1198 BC) as the second king of the 20th dynasty, disunity had begun to set in. The empire continued to shrink, and Egypt was subsequently subjected to attack from outsiders. This was the state of affairs when Alexander the Great arrived in the 4th century BC.

Greek Rule (332-30 BC)

Egypt was a mess when Alexander arrived in 332 BC. Over the previous several centuries Libyans, Ethiopians, Persians and Assyrians had invaded the country at different times. Alexander promptly established a new capital, which he named Alexandria after himself. After his death, Egypt was ruled by a Macedonian general, Ptolemy I, who established the Ptolemaic dynasty. Under this new dynasty, which lasted for 300 years, Alexandria became a great Greek city, housing, among other things, a famous library. The temples of Dendara, Philae and Edfu, which were built further south, are still in excellent shape, with most of their walls and roofs

Cleopatra protected Egypt from Roman rule for almost two decades. Her legendary death, by means of an asp, concluded the Ptolemaic dynasty and over 3000 years of Pharaonic rule.

extant. There was a melding of the Greek and Egyptian religions.

Despite the prosperity, however, the Ptolemies' rule was not without its share of murder, intrigue and threats from abroad. While they bickered, expelled and assassinated one another, the overall weakness and instability of their reign attracted the interest of the rulers of the expanding Roman Empire. For a while, the Romans supported various Ptolemies, but this seemed to lead to more rivalry and assassination rather than peace and stability. The litany of events leading to complete Roman rule over Egypt reads like a bloody soap opera.

From 51 to 48 BC Cleopatra VII and her younger brother Ptolemy XIII together ruled Egypt, under Roman protection. Pompei, one of Julius Caesar's rivals, was sent from Rome to watch over them. Ptolemy had Pompei killed and Cleopatra banished. However, in the same year (48 BC), Caesar gave his all to Cleopatra and on arrival in Egypt threw Ptolemy in the Nile, appointing another of Cleopatra's brothers, Ptolemy XIV, as co-ruler. Cleopatra gave birth to

Julius Caesar's son in 47 BC and had her brother killed in 45 BC. A year later Caesar was also assassinated. (Are you lost yet?) Marc Antony arrived from Rome, fell in love with Cleopatra, and moved in with her for 10 years of bliss, an arrangement the Roman senate wasn't too thrilled about. They declared Antony an enemy of the people and sent Octavian to deal with him. Antony and Cleopatra preferred bliss to captivity. They both committed suicide in 30 BC and Egypt became a Roman province.

Roman & Byzantine Rule (30 BC-638 AD)

Octavian was the first Roman ruler of Egypt. He ruled as Emperor Augustus for a few years and made Egypt the granary of the Roman Empire. Except for a brief invasion by Ethiopia in 24 BC, Egypt was basically stable and peaceful for about 30 years.

Although the Bible tells us that Mary, Joseph and their young baby fled from Bethlehem to Egypt, where Jesus grew up before returning to Palestine to spread the word of God, it was not until St Mark started preaching the gospel, around 40 AD, that Egyptians began converting to Christianity. The Roman emperor Nero capitalised on this renewed sense of religious unity by developing Egypt as a trade centre between Rome and India in 54 AD.

A national Egyptian, or Coptic, Church was founded, despite the persecution of Christians throughout the Roman Empire during the following centuries. Egypt prospered, but by the 3rd century the Roman Empire had begun to succumb to war, famine and power struggles. In the 4th century, not long after Christianity was declared the state religion, the Roman Empire cracked in half. The eastern half became what was later known as the Byzantine or Eastern Empire. It was ruled from Constantinople (now Istanbul), while the Western Roman Empire remained centred in Rome.

The empire was too weak to rule its dominions effectively, so Egypt was left to invaders – Nubians from the south and North Africans from the west. Egypt was also left

to develop the Coptic Church independently of the Byzantines. The Copts' adoption of a Monophysitic doctrine (the belief that Christ is divine, rather than both human and divine) was deemed heretical by the Byzantine and Roman orthodoxy, so they expelled the Coptic Church from the main body of Christianity. That doctrine, however, and a tradition of monasticism, greatly influenced later developments in European Christianity and are still an integral part of the Christian church in Egypt.

Aside from a few wars with Nubians, a famine and a couple of Persian invasions, life in 'Byzantine' Egypt was relatively sedate. Then, in 640 AD, the Arabs arrived.

The Arab Conquest & the Mamluks (640-1517)

The Arab conquest brought Islam to Egypt. By 642 the new Arab rulers had established Fustat as a military base and seat of government – the precursor of Cairo. Although it didn't last long as the seat of government, it grew quickly as a city of Muslims. The ruins of Fustat can still be seen just south of central Cairo.

In 658 the Omayyads, an Arab dynasty based in Damascus, snatched control of Egypt and stayed until 750. During the 92 years of their rule, Islamic faith and the Omayyad Empire extended from Spain all the way to central Asia. Theological splits were inevitable in such a large empire. One of the main splits concerned the spiritual leadership of the descendants of Ali, the Prophet Mohammed's son-in-law. Two groups – the Sunni and the Shi'ite – evolved because of this dispute, and conflict between them continues today (for more details see the boxed story Sayyidna Al-Hussein in the Cairo chapter). More than 1200 years ago, this same conflict led to the downfall of the Omayyad dynasty and the decapitation of Marwan, the last Omayyad caliph, or ruler. Persian troops paraded his head around the burnt remains of Fustat. For the next 108 years Egypt was ruled by the Baghdad-based Abbassid dynasty.

The Abbassids ruled Egypt differently

from their predecessors. They brought in outsiders, Turkish-speaking soldier slaves known as Mamluks, to protect their interests throughout the empire. One of these fighting nomads, Bayikbey, eventually gained enough power and influence to become a threat to the caliph. The caliph gave him Egypt, but Bayikbey preferred to remain in Turkey, where the caliph eventually had him killed. Bayikbey's stepson Ibn Tulun (Son of Tulun) was sent to Egypt as governor in his place.

Ibn Tulun wanted Egypt to be an independent state, not an Abbassid province, so he fought and defeated the Abbassids and established a dynasty. He erected one of the largest mosques in the Middle East: the Mosque of Ibn Tulun was big enough to accommodate all his cavalry – both horses and men.

After Ibn Tulun's death, Egypt was unable to keep its independence. Various leaders and invaders followed, including the Abbassids, Byzantines, Ikhshids and, finally, the Fatimids. The Fatimids came from a kingdom of rulers in north-west Africa who claimed descent from Mohammed's daughter, Fatima, and her husband, Ali. They quickly established a dynasty of independent caliphs which lasted for just over 200 years (968 to 1169).

Egypt flourished under the first Fatimid rulers. At the behest of the mysterious caliph Al-Muizz, a Greek named Gawhar spent four years building the new city of Al-Qahira, or Cairo. Desmond Stewart writes in his book *Great Cairo: Mother of the World* that Al-Muizz:

ruled mysteriously, as befitted an imam, from behind the curtain of awe. For Fatimid power was based on an idea: the sense that God allows an aspect of himself to be incarnate in an infallible ruler.

Gawhar's construction work in Cairo befitted an imam imbued with godliness, and his greatest work was the Al-Azhar Mosque. This immense structure, which resembles a fortress, became one of the world's greatest centres of Islamic studies. Today it continues to function as both a mosque and a major university. After the death of Al-Muizz, Egypt continued to flourish under his son, Al-Aziz, but the good times ended with the rule of Al-Aziz's crazy son, Al-Hakim (996 to 1021).

At first, Al-Hakim ruled Egypt as an absolute monarch with beneficence and grace. A magnificent mosque was built at the northern wall of Cairo between the gates of Bab al-Futuh and Bab an-Nasr. Al-Hakim began to share his rule with a council of advisers and also attempted to understand the problems of Cairenes by touring the city on his mule and talking to his people. All of this paled into insignificance, however, when the young Al-Hakim began ruling like a lunatic (for details see the boxed story about Al-Hakim in the Cairo chapter). His reign continued until one night in 1021 when Al-Hakim rode off into the Moqattam Hills near Cairo and disappeared. He was never seen again.

Over the next 150 years several Fatimid caliphs ruled Egypt. Apart from a relatively brief spate of plague and famine, and a few power squabbles, battles and wars, Egypt was prosperous. Food was plentiful in the *souqs*, or markets, and apartment buildings with as many as 10 floors (sometimes more) rose in Cairo. This prosperity, however, could not be maintained in those parts of the empire outside Egypt.

Around this time the Christians of western Europe began a crusade to spread Christianity and rescue the Holy City of Jerusalem from the Muslims.

The Crusaders seized Jerusalem from the Fatimids in 1099. Tripoli, in Lebanon, fell in 1109 and so did several other parts of the Fatimid Empire. By 1153 all of Palestine was under Christian control, and rather than suffer a similar fate the weakened Fatimid state decided to cooperate with the Crusaders. The Muslim Seljuk dynasty of Syria was not happy about this, as the balance of power was upset – a balance which had begun to tip increasingly in their favour. So the Seljuks sent in an army led by a Kurdish warrior named Shirkoh and his nephew Salah ad-Din (known to the west as Saladin).

Salah ad-Din eventually gained control of Egypt and founded his own dynasty, the Ayyubids, in 1171. The Crusaders attacked and partly burned Cairo in 1176, so Salah ad-Din immediately began fortifying the city. He built part of the city walls and the citadel; the latter became a small town of shops, stables and workshops. His reign marked the heyday of medieval Egypt and in 1187 he drove the Crusaders from Jerusalem.

Above all, Salah ad-Din sought power. He purchased Mamluks (whose name comes from an Arabic word for 'owned' or 'held') to assist him. Most Mamluks were Turkish mercenaries, sold by their parents when they were boys, to be trained solely to fight for the sultan. In his book *Travels through Syria & Egypt in the Years 1783, 1784 & 1785*, M Volney describes the Mamluks as follows:

strangers among themselves...Without parents...the past has done nothing for them; they do nothing for the future. Ignorant and superstitious by upbringing, they become fierce through murders, mutinous through tumults, deceitful through intrigues, corrupt through every species of debauch.

After a certain period of servitude and military service, many Mamluks were free to own land and raise families. Despite their violent nature some did choose to settle down quietly. Other Mamluks, however, began to seek positions of power and influence within the state. Their efforts brought about the demise of Shagarat ad-Durr, the last Ayyubid ruler and the first woman to reign over Egypt since Cleopatra (for more information see the boxed story about Shagarat ad-Durr in the Cairo chapter), and ushered in more than two and a half centuries of Mamluk rule.

Two dynasties of Mamluks ruled Egypt. The Bahri Mamluks were the first: in their 132 years of rule there were more than 25 sultans. Murder, intrigue and war were rife. In-between fighting and conspiring, however, the Mamluks developed a distinctive style of architecture, and several mosques were built, including those of Sultan Hassan, Az-Zahir and Qalaun.

The sultans of the next dynasty were equally given to construction. This dynasty began when a Circassian slave named Barquq seized power from the Bahri ruler, a six year-old Mamluk. More than 21 Circassian Mamluks became sultan before Egypt fell to the Turks in 1517.

Turkish Rule (1517-1882)

Since most of the Mamluks were either of Turkish descent or from Turkey and the surrounding areas, rule over Egypt by the Ottoman sultans of Constantinople was not difficult. In fact, their rule basically consisted of collecting taxes from Egypt, while the rest of the governing business was left to the Mamluks. This continued until Napoleon invaded Egypt in 1798.

Napoleon and his army routed the Mamluk army, supposedly as a show of support for the Ottoman sultan. In reality, Napoleon wanted eventually to strike a blow at British trade in the Indian Ocean by gaining control of the land and sea routes to India. He was also keen to 'civilise' Egypt.

Napoleon established a French-style government, revamped the tax system and implemented public works projects – canals were cleared, streets were cleaned of garbage and temporary bridges spanned the Nile. Through his Institut d'Égypte he put a variety of French intellectuals to work on a history of ancient Egypt and a record of the ancient monuments. The French were also responsible for the planting of new crops, establishing a new system of weights and measures, and reorganising the hospitals. However, as Alan Moorehead writes in his book *The Blue Nile*:

Everything these new conquerors proposed was a strain; it was a strain *not* to throw rubbish in the streets, *not* to bribe witnesses and officials, and it was upsetting to be obliged to undergo medical treatment where prayers had always served in the past. The Egyptians had been getting on very well, they felt, as they were before. They had no need for new canals, new weights and measures, and new schools...They did not believe Bonaparte's protestations of his respect for Muhammad, nor were they much impressed by his dressings-up in turban and caftan...

Napoleon's Egyptian adventure seemed doomed from the beginning. Less than a month after he arrived, the British navy, under Admiral Nelson, appeared off the coast of Alexandria. Nelson quickly destroyed the French fleet and cut off Napoleon's forces from France. A year later the British sent an army of 15,000 Turkish soldiers to expel the French from Egypt. The resulting battle at Abu Qir near Alexandria was a victory for the French; 5000 Turks were killed. Nevertheless, the British returned in 1801 and compelled the French to leave.

Although brief, the French occupation significantly weakened Egyptian political stability. After a period of internal strife, the headstrong Mohammed Ali became khedive (viceroy). A lieutenant in the Albanian contingent of the Ottoman army, he rose to power after the Albanian soldiers mutinied against their Turkish rulers. With Mamluk help, he temporarily expelled the British from Egypt. The Mamluk leaders, however, also posed a threat to Mohammed Ali, so he invited them to a sumptuous banquet and then had them massacred on their way home. A charming host!

Mohammed was power-hungry. He sent his troops on successful forays into Sudan, Greece, Syria and Arabia, and by 1839 he controlled most of the Ottoman Empire. However, the British intervened again and forced him into sharing power with the sultan in Istanbul. Mohammed died in 1848 and was succeeded by his grandson Abbas, who was in turn succeeded by his son Said Pasha.

Said Pasha began implementing many government reforms and projects, foremost of which was the establishment of the railway system and the digging of the Suez Canal.

Pasha Ismail succeeded Said, and followed in his path by establishing factories, a telegraph and postal system, canals and bridges. The fledgling cotton industry of Egypt prospered as the American Civil War disrupted cotton production in America's southern states. Ismail opened the Suez Canal in 1869 and achieved political independence for Egypt in 1873. Having gained independence, Ismail confidently spent more state money than he had. The national debt became so great that he was forced to abdicate in 1879.

British Occupation (1882-1952)

The debt and abdication brought greater British control over Egyptian affairs. With pressure from the British, Ismail's son Tawfiq reorganised Egypt's finances, and British and French controllers installed themselves in the government.

With the outbreak of WWI the Egyptian government threw in its lot with the Allies. When Turkey entered the war on the side of Germany, and made an abortive attack on the Suez Canal, the British Foreign Office placed Egypt 'under the protection of His Majesty', effectively terminating the suzerainty of Turkey over Egypt. The khedive, Abbas Hilmi, was deposed for his Turkish sympathies, Prince Hussein Kamil became sultan and martial law was proclaimed throughout the country.

During this time, several groups in Egypt, in particular the Ulama, or Muslim elite, and Egyptian civil servants, military officers and landowners, were disturbed by the increase in foreign influence, especially within the Egyptian government and civil service. A movement to expel Europeans from these areas evolved from a coalition of opposition groups, but the plan backfired and the British remained in such positions until 1952.

The British did, however, eventually allow the formation of a nationalist political party, called the Wafd (Delegation), and a monarchist party. The first elections were held in 1922, independence was granted, and King Fuad I was elected to head a constitutional monarchy. For the next 30 years the British, monarchists and Wafdists jockeyed for power and influence. Egypt played a strategic role in WWII, serving as a vital British base in the Middle East. It was here, too, following the Battle of El Alamein, that the tide of the war was turned. Towards the end of WWII, the Arab League was founded by seven countries, including Egypt, in order to strengthen regional relations. Egypt, however, was left in chaos following WWII and defeat in Israel's 1948 War of Independence. By 1952 only a group of dissident military officers had the wherewithal to take over the government.

Post-Revolution Egypt & Suez Crisis
The Free Officers, led by Colonel Gamal Abdel Nasser, overthrew King Farouk, Fuad's son, in a bloodless coup on 23 July 1952. Three days later the king abdicated (and the 26th July became the name of many streets). The coup was quickly dubbed the Revolution of 1952. The first independent Arab Republic of Egypt was formed and Nasser, who after some manoeuvring became head of state, wasted no time in getting embroiled in international politics.

He became one of the architects of the Nonaligned Movement, an association of countries that sought to distance itself from the western and eastern blocs and establish a third force in world politics. Through his role in the movement Nasser criticised the west; this and his growing economic ties with eastern Europe cost him western assistance in building the Aswan High Dam, so he turned to the Soviets instead. As the western powers had given Egypt's doubtful capacity to pay a reasonable share of the costs of the dam as one reason for pulling out, Nasser nationalised the Suez Canal Company in 1956, ostensibly to raise the necessary money. The British and French, anxious to maintain some degree of control over the waterway, secretly agreed to cooperate in an attack with the Israelis, who invaded on 29 October. The French and British 'intervened' two days later, and landed paratroops at Port Said on 5 November. Despite the Soviet invasion of Hungary in the same month, the USA and Moscow found themselves on the same side just for once in opposing the Anglo-French actions, and the United Nations had little trouble urging the invaders to leave and installing a UN peacekeeping force to guarantee safe passage through the canal. Nasser became a hero, especially in the Arab world.

Six Day War & October War
The Suez Crisis of 1956 made Nasser head of a pan-Arab nationalist movement that emphasised Arab unity. Unsuccessful attempts were made to unite Egypt, Syria and, for a short while, Yemen in a United Arab Republic (UAR). Amid a growing feeling that Egypt was getting too strong a say in Syrian affairs, Damascus pulled out of the UAR in 1961. There were further attempts at union with Syria and Iraq during the 1960s, all of them fruitless. At the same time, at a meeting in Cairo in 1964, the Arab League pledged funds to help set up the Palestine Liberation Organisation (PLO).

As Egypt's economy worsened under Gamal Abdel Nasser's 'Arab socialist' policies of nationalisation, he began diverting attention from the internal problems by emphasising Arab unity and making Israel a scapegoat. As tension increased on the Israeli-Syrian border, Nasser asked the UN force to leave Sinai and closed the Straits of Tiran, Israel's only outlet to the Indian Ocean. Soon after, Jordan and Iraq signed defence pacts with the UAR. On 5 June 1967 Israel attacked, and in just six days destroyed the Egyptian air force, captured Sinai and closed the Suez Canal, as well as taking the Golan Heights from Syria and the West Bank from Jordan. Despite this devastating defeat, the Egyptian people insisted that Nasser remain in power, which he did until his death in 1970. Arabs continue to revere him, and his photograph can still be found in many homes and shops.

Anwar Sadat, Nasser's vice president, took over the presidency and tried to repair Egypt's economy by becoming friendlier with the west, particularly the USA, at the expense of relations with the USSR. He also realised that to truly revitalise Egypt's economy he would have to deal with Israel – but first he needed bargaining power, a basis for negotiations. So, on 6 October 1973, the Jewish holiday of Yom Kippur, he launched a surprise attack across the Suez

Canal. Although Egypt actually lost the war, thanks mainly to massive US resupply of Israeli war material, Sadat's negotiating strategy succeeded. He also managed to get back the east bank of the Suez Canal under the ensuing cease-fire terms.

Peace with Israel

On 19 November 1977, Sadat travelled to Jerusalem to begin making peace with Israel, and a peace treaty based on the Camp David Agreement was eventually signed in 1979. In this, Israel agreed to withdraw from Sinai while Egypt recognised Israel's right to exist. Most of Sinai was returned to Egyptian control by 1982 and relations between Egypt and Israel were normalised. This independent peace deal did not, however, resolve the Palestinian issue. It also meant that Egypt was immediately ostracised by the rest of the Arab world and most socialist and developing countries. The seat of the Arab League was transferred from Cairo to Tunis and relations with Libya in particular – already strained (although the two countries had discussed union in the early 1970s) – rapidly worsened. By 1980, Egypt had turned the border area into a security zone and Libya had built fortresses and airfields on its eastern frontier.

For most Egyptians the treaty with Israel promised future peace and prosperity. However, radical groups of fundamentalist Muslims were opposed to the price of peace: normalisation of relations with Israel and alignment with the west (Sadat had expelled thousands of Soviet advisers and later 40 diplomats). A member of one such group, the Islamic Jihad, assassinated Sadat during a military parade on 6 October 1981.

Mubarak in Power

Hosni Mubarak, Sadat's vice president since 1974, was sworn in as president. He has since managed, to the surprise of some, to carry out a balancing act on several fronts, abroad and at home.

In the three to four years after taking over as president, Mubarak was able, to the irritation of more hardline states like Syria and

Libya, to break through Egypt's isolation in the Arab world without abandoning the treaty with Israel, although the latter's invasion of Lebanon in 1982 put relations between the two states under heavy strain. From then until late 1986, Egypt had no ambassador in Tel Aviv. From 1984, Egypt began to re-establish relations with moderate Arab countries, and used its unique position through the 1980s and 1990s to promote the Middle East peace process in Israel and the Arab countries. The Arab League headquarters were returned to Cairo in 1990. An exception to his foreign policy success were the continued poor relations with Libya. On the superpower front he proved equally adept, reopening relations with Moscow, letting experts return, and at the same time becoming the region's second biggest recipient of US aid after Israel.

Internally, he inherited the twin problems of an economy unable to match the growing demands of an exploding population – violent riots over price rises in September 1984 were a sharp reminder – and the ever-

Sworn in as president after the assassination of Sadat in 1981, Hosni Mubarak is currently serving his third term.

present threat to secular rule posed by Islamic groups demanding rule by *shari'a*, or Islamic law. Mubarak has attempted to keep a lid on the problem with a combination of limited democracy and tolerance and heavy-handed crackdowns on purported Muslim activists. In the last presidential elections in October 1993, Mubarak won his third presidential term for another six years. He was the only candidate.

Parliamentary elections in 1987, 1990 and 1995 resulted in overwhelming victory for his National Democratic Party (NDP), but opposition parties continue to protest against what they claim is electoral fraud.

Into the 1990s
Egypt joined Syria in throwing its weight behind the UN alliance aimed at Iraq after the latter's invasion of Kuwait in August 1990. About 35,000 Egyptian troops participated in the fighting in the Gulf War in January and February, and despite dire warnings that the essentially pro-western stance would bring domestic violence, Mubarak's move turned out to be an astute one. It enhanced his position as arbiter in the Middle East and as reliable partner of the west, which brought an immediate reward in the form of US$14,000 million of debt being cancelled. Relations with Libya also improved from the end of 1989 – the borders were opened and ambassadors exchanged.

However, relations with another neighbour, this time Sudan, deteriorated, due in part to the continuing dispute over the jointly administered Halaib region in the south-east corner of Egypt. In 1992, Sudan issued permits for oil exploration to a Canadian consortium in the Halaib region. Egypt declared this illegal after which some shooting broke loose. The dispute heated up in 1993, when Egypt claimed plans were afoot to allow Iran to use Port Sudan as a naval base, and Egyptian troops were reinforced in the Halaib.

It was the failed assassination attempt on Mubarak in July 1995, however, that plunged relations between Egypt and Sudan to an all-time low. The Egyptian government

has long accused Sudan of aiding Islamic militants in Egypt. Following the attempted murder, fighting broke out in the Halaib region and two soldiers were killed. Mubarak meanwhile warned the Sudanese government that Egyptian forces would win swiftly if war erupted. In early 1996, the United Nations Security Council charged Sudan with supporting terrorism and demanded the extradition of three men suspected of involvement in the assassination attempt. Sudan's refusal to comply has further widened the rift.

Pressure at home from Islamists grew in the early 1990s, partly for the usual economic reasons never far below the surface but also, in more recent times, due to the government's repressive crackdown against Islamists. About 150 people, including one British tourist, were killed in violence in 1992, mostly between Islamic fundamentalists and Coptic Christians in Upper Egypt. In response to this security forces carried out massive raids to round up suspects. In one of the most spectacular, 12,000 troops were sent into the Cairo slum of Imbaba.

The Gama'a al-Islamiyya (Islamic Association) and Islamic Jihad (holy war) groups declared war on tourism. Several groups of foreign tourists were shot at or bombed in the last months of 1992 and into 1993. Clashes between the security forces and members of the Islamic fundamentalist groups escalated and, by the end of 1993, another 275 people had died.

At a time when the domestic economy was showing some signs of improvement, the threat to the country's single biggest foreign currency earner encouraged Mubarak to come down hard against the fundamentalists. Waves of arrests led to renewed protests from human rights groups over abuses in Egypt. Amnesty International claims thousands of people, mostly Islamic fundamentalists and other opposition figures, have been arrested under state-of-emergency laws set in place in 1981. In 1994, these laws were extended until mid-1997. Repeated allegations of torture, deaths in custody, and summary executions have been denied by the government.

Despite opposition from human rights groups, the government in 1992 introduced the death sentence for crimes related to terrorism, and trials of suspects were handed over to military courts. By 1995, 66 death sentences had been handed down, and 48 of those had been carried out.

In February 1994, foreign investors and tourists were warned by the Gama'a al-Islamiyya to leave Egypt following a police raid in Cairo in which seven members of the group were killed. Over the next two months, tourist trains and Nile cruisers in Upper Egypt were shot at, bombs exploded in Cairo and a leading politician was killed. Once again, the government responded with a lightning crackdown on suspects, and some 29,000 people were jailed, many in a new purpose-built prison in the desert near Kharga Oasis.

Assuring the world that the 'militants' at home had been all but wiped out, the government turned its attention to the international arena and signed extradition treaties with Pakistan and various other countries in a bid to curtail the activities of Islamists abroad. But the attempt in mid-1995 to assassinate Mubarak while on a visit to Addis Ababa, Ethiopia, followed five months later by the bombing of the Egyptian embassy in Islamabad, Pakistan (in which 15 diplomats and one guard were killed), undermined official claims that the 'militants' were being defeated. They had, instead, simply moved abroad. The Islamic Jihad claimed responsibility for both incidents.

In April 1996, 18 foreign tourists were killed when gunmen opened fire on a hotel in Cairo. The attack further weakened the government's claim that the Islamists had been 'utterly crushed'.

GEOGRAPHY

Egypt is almost square in shape and covers roughly one million sq km. The distance from north to south is 1030 km (640 miles); from east to west in the north it's 965 km (600 miles) and 1240 km (770 miles) in the south.

For most Egyptians the Nile Valley – a strip of fertile land which, for the most part, ranges from 20 to 30 km in width – is Egypt. To the east of the valley is the Eastern (Arabian) Desert – a barren plateau bounded on its eastern edge by a high ridge of mountains which rise to over 2000m and extend for some 800 km. To the west is the Western (Libyan) Desert – a plateau punctuated by huge clumps of bizarre geological formations and luxuriant oases.

North of Cairo, the Nile splits into several tributaries, the main two being the Rosetta and the Damietta branches. Here the valley becomes a 200 km-wide delta, a vast green fan of fertile countryside, and the tributaries eventually flow into the Mediterranean. It is believed that the Delta is what remains of a Mediterranean bay that may once have extended as far south as modern Cairo.

Along the northern coast to the west of Alexandria there are hundreds of km of brilliant white-sand beaches. Some have been, or are being, developed as resorts, but a good deal of this coast is still fairly isolated. Land mines, however, are a danger along this stretch of coast (as they are in parts of Sinai). For more details see the Dangers & Annoyances section in the Facts for the Visitor chapter.

To the east, across the Suez Canal, is Sinai. Terrain here slopes from the high mountain ridges, which include Mt Sinai and Mt Catherine (or Gebel Katherina – the highest in Egypt, at 2642m), in the south to desert coastal plains and lagoons in the north. The jagged mountains and wadis (watercourses) around Mt Sinai appear to change shape and colour as the sun passes overhead, and a climb to the top offers a commanding view of this spectacle. Moses certainly chose the right mountain to climb.

CLIMATE

Egypt's climate is easy to summarise. Most of the year, except for the winter months of December, January and February, it is hot and dry. Temperatures increase as you travel south from Alexandria. Average temperatures range from 20°C (68°F) on the

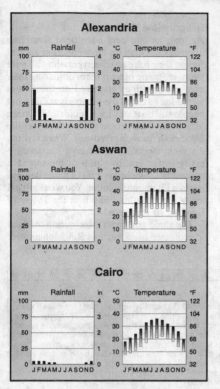

Alexandria

Rainfall — Temperature

Aswan

Rainfall — Temperature

Cairo

Rainfall — Temperature

often dusty wind that can blow in from the parched Western Desert at up to 150 km per hour.

ECOLOGY & ENVIRONMENT

It is unfortunate and ironic that so many of those animals worshipped by the ancients are extinct in modern Egypt.

Richard Hoath

Despite being a signatory to various international conventions aimed at protecting vulnerable or endangered species, Egypt still has a significant way to go as far as awareness and protection of the environment is concerned.

Migrating birds are being killed in massive numbers while en route through this corner of the African continent, despite Egypt having signed the Bonn Convention (to protect migrating birds). Ivory is still traded in shops, even though Egypt agreed to the Convention on the International Trade in Endangered Species of Wild Fauna and Flora (CITES) which outlawed the sale of elephant products in 1989. And, in blatant disregard to the Convention on Wetlands of International Importance (better known as RAMSAR), which was ratified in 1971, waterfowl are hunted in a protected breeding area.

Furthermore, reefs of the Red Sea are under enormous threat from irresponsible tourism and opportunistic development. Landfilling has been one of the biggest causes of reef destruction, with earth being dumped onto fringing reefs (a side effect of this practice is that sediments settle on and choke the millions of polyps that comprise the reef). Freshwater lakes are being poisoned by industrial and agricultural toxins, and air pollution in Cairo is so thick that it's eating away at the antiquities.

Very little is being done by the government to tackle these problems, although the Egyptian Environmental Affairs Agency (EEAA) is becoming more and more vocal over issues such as the development of a sustainable wildlife strategy in Egypt and the protection of the Red Sea reefs. Neverthe-

Mediterranean coast to 26°C (80°F) in Aswan. Maximum temperatures for the same places can get up to 31°C (88°F) and 50°C (122°F) respectively. At night in winter the temperature sometimes plummets to as low as 8°C, even in the south. It can get quite chilly in Cairo, and downright cold along the Mediterranean coast in winter – even well into spring. In the desert it's even more extreme – often scorching in the day and bitterly cold at night (for details on Sinai see that chapter).

Alexandria receives the most rain – approximately 19 cm a year – while far to the south in Aswan the average is about 10 mm in five years.

Between March and April, the outstanding phenomenon is the *khamsin*, a dry, hot and

less, it took a small nongovernmental organisation, known as HEPCA, to enlist the support of the USA before the Egyptian government even acknowledged that there was a problem at the Red Sea (for more details see the boxed story Rescuing the Red Sea in the Suez Canal & the Red Sea Coast chapter).

On a more positive note, the government has started to designate protected zones, such as the Elba region on the Red Sea coast and the coastal regions of Nabq, Ras Abu Gallum and Dahab in Sinai. However, with the exception of Ras Mohammed National Park on the tip of the Sinai peninsula, where rangers are on patrol, there is still precious little active enforcement of protection laws within these zones.

Responsible Tourism

As long as outsiders have been stumbling upon or searching for the wonders of ancient Egypt, they have also been crawling all over them, chipping bits off them or leaving their own contributions engraved on them. It is forbidden to climb the pyramids at Giza, but people still do it, and local 'guides' will make 'exceptions' for people willing to pay a little baksheesh for such privileges. When visiting the monuments, consider how important it really is for you to climb to the top of a pyramid or take home a bit of stone belonging to a Pharaonic column. You wouldn't get away with anything like it at the Tower of London, so why here?

The same goes with adventuring off-road in protected areas such as Ras Mohammed,

Migratory Birds Under Threat

It is estimated by Egyptian conservationists that some 540,000 small migratory birds are netted each autumn along Egypt's Mediterranean coast between Alexandria and Marsa Matruh. This figure does not include those caught on the return migration in spring, nor bigger birds, nor those captured between Alexandria and Rafah. It's a problem which Egypt must tackle if it is to honour its commitment to safeguarding these migrating birds – many of which are becoming increasingly rare in Europe.

Egypt's Mediterranean coastline is the first port of call for most of these smaller birds as they make their way south to the warm climes of Africa after spending the summer in Europe. For hundreds of thousands of these birds, their first stop on the African continent is also their last. Weary from the long flight across the Mediterranean Sea and eager to touch ground, the birds are easy prey and are caught in well-camouflaged quail nets draped over bushes or set up on the ground. Once netted, the birds' wing feathers are plucked out to prevent them from flying and they are sold live as food at markets in towns throughout the Delta region.

Some of these species, including many of the warblers and shrikes, are protected not only by international conventions but also by Egyptian law. They eat insects and vermin and thus help maintain the region's ecological balance.

Those that escape the nets make prime targets for local hunters. It's not uncommon in rural areas and in towns along the Mediterranean coast to see men and boys shooting at anything that flies past.

The Houbara bustard – protected under Egyptian law.

On the international scene, Egypt is a popular destination for hunters from Italy, Malta and the Gulf States. Gulf princes come for gazelles as well as for the Houbara bustard, a large bird which is extinct in the Gulf States and which is considered by some to be an aphrodisiac when eaten. Both creatures are protected under Egyptian law. In 1995 the government took a stand and banned all foreign hunting expeditions into Sinai and Western Deserts. The result was that less hunters came!

Falcons are also victims of this sport, as many are trapped in Egypt for eventual sale in Saudi Arabia where they're used to hunt game birds. ■

the country's only national park. Don't be swayed by comments like: 'We're in the middle of nowhere and who's going to know anyway'. It's illegal to drive off the beaten tracks and the fragile desert environment needs you to enforce this law.

Rubbish: there's lots of it in Egypt, and tidy-town awards do not feature here. Some of the refuse – plastic mineral water bottles for instance – is actually recycled in many ways, so don't be too quick to point an accusing finger at the Egyptians. However, there is no doubt that inadequate waste disposal and little regard for the environmental issues that have become so popular in the west in the past 20 years produces some ugly sights. More than one traveller has reported being disgusted by the garbage left behind by visitors climbing Mt Sinai. Try not to add to this.

When discussing the problem of waste, it's not surprising that toilets should come up. For a few tips on good toilet practices while you're travelling, see the Toilets section in the Facts for the Visitor chapter.

One of the worst things to happen environmentally in Egypt lately is the discovery of the plastic cup. Coke stands are springing up all over the country and selling the drink in these wasteful containers. It's probably a losing battle, but why not stick to the cheaper bottled stuff? You have a drink and hand the bottle back – much cleaner. You could also consider carrying around your own cup to produce at these stands.

Reef Protection
The natural wonders of the Red Sea parallel (many would say surpass) the splendours of Egypt's pyramids, but, again, care is needed if the delicate world of coral reefs and fish is not to be permanently damaged. Divers and snorkellers should heed the requests of instructors *not* to touch or tread on coral. If you kill the coral, you'll eventually kill or chase off the fish too.

The same principle applies with paying baksheesh to do something you shouldn't be doing, such as breaking off a bit of coral to take home as a souvenir. Doing so is illegal and you can be prosecuted. Don't be tempted to flaunt these rules just because you can bribe someone to get around them.

The boxed Code of Ethics for Reef Protection is a code that everybody needs to have in mind before leaving land – *Take nothing with you, leave nothing behind.*

FLORA & FAUNA
Egypt is often described as being made up of about 94% desert. Such a figure conjures up images of vast, barren wastelands where nothing can live. But that's not necessarily the case. While there are areas which are

---

Code of Ethics for Reef Protection

- Do not collect, remove or damage any material, living or dead (including, for example, coral, shells, fish, plants, fossils).
- Do not touch, kneel on or kick corals. Corals are delicate creatures that are damaged when touched.
- Do not stir up sand as corals use a lot of energy to remove sand particles and this, in turn, interferes with their feeding and reduces their growth.
- Do not disturb any part of the reef community by, for example, picking up and playing with sea creatures.
- Do not litter.
- Do not walk or anchor on any reef area. Try to time snorkelling with the high tide, so that you can swim, rather than walk, over the living reef to get to a good drop off.
- Do not feed fish. This disturbs the reef's ecological balance and can upset the digestive system and natural behaviour of marine creatures.
- Do not fish or spearfish, but do report spearfishing.

extremely arid and incapable of supporting life, there are also plenty of desert regions where fragile ecosystems have adapted over millennia to extremely hostile conditions. For more information on desert flora, see the boxed story Balancing Sinai's Ecosystem in the Sinai chapter.

If you're only on a brief visit to Egypt, it may be worthwhile getting hold of Richard Hoath's column entitled Nature Notes, which is published in the *Egypt Today* magazine monthly. His column generally features creatures – many of them migratory – which you might see in Egypt at that particular time of the year.

Flora

The lotus that symbolises ancient Egypt can be found, albeit rarely, in the Delta area, but the papyrus reed, depicted in ancient art as vast swamps where the Pharaohs hunted hippos, has been lost. Except for one clump found in 1968 in Wadi Natrun, papyrus can only be found in botanical gardens or places like Dr Ragab's Papyrus Institute in Cairo.

More than a hundred kinds of grasses thrive in areas where there is water, and the date palm is to be seen in virtually every cultivable area. Along with tamarisk and acacia, the imported jacaranda and poinciana (red and orange flowers) have come to mark Egyptian summers with their vivid colours. You'll also see a water hyacinth, known as the 'Nile rose', choking parts of the Nile and many canals.

In Ras Mohammed National Park in Sinai, there is a stand of mangroves which, according to environmentalists, is the second most northerly mangrove group in the world. These trees live in salt water and are extremely important to the area's ecosystem.

Plants and herbs with medicinal properties are used for trade among the Bedouins.

Papyrus

Cyperus papyrus is a tall aquatic plant which grows on river banks and marshes in tropical Africa and in the south-eastern corner of the Mediterranean region. In early times, the stem marrow was eaten and the narrow stem itself used for wickerwork or, since about 2400 BC, for writing material. For producing the latter, the stem of the papyrus was cut into pieces, split lengthwise and folded open. Several of these strips were joined using plant sap, and then a second layer was applied across the first, after which it was pressed, dried and polished. The side with the horizontal fibres was used to write on. Papyrus was commonly used in this form by the ancient Egyptians, as well as the Greeks, Romans and Phoenicians. ■

The papyrus reed – once commonly found throughout the Nile Valley.

Fauna

Mammals Egypt is home to about a hundred types of mammals. There are still a few exotic species about, however, the most common critters are house mice, black and brown rats, and bats. Besides these, you'll be lucky to see anything other than camels, donkeys, and to a lesser extent domesticated horses and buffalo.

Egypt's deserts used to be sanctuaries for an amazing variety of larger mammals, such as leopards, cheetahs, oryx, aardwolves (which feed on termites), striped hyenas and caracals (a desert lynx with long black ear tufts). All of these, however, have been brought to the brink of extinction due to persecution by hunters. In fact, there's only one known family of cheetahs still living in Egypt, and many years have passed since a leopard was sighted. Other creatures such as the sand cat (the soles of whose feet are covered in fur to aid hunting), the Fennec fox (the world's smallest vulpine) and the Nubian ibex (the males of this species have long, back-swept horns) are sighted, albeit rarely.

There are three types of gazelle in Egypt – the Arabian, dorcas and white. The first species is thought to be extinct, and of the other two groups only individual sightings are made these days, despite the fact that herds of Dorcas gazelle were, up until 30 or so years ago, common features of the desert landscape.

The zorilla, a kind of weasel, lives in the Gebel Elba region while in Sinai you may see rock hyraxes – small creatures about the size of a large rabbit which, like elephants (whom they're most closely related to!), live in large groups and are extremely sociable.

Birds Bird life is rich, with about 430 species having been sighted in Egypt. About one third of these species actually breed in Egypt while most of the others are passage migrants or winter visitors. Each year, an estimated one to two million large birds migrate via certain routes from Europe to Africa through Egypt. Most large birds, including flamingo, storks, cranes, herons, and all large birds of prey are protected under Egyptian law.

The most ubiquitous birds are the house sparrow and the hooded crow, however, one of the most distinctive is the hoopoe. This cinnamon-toned bird has a head shaped very much like a hammer and, when excited, it extends its crest. Hoopoes are often seen hunting for insects in gardens in central Cairo, though they're more commonly found in the countryside.

Bird-watchers should keep their eyes open in particular during autumn and spring, however, at any time of the year, Lake Qarun in the Al-Faiyum region is a good place for watching, with birds ranging from spoon-bills to marsh sandpipers. The saltwater lagoons in the northern Delta and the Zaranik Reserve on Lake Bardawil in northern Sinai are home to such creatures as the greater flamingo, white pelicans and spoonbills (all winter visitors). It's also possible to see huge flocks of pelicans around the small lakes near Abu Simbel in southern Egypt. On star-filled nights in the desert you may see, or hear,

eagle owls. The Gebel Elba region is renowned for tropical birds such as the shining sunbird, the Nubian nightjar and the Sudanese golden sparrow.

The sacred ibis, worshipped by the ancient Egyptians as the living image of Thoth, can still be found in Sudan but it is extinct in Egypt.

Marine Life The Red Sea is teeming with an amazing spectacle of colour and form. Reef sharks, stingrays, turtles, dolphins, colourful corals, sponges, sea cucumbers and a multitude of molluscs all thrive in these waters.

Coral is what makes a reef and, though thought for many centuries to be some form of flowering plant, it is in fact an animal. Both hard and soft corals exist, their common denominator being that they are made up of polyps – tiny cylinders ringed by waving tentacles that sting their prey and draw it into the stomach. During the day corals retract into their tube and only at night do they display their real colours.

There are about a thousand fish species in the Red Sea, many of them are endemic. Most of them are closely associated to the coral reef, and live and breed in the reefs or nearby beds of seagrass. These include grouper, wrasse, parrotfish and snapper. Others, such as the shark and barracuda species, live in open waters and usually only venture into the reefs to feed or breed.

When snorkelling or diving, the sharks you're most likely to encounter include white or black-tipped reef sharks. Tiger sharks, and the huge, plankton-eating whale sharks, are generally found in deeper waters only. No divers or snorkellers have ever been killed by sharks in the Red Sea, and there are no sea snakes here.

The most common type of turtle in these waters is the green turtle, although the leatherback and hawksbill are occasionally sighted. Turtles are protected in Egypt and, although they're not deliberately hunted, they are sometimes caught in nets and end up on menus in restaurants in Cairo and along the coasts.

As pretty as they seem to be, there are

some creatures that should be avoided, especially sea urchins, blowfish, fire coral, feathery lionfish, moray eels, turkeyfish, stonefish, triggerfish and, needless to say, sharks. Familiarise yourself with pictures of these creatures before snorkelling or diving. Providing you don't touch things, or stand on the reef or attempt to feed a moray eel, you shouldn't have too many worries with these creatures.

Other Creatures Some 34 species of snakes live in Egypt. The best known is the cobra, which featured on the headdress of the ancient Pharaohs. Another one to keep an eye on is the horned viper, a thickset snake which has horns over its eyes to keep the sand out when it buries itself.

There are plenty of scorpions throughout the country and, although some are capable of a fatal sting, they're largely nocturnal and rarely seen. Be careful if lifting up stones as they like to burrow into cool spots.

Once plentiful up and down the length of the Nile, crocodiles have been extinct north of the Aswan Dam since 1891 when the last one was shot by a British officer. These days they are protected, and live only in Lake Nasser south of the High Dam near Aswan.

National Parks & Protected Areas

Egypt's only national park is Ras Mohammed (for details see the Sinai chapter), however, there are about 18 other 'protected' regions dotted throughout Egypt including Nabq, Ras Abu Gallum and Dahab.

Gebel Elba, the only habitat in Egypt for birds from the African tropics, has been protected since the mid-1980s as has the Zaranik Reserve on Lake Bardawil. The latter is an important waterfowl habitat and the only wetlands area in Egypt which is protected under the RAMSAR convention. Despite this, however, bird netting was carried out here in 1995.

A cluster of islands just south of Aswan is also protected as it boasts the only original Nile vegetation remaining in Egypt. Elsewhere, about 95% of the vegetation has been introduced.

GOVERNMENT & POLITICS

The present constitution was introduced in 1971, although it has been amended since. The bulk of power is concentrated in the hands of the president, who is nominated by the People's Assembly and elected by popular referendum for six years. This term can be renewed at least once, although Mubarak decided to go for a third term in 1993. The president appoints vice presidents and ministers, as well as 10 members of the 454-member People's Assembly and 70 of the 210-member Majlis ash-Shura (Advisory Council).

In the elections of 1984 and 1987, parties had to achieve at least 8% of the vote to enter parliament, which discriminated against small parties and independents (both these elections were declared unconstitutional and the parliaments did not sit for their full term). The two most recent elections in 1990 and 1995 have not been run on party lists. Instead, candidates stand as independents and parties may endorse them as they please.

Elections are supervised by the Ministry of the Interior, and President Mubarak's National Democratic Party (NDP) won an overwhelming majority of seats in the assembly in 1995. An independent monitoring group, however, claimed the election was rigged and clearly biased towards the NDP.

Mubarak himself admits democracy in Egypt is 'limited', although he has loosened controls on opposition parties considerably since he came to power in 1981. All political parties had been banned in 1953 and only allowed to operate again by Anwar Sadat in 1977. The government NDP was formed the following year.

The main opposition party is the Wafd, followed by the Muslim Brotherhood. As a religious group, the Muslim Brotherhood is outlawed but officially tolerated. Its relations with the government improved slightly in the early 1990s as the group is seen as a comparatively moderate Islamic force. However, in 1995, the government once again cracked down on the group and, immediately prior to the 1995 election, many nonviolent members, including doctors and lawyers, were rounded up and sentenced to imprisonment with hard labour for holding 'secret meetings'.

The republic is divided into 25 *muhafazat*, or governorates, for administrative purposes.

The Egyptian flag is composed of three horizontal bands: red, white and black. In the white band stands an eagle (before 1984 it was a falcon and before that a star).

ECONOMY

Initiated by Anwar Sadat, a process of gradual economic reform has been continued by Hosni Mubarak, in an attempt not only to reduce the Nasserist state-run sector and huge subsidies, but to ease Egypt into a market economy and reduce dependence on foreign aid. Responding to oft-repeated frustration on the part of the International Monetary Fund (IMF) and others at the slow pace of reform, Mubarak has said too rapid a change to a free economy would do more harm than good, and pointed to the experience of eastern European economies, which have so precipitately dived into the free market whirlpool since 1989.

The slowly-slowly approach has not been without fruit. The Public Enterprise Office is in charge of putting about US$50,000 million of state assets up for sale. The sale of some top hotels to private enterprise, as well as two bottling companies in 1994, is seen as a sign of growing foreign interest in investment in Egypt. Exchange, tax and banking laws are being relaxed, and the Egyptian pound is all but fully convertible. What has surprised most observers is that it has managed to remain largely unchanged against hard currencies since about mid-1991.

Nasser's legacy was not all bad. The High Dam at Aswan, for instance, greatly increased the amount of land available for regular cultivation and doubled Egypt's power generation capacity. Begun in 1961 and in commission by 1971, it had already paid for itself by 1974.

A less happy result of Nasser's socialism was the growth of an enormous bureaucracy, stacked with people without anything to do,

and a system of subsidies for a whole range of basic and not-so-basic products.

Of a total official workforce of about 15 million, some five million are employed by the state. The 20% official unemployment rate was exacerbated by the return of 600,000 Egyptians from Iraq and Kuwait during the Gulf War, who not only swelled the ranks of the jobless, but were no longer sending remittances home. If any serious attempt were made to streamline the public sector, unemployment would soar.

The subject of subsidies is the thorniest. With an eye to a population already hard pressed, successive governments have been loath to attack this side of the economy with too much zeal. Under pressure from the IMF, however, Mubarak has systematically reduced the subsidies and so seen prices rise without exciting, yet, too much trouble among the populace. In spite of the price rises, inflation has dropped from more than 30% in the 1980s to about 11% by 1994.

Circumstances have also played in Egypt's favour. The loss of business and aid from Kuwait because of the Gulf War was not nearly as bad as expected. Although lost tourist trade and remittances cost an estimated US$2.4 billion in 1990, Gulf and western states agreed to wipe about US$14 billion (a quarter) of Egypt's debt for services rendered in the war.

Egypt is a big exporter of cotton, selling 1½ times what the USA sells overseas. However, the industry is facing trouble as farmers turn to other crops such as wheat, which is a popular alternative, although Egypt is still a large net importer of the grain. The wheat crop in 1991 was a record 5.2 million tons, sufficient to cover just over half of the country's consumption. The growing population's demands are being aggravated by higher per capita consumption. Other important crops include various fruits, especially citrus, as well as vegetables, rice and sugar cane.

The limits on available land are being pushed as far as possible, with intense crop rotation and complex irrigation (a project launched in 1992 and expected to be finished in 1997, the 'Suez Siphon', envisages diverting Nile water under the Suez Canal to Sinai). Areas to the south-west of Alexandria, around the Delta and the belt of oases, are also targeted for greater irrigation programmes.

Industry still lags behind. Textiles account for 16% of output. Cement, steel, iron, arms and vehicles are all produced.

Egypt is a net exporter of oil, and more oil and gas finds in the Western Desert have boosted hopes of continuing export profits to be made from that sector. Other raw materials mined include iron ore, manganese, phosphates, chromium and small amounts of coal. Some uranium has also been found in Sinai.

The Suez Canal is Egypt's largest single foreign currency earner. In 1994, the Suez Canal was widened to accommodate bigger ships, however, the second stage of the expansion, which will permit it to handle the biggest tankers and cargo vessels plying the world's waters, has been delayed. Although an expensive undertaking, it may well eventually pay for itself. Dues from commercial users now amount to more than US$2 billion per year.

A rapidly expanding sector is tourism and, by the end of 1997, Egypt hopes to have increased the number of hotel rooms from 70,000 to 110,000; by the year 2000, authorities hope the annual number of tourists will have reached six million. In 1992, just under three million tourists piled in. However, attacks by Islamic extremists on tourists between 1992 and 1994 put a brake on foreign visitors. Tourist numbers fell by an estimated 40% in 1993 as tour operators pulled out and travellers stayed away in droves. With the prospect of continued growth in tourism revenue (it was almost US$1 billion in 1990 and 1991) suddenly under threat, the authorities tried, as they sent thousands of troops off on the hunt for suspects, to calm fears by saying most of the attacks had occurred in out-of-the-way places. A series of shooting and bombing attacks in Cairo, Luxor and Hurghada gave the lie to that claim, but the Egyptian press

maintained (perhaps rightly) that Cairo was still a much safer place for a foreigner than New York or London.

Despite the continuing violence, tourism is again on the increase. The government reported a 20% growth in tourist numbers in 1995 compared with the previous years. However the shooting of 18 tourists in April 1996 could once again put the brakes on the tourist sector.

POPULATION

Egypt is the most populous country in the Arab world and has the second highest population in Africa after Nigeria. Its population has, in a sense, become its greatest problem. From about 6½ million people at the first census in 1882, the population was estimated at around 60 million in 1995. It is predicted by some to reach 65 million by the year 2000. With annual growth of about 2.3% (down from 2.8% in the 1980s) – something more than a million every year – it hardly seems to matter what Egypt does to improve its economic situation; the gains are always eaten up by the extra mouths to feed and people to house.

About 18 million (some estimates say 22 million) people live in the greater Cairo area and about a further five million in Alexandria and outlying zones. One result of the rapid population growth is that half the population is now under 18 years, and the government hasn't been able to construct schools and train teachers quickly enough to keep up. Something like 99% of the population occupies only 4 to 6% of the total surface area of the country, which corresponds to the cultivable area, although various projects are in place to expand this and make it more productive.

PEOPLE

Anthropologists divide the Egyptian people very roughly into three racial groups, of which the biggest is descended from the Hamito-Semitic race that has peopled the Nile (as well as many other parts of north Africa and neighbouring Arabia) for millennia. Included in this race are the Berbers, a minority group who settled around Siwa in the country's Western Desert. The second group, the truly Arab element, is made up of the Bedouin Arab nomads who migrated from Arabia and who also live in desert areas, particularly Sinai. The third group are the Nubians, in the Aswan area. Of course there has been much intermingling and many other peoples have come and gone, leaving their own contributions.

Berbers

A small number of Berbers who settled in the west of the country, particularly in and around Siwa, have retained much of their own identity. They are quite easily distinguished from other Egyptians by, for instance, the dress of the women – usually *melayas* – head-to-toe garments with slits for the eyes. Although many speak Arabic, they have preserved their own language.

Bedouins

Nearly 500,000 Bedouins survive in the harshest, most desolate parts of the Western and Eastern deserts and Sinai. But, despite being the country's most isolated population group, Egypt's economic problems have also begun to affect the Bedouins. The Western Desert oases have long been slated for massive agricultural development and resettlement to ease urban overcrowding, and there are also plans to increase tourism in this region. Likewise, in Sinai, plans to start resettlement programmes are being drawn up, and tourism has already taken off, particularly in the south-eastern coast, which is rapidly becoming a stretch of tourist resorts. With the influx of outsiders into their previously isolated domains, the Bedouins are gradually becoming more settled and less self-sufficient. For more details on these people, see the boxed story in the Sinai chapter.

Nubians

The original people of Nubia, the region between Aswan in the south of Egypt and Khartoum in Sudan which was known in ancient times as Cush, had for millennia inhabited the middle reaches of the Nile. Their traditional way of life – based on agriculture, fishing and the transport of goods up and down the Nile – existed virtually unchanged until early this century when the Aswan Dam was built. As the waters gradually rose, the Nubians' homeland was consumed; the final assault came with the building of the High Dam near Aswan in 1971, which entirely devoured their traditional lands. Many of the 60,000 or more displaced people were resettled in Aswan and around Kom Ombo, while others were repatriated to Sudan.

EDUCATION

Although nine years of primary school education are supposedly compulsory in Egypt, and about 97% of children from six to 15 attend school, the adult illiteracy rate was estimated by UNESCO to be 50% in 1992. To westerners that may seem startlingly high, but 16 years earlier the level was 61.8%! Two-thirds of Egypt's illiterates are women.

Those who are literate have usually received inferior education because classes are often too large for individual attention.

Secondary education lasts for six years, beginning at 11 years of age. There are 13 universities. Education is free at all levels, which is perhaps why it is not uncommon to find lawyers, engineers and other professionals working for their 'brother's factory' or shops in tourist areas – there is often nothing for Egypt's educated to do. Many of its professionals (and a good number of its less educated people) are compelled to seek work in other Arab countries – more than two million are said to be abroad, the bulk of them in the Gulf States, Libya and, despite harassment, in Iraq.

Males are generally subject to three years' military service, but those who complete high school are permitted to complete only two years, and university students only one.

ARTS
Painting

Painting was first incorporated into Egyptian

tomb art in the 24th century BC in the Pyramid of Unas at Saqqara. However, it was the Pharaohs of the New Kingdom era (1550 to 1150 BC) who really brought this art to the fore, adorning the interiors of their tombs with spectacular images of the netherworld and resurrection. You'll find no better example of this than the reliefs in the Tomb of Nefertari in the Valley of the Queens near Luxor.

Contemporary Egyptian painting continued to be heavily influenced by foreign artists right up until the mid-1900s. It wasn't until 1946, when the Contemporary Egyptian Art Group was formed by a group of leading artists such as Hamid Nada and Abdel Hadi al-Gazzar, that modern art emphasised local themes drawn from the country's heritage rather than foreign concepts.

Some of the better known contemporary female artists include Gazbia Serri and Inji Eflatoun (who died in 1989), while male artists of note include Abdel Wahab Morsi, Adel el-Siwi and Wahib Nassar. The latter lives in the Netherlands and paints under the name of the rebellious Pharaoh, Akhenaten.

For more on contemporary artists, Fatma Ismail's *29 Artists in the Museum of Egyptian Modern Art* explores the 1960s to the early 1990s.

Music

Up until the 1980s, popular Egyptian music centred around the voice of Om Kolthum, or the 'mother of Egypt' as she was also known. In fact, Om Kolthum's following was much wider than just Egypt and when she died in 1975, leaders from all over the Arab world descended on Cairo to pay homage. Her music, based on poetry and operettas that seemingly meandered for hours, lives on and, for westerners, it epitomises and simplifies the mystery and complexity of Arabic music.

While Om Kolthum remains top of the tree, there are many other popular names in the often parallel worlds of Egyptian and Arab music. Abdel Halim al-Hafez (1927 to 1977), dubbed the 'dark nightingale' and

Mohammed Abd el-Wahaab (1910 to 1991) were two of Om Kolthum's highly respected contemporaries, as was Fareed al-Atrash, whose voice is almost as well known and universally loved as that of Om Kolthum. Fairouz and Dalida (actually French) have also left a lasting imprint on Egypt's musical heritage and that of the Arab world.

More contemporary popular music retains its essential Middle Eastern characteristics but, increasingly, is being influenced by western pop. It appears to be an acquired taste, and many westerners find it pretty awful stuff. However, among the Egyptian youth, music known as *al-jeel* and *shaabi* have found mass support. Al-jeel is basically Egyptian pop and two of the names to look for are Iheb Tawfik and Mohammed Fouad. Shaabi is the music of the overcrowded, working-class quarters of Cairo and other large cities and is typically humorous and provocative – both politically and socially – which means many lyrics in these songs don't get past the censors. The charismatic Ahmed Adaweea was one of the founders of this genre.

Traditional Egyptian music is as diverse as the country's ethnic groups, with the Bedouins, Nubians and Sufis all having their own distinct instruments and music. Popular folkloric music centred around the *nay* (flute), the *oud* (lute) and the *tar* (tambourine). These instruments would be used by *chaer*, or itinerant musicians, who would wander from festival to festival, gripping audiences for hours with their songs and stories.

Dance

Dancing is generally considered promiscuous by Egyptians although at weddings, private parties and other family gatherings, dancing comprises a large part of the fun. In contrast, one sector of society that totally embraces dancing are the Sufis, adherents of a Muslim mystical order which emphasises dancing as a direct personal experience of God.

There are a few Egyptian dance troupes of both men and women that perform in Cairo,

Luxor and Aswan during the winter and in Alexandria during the summer. Otherwise, belly-dancing shows, put on at most of Cairo's major hotels and in resorts along the coasts, are about it. When watching one you will think you have landed on a Hollywood movie set. Many of the dancers will be European or American, because it is considered improper for an Arab woman to dance in public. In fact, in recent times, many belly dancers have chosen to cover their voluptuous stomachs in order to diminish the threat of attack from Islamic fundamentalists. Star dancers like Fifi Abdou have also taken to hiring bodyguards.

It comes as no surprise that the audiences are made up mainly of men, although by western measures of the erotic, the performances are tame. As the dancer swirls around in front of a full band, with the odd inebriated local getting up to join in, a male singer croons in the background. He or a presenter usually takes care of business, raking in the cash tributes pouring in from the men in the audience. At the big hotels and nightclubs along Pyramids Rd in Cairo, Gulf Arabs have been known to literally shower dancers with money.

Cinema & TV

Foreigners learning Arabic are often advised to learn the Egyptian dialect, as it is supposed to be understood in most parts of the Arab world. The reason is simple. Most of the TV shows Arabs watch and Arabic-language movies that have hit the screens over the past six decades have come from Egypt.

Om Kolthum's popularity extends across the Arab world due in part to her movies – often Egyptian versions of the musicals that used to pour out of Hollywood. Another famous face is that of Fareed al-Atrash, Om Kolthum's male equivalent. Old B&W musicals starring one, the other or both regularly appear on Egyptian TV.

Egypt's first locally produced film was *Laila* (1927) by female producer, Aziza Amir. In the wake of Om Kholthum's popularity, the number of films produced skyrocketed and, by the 1960s, some 300 movies a year were being produced. While many of them were melodramatic musicals, which either started or ended with a wedding party complete with belly dancers, others were realistic portrayals of society.

One of the nation's best known contemporary film-makers is Youssef Chahine, who emerged during the 1940s and whose films are fairly accessible to western audiences. His international breakthrough came with *Heaven or Hell*, starring Egypt's premier acting export, Omar Sherif, and was followed by notable works such as *The Sparrow* (1973) and, more recently, the controversial *El-Mohager* (The Emigrant). Those wondering what happened to Omar Sherif may be interested to know that he's still making films in Cairo.

These days, Egypt's film industry is unfortunately in a slump. The number of films being made has fallen greatly in recent years and quality, too, has declined, with cheap, melodramatic films back in fashion.

Literature

Egypt's most well-known writer in the west is Naguib Mahfouz, the Nobel laureate who has captured people's imagination with his stories, often of very ordinary lives in the poor parts of central Cairo, his stamping ground (for more details see the boxed story Naguib Mahfouz – Cairo's Dickens & Nobel Laureate, following).

Edward Kharrat, an Alexandrian, is another writer beginning to command more attention outside his own country. Kharrat is much more of a stylist, his work informed by the classics of Arabic literature, mainly its rich tradition in poetry and the Qur'an (Koran) itself.

The writings of Taha Hussein, a blind author and intellectual who spent much of his life in trouble with whichever establishment happened to be in power, reflect in great part his desire to marry the best of the west with the east.

Other leading authors include Tawfiq al-Hakim, Yahya Haqqi and the late Yusuf Idris, who told powerful short stories which reflected experiences in his own life (two to

꓄ ꓄ ꓄ ꓄ ꓄ ꓄ ꓄ ꓄ ꓄ ꓄ ꓄ ꓄ ꓄

Naguib Mahfouz – Cairo's Dickens & Nobel Laureate

Naguib Mahfouz was awarded the 1988 Nobel Prize in Literature for *The Cairo Trilogy* (comprising *Palace Walk*, *Palace of Desire* and *Sugar Street*), works that many compare to those of Dickens or Balzac. According to the Swedish Academy, his novels are 'rich in nuance – now clear-sightedly realistic, now evocatively ambiguous...his work speaks to us all'. Mahfouz takes pleasure in using the language of the people, dialect and slang, to make his characters live. By 1996, he had 40 novels and short-story collections and 30 screenplays to his name.

Other works by Mahfouz which provide insightful perspectives on life in Egypt include *Midaq Alley*, *Miramar* and *The Thief & the Dogs*. *Midaq Alley* portrays a poor back-alley neighbourhood in Islamic Cairo. The book focuses on the life of a girl who gets engaged to the local barber but becomes a prostitute while her fiancé is off earning money for their future together. *Miramar* presents a microcosm of Egyptian society through the story of a young girl from the countryside who flees to Alexandria to avoid an arranged marriage. *The Thief & the Dogs* is a critical, somewhat cynical, psychological study of a man who was wrongfully imprisoned for several years and then set free. His new life becomes a symbolic quest for justice.

While the west has embraced Mahfouz's works, at home his popularity is polarised. His 1959 novel, *The Sons of Gaballawi*, is banned in Egypt as the authorities consider it blasphemous. Others, it seems, rate it worse than that. In 1994, the then 83-year-old author was stabbed as he walked down a street in Cairo. Although no-one claimed responsibility, it's believed his attacker was attempting to carry out a death sentence ordered by Omar Abdel Rahman, the spiritual leader of Gama'a al-Islamiyya who, in early 1996, was sentenced to life imprisonment by a court in the US for masterminding a plan to blow up several New York landmarks, including the UN headquarters. In 1989, Rahman announced that Mahfouz should be killed unless he repented for writing the book. ■

꓄ ꓄ ꓄ ꓄ ꓄ ꓄ ꓄ ꓄ ꓄ ꓄ ꓄ ꓄ ꓄

women means her popularity is considerably less widespread at home). El-Saadawi is a psychiatrist, feminist, novelist and writer of nonfiction. *The Hidden Face of Eve: Women in the Arab World* was the first of her numerous works to be translated into English. It considers the role of women in world history, Arab history and literature, and contemporary Egypt. All her books, many of which have been translated into several languages, are well worth reading for the insight they provide into the lives of women in the Arab world. Her most recent title is *The Innocence of the Devil*, published in 1994, but her most acclaimed works are *Point Zero*, *The Fall of the Imam* (banned in Egypt) and *Death of an ex-Minister*.

Islamic Architecture

Pharaonic monuments and the work behind them are discussed at length throughout the book, as well as in the Pharaonic Egypt section, but there is another side to monumental Egypt that often passes less noticed. Cairo is one of the greatest repositories in the world of Islamic, and especially medieval, architecture.

The earliest construction efforts undertaken by Muslims – more often than not mosques – inherited much from Christian and Graeco-Roman models. However, various styles soon developed and owed increasingly less to their architectural forebears.

Mosques are generally built around an open courtyard, off which lie one or more *iwan* (covered halls). The iwan facing Mecca is the focal point of prayer. A vaulted niche in the wall called the mihrab indicates the kibla (the direction of Mecca, which Muslims must face when they pray). Islam does not know priests as such, but the closest equivalent is the mosque's imam, a man schooled in Islam who often doubles as the muezzin, who calls the faithful to prayer. At the main Friday prayers in particular, the imam gives a *khutba* (sermon) from the *minbar* – the pulpit raised above a narrow staircase, better examples of which are ornately decorated.

look out for are *The Cheapest Nights* and *Rings of Burnished Brass*).

On a more rebellious note is Nawal El-Saadawi, arguably Egypt's best known writer abroad after Mahfouz (though her constant championing of the rights of

The mosque also serves as a kind of community centre, and often you'll find groups of children or adults receiving lessons (usually in the Qur'an), people in quiet prayer and others simply sheltering in the tranquil peace of the mosque.

The minaret (from the word *manara*, meaning lighthouse) most often consists of a square base leading to more slender cylindrical or hexagonal stages. Most have internal staircases for the muezzin to climb (the advent of the microphone saves them that effort now) to the top.

The decoration of mosques and many other public buildings is an exercise in geometric virtuosity. As Islam frowns on the artistic representation of living beings, the art of carving out complex arabesques of vines, palms and other flora in various deceptive designs merged with a growing tradition of highly intricate decorative calligraphy. Much of the decoration along the top end of walls is more or less stylised verses from the Qur'an. The phrase *la illah illa Allah* (there is no God but Allah), appears in a seemingly unlimited variety of designs as an integral part of decoration, fusing religious precept and the very reference to God with the art that exalts Him.

The carved woodwork ceilings in some iwans sometimes display painstaking, again largely geometric, and graceful decoration.

The same guidelines in decoration influenced domestic building as well, and can be seen in some of the grander Ottoman residences that have survived in Cairo and other cities. The most outstanding feature of these is the *mashrabiyyah*, the intricately carved wooden screen most often used on balconies and windows to hide women while they looked out upon the goings on in the streets below them.

The biggest concentration of medieval Islamic architecture is to be found in the area known as Islamic Cairo (see the Islamic Cairo section in the Cairo chapter).

SOCIETY & CONDUCT
Traditional Culture
The main events of life – birth, marriage and death – and principal daily concerns – family, friends and food – are most important in Egyptian society. The future is not, because it will not be much different from the past or present. This apparent nonchalance, fatalism, apathy – call it what you wish – seems to come from a centuries-old capacity for letting life flow by, a little like the Nile, in its own inevitable way. From plagues to invasion, floods to drought, Egypt and its people have seen it all, and it is as though the present generations had inherited a seen-it-all-before attitude from their forbears. There are three commonly used words which seem to sum up this attitude: *insha-allah* (if God wills it); *bukra* (tomorrow); and *maalesh* (never mind, it doesn't matter, or pardon).

Egyptians of both sexes dress conservatively, whether they be in rural or urban areas. Rural men usually get around in long, flowing robes known as *galabiyyas*; their urban counterparts dress in long pants and shirts. You'll rarely see an Egyptian man wearing shorts except perhaps at the beach. Women, too, are almost always well-covered, even the rare ones who frolic in the waves along the Mediterranean coast. And, while many women in the 1980s discarded their *hejab* (head covering), the success of recent demands by Islamists that women dress more modestly is becoming obvious, as increasing numbers of women in Cairo once again adopt the hejab and long-sleeved blouses.

While westerners find female circumcision barbaric and incomprehensible, for many Egyptians it is still a part of their culture. The government and many parents supposedly try to discourage it; they are, however, fighting an age-old tradition. Circumcision is normally carried out by a midwife on girls between about the ages of seven and 12. It's difficult to estimate how many girls are circumcised these days, however, Jan Goodwin in her book, *Price of Honour*, reports that 80% of rural girls and 40% of urban ones are still subject to this custom. In 1995, the government announced that public hospitals would designate one day a week for female circumcision in order to improve the hygienic conditions in which many of the these operations take place.

For information about the nuances in body language between Egyptians and westerners, see the boxed story Understanding Body Language.

Western technology and lifestyles have gained influence in Egypt. The fellahin (peasant farmers) in the countryside, who make up the majority of Egypt's population, have begun using tractors and diesel-powered irrigation pumps in place of ploughs and *sakieh*, the ancient waterwheels powered by buffalo or donkeys (who are sometimes blinded to prevent dizziness).

TV programmes from the west, particularly the USA, have had an incredible impact. At the flick of a switch, a family of fellahin is transported from a mud-brick house in an Upper Egypt village to places like the streets of San Francisco or the living rooms of American families. A lifestyle of previously unimaginable luxury suddenly comes alive on a little screen in front of them and the seed of possibility, the chance of living a 'better' life, is planted. Such images have helped feed a tide of rural migration to the already overcrowded cities, and in some cases enticed Egypt's best educated to seek that better life abroad. These same images have also promoted some pretty distorted ideas about western women and sex (see the Women Travellers section in Facts for the Visitor).

TV and tractors aren't the only western imports. Some people feel Egypt is being 'Coca-Cola-ised' by the trappings of western life. Coca-Cola, colour TVs, VCRs and blue jeans are popular not only for what they are but, more importantly, for what they symbolise – a slice of the 'good' life. Such material goods, and other more ambitious targets, are

---

Understanding Body Language

Walking down a crowded street, you suddenly hear what sounds like a snake hissing copious amounts of spittle in your direction. On turning around, you'll probably find someone on a bicycle is trying to get by – there are few bicycle bells in Egypt. It takes a while to get used to, but it's nothing personal.

There's another kind of hissing, which is the local version of a wolf whistle – there's everything personal about that. Arabs gesticulate a lot in conversation, and some things can be said without uttering a word. Certain expressions also go together with particular gestures.

Egyptians, like most Arabs, often say 'No' merely by raising the eyebrows and lifting the head up and back. This is often accompanied by a 'tsk tsk' noise and it can all be a little off-putting if you're not used to it – don't take it as a snub.

Shaking the head from side to side (as westerners would to say 'No') means 'I don't understand'. Stretching out the hand as if to open a door and giving it a quick flick of the wrist is equivalent to 'What do you want?', 'Where are you going?' or 'What's your problem?'. A combination of the two probably means your interlocutor has not got the foggiest idea of what you're going on about.

Getting flustered invariably excites the mirth of locals, and at the very least an admonition to slow down or take it easy *(shwayya)*, along with a hand signal – palm up, all the fingers and thumb drawn together.

Guys asking directions should not be surprised to be taken by the arm or hand and led along. It is quite natural for men to hold each other by the hand and, despite what you may think, rarely means anything untoward is happening. Which is not to say it *doesn't* happen – and judging between the two kinds of situation requires some subtle thinking, or plain luck! Women should avoid such helpfulness, as more often than not it can spell trouble.

A right hand over your heart means 'no thanks' when you are offered something. When you've had enough tea, Turkish coffee or anything else to drink, you put your hand over the cup.

As the left hand is associated with toilet duties it is considered unclean and so you should always use the right hand when giving or receiving something.

Arrival in one piece is always something to be grateful for. Relieved passengers will often be heard to mutter *ilHamdu lillah 'as-salaama* – 'Thank God we arrived in safety'. ∎

spawning greater motivation to succeed in one way or another, but also contribute to growing anger at the manifest shortcomings in the economy that frustrate people's attempts to improve their lot.

While some Egyptian Muslims have welcomed modernisation, the vast majority, the Muslim fellahin, are distressed by the possibility of sudden changes in a way of life that has remained virtually unaltered for centuries. Some, especially those faced with being at the bottom of Egypt's socioeconomic pyramid, are turning to the extreme Islamic groups. 'Islam is the Solution' is the common cry – to precisely what, one might ask.

Dos & Don'ts

Although increasingly used to the antics of westerners, Egyptians have a different code of behaviour on many subjects and find western ways at best curious or at worst offensive. Dress is the first obvious point. Men will usually have little trouble in (long) shorts, although full-length trousers must be worn in mosques (and often in churches for that matter). Wearing singlets on sunny days may seem the most enjoyable way of dealing with the heat; choose your location. On the main tourist beaches, say in Sinai, and in the larger hotels men will have no trouble. Use your own judgement in the big cities like Cairo, but wear something more modest in the smaller places. The sight of underarms and hairy legs is offensive to Muslims.

Women should pay much greater attention. Wandering around the Khan al-Khalili in short pants and a loose top is the perfect way to attract a maximum of just the kind of attention you don't want. Unless you want hands in all sorts of places, or even worse, cover up. At least knee-length skirts or trousers and, in the more out-of-the-way or conservative places, elbow-length shirts. Covering your hair may help too. There is a constant stream of complaints about Egyptian men, often justified, but there's little point in attracting trouble – see the Women Travellers section in Facts for the Visitor.

Alcohol is quite freely available in Egypt – getting stonkered is not a widespread national pastime, however, so it is advisable not to find yourself reeling around the streets. Just use a little common sense.

If you're invited to someone's home for dinner, you should remove your shoes before entering, as you would before going into a mosque (see the following Religion section). It's polite to offer your host a gift, such as tea or some sweet pastries, and remember not to eat with your left hand.

RELIGION
Islam

Islam is the predominant religion of Egypt. It shares its roots with two of the world's other major religions – Judaism and Christianity. Adam, Abraham (Ibrahim), Noah, Moses and Jesus are all accepted as Muslim prophets, although Jesus is not recognised as the son of God. Muslim teachings correspond closely to the Torah (the first five chapters of the Old Testament and the foundation of the Jewish religion) and the Gospels. However, the essence of Islam is the Qur'an, or Koran, and the prophet Mohammed who was the last and truest prophet to deliver messages from Allah (God) to the people.

Islam was founded in the early 7th century by Mohammed, who was born around 570 AD in Mecca (now in Saudi Arabia). Mohammed got his first revelation at about the age of 40, in the form of a voice telling him to recite. The revelations continued for the rest of Mohammed's life, and the oral recitations were, during and after his lifetime, written down in the Qur'an. To this day not one dot has been changed in the holy Qur'an, and foreign translations are never definitive, merely introductory.

Mohammed began to preach against the idolatry that was rampant in the region, particularly in Mecca, and proved to be a powerful and persuasive speaker. He quickly gained a devoted following. When he died in 632, the new religion continued its rapid spread. Within a decade it had reached Egypt and, within two decades of the Prophet's death, most of Arabia had converted to Islam. In succeeding centuries it spread over three continents. Mecca became Islam's holiest city because it was there that Abraham built the first shrine to Allah.

Islam means 'submission' and this principle is very visibly present in the daily life of Muslims. The faith is expressed by observance of the five so-called pillars of Islam. Muslims must:

Publicly declare that 'there is no God but Allah and Mohammed is his Prophet'.

Pray five times a day: at sunrise, noon, mid-afternoon, sunset, and night.

Give *zakat*, or alms, for the propagation of Islam and for help to the needy.

Fast during the day for the month of Ramadan.

Make the haj (pilgrimage to Mecca).

The first pillar is accomplished through prayer, which is the second pillar. Prayer is an essential part of the daily life of a believer. Five times a day the muezzins bellow out the call to prayer through speakers on top of the minarets. It is perfectly permissible to pray at home or elsewhere – only the noon prayer on Friday should be conducted in the mosque. It is preferred that women pray at home.

The act of praying consists of a series of predefined movements of the body and recitals of prayers and passages of the Qur'an, all designed to express the believer's absolute humility and God's sovereignty. Before entering the mosque, believers take off their shoes and carry them, sole to sole, in the left hand. They enter with the right foot first and then wash to demonstrate the will to be purified – there are fountains or ablutions pools in mosques for this purpose. They then go to

Moulid Celebrations

Literally meaning 'birth', a moulid celebrates the birthday of a local saint or holy person. These annual events are held throughout Egypt by both Muslims and Copts. Those who attend aim to receive *baraka* (blessing), as well as to have a lot of fun. In larger cities, moulids are often riotous affairs, with hundreds of thousands of people coming from far and wide to take part in a frenzy of celebrations ranging from fasting and feasting to prayer and performing *zikrs*.

A zikr (literally mentioning or remembrance) is the communal recitation of the name of God in a bid to reach enlightenment. More often than not it's performed by a group of Sufi believers, known as *mugzzabin* (meaning those drawn in), and can either be a very restrained event or one charged with energy. In the former, mugzzabin stand in straight lines and sway from side to side to the rhythm of clapping. As the clapping gains momentum, the zikr reaches its peak and the mugzzabin, having attained oneness with God, awake sweating and blinking from their trance-like state. Other zikrs are formidable endurance tests where troupes of musicians perform for hours in the company of ecstatic dancers. This sort of zikr occasionally takes a more extreme turn, with people pushing needles and skewers into parts of the face (nose, cheeks) and withdrawing them again leaving no trace and apparently feeling no pain.

Moulids generally take place around the tomb of the venerated saint and the whole scene usually resembles a fair. Those from out of town set up camp in the streets close to the saints' tomb. Childrens' rides, sideshows and food stalls are erected, and *tartours* (cone-shaped hats) and *fanous* (lanterns) are made and sold to passers-by. Much of this infrastructure is provided by 'professional' moulid people who spend their lives going from one moulid to another. Most moulids last for about a week, and climax with the *leila kibeera* (the big night).

For visitors, the hardest part about attending a moulid is ascertaining dates. Events are tied to either the Islamic or Gregorian calendars, and dates can be different each year (see the Public Holidays & Special Events section in the Facts for the Visitor chapter). Also, you'll need to be prepared for immense crowds (hold onto your valuables or, better still, leave them behind) and women should be escorted by a male.

Cairo hosts three of the country's biggest moulids: the Moulid an-Nabi (held during the Islamic month of Rabei al-Awal); the Moulid of Sayyida Zeinab (during Ragab) and the Moulid of el-Hussein (in Rabei at-Tani). Even bigger is the Moulid of Sayyid Ahmed al-Badawi in the Delta town of Tanta which follows the October cotton harvest. The Moulid of Abou el-Haggag in Luxor is also worth catching. ■

the place of prayer, orientate themselves towards Mecca – the proper orientation is indicated by the alignment of the mosque – and perform one or more *rakats*, or cycles of prayer, during which they recite certain passages of the Qur'an, pray, bow and lie prostrate in a series different for each of the day's five prayer times.

About 90% of Egypt's population is Muslim, and almost all are from the Sunni group. Muslims are forbidden to marry Copts or to convert to another religion.

Visiting Mosques Before traipsing through mosques there are a few rules you should be aware of. You cannot visit during prayer time, but any other time is fine. Nor can you visit all mosques; some of those not designated by the Ministry of Tourism as 'tourist sites' are off limits. You'll know if you have stumbled into one of these because someone will probably tell you to leave.

You must dress modestly. For men that means no shorts; for women that means no shorts, tight pants, shirts that aren't done up, or anything else even remotely suggestive. Just use your common sense. Women may also be asked to cover their hair. Lastly, you must either take off your shoes or use the shoe coverings available for a few piastres (pt) at most mosques.

Egyptian Coptic Christianity
Before the arrival of Islam, Christianity was the predominant religion in Egypt. St Mark, one of the 12 apostles of Jesus, began preaching Christianity in Egypt in 35 AD, although it didn't become the official religion of the country until the 4th century. The term 'Copt' is derived from the Greek word 'Aegyptios' (meaning Egyptian), which the Arabs transliterated and eventually shortened to Copt. The term 'Coptic Church' originally referred to the native Egyptian Christian Church, but by the 5th century a different meaning had evolved.

Egyptian Christians split from the orthodox church of the Eastern (or Byzantine) Empire, of which Egypt was then a part, after the main body of the church described Christ

as both human and divine. Dioscurus, the patriarch of Alexandria, refused to accept this description. He embraced the theory that Christ is totally absorbed by his divinity and that it is blasphemous to consider him human. Since that time, Egyptian Christians have been referred to as Coptic Christians.

The Coptic Church is ruled by a patriarch, other members of a religious hierarchy, and an ecclesiastical council of laypeople. It has a long history of monasticism and can justly claim that the first Christian monks, St Anthony and St Pachomius, were Copts. The Coptic language is still used in religious ceremonies, sometimes in conjunction with Arabic for the benefit of the congregation. It has its origins in a combination of Egyptian hieroglyphs and Ancient Greek. Today, the Coptic language is based on the Greek alphabet with an additional seven characters taken from hieroglyphs.

The Copts comprise about 13% of Egypt's population. The precise number has been a subject of much controversy. The Muslims and the Copts have each done a census and come up with very different figures. Muslim extremists have continuously harassed the Copts. In the late 1970s the government further Islamicised the legal system, a move that infuriated the Copts but pleased Muslim extremists. By 1981 relations between the two were very tense. A Coptic church in Cairo was bombed, and to avoid further conflict Sadat sent the Coptic pope, Shenuda III, into internal exile. He stayed at one of the monasteries of Wadi Natrun until Mubarak allowed him to return in early 1985.

Tension eased a little in the late 1980s, but again reached new heights in the early 1990s as the extremist Gama'a al-Islamiyya, which embarked on a campaign of antigovernment and antitourist terrorism, also stepped up attacks on Christians, particularly in the Dairut-Asyut area. More than 500 have died in the violence since 1992, including two Coptic priests who were shot dead at the gates of Deir al-Muharraq, a monastery near Al-Qusiya, in 1994.

Despite all this, the Copts have long provided something of an educated elite in

Egypt, filling many important posts in government and bureaucracy. They have always been an economically powerful minority. Internationally, the most famous Copt today is the United Nations secretary-general, Boutros Boutros-Ghali.

Other Christians

Many Christian denominations are represented in Egypt, each by a few thousand adherents, or sometimes fewer. In total, there are about one million members of other Christian groups. Among Catholics, apart from Roman Catholics of the Latin rite, the whole gamut of the fragmented Middle Eastern rites is represented, including the Armenian, Syrian, Coptic, Chaldean, Maronite and Melkite rites. The Anglican communion comes under the Episcopal Church in Jerusalem. The Armenian Apostolic Church has 10,000 members, and the Greek Orthodox church is based in Alexandria.

Judaism

Until 1948 more than 80,000 Jews lived in Egypt. However, with the independence of Israel and subsequent wars between the two countries, many Jews had to leave. Today, there are fewer than 500 Jews, mostly elderly, scattered through Alexandria, Cairo and Al-Minya. The marble-pillared synagogue of Cairo is open to the public (the one in Alexandria is generally closed) – an interesting vestige of what must once have been a thriving community.

Pharaonic Religion

The religion of Pharaonic Egypt is difficult to describe because so much about it is still unknown. The stories behind the many gods and goddesses depicted in hieroglyphs tell more about how, rather than what, ancient Egyptians actually worshipped. But Egyptologists have been able to solve a few of the mysteries and, at the very least, it is known what most of the ancient deities symbolised. The illustrated section on Gods and Goddesses in Tomb & Temple Art in Pharaonic Egypt covers this in more detail.

LANGUAGE

Arabic is the official language of Egypt. However, the Arabic spoken on the streets differs greatly from the standard Arabic written in newspapers, spoken on the radio or recited in prayers at the mosque.

Egyptian Colloquial Arabic (ECA) is fun, but difficult to learn. It is basically a dialect of the standard language, but so different in many respects as to be virtually like another language. As with most dialects, it is the everyday language that differs the most from that of Egypt's other Arabic-speaking neighbours. More specialised or educated language tends to be pretty much the same across the Arab world, although pronunciation may vary considerably. An Arab from, say, Jordan or Iraq, will have no problem having a chat about politics or literature with an Egyptian, but might have more trouble making himself understood in the bakery.

There is no official written version of colloquial Arabic (although there is no real reason why it could not be written with Arabic characters – Nobel Prize-winning author Naguib Mahfouz has no trouble writing out whole passages using predominantly Egyptian (or Cairene) slang).

For some reason though, foreigners specifically wanting to learn the Egyptian dialect (instead of Modern Standard Arabic, or MSA, the written and spoken lingua franca understood by most, and in fact not so far removed from the daily language of the Arab countries of the Levant) are told that it *cannot* be written, and then presented with one system or other of transliteration as a poor substitute – none of them totally satisfactory. For the student of MSA, such systems can be a hindrance rather than a help. An esoteric argument flows back and forward between those who say you should learn MSA first and then a dialect (which could mean waiting a very long time before you can converse adequately with shopkeepers), and those who argue the opposite. If you're getting a headache now, that will give you some idea of why few non-Arabs and non-Muslims embark on the study of the language.

Nevertheless, if you take the time to learn even a few words and phrases, you will discover and experience much more while travelling through the country.

Pronunciation

Pronunciation of Arabic can be somewhat tongue-tying for someone unfamiliar with the intonation and combination of sounds. Pronounce the transliterated words and phrases slowly and clearly.

The following guide should help, but it isn't complete because the myriad rules governing pronunciation and vowel use are too extensive to be covered here.

Vowels In spoken Egyptian Arabic, there are five basic vowel sounds that can be distinguished:

a	as the 'a' in 'had'
e	as the 'e' in 'bet'
i	as the 'i' in 'hit'
o	as the 'o' in 'hot'
u	as the 'oo' in 'book'

A macron over a vowel gives the vowel a long sound:

ā	as the 'a' in 'father'
ē	as the 'e' in 'ten', but lengthened
ī	as the 'e' in 'ear', only softer
ō	as the 'o' in 'for'
ū	as the 'oo' in 'food'

Combinations Certain combinations of vowels with vowels or consonants form other vowel sounds:

aw	as the 'ow' in 'how'
ay	as the 'i' in 'high'
ei	as the 'a' in 'cake'

These last two are tricky, as one can slide into the other in certain words, depending on who is pronouncing them. Remember these rules are an outline, and far from exhaustive.

Consonants Most of the consonants used in this section are the same as in English.

However, a few of the consonant sounds must be explained in greater detail.

'	glottal stop – the sound you hear between the vowels in the expression 'Oh oh!'. It is a closing of the glottis at the back of the throat so that the passage of air is momentarily halted.
gh	the 'rayn' – tighten the muscles at the back of the throat and growl this sound; like a French 'r'.
'	the 'ayn' – gag muscles at the back of the throat as when puking; like the 'u' in 'but' but closed. When this occurs before a vowel, the vowel is 'growled' from the back of the throat. If it's before a consonant or at the end of a word, it sounds like a glottal stop. The best way to learn this sound is to listen to a native speaker.

Other common consonant sounds include the following:

g	as the 'g' in 'gain' (Egyptian Arabic is the only Arabic dialect with this sound – the others have a 'j' sound, as in 'John'. The Egyptians have in fact introduced an extra letter for the rare occasion when they need a 'j' sound, as in 'garage', which is pronounced as in English).
H	a strongly whispered 'h', almost like a sigh of relief.
kh	a slightly gurgling sound, like 'ch' in the Scottish 'loch'
q	strong guttural 'k' sound. In Egyptian Arabic, often pronounced as a glottal stop. Often transcribed as 'k', though there is another letter in the Arabic alphabet which is the equivalent of 'k' (see Transliteration section)
r	a rolled 'r', as in Spanish 'para'
s	pronounced as in English 'sit', never as in 'wisdom'
sh	as in 'shelf'
ž	as the 's' in 'pleasure'; rarely used in Egyptian Arabic

Double Consonants In Arabic, double

consonants are both pronounced. For example, the word *istanna*, which means 'wait', is pronounced 'istan-na'.

Transliteration

Converting what for most outsiders is just a bunch of squiggles into meaningful words (ie, those written in the Latin script) is a tricky business – in fact no really satisfactory system of transliteration has been established, and probably never will be. For this edition, an attempt has been made to standardise some spellings of place names and the like. There is only one word for 'the' in Arabic: 'al'. (Before certain consonants, it modifies: in Arabic, Saladin's name is Salah ad-Din, meaning 'righteousness of the faith'; here, 'al' has been modified to 'ad' before the 'd' of 'Din'.) Nevertheless, 'el' is often used. This has been left only in a few circumstances such as well-known place names (El Alamein, Sharm el-Sheikh) or where locals have used it in, say, restaurant and hotel names. Riverside boulevards in Nile cities are often called Corniche el-Nil (pronounced Corniche an-Nil). Whichever way you see these little blighters spelt, either in the book or in the signs you come up against, remember that they are all the same word.

The whole business is fraught with pitfalls, and in a way there are no truly 'correct' answers. The locals themselves can only guess at how to make the conversion – and the result is often amusing. The fact that French and English have had a big influence (though the latter has all but 'conquered' the former in modern Egypt) has led to all sorts of interesting ideas on transliteration. Don't be taken aback if you start noticing half a dozen different spellings for the same thing. The high rate, among Egyptians, of illiteracy in their own language does not help.

For some reason, the letters 'q' and 'k' have caused enormous problems, and have been interchanged willy-nilly in transliteration. For a long time, Iraq (which in Arabic is spelled with what can only be described as its nearest equivalent to the English 'q') was written, even by scholars, as 'Irak'. Other examples of an Arabic 'q' receiving such

treatment are souq (market), often written souk; *qasr* (castle), sometimes written 'kasr'; and the Cairo suburb of Doqqi, which is often written Dokki, although the Egyptian habit of swallowing 'q' and pronouncing the place 'Do'i' is a dead giveaway. It's a bit like spelling English 'as she is spoke' – imagine the results if Australians, Americans, Scots and Londoners were given free rein to write as they pronounce!

Greetings & Civilities

Arabic is more formal than English, especially with greetings; thus even the simplest greetings, such as 'hello', vary according to when and how they are used. In addition, each greeting requires a certain response that varies according to whether it is being said to a male, female or group of people.

Hello.
salām 'alēkum
(lit: peace upon you)
And hello to you.
wa 'alēkum es salām
(lit: and peace upon you)
Hello/Welcome.
ahlan wa sahlan
Hello. (in response)
ahlan bīk (to m)
ahlan bīkī (to f)
ahlan bīkum (to grp)
Pleased to meet you. (when first meeting)
tasharrafna (formal)
fursa sa'īda (familiar)
How are you?
izzayyak? (to m)
izzayyik? (to f)
izzayyukum? (to grp)
Fine. (lit: fine, thanks be to God)
kwayyis ilHamdu lillah (m)
kwaysa ilHamdu lillah (f)
kwaysīn ilHamdu lillah (grp)
(On their own, *kwayyis*, *kwaysa* and *kwaysīn* literally mean 'good' or 'fine', but they are rarely heard alone in response to 'How are you?')
Good morning.
sabāH al-khēr

Good morning. (in response)
sabāH an-nūr
Good evening.
misa' al-khēr
Good evening. (in response)
misa' an-nūr
Good night.
tisbaH 'ala khēr (to m)
tisbaHī 'ala khēr (to f)
tisbaHu 'ala khēr (to grp)
Good night. (in response; also used as 'Good afternoon' in the late afternoon)
wenta bikhēr (to m)
wentī bikhēr (to f)
wentū bikhēr (to grp)
Goodbye. (lit: go in safety)
ma'as salāma
Excuse me.
'an iznak, esmaHlī (to m)
'an iznik, esmaHīlī (to f)
'an iznukum, esmaHūlī (to grp)
Thank you.
shukran
Thank you very much.
shukran gazīlan
You are welcome.
'afwan, al-'affu
No thank you.
la' shukran
Sorry.
'assif

There are three ways to say 'Please' in Egyptian Arabic, each of which is used somewhat differently:

When asking for something in a shop, say:
min fadlak (to m)
min fadlik (to f)
min fadlukum (to grp)

Under similar, but more formal, circumstances (eg when trying to get a waiter's attention), say:
law samaHt (to m)
law samaHī (to f)
law samaHtu (to grp)

When offering something to someone, for example a chair or bus seat, or when inviting

someone into your home or to join in a meal, say:
tfaddal (to m)
tfaddalī (to f)
tfaddalū (to grp)

The same words beginning with 'i' (eg *itfaddal*) can be used to mean much the same thing or 'Please, go ahead' (and do something).

Small Talk
My name is ...
ismī ...
What is your name?
ismak ēh? (to m)
ismīk ēh? (to f)
I understand.
ana fāhem
I don't understand.
ana mish fāhem
Do you speak English?
enta bititkallim inglīzī? (to m)
entī bititkallimī inglīzī? (to f)
Yes.
aywa
na'am (more formal)
No.
la'

One of the most useful words to know is *imshī*, which means 'Go away'. Use this at the pyramids or at other tourist sites when you are being besieged by children. Do not use it on adults; instead, just say, *'la' shukran'* ('No thank you').

Accommodation
Where is the hotel ...?
fein al-funduq ...?
Can you show me the way to the hotel ...?
mumkin tewarrīnī at-tarīq lil-funduq ...?
I'd like to see the rooms.
awiz ashūf al-owad
May I see other rooms?
mumkin ashūf owad tānī?
How much is this room per night?
kam ugrat al-odda bil-laila?

Do you have any cheaper rooms?
fī owad arkhas?
That's too expensive.
da ghālī 'awī
This is fine.
da kwayyis
air-conditioning
takyīf hawa

Getting Around

Where is the ...?	*fein ..?*
bus station	*maHattat al-otobīs*
railway station	*maHattat al-'atr*
ticket office	*maktab at-tazāker*
street	*ash-shāri'*
city	*al-medīna*
village	*al-qarya*
bus stop	*maw'if al-otobīs*
station	*al-maHatta*

How far is ...?
kam kilo li ...?

When does the ... leave/arrive?	*emta qiyam/ wusuul...?*
bus	*al-otobīs*
train	*al-'atr*
boat	*al-markib*

Which bus goes to...?
otobīs nimra kam yerūH...?
Does this bus go to ...?
al-otobīs da yerūH ...?
How many buses per day go to ...?
kam otobīs fil yōm yerūH...?
Please tell me when we arrive ...
min fadlak, ullī emta Hanūsel ...
I want to go to ...
ana 'ayiz arūH ...
What is the fare to ...?
bikam at-tazkara li ...?
Stop here, please.
wa'if (or hassib) hena, min fadlak
Please wait for me.
mumkin tantazarnī
May I/we sit here?
mumkin eglis/neglis hena?
Where can I rent a bicycle?
fein e'aggar 'agala?

Wait!	*istanna!*
Where?	*fein?*
north	*shimāl*
south	*ganūb*
east	*shark*
west	*gharb*
airport	*matār*
bicycle	*'agala, bīcīklēt*
boat	*markib*
camel	*gamal*
car	*sayyāra/'arabiyya*
crowded	*zaHma*
daily	*kull yōm*
donkey	*Humār*
early	*badrī*
ferry	*ma'atiya*
here	*hena*
horse	*Husān*
late	*mut'akhar*
left side	*'ala ash-shimāl*
there	*henek*
this address	*al-'anwān da*
ticket	*tazkara*

Around Town

Where is the ...?	*fein ...?*
bank	*al-bank*
barber	*al-Hallē'*
beach	*al-plā/ash-shaata*
citadel	*al-'ala*
embassy	*as-sifāra*
ladies' room	*twalēt al-Harīmī*
market	*as-sūq*
men's room	*twalēt ar-ragel*
monastery	*dēr*
mosque	*al-gāme'*
museum	*al-matHaf*
old city	*al-medīna al-'adīma*
palace	*al-'asr*
police station	*al-bolīs*
post office	*al-bōsta/maktab al-barīd*
restaurant	*al-mat'am*
synagogue	*al-ma'bad al-yehūdī/al-kinees*
university	*al-gam'a*
zoo	*Hadīqat al-Haywān*

Money

The Egyptians have a collection of names for their own money, used in most everyday transactions.

pound	*guinay*
half pound (50 pt)	*nuss guinay*
quarter pound (25 pt)	*ruba' guinay*
20 pt	*riyal*
10 pt	*barisa*
5 pt	*shilling*

I want to change ...	*ana 'ayiz usarraf ...*
money	*fulūs*
US$	*dolār amrikānī*
UK£	*guinay sterlīnī*
A$	*dolār ustrālī*
DM	*mārk almānī*
travellers' cheques	*shīkāt siyaHiyya*

Shopping

Where can I buy ...?
  fein mumkin ashtirī ...?
How much is this/that ...?
  bikam da ...?
It costs too much.
  da ghālī 'awī
Do you have?
  fī 'andak?

Time & Dates

What time is it?	*sā'ah kam?*
When?	*emta?*
day	*yom*
month	*shaher*
today	*el nharda*
tomorrow	*bokra*
week	*esbuwa*
year	*sana*
yesterday	*mberrah*

Numbers

0	*sifr, zero*
1	*wāHid*
2	*itnein*
3	*talāta*
4	*arba'a*
5	*khamsa*
6	*sitta*
7	*sab'a*
8	*tamanya*
9	*tis'a*
10	*'ashara*
11	*Hidāshar*
12	*itnāshar*
13	*talattāshar*
14	*arba'tāshar*
15	*khamastāshar*
16	*sittāshar*
17	*saba'tāshar*
18	*tamantāshar*
19	*tisa'tāshar*
20	*'ishrīn*
21	*wāHid wi 'ishrīn*
22	*itnein wi 'ishrīn*
30	*talatīn*
40	*arba'īn*
50	*khamsīn*
60	*sittīn*
70	*sab'īn*
80	*tamanīn*
90	*tis'īn*
100	*miyya*
101	*miyya wi wāHid*
110	*miyya wi 'ashara*
1000	*'alf*
2000	*'alfein*
3000	*talattalāf*
4000	*arba'talāf*
5000	*khamastalāf*

Ordinal Numbers

first	*'awwal*
second	*tānī*
third	*tālit*
fourth	*rābi'*
fifth	*khāmis*

Days of the Week

Sunday	*(yōm) al-aHadd*
Monday	*(yōm) al-itnīn*
Tuesday	*(yōm) at-talāt*
Wednesday	*(yōm) al-arba'a*
Thursday	*(yōm) al-khamīs*
Friday	*(yōm) al-gum'a*
Saturday	*(yōm) as-sabt*

Months of the Year

East of Egypt, in addition to the Hjira calendar, there is also another set of names for the Gregorian calendar. In Egypt the names of the months are virtually the same as their European counterparts and easily recognisable.

January	*yanāyir*
February	*fibrāyir*
March	*māris*
April	*abrīl*
May	*māyu*
June	*yunyu*
July	*yulyu*
August	*aghustus*
September	*sibtimbir*
October	*'uktoobir*
November	*nufimbir*
December	*disimbir*

For a list of Hjira calendar months, see the Public Holidays & Special Events section in the Facts for the Visitor chapter.

Health & Emergencies

I need a doctor.
'awiz doktōr

My friend is ill.
sadīqi 'ayan

I'm allergic to antibiotics/penicillin.
'andī Hasasiyya dodd el entībiyotik/ el binisilīn

I'm ...	*'indī ...*
asthmatic	*hasāsiyya fi sad*
diabetic	*sukkar*
epileptic	*sar'*

antiseptic	*mutahhir*
aspirin	*asbirin*
Band-Aids	*blāstir*
condoms	*kabābīt*
diarrhoea	*is-hāl*
fever	*sukhūna*
headache	*sudā'*
hospital	*mustashfa*
pharmacy	*agzakhana*
pregnant	*Hāmel*
prescription	*roshetta*
stomachache	*waga' fil batn*
tampons	*hifāz al-'āda al-shahriyya*

PHARAONIC EGYPT

TOMB & TEMPLE ARCHITECTURE

Ask anyone what they'd like to see when they visit Egypt and nine times out of 10 they'll mention the pyramids at Giza, the tombs in the Valley of the Kings or the ruined temples at Luxor and Karnak. It is hardly surprising that people today are fascinated by Egyptian architecture. For 5000 years, since Zoser founded the tradition of monumental stone architecture at Saqqara, people have been gazing in awe, wonder and disbelief at the tombs and temples of ancient Egypt. However, despite the extreme antiquity of these monuments, scholars believe that they can accurately trace the gradual development of architectural techniques and styles all the way back to the dawn of Egyptian civilisation.

Early Buildings

When the people of Egypt first settled beside the Nile, they quite naturally built their homes from the reeds, mud and palm trees that were all around them. The influence that these materials – still used in many villages today – exerted over the form and decoration of almost all later ancient Egyptian architecture is quite staggering. In fact, the origin of many of the characteristic features of Egypt's stone temples and tombs, such as columns, battered walls, cavetto cornices and *kheker* friezes, can all be traced back to the way in which the Predynastic wattle-and-daub mud houses were constructed.

These simple mud houses – now largely known from models and hieroglyphic depictions – were made from intertwined bundles of rushes and reeds plastered over with mud. The plant stalks that protruded from the wall tops were tied into bundles that later inspired the design of the *kheker* frieze and cavetto cornice, which were often used to decorate the walls of stone buildings.

To stabilise and strengthen these early structures, the battered wall was used – its base was deliberately thickened so that the outer wall face sloped inwards. Battered walls continued to be a feature of all later Egyptian Dynastic buildings, even those constructed in stone – as a glance at the sloping walls of the massive pylons at the temples of Karnak and Luxor will show. Columns made from palm trunks, or bundles of tall papyrus stems, were often used to support the flat roofs. Their splaying tops were bound with cords and ropes to prevent them splitting under the weight. Later stonemasons faithfully imitated these columns, first naturalistically but gradually in more stylised forms.

The kheker frieze was inspired by the Predynastic wattle-and-daub mud houses. It represents the bundled plant stalks that protruded from the mud wall tops.

By the Early Dynastic period, larger and more complicated buildings made of mud brick had begun to appear. Versatile and easy to manufacture, sun-dried mud bricks are one of the most enduring building materials to be used in the Middle East. Mud-brick architecture dominated until the 3rd dynasty, when the desire to build monuments that would 'endure forever' meant that stone began to replace mud brick for the construction of temples and tombs. However, domestic architecture, royal palaces, fortresses and the walls of temple precincts and towns continued to be built of mud brick.

One of the most enduring decorative forms that developed from the Early Dynastic mud-brick architecture was the palace-facade niche design. Originally derived from the buttressed mud-brick exteriors of early royal palace entrances, this design, consisting of a succession of square towers projecting either side of a false entrance portal, later also became a popular decorative feature of funerary monuments such as mastabas. The great plaza and token palace in front of the Step Pyramid complex at Saqqara is one of the best examples of this design translated into stone.

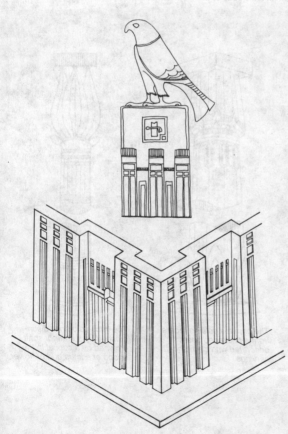

The palace-facade niche design is one of the most enduring decorative forms that developed from the Early Dynastic mud-brick architecture. It is represented here as a popular decorative motif featured on funerary monuments (top) and in its structural form (bottom).

Columns

The first stonemasons imitated the forms of early organic columns, even down to reproducing their swelling bases and rope-bindings, splaying fronds and lotus and papyrus buds in the capitals. Over time, the column shaft's moulding was gradually replaced by inscriptions and the elaborate decoration became confined to the capitals, where numerous stylistic variations appeared.

One of the earliest types of columns, common in both the Old Kingdom and the later Ptolemaic period, is the palm column, which actually represents eight palm fronds gathered and bound to a cylindrical column shaft. Other early columns were the papyrus-bundle and lotus columns. The former, with a tapering shaft whose thickened base was decorated with plants representing those of the primeval marshes can be seen in colonnaded temple courts and hypostyle halls. A variation of this, the open papyrus column with its bell-shaped capital, appeared in the New Kingdom. The lotus column, which has a straight shaft surmounted by a capital in the form of lotus buds or flowers, is more common in domestic constructions.

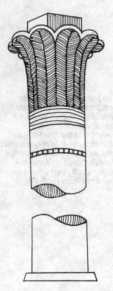

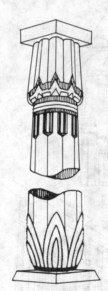

The palm column represents eight palm fronds that are gathered and bound, curving to a slender capital.

The papyrus column tapers from a thickened base decorated with stem sheath carvings.

The lotus column is distinguished by a straight shaft crowned by a capital in the shape of a lotus bud or flower.

By the Middle Kingdom, other types of column were also developing, such as the polygonal column, Osiride pillar and Hathor, or sistrum, capital. All probably had their origin in the large, stone blocks used to support the roofs of the earliest stone temples. Eight or 16 sided polygonal columns were created by cutting and shaping the pillar's corners. The Osiride pillar retained its square shape, as its name suggests, but with the addition of a carved mummiform statue of the king in the form of Osiris standing in front. The Hathor or sistrum capital (so-called because of its similarity to Hathor's musical rattle, the sistrum), found on both columns and pillars, is also square with each side depicting the face of the goddess supporting a miniature temple on her head.

The elaborate composite capital, composed of bound bunches of lotus and papyrus flowers, wheat, grapes and leaves, was a development of the Ptolemaic period.

The Osiride pillar is carved with a statue of the king in the form of Osiris.

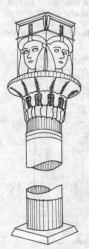

The Hathor capital is carved with the face of the goddess supporting a miniature temple on her head.

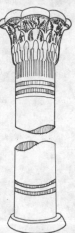

The composite capital is the most elaborate of the capitals, comprising a bunch of lotus and papyrus flowers, wheat, grapes and leaves.

Funerary Architecture

The earliest Egyptian burials were a far cry from their well known dynastic descendants, being little more than shallow pits in the desert containing few, if any, grave goods. Over time, with the desire to create a more protected dwelling for the dead, the graves became deeper and were covered with a mound of rocks and sand. For the majority of the population this continued to be the standard type of burial until modern times. However, with the rise of the belief that the tomb was the 'house of eternity' for the spirit of the deceased, the graves of the wealthy slowly became more and more elaborate in order to create a satisfactory eternal dwelling for their spirit bodies.

In order to both protect the body from grave robbers and create a more comfortable abode for the afterlife, the burial pits of wealthy graves became deep shafts lined with matting, mud brick or wood, and more chambers were added to house growing collections of grave goods. The simple covering mound also grew greatly in size and developed a low rectangular mud-brick superstructure which, because of its resemblance to the mud-brick seat found outside many Egyptian peasant houses, was given the name mastaba, which means bench in Arabic.

Mastabas

The building of mastabas, used to house the dead of the affluent, was well established by the beginning of the 1st dynasty. By this time, the tomb's enclosing mud-brick superstructure regularly rose to a height of six metres and inside contained a labyrinth of storage rooms for burial goods and subterranean burial chambers. Royal tombs could be easily distinguished from those of the nobles which surrounded them by their size and by the elaborate palace-facade motif dominating their retaining walls.

A stone, or less frequently wood, stele was placed against one of the faces of early mastabas, acting both as a tombstone and as the focus of the funerary cult of the deceased. Priests and relatives could come here on certain days and leave offerings on a small altar near the stele. In time, with the development of the palace-facade niche design, these stelae were

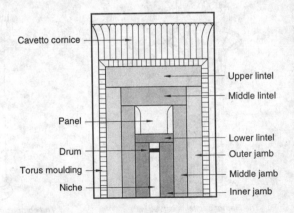

Cavetto cornice
Upper lintel
Middle lintel
Panel
Lower lintel
Drum
Outer jamb
Torus moulding
Middle jamb
Niche
Inner jamb

Evolving from the 'tombstone' stelae of early mastabas, the false door stele, it was believed, allowed the ka to pass between the burial chamber and the world of the living.

moved to the southernmost niche in the mastaba's eastern external wall. This was the origin of the false door stele, the 'dummy' door through which the ka or spirit could pass between the tomb and the world of the living.

With the rise to power of the 3rd dynasty and the introduction of stone as a building material at the Step Pyramid complex at Saqqara, more extensive changes to mastaba design developed. Stone replaced the mastaba's mud brick outer-casing and the external offering niche was moved to become the focus of a chapel built inside the mastaba super-structure. The contents of the stelae, depicting the deceased sitting at a table laden with offerings of food and beer or lists of grave goods, were transferred to a panel above the false door, which had itself become more elaborate in design and decoration. Sometimes a ka-statue (substitute body) of the tomb owner stood in front of the false door. Both it and the increasingly detailed reliefs decorating the tombs were meant to ensure that the deceased enjoyed a comfortable existence in the afterworld. Statues were also sometimes placed in a small room near the chapel called a serdab. This chamber was completely sealed except for a small window through which the statue (and thus the deceased inhabiting it) could view the commemorative offering ceremonies.

Artwork in tombs represented much more than just a decorative record of each individual's life. Each carving, painting and statue was meant to guarantee that everything depicted in the tomb would come to life in the afterworld. This had a very practical reason behind it, for if the mummy was destroyed, the ka could continue to survive through the likenesses of the deceased as represented in stone and wood. In order to make this possible, priests performed a ritual in the tomb after all the carving and painting was finished, which caused everything depicted in the tomb 'to come to life' and fulfil their role in the afterlife.

Over time, the walls of these mastaba tombs were elaborately decorated with fine painted bas-reliefs. The floor plan also became more complex comprising the burial shafts, chapels and storage rooms of other family members. One particular mastaba at Saqqara, belonging to Mereruka, a vizier of the first king of the 6th dynasty, had 31 rooms – 21 for his own funerary purposes and the rest for his wife and son.

Pyramids

It was not an obsession with death, or a fear of it, on the part of the ancient Egyptians that led to the construction of these incredible mausoleums; it was their belief in eternal life and their desire to be one with the cosmos. A Pharaoh was the son of a god, and the sole receiver of the ka, or life force, that emanated from the god. The Pharaoh, in turn, conducted this vital force to his people, so in life and death he was worshipped as a god.

A pyramid was thus not only an indestructible sanctum for the preservation of a Pharaoh's ka, nor simply an incredible, geometric pile of stones raised over the mummified remains of a Pharaoh and his treasures to ensure his immortality. It was the apex of a much larger funerary complex that provided a place of worship for his subjects, as well as a visible reminder of the absolute and eternal power of the gods and their universe.

Architecturally, the pyramid exemplified the culmination of the mortuary structures developed from the Early Dynastic period. Egypt's first pyramid, in Pharaoh Zoser's mortuary complex at Saqqara, was a 62m-high marvel of masonry completed in the 27th century BC. It was a product of the technical brilliance of Imhotep, the Pharaoh's chief architect. In this early model, a series of stone mastabas were placed on top of one another in a graduated design, and finally sheathed in fine limestone. This was the first time stone had been used to such an extent and with such artistry and precision. It became known as the Step Pyramid. (For further details, see Saqqara in the Around Cairo chapter.) Other step pyramids were built shortly after Zoser's reign, and have been found at Zawiyet el-Mayitin, Sheila, el-Kula, Edfu and at Elephantine Island.

The first true pyramid was built at Meidum at the end of the Third Dynasty, however, the style attained its highest form in the great pyramids at Giza. The pyramid complex at Giza is the best known and most visited today. Erected by Cheops, the Great Pyramid is the only surviving wonder of the ancient world. Its base covers 13 acres, and its positioning reflects the religious and astronomical beliefs of the age. (For further information on the pyramids at Giza, see the boxed story in the Cairo chapter.)

The planning and building of the pyramid was a long, involved process. First a site had to be chosen. A firm base capable of holding the weight of the construction was of paramount importance. Once selected by architects and artists, the site would be levelled and the foundation cleared. Foundation stelae and inscriptions contained in the foundations of many pyramids indicate that dedication rituals were common. Digging of the underground chambers and passageways would follow.

Different theories exist regarding how the pyramids were constructed. Some pyramids, like Imhotep's step pyramid, were solid stone; others had initial walls supported by masonry and filled with rubble, mud and sand. It is thought that ramps were used to build each level, and were extended as the pyramid rose in height. Another possibility is that mounds rather than ramps were attached to the sides of the construction and dismantled upon the pyramid's completion. Stones were apparently moved with levers and rollers, while pulleys were used to lift the stone blocks which sealed the entrance and passageways. Once the structure was completed – capped by the pyramidion, finished with casing, and the chambers decorated and inscribed – the funeral of the deceased commenced at the site.

A total of about 70 pyramids stretch the length of the Nile as far south as Sudan. Although the age of the pyramids lasted only a few hundred years, for four and a half millennium these ancient structures have inspired, awed and baffled.

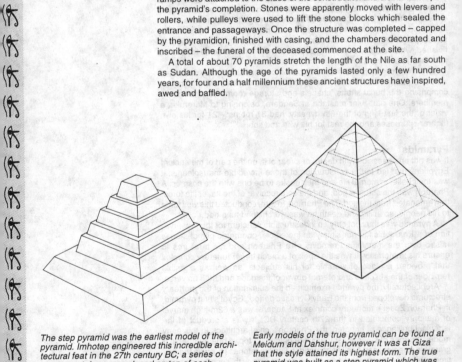

The step pyramid was the earliest model of the pyramid. Imhotep engineered this incredible architectural feat in the 27th century BC; a series of stone mastabas were placed on top of each other in graduated design, and then sheathed in fine limestone.

Early models of the true pyramid can be found at Meidum and Dahshur, however it was at Giza that the style attained its highest form. The true pyramid was built as a step pyramid which was then cased in polished stone.

Rock-Cut Tombs

By the end of the Old Kingdom, an alternate type of tomb architecture was developing in Middle and Upper Egypt to the south of the Giza plateau at places such as Beni Hasan and Aswan. Since the narrow band of the Nile valley left little superfluous room to build pyramids or mastabas, the people living in these regions cut their tombs into the rock of the cliffs overlooking the Nile. Originally, most of these tombs were very simple, with only a single chamber. However, like mastabas, in an attempt to imitate a more home-like environment for their spirit, the Egyptians gradually developed a more elaborate plan, consisting of an open courtyard and entrance facade, which they excavated out of the cliff wall, enclosing an offering chapel. An undecorated burial chamber was at the bottom of a shaft connected to the court or chapel. For the purpose of performing rituals, the living could reach the tomb via a staircase or causeway cut into the cliff face. By the Middle Kingdom, rock-cut tombs had become the norm in Upper Egypt, reaching their peak with the elaborately decorated royal tombs of the New Kingdom.

The basic plan of New Kingdom rock-cut royal tombs differed little from their predecessors except that they were more elaborate in both their decoration and floor plan. Often comprising a labyrinth of corridors and chambers tunnelling deep into the cliff, they were covered with images and religious texts meant to smooth the king's passage into the underworld and symbolise his deification. The Tomb of Seti I, 2nd king of the 19th dynasty, is one of the most striking examples from this period, extending 100m into the hillside and containing an impressively decorated barrel-vaulted burial chamber, intended to represent the vault of heaven.

One of the most original developments of the New Kingdom was the decision of the kings of the 18th and 19th dynasties to bury their dead in a remote valley near Thebes, now known as the Valley of the Kings. It seems that the original motive behind the conception of the Valley of the Kings

The high cliffs opposite Aswan are honeycombed with the corridors and chambers of the Tombs of the Nobles.

Tomb of Nakht

Nakht was one of Amun's astronomers. His tomb, on the west bank of Luxor, represents a very basic plan typical of the smaller New Kingdom rock-cut tombs. It is noted particularly for its detailed artwork.

necropolis was tomb security. Unlike earlier funerary architecture, the location of these tombs was meant to be secret – the tomb would be concealed and never visited by relatives or members of the funerary cult. Funeral cult rituals were carried out instead at a separate mortuary temple which supplanted the tomb's role as a memorial monument – a radical departure from tradition. However, when it became evident that any efforts to maintain any secrecy about the tomb's location was fruitless, the Pharaohs of the 20th dynasty again marked their tombs with impressive facades.

Tombs of this type continued to be cut until the middle of the 1st millennium BC, when production slowly ceased. Instead existing rock-cut tombs were reused, becoming the repository for mass burials, initially by descendants of the tomb's original owner, but later by just anyone. By the Graeco-Roman period, it was not unusual for one small tomb to contain 50 bodies.

Temple Architecture

It is generally accepted, based on hieroglyphic depictions, that the earliest shrines differed little in their outward form from the early houses. Rectangular in plan with their eaves and corners embellished with a concave cornice of tied plant stem bundles, these early temples were identifiable by coloured pennants hanging from wooden flagpoles at their entrances. The tendency of the ancient Egyptians to build later temples at the sites occupied by these early shrines, as well as the habit of each Pharaoh to add his own 'personal touch' to the existing structures, has meant that little of the temple architecture that survives to this day actually predates the New Kingdom – the enormous Temple of Amun at Karnak was the culmination of at least 2000 years of architectural reconstruction, from the 12th dynasty onwards. However, the tendency of the ancient Egyptians to archaise means that even the more recent Graeco-Roman temples can be considered imitations of the earlier structures.

Two distinct types of temple developed in ancient Egypt: cult temples, the house of the principal god of the region; and mortuary temples, dedicated to the worship of the dead king. Originally a simple structure connected to the king's pyramid, mortuary temples developed into huge elaborate complexes during the New Kingdom when they were built at a separate location to the Pharaoh's tomb. Because they were consistently new foundations and subject to the whims of individual monarchs, mortuary temples do not show the same conformity to a regular plan as do the cult temples. One of the most original and beautiful is Queen Hatshepsut's temple at Deir al-Bahri, near Luxor.

Cult Temples

Cult temples were quite literally the god's house on earth, so like tombs, they readily adopted the most enduring building material available – stone – so that they would last for eternity. A massive mud-brick enclosure wall separated the temple precincts from its surroundings, protecting the consecrated ground from intrusion, both human and supernatural. Inside this wall lay the temple itself, the priest's residences, the temple workshops and storehouses and the sacred lake, used for ritual ablutions. In the Graeco-Roman period, a *mammisi* or birth house, originally located on the temple roof and dedicated to Osirian rituals of rebirth, was also moved into the grounds.

Art was an integral feature of temple architecture and, as in tomb architecture, was functional as well as decorative. The reliefs and paintings acted both as magical protection against evil influences and also as a measure to guarantee that temple rituals were continually enacted. The various rooms of the temple were decorated in a style that reflected the

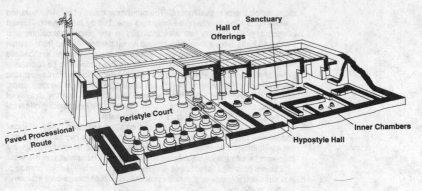

Sanctuary

Hall of Offerings

Peristyle Court

Paved Processional Route

Inner Chambers

Hypostyle Hall

room's function and ritual significance, for example the scenes in the brightly lit outer precincts tend to show the king performing public acts and duties, but in the inner regions the scenes change, emphasising the intimate relationship between the king and the god.

Access to the temple and its different sectors was based on an individual's status, so whilst the priests and a few privileged lay people could gather in the temple forecourt, only the king and members of the priesthood were allowed to progress into the temple's darker heart – the domain of the god.

To enter the temple, worshippers would travel along a paved **processional route** – sometimes lined with sphinxes as at the Temple of Amun at Karnak – that led up to the massive pylons guarding the main gateway. Carved with gigantic reliefs of the king smiting Egypt's foes, this huge entrance, the largest part of the temple, served both as a focal point for public processions and as a powerful tool to reinforce the power of the king and his link with the gods. As at the earlier shrines, tall wooden flagpoles sporting brightly coloured pennants that symbolised guardian deities, were placed in niches in front of the pylons.

The majority of Egyptian religious rituals were processional in nature. This is clear from the single axis upon which temples were built. On festival days, worshippers could congregate in the paved courtyard in front of the pylons, or, for the privileged few, pass through the pylons to assemble in the peristyle court.

The **peristyle court** consisted of an open courtyard surrounded on three of its sides by a covered colonnade. As a semi-public area, the decoration of this court often featured coronation scenes.

The priestly procession would then move through the three other main temple areas: the hypostyle hall, the inner chambers and the sanctuary or *naos*. Architecturally, the design of the temple changed noticeably as one moved from the bright peristyle court into the succeeding rooms. The temple was planned so that the rooms became smaller, darker and more mysterious as the sanctuary was approached. This effect was achieved by gradually raising the height of the floor, lowering the ceiling and narrowing the doorways.

Separated from the peristyle hall by either a screen wall or raised portico was one of the most imposing parts of the temple, the **hypostyle hall**. This hall, with its massive, towering plant columns lit only by slashes of clerestory lighting, was designed to resemble the primitive ancient forest and marsh

Cult temples were constructed so that rooms became smaller, darker and more mysterious as the sanctuary was approached. Floor heights were raised, ceilings lowered and doorways narrowed to achieve this effect.

surrounding the primeval mound. The number and size of such halls varied – most New Kingdom temples only had one, but by the Graeco-Roman period, a second such hall was included in the plan. The columns of hypostyle halls were cleverly positioned so that, when viewed from certain angles, there seems to be no space between them. This hall symbolises the primeval marsh of creation and its decoration is meant to be representative of the whole world: the column capitals and bases display aquatic plants; the architraves and ceiling are covered in reliefs of winged discs, stars or astronomical calendars, representing the sky; and the activity of the world, scenes of people bringing offerings and the king making offerings and performing rituals to the god, covers its walls.

From the hypostyle hall a door led into the temple's dimly lit **inner chambers**. On the main axis, often directly behind the hypostyle hall was the small, often columned, **hall of offerings**. Here the daily offerings were prepared before they were offered to the god. The decoration on the walls of different offerings reflects this. Side doors from this hall led, via corridors, into subsidiary chapels, a maze of rooms used for storage and stairways leading to the roof and the crypts.

Representing both the god's home and the primeval mound, the **sanctuary** stood at the highest and most remote part of the temple. This unlit, free-standing shrine, was only accessible to the king or high priest. Inside was the stone naos which supported the god's statue as well as a pedestal for the sacred barque – a boat-shaped shrine in which the god was carried in processions. Its walls were covered with reliefs depicting the king performing every stage of the offering ceremonies, that occurred twice each day.

In conception and design, the well-preserved Temple of Horus, Edfu, follows the traditions of authentic Pharaonic architecture, with the same basic plan, scale and ornamentation. Built under the Ptolemies, it is in fact a 2000 year old replica of an architectural style already archaic during Ptolemaic times.

GODS & GODDESSES IN TOMB & TEMPLE ART

Ancient Egypt produced a wealth of gods and goddesses, animal deities and magical practices that has both captured modern imagination and defied attempts to create for it neat and tidy categories. Ancient Egyptian deities could be local or universal or both; they could assume the characteristics of one another; they could be at once destructive and beneficial, evil and good. The ancients themselves seemed to have accepted such contradictions with equanimity. In their world, the sun brought light and life to the world, but its rays could also scorch and kill.

The deities, on whom the preservation of cosmic order depended, required constant attention, which meant for mortals strict adherence to rite and ritual. Detailed descriptions of how particular rituals were to be carried out are today the major source of information we have on religion in Pharaonic times, the thinking behind them having been largely lost. Nevertheless, the impression gained is of a people to whom order was everything; as they saw it, their world rose out of chaos and was daily in danger of returning to it. Their intermediary between the cosmic and the mortal worlds was the Pharaoh (regarded as a god himself - the living Horus) and in theory (if not in practice) he was responsible for ensuring the necessary rituals were performed. His reward for successfully fulfilling this role was wealth and power in this world, and a safe passage to the next.

Describing the gods, goddesses and belief systems of Ancient Egypt is a tricky business. First is the sheer amount of time to consider - its history spanned some 3000 years. It's little wonder that, looking back from our vantage point today, what we tend to see is a chaos of conflicting ideas. Next is the proliferation of local deities and the tendency over time for some of these to assume the characteristics of others. Then there are the deities' various manifestations; one god could take many forms. At least four cosmogonies provide slightly different explanations of how the world began (see the Ancient Egyptian Cosmogonies boxed story in the Cairo chapter). In addition, there are a number of myths (for example, the struggle between the brothers Horus and Seth for control of the world) which may well echo an even more distant past and the struggle between Upper and Lower Egypt for supremacy. Then there are the magic spells, charms and amulets (for example, the udjat eye which protected against evil), many of which retain a certain currency today.

Listed below are some of the major deities and how they are depicted in tomb and temple art. The emphasis is on 'some'. If you are interested in delving deeper into the subject, there are many books that can enlighten. They include: *Egyptian Religion* by S Merenz (translated by A Keep); *Egyptian Mythology* by Veronica Ions; *Reading Egyptian Art* by RH Wilkinson; *Atlas of Ancient Egypt* by John Baines & Jaromir Malek; *A Dictionary of Egyptian Gods and Goddesses* by George Hart.

Aker

An earth-god who watched over the western and eastern gates of the underworld *(duat)*. Shown with a lion's head or with two human heads facing opposite directions.

Amun (Amen)

Anubis

Amun (Amen)

The hidden one. Amun is portrayed as a man with blue-coloured flesh. He is sometimes depicted with ram's horns (the ram being one of his sacred animals, along with the goose), but more often he is shown wearing a crown topped with two tall plumes and holding a crook and a flail (symbols of sovereignty).

Amun was initially a minor deity in Thebes, but during the Middle Kingdom began to eclipse and assimilate other gods, such as the Theban god of war, Montu, and the fertility-god Min. In the New Kingdom Amun became associated with the sun-god Ra. As Amun-Ra he was regarded as King of the Gods and father of the Pharaoh, and so he remained for almost the entire Pharaonic period.

Anubis

God of cemeteries and of embalming, and patron of embalmers. Anubis is depicted as a man with a canine head, or as a reclining dog, often thought to be a jackal. His coat is black, and it is suggested this represents the discolouration of the corpse after it has been treated with natron (a mineral of hydrated sodium carbonate) and other substances during mummification. It could also be symbolic of renewed life, a reference to the rich, dark Nile silt vital for crops.

In the *Book of the Dead* Anubis, in the presence of 42 assessor gods, weighs the deceased's heart (regarded as the centre of the intellect and emotions) against the feather of truth (the symbol of Maat, goddess of truth, justice and cosmic order).

Apis

Sacred bull and herald of Ptah, god of Memphis. According to the Greek writer Herodotus, an Apis calf was singled out for deification because of its special markings. It had to be black with a white diamond on its forehead and have double hairs on its tail, carry the image of a crescent moon on its right flank and the mark of a scarab on its tongue. The Apis bull is depicted with a sun disc between its horns and, on its back, the protective wings of the vulture-goddess Nekhbet.

When an Apis bull died it was mummified (some of the alabaster tables used for the purpose can still be seen at Memphis) and buried at Saqqara. The vast, subterranean catacombs, now known as the Serapeum, were discovered in 1851 by Auguste Mariette.

Apophis

Snake god. Embodiment of darkness, symbolic of chaos and enemy of the sun-god Ra. As Ra enters and leaves the underworld (duat) in his solar boat he is attacked by Apophis, who is in turn beheaded (some versions of the legend say by the cat-goddess Bastet, others, Seth), his blood staining the morning and evening skies as the struggle is endlessly repeated.

Aten (Aton)

An aspect of the sun-god Ra. The sun at noon. Aten is depicted as a disc from which rays extend ending in outstretched hands. Those pointing towards the king or queen clutch ankhs (the hieroglyph for life). At the base of the disc is the uraeus (a symbol of sovereignty). Under the 18th-dynasty Pharaoh Akhenaten, Aten enjoyed a brief spell as the kingdom's supreme god (the Pharaoh being his only priest). But after Akhenaten's death and the accession of the boy-king Tutankhamun, Amun-Ra was restored to his former glory and Aten's temples were sacked.

Atum

Creator god of Heliopolis and identified from earliest times with the sun-god Ra (generally an aged aspect of the sun; the setting sun). Atum embodies the notion of completeness and is generally depicted as a man wearing the crowns of both Upper and Lower Egypt. Atum was said to have arisen from Nun (chaos or primordial ocean) and to have formed from himself both men and gods. According to the Heliopolitan cosmology (which eventually became the most widely accepted), Atum created the sky deities Shu (air) and Tefnut (moisture). They in turn produced Geb (earth god) and Nut (sky goddess). From them came Osiris, Seth, Isis and Nephthys. The entire 'family' is often referred to as the divine ennead (nine).

Bastet

Cat goddess and daughter of sun-god Ra. Her cult centred on Bubastis in the north-east Delta. Bastet could be ferocious, associated as she was with the sun's vengeance, but she was more usually regarded as a friendly deity and associated with joy.

Bastet

Bes

Despite his grotesque appearance, dwarfish, bandy-legged Bes was a benign character fond of music and dancing. He protected women in childbirth by frightening away evil spirits (see Taweret below) and watched over newborns.

Bes

Geb

Earth-god Geb was married to his sister, the sky-goddess Nut. He is usually depicted as a reclining man. According to legend, Geb divided Egypt in two, giving one son, Horus, the lower half and another son, Seth, the upper.

Hapy

Hapy symbolised the Nile's annual flood. He appears as a man and, as he embodies fertility and abundance, often possesses female breasts and a rounded abdomen, and wears aquatic plants on his head.

Hathor

Hathor, daughter of the sun-god Ra, was goddess of joy and love. She also protected women and travellers, although one myth depicts her as very violent, wishing to destroy humankind. She is often represented as a cow, or as a woman with cow's ears or horns between which sits a sun disc.

Hathor

Horus

Sky god and Lower Egyptian counterpart of Seth. Horus came to be acknowledged as the son of Osiris and Isis. He sometimes appears as a hawk, but more often as a man with a hawk's head. Horus' antagonist Seth (god of chaotic forces and indeed Horus' own brother), during one of their legendary conflicts, cut out Horus' eyes. Restored with royal saliva, the eyes came to symbolise perfection (the udjat eye). The udjat, represented as a human eye with hawk-like markings, was considered potent protection against evil. As one of the earliest state gods, Horus was closely connected with the king. In fact, the king was regarded as the living Horus (a notion that makes sense in the context of the story of Osiris) and from the earliest times he took a Horus name or ka name (one of five names) that declared his divine status.

Horus

Isis

Isis, sister/wife of Osiris, mother goddess and (as mother of Horus) symbolic mother of the king, possessed great magical powers. Isis is depicted as a woman wearing either a throne on her head or a sun disc flanked with cow's horns. Sometimes she appears (along with her sister Nephthys) as a kite, mourning the dead.

She used her magical powers to restore Osiris to life and to protect the young Horus. Those seeking protection or healing for children therefore appealed to her for assistance.

Khepri

The rising sun. Khepri was regarded as self-created and depicted as a scarab beetle, whose habit of rolling balls of dirt over the ground could be viewed as analogous to the divine task of pushing the sun disc up from the underworld to begin its journey across the sky. Hence the symbol of daily resurrection when incorporated into funerary jewellery. Small stone or faience scarabs were made in their thousands as amulets and stamp seals.

Isis

Khnum

Khnum's cult centred on Elephantine (near modern-day Aswan). Khnum had two roles: controlling the annual flood of the Nile and, as a potter, creating both gods and men. He is depicted with a ram's head.

Khons

Moon-god Khons (wanderer or traveller) is depicted as a man (sometimes with a hawk's head), wearing a crown topped with a crescent moon cradling a full moon. As the son of Amun and Mut, he also appears wearing the lock of youth.

Maat

Personification of cosmic order (truth, justice, harmony). Maat is depicted as a woman wearing an ostrich feather on her head, although sometimes she is symbolised solely by the feather (she is represented as such during the weighing of the heart ceremony).

Khepri

Khnum

Khons

Maat

Meretseger

Cobra goddess. Her name means 'she who loves silence'. She appears as a coiled cobra or with a snake's body and a woman's head. Meretseger protected the Theban royal tombs and her venom was said to blind dishonest necropolis workers. Only those who repented could appeal to her curative powers.

Min

Fertility god and protector of mining areas in the Eastern Desert. Min is depicted wrapped in mummy bandages, standing with his right arm extended and bent upwards at the elbow. In his left hand he clutches a royal flail. He wears a crown topped with two tall plumes.

Min

Montu

Falcon-headed Theban god of war. He is depicted wearing a sun disc on his head with two tall plumes.

Mut

A symbolic mother of the king, Amun's consort and Thebes' principal goddess. She appears as a slender woman wearing a vulture-shaped headdress. Sometimes she appears with the head of a lion.

Montu

Neith

An ancient deity associated with hunting or war and creator goddess of Sais, capital of Egypt around 700 BC. She appears as a woman wearing the red crown of Lower Egypt.

Nekhbet

Vulture goddess of Nekheb (el-Kab). Nekhbet appears as a vulture clutching the symbol for eternity in her talons. She is often included in the Pharaoh's crown (as the wadjet), and represents Upper Egypt.

Mut

Nephthys

Daughter of Geb and Nut. Mother of Anubis. On her head Nephthys wears hieroglyphs symbolising her name, which is 'lady of the mansion'. In the form of a kite she stands guard over the deceased.

Neith

Nephthys

Nun

Represents the primordial, chaotic waters from which arose the first god.

Nut

Sky goddess and both sister and wife of the earth-god Geb. Mother of Osiris, Isis, Seth and Nephthys. She usually appears as a woman, but sometimes as a cow, and is often depicted stretched across the ceilings of tombs, swallowing the sun and creating the night.

Nut, Geb and Shu are often depicted together. The sky goddess, Nut, is supported by Shu, god of air and light, who separates her from the reclining earth god Geb.

Osiris

God of the underworld and of fertility. He generally appears in mummy wrappings holding the crook and flail (representing kingship) and wearing a conical headdress that includes a pair of ram's horns and a tall plume. He is the brother of Isis and father of Horus. (Refer to the Osiris Cult boxed story in the Nile Valley – Beni Suef to Qus chapter.)

Ptah

Anthropomorphic creator god of Memphis. Ptah was also regarded as a skilled artisan and leader of craftsmen. He appears wearing a tight cap on his shaven head and he carries a sceptre (*was*) on which are the emblems of power, life and stability. Ptah is sometimes linked with the solar-god Sokar.

Osiris

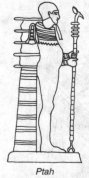

Ptah

Ra

Ra

Sun god and creator god of Heliopolis. Ra takes many forms (for example, as Khepri, Aten), and other deities also merge with him, enhancing their own powers (for example, Amun-Ra). He is generally shown as a man with a falcon's head upon which rests a sun disc. The ancient Egyptians believed that Ra traversed the sky in a solar boat, rising from the underworld in the east and re-entering it in the land of the dead in the west.

Renenutet

Cobra goddess and protector of the Pharaoh. She appears on the king's headdress in the form of a rearing cobra (uraeus). In this role she is ever-ready to strike down those who threaten the king.

Sekhmet

Lion goddess and daughter of sun-god Ra. Sekhmet's name means 'powerful' and she represents the burning heat of the sun. According to legend, the sun-god Ra sent Sekhmet (his 'eye') to punish an irreverent humankind.

Sekhmet

Selket

Represented as a woman with a scorpion on her head, Selket is associated with funerary rites and helps protect the dead.

Seth

Worshipped from very early times. Upper Egyptian counterpart to Horus. Seth is often seen as synonymous with evil. His birth was indeed violent (he wrenched himself apart from Nut, his mother) and one of ancient Egypt's most enduring legends relates his ferocious fights with his brother, Osiris, who he eventually murders. God of chaotic forces (and associated with wind, rain, storms and thunder), Seth has some redeeming features. For example, sitting in the prow of Ra's solar boat, he spears the evil snake Apophis as the boat begins its entry from the western horizon into the underworld.

Seth

Shu

God of air and light, Shu supported the heavens. He is depicted as a kneeling man bearing the sky-goddess Nut in his upraised arms, separating her from the earth-god Geb.

Sobek

Crocodile deity and symbol of royal power.

Taweret

Like Bes, Taweret protected women in childbirth, her eccentric appearance (hippo head, lion legs and arms, crocodile tail and pendulous breasts) supposedly scaring off evil forces.

Sobek

Tefnut

Daughter of sun-god Atum, Tefnut personified moisture. She is also sometimes referred to as the 'eye of Ra'.

Thoth

God of writing and counting, and patron of scribes. Thoth was worshipped in the form of a baboon or an ibis. He is usually depicted during the weighing of the heart ceremony as poised to record the results before the assessor gods.

Thoth

Facts for the Visitor

PLANNING
When to Go
Planning the best time to head to Egypt depends to some extent on whereabouts you want to go. Winter is without doubt the most comfortable time to be in Upper Egypt, and wandering around the sights at Luxor and Aswan. These places become insufferably hot in the summer months (June to August). The same goes for the oases.

Spring and autumn are the most pleasant times to be in Cairo, as it can get a bit nippy in winter. The Red Sea is pleasant in winter, but many people still come in the summer as well. The Mediterranean coast is at its most popular with Egyptians in summer, which is a good reason for not being there at that time of year – the crowds can be oppressive and obviously accommodation becomes tighter. It can still be quite cool on the coast and in Alexandria as late as April however, so a sense of timing – from mid-May to mid-June – and luck with the sun will get you the advantages of warm, sunny days without the full brunt of the local summertime rush.

Maps
Lonely Planet's *Egypt Travel Atlas* covers the country across about 40 pages of detailed maps (scales 1:900,000 and 1:1,800,000) and so provides unrivalled coverage. It's fully indexed and the book format means it is easy to refer to, especially on buses and trains.

Kümmerly & Frey has a map covering all of Egypt on a scale of 1:950,000, which sells for US$9. It also produces a separate map of Sinai and a pictorial (but fairly useless) map of the Nile for about US$7.50.

The Freytag & Berndt map includes a plan of the Great Pyramids of Giza and covers all of Egypt except the western quarter on a scale of 1:1,000,000. It includes small insets of Cairo and central Alexandria.

Nelles Verlag has one of the most complete, though dated, general maps of Egypt (scale 1:2,500,000) including, on the reverse side, a map of the Nile Valley (scale 1:750,000) and a good enlargement of central Cairo.

The Macmillan Publisher's *Map of Egypt* (scale 1:1,000,000) has a map of the Nile Valley and a small map of the whole of Egypt, plus good maps of Cairo and Alexandria, and a variety of enlargements, temple plans and the like for around US$7.

Clyde Surveys, of England, has an excellent map of eastern Egypt. It covers the Nile region from the coast to Aswan, and has detailed maps of Cairo, Alexandria, Luxor and Thebes, and the Great Pyramids of Giza, with notes in English, French and German. It is entitled *Clyde Leisure Map No 6: Egypt & Cairo.*

One of the best maps of Sinai is Tzofit's *South Sinai* (1:250,000) map. It's produced in Israel and is available at the Red Sea Diving College in Na'ama Bay, Sinai.

The Bartholomew *World Travel Map of Egypt* (scale 1:1,000,000) is a tad simplistic and it's missing a large part of the Western Desert. On the same scale is the French IGN map which concentrates on the Nile Valley. Michelin map No 954 (scale 1:4,000,000) covers north-east Africa as well as other parts of the Middle East.

The Egyptian Survey Department (☎ 348-4853) in Giza has topographic maps covering every nook and cranny in Egypt. It's open daily except Friday from 8.30 am to 1 pm and you can get copies of these maps for E£10 each.

There is an expanding plethora of maps of Cairo (or Cairo suburbs) available in the city's better bookshops. Some are OK, others pathetic and most of little interest to the traveller passing through. Falk produces a detailed map of Cairo (scale 1:13,000) with a small Alexandria addition and a booklet packed with details about the two cities. But you have to appreciate Falk's style of unravelling map – you either like it or you hate it.

It costs about US$8.50, or E£33 in Cairo bookshops.

If you're spending a long time in Cairo you'll probably find the *Cairo A-Z* helpful – a 150 page street directory which includes a useful information section (though it's a bit out of date).

The Society for the Preservation of the Architectural Resources of Egypt (SPARE) has designed a couple of maps covering parts of Islamic Cairo.

What to Bring

Bring sunglasses, a flashlight (torch), a collapsible drinking cup, a water bottle/canteen, sun screen (anything above factor eight is hard to find anywhere in Egypt), a hat, a flat drain stopper (not a plug), a pocket knife, two to three metres of nylon cord, plastic clothes pegs (pins), a day pack, a small sewing kit and a money belt or pouch (leather pouches can be made to order in the bazaars).

Be prepared for the temperature extremes. Sweaters are useful in the evenings throughout the country in winter. It can get bitterly cold in the night-time desert.

Although most toiletries can be found in Cairo, Luxor and Aswan (especially at major hotels), certain items can be expensive or difficult to find in Egypt, so you may want to bring your own contact lens solution, tampons (Tampax are about the only kind available), contraceptives (Tops condoms are available – to men – but apparently have a distressingly high failure rate; the pill is actually possible to get, but not easily) or shaving cream in a can (in a tube it's readily available). Women living in Egypt suggest it is better to bring your own sanitary pads and panty liners, although they are available.

See the Health appendix for a list of necessary medical items.

SUGGESTED ITINERARIES

Egypt offers a rich variety of attractions, from Pharaonic ruins to the underwater wonders of the Red Sea to the wild beauty of blossoming oases surrounded by thousands of km of harsh desert. It's a big country and, unless you've got the money to fly, getting around takes time. If you don't mind rushing, you can cover a lot, though many people get a bit tired of tombs and temples after a week or so. The following itineraries assume you're not taking internal flights.

One Week

You can see many of Egypt's most famous sights in a week's whirlwind tour. You'll need two days in Cairo to cover the pyramids and the Egyptian Museum, after which you could take the overnight train to Luxor and spend two days visiting the ancient necropolis of Thebes and the sites in Luxor itself. Jump on a morning bus to Aswan (five hours) and you'll be able to spend the afternoon sailing on a felucca on the Nile. Real travel buffs could fit in a trip to Abu Simbel the next day, before hightailing it by train or bus back to Cairo.

Two Weeks

A fortnight will give you enough time to explore parts, but not all, of Egypt. If ancient monuments are your thing, just stick to combing the Nile Valley.

Those who like a cocktail of sights could consider three days in and around Cairo, two days in Luxor and another two days in Aswan, taking in Abu Simbel and the Temple of Philae, before moving into relaxation mode with two nights on a felucca from Aswan to Edfu followed by a couple of days snorkelling around Hurghada on the Red Sea. If you prefer to concentrate less on temples and tombs, head straight to Luxor after Cairo and then backtrack across the Eastern Desert to Hurghada. From there you can get a ferry across the Red Sea to southern Sinai where you can delight in the underwater world before climbing to the peak of Mt Sinai.

Desert buffs have plenty of scope. You could take in Cairo and its surrounds before heading west for a leisurely circuit of the oases of Bahariyya, Farafra, Dakhla and Kharga, finishing up with a couple of days in either Luxor or Hurghada. Alternatively, head west via Alexandria to Siwa, spend three or four days there, and then hightail it east to do a week-long circuit of southern Sinai.

One Month
In a month you could cover most of Egypt's main sites, however, to do so, you'd still have to travel at a pretty steady pace. You could easily fill in four days in and around Cairo before hightailing it west to Siwa. After two days in this tranquil haven, backtrack along the Mediterranean coast, stopping overnight at Marsa Matruh (where the colour of the sea is at its most sublime) and then spend two days in Alexandria. Take an early morning bus from Alexandria to Cairo and you'll be in time to get the bus to Bahariyya or Farafra Oasis, where you can arrange an overnight trip in the White Desert – there's nothing like sleeping under a star-studded sky. Finish the oasis circuit with two days in Dakhla Oasis. From here you can bus it to the Nile Valley, and then spend a week or so exploring the multitude of sights between Qena and Aswan. You'll need another day for Abu Simbel. Then head east to Port Safaga or Hurghada on the Red Sea Coast. Two nights in one of these coastal towns would easily allow you time to recharge your batteries and look around before getting the ferry across the Red Sea to Sharm el-Sheikh. You'll then have another six or so days to explore the delights of Sinai.

Two Months
This would give you enough time to leisurely look around the whole country. However, even with time on your side, you'll probably find yourself backtracking at some stage, as it's almost impossible to do a continuous circuit around Egypt. As a rough guide, consider the following tour: One week in and around Cairo; four days in the Delta region and along the Mediterranean coast; five days in Siwa including a three day camel safari into the desert; backtrack to Cairo and then spend five days doing the circuit of the Bahariyya, Farafra and Dakhla oases; two weeks combing the Nile valley from Asyut to Abu Simbel; three days on a felucca coming back from Aswan to Edfu; six days

on the Red Sea coast including two nights at either the Monastery of St Anthony or St Paul; one week in Sinai (where many people like to relax at the end of an Egyptian tour) during which you could do a scuba-diving course; and three days back in Cairo to revisit the Egyptian Museum and hunt for some last minute souvenirs.

HIGHLIGHTS
The first thing to spring to mind when evoking images of Egypt are the **pyramids**. These extraordinary testimonies to the power and science of the ancient Egyptians are still without doubt one of the world's great tourist attractions. But perhaps because they are such a familiar image, some people are touched by a slightly uneasy feeling of disappointment – the feeling of overpowering elation at finally seeing them does not always come and the hordes of tourists and hustlers don't help.

Perhaps any disappointment felt makes the discovery of Cairo's other, lesser known wonders all the more satisfying. The tumble-down medieval labyrinth of so-called **Islamic Cairo** is for many the most powerfully evocative of places the foreigner encounters. Here the modern and the centuries-old are melded in a breathtaking way unknown in many other cities with long histories. Where medieval city centres of Europe have been carefully preserved and sanitised, here you get the feeling that, apart from the addition of cars, radios and electricity, little has changed over the centuries. Even the most touristy parts of the **Khan al-Khalili** are not completely bereft of this chaotic magic.

Of all the Pharaonic gifts to the present, the collection of sites from **Luxor** south to Abu Simbel is not to be missed. Bathed in the bright light of the winter sun (summer is oppressively hot), the temples of Luxor and in particular **Karnak** tower above their admirers. The west bank offers everything from the **Valley of the Kings** and other tombs – such as the newly opened masterpiece, the **Tomb of Nefertari** – to startling monuments such as the unique **Temple of**

Hatshepsut. You could easily spend many days exploring all there is to be seen here. **Abu Simbel** is as impressive for the salvation work done to move it out of reach of the rising waters of **Lake Nasser** as for its own grandiose dimensions.

For those left cold by the big cities or monument-gazing, the seascape of the **Red Sea** may be the high point – the splendid coral gardens, with fish of every imaginable shape, size and brilliant colour, provide a stunning visual feast. There are numerous places along the coast, from **Hurghada** to towns in Sinai. Most divers seem to agree that the area around **Sharm el-Sheikh** and **Ras Mohammed** in the south of the Sinai peninsula offers the cream of the country's easily accessible diving. Some just prefer the tranquillity of hanging around **Dahab.**

The **oases** present a unique escape from the madding crowds and frenetic tourism. There's not a lot to do, but that can be the whole pleasure of being there in the first place. Despite its growing popularity, **Siwa** is probably still the pick of that crop.

TOURIST OFFICES

The Egyptian government has tourist information offices throughout Egypt and in 12 other countries. The tourist offices outside Egypt tend to be better than the ones within.

Local Tourist Offices

Following is a list of the tourist offices within the country:

Cairo
Administrative Headquarters: Misr Travel Tower, Midan Abbassiya (☎ 820283; fax 830844)
Head Office, 5 Sharia Adly (☎ 391-3454)
Old Airport Office (☎ 667475)
New Airport Office (☎ 291-4255/2223)
Pyramids Office, Pyramids Rd, near Hotel Mena House (☎ 385-0259)
Railway Station Office, Ramses Square
Manyal Palace
Al-Arish
Sharia Fouad Zekry
Alexandria
Midan Saad Zaghloul (☎ 807-9885)
Airport Office (☎ 425-8764)

Maritime Station (☎ 492-5986)
Masr Railway Station Office (☎ 492-5985)
Al-Minya
Governorate building (☎ 320150)
Aswan
Railway Station Office (☎ 312811)
Office one block in from Corniche el-Nil (☎ 323297)
Asyut
Governorate building (☎ 310010)
Hurghada
Just off Sharia an-Nasr beside the Ritz Hotel (☎ 546513)
Ismailia
Governorate building (☎ 321074 ext 284)
Kharga Oasis
Midan Nasser (☎ 901205)
Luxor
Tourist Bazaar, across from the Luxor Temple (☎ 373294)
Marsa Matruh
Governorate building (☎ 931841)
Port Said
43 Sharia Palestine (☎ 223868)
Suez
Port Tawfiq Office (☎ 221141)

Tourist Offices Abroad

Following is a list of Egyptian tourist offices outside the country:

Austria
Aegyptisches Fremdenverkehrsamt, Elisabethstrasse 4, Pornringhof, 1010 Vienna (☎ (1) 587-6633; fax (1) 587-6643)
Canada
Egyptian Tourist Authority, 1253 McGill College Ave, Suite 250, Montreal, Quebec H3B 2Y5 (☎ (514) 851-4606; fax (514) 861-8071)
France
Bureau de Tourisme, Ambassade de la RAE, 90 Ave des Champs-Élysées, Paris (☎ (01) 45 62 94 42; fax (01) 42 89 34 81)
Germany
Aegyptisches Fremdenverkehrsamt, 64A Kaiserstrasse, 60329, Frankfurt/Main (☎ (69) 252319; fax (69) 239876)
Greece
Egyptian Tourist Authority, 6th floor, 10 Amerikas St, Athens 10671 (☎ (1) 360-6906; fax (1) 363-6681)
Italy
Ufficio Turistico Egiziano, 19 Via Bissolati, 00187 Rome (☎ (6) 482-7985; fax (6) 487-4156)
Japan
Egyptian Tourist Authority, Akasaka 2-Chome Annex, M-S Akasaka, Minato Ku, Tokyo (☎ (3) 35 89 06 53; fax (3) 35 89 13 72)

Spain
    La Toree de Madrid, Planta 5, Oficina 3, Plaza de
    España, 28008 Madrid (☎ (1) 559-2121; fax (1)
    547-5165)
Sweden
    Egyptian Tourist Office, Drottnin 99 Atan 65,
    11136 Stockholm (☎ (8) 102548; fax (8) 102
    5412)
Switzerland
    Office du Tourisme d'Égypte, 9 Rue des Alpes,
    Geneva (☎ (22) 732-9132; fax (22) 738-1727)
UK
    Egyptian Tourist Authority, 3rd Floor West,
    Egyptian House, 170 Piccadilly, London W1V
    9DD (☎ (0171) 493-5282; fax (0171) 408-0295)
USA
    Egyptian Tourist Authority, 630 5th Ave, Suite
    1706, New York, NY 10111 (☎ (212) 332-2570;
    fax (212) 956-6439)
    Egyptian Tourist Authority, Suite 215, 83 Wil-
    shire Boulevard, Wilshire San Vincente Plaza,
    Beverly Hills, CA 90211 (☎ (213) 781-7676; fax
    (213) 653-8961)
    Egyptian Tourist Authority, 645 North Michigan
    Ave, Suite 829, Chicago, IL 60611 (☎ (312) 280-
    4666; fax (312) 280-4788)

VISAS & DOCUMENTS
Passport
Your most important travel document is a
passport, which should remain valid until
well after your trip. If it's just about to expire,
renew it before you leave as some countries
insist your passport remains valid for a specified period. Also, make sure it has enough
space to cover all the countries you'll be
visiting – what with the visa and all the
associated stamps you'll need two full pages
for Egypt alone.

Visas
A visa is a stamp in your passport permitting
you to enter the country in question and stay
for a specified period of time. All foreigners
entering Egypt, except nationals of Malta
and Arab countries, must obtain visas from
Egyptian consulates overseas or at the
airport or port upon arrival. As a general rule,
it is cheaper to get one upon arrival at Cairo
airport, but this depends on your nationality
and where you apply for the visa.

Processing of visa applications varies. In
the USA and the UK, processing takes about
24 to 48 hours if you drop your application

off in person, or anything from 10 days to six
weeks if you mail it.

You need to fill in one application form
and attach one passport-size photo. If you are
mailing your application, include a money
order (cheques are not accepted), a stamped
self-addressed envelope with enough
postage to send it registered (if you are
mailing it) and, of course, your passport. You
must pay cash if applying in person.

The single-entry visa is valid for three
months and entitles the holder to stay in
Egypt for one month. Multiple-entry visas
(for three visits) are also available for a little
extra money, but although good for presen-
tation for six months, still only entitle the
bearer to a total of one month in the country.

Costs vary depending on your nationality
and the country where you apply. As an
example, a single-entry tourist visa costs
most western applicants the equivalent of
UK£15 (about US$22) in the UK.

In Jordan, visas cost JD17 and you need
one photo. To find the embassy in Amman,
head towards 5th Circle from 4th Circle and
take the fifth street off to the right. The
embassy is next to the distinctively yellow
Dove Hotel. Applications are accepted, if
you can fight your way through the crowds,
between 9 am and noon, and visas are generally issued on the same day at 3 pm. You
need one photo.

The consulate in Aqaba is much quieter,
and visas here are issued on the spot for
JD12. It is open from 9 am to noon daily
except Friday. The consulate in Aqaba is in
the new part of town, about 20 minutes walk
from the centre.

It is also possible to be issued with a visa
in Nuweiba upon arrival (by ferry), but the
Egyptian officials make a bit of a song and
dance about it, and will want payment in US
dollars.

If you are coming from Israel, remember
that you cannot get a visa on the Israeli-
Egyptian border. The embassy in Tel Aviv
(☎ 546-4151) is open for applications from
9 to 11 am from Sunday to Thursday. Single-
entry, one month visas cost 40 NIS for most
nationalities, and are ready to be picked up

at 1 pm on the same day. Israelis pay 60 NIS and must wait about a week. You need a photo. The Egyptian consulate in Eilat also issues visas.

Bear in mind that evidence of having been in Israel renders your passport useless for travel in any other Arab countries, with the exception of Egypt and Jordan. Although the Israelis generally comply with requests not to stamp passports on entry or exit (they stamp your entry card instead), you will still get an Egyptian stamp bearing the name of the border post (Taba or Rafah) – which is enough evidence if it is noticed by visa authorities of other Arab countries. 14-day Sinai permits are an exception to this rule (see Sinai, following).

In Sudan you can obtain a visa on the same day at the Egyptian consulate in Sharia al-Gomhurriya, Khartoum. It costs between US$12 and US$16, and you need one photo.

If, within your one month stay, you plan to return to Egypt after, for example, visiting Israel, Jordan or Sudan, you should request the multiple-entry visa. Otherwise, you will have to arrange to get a re-entry visa while in Cairo (see Visa Extensions & Re-Entry Visas, following) or get a new visa to return.

You can get a visa on entering the country at some points. At the new Cairo airport terminal, where most visitors arrive, the process is simple and generally cheap. Thomas Cook or some of the other 24 hour exchange booths you pass just before passport control will sell you the required stamps for the visa on the spot, and no photo is required. Most nationalities pay US$15 or UK£10. Citizens of countries in sub-Saharan Africa require evidence of an AIDS test before entering Egypt.

Sinai It is possible to visit the Sinai area between Sharm el-Sheikh and Taba (on the Israeli border) without a visa. You are also permitted to visit St Catherine's Monastery, but divers should note that a full visa is required to get to Ras Mohammed, south of Sharm el-Sheikh. On arrival, you are issued with an entry stamp free of charge allowing you up to 14 days in the area. If coming from Israel, you can have the stamp put on a separate piece of paper.

Valid points of entry for such visa-free stamps are Taba, Nuweiba and Sharm el-Sheikh (airport or port).

Registration You must register with the police within one week of your arrival in Egypt. Most hotels will take care of this, some for a small fee. The bigger hotels complete the registration formality without being asked to do so – most package tourists don't even know it happens. Late registration incurs a fine of E£25.40 plus E£3 in government stamps.

In Cairo, you must register at the Mogamma on Midan Tahrir (see the Information section in the Cairo chapter for details). Most of the main entry points, including Alexandria, Luxor, Aswan, Suez, Port Said, Sharm el-Sheikh and Hurghada, have passport offices where you can also register. For addresses of these offices, see the Information section of the appropriate city or town.

Visa Extensions & Re-Entry Visas Extensions of your visa beyond the first month can be obtained for either six or 12 months and cost E£12.10/38.10 respectively. You need one photograph and a modicum of patience.

If you do not have a multiple-entry visa, it is also possible to get a re-entry visa, valid to the expiry date of your visa and any extensions, at most passport offices including the Mogamma in Cairo. A single/multiple re-entry visa costs E£10.10/13.10.

Note that there is a two week grace period beyond the expiry date of your visa. (In other words, a one month stay is to all intents and purposes six weeks.) If you stay beyond that, a fine of E£60 is imposed on exit, and there are also the costs and hassles of getting an extension. If you are caught at the airport in this situation, you could well have to kiss your flight goodbye.

You can get visa extensions and re-entry visas at most points of entry (for example, Aswan, Luxor, Alexandria and Suez). It is often less of a hassle outside Cairo.

Photocopies

It's a good idea to make photocopies of all vital documents – such as the data pages of your passport, your birth certificate, credit cards, airline tickets, the serial numbers of your travellers' cheques and other travel documents – and keep them separate from your real documents. Add to this an emergency stash of about US$50. Also leave copies of all these things with someone at home.

Travel Permits

Travel permits are no longer required for travel westward past Marsa Matruh or to Siwa Oasis. This is a result of the easing of relations between Egypt and Libya since 1989, but it is not a guarantee, in what is after all a volatile area, that the need for permits might not be reimposed if the two countries again find themselves at loggerheads – it would not be the first time in their postwar history.

Military permits issued by the Ministry of Interior in Cairo are required for travel south beyond Marsa Alam on the Red Sea coast. They are very hard to come by, particularly as long as Egypt and Sudan continue to squabble about the Halaib region. This situation is always subject to change.

A permit used to be required to visit the pyramids of Dahshur, south of Saqqara, however, this regulation was lifted in mid-1996.

Travel Insurance

However you're travelling, it's worth taking out travel insurance. Work out what you need and consult your travel agent for the most appropriate policy. You may not want to insure that grotty old army surplus backpack – but everyone should be covered for the worst possible case: an accident, for example, that will require hospital treatment and a flight home. Check out the details. In most cases you need to pay extra to cover you for 'dangerous sports' such as diving. Also, you often need to pay a surcharge for expensive camera equipment and the like.

It's a good idea to make a copy of your policy, in case the original is lost. If you are planning to travel for a long time, the insurance may seem very expensive – but if you can't afford it, you certainly won't be able to afford to deal with a medical emergency overseas. For more details, see the Health section later in this chapter.

Driving Licence & Permits

If you plan to drive in Egypt you should obtain an international driving permit from your local automobile association before you leave home – you'll need a passport photo and a valid licence. For information about driving in Egypt, see the Getting Around chapter.

Hostel Card

Some Egyptian hostels don't require that you be a hostelling member, but often charge a pound or two less if you have a card. Occasionally they'll issue a membership card on the spot, otherwise they're available at the Hostelling International (HI) office in Cairo (see the Accommodation section later in this chapter for details).

Student Cards

For years, it has been notoriously easy to get a legitimate International Student Identification Card (ISIC) in Cairo. At the time of writing they were available from two places – the Medical Scientific Centre (MSC) and the Faculty of Engineering at Cairo University. These locations are prone to change so ask around before you set off.

The MSC (☎ 363-8815) is at 103 Sharia al-Manial on Roda Island and is open daily except Friday from 8 am to 8 pm. Cards are issued in a matter of minutes and cost E£20; no proof is needed but you'll require a passport photo (preferably colour).

Finding the office at the Faculty of Engineering on Sharia Gamiat al-Qahira in Giza is a tad more difficult and cards issued from here are more expensive – E£30 for foreigners studying outside Egypt and E£21 for those studying in Cairo. The tiny office is next to the (empty) swimming pool at the rear of the grounds – ask any of the Egyptian students to point the way. The office is open from 9.30 am to 1.30 pm Saturday to Thursday, and from 10 am to noon on Friday.

Given the benefits, it is well worth having a student card as it entitles you to a 50% discount on admission to almost all of the antiquities and museums, as well as significant reductions on train travel.

Travellers have reported using a whole range of other cards to get student discounts for museum entry and transport, from Hostelling International (HI) cards to Eurail cards.

International Health Card
You'll need this yellow booklet proving that you have been vaccinated for yellow fever and/or cholera only if you are coming from an infected area (such as most of sub-Saharan Africa and South America). Yellow fever is not endemic in Egypt.

See the appendix on Health for further information.

Other Documents
An antiquities permit is a useful thing to have, as it allows you easier access to many of Egypt's archaeological sites, especially sites usually closed to tourists. Getting the permit, however, is not so easy. They are supposedly issued from the Department of Antiquities in Abbassiya (behind the Misr Travel Tower), however it seems to depend on the mood of the person in charge whether applications are approved or not. A letter from the archaeology department of any university and a good deal of patience may help.

A business card can give you a certain degree of credibility in Egypt and, depending what's on it, can be a great help in obtaining assistance.

It's a good idea to carry some spare passport photos with you, although these can easily be obtained in Cairo and other large cities.

EMBASSIES
Egyptian Embassies Abroad
Following are the addresses and telephone numbers of Egyptian embassies and consulates in major cities around the world:

Australia
  Embassy: 1 Darwin Ave, Yarralumla, Canberra, ACT 2600 (☎ (06) 273-4437/8)
  Consulates: 9th floor, 124 Exhibition St, Melbourne, Vic 3000 (☎ (03) 9654-8869/8634)
  335 New South Head Rd, Double Bay, Sydney NSW 2028 (☎ (02) 9362-3483)
Belgium
  44 Ave Léon Herrera, 1180 Brussels (☎ (2) 345-5015)
Canada
  Embassy: 454 Laurier Ave East, Ottawa, Ontario K1N 6R3 (☎ (613) 234-4931/35/58)
  Consulate: 1 Place Sainte Marie, 2617 Montreal, Quebec H3B 4S3 (☎ (514) 866-8455)
Denmark
  Kristianiagade 19, 2100 Copenhagen (☎ 3543-7070, 3543-7152)
France
  Embassy: 56 Ave d'Iena, 75116 Paris (☎ (01) 47 23 06 43, 53 67 88 30)
  Consulates: 58 Ave Foch, 75116 Paris (☎ (01) 45 00 49 52, 45 00 77 10)
  166 Ave d'Hambourg, 13008 Marseilles (☎ 91 25 04 04)
Germany
  Embassy: Kronprinzenstrasse 2, Bad Godesberg, 53173 Bonn (☎ (228) 956-8311/2/3)
  Embassy branch: Waldstrasse 15, 13156 Berlin (☎ (30) 477-1048)
  Consulate: Eysseneckstrasse 34, 60322 Frankfurt/Main (☎ (69) 590557/8)
Greece
  3 Vasilissis Sofias, 106 71 Athens (☎ (1) 361-8612/3)
Ireland
  12 Clyde Rd, Dublin 4 (☎ (1) 660-6566, 660-6718)
Israel
  Embassy: 54 Rehov Basel, Tel Aviv (☎ (3) 546-4151/2)
  Consulate: 68 Afraty St, Bna Betkha, Eilat (☎ (7) 597-6115)
Japan
  4-5, 1 Chome, Aobadai, Meguro-Ku, Tokyo 153 (☎ (3) 37 70 80 22)
Jordan
  Embassy: Karbata Ben El-Dawar St, 4th floor, Amman or PO Box 35178 (☎ (6) 605202; fax (6) 604082)
  Consulate: Al-Wahdat al-Jarbiyya, al-Istiqlal St, Aqaba (☎ (3) 316171/81)
Libya
  Omar Khayam Hotel, 5th floor, Benghazi (☎ (61) 92488; fax (61) 96291)

Netherlands
> Badhuisweg 92, 2587 CL, The Hague (☎ (70) 354-2000)

Sudan
> Embassy: Sharia al-Gama'a, al-Mogran, Khartoum (☎ (11) 778741; fax (11) 778741)
> Consulate: Sharia al-Gomhurriya, Khartoum (☎ (11) 772191)

Sweden
> Strandvägen 35, Stockholm (☎ (8) 660-3145, 662-9603/9687)

UK
> Embassy: 26 South St, Mayfair London W1Y 6DD (☎ (0171) 499-2401)
> Consulate: 2 Lowndes St, London SW1 (☎ (0171) 235-9777/9719)

USA
> Embassy: 3521 International Court NW, Washington DC 20008 (☎ (202) 232-5400, 224-5131)
> Consulates: 1110 2nd Ave, New York, NY 10022 (☎ (212) 759-7120/1/2)
> 3001 Pacific Ave, San Francisco, CA 94115 (☎ (415) 346-9700/2)
> 1990 Post Oak Blvd – Suite 2180, Houston, TX 77056 (☎ (713) 961-4915/6)
> 500 N Michigan Ave – Suite 1900, Chicago, IL 60611 (☎ (312) 828-9162/64/67)

Foreign Embassies in Egypt

The addresses of some of the foreign embassies and consulates in Egypt are:

Algeria
> 14 Sharia al-Brazil, Zamalek, Cairo (☎ 341-8527, 341-1520)
> Visas cost E£102 for a stay of one month or E£170 for three months. Applications are accepted between 10 am and noon on Sunday and Monday only, and take anywhere between one and four weeks to process. You'll need four passport photos.

Austria
> El Riyad Tower, 5th floor, Sharia Wissa Wassef, Giza (☎ 570-2975)

Australia
> World Trade Centre, 11th floor, 1191 Corniche el-Nil, Cairo (☎ 575-0444; fax 578-1638); hours are 8 am to 3 pm, Sunday to Thursday

Belgium
> 20 Sharia Kamel ash-Shennawi, Garden City, Cairo (☎ 354-7494)

Canada
> 3rd floor, 4 Sharia Kobra, Garden City, Cairo (☎ 354-3110); hours are from 8.30 am to 4.30 pm, Sunday to Thursday

Cyprus
> 23 Sharia Ismail Mohammed, Zamalek, Cairo (☎ 341-1288)

Denmark
> 12 Sharia Hassan Sabri, Zamalek, Cairo (☎ 340-2503)

Eritrea
> 13 Sharia Mohammed Shafik, Mohandiseen, Cairo (☎ 303-0517)
> Visas valid for a month are issued within 24 hours. You need a letter of introduction from your embassy and two photos. Visas cost E£135, and you have the option of a single or multiple entry. If you are going via Sudan, you can obtain an Eritrean visa in Khartoum (☎ 451019/37; fax 452256), PO Box 8129.

Ethiopia
> 3 Sharia Ibrahim Osman, Mohandiseen, Cairo (☎ 347-7805)
> People have had varying experiences here. A letter of introduction and one photo are required for visas that cost around E£60; it takes one to two days. However, some people have been refused visas without an air ticket showing an onward flight. Hours are from 8.30 am to noon daily except Friday.

France
> Embassy: 29 Sharia al-Giza, Giza (☎ 728649, 728346)
> This street has changed names several times, so there are variations. It's also known as Sharia Taha Hussein, Sharia el-Nil and Sharia Bahyi ad-Din Barakat, which is actually an extension southward of Sharia al-Giza.
> Consulate: 5 Sharia Fadl (off Sharia Talaat Harb), Cairo (☎ 393-4645)
> Consulate: 2 Midan Orabi, Mansheya, Alexandria (☎ 482-7950); open Sunday to Thursday from 8.30 am to 3 pm

Germany
> Embassy: 8 Sharia Hassan Sabri, Zamalek, Cairo (☎ 341-0015)
> Consulate: 5 Sharia Mena, Rushdy, Alexandria (☎ 545-7025); open weekdays from 8 am to 4 pm

Greece
> Embassy: Sharia Aisha Taymouria, Garden City, Cairo (☎ 355-1074)
> Consulate: Sharia Iskander al-Akbar, Alexandria (☎ 483-8454); open weekdays from 9 am to 1 pm

Ireland
> 7th floor, 3 Sharia Abu al-Feda, Zamalek, Cairo (☎ 340-8264)
> Consulate: Honourary Consul, Hisham Helmy, 36 Sharia Kafr Abdu, Rushdy, Alexandria (☎ 546-4686); open Sunday to Thursday from 9 am to 3 pm

Israel
> Embassy: 18th floor, 6 Sharia Ibn al-Malek, Giza (☎ 361-0528); open from 10 am to 12.30 pm Sunday to Thursday
> Consulate: 207 Sharia Abdel Salem Aref, Alexandria (☎ 586-0492)

Italy

Embassy: 15 Sharia Abdel Rahman Fahmi, Garden City, Cairo (☎ 354-3195)

Consulate: 52 Tariq al-Hurriya, Alexandria (☎ 482-7292); open from 8.30 am to 2.30 pm daily except Sunday

Japan

Embassy: Cairo Centre building, 3rd floor, 2 Sharia Abdel Kader Hamza, Garden City, Cairo (☎ 355-3962)

Consulate: 41 Sharia Mustapha Abu Heif, Saba Pasha, Ramla, Alexandria (☎ 587-1859)

Hours are from 8.30 am to 3.30 pm, Sunday to Thursday.

Jordan

6 Sharia Gohainy, Doqqi, Cairo (☎ 348-5566)

Hours are from 9 am to 3 pm, Saturday to Thursday. The embassy is two blocks west of the Sheraton Hotel. Visas cost from nothing for Australians to E£63 for UK citizens, E£77 for Americans and E£91 for Canadians. You apply in the morning and come back to collect the visa at 2 pm. You'll need one photo. It is generally quite easy, and cheaper, to get a Jordanian visa on entering the country (JD10 for UK and USA citizens; free for Australians). At Aqaba, there is a police and immigration station at the passenger ferry terminal, where visas are issued on the spot, although they can keep you waiting a bit.

Kenya

7 Sharia al-Mohandis Galal, Mohandiseen, Cairo (☎ 345-3907)

Visas valid for three months and good for travel in Kenya for a month cost E£26 for most western nationalities. You need one photo. The embassy is open from 8 am to 2 pm, but closed on Saturday and Sunday.

Libya

Embassy: 7 Sharia As-Saleh Ayoub, Zamalek, Cairo (☎ 340-1801)

It is possible to visit Libya, but generally only 10 day visas are being issued. Visas cost US$30 and are supposedly issued in three days, however, the process has been known to take much longer. Two photos are required and you may need a translation into Arabic of your passport details, authenticated by your embassy, along with a letter of recommendation from your embassy.

Consulate: Sharia Lumumba, Alexandria (☎ 494-0297); hours are from 8 am to 2 pm, daily except Friday

Netherlands

Embassy: 18 Sharia Hassan Sabri, Zamalek, Cairo (☎ 340-1936)

Consulate: 3rd floor, 18 Sharia al-Hurriya, Alexandria (☎ 482-9044, 483-4210)

New Zealand

New Zealand's affairs are handled by the UK Embassy.

Norway

8 Sharia el-Gezirah, Zamalek, Cairo (☎ 340-8046)

Saudi Arabia

Embassy: 2 Sharia Ahmed Nessim, Giza (☎ 349-0797)

You'll have little joy trying to get a visa here; the consulate in Suez supposedly issues transit visas for those going by ferry from Suez to Port Sudan in Sudan but some travellers have found even these impossible to get.

Consulate: 9 Sharia Batalsa, Alexandria (☎ 482-9911); open from 9 am to 2.30 pm, daily except Friday

Consulate: Port Tawfiq (around the corner from the tourist office), Suez (☎ 222461); open from 9 am to 3 pm daily except Friday

Spain

41 Sharia Ismail Mohammed, Zamalek, Cairo (☎ 340-6397)

South Africa

21-23 Sharia al-Giza, Giza, Cairo

Sudan

Embassy: 4 Sharia al-Ibrahimy, Garden City, Cairo (☎ 354-5043)

Consulate: 1 Sharia Mohammed Fahmy as-Said, Garden City (☎ 354-9661)

The consulate is around the corner from the embassy and is open roughly from 10 am to 1 pm Saturday to Thursday. It's probably best to get there as early as possible. You can't miss it; there will probably be plenty of Sudanese negotiating their way past a black grill gate. You will probably be ushered straight in. Five copies of the application, five passport-size photos, and a letter of recommendation from your embassy are required before the visa can be issued. At the time of writing, it was taking anything up to a month to issue a visa. Mention of being a journalist or similar profession may not enhance your chances. They do *not* take your passport while processing your application. You pay US$50 cash (they will not accept other currencies) on receipt of the visa, which is valid for use within a month and good for a month's stay.

Sweden

Embassy: 13 Sharia Mohammed Mazhar, Zamalek, Cairo (☎ 341-4132)

Consulate: 55 Sharia 26 July, Alexandria (☎ 483-3755)

Switzerland

10 Sharia Abdel Khaliq Sarwat, Central Cairo (☎ 5758133)

Syria

18 Sharia Abdel Rahim Sabri, Doqqi, Cairo (☎ 377-7020)

Visas are usually issued within three days; two photos and a letter of recommendation from your embassy are required. For Australians it is free,

Americans pay E£116, and most other nationalities pay E£185.

Tunisia
26 Sharia al-Gezira, Zamalek, Cairo (☎ 340-4940)
Visas can be obtained with relatively little sweat. You need two photos. EC citizens pay nothing, others E£23. The visa is valid for one month.

Turkey
Embassy: 25 Sharia al-Falaki, Central Cairo (☎ 356-3318)
Consulate: 11 Sharia Kamel el-Kilani (☎ 493-9086); open Sunday to Thursday from 9 am to 3 pm

Uganda
9 Midan al-Missaha, Doqqi, Cairo (☎ 348-6070)

UK
Embassy: 7 Sharia Ahmed Ragheb, Garden City, Cairo (☎ 354-0850); hours are from 7.30 am to 2 pm, Sunday to Thursday
Consulate: 3 Sharia Mena, Rushdy, Alexandria (☎ 546-7001/2); open Sunday to Thursday from 8 am to 1 pm

USA
Embassy: 5 Sharia Latin America, Garden City, Cairo (☎ 355-7371); open Sunday to Thursday from 8 am to 4.30 pm
Consulate: Unit 64904, 110 Tariq al-Hurriya, Alexandria (☎ 482-1911); open from 8.30 am to 4.30 pm, Sunday to Thursday

CUSTOMS

A grand total of E£1000 can be imported into or exported out of the country. If you have more than this on leaving the country, there is a slim chance you might have the excess confiscated. There are no restrictions on the import of foreign currencies, although you are supposed to declare all you have when you enter. You are not supposed to take out more than you have brought in and declared.

Sometimes the Customs Declaration Form D is given to arriving tourists to fill out. You are supposed to list all cameras, jewellery, cash, travellers' cheques and electronics (personal stereos, computers, radios, VCRs, etc). No-one ever seems to be asked for this form on departure, and few tourists are given it on arrival. Travellers are, however, regularly asked to declare and register their video cameras.

There are prohibited and restricted articles including books, printed matter, motion pictures, phonographs and materials which the government considers 'subversive or constituting a national risk or incompatible with the public interest'. Articles for espionage or 'intelligence activities' are banned, as are explosives.

The duty-free limit on arrival is one litre of alcohol, one litre of perfume, 200 cigarettes and 25 cigars. On top of that, you can buy another three litres of alcohol plus a wide range of other duty-free articles anytime within the next 30 days. For details on duty-free shopping see the Things to Buy section later in this chapter.

MONEY
Costs

It's difficult to say what travelling around Egypt will cost you. It depends on where you stay, what you eat, what you want to see and how you travel. However, whatever budget you decide to travel on, you'll find Egypt great value compared to western countries.

It is still quite possible to get by on US$10 a day or even less if you're willing to stick to hostels or cheap hotels (E£5 to E£10), eat the staple snacks of fuul or ta'amiyya, limit yourself to one historic site per day and take 3rd class trains packed to the hilt with screaming babies, chicken cages and half the Egyptian army.

At the other extreme, if you stay in luxury hotels, fly from place to place and want to see all the top sites in a relatively short period of time you'll spend a lot. Egypt has plenty of hotels at US$50 to US$150 or more per day.

Most travellers will probably be looking for something between the extremes. In this case, if you stay in a modest hotel and have a room with a fan and private bathroom, eat in regular restaurants but have the occasional splurge, travel on buses or service taxis, and aim to see a couple of sites each day, you'll be looking at between US$15 toUS$25 a day.

To give some indication of daily costs, a fuul or ta'amiyya sandwich costs about 35 pt while a meal in a cheap restaurant will set you back E£4 to E£8. A cup of tea/coffee is 30/50 pt, a beer retails for around E£5 and a bottle of mineral water is E£1.50. A kg of apples, a relatively expensive fruit in Egypt, will cost E£8 to E£12; on the other side of the scale, a kg of bananas is just E£1.50. Local phone calls cost just 10 pt and a newspaper is 50 pt. Luxuries like a *shisha* (water pipe) is 60 pt and a shoeshine is 50 pt.

The major expense will be transport and entry fees to the ancient sites. Since the last edition, entry fees have risen drastically. The Egyptian Museum in Cairo, for instance, costs a whopping E£60; the newly opened Tomb of Nefertari near Luxor is an incredible E£200. Luckily, students get half price on almost all ancient sites. Egyptians too, it may be noted, pay much less than foreigners for admission to sites (sometimes as little as one tenth) as well as for rooms in hotels. However, before you complain, bear in mind that, with an average monthly wage of about E£200, an Egyptian teacher with a family would find a trip to the museum at E£60 almost prohibitive.

A service charge of 12% is applied in restaurants and hotels and, in recent years, has been accompanied by a 5 to 7% sales tax. In addition, some governorates levy an additional tax of anywhere between 1 to 4% for rooms in luxury hotels. In other words, the price you're quoted for a mid-range or top-end hotel could be slugged with 23% tax by the time you come to pay.

Those heading for Sinai should note that most things are more expensive there than anywhere else in Egypt (see the Information section at the start of the Sinai chapter for details).

Carrying Money

A money pouch worn under your clothing is the most secure way to carry money. Avoid leaving your wallet in your back pocket and be careful about carrying around a lot of cash, as pickpockets are a definite problem at the more popular sights and in the big cities (see the Dangers & Annoyances section later in this chapter).

Organising Your Money

There seems little point in buying Egyptian currency before you leave home. Aside from the fact that importing more than E£1000 is illegal (even if they don't seem to check what you're carrying), you may well lose out. Thomas Cook in London was quoting a rate 10% inferior to that available in Cairo at the time of research.

Most foreign hard currencies, cash or travellers' cheques, can be readily changed in Egypt, although in smaller places, US dollars, UK pounds and Deutschmarks are probably the safest bet. It's best to vary the forms of money and the currencies that you bring – by having cash in one currency and travellers' cheques in another, you can take advantage of whichever has the better exchange rate. Well-known brands of travellers' cheques are best and, ideally, you should back them up with a credit card or Eurocheques. Eurocheques can be cashed at some banks – you need your Eurocheque card and passport. Cheques issued on post office accounts (common in Europe) or cards linked to such accounts cannot be used in Egypt. Banks sometimes have a small handling charge on travellers' cheques, something in the order of 50 pt, plus E£2 to E£3 for stamps. Always ask about commission as it can vary. Recently, some travellers have reported that banks and exchange bureaus will not cash US$100 notes for fear of them being counterfeit. It may be wise to avoid bringing these notes.

A host of foreign banks are represented in Cairo (see the Information section in the Cairo chapter for addresses) and some in Alexandria, should you need specialised services of any kind. Check with your bank before you leave home if it has a particular partner in Cairo through which it effects money transfers.

It is also possible to have money wired from home through American Express. This service operates through most of its branches, and can be used by anyone, regardless of whether you have one of their cards or travellers' cheques. You simply need to arrange for someone from home to send whatever amount you need to a nominated office in Egypt. The charge for this service is about US$80 per US$1000, payable in the country from where the money is sent.

You can obtain hard currency or travellers' cheques from American Express using an American Express card or, with a Visa or MasterCard, from Thomas Cook. The limit appears to be only the conditions on your card and the availability of cash. Only the bigger branches of Banque Misr in the main centres will sell hard currency. All of these places will usually oblige you to change first into local currency and then back into the hard currency.

Credit Cards American Express, Visa, MasterCard, JCB cards and Eurocard can be used for purchases in a wide range of stores displaying the appropriate signs.

Visa and MasterCard can be used for cash advances from many branches of Banque Misr and the National Bank of Egypt as well as Thomas Cook. Banque Misr generally charges no commission for cash advances, and the limit appears to depend on the terms of your particular card. Outside the big cities and tourist hubs, cash advances are often impossible, so keep some travellers' cheques and/or cash handy.

Currency
The official currency of Egypt is called the pound (E£). In Arabic it is called a *guinay*. A pound = 100 piastres (pt – sometimes indicated by ⌒ or 1000 millims. The Arabic word for piastre is *irsh* or *girsh*. There are notes in denominations of 25 and 50 pt and E£1, E£5, E£10, E£20, E£50 and E£100 (the latter is rarely seen). Many of the notes are extremely dilapidated.

Coins in circulation are for denominations of 1, 5, 10, 20 and 25 pt. The locals have colloquial names for the coins – see Language in the Facts about the Country chapter.

Prices can be written with or without a decimal point. For example, E£3.35 can also be written as 335 pt. Some places still write prices in millims, or a combination of pounds and millims, which gives you three figures after the decimal point.

There is a severe shortage of small change in Egypt. The 25 and 50 pt notes, which are useful for tipping, local transport and avoiding the painfully repetitious incidence of not being given the correct change, are not always easy to come by – they should be hoarded. Sometimes you're offered 'change' in the guise of boxes of matches, sweets, aspirins and the like, although more often than not they pocket the difference. The only answer is to be ruthless: when you're told there's no change, don't scrape around and find it yourself – insist that they find it. Taxi drivers are rarely going to have change if the fare can be rounded up against you. An E£8 taxi fare will often be E£10 if you don't have exactly E£8 to give the driver.

Currency Exchange
The Egyptian pound was partly floated in 1987, so that it fluctuates in value according to economic conditions – it seems closely tied to the US dollar. Much to the surprise of many, the pound has remained fairly steady since late 1990.

Exchange rates for a range of foreign currencies were as follows at the time of research. Check with your bank for the latest rates.

Australia	A$1	=	E£2.66
Canada	C$1	=	E£2.47
France	F10	=	E£6.76
Germany	DM1	=	E£2.29
Greece	Dr100	=	E£1.44
Israel	NIS	=	E£1.05
Japan	Y100	=	E£3.14
Jordan	JD1	=	E£4.18
UK	UK£1	=	E£5.29
USA	US$1	=	E£3.39

Changing Money
Money can be officially changed at American Express and Thomas Cook offices, commercial banks, foreign exchange (forex) bureaus and some hotels. Note that rates can vary quite a bit between banks though the variations seem to be minimal on the US

Tips on Tipping: Mastering the Payment of Baksheesh

Tipping in Egypt is called baksheesh, although it is more than just a reward for having done a service properly. Salaries and wages in Egypt are much lower than in western countries, so baksheesh is regarded as a means of supplementing income – an often essential means. For example, cleaners in a one or two star hotel earn only about E£60 per month, so E£1 a day in baksheesh would mean quite a lot to them. Public servants generally earn only about E£200 a month.

For western travellers who are not used to almost continual tipping, demands for baksheesh for doing anything from opening a door to guiding you, against your will, through an ancient site can be quite irritating. But it is the accepted way of getting things done in Egypt. Don't be intimidated into paying baksheesh when you don't think the service warrants it, but remember that more things warrant baksheesh here than anywhere in the west.

In hotels and restaurants, a 12% service charge is included at the bottom of the bill, but the money goes into the till rather than into the pocket of the woman who cleaned your room or the waiter. If you want to tip someone, you'll have to do so directly. Services such as opening a door or carrying your bags warrant 25 or 50 pt. A guard who shows you something off the beaten track at an ancient site should receive about E£1. Baksheesh is not necessary when asking for directions, although in Cairo there seems to be a band of professional direction-givers who ask for baksheesh practically before they have led you down the street you never wanted to know about anyway. Many of these guys profess to be English teachers or other such professionals – what you give them or how you get rid of them is up to you!

In tombs and temples, if you're alone or with one or two others, the guards will whisper to you about some supposedly Pharaonic secret that they want to reveal only to you. Their English usually amounts to only a few words, which means that they can't really explain anything they're showing you. You might be taken by the arm and shown a deteriorating panel of hieroglyphs depicting a fire, a basket of fruit or a couple of dogs. The guard will look around to make sure no-one else is listening and whisper, 'Ah food. Ah dog. Yes', and smile with conspiratorial delight. Such Pharaonic 'secrets' can cost a pound.

Unfortunately, in several tourist areas, many children have become baksheesh brats. They scream and claw at you, demanding baksheesh and pens. How you handle this is up to you – there's no 'right answer' and it's unlikely that anything is going to reverse the phenomenon. If you do want to give money or gifts to impoverished children, you'll have a much greater impact by making a donation through a school, orphanage, medical clinic or any number of other social welfare organisations.

One last tip: carry lots of small change with you, but keep it separate from bigger bills, so that baksheesh demands don't increase when they see that you could supposedly afford more. ■

---

dollar. The hotels sometimes charge higher commissions than the other institutions. The forex bureaus often offer slightly better rates than the banks for cash, but sometimes don't accept travellers' cheques. You may find some banks reluctant to cash travellers' cheques or even foreign cash if they can fob you off to the local branch of American Express or Thomas Cook. Both companies have slightly lower exchange rates than the banks. Whatever method you use for changing money, make sure you have your passport with you, as you'll nearly always need it.

At the time of writing it was not possible to change Sudanese currency in Egypt. You may also have difficulty finding somewhere to exchange Jordanian dinars.

Excess Egyptian pounds can be changed back into hard currency at the end of your stay, or during if you wish, at some banks, forex bureaus and Thomas Cook and American Express offices.

See Business Hours later in this chapter for opening hours of banks and other institutions.

Black Market

The black market for hard currency is negligible and few travellers can be bothered hunting it out for the fraction of the difference it makes.

Bargaining

Bargaining is part of everyday life in Egypt. Almost everything is open to haggling –

from hotel rooms to the fruit juice you buy at a local stand or the felucca which takes you off down the Nile. How hard you go about it is up to you. When buying souvenirs in bazaars like Cairo's famous Khan al-Khalili, don't start bargaining until you have an idea of the true price, and never quote a price you're not prepared to pay. Most of all, take your time, have some fun, accept the tea or coffee they offer and play along with them. You're not obliged to buy and they won't be offended if you don't – though no doubt they'll keep up the sales pitch.

POST & COMMUNICATIONS

The Egyptian postal system is improving and eventually most mail gets to its destination. Letters can be slow in coming and going; postcards are even slower; and packages...well, bring out the camel express.

Postal Rates

Postcards and letters up to 15g cost 55 pt to Arab and some African countries and 80 pt to all other countries, although sometimes 70 pt seems to suffice for postcards. Stamps are available at post offices, and some souvenir kiosks, shops, newsstands and the reception desks of some major hotels. Stamps bought outside the post office generally cost a little more than their face value.

Sending Mail

Post offices are generally open from 8.30 am to 3 pm daily except Friday. Letters and postcards can take anywhere from four to 10 days to get to the UK and one to three weeks to get to the USA or Australia. Sending mail from the post boxes at major hotels instead of from the post offices seems to be quicker. If you use the post boxes, blue is international airmail, red is internal mail and green internal express mail.

Packages

Packages going by normal sea mail or airmail normally have to be sent from the GPO, although in Cairo they can only go from the huge post office branch at Midan Ramses. As an indication of fees, a parcel to Australia costs E£32.50 per kg for airmail;

E£16 to the UK. Sea mail to both is E£8.35 (and arrival times impossible to guess). Parcels of more than 20 kg for Western Europe and Africa, and 30 kg to the USA, will not be accepted. Nor should they be bigger than one metre long and deep, and half a metre wide.

There is usually a long and complicated process of customs inspection and form filling to be withstood – don't close the parcel until the procedures are over. You may have to get export licences or have goods inspected, depending on what they are. Printed matter and audio and visual material will be checked and foodstuffs (except dried food) and medicines also need clearance.

The easiest way to send a package is to pay someone else a small fee and have them do it for you. Some shopkeepers will provide this service, especially if you've bought the article in their bazaar. It should include obtaining an export licence, packaging and mailing.

Express Mail Service It is possible to send a letter of up to 100g by Express Mail Service (EMS). There are several branches of this service around the main cities. Such a letter to the UK would cost E£20 and arrival is 'guaranteed' by the following day. Parcels of up to 10 kg to Australia cost E£259 and take at least three days to arrive. To the UK, parcels of 500g cost E£34 while parcels weighing one/10 kg cost E£45/243; they supposedly take only two days to arrive.

A local fellahin sends registered mail from the post office on the west bank in Luxor, near the Tomb of Ramose.

In addition to the EMS fast mail service, you could try DHL, TNT Skypack or various other courier services. Their addresses are listed under Post in the Information section of the Cairo chapter.

Receiving Mail

Letters take one to two weeks to arrive from Europe, and one to three weeks from Australia and the USA. Mail can be received at American Express offices or at the poste restante in most Egyptian cities. American Express offices are the better option and you don't need to have an American Express card or travellers' cheques to use the mail pick-up service. In Cairo, have mail sent to its office at 15 Sharia Qasr el-Nil, Cairo, Egypt. Bring your passport.

The poste restante in Egypt functions remarkably well and is generally free (though in Alexandria there's a small fee to collect letters). If you plan to pick up mail there, ensure that the clerk checks under Mr, Ms or Mrs in addition to your first and last names.

Some embassies will hold mail for their nationals, but check this first with your representatives.

If you receive a package, you'll probably get a card (written in Arabic) telling you to pick it up from the GPO or one of the other main branches. As anyone who has tried it will attest, having a package sent to you in Egypt is slow torture – you could wait in vain for months.

Telephone

The phones in Egypt can be a test of one's patience, but they're a lot better than they used to be. In 1986 the government began revamping the system and lines and connections are still being upgraded around the country.

In Cairo, the central telephone and telegraph offices at Sharia Adly, Midan Tahrir and Sharia Alfi Bey are open 24 hours a day, seven days a week. Other telephone offices, such as the one on Sharia Ramses in Cairo, are generally open from 8 am to 10 pm.

Telephone Codes

If you're calling Egypt from abroad, the country code is 20.

The international access code (to call abroad from Egypt) is 00.

Area codes for some cities and towns within Egypt are:

'Ain Sukhna	062
Al-Arish	068
Al-Balyana	093
Al-Faiyum	084
Al-Minya	086
Al-Quseir	088
Alexandria	03
Aswan	097
Asyut	088
Baltim	047
Beni Suef	082
Cairo	02
Dahab	062
Dakhla Oasis	092
Damietta	057
El Alamein	03
El-Tor	062
Farafra Oasis	010+1405
Gamasa	057
Hurghada	065
Ismailia	064
Kharga Oasis	092
Kom Ombo	097
Luxor	095
Marsa Matruh	03
Na'ama Bay	062
Nuweiba	062
Port Safaga	065
Port Said	066
Qena	096
Ras al-Bar	057
Ras as-Sudr	062
Sharm el-Sheikh	062
Sidi Abdel Rahman	03
Siwa	03+934026
Sohag	093
Suez	062
Taba	062
Tanta	040

Offices elsewhere around the country tend to set their own opening hours.

For general enquiries call ☎ 140.

Local Calls Local telephone calls from pay phones cost 5 pt or 10 pt for anywhere between 30 seconds and three minutes depending on the mood of the phone. You'll usually hear a beep before it cuts off. Only the silver-coloured 5 pt and 10 pt coins can be used (the copper-toned coins of the same denomination are too thick). The public phones (which come in a variety of colours, including red, yellow and green) are usually in front of telephone offices or, in Cairo, in metro stations. There's often a queue and many of them don't work. Many kiosks and small shops have telephones for public use, for 50 pt per local call. Major hotels usually charge E£1.

National & International Calls Long-distance calls can be made from some home phones, but most are made from hotels or telephone offices. Many hotels, but not the very cheap ones, have direct international lines, but they'll charge more than the telephone offices (sometimes as much as double).

Card phones are increasingly coming into use though they're still scarce in smaller towns and the cards themselves are sometimes in short supply. You'll find these bright orange phones mainly in telephone offices, where you can buy phone cards valued at E£15 (135 units). You get approximately the same amount of time as you would for a call placed through the exchange, but you can simply call direct anywhere in Egypt or internationally. Dial 00 and the country code for international calls. If you're heading to Sinai, buy your phone cards in Cairo before you leave, otherwise you'll pay a lot more for a card.

Calls booked at telephone offices must be paid for in advance and there is a three minute minimum. They can either be taken in a booth at the office or directed to an outside number such as a private home or hotel. If you opt for the latter, keep the receipt just in case you need a refund for an incomplete call.

There are different rates for day (8 am to 7.59 pm) and night (8 pm to 7.59 am) calls. As an example, a three minute call to the USA costs E£21/11 at the day/night rates respectively; to Australia E£27/23.50; to the UK and Europe E£18.50/12.80.

The big news is that collect calls can now be made from Cairo, but only to those countries – such as Canada, Italy, South Korea and the UK and USA – which have set up Home Country Direct phones. With this service, you can get through to an operator in one of the above mentioned countries and then reverse the charges or, depending on the service, charge the call to a credit card. At the time of writing, this service was offered by only a few places in Cairo such as the Marriott or Semiramis InterContinental hotels, the telephone office in the departure hall at the new airport terminal, or at British Airways (calls to the UK only).

Fax & Telegraph

Fax machines are available for sending and receiving documents at the main telephone and telegraph offices in the big cities, at EMS offices, at most three to five star hotels, and at some of the smaller hotels as well. You can receive a fax for free at American Express offices but it's not possible to send faxes from there.

From a telephone office, a one page fax to the UK or USA costs about E£14, and E£20.25 to Australia. Hotel rates are quite a bit more. The minimum from the Nile Hilton to the UK is E£38.50, and E£51.25 to Australia. Receiving a fax message costs E£6 at a telephone office, or E£5.50 at an EMS office.

Telegrams in English or French can be sent from the telephone and telegraph offices in central Cairo. The rates to the UK, USA and Europe are 67 pt per word and to Australia 84 pt per word. Each word in an address is also counted. Major hotels also offer this service but rates vary.

BOOKS

The following is a short list of books which can further introduce you to Egypt and the Egyptians. Most can be found at bookshops in Egypt or in the library and bookshop of the American University in Cairo. Outside Egypt, many of them can be ordered through local bookshops.

Most books are published in different editions by different publishers in different countries. As a result, a book might be a hardcover rarity in one country while it's readily available in paperback in another. Fortunately, bookshops and libraries search by title or author, so your local bookshop or library is best placed to advise you on the availability of the following recommendations.

Lonely Planet

It's pleasing to be able to claim that for more information on Egypt's neighbours and for travel beyond Egypt, most of the best guides come from Lonely Planet. Our *Israel & the Palestinian Territories* and *Jordan & Syria* guides comprehensively cover the three countries immediately to the east of Egypt, while *Arab Gulf States* is our guide to Bahrain, Kuwait, Oman, Qatar, Saudi Arabia and the United Arab Emirates. For an overview of all these areas and more, pick up our *Middle East on a shoestring*. Heading west, our *North Africa* guide will take you through Libya, Algeria, Tunisia and Morocco, while long-haulers will want to get their hands on our *Africa* book which covers every country in the continent.

Guidebooks

The Blue Guide, by Veronica Seton-Williams & Peter Stocks, is one of the most comprehensive guides to Egypt. This massive tome describes every place of even the slightest historical interest and has excellent sections on Egypt's natural history. However, it is a bit heavy to lug around.

Egypt, *The Nile* and *Cairo* are three separate books produced by Insight Guides. Put together by a team of specialists, they are colourful journey companions in essay style rather than practical guides.

Let's Go's *Israel & Egypt* is researched and compiled by Harvard University students. This guide also briefly covers Jordan, the West Bank & parts of Syria.

Islands of the Blest by Cassandra Vivian is a comprehensive guide to the five Western Desert oases as well as to Wadi Natrun, El Alamein and the Qattara Depression. It gives scant detail to practical information but provides a lot of cultural background and has seven pull-out maps.

The *Guide to Alexandrian Monuments* describes the main attractions and details the city's history; it's intermittently available at the Graeco-Roman Museum in Alexandria.

Cairo: A Practical Guide was published by the American University in Cairo Press in 1988. Almost every bit of practical information from auctions to toy shops is contained in this guide, however, much of it is now way out of date and it's doubtful whether it's worth the E£30. The maps are some of the best you will find.

The Red Sea & Sinai

Guide to the Exploration of the Sinai by Alberto Siliotti is one of the best guides available to the peninsula, though the maps are not that good.

The Red Sea Coasts of Egypt – Sinai & the Mainland by Jenny Jobbins has good route descriptions of the coastal road around Sinai.

There is a range of books aimed at divers. One of the best is the *Red Sea Divers Guide (Volume 2)* by Shlomo & Roni Cohen which is available in English, German and Italian. It covers the area from Sharm el-Sheikh to Hurghada and is indispensable to all divers, with information on the best wrecks and dive sites, as well as on marine life. Don't mix it up with volume one which isn't nearly as comprehensive.

The Egyptian Red Sea – A Diver's Guide by Eric Hanauer is another comprehensive guide to what to look for and where to find it.

A more specific guide to the marine life of the area is the bilingual German-English *Red Sea Underwater Guide* by Helmut Debelius.

Travel

Gerard de Nerval's *Journey to the Orient* was first published in the 19th century. This book will prime you for exploration of the mysteries of Egypt.

Egypt – A Traveller's Anthology, compiled by Christopher Pick, is a collection of literary titbits from some of Egypt's more illustrious visitors such as Flaubert, EM Forster, Freya Stark and Howard Carter.

An Egyptian Journal by William Golding is an often negative account of Golding's observations as he lays on his bunk cruising up and down the Nile.

A Thousand Miles up the Nile by Amelia Edwards is a well-known but long-winded chronicle of this Englishwoman's travels in 1873-74.

The Other Nile by Charlie Pye-Smith is a highly readable and incisive narrative of a leisurely ramble up the Nile through Egypt and into Sudan, where internal strife stopped the author going any further. He contrasts the trip with an earlier one he made right through Sudan and Ethiopia in the mid-1970s.

Douglas Kennedy's *Beyond the Pyramids* is one of the few travelogues written about Egypt in recent years and is an entertaining, often humorous read.

EM Forster's *Alexandria: A History & A Guide*, written during WWI, is still regarded as the best historical guide to the city. In a collection of short essays, Forster recreates the more than 2000 years of Alexandria's existence and then takes the visitor on a guided tour of the city's attractions as they were early this century. An annotated edition of the book recently published by Michael Haag Ltd brings the guide up to date for the modern traveller.

Lawrence Durrell's *The Alexandria Quartet* offers a fascinating insight into the cosmopolitan community of Alexandria before and during WWII.

Mike Asher's book *In Search of the 40 Days Road* recounts his search for the trail which Sudanese camel traders follow when taking their camels north to Egypt.

History & Politics

Arab & Islamic History For those wanting to become generally acquainted with the wider Arabic-speaking world, there are several books to recommend. Philip Hitti's work, *History of the Arabs*, now regarded as something of a classic and highly readable, is one.

A more recent but equally acclaimed work is Albert Hourani's *A History of the Arab Peoples*. Peter Mansfield has written several insightful works, including *A History of the Middle East* and *The Arabs*.

If it's weightier stuff you're after, or a pretty comprehensive reference source (although it's weak on more recent history) not just on the Arabs but on the whole Muslim world, you could try delving into the two hardback or four paperback volumes of *A Cambridge History of Islam*.

Al-Fustat, by Wladislaw B Kubick, is a slim volume dealing with the Muslims' first settlement in what would one day come to be known as Cairo.

The Citadel of Cairo, by William Lyster, traces the history of the most visible feature of Cairo's landscape.

Egyptian History *The Penguin Guide to Ancient Egypt* by William J Murnane is one of the best overall books on the life and monuments of ancient Egypt. There are plenty of illustrations and descriptions of almost every major monument in the country.

The British Museum Book of Ancient Egypt, edited by Stephen Quirke and Jeffrey Spencer, gives an authoritative overview of ancient Egypt, but is surprisingly short on plans and diagrams of monuments.

Sakkara and Memphis, by Jill Kamil, is full of plans, photos and descriptions of these sights. *Luxor*, also by Jill Kamil, may also be of interest.

The Ancient Egyptians: Religious Beliefs & Practices by Rosalie David is one of the first books to trace the evolution of religious beliefs and practices in ancient Egypt. It is a very thorough and comprehensible treatment of a complex subject.

The Gods & Symbols of Ancient Egypt by Manfred Lurker is an illustrated dictionary which offers brief explanations and descriptions of the most important aspects of ancient Egypt. It can be helpful in understanding some of the hieroglyphs.

An excellent reference on Pharaonic deities is George Hart's *A Dictionary of Egyptian Gods and Goddesses*. It's portable and is extensively illustrated with line drawings.

Discovering Egyptian Hieroglyphics, by Karl Theodor Zangich, explains in depth the Egyptians' ancient system of writing, which long baffled the modern world before the Rosetta stone helped shed light on it.

For information on the stone itself there's *The Rosetta Stone*, published by the British Museum, which tells where it all began and how the text was deciphered.

Richard H Wilkinson's *Reading Egyptian Art* is an excellent encyclopedia of the signs and symbols incorporated in ancient Egyptian painting and sculpture, but it's way too heavy to carry around.

The Complete Tutankhamun by Nicholas Reeves is a large, superbly illustrated hardcover book which gives you just what its title proclaims.

The Blue Nile and *The White Nile*, by Alan Moorehead, are classics which cover the history of the Nile during the 19th century. *The Blue Nile* deals with the period 1798 to 1856; *The White Nile* is concerned with events from 1856 to the end of the century. Moorehead's detailed descriptions of events and personalities are superb. These two should definitely be read.

Great Cairo: Mother of the World, by Desmond Stewart, covers 55 centuries of Cairo's history; the descriptions of the many diabolical rulers are wonderful.

Nagel's Encyclopedia Guide to Egypt is an expensive but extremely thorough guide to Egypt's ancient monuments.

Modern History *In Search of Identity* is the autobiography of Anwar Sadat. It is a good introduction to the events leading up to and following Egypt's 1952 Revolution.

Nasser – The Final Years, by Abdel Magid Farid, records events following the October 1967 war to 27 February 1970, the day before Nasser died. It consists largely of transcripts of meetings between Nasser and various world leaders.

The History of Egypt, P J Vatikiotis, is one of the best books on the history of Egypt. It emphasises the 19th and 20th centuries with a focus on political and social development since 1805 and the 'new social order' that has evolved since the 1952 Revolution.

A Short History of Modern Egypt is by Afaf Lutfi al-Sayyid Marsot, one of Egypt's foremost historians. It's for those after a more concise history of Egypt from 639 AD.

General
For information on Egyptian authors and their works, see the Arts section in the Facts about the Country chapter.

People & Society Amitav Ghosh's *In an Antique Land* is a superb account of life in a Nile Delta village.

Richard Critchfield's *Shahhat: An Egyptian*, , is an in-depth portrait of a young man named Shahhat and of his life in an Egyptian village. Critchfield lived and worked for an extended period in a west bank village near Luxor to write this.

Egypt: Burdens of the Past, Options for the Future by John Waterbury is an excellent comprehensive portrayal of Egyptian society by a leading scholar of North Africa.

An Account of the Manners & Customs of the Modern Egyptians by Edward Lane is a wonderful classic, first published in 1839, which continues to offer insight into the traditional Arab culture of Egypt.

Khul-Khaal: Five Egyptian Women Tell their Stories, edited by Nayra Atiya, is the life stories of five contemporary Egyptian women from a variety of backgrounds. Fascinating information for anyone interested in understanding Egyptian life.

Daughters of Isis – Women of Ancient Egypt by Joyce Tyldesley is a vivid portrait of daily life in ancient Egypt from a feminine perspective. According to Tyldesley, women of this era enjoyed a 'legal, social and sexual independence unrivalled by their Greek and Roman sisters'.

Women in Egyptian Public Life, by Earl A Sullivan, gives a different insight again into what some extraordinary women have achieved in Egypt.

Baladi Women in Cairo by Evelyn A Early is a discussion on everyday matters with women living in the overcrowded Cairo suburb of Bulaq.

John H Taylor's *Egypt & Nubia* is an attractively illustrated and informative history of ancient Nubia.

Coptic Egypt, by Jill Kamil, gives an historical outlay to Coptic art, the monasteries and the life of the Copts.

Monks and Monasteries in the Desert, by Otto Meinardus, offers information on a little discussed aspect of Egyptian religious life that could be of interest.

Siwa Oasis by Ahmed Fakhry takes a close look at a part of Egypt that is really quite un-Egyptian. It's the first volume of a trilogy about the Western Desert oases entitled *The Oases of Egypt* which Fakhry was writing when he died (the third volume was never finished).

Bedouin of the Sinai by Paola Crociani is a photographic essay of traditional Bedouin life. It's a large coffee-table style book filled with B&W photos.

Wildlife *Natural Selections: A Year of Egypt's Wildlife*, written and illustrated by Richard Hoath, is an insightful and passionate account of the birds, animals, insects and marine creatures that make Egypt their home. The lively text is backed up by many captivating drawings.

Look out also for Hoath's *Field Guide to the Mammals of Egypt* which should be out in 1997.

Food Samia Abdennour's *Egyptian Cooking – A Practical Guide* is a modest, inexpensive cookbook published locally which has more than 300 recipes from mezzes to main courses and drinks.

For a broader, more costly book you could try *Middle Eastern Food*, by Claudia Roden.

Language Those who want a comprehensive guide to Modern Standard Arabic or colloquial Egyptian Arabic should check at the American University in Cairo Bookstore for the latest textbooks.

Otherwise, Lonely Planet's *Egyptian*

Arabic phrasebook should suffice. It's small enough to easily fit in your pocket.

ON-LINE SERVICES

For the latest travel information, visit Lonely Planet's web site. This award-winning site contains updates, recent travellers' letters and a useful travellers' bulletin board.

http://www.lonelyplanet.com

There are many Egypt sites on the internet. For some links, go to Ahmed Khalil's Little Corner in Cyberspace.

http://www.ionet.net/usarch/ak-me-eg.shtml

For a longer list of links, for visitors, academics and general interest, try Egypt Interactive.

http://www.channel1.com/users/mansoorm/index/html

The Egypt Tourism Authority has a site, Egypt Has it All, with pictures and information on the major attractions.

http://163.121.10.41/tourism

If you have time on your hands, load the Brighton Health Care report on the 3D reconstruction of a mummy using CT scanning.

http://www.pavilion.co.uk/Health Services/BrightonHealthCare/mummy.htm

If you're interested in Egyptology, there are some excellent links at:

http://www.sirius.com/reeder/links.html

NEWSPAPERS & MAGAZINES

By Middle Eastern standards, the press in Egypt suffers under a moderate level of censorship. Under President Mubarak, the reins have been loosened somewhat, and there is some reasonably lively debate in the papers and magazines. Total freedom there is not.

The *Egyptian Gazette* is Egypt's daily English-language newspaper. It is difficult to find outside of Cairo and Alexandria, and the news coverage can be pretty mediocre due, in part, to government censorship. The Saturday issue is called the *Egyptian Mail*. The French-language equivalents are the daily *Le*

Progrès Égyptien and Sunday's *Progrès Dimanche*. All are good entertainment for lovers of typos and quirky expressions.

Since 1990, a weekly summary of the Arabic-language daily, *Al-Ahram*, has been providing some decent competition for the daily English-language stalwarts. The English can be a little awkward, however, it has a comprehensive listings guide covering cinema, theatre, classical music, the arts and lectures. It costs 50 pt and is published on Thursday. On Wednesday, Al-Ahram puts out a new weekly French edition, *Hebdo*.

The *Middle East Times* is a weekly English-language newspaper, out every Sunday, that offers quite good coverage of events and issues in Egypt and the rest of the Middle East.

Many major western newspapers and news magazines can be found in Cairo and Alexandria, including *Newsweek* and *Time*. They're available in major hotels and at a few newsstands and bookshops. In Cairo they tend to be a day old. You can even find a selection of western papers as far away as Aswan, where they are usually two or three days old.

The Middle East is a bimonthly magazine published in England which covers news and current events.

Egypt Today, a local English-language publication, is a monthly magazine that covers a variety of subjects including the arts and nature in Egypt. Feature articles regularly focus on different parts of Egypt. Every issue has a guide to nightlife in both Cairo and Alexandria, as well as a few of the main tourist destinations.

Of less interest is *Cairo's*, a flimsy entertainment guide that's essentially a waste of E£4 – most of the listings you'll find in Al-Ahram anyway.

A few other magazines to keep an eye out for are: *Egypt Magazine* a bimonthly which covers contemporary issues and cultural items; *Sports & Fitness Egypt*, a glossy monthly which generally highlights Red Sea dive spots; and *Business Today*, covering business related issues on Egypt and the world.

RADIO & TV

The most interesting development in Egypt is the arrival of satellite and, more recently, cable TV. Many hotels have satellite TV, even some of those towards the lower end, and it has revolutionised viewing possibilities.

The local offering, apart from some good old movies, remains painful. During Ramadan it's throat-slitting, for most westerners anyway. There are three TV channels that are state-controlled. Channels 1 and 3 are predominantly Arabic. Channel 2 has daily English-language programmes and often screens foreign movies, (usually subtitled in Arabic but occasionally dubbed), at 4 pm and 11.30 pm. News in French is broadcast at 7 pm and in English at 9 pm.

Local radio offerings are not much better. Normally, the news can be heard in English on FM95, radio frequency 557 kHz, at 7.30 am, 2.30 pm and 8 pm. This is the European-language station, broadcasting from 7 am to midnight, and, in addition to English, it has programmes in French, German, Italian, and Greek.

Check the *Egyptian Gazette* for the latest radio and TV (both local and satellite) programme information. For a selection of the month's satellite and cable TV highlights, pick up *Egypt Today* magazine.

BBC and Voice of America (VOA) broadcasts can be picked up on medium wave at various times of the morning and evening. The BBC can be heard on 639 kHz and 1320 kHz, and VOA on 1290 kHz. Radio Monte Carlo sometimes has English and French-language programmes in addition to its Arabic broadcasts – it can be picked up on medium wave bands in the evening.

PHOTOGRAPHY & VIDEO
Film & Equipment

Film generally costs as much as, if not more than, it does in the west, so you may as well bring it with you. If you do buy in Egypt, check the expiry dates. As an example of prices, Kodacolor 100/200 (36 exposures) costs about E£15, and Kodacolor 400 (24 exposures) E£14. For Kodachrome 100 slide film, you'll pay E£24 (36 exposures). Colour print processing costs from E£2 to E£4 depending on whether it's a one hour or overnight service, plus from 50 to 135 pt per print depending on print size. B&W processing is not recommended, but colour processing is usually adequate for nonprofessional purposes. Developing a roll of slide film costs between E£10 and E£13. There are quite a few labs and one hour processing places in the big cities and tourist centres, and many of these outlets also do passport photos.

Photography

Egypt is full of opportunities for great photography. Early morning and late afternoon are the best times to take photographs. During the rest of the day, the sunlight can be too bright and the sky too hazy and your photos will look washed out. There are a few remedies for this: a polarisation filter will cut glare and reflection off sand and water; a lens hood will cut some of the glare; Kodachrome film with an ASA of 64 or 25 and Fujichrome 50 and 100 are good slide films to use when the sun is bright.

Cameras and lenses collect dust quickly in Egypt. Lens paper and cleaner are difficult to find, so bring your own. A dust brush is also useful.

Photography is allowed in many of the ancient sites, however, flash photography is banned in some of the tombs to help preserve the paintings. You can take photos of the interior of mosques and temples, although at an increasing number of sites the government now charges E£5 to E£15 for the privilege.

Video

Outrageous fees have been introduced for taking videos in many ancient sites. In most cases it's around E£25, but fees of E£100 are becoming standard fare, and at the Manyal Palace Museum in Cairo the charge is E£150.

Restrictions

Be careful when taking photos of anything other than tourist sites, the Nile, the Suez Canal and beaches. It is forbidden to photograph bridges, railway stations, anything military, airports and other public works. Signs are usually posted.

Photographing People

It can sometimes be tricky taking photos of people, so it's always better to ask first. Children will almost always say yes, but their parents or other adults might say no. Some Muslims believe that by taking photos of children you might be casting an 'evil eye' upon them. Similar attitudes sometimes apply to taking photos of women, especially in the countryside.

Egyptians are also sensitive about the negative aspects of their country. It is not uncommon for someone to yell at you when you're trying to take photos of things like a crowded bus, a donkey cart full of garbage or a beggar – so exercise discretion.

TIME

Egypt is two hours ahead of GMT/UTC and daylight saving time is observed (it begins on 1 May and ends on 30 September). So, without allowing for variations due to daylight saving, when it's noon in Cairo it is: 10 am in London; 5 am in New York and Montreal; 2 am in Los Angeles; 1 pm in Moscow; and 7 pm in Melbourne and Sydney.

ELECTRICITY

Electric current is 220 volts AC, 50 Hz. Alexandria and the Cairo suburbs of Maadi and Heliopolis used to have current of 110 to 120 volts, 50 Hz, but they all seem to have been brought into line with the rest of the country. Wall sockets are the round, two pin European type (though for some strange reason the socket holes are often too narrow to accept European plugs). Bring adapter plugs and transformers if necessary; travel-size transformers are difficult to obtain in Egypt.

WEIGHTS & MEASURES

Egypt is on the metric system. Basic conversion charts are given on the inside of the back cover of this book.

LAUNDRY

There are a few self-service laundries around Cairo but virtually none elsewhere. Another option is to take your clothes to one of Egypt's many 'hole-in-the-wall' laundries where they wash and iron your clothes by hand. The process is fascinating and entertaining to watch. The *mukwagee* (ironing man) takes an ancient iron which opens at the top, places hot coals inside and then fills his mouth with water from a bottle on the table. The water is sprayed from his mouth over the clothes as he vigorously irons. Most hotels can organise to have your washing done.

In a few of the places where travellers hang out, like Luxor and Dahab, some of the cheaper hotels lure guests with advertisements about 'washing machines'. Don't be fooled into thinking they've got the latest Hoover stashed away in a back room. The reality is a humble machine that lethargically twists your clothes around and leaves you to do the rinsing and wringing out. These machines are almost as laborious as your last – and most common – option, which is to do your own washing by hand.

HEALTH

Travel health depends on your predeparture preparations, your day-to-day health care while travelling and how you handle any medical problem or emergency that does develop. While the list of potential dangers can seem quite frightening, with a little luck, some basic precautions and adequate information few travellers experience more than upset stomachs. Refer to the Health appendix for detailed advice, information and recommendations.

TOILETS

Public toilets are bad news: fly-infested, dirty and smelly. Some toilets are still of the squat-over-a-hole-in-a-little-room variety. Only in mid-range and top-end hotels will toilet paper be provided; most toilets simply come equipped with a water squirter for

washing yourself when you're finished. It's a good idea to adopt this practice if you can as toilets in Egypt are not capable of swallowing much toilet paper and it's not uncommon to find toilets in hotels frequented by westerners absolutely choked with the stuff. If you do use toilet paper, put it in the bucket that's usually provided.

While on the subject of ablutions, when trekking in the desert, climbing Mt Sinai or camping out on a beach somewhere please do not leave used toilet paper lying around. At the very least bury it or, better still, take a spare plastic bag with you and put it in there, to be thrown in a bin later on. In places like the rocky Mt Sinai, where it's difficult to bury anything, the latter option is definitely preferable. There's nothing worse for future travellers than finding a pristine spot of nature that's been defiled by shit.

WOMEN TRAVELLERS

Egyptians are conservative, especially about matters concerning sex and women; Egyptian women that is, not foreign women.

An entire book could be written from the comments and stories of women travellers about their adventures and misadventures in Egypt. Most of the incidents are nonthreatening nuisances, in the same way a fly buzzing in your ear is a nuisance: you can swat him away and keep him at a distance, but he's always out there buzzing around.

Attitudes to Women

Most Egyptian women don't wear veils but they are still, for the most part, quite restricted in what they can do with their lives. They do not have the same degree of freedom, if any at all, that western women enjoy. Egyptian men see this not as restraint and control, but as protection and security – many of the women seem to see it that way too.

For many Egyptians, both men and women, the role of a woman is specifically defined: she is mother and matron of the household, and it is this which the men seek to protect – they don't want their wives to have to work. Ironically, in maintaining this position a woman actually works very hard. Even if she can afford domestic help and doesn't do any household work herself, her husband's view is still that she should not have to work for a wage. It is *his* role to provide for the family.

It is difficult for westerners to make balanced judgements about a whole social structure they little understand. It certainly appears that any Egyptian women wanting to go beyond the family roles allotted to them are going to have a very hard time. On rare occasions outstanding and determined individuals – almost exclusively in the upper classes – succeed in carving out some such niche for themselves. The vast majority continue to be raised in and embrace the traditional roles. This is an important consideration – women take the division of roles as seriously as men. And the men are quick to assert that, within the family, women have far greater power than is at first apparent.

Premarital sex is a taboo subject in Egypt, although, as in any society that disapproves of what is considered promiscuous activity, it happens. Nevertheless, it is still rather the exception than the rule – and that goes for men as well as women. The presence of foreign women presents, in the eyes of some Egyptian men, a chance to get around the local norms with greater ease. That this is even possible is heavily reinforced by distorted impressions gained from western TV and, it has to be said, the behaviour of some foreign women in the country.

The belief that the western woman is ready and willing to hop into bed with the nearest male has produced in some Egyptian men the belief that they are all candidates for immediate gratification by any western woman who walks down the street. At the very least, pinching bottoms, brushing breasts or making lewd suggestions seem to be considered by some perfectly natural means of communication with the unknown foreign woman. Flashing and masturbating in front of the victim are not unknown, but serious physical harassment and rape are not significant threats in Egypt.

Safety Tips for Women Travellers

- Wear a wedding band. Generally, Egyptian men seem to have more respect for a married woman (this seems not always to work; sometimes Egyptians assume you are not really married).
- If you are travelling with a man, it may be better to say you're 'married' rather than 'just friends'.
- Avoid direct eye contact with an Egyptian man unless you know him well; dark sunglasses could help.
- Try not to respond to an obnoxious comment from a man – act as if you didn't hear it.
- Be careful in crowds and other situations where you are crammed between people, as it is not unusual for crude things to happen behind you.
- On public transport, sit next to a woman if possible. This is not difficult on the Cairo metro where the first compartment is reserved for women only.
- If you're in the countryside (off the beaten track) it's often a good idea to wear a scarf over your hair.
- Be very careful about behaving in a flirtatious or suggestive manner – it could create more problems than you ever imagined.
- If you need help for any reason (directions etc), ask a woman first. Egyptian women are very friendly and will not threaten or follow you.
- Be wary when horse or camel riding, especially at touristy places. It's not unknown for a guy to ride close to you and grab your horse, among other things. Riding in front of a man on a camel is simply asking for trouble.
- Egypt is not the place for acquiring a full suntan. Only on private beaches in the top-end resorts along the Red Sea and the southern Sinai peninsula are you likely to feel comfortable stripping down to a bikini. Along the Mediterranean coast and in oases pools, you'll have to swim in shorts and a t-shirt, at the very minimum, and even then you'll attract a flock of male onlookers. Egyptian women rarely go swimming; when they do, they swim fully clothed, scarf and all.
- You may find it handy to learn the Arabic for 'don't touch me' *(lā tilmasni)*.
- Being befriended by an Egyptian woman is a great way to learn more about life in Egypt and, at the same time, have someone totally nonthreatening to guide you around. Getting to know an Egyptian woman is, however, easier said than done. You won't find them in cafes or teahouses and, while many do speak at least some English, fewer women speak English than men.

What to Wear

Away from the Sinai beaches, Egyptians are, to a greater or lesser degree, quite conservative, especially about dress. The woman wearing short pants and a tight T-shirt is, in some people's eyes, confirmation of the worst views held of western women. And don't think this goes for women alone. In places less used to tourists, the sight of a man in shorts and singlet is considered offensive. Count the number of Egyptian men in shorts.

Generally, if you're alone or with other women, the amount of harassment you get will be directly related to how you dress: the more skin that is exposed, the more harassment you'll get. As hot as it gets in Egypt, you'll have fewer hassles if you don't dress for hot weather in the same way as you might back home. Unfortunately, although dressing conservatively should reduce the incidence of any such harassment, it by no means guarantees you'll be left alone.

GAY & LESBIAN TRAVELLERS

Homosexuality among males in Egypt is not uncommon. It is, however, clandestine. No man will attest to being gay as Egyptians in general perceive gay men to be weak and feminine. (Indeed, this very perception has been exploited in recent times to demoralise many of those arrested en masse during purges against suspected Islamic fundamentalists. New prisoners are reportedly stripped of their rightful title, allocated a feminine name and are often subject to rape.)

There is no mention in the law of sexual behaviour between consenting adults of the same sex being a criminal offence, however, discretion is advisable.

No national support group exists, and only in Cairo will you find gay bars. The Taverne du Champs de Mars and Jackie's Disco, both in the Nile Hilton Hotel in Cairo, are popular gay hang-outs, as is L'Amphitrion cafe on Sharia Al-Ahram, Heliopolis, Cairo.

DISABLED TRAVELLERS

Egypt is not well equipped for travellers with a mobility problem; ramps are few, public facilities don't necessarily have lifts, and gaining entrance to some of the ancient sites – such as the Pyramids of Giza or the tombs on the west bank near Luxor – is all but impossible due to their narrow entrances and steep stairs. Temples tend to be more accessible as they're generally built on level ground, and some museums have ramps or lifts.

If you have a physical disability, you should get in touch with your national support organisation (preferably the 'travel officer' if there is one) before you leave.

You may also like to contact ETAMS (☎ 575-4721; fax 575-4191), at 13 Sharia Qasr el-Nil, in central Cairo. This tour company specialises in custom-made tours, accommodation and sightseeing in specially equipped buses for disabled individuals and groups, and it also has information on hotels claiming to have facilities catering to the disabled.

SENIOR TRAVELLERS

Unlike in many western countries, there are no discounts on things like public transport, museum admission fees and the like for senior travellers in Egypt.

If you plan to stay in cheap hotels, you'll need to be fit enough to cope with numerous flights of stairs. Many tombs are also accessed by stairs, some of which are steep. The corridors inside tombs are sometimes very low, forcing you to bend over double; some people find this, coupled with the heat and dim lights inside the tombs, quite claustrophobic.

TRAVEL WITH CHILDREN

Successful travel with young children requires planning and effort. Don't try to overdo things and make sure the activities include the kids as well – balance the Egyptian Museum with a camel ride or sailing a felucca. Include children in the trip planning; if they've helped to work out where you will be going they will be much more interested when they get there. In general, Egyptians are delighted to see western children and will often demonstrate this with a lot of touching or an eagerness to keep them amused. See Lonely Planet's *Travel with Children* by Maureen Wheeler for more information.

DANGERS & ANNOYANCES

Egypt is generally a safe place to be, although the continuing violence directed by Islamists at the authorities and tourists, in what appears to be an attempt to overthrow the present regime, has added a degree of uncertainty to travel.

This aside, the amount of violent crime of any kind is negligible compared with its incidence in many western countries. That may be due to a heavy-handed Security regime or the nature of Egyptian society, or more probably a combination of both. This does not mean it does not exist at all, and common sense dictates you don't take anything for granted. In all, even taking the low risk of terrorist attack into account, Cairo is a much safer place to wander around at night than, say, New York.

Terrorism

What began as one or two isolated incidents in 1992 took on all the signs of a concerted campaign against tourism in early 1993 and then seemed to subside again as Islamists turned their attention to killing police. A bomb blast in a central Cairo cafe often frequented by travellers brought home the risk to many with greater force than the several attacks on tour buses had until that point. Subsequent blasts at the Egyptian Museum and on the road to the pyramids rammed the message home further – violence that had been confined largely to Upper Egypt was now possible anywhere.

Although the bulk of the attacks has been directed against the security forces (which have carried out repeated raids in areas as far apart as Aswan and the Cairo suburbs of Shubra and Imbaba), members of al-Gama'a al-Islamiyya have declared attacks on the tourist industry (and hence on tourists) to be a legitimate strategy in the fight to establish an Islamic state. In a more recent development, an Egyptian group has threatened to kidnap American citizens in a bid to pressure

the US government into releasing Sheikh Omar Abdel Rahman, the spiritual leader of al-Gama'a al-Islamiyya, who was sentenced to life imprisonment in 1996 for planning to blow up the UN headquarters.

The authorities have embarked on campaigns to reassure the world as to how safe Egypt is, but the danger of being caught in the cross-fire, however statistically slight, should at least be borne in mind. Many people went one step further and, between 1992 and 1994, stayed away in droves. As the threat of violence remains, security checks are now in force at many government buildings, offices, and even some hotels and tourist sights such as the Egyptian Museum in Cairo. Travellers are advised to keep abreast of regional and local news as this can signal changes in the security situation.

Land Mines

A leftover from the Israeli-Egyptian wars, and from WWII, land mines are still littered along the Red Sea and Mediterranean coasts and throughout Sinai. If you're a sun worshipper in search of the perfect beach or simply an off-road adventurer, think twice about wandering off the beaten track. And don't rely on tourist operators, signs or barbed wire to alert you to a potentially dangerous area. Two American tourists were killed in mid-1995 after going off road in southern Sinai, a region many tourist operators previously considered safe. The coast from El Alamein to the Libyan border – the scene of the WWII standoff between field marshals Rommel and Montgomery – is still peppered with unexploded mines despite requests from Egypt to the British and German governments for aid to clean up the area.

Drugs

Marijuana and hashish are fairly freely available in certain places around Egypt where travellers gather – most notably Aswan and Dahab. Harder drugs are also in circulation in Dahab. Remember that the authorities take a dim view of drug use and do not feel overly indulgent towards anyone caught with the stuff – westerners have been arrested in Dahab for possession and jailed. Use common sense and try to be discreet. If you are not interested in smoking and are trying to organise yourself into a group for a felucca ride, say, from Aswan, it might be an idea to find out what the intentions of the other passengers are. If it makes you uneasy, it'll be a bit late once you're sailing. Penalties for smuggling and dealing include 25 years' jail or death by hanging.

Theft

Petty crime can be a problem. Pickpockets like money. In fact, some like it so much they are brave and deft enough to search and empty your pockets while standing in front of you on a crowded bus – and you probably won't even realise what's happening until it's too late.

Be careful about carrying money and valuables in a day pack or handbag. Razor blades work wonders on bags when the dastardly perpetrator is standing behind you in a queue or on a crowded bus. Passengers on the bus from Midan Tahrir to the Pyramids of Giza are a favourite target for these stealthy fingers. Money belts and pouches around your neck keep your money where it belongs. Another protective measure is to carry travellers' cheques; they can be replaced if stolen or lost.

Smoking & Pollution

Egyptian men are prolific smokers and non-smokers may find long journeys on air-conditioned buses to be a hazy nightmare of endless smog, despite the fact that many buses actually sport 'no smoking' signs. Protesting may make the guy next to you stop, but it's unlikely to change the habit of the rest of those on board.

Breathing, in general, can sometimes be troublesome in Egypt. The lack of humidity, the contrast of heat outside and air-con indoors, and the abundance of dust and pollution can aggravate your eyes, nose and throat. Eyedrops and throat lozenges can be helpful.

Marine Creatures

For a brief introduction to some of the potentially dangerous marine creatures you may encounter, see Diving & Snorkelling in the Activities section later in this chapter.

Hawkers

In the bazaars you expect it, but the chitchat in the streets of central Cairo can be a real pain. Take a large dose of patience combined with firmness. Foreigners wandering around in ones and twos inevitably win 'instant' friends who often coincidentally have a papyrus 'factory' they'd like to show you. Everyone works out their own strategy for reducing this to a minimum. Try to smile and just walk on by. Some people try mumbling words in what they hope will be a little-known language – but it's amazing how many languages these guys seem to latch on to, even if only in a limited way.

Women, as already mentioned, will have to be prepared to deal with possible harassment, ranging from declarations of love to lightning gropes. Not everyone encounters this sort of thing, but there is little point in pretending it doesn't happen.

The unfortunate thing about all this is that often people are just being genuinely friendly and curious. It can be hard to know what you are dealing with and inevitably some locals feel offended by the apparent brusqueness of their foreign guests. Keep an open mind and remember that Egyptians, like the bulk of Arabs, take hospitality to strangers seriously.

LEGAL MATTERS

For information on driving laws, see Road Rules in the Getting Around chapter. As previously mentioned, marijuana, hashish and harder drugs are available but penalties for smuggling, dealing and even possession are high (see the Dangers & Annoyances section of this chapter).

Foreign travellers are subject to Egyptian laws – you'll get no special consideration just because you're not Egyptian. If arrested, you have the right to immediately telephone your embassy.

BUSINESS HOURS

Banking hours are from 8 or 8.30 am to 2 pm from Sunday to Thursday. Many banks in Cairo and other cities open again from 5 or 6 pm for two or three hours, largely for foreign exchange transactions. Some of them also open on Friday and Saturday for the same purposes. Banque Misr at the Nile Hilton and Shepheard's hotels in Cairo are open 24 hours, and there are 24 hour banking services at Terminal II of Cairo airport. Foreign banks are shut on both Friday and Saturday. During Ramadan, banks are open between 10 am and 1.30 pm. Foreign exchange offices, or forex bureaus, are generally open right through the day.

Most government offices operate from about 8 am to 2 pm, Sunday to Thursday, but tourist offices are exceptions (for details see the relevant city section).

Shops generally have different hours at different times of the year. In summer most shops are open from 9 am to 1 pm and from 5 to 8 pm. Winter hours are from 10 am to 6 pm. Hours during Ramadan are from 9.30 am to 3.30 pm and from 8 to 10 pm. There are no real hard and fast rules however, and even on Fridays, it is not uncommon to see shops open for much of the day.

PUBLIC HOLIDAYS & SPECIAL EVENTS

Egypt's holidays and festivals are primarily Islamic or Coptic religious celebrations.

The following are public holidays in Egypt:

New Year's Day
  1 January
Sinai Liberation Day
  25 April
May Day
  1 May
Revolution Day
  23 July
National Day
  6 October

Ras as-Sana and Moulid an-Nabi are also public holidays (see Islamic Holidays, following). National Day is a day of military parades and air displays.

Islamic Holidays

Because the Islamic, or Hjira ('flight', as in the flight of Mohammed from Mecca to Medina in 622 AD), calendar is 11 days shorter than the Gregorian (western) calendar, Islamic holidays fall 11 days earlier each year. Thus 4 October 1995 was 9 Gamada al-Awal 1416 AH. The 11 day rule is not entirely strict – the holidays can fall from 10 to 12 days earlier. The precise dates are known only shortly before they fall, dependent upon the sighting of the moon. The Hjira (or Higra in Egyptian Arabic) calendar has 12 lunar months, which are:

1st	Moharram
2nd	Safar
3rd	Rabei al-Awal
4th	Rabei at-Tani
5th	Gamada al-Awal
6th	Gamada at-Taniyya
7th	Ragab
8th	Sha'aban
9th	Ramadan
10th	Shawal
11th	Zuu'l Qeda
12th	Zuu'l Hagga

The following is a list of the main Muslim holidays (for details about moulids see the

---

On the Road During Ramadan

It is more difficult to travel around Egypt during Ramadan than during the rest of the year. Almost everything closes in the afternoon or has shorter daytime hours; this does not apply to businesses that cater mostly to foreign tourists, but some restaurants and hotels may be closed the entire month of Ramadan.

Transportation schedules, which are usually erratic even at the best of times, become even crazier and sometimes it is more difficult to buy reserved seats. *Never* travel during Eid al-Fitr, which marks the end of Ramadan. All of Egypt is travelling at that time, so practically all buses and trains are dangerously crowded – especially on the last day of the *eid* (feast) when everyone is returning home. ■

꙳ ꙳

Islamic Holidays

Hjira Year	New Year	Prophet's Birthday	Ramadan Begins	Eid al-Fitr	Eid al-Adhah
1417	19.05.96	28.07.96	10.01.97	10.02.97	18.04.97
1418	09.05.97	18.07.97	31.12.98	31.01.98	08.04.98
1419	28.04.98	07.07.98	20.12.99	20.01.99	28.03.99
1420	17.04.99	26.06.99	–	–	–

꙳ ꙳

boxed story Moulid Celebrations in the Facts about the Country chapter):

Ras as-Sana
New Year's Day; celebrated on 1 Moharram
Moulid an-Nabi
Birthday of the prophet Mohammed; celebrated on 12 Rabei al-Awal. The streets of Cairo are a feast of lights and food on this day.
Ramadan
The ninth month of the Islamic calendar, Ramadan is considered the fourth of Islam's five fundamental pillars of faith. It was during this month that the Qur'an was revealed to Mohammed and, for the entire month, faithful Muslims fast from dawn to sunset in order to gain strength against evil spirits. No food and water are allowed until sunset. The *iftar*, or breaking of the fast, occurs the moment the sun has set and it's a festival occasion – try to attend an iftar at an Egyptian family's home.
Eid al-Fitr
The end of Ramadan fasting; the celebration lasts from 1 to 3 Shawal.
Eid al-Adhah (Bairam)
The time for Muslims to fulfil the fifth pillar of Islam, the pilgrimage to Mecca. Every Muslim is supposed to make the haj at least once in his or her lifetime. This special period for making the haj lasts from 10 to 13 Zuu'l Hagga.

Coptic Christian Holidays

These are a mixture of religious and commemorative holidays.

Christmas
7 January
Epiphany
19 January; celebrating the baptism of Jesus
Annunciation
23 March

Easter
This is the most important date on the Coptic calender. It's preceded by 55 days of fasting, and is celebrated on different dates each year.
Sham an-Nessim
A special Coptic holiday with Pharaonic origins, it literally means 'the smell of a fresh wind'. It falls on the first Monday after the Coptic Easter and is celebrated by all Egyptians, with family picnics and outings.

ACTIVITIES
Diving & Snorkelling

Many visitors to Egypt rarely have their heads above water. Small wonder, as some of the best scuba diving and snorkelling in the world is to be found along the Red Sea coast.

The pick of the crop is along the southern stretch of the Red Sea coast towards the border with Sudan and along the southern coast of the Sinai peninsula. The former region is accessible only by boat – diving safaris called 'liveaboards' are organised through some dive clubs. The latter region, from the Straits of Tiran to Ras Mohammed, is a marine nature reserve on the tip of the peninsula and is easily accessed from nearby (but pricey) resort towns. Away from the expensive resort atmosphere, there are other possibilities further north, such as in Dahab. Alternatively, you can cross the Gulf of Suez to Hurghada.

The Red Sea reefs have suffered a lot of destruction in recent years due to the demand placed on them by tourist activities. In order to help conserve them, there are a few important things to remember when you're out on the reefs – see Reef Protection in the Ecology & Environment section of the Facts about the Country chapter. You should also be aware of potential dangers – see the following Marine Hazards section.

Snorkellers should also be aware that the best places to dive are not always so great for snorkelling. Reef walls which run to about five metres in depth usually offer spectacular views for snorkellers. However, there's not much point paying to go out on a dive boat to a site with a 30m drop off as you won't be able to see more than five metres below you anyway. Also, try to snorkel at high tide to avoid walking across reefs and killing the corals. You'll be looking at about E£6 to E£10 for daily rental of a mask, snorkel and fins.

Dive Clubs & Courses There's a plethora of dive operators in Sinai (at Na'ama Bay, Sharm el-Sheikh, Dahab and Nuweiba) and on the Red Sea coast (Hurghada, Port Safaga and Al-Quseir); Na'ama Bay and Hurghada have the greatest concentration. Many have set up in recent years simply to make money out of this boom sector of the country's tourism industry, and some are shonky backyard businesses which are best avoided.

There are certain things you should know before choosing your club. Find out the student-instructor ratio (obviously the fewer students there are, the more attention you'll get – four students or less is ideal); ask how trained the instructors are; and ascertain whether there is oxygen and a VHF radio on the club's dive boat, in case of an accident. Try to choose a dive club whose instructors are interested in the reef and who take the time to explain some of the vagaries of marine life, like, for instance, why a trigger fish blow holes in the sand. See the boxed story Choosing a Dive Club in the Hurghada section of the Suez Canal & Red Sea Coast chapter for more information on this topic.

Most of the clubs offer every possible kind of dive course. The average open-water certification course for beginners, either with CMAS, PADI or NAUI, takes about five days and usually includes several dives. The total cost varies between US$280 and US$400 depending on the operator and location. Make sure you ask whether the log books, manual and certificate are included in the price – if not you will be looking at about US$70 extra.

An introductory dive including equipment costs between US$45 and US$60. Also on offer are a number of packages for more experienced divers, such as an advanced open-water course including equipment for US$180 to US$280. Other courses, such as Divemaster, Rescue and Medical First Aid, are offered by some of the dive clubs. Full-day diving trips (two dives) including equipment and air fills cost from US$50 to US$95. A seven day liveaboard safari (including food, two daily dives and one night dive), could set you back at least US$1000. All equipment is available including regulators, buoyancy compensators, tanks, wet suits and so on, and can be hired for about US$20 per day.

Dive clubs in Dahab have started organising camel/diving safaris whereby you spend a few hours (or longer if it's a three day safari) trekking by camel to a secluded dive site, followed by two dives. Prices range from E£80 to E£115 per day, all inclusive.

If you plan to do some diving, it's a good idea to contact the Cairo Divers Group before you leave Cairo. This group actively participates in conserving the Red Sea reefs and can provide plenty of information on dive sites. It organises monthly trips, rents equipment and, in addition, members are entitled to discounts with various dive clubs in Sinai. See the Dive Club section in the Cairo chapter for details on this group.

Decompression Facilities There are decompression chambers in Hurghada and Sharm el-Sheikh. For details see those sections.

Marine Hazards Don't be completely fooled by the undeniable beauty of the Red Sea coast's blue-green waters and coral reefs – they do have their share of hazards. Avoid bumping into sea urchins and coral, especially fire coral, as it is extremely sharp and can cause a painful, burning sensation where it breaks your skin. The best policy for your own protection and that of the reef is simply not to touch, kneel or kick the reef.

Before diving or snorkelling, you should learn to recognise potentially dangerous creatures such as the stonefish, lionfish and scorpionfish. Barracuda and moray eels are also prevalent, although seldom threatening. There are sharks in the Red Sea, however, it has been a long time since sharks have bothered humans in Sinai waters. If you do see one, don't panic – nothing attracts sharks more than a terror-stricken human flailing about in their territory.

COURSES
Language
Various institutions in Cairo offer Arabic courses. One of the most expensive is the Arabic Language Institute (☎ 357-5055) at the American University in Cairo (AUC). This independent wing of the AUC offers intensive instruction in Arabic language at elementary, intermediate and advanced levels. The courses incorporate both Egyptian Colloquial Arabic (ECA) and Modern Standard Arabic (MSA), with a firm emphasis on the latter. (For information about these two versions of Arabic, see Language in the Facts about the Country chapter.) At the time of research the intensive course cost US$4500 per semester (20 hours per week over 14 weeks). The institute also offers intensive summer programmes (20 hours per week for six weeks) in which class time is divided equally between ECA and MSA. These courses cost US$2240.

If you're wanting a cheaper Arabic course than the AUC programmes detailed above, you might want to try the British Council (☎ 345-3281), at 192 Sharia el-Nil in Cairo. It appears to be the most popular place to do a range of intensive and other courses in ECA and MSA.

The International Language Institute (ILI) has two offices in Cairo – one (☎ 346-3087) at 3 Sharia Mahmoud Azmy, Sahafayeen and the other (☎ 291-9295) at 2 Sharia Mohammed Bayoumi, in Heliopolis. They charge E£350/390 for a 60 hour programme of ECA/MSA. They also offer residential summer courses (running from late June to late July) ranging from E£275 for 40 hours of tuition to E£500 for 100 hours.

For details of other places to learn Arabic in Cairo, refer to Language Courses in the Cairo chapter.

Studying at the American University
The AUC is one of the premier universities in the Middle East. Some 4300 students, the bulk of whom are Egyptian, study at its campus on Midan Tahrir in the heart of Cairo. The curriculum, and a third of the full-time faculty of 275, are American and accredited in the USA.

The AUC offers degree, nondegree and summer-school programmes. Any of the regular courses offered can be taken. Popular subjects include Arabic Language and Literature, Arab History & Culture, Egyptology, Islamic Art and Architecture, Middle East Studies and Social Science courses on the Arab world. Up to 15 unit hours can be taken per semester at the undergraduate level.

Summer programmes offer similar courses. The term lasts from mid-June to the end of July. Two three unit courses can be taken and several well-guided field trips throughout Egypt are usually included.

The largest programmes at the AUC are for bachelor's and master's degrees; they offer more than 29 subjects ranging from Anthropology to Teaching English as a Foreign Language.

Applications for programmes with the Arabic Language Institute (previously detailed) and undergraduate and graduate studies at the university are separate. Specify which you want when requesting an application form. A catalogue and programme information can be obtained from: The Office of Admissions, The American University in Cairo, 866 United Nations Plaza, New York, NY 10017 (☎ (212) 421-6320; fax 688-5341); or you can write to PO Box

2511 in Cairo (☎ 354-2964, ext 5011/2/3 or fax 355-7565).

Egyptian Universities

It is also possible to study at Egyptian universities such as Al-Azhar, Alexandria, 'Ain Shams and Cairo. Courses offered to foreign students include Arabic Language, Islamic History, Islamic Religion, and Egyptology. For information on courses, tuition fees and applications, contact: The Cultural Counsellor, The Egyptian Educational Bureau (☎ (202) 296-3888), 2200 Kalorama Rd NW, Washington DC 20008. In London, contact the Cultural Affairs Office (☎ (0171) 491-7720).

Dive Courses

For information on the various dive courses offered in Egypt see the previous Activities section.

WORK

More than 40,000 foreigners live and work in Egypt. That figure alone should give you some idea of the immense presence foreign companies have in the country. It is possible to find work with one of these companies if you are committed and motivated. Begin your research before you leave home. *Cairo: A Practical Guide*, published by The American University in Cairo Press, has lists of all foreign companies operating in Egypt, however it's quite out of date. There's also a two volume directory listing all foreign companies, subsidiaries and representatives in Egypt that's available in most hotel bookshops, however at E£300 you'll need a job just to be able to afford it. If you know some Arabic, you will definitely be in an advantageous position. Once you have an employer, securing a work permit through an Egyptian consulate or, in Egypt, from the Ministry of the Interior, should not be difficult.

Teaching English

There are many opportunities for teaching English as a second language. The first preference should be the recognised schools. They pay better and are usually better

equipped and have some interest in the progress of their students. The down side is that you will need a qualification. The RSA Teaching English as a Foreign Language to Adults (TEFLA) Certificate is the minimum requirement. If you have that and some experience, try the British Council (☎ 345-3281) at 192 Sharia el-Nil, the Centre for Adult & Continuing Education (☎ 354-2964) at the American University in Cairo, or one of the International Language Institute's (ILI) two offices – one (☎ 346-3087) at 3 Sharia Mahmoud Azmy, Sahafayeen and the other (☎ 291-9295; fax 418-7275) on 2 Sharia Mohammed Bayoumi, in Heliopolis. Full-time teachers (100 hours per month) at the ILI earn E£2450. The British Council pays higher rates but only UK citizens can get full-year contract packages there, though other nationals often work part time.

If you have no qualification or experience, you could try some of the schools in Cairo and Alexandria that are listed in *Egypt Today*. Some of them are what the trade knows as 'cowboy outfits' – you work hard for little return and often with only minimal interest taken in the progress of students. Check with recognised institutions such as the AUC and British Council for advice.

The British Council and, above all, the ILI run RSA certificate and diploma courses throughout the year.

Journalism

Another possible source of work for English speakers is in copy-editing or writing on one of the various English-language publications in Cairo. *Al-Ahram* and *Egypt Today* sometimes have openings, or at least may be interested in freelance contributions. The pay is nothing terrific, and they are at pains to make clear that beginners need not apply.

Film & TV Extras

If you look European and want to earn a few extra pounds in Egypt while you're travelling, you can appear in Egyptian TV commercials or even in films, as the local advertising agencies are always looking for western faces. For what can sometimes boil down to a few minutes work you can earn as much as E£50 – not bad at all.

Notices for cameo parts in commercials and TV soap operas are sometimes put on the bulletin board at the Oxford Pensione. People have been known to be offered this kind of work by middlemen plying Sharia Talaat Harb, especially in the vicinity of the Amira Restaurant. Beware of shysters.

Dive Instructors

The Red Sea's booming tourist industry has created quite a lot of work for experienced scuba diving instructors, especially during the peak season (winter). If possible, contact some of the clubs before you get to Egypt. Otherwise start door knocking once you get to Na'ama Bay or Hurghada.

ACCOMMODATION

Accommodation in Egypt ranges from cheap to expensive and rough to luxurious. There are resorts, hotels, flotels (Nile cruisers), pensions, youth hostels and a few camping grounds.

On the specific subject of hotels, as a general rule there is a review of prices each year in October. On average, prices rise by about 15% but it can be higher. You tend to find cheaper accommodation and get more for your money outside Cairo.

Residents in Egypt are often entitled to something closer to the local rate for rooms in the bigger hotels. Yes, there is one rate for foreigners and another for locals. If you are a resident, make a point of asking about resident rates, as they entail a considerable saving.

One thing that's available to everyone is bargaining. Just because a hotel has its room rates displayed in a glass frame on the wall, doesn't mean they are untouchable. In off-peak seasons haggling will often get you significant discounts, even in mid-range places. Also, many hotels offer left-luggage facilities for a few pounds per day.

And a note of warning...the majority of travellers arriving in Egypt fly first to Cairo. On arrival at the airport, if you're not with a group, the chances are that you'll be

approached by a man or woman with an official-looking badge that says 'Egyptian Chamber of Tourism' or something similar. Such people are not government tourism officials, they are hotel touts, and the methods they use to drum up trade can be quite devious. They'll tell you all sorts of porkies like, for example, the hotel that you want to stay in is 'no good', or 'full' or that it has quadrupled its prices. Unless you want to be taken for a ride, it's best to steer clear of these people.

Camping

Officially, camping is allowed at only a few places around Egypt such as at Harrania near Giza in Cairo, Luxor, Aswan, Farafra Oasis and Ras Mohammed National Park. At official sites, facilities tend to be rudimentary. A few private hotels around the country also allow campers to set up in their backyard, such as at Abu Simbel, Kharga Oasis, Nuweiba, Basata, Qena and Abydos. Facilities in most of these places are also pretty basic.

Hostels

Hostels are among the cheapest places to stay in Egypt, although you can find the odd hotel that outdoes them. There are 15 recognised by Hostelling International (HI), located in Cairo, Alexandria, Al-Faiyum, Aswan, Asyut, Damanhur, Hurghada,. Ismailia, Luxor, Marsa Matruh, Port Said, Sharm el-Sheikh, Sohag, Suez and Tanta and they generally range in price from about E£3 to E£10. The one in Ismailia has beds as expensive as E£16 – it's virtually a hotel. In some cases the price includes breakfast. Having an HI card is not absolutely necessary, as non-members are admitted. A card will save you between E£2 and E£4, depending on the hostel. The youth hostels tend to be noisy, crowded and often a bit grimy. In some there are rooms for mixed couples or families, but on the whole the sexes are segregated. Reservations are not usually needed.

The Egyptian Hostelling International office (☎ 575-8099) at 7 Sharia Dr Abdel Hamid Said (opposite the Odean Palace

Hotel), Cairo, can give you the latest information.

Hotels

At the five star end of the price range are hotels representing most of the world's major chains. Prices typically start at about US$100 per night, not including a series of taxes and service charges of between 19 and 23%. There are also a few privately owned Egyptian hotels in this range. Although all five star and many much cheaper hotels still quote prices in US dollars, it is usually no problem paying in pounds. Some top-end hotels offer rooms on a 'day use' basis which means you can use a room and the hotel's swimming pool from about 9 am to 6 pm, however, it's a pretty expensive way to cool off.

In the next price range – four stars – there are mostly Egyptian managed and owned hotels which range upwards in price from about E£100 per night and add similar charges and taxes.

Next come the three star hotels. They are generally clean, comfortable and relatively good value and range from E£50 to E£100 per night. Taxes and service charges may be only two of the 'extras' that get added on to your final bill. Egyptian hotels are very keen on giving you breakfast but it's often 'compulsory' rather than included. Sometimes you are charged extra for the fridge and TV in your room as well. In this way you can take an ordinary double room, add E£4 each for two breakfasts, E£2 for the fridge you never used and E£2 for the TV you never turned on, whack 12% service on the whole lot and then 5% sales tax and possibly a government tax on top of that, and your E£30 room suddenly costs you E£50 a night.

Some of the mid-range and top-end hotels in the various coastal resorts offer rooms on a 'half-board' basis which means breakfast and either lunch or dinner is included in the price. In peak seasons, this is sometimes obligatory.

The two, one and no-star hotels form the budget group. Often the ratings mean nothing at all, as a hotel without a star can be as good as a two star hotel, only cheaper. You can spend as little as E£10 a night for a clean single room with hot water or as much as E£40 or more for a dirty double room without a shower. Pensions are in this range and tend to be fairly good. Generally the prices quoted include any charges and quite often breakfast. Don't have great expectations about these breakfasts as they usually consist of no more than a couple of pieces of bread, a chunk of frozen butter, a dollop of jam, and tea or coffee. Beyond this, you have to pay extra.

A word on hot water (and remember, in the top half of the country this can be a consideration in winter). Most hotels will tell you they have it when they don't. Don't take assurances of steaming hot baths at face value – turn the tap on and check for yourself or keep an eye out for an electric water heater when viewing the bathroom. Other things to keep an eye (or ear) out for are peepholes (you'll be amazed how many doors have holes drilled though them), the proximity of mosques and noisy streets. If there's no plug in your bathroom sink and you forgot to bring your own, then try using the lid of a Baraka mineral water bottle. According to one ingenious traveller, they fit 90% of the time.

The hotel's location is another consideration. Many of the cheaper abodes in Cairo and Alexandria are on the top floor of old apartment blocks. While most have elevators, these rickety contraptions tend to allow you to ride up but not down, which means a dizzy descent down nine or so flights every time you want to go out.

You get what you pay for – and the great Egyptian budget bed is one of the delights found not always exclusively at the very bottom rung. A thin mattress and nice hard planks can be the perfect combination for acquiring a sizeable backache. Also, many bottom-end establishments seem to be economising on sheets, putting either one or sometimes none between you and blankets that may never have been washed since they were acquired. A sleeping sheet is a good antidote. If you don't have one of these, then just politely ask for clean sheets – in most cases they'll be readily supplied.

Most hotels quoting prices in dollars will accept most credit cards, particularly Visa, MasterCard and American Express. Even many smaller places will accept credit cards.

FOOD

Egyptian food varies from the exotic to mundane, and sampling the various types of food should be part of the adventure of your visit. Be open-minded, don't look at the kitchens, and remember that you can have a uniquely great meal here for very little money.

In the cities you'll find plenty of restaurants and cafes as well as fast-food outlets. In Cairo, the Delta and Alexandria region you may also come across restaurants called *casinos*. These places have nothing to do with gambling – they're simply large restaurants where families often congregate for a meal and some music.

Snacks

Fuul and *ta'amiyya* are unofficially the national staples of Egypt. Fuul is fava beans, with a variety of things such as oil, lemon, salt, meat, eggs and onions added to spice it up. Ta'amiyya is a concoction of mashed chickpeas and spices fried into little balls, similar to felafel. A fuul and ta'amiyya sandwich on pita bread with a bit of tomato makes a tasty snack or light lunch.

It's also popular to substitute *tahina* for fuul in pita bread sandwiches. Another national staple, tahina is a delicious sesame spread spiced with oil, garlic and lemon. In addition to putting it on ta'amiyya, you can also order a plate of tahina to eat as a dip with pita bread. Together with a few other such *mezzes* (hors d'oeuvres) like *hoummos* and *baba ghanoug*, this can make a decent meal. Hoummos is a chickpea spread which is especially tasty with a bit of oil and a few pinenuts on top. Baba ghanoug is a mix of mashed eggplant and tahina.

Sandwich stands also serve – you guessed it – the *sandweech*. Most Egyptian sandwiches are small rolls with an equally small piece of meat, cheese or *basturma*, a smoked meat which resembles pastrami. Nothing else. Add some mustard to perk it up. Other popular sandwiches include grilled, crumbed or fried *kibda* (liver) served with spicy green peppers and onions; *mokh*, or crumbed cows' brains; and tiny shrimp.

Shawarma is also good for sandwiches and is the Egyptian equivalent of the Greek *gyros* sandwich. Throughout Egypt you will see lamb roasting on rotating shawarma spits. Hot strips of lamb are cut from the spit and placed in a pocket of pita with tomatoes to make a sandwich which is often accompanied separately by *torshi*, a mixture of pickled vegetables such as radishes, carrots and cucumbers. They look somewhat strange and discoloured but taste great if they're pickled properly.

There are several other quick, cheap dishes available: *Fiteer* is a cross between pizza and pastry and is served at a place called a *fatatri*. It's flat and flaky, and contains sweet things like raisins, nuts and powdered sugar, or something spicy like white cheese, olives, ground meat or eggs. One fiteer is almost filling enough to be an entire meal, and should cost no more than E£4 to E£5 depending on the toppings.

Makarone is a clump of macaroni baked into a cake with ground meat and tomato sauce inside and *pashamel* (white sauce or gravy). It is very filling and costs from 50 pt to E£1.

Mahshi are various vegetables such as vine leaves (in summer), cabbage (in winter), tomatoes, and white and black aubergines, usually stuffed with minced meat, rice, onions, parsley, green herbs and, sometimes, tomatoes.

For in-between meals, you can join the national passion of chomping on roasted watermelon and pumpkin seeds (like everyone else, you should spit out the husk). They're bought in a paper cone from nut and seed shops everywhere. Bakeries and patisseries are another delight – you can always smell these places way before you see them. Typical products are tiny French loaves and sesame-covered bagels, almond or date biscuits, big pastries dripping with honey, chocolates and an assortment of other things for those looking for intense sugar highs.

Main Dishes

Kofta and *kebab* are two of the most popular dishes in Egypt. Kofta is ground meat peppered with spices, skewered and grilled over a fire just like shish kebab. Kebab is similar, but the meat isn't ground. Grilled tomatoes and onions are also served. Both dishes are ordered in Egyptian restaurants by weight. *Moza* is basically a plate of roast lamb on rice.

Firakh, or chicken, is something you'll probably be eating quite often. It is usually grilled or stewed and served with a vegetable. Takeaway spit-roasted chickens are available from many small restaurants for about E£4 to E£8 depending on the weight.

Vegetarians shouldn't have too much trouble finding things to eat. *Musaga* is one delicious dish to try. It's a mixture of eggplant, tomatoes, garlic, oil and an assortment of spices baked in the oven. *Molokhiyya* is also very popular and is one of the few truly Egyptian dishes. It's a green, slimy, delicious soup made by stewing a strange leafy vegetable, rice and garlic. The soup base is often made from a chicken or beef stock.

Shakshooka is a mixture of chopped meat and tomato sauce with an egg tossed on top and baked in the oven. It's rather like a Spanish omelette with meat, though you can also get vegetarian versions.

The best *samak* (fish) comes from the Mediterranean and south Sinai coasts and is often served grilled. The restaurants along the Mediterranean serve their fish by the kg. You choose it yourself from a large ice tray near the kitchen and the price usually includes a salad, bread and dips like tahina and baba ghanoug. Remember, fish spoils quickly in the summer heat. Before ordering, be sure that it's fresh. It shouldn't smell like the inside of a locker room and shouldn't feel spongy.

Another grilled dish is *hamam*, or pigeon. Pronounce the word carefully because another 'm' makes the word *hammam*, which means bathroom. Hamam is served grilled on charcoal or sometimes filled with *freek* (wheat stuffing). It's also served as a stew cooked with onions, tomatoes and rice or freek in a deep clay pot known as a *tagen*.

Another popular dish, and good for vegetarians, is *kushari*, a combination of noodles, rice, black lentils, fried onions and tomato sauce. Each item is cooked separately and piled high in the windows of kushari joints, which are never street stands because the tomato sauce spoils quickly in the sun. A bowl of kushari is healthy and very filling and costs only about E£1. The fried onions are usually extra.

For those who find themselves on long train or bus rides, it is also essential to know about bread and cheese – the easily transportable staple of the traveller. Bread, including pita, is called *aysh*. In Egypt aysh also means 'life'. Egyptians say that life without aysh isn't life. Most of the aysh which you'll see and eat is *aysh baladi*, also called country bread or pita. The other main type is called *aysh fransawi*, or French bread.

There are also two main types of cheese: *gibna beyda*, or white cheese, which tastes like Greek feta; and *gibna rumi*, or Roman cheese, which is a hard, sharp, yellow-white cheese.

The following words will also come in handy as you eat your way around Egypt:

Soup

soups	*shurba*
lentil soup	*shurbat 'ads*
chicken soup	*shurbat firakh*
tomato soup	*shurbat tamatim*

Fish & Shellfish

fish	*samak*
Nile perch (try it grilled)	*ishr bayad*
flatfish	*samak musa*
red mullet	*mourgan*
fried fish	*samak maklee*
crab	*kaboria*
prawns, shrimps	*gambari*
squid	*calamari*

Vegetables

aubergine	*badingan*
cabbage	*khroumbe*
carrots	*gazar*
cauliflower	*arnabeet*
green vegetables	*khudrawat, khudar*
green beans	*fasooliyya*
lentils	*'ads*
maize	*durra*
(try it charcoal grilled from a sidewalk vendor)	
okra	*baamiyya*
peas	*baseelah*
potatoes	*batatas*
turnips	*lift*
dry green wheat	*fareek*

Salad Items

salad	*salata*
cucumber	*khiyaar*
garlic	*tum*
lettuce	*khass*
onion	*bassal*
green winter pepper	*sabanekh*
(great source of iron)	
hot pepper	*shattah*
sweet pepper	*filfil*
tomato	*tamatim, uta*

Meat & Poultry

meat	*al-luhum*
beef	*lahma kanduz, lahma ba'aree*
camel	*lahma gamali*
chicken	*firakh*
kidney	*kalawi*
lamb	*lahma danee*
liver	*kibda*
turkey	*deek roumee*
(found mainly at Christmas)	
veal	*lahma beetalu*

Desserts

cornflour pudding	*mahalabiyya*
ice cream	*ays krim*
semolina cake	*basboosah*
Turkish delight	*malban*
milk dish with nuts, raisins & wheat	*bilaylah*

flaky pastry & nuts in honey	*baqlawah*
shredded wheat, pastry with nuts	*atayf*
pastries dipped in rosewater	*zalabiyyah, lomet al-addee*
cornflour pudding with nuts, coconut, cinnamon & cream and served hot	*om ali*
stringy pastry with honey & nuts	*kounafa*
baked rice & milk pudding	*ruz bi laban*
flaky pastry with nuts & honey or cheese	*ghoulash*

Fruit & Seeds

fruit	*fawakah, fak-ha*
apricots	*meesh-meesh*
apples	*tooffah*
bananas	*mohz*
dates	*balah*
figs	*teen*
grapes	*einab*
guavas	*guafa*
limes	*limuun*
mangoes	*manga*
oranges	*burtuaan*
peaches	*khukh*
pears	*kumitrah*
pomegranates	*rumman*
strawberries	*farawleh*
tangerines	*yusuf affandi*
watermelons	*batteekh*
seeds	*libb*
pumpkin seeds	*libb abyad*
watermelon seeds	*libb batteekh*

Miscellaneous Items

bread	*aysh, khubz*
pita bread	*aysh baladi*
butter	*zibda*
cheese	*gibna*
cream	*ishta*
eggs	*bayd*
jam	*murabbah*
honey	*asal*
milk	*laban*

mint	*nana*
salt	*malh* (pronounced almost as 'malha')
sugar	*sukkar*
yoghurt	*zabadi*
water	*mayya*

DRINKS

Nonalcoholic Drinks

Tea & Coffee *Shay* and *ahwa* – tea and coffee – head the list of things to drink in Egypt. Both are usually made strong enough to be major contenders for the title of most caffeinated drink in the world.

Tea is served in glasses at traditional Egyptian teahouses and in teacups at western-style restaurants. At teahouses, the tea leaves are boiled with the water; in other places you'll probably get a teabag.

Specify how much sugar you want, otherwise two or three big teaspoons of the stuff will be automatically plopped into your glass. If you only want a bit of sugar in your tea, ask for *shay ma'a shwayya sukkar*. If you don't want any sugar at all ask for *shay min gheer sukkar*. Egyptians are always amazed that westerners don't like as much sugar as they do. Try *shay bi-nana* (mint tea) or *shay bi-laban* (tea with milk).

If you ask for coffee, you will probably get *ahwa turki* (Turkish coffee), which is served throughout the Middle East. It bears a strong resemblance to mud and it's quite a surprise to find your spoon doesn't actually stand up in it. Don't be deceived by the size of the tiny porcelain cups; this coffee is *very* strong. Let the grains settle before drinking it, in small sips. As with tea, you have to specify how much sugar you want if you don't want to suffer an overdose. *Ahwa ziyadda* is for those who seek the ultimate sugar and caffeine high – it is extra sweet. *Ahwa mazboota* comes with a moderate amount of sugar but is still fairly sweet and *ahwa saada* is without sugar. Egyptians drink the latter when a relative or close friend has died. Should you find that the coffee has an unusual aroma and taste, it's likely to have been mixed with cardamom.

Western-style instant coffee is called Nescafe. It comes in a small packet with a cup of hot water.

Another popular hot drink is *hoummos ash-shem*, which is made from boiled chickpeas, tomato sauce, lemon and cumin.

Fruit Juices On practically every street corner in every town throughout Egypt there is a juice stand, where you can get a drink squeezed out of just about any fruit or vegetable that is in season. Standard *asiir*, or juices, include:

banana	*mohz*
guava	*guafa*
lime	*limuun*
mango	*manga*
orange	*burtuaan*
pomegranate	*rumman*
strawberry	*farawleh*
sugar cane	*asiir asab*
tamarind seed	*tamr hindi*
tangerine	*yusuf affandi*

Other Nonalcoholic Drinks Soft drinks are extremely popular in Egypt and most major brands are sold here, as are local varieties like Mirinda (an orange soda) and Teem (virtually Seven-Up). If you drink at the soda vendor's stand, you won't have to pay a deposit on the bottle. Soft drinks are cheap – only 35 to 50 pt depending on the size of the bottle – but it's not unusual to pay anything from E£1 to E£4 in hotels and at tourist sites. A can of drink can cost at least a E£1 because the can isn't reusable. Diet soft drinks are becoming quite popular. Remember that when it's hot, a soft drink will not quench your thirst. In fact, if anything, the sugar in it will make you more thirsty.

Sahleb is a sweet, milky drink made from rice flour, grapes, coconut and various nuts, including hazelnuts and pistachios. Cheap juice stands sell a simpler version.

A few other *mashrubat*, or drinks, which you might encounter are:

aniseed	*yansun*
caraway seed	*karawiyya*
carob	*carob*

cocoa	*kakaw*
fenugreek	*helba*
hibiscus	*karkaday*
licorice	*arasus*

Bottles (1½ litres) of Baraka and Siwa mineral water can be bought from most corner stores and cost about E£1.25. In Sinai, you'll pay up to E£2. Tap water is generally safe to drink throughout Egypt. However, some travellers prefer to begin drinking it gradually rather than immediately. See the Health section in this chapter for more details.

Alcoholic Drinks

Egypt has several indigenous alcoholic beverages. Most drinks are cheaper if you buy them in the liquor stores.

Beer Egyptian beer, which to most palates is a little on the watery side, is called Stella, and it is served in 75 cl bottles. There is also Stella Export, which comes in smaller bottles, has double the alcohol content of regular Stella and costs more, at E£5.50 in liquor stores and anywhere up to E£15 in restaurants and hotels. Few things (available) can beat a cold bottle of Stella on a hot day. It costs about E£4 from a liquor store (plus a returnable deposit of 50 pt), or from E£5 to E£9 in most bars or cafeterias. Be wary of expiry dates, however. In spring and autumn, a dark beer, a bit like stout, sometimes makes an appearance. They have given it the German name Marzen Bier. It seems a bit of a rarity, but anyone who likes beer who has tried it has sung its praises – at least it's different.

A nonalcoholic beer called Birelli (or Bireel) is also available, but it seems to be little more than a concoction of hops and soda water. It's often used as a prescribed remedy for people with kidney stones.

Wine One of the best medium-dry white Egyptian wines is called Gianaclis Village; it comes from a village of the same name in the Nile Delta. A good dry white wine is Patalomai. A sweeter wine is Reine Cléopatra. There's only one type of rosé wine – Rubis d'Égypte – and it's pretty awful. If it's red wines you're after, the best dry one is Omar Khayyam, the best medium-dry is Gianaclis Château, and the sweetest is Nefertiti. They don't exactly compare with western wines and they're pretty expensive at E£30 a bottle (or E£7 for a glass in a restaurant), but they aren't too bad. Most come from the Gianaclis vineyards in the Nile Delta.

Liquor For hard liquor, you can get quite expensive western brands in the major hotels and some nightclubs, but the Egyptians, apart from creating their own series of drinks with labels that look almost like the real McCoy (Black Jonny or Gardan's gin for instance!) to fool whomever will be fooled, also do a few honest, if not high-class, drops. A couple of brandies are available, including Vat 20 and its stronger relative Vat 1884. There is also an Egyptian version of *araq* or *raqi* (the Greek version is ouzo) called *zibiba*. You can get it in the small liquor stores and some supermarkets like Sunnys.

There is also an odd-tasting sweet liqueur, Abu Simbel, which contains iron – recommended by some as an agent against anaemia!

ENTERTAINMENT
Cinemas

Going to a movie in Egypt can be an interesting and inexpensive cultural experience. Most foreign-language movies have subtitles in Arabic, but because the audience doesn't have to listen to the soundtrack they often talk all the way through the movie. Also, don't be surprised if a scene in a movie suddenly disappears. Censorship is common in all movies except those shown at the Cairo International Film Festival in late November, and even then it has been known to happen.

It is quite possible to catch a good and recent mainstream movie in either Cairo or Alexandria. Cinemas fall roughly into two categories – those showing the kind of movies you might want to catch at home and others showing either local product or the action/martial arts genre that seems to appeal to a lot to male audiences in the Arab world. Those in the latter category generally cost about E£4. The former are screened in a handful of cinemas and usually subtitled, not dubbed, in Arabic. A seat costs about E£7 in the stalls or E£10 in the balcony.

There are generally five screenings a day at roughly the same times: 10 am and 1, 3, 6 and 9 pm. There are sometimes midnight screenings on Thursday and Saturday.

Discos, Nightclubs & Bars

Most of the discos of the western variety are in the middle to top-range hotels. They're predominantly pick-up joints rather than somewhere to go to simply dance and have a good time. Nightclubs of this variety are often pretty disappointing and tacky.

Many discos and nightclubs have a 'minimum charge' policy. Depending on the venue this either means each person must purchase a certain amount worth of drinks (basically a deterrent for riffraff and to makes sure you spend enough), or it acts as a cover charge and by paying it you get a 'free' beer or soft drink.

In Cairo and a few other tourist centres it is possible to see belly dancing. There is also an assortment of bars around the capital, but outside the main cities you're limited to bars in the top-end hotels. In addition, Cairo has another particular breed of bar, called a cafeteria. See the Entertainment section in the Cairo chapter for more details on all of these.

Casinos

A number of Cairo's five star hotels and a few resorts on the coasts have casinos, open to non-Egyptians only. All games are conducted in US dollars or other major foreign currencies, with minimum stakes of US$1. Smart casual attire is required. These casinos are not to be confused with local *casinos*, the name given for certain restaurants popular with families on a day out.

Coffee & Tea Houses

There are simply thousands of tea/coffee houses all round Egypt where you can sit over a glass of tea or a sludgy coffee, play a game of chess or backgammon, suck on a shisha and watch life pass by. Though predominantly male establishments, foreign women should have no hesitation drinking in them. Likewise, you'll never see a local woman smoking a shisha in a teahouse, though female travellers occasionally do.

SPECTATOR SPORT

Football (or soccer to some) is king in Egypt. On the subject of imports, this is one that has been fully incorporated into most of Arab society. Of the Arab countries, Egypt is the one country with players of international capacity, and although they have yet to win a World Cup, they do at least manage to qualify. The premier teams – Zamalek and Al-Ahly in Cairo and Ittihad in Alexandria – arouse greater passions, it seems, than any discussion of war or peace, secularism and religion. The season begins in September and continues until May. Big matches are held in the Cairo stadium at Medinet Nasr.

THINGS TO BUY

Egypt is a budget souvenir and kitsch-shopper's paradise. Hieroglyphic drawings of Pharaohs, queens, gods and goddesses embellish and blemish everything from ashtrays to engraved brass tables. Jewellery, leather, woodwork, basketry, copperware, brassware, ceramics and, of course, the ubiquitous papyrus are just some of the possibilities. Although markets abound all over the country, there is no doubt that the greatest range is to be found in Cairo, especially in the medieval labyrinth of Islamic Cairo. The Khan al-Khalili is the heart of this shopper's paradise, but often the source of the greatest rip-offs. If you're after alabaster, it's best bought in Luxor.

Benetton and the trendy Paris chain Naf Naf have got stores in various places around Egypt and some travellers have reported filling their luggage with European-designed items made in Egypt at prices well below those in Europe.

In Search of that Special Souvenir

The best thing about souvenir hunting in Egypt is not the souvenirs. They are secondary to the excitement of the expedition up and down the back alleyways of the bazaars, past pungent barrels of basil and garlic and through medieval caravanserais. Take your sense of humour and curiosity with you, and if you want to buy something, be prepared to bargain for it; it is expected.

Everyone seems to have a different bargaining strategy. Don't show too much interest in the thing that you want to buy. Start the bargaining with a price much lower than you are really prepared to pay and then barter up to that point. When you state your first price the shopkeeper will inevitably huff about how absurd it is and then tell you his 'lowest' price. If it is still not low enough, be insistent and keep smiling. Tea may be served as part of the bargaining ritual; accepting it doesn't place you under obligation to buy. If you still can't get your price, just walk away. There are hundreds of shops in the bazaars. ■

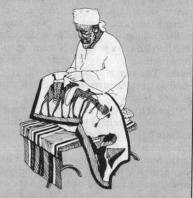

Handicrafts are a speciality among the treasures to be found in Egypt's souqs and bazaars.

Jewellery

Gold and silver jewellery can be made to specification for not much more than the cost of the metal. A cartouche with the name of a friend or relative spelled in hieroglyphs makes a great gift.

Although gold shops are concentrated in the centre of the Khan al-Khalili, gold can be bought all over Islamic Cairo. It is generally sold by weight. Buying gold and jewellery is always a little fraught. The Assay Office in Birmingham, UK, says that hallmarking for gold of at least 12 carats and silver of 600 parts per thousand or more is compulsory in Egypt – verifying this is another matter. The hallmark contains a standard mark showing where a piece was assayed and a date mark in Arabic. Foreign goods cannot be resold, in the UK at least, unless they are first assayed there. Storekeepers have an irritating habit of weighing the gold out of sight. Insist that they put the scales on the counter and let you see what's happening. This doesn't eliminate the chances of cheating, but does reduce them. Another precaution may be to check the day's gold prices in the *Egyptian Gazette*.

Much the same cautionary rules apply to silver and other jewellery. An endless assortment of rings, bracelets, necklaces and the like can be found all over Islamic Cairo. Hunt around, and beware of the 'antiques' made to look so.

Papyrus

You can pick up cheap bits of poor quality papyrus all over Egypt for virtually nothing (a distressing number of well-heeled visitors part with ridiculous sums of money for garbage or, better still, banana leaf substitutes). Look long and hard at what you are getting. Good papyrus will not be damaged by rolling and the quality of designs varies from the sloppy machine print to masterful hand painting. The name Dr Ragab has long been associated with papyrus, and he has 'institutes' and shops all over the country. His stuff is expensive however. One alternative is Said Delta Papyrus Centre, in Islamic Cairo. See the appropriate entry in the Islamic Cairo section of the Cairo chapter.

Cotton Goods

Since cotton is one of Egypt's major crops it is no surprise that cotton clothing is very popular. Cotton shirts, pants and *galabiyyas* (the loose gowns worn by many Egyptians) can be made to your specifications. Many Cairene tailors can work from photographs of the clothing. The area between Al-Azhar and Bab Zuweila in Cairo is teeming with shops selling galabiyyas, ready and tailor-made. You can also try at the village of Kerdassa, near the pyramids. T-shirts abound all over the country.

A lot of travellers have found it extremely cheap to have suits and other clothes tailor-made in Egypt, at prices that are ridiculously low by western standards.

On Sharia Khayamiyya in Islamic Cairo you can pick up some beautiful applique cotton wall hangings, cushion covers and similar items decorated with Islamic, Pharaonic and folkloric designs. Some of the more intricate Islamic patterns on big items take a week's work or more and can cost as much as E£1000. Mostly the work and prices are far more moderate (a typical cushion cover will costs between E£15 to E£20), and fierce bargaining remains the first rule. You can also buy the printed applique material so often used to decorate booths and stands for major festivals, and especially during Ramadan. The masters' work seems to be concentrated at the southern end of this part of the market. Look closely at the stitching.

In Dahab, in Sinai, cotton trousers and printed shirts are quite popular. A pair of light, simple trousers will cost around E£8. The Bedouins also make up traditional clothing for sale. Canvas bags are also cheap and popular, usually around E£5 depending on size and quality.

For those into hand-woven silk and cotton, the place to buy these is Achmin near Sohag (see the Nile Valley chapter).

Fezzes

There are only two fez shops left in Cairo, just south of Al-Azhar on Sharia al-Muizz li-Din Allah. Introduced by the Turks and once worn as a sign of having made it in society, hardly anybody wears the red *tarboosh* any more. Bargaining may get you one for E£5.

Tapestries & Carpets

As with a lot of items, you can find carpets and rugs all over the place, but if you have time and happen to be in the pyramids area, it would be an idea to visit some of the carpet and tapestry schools along Saqqara Rd. The Wissa Wassef school is particularly interesting (see the Cairo chapter for details).

In Dahab there's a plethora of shops selling cheap, colourful cotton rugs made by the Bedouins.

Leather

Leather is another popular buy. However, you will generally be offered items in the soft leather of gazelle hide and these creatures are protected and are becoming quite rare in Egypt.

Copperware & Brassware

Plates, coffeepots and a variety of other objects make nice gifts, and are often fairly cheap. Engraved trays and plates start at around E£15, depending on their intricacy and age. Watch for the quality of any engraving work and be wary of claims that the object in your hand is a hundred years old – more often than not it rolled off the production line a couple of weeks ago.

Basketware

Especially good in Al-Faiyum and Siwa, basketware is a cheap but awkward souvenir. Many of the baskets are nicely decorated and often sturdy and well made. For some reason, a bunch of polyglot young girls hang around the Tell al-Amarna site in Upper Egypt trying to flog this kind of thing to tourists as soon as they get off the Nile ferry. You can pick up a big basket for as little as E£5.

In Cairo, a guy often sets up a basketware stall at the entrance to Sayyida Zeinab metro station.

Inlay & Woodwork

Along with papyrus, inlaid backgammon boards (some with chess on the reverse side) and jewellery boxes are a popular buy. Small jewellery boxes start at about E£5. So long as you don't believe the stories about them all being done with mother-of-pearl, they make an attractive and typically Egyptian souvenir.

Spices

Every conceivable herb and spice, and many you will never have heard of or seen, can be bought in most markets throughout the country. Generally they are fresher and better quality than any of the packaged stuff you'll find in the west, and four to five times cheaper. How much cheaper will depend on your bargaining.

Perfumes

Egypt is a big producer of many of the essences that make up French perfume, hence it's no surprise that part of Cairo's Khan al-Khalili is devoted to a perfume bazaar. Here you can buy pure essence (anywhere from E£8 to E£20 an ounce) as well as cheaper substances diluted with alcohol or oil. Intricate perfume bottles are also a big seller but, once again, there are expensive and cheap varieties. Small glass bottles start at about E£3; the heavier and more durable pyrex bottles cost from E£10. Some of the perfume traders have price tags on their goods, but that doesn't mean you can't haggle.

Musical Instruments

Traditional musical instruments such as an *oud* (lute), *kamaan* (violin), *nay* (flute), *tabla* (drum) and various others are made and sold in about a dozen shops in Cairo on Sharia al-Qala'a (also known as Sharia Mohammed Ali) which runs south-east from Midan Ataba to the Museum of Islamic Art. One such shop is that of Gamil Georges at No 170. Ouds, ranging from E£150 to E£300, have been made and sold here since 1906. The owner, the son of the original Gamil Georges, is a kindly man who will show you the process and perhaps even play a tune.

Duty-Free Shops

It is possible to buy a wide range of articles duty-free, either on entering the country or within a month of entry. Good liquor and cigarettes are the main items worth inspection. The liquor is very expensive in the stores so it is easy to make a little profit by reselling well-known brands of whisky and cognac to the hustlers in front of the Egyptian Museum in Cairo. Alternatively, you may be approached by locals in some of the cheaper hotels to buy alcohol for them using your duty-free allowance; naturally, you'd expect some baksheesh for this kind of service.

There are several branches of the Egypt Free Shops Company scattered around the country. A bottle of Johnny Walker Red or Black Label costs from US$16 to US$27 in one of these duty-free shops. Take your passport and the air or ferry ticket you came with (the latter may not be necessary). You can buy up to US$100 worth of these items (this is the tax, not pretax, value of the item).

Branches can be found at:

Cairo
    106 Sharia Gamiat ad-Dowal al-Arabiyya, Mohandiseen (☎ 349-7094)
    19 Sharia Talaat Harb, Central Cairo (☎ 393-1985) – alcohol and cigarettes are not sold at this branch.
    17 Sharia al-Gomhurriya, Central Cairo (☎ 391-5134)
    Cairo Sheraton Hotel (☎ 348-9059)
Alexandria
    513 Tariq al-Hurriya (☎ 586-8546)
    16 Sharia Salah Salem (☎ 483-3429)
    Maritime station, Alexandria (☎ 422-7808)
Luxor
    Just off Sharia al-Karnak, one block north of the Emilio Hotel
Port Said
    Sharia al-Gomhurriya (☎ 325151)

It is also possible to buy duty-free in Aswan (at the New Cataract Hotel), Hurghada (opposite Banque Misr on the resort strip), Na'ama Bay (at the Aquamarine Hotel) and in Nuweiba (port area).

Things to Avoid

Unfortunately, there is a number of animal products which are still sold in Egypt's souvenir shops despite national and international bans to protect the creatures.

Ivory is one such product. Most of the ivory comes from Sudan and Kenya, where the elephant populations were decimated in the 1970s and 1980s in order to meet demands for ivory jewellery and trinkets. The slaughter prompted an indefinite worldwide ban on the trade of ivory which was imposed at the Convention on the International Trade in Endangered Species (CITES) in 1989. Ivory brought into Australia without a permit from Australian National Parks &

Wildlife *and* the country of origin will be detained by customs.

Other animals which have fallen victim to illegal trading are birds and desert creatures. You'll see plenty of these stuffed and sold at Kerdassa, a village near the pyramids in Cairo, as well as in Khan al-Khalili. Marine curios are sold from street stalls in Hurghada, turtle shells in Port Said, and stuffed crocodiles in Aswan. If people stopped buying these things, the slaughter might end.

Getting There & Away

If you're heading to Egypt from Europe, you have the choice of either flying direct or going overland to one of the Mediterranean ports and taking a ferry to North Africa. If you're coming from any other continent, it can sometimes be cheaper to fly first to Europe, and then make your way to Egypt, than to fly direct. There are also the overland combinations of bus, taxi and ferry from other countries in Africa, and from Jordan, Kuwait, Saudi Arabia, Israel and Libya.

Whichever route you take there is always the inescapable search for the cheapest ticket and the certainty that no matter how great a deal you find, there's always someone out there with a better one.

AIR
Airports & Airlines
Egypt's international and national carrier is EgyptAir. The country is also serviced by many airlines from Europe, as well as some from Africa and the Middle East.

EgyptAir planned to introduce a smoking ban on all international flights of less than six hours in 1996. By July 1997, all their flights are expected to be smoke free.

Egypt has a handful of airports but only six are international ports of entry: Cairo, Alexandria and, increasingly gaining status, the 'international' airports at Luxor, Aswan, Hurghada (Al-Ghardaka) and Sharm el-Sheikh. Most air travellers enter Egypt through Cairo. The other airports tend to be serviced from outside Egypt by charter and package-deal flights in the high season only.

EgyptAir and Air Sinai have internal flights linking at least nine destinations within Egypt. See the Getting Around chapter for details.

Cairo The airport is 25 km, or a 45 to 60 minute drive, to the north-east of central Cairo. There are two terminals about three km apart, and plans to build a third. The new terminal, known as Terminal II, services most international airlines. The old Terminal I is mainly used by EgyptAir (domestic and international flights).

Arriving at Terminal II, you'll pass a couple of duty-free shops, exchange offices, several banks and a Thomas Cook office before arriving at customs control. The exchange offices are right next to each other and their rates are about the same. They can also issue stamps for a visa (see the Visas & Documents section in the Facts for the Visitor chapter for details). Similar banking facilities are available at Terminal I. There's also a (quite useless) tourist information office at Terminal II.

The departure lounge at Terminal II has a handful of duty-free shops (E£ are not accepted) and a post & telephone office. Card phones and a Home Country Direct telephone are available, as are telex and telegraphic services.

✈ ✈ ✈ ✈ ✈ ✈ ✈ ✈ ✈ ✈ ✈ ✈ ✈

Things Change
The information in this chapter is particularly vulnerable to change: prices for international travel are volatile, routes are introduced and cancelled, schedules change, special deals come and go, and rules and visa requirements are amended. Airlines and governments seem to take a perverse pleasure in making price structures and regulations as complicated as possible. You should check directly with the airline or a travel agent to make sure you understand how a fare (and ticket you may buy) works. In addition, the travel industry is highly competitive and there are many lurks and perks.

The upshot of this is that you should get opinions, quotes and advice from as many airlines and travel agents as possible before you part with your hard-earned cash. The details given in this chapter should be regarded as pointers and are not a substitute for your own careful, up-to-date research. ∎

✈ ✈ ✈ ✈ ✈ ✈ ✈ ✈ ✈ ✈ ✈ ✈ ✈

Between the arrival and departure lounges is a left-luggage room which is open 24 hours. It charges E£3 for items less than 25 kg, and E£6 for those weighing more.

Most major car rental companies have booths in the arrivals hall. Outside Terminal I is a lost-and-found booth. For details on getting between the airport and central Cairo, see the Getting Around section in the Cairo chapter.

Warning Many travellers arriving at Cairo airport are met by the infamous 'tourist officials'. For more on the tactics of these touts, see the Accommodation section in the Facts for the Visitor chapter.

Alexandria The international airport in Alexandria is much smaller than in Cairo. Only Lufthansa and Olympic Airways have direct flights between Alexandria and Frankfurt and Athens respectively. For details on transport between the airport and central Alexandria, refer to the Getting Around section in the Alexandria chapter.

Luxor & Aswan Charter companies fly directly from Europe, especially Germany, to Luxor airport, and increasingly also to Aswan. EgyptAir has also started direct flights from Luxor to London, Zürich, Frankfurt and Paris (for details see the Luxor Getting There & Away section in The Nile Valley – Luxor chapter).

Hurghada & Sharm el-Sheikh There are charter flights between these Red Sea tourist resorts and European destinations, also invariably part of package deals.

Buying Tickets

The plane ticket will probably be the single most expensive item in your budget, and buying it can be an intimidating business. There is likely to be a multitude of airlines and travel agents hoping to separate you from your money, and it is always worth putting aside a few hours to research the current state of the market. Start early: some of the cheapest tickets have to be bought

months in advance, and some popular flights sell out early. Talk to other recent travellers – they may be able to stop you making some of the same old mistakes. Look at the ads in newspapers and magazines (not forgetting the press of the ethnic group whose country you plan to visit), and watch for special offers. Then phone round travel agents for bargains. (Airlines can supply information on routes and timetables; however, except at times of inter-airline war they do not supply the cheapest tickets.) Find out the fare, the route, the duration of the journey and flexibility of the ticket. (See Restrictions in the Air Travel Glossary.) Then sit back and decide which is best for you.

You may discover that those impossibly cheap flights are 'fully booked, but we have another one that costs a bit more...'. Or the flight is on an airline notorious for its poor safety standards and leaves you in the world's least favourite airport in mid-journey for 14 hours. Or they claim only to have the last two seats available for that country for the whole of July, which they will hold for you for a maximum of two hours. Don't panic – keep ringing around.

Use the fares quoted in this book as a guide only. They are approximate and based on the rates advertised by travel agents at the time of going to press. Quoted airfares do not necessarily constitute a recommendation for the carrier.

If you are travelling from the UK or the USA, you will probably find that the cheapest flights are being advertised by obscure bucket shops whose names haven't yet reached the telephone directory. Many such firms are honest and solvent, but there are a few rogues who will take your money and disappear, to reopen elsewhere a month or two later under a new name. If you feel suspicious about a firm, don't give them all the money at once – leave a deposit of 20% or so and pay the balance when you get the ticket. If they insist on cash in advance, go somewhere else. And once you have the ticket, ring the airline to confirm that you are actually booked onto the flight.

You may decide to pay more than the

rock-bottom fare by opting for the safety of a better-known travel agent. Firms such as STA, who have offices worldwide, Council Travel in the USA or Travel CUTS in Canada are not going to disappear overnight, leaving you clutching a receipt for a non-existent ticket, but they do offer good prices to most destinations.

Once you have your ticket, write its number down, together with the flight number and other details, and keep the information somewhere separate. If the ticket is lost or stolen, this will help you get a replacement.

It's sensible to buy travel insurance as early as possible. If you buy it the week before you fly, you may find, for example, that you're not covered for delays to your flight caused by industrial action.

Air Travellers with Special Needs

If you have special needs of any sort – you've broken a leg, you're vegetarian, travelling in a wheelchair, taking the baby, terrified of flying – you should let the airline know as soon as possible so that they can make arrangements accordingly. You should remind them when you reconfirm your booking (at least 72 hours before departure) and again when you check in at the airport. It may also be worth ringing round the airlines before you make your booking to find out how they can handle your particular needs.

Airports and airlines can be surprisingly helpful, but they do need advance warning. Most international airports will provide escorts from the check-in desk to the plane where needed, and there should be ramps, lifts, accessible toilets and reachable phones. Aircraft toilets, on the other hand, are likely to present a problem; travellers should discuss this with the airline at an early stage and, if necessary, with their doctor.

Guide dogs for the blind will often have to travel in a specially pressurised baggage compartment with other animals, away from their owner; though smaller guide dogs may be admitted to the cabin. All guide dogs will be subject to the same quarantine laws (six months in isolation etc) as any other animal when entering or returning to countries currently free of rabies such as Britain or Australia.

Deaf travellers can ask for airport and in-flight announcements to be written down for them.

Children under two travel for 10% of the standard fare (or free, on some airlines), as long as they don't occupy a seat. They don't get a baggage allowance either. 'Skycots' should be provided by the airline if requested in advance; these will take a child weighing up to about 10 kg. Children between two and 12 can usually occupy a seat for half to two-thirds of the full fare, and do get a baggage allowance. Push chairs can often be taken as hand luggage.

The USA & Canada

The *New York Times*, the *LA Times*, the *Chicago Tribune* and the *San Francisco Examiner* all produce weekly travel sections in which you'll find any number of travel agents' ads. Council Travel and STA Travel have offices in major cities nationwide.

The magazine *Travel Unlimited* (PO Box 1058, Allston, Mass 02134) publishes details of the cheapest air fares and courier possibilities for destinations all over the world from the USA.

In Canada, Travel CUTS has offices in all major cities. The *Toronto Globe & Mail* and the *Vancouver Sun* carry travel agents' ads. The magazine *Great Expeditions* (PO Box 8000-411, Abbotsford BC V2S 6H1) is useful.

The cheapest way from the USA or Canada to the Middle East and Africa is usually a return flight to London and a bucket-shop deal from there.

A Round-the-World (RTW) ticket including a stopover in Cairo is a possibility. Check the travel sections of Sunday newspapers for the latest deals.

EgyptAir flies from New York and Los Angeles to Cairo. The cheapest advance purchase tickets are for a minimum stay of seven days and a maximum stay of two months. Regular fares from New York and Los Angeles are approximately US$1280/2176 one way/return and US$1630/3358 one way/return, respectively. EgyptAir has no connections to Canada.

Lufthansa has connections to Cairo via Frankfurt from many cities in the USA. Advance purchase fares are available. From Los Angeles, the return fare is US$2032, and also entails a minimum stay of seven days and a maximum of two months. A one-way ticket is US$1718. From New York, the same two tickets are US$1606 and US$1088 respectively.

The UK

London is one of the best centres in the world for discounted air tickets. The price of RTW tickets, especially, is about the best available anywhere and tickets can be had for well under UK£1000, although Cairo is not a very common stop on such a ticket and may lift the price considerably.

Trailfinders in west London produces a lavishly illustrated brochure which includes air fare details. STA also has branches in the UK. Look in the listings of the *Time Out* and *TNT* magazines as well as the Sunday papers and *Exchange & Mart* for ads. Also look out for the free magazines widely available in

---

Air Travel Glossary

Apex Apex, or 'advance purchase excursion' is a discounted ticket which must be paid for in advance. There are penalties if you wish to change it.

Baggage Allowance This will be written on your ticket: usually one 20 kg item to go in the hold, plus one item of hand luggage.

Bucket Shop An unbonded travel agency specialising in discounted airline tickets.

Bumped Just because you have a confirmed seat doesn't mean you're going to get on the plane – see Overbooking.

Cancellation Penalties If you have to cancel or change an Apex ticket there are often heavy penalties involved. Insurance can sometimes be taken out against these penalties. Some airlines impose penalties on regular tickets as well, particularly against 'no show' passengers.

Check In Airlines ask you to check in a certain time ahead of the flight departure (usually 1½ hours on international flights). If you fail to check in on time and the flight is overbooked the airline can cancel your booking and give your seat to somebody else.

Confirmation Having a ticket written out with the flight and date you want doesn't mean you have a seat until the agent has checked with the airline that your status is 'OK' or confirmed. Meanwhile you could just be 'on request'.

Discounted Tickets There are two types of discounted fares – officially discounted (see Promotional Fares) and unofficially discounted. The lowest prices often impose drawbacks like flying with unpopular airlines, inconvenient schedules, or unpleasant routes and connections. A discounted ticket can save you other things than money – you may be able to pay Apex prices without the associated Apex advance booking and other requirements. Discounted tickets only exist where there is fierce competition.

Full Fares Airlines traditionally offer 1st class (coded F), business class (coded J) and economy class (coded Y) tickets. These days there are so many promotional and discounted fares available from the regular economy class that few passengers pay full economy fare.

Lost Tickets If you lose your airline ticket an airline will usually treat it like a travellers' cheque and, after inquiries, issue you with another one. Legally, however, an airline is entitled to treat it like cash and if you lose it then it's gone forever. Take good care of your tickets.

No Shows No shows are passengers who fail to show up for their flight, sometimes due to unexpected delays or disasters, sometimes due to simply forgetting, sometimes because they made more than one booking and didn't bother to cancel the one they didn't want. Full fare passengers who fail to turn up are sometimes entitled to travel on a later flight. The rest of us are penalised (see Cancellation Penalties).

On Request An unconfirmed booking for a flight, see Confirmation.

Open Jaws A return ticket where you fly out to one place but return from another. If available this can save you backtracking to your arrival point.

London – start by looking outside the main railway stations.

Most British travel agents are registered with ABTA (Association of British Travel Agents). If you have paid for your flight to an ABTA-registered agent who then goes out of business, ABTA will guarantee a refund or an alternative. Unregistered bucket shops are riskier but also sometimes cheaper.

The Globetrotters Club (BCM Roving, London WC1N 3XX) publishes a newsletter called *Globe* which covers obscure destinations and can help in finding travelling companions.

The Africa Travel Shop (☎ (0171) 387-1211), at 4 Medway Court, Leigh St, London WC1, caters to the growing number of travellers interested in Africa. It is ABTA bonded, has a free video library and can organise overland safaris and most other travel requirements. As an example of 1995 fares, it has a UK£299 return fare with British Airways (valid for 35 days), while regular return tickets without restrictions (valid for one year) cost UK£320.

Travellers planning to head further into Africa might be advised to get a ticket to, say, Nairobi in Kenya with a stopover in Cairo. Air fares are generally expensive within Africa. The Africa Travel Shop has one-way

---

Overbooking Airlines hate to fly empty seats and since every flight has some passengers who fail to show up (see No Shows) airlines often book more passengers than they have seats. Usually the excess passengers balance those who fail to show up but occasionally somebody gets bumped. If this happens guess who it is most likely to be? The passengers who check in late.

Promotional Fares Officially discounted fares like Apex fares which are available from travel agents or direct from the airline.

Reconfirmation At least 72 hours prior to departure time of an onward or return flight you must contact the airline and 'reconfirm' that you intend to be on the flight. If you don't do this the airline can delete your name from the passenger list and you could lose your seat. You don't have to reconfirm the first flight on your itinerary or if your stopover is less than 72 hours. It doesn't hurt to reconfirm more than once.

Restrictions Discounted tickets often have various restrictions on them – advance purchase is the most usual one (see Apex). Other restrictions are on the minimum and maximum period you must be away, such as a minimum of 14 days or a maximum of one year. See Cancellation Penalties.

Standby A discounted ticket where you only fly if there is a seat free at the last moment. Standby fares are usually only available on domestic routes.

Tickets Out An entry requirement for many countries is that you have an onward or return ticket, in other words, a ticket out of the country. If you're not sure what you intend to do next, the easiest solution is to buy the cheapest onward ticket to a neighbouring country or a ticket from a reliable airline which can later be refunded if you do not use it.

Transferred Tickets Airline tickets cannot be transferred from one person to another. Travellers sometimes try to sell the return half of their ticket, but officials can ask you to prove that you are the person named on the ticket. This is unlikely to happen on domestic flight; on an international flight tickets may be compared with passports.

Travel Agencies Travel agencies vary widely and you should ensure you use one that suits your needs. Some simply handle tours while full-service agencies handle everything from tours and tickets to car rental and hotel bookings. A good one will do all these things and can save you a lot of money but if all you want is a ticket at the lowest possible price, then you really need an agency specialising in discounted tickets. A discounted ticket agency, however, may not be useful for other things, like hotel bookings.

Travel Periods Some officially discounted fares, Apex fares in particular, vary with the time of year. There is often a low (off-peak) season and a high (peak) season. Sometimes there's an intermediate or shoulder season as well. At peak times, when everyone wants to fly, not only will the officially discounted fares be higher but so will unofficially discounted fares or there may simply be no discounted tickets available. Usually the fare depends on your outward flight – if you depart in the high season and return in the low season, you pay the high-season fare. ■

tickets with EgyptAir to Nairobi including a stop in Cairo for UK£295 – much better than anything you'll find in Cairo.

For shorter trips, it's worth looking into package trips or combined air fare and hotel deals. Charters to Luxor and leaving from Cairo, with accommodation in two to three star hotels, can come to about UK£350 for two weeks.

The cheapest, but most unpredictable, way to fly to Cairo from London may be as a courier for DHL or another air courier service.

Continental Europe

Germany One of the most popular European carriers for flights between North Africa and the rest of the world is Lufthansa. If your trip is originating in Germany, or if you wish to stop over in Germany before or after visiting Egypt, Lufthansa and its charter subsidiary Condor offer some of the most frequent connections with flights to and from Egypt. There are direct scheduled flights from Frankfurt to Cairo and Alexandria. During the high season (October to April), there are several flights weekly to Sharm el-Sheikh and Luxor.

In Munich, a great source of travel information and gear is Travel Overland (☎ (89) 280864) at Theresienstrasse 66, D-8000, Munich 2. Aside from producing a comprehensive travel equipment catalogue, it also runs an 'Expedition Service' with current flight information available.

In Berlin, Kilroy (☎ (30) 410-0040), at Hardenbergstrasse 9, near Berlin Zoo (with five branches around the city), is a popular travel agency.

Netherlands Amsterdam is a popular departure point. Some of the best fares are offered by the student travel agency NBBS Reiswinkels (☎ (20) 679-9337). It has seven branches throughout the city, with fares comparable to those of London bucket shops. NBBS Reiswinkels has branches in Brussels, Belgium, as well.

France Paris is not a bad place to organise a

trip to Egypt from. It seems to abound with Egypt and desert specialists. Voyageurs en Egypte et au Proche Orient (☎ 42 86 17 19) at 55, rue Sainte-Anne, 75002 Paris, has a return flight on EgyptAir for 2314FF.

There are a few other places worth looking at, particularly if you are looking for something more organised on the ground or desert expeditions. Explorator (☎ 42 66 66 24), 16, Place de la Madeleine, 75008 Paris, offers one week in Sinai for 7900FF. The price includes everything except visas and insurance. They also have a one week Western Deserts Tour from Cairo to the Libyan border.

Esprit d'aventure (☎ 53 73 77 99) at 12, rue Saint-Victor, 75005 Paris, offers an all inclusive 10 day tour for 9600FF, and a 15 day tour to Jerusalem-Sinai-Petra for 13,200FF, everything included. Allibert (☎ 76 45 22 26), route de Grenoble, 38 530 Chaparcillan (in the Alps, near the Swiss border) has an eight day Sinai trip (six days of walking; tents) for 7800FF. Also worth trying is Déserts (☎ 46 04 88 40), 6-8 Rue Quincampoix, 75004 Paris.

Greece Bucket shop agencies around the Plaka and Syntagma Square in Athens charge about the lowest fares you can find for flights from Athens to Cairo. Fantasy Travel at 10 Xenofontas St (near Syntagma Square), Speedy Ways Travel Agency and Lin Travel (☎ 322-1237), at 39 Nikis St, have been recommended by travellers.

From Cairo or Alexandria, the one-way flight with Olympic Airways costs E£1193, or E£664 for the student fare; EgyptAir is slightly more expensive.

Turkey A similar crowd of bucket shops is also clustered around the Sultan Ahmet area of Istanbul.

Middle East

Israel Air Sinai and El Al regularly fly between Cairo and Tel Aviv for about E£637 one way or E£907 return (valid for one month). If you have the time, however, travelling overland between Egypt and Israel is much cheaper and more adventurous.

Jordan There are daily flights with Royal Jordanian Airlines and EgyptAir between Cairo and Amman, but there is no discounting. Amman to Cairo is JD84 one way and double that for a return. Going the other way, the fare is E£571 one way and E£1010 return. There are no student reductions.

Africa
Libya At the time of writing, international flights to and from Libya had been suspended as a result of the UN air embargo imposed on Libya following its refusal to hand over two suspects accused of bombing a Pan-Am flight over Lockerbie in Scotland in 1988.

Sudan Sudan Airways and EgyptAir both have two flights a week between Cairo and Khartoum. The 2½ hour flight costs E£1326 one way or E£1444 return (valid for one month). Sudan Airways also has a youth fare (for those under 25 years) which costs E£849 one way or E£1565 return (open for one year). However, one-way tickets will not be sold unless you can show a ticket from Sudan to your home country, and no ticket will be issued until you've got your Sudanese visa.

Tunisia Tunis Air and EgyptAir offer student discounts on flights between Cairo and Tunis, but that doesn't make it cheap. The one-way fare is E£840. If you're over 31, it will come to E£1550. Consult the offices of each airline for the latest information.

Other African Countries As you will have gathered from the information on flights to Tunis and Khartoum, there is nothing cheap about travelling by air between African capitals. About the best you can do to Nairobi is E£2129 one way with Kenyan Airways (or E£1678 for a student fare). A return ticket, valid for two months, costs E£2835. The flight to Addis Ababa in Ethiopia is E£1820

one way (or E£2545 return) with Ethiopian Airlines. However, one-way tickets can only be purchased if you can show a credit card or travellers' cheques to cover the cost of a return ticket.

Australia & New Zealand
STA and Flight Centres International are major dealers in cheap air fares from Australia and New Zealand. Check the travel agents' ads in the Yellow Pages and ring around.

EgyptAir commenced flights between Cairo and Sydney in November 1995. As an example of fares, it costs E£6000/8625 to fly one way/return from Cairo to Sydney; in the other direction, tickets cost A$1220/1830. RTW fares with a stopover in Cairo start from A$2080 but vary according to season.

Asia
Hong Kong is the discount plane ticket capital of the region. Its bucket shops, however, are at least as unreliable as those of other cities. Ask the advice of other travellers before buying a ticket.

STA, which is reliable, has branches in Hong Kong, Tokyo, Singapore, Bangkok and Kuala Lumpur.

From Bangkok, EgyptAir offers a one-way fare for US$1015; the return fare costs US$2018.

To Bombay, the EgyptAir fare is E£2230 one way.

LAND
Your Own Transport
Drivers of cars and riders of motorbikes will need the vehicle's registration papers, liability insurance and an international drivers' permit in addition to their domestic licence. Beware: there are two kinds of international permits, one of which is needed mostly for former British colonies. You will also need a *Carnet de passage en douane*, which is effectively a passport for the vehicle, and acts as a temporary waiver of import duty. The carnet may also need to have listed any more expensive spares that you're planning

to carry with you, such as a gearbox. This is necessary when travelling in many countries in Asia, Africa and Central and South America, and is designed to prevent car import rackets. Contact your local automobile association for details about all documentation.

At the Egyptian border, you will be issued with a licence valid for three months (less if your visa is valid for less time). You can keep renewing the licence every three months for a maximum of two years but you'll have to pay a varying fee each time (somewhere between 5 and 10% of customs duty). The cost of the initial three month licence ranges between E£500 and E£1000. After paying this, you'll be issued with Egyptian number plates. It is forbidden for a carnet vehicle to be sold in Egypt – you must take it out when you leave.

Liability insurance is not available in advance for many out-of-the-way countries, but has to be bought when crossing the border. The cost and quality of such local insurance varies wildly, and you will find in some countries that you are effectively travelling uninsured.

If you are coming by sea, check with the ferry company that you are covered for any letters of guarantee that may be required by customs. If you are staying for more than six months, proof of payment for road tax and customs duties, refundable on departure, is supposedly required.

The Egyptians themselves give conflicting advice on whether or not diesel-powered vehicles may enter the country. The latest advice is that they can be brought in but only through the port at Alexandria. People wishing to bring in 4WD cars should check at an Egyptian embassy first, as the rules governing these vehicles are contentious. For further information try contacting the Automobile and Touring Club of Egypt (☎ 574-3355), 10 Sharia Qasr el-Nil in Cairo, which is open daily except Friday from 9 am to 1.30 pm.

Anyone who is planning to take their own vehicle with them needs to check in advance what spares and petrol are likely to be available. In Egypt, lead-free was introduced in 1995 but is available only in Cairo and Alexandria. You are also likely to have trouble finding every little part for your car.

Cycling is a cheap, convenient, healthy, environmentally sound and above all fun way of travelling. One note of caution: before you leave home, go over your bike with a fine-toothed comb and fill your repair kit with every imaginable spare. As with cars and motorbikes, you won't necessarily be able to buy that crucial gismo for your machine when it breaks down somewhere in the back of beyond as the sun sets.

Bicycles can travel by air. You *can* take them to pieces and put them in a bike bag or box, but it's much easier simply to wheel your bike to the check in desk, where it should be treated as a piece of baggage. You may have to remove the pedals and turn the handlebars sideways so that it takes up less space in the aircraft's hold; check all this with the airline well in advance, preferably before you pay for your ticket.

Israel & Palestinian Territories

There are two crossing points between Egypt and Israel: Taba on the Gulf of Aqaba coast and Rafah (also spelt Rafiah) on the southern edge of the Gaza Strip.

Taba, just four km south of central Eilat, is the most convenient place to cross if you are planning a visit to Sinai. While there are no organised buses from Eilat into Egypt a solo crossing is simple enough and once over the border it's possible to pick up local Egyptian transport both for Sinai destinations and for Cairo.

The border is open 24 hours but this is subject to occasional change and you will want to cross when there's transport on the other side. It's normally possible to stroll through the formalities at Taba in around 30 minutes.

Once on the Egyptian side, change money at the Taba Hilton and then it's a further one km walk to the small tourist village and bus stop.

At Rafah, waits of anything up to four or five hours are common as it's a more heavily used crossing and all holders of Egyptian and Israeli passports are scrutinised and checked against computer records. You can change money at the border.

Departure and entry fees vary between Taba and Rafah, see Departure Taxes later in this chapter.

Egyptian visas can be obtained from the embassy in Tel Aviv or the consulate in Eilat. For more information see the section on Visas in the Facts for the Visitor chapter. No visa is required for most nationalities entering Israel.

Bus Tour operators provide coach services from Tel Aviv and Jerusalem non-stop to Cairo via the border at Rafah (where there is a change of bus). The journey takes roughly 10 hours; a ticket from Tel Aviv or Jerusalem is about US$30 one way, US$45 return.

There are two main operators: Egged Tours (☎ (03) 371 101) at 59 Ben Yehuda St, Tel Aviv has daily departures at 8.30 am. In Jerusalem (☎ (02) 304 883), 224 Jaffa Rd, their buses depart Thursday and Sunday at 6.30 am.

Mazada Tours (☎ (03) 544 4454), 141 Ibn Gvirol St, Tel Aviv, has daily buses departing at 9 am, arriving in Cairo at 7 pm. There are also Tuesday, Thursday and Sunday overnight buses departing at 8.30 pm, arriving 7 am the next morning. In Jerusalem (☎ (02) 235 7777), 9 Koresh St, buses depart Monday to Friday at 7.30 am. There are also overnight services on Tuesday and Thursday, departing at 7 pm.

Alternatively, you can do it yourself from Tel Aviv. An Egged bus departs for Rafah at 9 am each day from the central bus station. The journey takes about two hours and costs 27 NIS. After passing through Israeli immigration, catch the shuttle bus (approximately US$2) over to the Egyptian hall. Once through procedures there, you can catch a local Egyptian bus or service taxi for Cairo, some five hours distant. Do not go via Rafah if you want to go directly to Sinai without first visiting Cairo.

On the return leg, the bus departs Rafah

for Tel Aviv at 3 pm each afternoon. If you miss that or arrive early in the morning then get a *sherut* (service taxi) to Beersheeba, 50 km distant, from where you can easily pick up an onward bus.

There is also a bus to Taba from Cairo, but it won't save you anything. You could try going first to Suez (E£5 by service taxi), and picking up the Taba bus from there (E£30).

On the Israeli side, the local bus No 15 from the border to Eilat costs 4 NIS (a taxi is 20 NIS). The Egged bus from Eilat to Tel Aviv costs 46 NIS. For more local transport information and possibilities, and border crossing formalities, see the Rafah and Taba Getting There & Away sections in the Sinai chapter.

Sudan

There are three potential ways to travel overland between Egypt and Sudan, but they're not very practical, and probably impossible, for foreign travellers. It's unwise to attempt any of these at present in view of the deteriorating relationship between Egypt and Sudan. The following, therefore is not a recommendation – the information is given simply to assist travellers in the event that conditions improve.

With a bit of negotiation and an adventurous spirit, you might be able to join a camel caravan from Sudan. The camel herders, following an age-old caravan route known as Darb al-Arba'in, or the 40 Days Road, bring their camels up from western Sudan through the desert to Daraw, where they sell them.

It may one day be possible to drive along the Red Sea coast between the two countries. However, you'd need a tough 4WD vehicle to do so, and you'd also want the Egyptian and Sudanese troops in the disputed Halaib region to have stopped shooting at each other.

The most common way of travelling between Sudan and Egypt used to be by steamer from Aswan up Lake Nasser to Wadi Halfa. However, this service has been indefinitely cancelled. People determined to drive into Sudan, or at least get their vehicles in, have occasionally negotiated for a boat to transport them from the docks at the High Dam, south of Aswan, to Wadi Halfa. For further details on this, refer to the Aswan Getting There & Away section.

Libya

There are direct buses running between Cairo, Benghazi and Tripoli (Tarabulus). You can also get buses to the same destinations from Alexandria. Fares from here tend to be slightly cheaper. For more details see the Cairo and Alexandria Getting There & Away sections. A more laborious, but even cheaper alternative would be to get local transport (buses, trains or service taxis) to Sallum and a service taxi to the border. From there you can get Libyan transport heading west. See the Sallum entry for details.

SEA

Europe

Menatours acts as the agent for the limited passenger-ship services that operate between Port Said or Alexandria and various Mediterranean destinations, including Beirut (Lebanon) and Antalya (Turkey). For details see the Port Said and Alexandria Getting There & Away sections.

Sudan

Other than flying, the easiest way to get to Sudan from Egypt is to go by sea ferry. Ferries bound for Port Sudan leave from Suez; the voyage, via Jeddah in Saudi Arabia, takes four days. Information and tickets are available from Yara Tours & Shipping (☎ 393-8861) at 38 Sharia Mohammed Sabri Abu Alam in central Cairo, as well as

---

Travelling by Freighter

Jumping a tramp freighter and enjoying some cheap and grungy travel is largely a thing of the past, thanks to the containerisation of most cargo services. There might be local services where a quiet chat with an officer can get you on boat, but for most long-distance travel you are limited to container vessels.

Some container lines take passengers, and while the voyage will cost considerably more than an economy class air ticket, the per-day cost isn't too outrageous. Think of it as an experience rather than a means of getting from A to B.

Ships can be well equipped, with gyms and swimming pools, and plenty of duty-free alcohol, and many operators offer unlimited personal luggage. Passengers generally eat with the officers, and the food is usually good. The number of passengers is usually less than 12, because if the ship carries more it must also carry a doctor.

The best source of information about routes and the shipping lines plying them is the *OAG Cruise & Ferry Guide* (it used to be call the *ABC*), published quarterly by Reed Travel Group (☎ (01582) 600111; fax 695230), Church St, Dunstable, Bedfordshire LU5 4HB, UK. Your travel agent might have a copy.

As would be expected, many operators service routes that travel via the Suez from ports throughout the world.

Following is a brief list of operators or their agents who take bookings for freighters:

UK
  Strand Cruise & Travel Centre, Charing Cross Shopping Concourse, Strand, London WC2N 4HZ (☎ (0171) 836 6363; fax 497 0078)
US
  Freighter World Cruises Inc, 180 South Lake Ave, Suite 335, Pasadena, CA 91101 (☎ (818) 449 3106; fax 449 9573)
Germany
  Frachtschiff-Touristik, Exhofter Damm 12, 24404, Maasholm (☎ (04642) 6068; fax 6767)
Australia
  Sydney International Travel Centre, Level 8, 75 King St, Sydney, 2000 (☎ (02) 9299 8000; fax 9299 1337)

from agents in Suez (for more details, see the Suez Getting There & Away section).

Jordan

Ferry or Speedboat There is at least one daily car ferry and a speedboat between Nuweiba, in Sinai, and Aqaba, Jordan's only port. The ferry (3 hrs) is supposed to leave Nuweiba at noon and 6.30 pm, with speedboat departures (1 hr) at 4 pm. Recent reports, however, show a different story: the ferries leave Nuweiba at noon and 6.30 pm on Sunday, and at 4 pm the rest of the week; the speedboat leaves at noon.

The speedboat costs US$42 return, US$27 one way (plus a 200 fils charge). Ferry tickets cost more from Egypt (US$32) than the other way (US$20), although you must add the Jordanian port tax (JD6). Tickets can be bought from the window of an apartment building about 400m from the Nuweiba port entrance (off to the right as you face the port) and must be paid for in US dollars. If you don't have US dollars, and the nearby banks prove useless, the police may lead you to some moneychangers in the port area. Note that Jordanian currency can rarely be changed in Egypt.

In Aqaba, tickets can be bought from the Arab Bridge Maritime Co and numerous travel agents, some of whom will accept Jordanian currency, in which case you pay JD13.500. Tickets can generally be bought for either passage on the day of travel. There is an Egyptian consulate in Aqaba and visas are issued with relatively little fuss on the same day.

Sometimes the ferries are often grossly delayed; they will also be delayed until all passport and customs formalities are completed. Nevertheless, you should be at the port two hours (one hour minimum) prior to the scheduled departure. The trip by ferry is meant to take three hours, but can often take much longer. Occasionally a southerly wind blows up that can oblige ferries coming to Nuweiba to wait until it subsides, but the problem is more likely to be chaos at one port or the other. Be prepared for a trip that could last as long as eight hours.

Although some travellers have reported the luxury of travelling on a nearly empty boat, the more common experience is of ferries packed beyond capacity. The busiest time is around the haj, the pilgrimage to Mecca, when traffic on both sides is swelled by hajjis (pilgrims) heading to and from Mecca in Saudi Arabia. At the peak of this period, they sometimes put on two extra boats. Foot passengers should have little problem getting a ticket.

Bus & Ferry You can book a ferry and bus combination ticket from Cairo or Alexandria through to Aqaba, or even on to Amman if you wish. From Cairo, the trip to Aqaba is US$23 plus E£40.20. You can also book a ferry and bus right through to Cairo at the JETT bus office in Aqaba. The ticket costs US$45, but you can pick up Cairo-bound buses on arrival at Nuweiba anyway. Beware of buying ferry tickets in Amman as you may be charged for nonexistent 1st class places. Remember that it is generally cheaper to pay for each leg as you go than to get a ticket for the whole trip.

Saudi Arabia & Kuwait

Ferry There are regular ferries from Jeddah to Suez (about 36 hours) and Port Safaga (about 24 hours). Several lines compete on the route and fares can vary from one agent to another but, generally, tickets start at around E£145 for deck class to E£300 for 1st class. Most of the ferries on the route also carry cars, at a significant cost. Bear in mind that getting a berth during the haj is virtually impossible.

You can get information at Misr Travel agencies, or buy a ticket directly from their office in Port Tawfiq, Suez. In Jeddah contact Al-Aquel Travel (☎ (02) 647-4208), just off Ba'najah and Al-Dahab Sts. For more details, see the Suez Getting There & Away section.

There are also passenger boats from Port Safaga to Duba and Jeddah, both in Saudi Arabia (see the Port Safaga Getting There & Away section).

Bus & Ferry In the same way that passage can be booked straight through to Aqaba and Amman, you can purchase tickets through to many destinations in the Gulf, either at the Abbassiya Sinai terminal, or at a couple of the other terminals in Cairo or in Alexandria. The fare to Riyadh is E£210 and to Kuwait E£380.

There are daily buses from Riyadh, Jeddah and Dammam to Cairo. SAPTCO, the Saudi Arabian bus company, has two buses per day from each city, one each via Aqaba, Jordan and via Dhuba, Saudi Arabia. Fares always include the ferry crossing. The Dhuba to Port Safaga crossing is shorter, and fares on this route tend to be a bit cheaper. In all cases tickets can be purchased at the main SAPTCO stations.

In Jeddah the station is just off the Corniche across from the GPO. Tickets to Cairo cost SR 290/US$80 via Dhuba and slightly more via Aqaba. In Riyadh the station is just off Al-Batha'a St. Tickets to Cairo cost SR 350/US$95 via Dhuba and SR 395/US$105 via Aqaba. Remember that if you opt for the Aqaba bus you will also need a Jordanian visa.

A bus travels from Kuwait across Saudi Arabia to Aqaba, Jordan. From Aqaba you can take the ferry to Nuweiba and then a bus to Cairo.

DEPARTURE TAXES

Exit fees seem to vary. There is a 50 NIS (US$16) Israeli departure tax to be paid at Taba as well as E£24 (US$8) Egypt entry tax. Visitors crossing to Taba only are exempt from these payments. Leaving Egypt there is no fee.

At Rafah, there is a 90 NIS (US$30) Israeli departure tax and an Egyptian entry fee of E£17. Going the other way, the Egyptian exit tax is E£17, but there is no Israeli entry fee.

Crossing the Libyan border from Egypt there is a E£2 exit fee.

Leaving Nuweiba by boat for Aqaba, the Egyptian departure tax is E£2. In the other direction, there is a port departure tax of JD6 from Aqaba.

Leaving Alexandria by ship there is a E£21 embarkation fee.

There is a E£21 airport departure tax which is incorporated into the price of air tickets.

ORGANISED TOURS

There are any number of tour possibilities to Egypt, and a plethora of agents dealing with everything from Nile cruises to overland safaris or diving trips. Figure out what kind of tour you want to do, or what area of Egypt you want to cover. A charter package to Sharm el-Sheikh won't do much for the Islamic architecture buff. On the other hand, the diving along the Nile is not the best either. If there is an Egyptian Tourist Authority in your city, it may be a good place to start. They should at least be able to provide you with brochures giving you an idea of what's where – don't fall for all the gushing propaganda though! They will usually have the names of several travel agents dealing with tours, and possibly save you time looking for more specialised tour operators (such as for diving in Sinai).

Some of the cheapest air fares with charter aircraft also come with short stays (see Air earlier in this chapter).

It should be remembered that the programmes on such trips are usually fairly tight, leaving little room for roaming around on your own, but they take much of the hassle off your plate. It pays to shop around. Check itinerary details, accommodation, who does the ticketing, visa and other documentation footwork, insurance and tour conditions carefully.

Nile Cruises & Other Packages

Many of the packaged trips to Egypt include a stint on one of the approximately 200 cruisers operating up and down the river. These vessels come in all shapes and sizes, but the big floating hotels ('flotels') seem to dominate. These beasts roam up and down the river in such numbers that smaller vessels, and feluccas especially, have to pay careful attention not to be capsized. There's something worrying about being asked in the dead of night by a felucca captain for a pocket flashlight to shine on the sail, in the hope of not being rammed by a cruiser – they are in fact not supposed to sail after dark.

A few companies you might want to investigate include:

Bales
> Bales House, Junction Rd, Dorking, Surrey RH4 3HB (☎ (01206) 885991). A well-known name in Middle East and African touring, Bales offers a wide range of tours, again the bulk of them involving cruises. They have combined air and land trips to the ancient sights and other tours combining Egypt with Jordan or even Kenya. They also have an escorted, eight day, budget tour starting at UK£499 (airfare and half board but no cruises included).

The Imaginative Traveller
> 14 Barley Mow Passage, Chiswick, London (☎ (0181) 742-3113). With offices around the world (including in the USA, Australia, Canada, New Zealand and South Africa), this company offers various programmes of differing duration in Egypt. Costs vary depending on season and country of departure, but a typical two week 'Sail-Trek' trip starting in Cairo and including four nights and days on a felucca can come to UK£345, excluding air fare.

Jasmin Tours
> High St, Cookham, Maidenhead, Berkshire SL6 9SQ, UK (☎ (01628) 531121). These folk run numerous tours to Egypt, mostly including cruises. A 10 day package – including six days cruising, all fares and meals – costs UK£900.

The Nile Cruise Centre
> 2 Cinnamon Row, Plantation Wharf, York Place, London SW11 3TW (☎ (0171) 978-5222, fax (0171) 924-3171). This company claims to be the only specialist of its kind, and offers advice on a range of cruises and one-off charters. Its cheapest offer is UK£600 for 10 days.

There are many Cairo-based tour operators with offices in several countries around the world, including the Egypt Travel Centre, Sphinx Tours and Gaz Tours, to name a few. With these you can also organise shorter cruises locally, rather than fully-organised tours from abroad (see the Getting Around chapter for more details on organising tours within Egypt).

Adventure & Overland Safaris

A popular mode of travelling through Africa and Asia is by overland truck. This is not everyone's cup of tea, as you spend a lot of time with the same group of people, travelling, camping and cooking. Organisers of these tours do take much of the hassle out of the bureaucratic footwork, helping out with visas and dodging a lot of the cross-border hassles. Egypt often features as a leg on one of these trips.

London, again, is teeming with places that organise such excursions. One is Top Deck (☎ (0171) 244-8641), Earls Court Rd, London SW5 9RH, which has branches in Sydney and Auckland as well. You could also inquire at the Africa Travel Shop (see the Air section earlier in this chapter).

For trips to Sinai, you might want to contact Wind, Sand & Stars (☎ (0171) 433-3684) at 2 Arkwright Rd, London NW3 6AD. It offers climbing and walking tours in Sinai, as well as bird-watching, sleeping under the stars and snorkelling in the Red Sea. You'll be looking at about UK£600/1500 for one/two weeks all inclusive.

There are a number of similar specialists based in Paris (see Continental Europe in the above Air section).

Diving Tours

It is possible to organise diving holidays to the Red Sea. The UK-based Travel Care (☎ (0181) 892-8164), 22 Church St, Twickenham TW1 3NW, offers a range of tours to Egypt, Israel, Jordan and Syria, including one and two week diving holidays.

Getting Around

Egypt has a very extensive public and private transport system. If you don't suffer from claustrophobia, and have plenty of patience and a tough stomach, you can travel just about anywhere in Egypt for relatively little money.

For a few tips about travelling around Egypt during Ramadan, see the boxed story On the Road During Ramadan in the Facts for the Visitor chapter.

AIR

In Egypt, air fares are about average by international standards, but probably out of the range of most low-budget travellers. There are two kinds of fare, one for foreigners and one for Egyptians. One guess who pays more. In general, it is only worth flying if your time is very limited.

EgyptAir is the main domestic carrier. Air Sinai, which to all intents and purposes is EgyptAir by another name, is the only other operator. Private airlines don't get much of a look in, as, by law, they are not allowed to fly the same routes as EgyptAir. You may still see a few signs around for an air company called ZAS which, until it folded under massive debts in early 1995, was Egypt's largest private sector airline.

During the high season (October to April), many flights are full. Since June 1994, smoking has been banned on all EgyptAir domestic flights.

Air Sinai has flights from Cairo to Sharm el-Sheikh (Ras Nasrany) for E£445/890 one way/return – slightly more expensive than EgyptAir's fare and Air Sinai only flies a couple of times per week. In winter only, it

EgyptAir Domestic Flights

Destination	Fare (one way)	Flight Time (hours)	Frequency
From Cairo to:			
Abu Simbel	E£708	2.10	daily
Al-Arish	E£328	1.00	two per week
Al-Kharga	E£399	2.00	two per week
Alexandria	E£214	0.35	daily
Aswan	E£497	1.45	daily
Hurghada	E£391	1.00	daily
Luxor	E£361	1.00	daily
Marsa Matruh	E£344	1.00	three per week
Sharm el-Sheikh	E£412	0.45	daily
From Luxor to:			
Aswan	E£163	0.30	daily
Hurghada	E£163	0.35	one per week*
Sharm el-Sheikh	E£412	0.45	two per week
From Aswan to:			
Abu Simbel	E£439 (return)	0.40 (one way)	daily
Hurghada (via Luxor)	E£323 (one way)		

* high season only

also flies twice a week to Taba (Ras an-Naqb) for E£430/853.

Flights to St Catherine's and Port Said have been suspended; the former since 1990, the latter since 1995.

BUS

Buses service just about every city, town and village in Egypt. Ticket prices are generally comparable with the cost of 2nd class train tickets. Intercity buses, especially on shorter runs and in Upper Egypt, tend to become quite crowded, and even if you are lucky enough to get a seat in the first place, you'll probably end up with something or somebody on your lap. It's one way to meet Egyptians!

Deluxe buses travel between some of the main towns. For instance, the Superjet and West Delta Bus companies run luxury buses between Cairo and Alexandria daily. Similar services are offered to other parts of the country, and air-conditioned, comfortable buses run between Cairo, Ismailia, Port Said, Suez, St Catherine's Monastery, Sharm el-Sheikh, Hurghada and Luxor. Tickets cost a bit more than on standard buses but they're still cheap. The bulk of buses running south of Cairo along the Nile tend to be more basic.

Often the prices of tickets for buses on the same route will vary according to whether or not they have air-con, video or any other 'luxuries'. Snacks are not included in the price of tickets for deluxe buses so, unless you want to pay from E£5 to E£10 for a cup of tea, cake and chips, it's best to decline the on-board service. There are no student discounts on bus fares.

A direct bus between Cairo and Aswan will cost E£50, and from E£15 to E£28 between Cairo and Alexandria. The direct buses from Cairo to Sinai destinations tend to be disproportionately expensive.

Tickets can be bought at windows at the bus stations or, often, on the bus. Hang on to your ticket until you get off, as inspectors almost always board the bus to check fares. It is advisable to book tickets, at least on very popular routes (such as to Sinai from Cairo) and those with few buses running (out to the

Western Oases from Cairo), a day or two in advance. Where you are allowed to buy tickets on the bus, you generally end up standing if you don't have an assigned seat with a booked ticket. On short runs there are no bookings and it's a case of first on best seated. You may find you end up with a fistful of tickets – each one has a certain amount printed on it, and the fare is made up of a combination of these.

The issue of timetables is a vexing one. Some lines are more reliable than others, but any specific departure times mentioned should be taken with a pinch of salt.

The basic buses can be grimy, dusty affairs, and their drivers occasionally seem a little too confident of their skills, but generally they do the job. On the other hand, buses with video, although cleaner, faster and more comfortable, are a serious threat to your ear drums. An overnight ride from Cairo to Luxor with nonstop Egyptian and Indian movies at high volume is great headache material.

You might find a sweater handy on overnight deluxe buses as the air-con brings the temperature down to a level where, according to one traveller, 'polar bears would feel at home'.

TRAIN

Trains travel along more than 5000 km of track to almost every major city and town in Egypt from Aswan to Alexandria, although the system needs substantial investment for modernisation. Now that there are two tracks as far south as Edfu, train timetables have become more reliable than in the past. Work is extending the second track to Aswan, which will see an end of trains shunting backwards to small sidings to allow others coming in the opposite direction to pass. A timetable for the main destinations, in shoddy English, is updated every year (valid to June 30) and is occasionally actually available for E£1.

If you have an International Student Identification Card (ISIC) discounts as high as 50% are granted on all fares except those for wagons-lits (cars with deluxe sleeper compartments). Some travellers report getting a 50% discount with International Youth Hostel Federation cards and Youth International Educational Exchange cards. It is possible to travel from Cairo to Aswan for only a few pounds if you have an ISIC and are willing to take a beating in the 3rd class cars.

One advantage (for a change) of being a woman here is that you go straight to the head of the queue for train tickets.

Classes

Services range from relatively cheap (compared to the USA and Europe) 1st class wagons-lits through 1st class sitting, 2nd class air-con and 2nd class ordinary to the ridiculously cheap 3rd class cars.

Wagons-Lits Trains with wagons-lits are the most comfortable and among the fastest in Egypt. The cars are the same as those used by trains in Europe and only sleeper compartments are available. Two wagon-lit trains used to travel between Cairo, Luxor and Aswan every day, but the number dropped to one a couple of years ago.

Wagon-lit trains have both 1st and 2nd class sections, are air-conditioned, and each compartment has hot and cold water. There are lounge cars, and dinner and breakfast are served in the compartments. A double 1st/2nd class compartment for the trip to Aswan costs E£451/293 one way per person, including the sleeper ticket, meals, service and taxes. A return ticket costs E£540 in 2nd class.

For details about how to make bookings, see the Getting There & Away section in the Cairo chapter.

Other Classes Regular night trains with and without sleeper compartments and meals included leave for Luxor and Aswan every day and cost much less than the wagons-lits, but for some time now the 1st class sleepers have not been available to anyone but Egyptians and Sudanese.

As an example of fares, the 1st/2nd class sitting fare to Luxor is E£48/28 (student

E£28/22). Reservations must be made in advance at Ramses station in Cairo. Unless you specify otherwise, you'll be issued with a ticket that includes meals on board. For this you'll pay, for example, an extra E£10 on the trip from Cairo to Luxor. Many travellers have said the food is tasteless and, for what you get, a waste of money so you may want to flout the rules and bring your own. Both 1st and 2nd class compartments have air-con and they can get chilly at night; have something warm to put on.

Non-air-conditioned trains are next down the scale. Classes here are divided into ordinary 2nd class, which generally has padded seats, and 3rd class, where seating is of the wooden bench variety. These trains tend to spend a lot of time at a lot of stations and can be subject to interminable delays.

The fastest trains are the sleek Turbos that run between Cairo and Alexandria nonstop three times a day.

Always check the timetables posted at stations – if you can make head or tail of them – for the latest train schedules.

TAXI
Service Taxi

Travelling by 'ser-vees' taxi (you'll occasionally hear them referred to rather quaintly as *bijoux* – don't let the French deceive you; they're generally anything but 'jewels'!) is the fastest way to go from city to city. In most places the service taxis and their drivers congregate near bus and railway stations. Each driver waits with his Peugeot 504 taxi (or increasingly Toyota microbus) until he has six or seven passengers; he won't leave before his car is full unless you and/or the other passengers want to pay more money. If you want to go somewhere these taxis don't usually go, you can either hire a whole taxi for yourself or coax other travellers into joining you. Taxis hired under these conditions are usually called 'special' taxis and cost more than service taxis.

Service-taxi rides can be a little hairy at times. Most of Egypt's main Nile road has only two lanes, so one ambling donkey cart can cause an immense traffic jam. This

Top: Selling oranges in Dendara's market, near Qena.
Middle: Serving juice at a typical bar in Cairo; a Bedouin guide prepares lunch for
            travellers; preparing a fiteer in a small restaurant in Cairo.
Bottom: Enjoying a leisurely game of backgammon – a favourite pastime in Egypt.

DAMIEN SIMONIS

KRISTIE BURNS

DAMIEN SIMONIS

DAMIEN SIMONIS

KRISTIE BURNS

KRISTIE BURNS

Egyptians are often pleased to be photographed, but it's wise and polite to always ask first. Clockwise from top left: fruit vendor, Cairo; village guard; boys playing; Asyut school children; camel trader; Nubian woman; camel dealer.

prompts everyone to try passing everyone else, even though the oncoming traffic usually prevents a clean, smooth pass. It's a modern joust where, fortunately, the jousters usually miss each other. Occasionally they don't, however, and the metal scraps of past accidents litter the roadside all over the country.

Microbus

A slightly bigger version of the service taxi is a van that would normally take about 12 people. More often than not they cram on as many as 22 – it can be done, but it is not very comfortable. These run on fewer routes than the service taxis, and generally cost the same. There are several types variously known as *meecrobus* (microbuses), *meecro*, *baas* or service taxi, depending on whom you ask. Microbuses are being increasingly used as service taxis for the simple reason that they can carry more people.

On either microbuses or service taxis, travellers are frequently charged extra for luggage; it's up to you whether or not you want to argue about it. Don't take it personally, the same applies to Egyptians. This is one advantage of the big buses, where luggage is dumped in the hold.

Pick-Ups

Toyota and Chevrolet pick-up trucks cover a lot of the routes between smaller towns and villages off the main roads. The general rule is to get 12 inside the covered rear of the truck, often with an assortment of goods squeezed in around feet on the floor. After that, it's a matter of how many can and want to scramble on to the roof or hang on at the rear – it's remarkable how many people you can get on to them if you try!

CAR & MOTORCYCLE

Driving in Cairo is a crazy affair, so think seriously before you decide to rent a car there. However, driving in other parts of the country, at least in daylight, isn't necessarily so bad. It would be great to have a car – or better still a 4WD – in Sinai, where the traffic

---

The Hazards of Night Driving

Driving at night is a particularly hazardous exercise, especially outside well-lit areas. Headlights are often not used or, if at all, only to warn oncoming traffic with a blinding flash. It should be noted that travelling as a passenger in a private car, service taxi or even bus at night can be risky. There appear to have been a few too many fairly gruesome nocturnal meetings; in late 1992, for example, a bus load of schoolchildren was virtually decapitated when a charging bulldozer with raised scoop managed to sheer the top off the bus, which had been left standing in the middle of the highway in Sinai without headlights on while the driver relieved himself. ■

---

is very light and there are lots of fascinating places to visit.

Motorcycle would be an ideal way to travel around Egypt. The only snag is that you have to bring your own and the red tape involved is extensive. Ask your country's automobile association and the Egyptian embassy about regulations. You must ride very carefully because the roads are often sandy and pocked with potholes.

Petrol is readily available. Normal, or *benzin aadi*, costs 90 pt a litre. *Mumtaz*, or super, is more expensive at E£1 a litre. Lead-free was introduced in 1995 but, with only six pumps in Cairo and Alexandria, there might be a queue.

Road Rules

Driving is on the right-hand side. The official speed limit outside towns is 90 km per hour (though it is often less in some areas) and 100 km per hour on four-lane highways such as the one between Cairo and Alexandria. A few roads, such as the Cairo-Alexandria Desert Highway and the road through the Ahmed Hamdi Tunnel (which goes under the Suez Canal near Suez), are subject to tolls of about E£1.25.

Many roads have checkpoints where police often ask for identity papers, so make sure you've got your passport and driving licence on hand or you may be liable for a US$100 on-the-spot fine.

For more information on road rules, suggested routes and other advice, it might be worth picking up a copy of *On the Road in Egypt – A Motorist's Guide* by Mary Dungan Megalli. It was printed in 1989, so it's starting to become outdated, but it's still available at the Lehnert & Landrock bookshop in Cairo.

Rental

Several car rental agencies have offices in Egypt, including Avis, Hertz and Budget (for addresses, see the Getting Around section in the Cairo chapter). Their rates match international charges and finding a cheap deal with local dealers is virtually impossible. No matter who you go with, make sure you read the fine print.

An international driving permit is required and you can be liable to a heavy fine if you're caught renting a car without one. Drivers should mostly be over the age of 25.

As an indication of prices, for a small car like a Suzuki Swift you'll be looking at about US$33 to US$40 per day, plus up to US$0.20 for each extra km. A Toyota Corolla is about US$56 to US$0.60 per day, plus around US$0.25 per km. These prices generally include insurance and the first 100 km, but check this before signing. For unlimited km, you'll be looking at about US$47/70 per day respectively for the above cars. Some companies set a minimum of seven days for unlimited-km rentals, in which case you'll be looking at about US$240 to US$275 per week for a Toyota Starlet. Remember there's a 10 to 17% tax to be added to your bill. It's usually possible to pay with travellers' cheques or by credit card.

Some companies, such as Europcar, offer the option of one-way rentals from, for example, Cairo to Sharm el-Sheikh. It's also possible to hire a car plus a driver for those who don't feel like tackling the Egyptian roads.

BICYCLE

Bicycles are a practical way of getting around a town and its surrounding sites. In most places, particularly Luxor, you can rent a bicycle quite cheaply; prices start at around E£4 per day. Bicycles are, however, somewhat impractical for covering long distances or for getting around in big cities. The biggest problem is the possibility of getting flattened by one of Egypt's crazy drivers, who are not the slightest bit accustomed to cyclists on the roads.

HITCHING

Hitching is never entirely safe in any country in the world, and we don't recommend it. Travellers who decide to hitch should understand that they are taking a small but potentially serious risk. Hitching is certainly not recommended for women travellers. Should you decide to hitch, you'll find many drivers expect to be paid for giving you a ride and therefore you probably won't save very much money by hitching anyway.

CAMEL

Yes, it is actually possible to travel around Egypt by camel. While the more intrepid travellers will probably want to buy their own 'ship of the desert', there are easier and less costly alternatives.

Camels are brought, in caravans, from Sudan to Egypt's two main camel markets – at Daraw, near Kom Ombo, and Birqash, north-west of Cairo. If you're serious about owning your own, note that the camels are cheaper at Daraw, as it's closer to the end of the caravan route. They can cost as little as US$400 there, while in Birqash the price rises to as much as US$1000 per animal. This US dollar price, of course, depends on the current exchange rate. Note that you might not be buying a great pedigree: the bulk of camels on sale are destined for the slaughterhouse.

Once you've purchased your camel you then have to buy a proper saddle and appropriate kit bags. It all gets somewhat costly and complicated. You'll also have to learn how to mount and ride your camel. Remember that a camel stands up in three jerky manoeuvres so hold on until it's standing tall.

For the inexperienced, camel riding can be a painful event and, unless you have something very soft to sit on, your thighs and backside can end up a suppurating mess after a few hours in the saddle. Thankfully, it tends to get better with a bit of practise.

It would be a good idea to try and get hold of an article by Rene Dee called 'Travel by Camel', which appeared in *The Traveller's Handbook*. For those who can read Dutch (or who can track down an English translation), there's also Anita Baaijens' novel, *Een Regen van Eeuwig Vuur* (A Rain of Eternal Fire), which describes this woman's solo camel journey through the Egyptian desert from Farafra Oasis to the Chephren quarries in the south. Another book for real camel buffs is Robyn Davidson's *Tracks*. Although set in Australia, this book will give you plenty of insight on travelling with camels.

If you're less adventurous (or more sensible!) there are easier and less physically and financially draining ways to realise your camel fantasies. It's easiest to hire a camel for a couple of hours to tour around the pyramids at Giza, the temple complex at Saqqara, along the banks of the Nile at Luxor or to the Monastery of St Simeon in Aswan. A guide usually accompanies you. It is also easy to arrange a camel safari in Sinai from near Nuweiba and Dahab, or from Siwa Oasis in the Western Desert. More information about such treks is given in the relevant chapters.

DONKEY & HORSE

Donkeys are a very popular means of transport and you'll see them everywhere in Egypt except, perhaps, in restaurants. *Don't* buy one of these critters. They are cheap enough to rent for a couple of hours, or a few days, for getting you around some of Egypt's ancient sites. Like camels, there's something of an art to riding these little beasts of burden, as is obvious when you watch young boys jigging along on the rumps of unsaddled donkeys.

Horses are a great way to cover the sandy stretches between the Pyramids of Giza, and can also be hired in various places in Sinai.

BOAT
Felucca
The ancient sailboats of the Nile are still the most common means of transport up and down the river. Sunset is one of the best times to take a felucca ride, but you can arrange a few hours' peaceful sailing at any time from just about anywhere on the Nile.

The best trip to make, however, is the journey between Aswan and Esna, Edfu or Kom Ombo; this takes from one to three days. See the Aswan Getting There & Away section for more information on how to arrange a trip.

Ferry
The only ferry likely to be of much use to travellers is the service between Hurghada on the Red Sea coast and Sharm el-Sheikh in Sinai. For details of this ferry, see the Hurghada Getting There & Away section.

Yacht
It is possible to take a yacht into Egyptian waters and ports. There are 12 designated ports of entry, including Alexandria, Port Said, Sharm el-Sheikh, Dahab, Nuweiba, Hurghada, Suez, and Ismailia. A security permit is required to enter the Nile River, and transit fees of US$10 per person and US$20 for the yacht need to be paid to negotiate the Suez Canal. These and other fees are liable to change.

You will need all the usual documentation for the yacht, plus six copies of the crew list. You will also need valid visas and a raft of other bits of paper, including health certificate, customs list of yacht's equipment and insurance policy (for the Suez Canal). You can get visas on arrival in your first port.

It is also possible to shelter in other 'nonentry' ports, but you cannot go ashore.

Fuel is available in all ports of entry, and navigational charts are available in Alexandria, Port Said and Suez (ask for 'Marinkart'). There are nine yacht clubs in

Egypt. For more details, contact your own yacht club before heading for Egypt.

Before departing, a departure permit has to be obtained from the Coast Guard and you are supposed to leave within 24 hours of obtaining it.

If you want to get a lift on a yacht heading down to the Red Sea or elsewhere, it can be best done in Suez or Port Said.

LOCAL TRANSPORT
Bus

Cairo and Alexandria are the only cities in Egypt with their own bus systems, although neither one ever seems to have enough vehicles. If this is your first visit to a developing country, it will probably be the first time you have ever seen buses as crowded as these.

You may find it more tempting to photograph than ride them, but this tends to anger the locals, who object to being treated like a tourist sight – so perhaps you should consider your reasons for doing so.

Besides large buses, there are also more comfortable and slightly more expensive government-run minibuses in Cairo and Alexandria.

Local buses seem to awaken an unusual level of energy in Egyptians. Typically laid back to the point of being aggravating, Egyptians, and Cairenes in particular, seem not to be able to get on to that bus fast enough. They stampede the entrance before the thing has even slowed down, and there can be an almighty lot of pushing and shoving to barge on – even when hardly anyone is using that particular service. In summer it is advisable not to get crowded buses. There are times when, crammed up the back with exhaust fumes billowing around you and ever more people squeezing on, asphyxiation seems perilously close.

Buses idling at bus stations are the perfect outlet for street vendors, and it's not unusual to find men and young boys wandering up and down the isle with a box of whatever it is they're selling – sweets, hair brushes, toiletries etc. The usual sales pitch is to drop one of their products into the lap of each passenger. If this happens to you, don't bother protesting or trying to give it back – just before the bus takes off, that same vendor will swoop around the bus retrieving all the unwanted bits and pieces while pocketing money for the items he has sold.

Metro

Cairo is the only city in Egypt (indeed in Africa) with a metro system. It's a single line that stretches for 43 km, however, at least two more lines are planned. Feasibility studies are being done for an underground train line in Alexandria.

The metro is fast, inexpensive and usually crowded only during peak hours. It seems to have significantly reduced traffic in central Cairo.

Tram

Cairo and Alexandria are also the only two cities in the country with tram systems. Alexandria's trams are relatively efficient and go all over the city but they also get quite crowded. Cairo's trams (actually known to Cairenes as the 'metro' – confused?) are similar, but only a handful of lines remain.

Taxi

There are taxis in most cities in Egypt. The most common and cheapest are the black and white taxis in Cairo and the black and orange ones in Alexandria, most of which are small four seaters. Almost all of them have meters but many of the meters don't work (at least that's what some drivers will tell you), so you have to pay what you think is right and be prepared to argue and bargain.

The best method for paying is to get out of the cab when you arrive at your destination, stick the money through the front passenger's side window and walk away. If you have to argue the price with the driver and he seems to be trying to cheat you, then just mention the police, and the taxi driver will probably accept your price to avoid any hassle. Don't be intimidated by the driver's yelling; it's usually just an act to get you to cough up more money. If he agrees with you about seeing the police, then the fare you offered is probably too low. Sometimes, as one traveller reports, the driver may even jump out of the car, rip open his shirt like Superman and pound on his chest. Fortunately, this sort of tactic is rarely used.

Don't be afraid to hop out just after getting in if, as sometimes happens, the driver names too high a fare. Simply tell him what you are prepared to pay and demand to be let out if he does not accept.

The taxis sometimes marked 'special' charge more than other taxis; these are almost always Peugeot 504s that can hold up to seven passengers. The advantage of these taxis is that you can get a group together and commandeer one for a long trip.

If you're uncertain about the fare, then first consult a local or, as a last resort, negotiate the price before you get in. If possible, however, the best strategy whenever you take a taxi is to pretend that you know the fare, and pay when you get out. Fares are usually 50% higher after midnight.

When you want a taxi, stand where a driver can see you and wave your arm. When he slows down, yell out your destination so that, if he feels like it, he can stop for you. It's quite common to share a taxi with other passengers, so don't be surprised if people hop in and out along the way.

Microbus Privately owned and usually unmarked microbuses (in the form of a minibus) shuttle around all the larger cities. For the average traveller, they can be difficult to use, as it is quite unclear where most of them go. The exception is the run from Midan Tahrir in Cairo to the pyramids. Most of the smaller cities and towns have similar microbuses doing set runs around town.

Pick-Ups As well as servicing routes between smaller towns, covered pick-up trucks are sometimes used within towns as local taxis. This is especially so in some of the oases towns and smaller places along the Nile. Should you end up in one of these, there are a couple of ways you can indicate to the driver when you want to get out: if you happen to be lucky enough to have a seat, pound on the floor with your foot; alternatively ask one of the front passengers to hammer on the window behind the driver; or, lastly, use the buzzer that you'll occasionally find rigged up.

Hantour

Also sometimes called a *caleche*, these horse-drawn carriages are popular tourist vehicles in some cities in Upper Egypt, such as Luxor and Aswan, and are also still used as a means of local transport in some towns in the Delta.

Careta

These donkey-drawn carts with plastic awnings and wooden seats are used as local taxis in some towns on the Mediterranean Coast and are a common sight in Siwa Oasis.

ORGANISED TOURS

There are numerous possibilities for organising tours in Egypt. As with those organised outside the country, the most popular tend to involve Nile cruises on one of the 200 or so 'flotels' which ply up and down the river.

Top-of-the-range cruises can be booked through many five star hotels. A single/double cabin, meals and sightseeing for about four days (three nights) start at around US$400/600. Some of the operators at this level include: Sheraton Nile Cruises (☎ 355-6664), Sharia Ahmed Naguib, Garden City; Misr Travel Co & Hilton International (☎ 383-3444), Misr Travel Tower, Abbassiya; Presidential Nile Cruises (☎ 340-0517), 13 Sharia Marashli, Zamalek (these cruises are also sold through the American Express office on Sharia Qasr el-Nil in Cairo); Travcotels (☎ 340-0959), 112-116 Sharia 26th of July, Zamalek; and Seti First Travel (☎ 341-9820), 16 Sharia Ismail Mohammed, Zamalek.

A host of Cairo travel agencies organise less luxurious tours of a similar duration. Many of these agencies, including Sphinx Tours (☎ 392-0704) and Eastmar Travel (☎ 753216), cluster around sharias Qasr el-Nil, Talaat Harb and Midan Talaat Harb.

Those enamoured by the thought of glimpsing the temples of Abu Simbel from the calm waters of Lake Nasser will be excited to know that it's now possible to relive the *belle époque* voyages of 19th century travellers. The new five star MS *Eugénie* sails from Aswan High Dam to Abu Simbel and back again once a week, visiting a few ancient sites along the way. The three day trip up (or alternatively down) Lake Nasser costs US$100/120 per person per day in a single/double cabin, including meals. The boat leaves Aswan every Saturday, and departs from Abu Simbel each Wednesday.

Information and reservations can be made through 17 Sharia Tunis, New Maadi, Cairo (☎ 352-4775; fax 353-6114).

Misr Travel has a lengthy programme of other less costly (and less romantic) tours, including four day trips to the New Valley (read oases) and a series of full-day excursions to Luxor (flying), Aswan, Alexandria, Al-Faiyum and Wadi Natrun.

For information on sightseeing tours of Cairo, see the Organised Tours section in the Cairo chapter.

Cairo is a seething, breathing monster of a city that swallows new arrivals and consumes those who return. All are destined to be captured and captivated in some small way by its incredible past and vibrant present. There are few, if any, cities in the world where the clash between old and new, modern and traditional, and east and west is more evident. Tall, gleaming hotels and office buildings overlook streets where cars and buses rumble and weave past donkey carts and their stubborn drivers. Less than one km from a computer store and supermarket in central Cairo there are mud-brick houses where goats still wander through 'living rooms' and water is obtained from spigots down the street.

Cairo is still the heart of Egypt and is allegorically called the Mother of the World. Since its rise in the 9th century under Ibn Tulun, Egyptians have known Cairo as Al-Qahira, which means 'the victorious', and Misr (or Masr), which also means 'Egypt'. For Egyptians it is the centre of the country and has been attracting them in increasing numbers for centuries. No-one is sure how many people have been drawn in from the countryside, even over the past few years, but the city is bursting at the seams. Some 62 slums and squatter settlements, such as Dar al-Salam and Sayyida Zeinab, are home to about five million people. And there are countless numbers of people living in the ancient cemeteries known as the Cities of the Dead. In total, Greater Cairo's population is estimated at between 18 and 22 million – roughly a quarter of Egypt's total.

The massive and continual increase in the number of people has overwhelmed the city. Housing shortages are rife; buses are packed to the hilt; snarled traffic paralyses life in the city; and broken pipes spew water and sewage into the streets. Everything is discoloured – buildings, buses and footpaths are brown and grey from smog and desert dust. Amidst this chaos, the city government is trying to do what it can. An underground metro has alleviated traffic problems – although for the first-time visitor that may be hard to believe – and a new line to further improve the situation is under construction. Satellite suburbs such as Nasser City, 6 October City and 10 Ramadan City have been, or are being, built to alleviate housing shortages, although people have not been as quick as was hoped to move into them.

HISTORY

The oldest reminder of Cairo's ancient beginnings is to be found in Fustat and what is now known as Old Cairo, south of the modern city's centre. Not far from here Seth and Horus are supposed to have engaged in combat. Around 500 BC, the Persians turned the area into a fortress, known as Babylon, and were later replaced by the Ptolemies, Romans and finally the Byzantines.

The local Byzantine commander, Cyrus, allowed himself to be lured out of the city into battle against the invading Muslim Arab forces of Amr Ibn al-Aas near Heliopolis in 640 AD. After his victory, Amr established himself at Fustat, outside the Christian city. The Christian and Jewish inhabitants, as People of the Book, were treated reasonably, and in the following two centuries Babylon and Fustat melded as the administrative centre of an important granary for the new Muslim world order.

Ibn Tulun, appointed by the caliph in Baghdad as governor of Egypt, eventually exploited internal weaknesses in the caliphate to establish his virtual independence and overrun Syria. After his death in 884, Syria was lost, but Egypt's autonomy within the Muslim world was untouched.

In June 969 the Fatimids, coming from the west, conquered Egypt. These Ismaili Shi'ites rejected the Sunni Abbassid caliphate in Baghdad and claimed the moral leadership of the whole Muslim world. The general Gawhar determined that a new city should be built north of Fustat. The area, it is said, was pegged out, and labourers waited for a signal from Moorish astrologers who were to ring bells attached to the ropes marking off the area when the right moment came. A raven landed on the rope and set off the bells, however, with the planet Mars (al-Qahir) in the ascendant. So work began and, to avoid evil, it was decided to call the city al-Qahira (Cairo): it became the capital of an independent empire stretching from North Africa and Sicily to Yemen. Fatimid rule soon degenerated. One of its more odd-ball products was Al-Hakim (see the boxed story later in this chapter) who, as a divine character, became the focus of what is now known as the Druse faith. He left an elegant mosque in the north of the Fatimid city, inside the two remaining medieval city gates in the north, Bab an-Nasr and Bab al-Futuh.

In 1171, Salah ad-Din (known to the Crusaders and later to the west as Saladin), restored Sunni rule in Cairo and established a new dynasty, the Ayyubids. This was a welcome change to Cairenes after the last days of confused Fatimid rule in which, fearing the city would fall to the advancing Crusaders, they destroyed the city of Fustat in a kind of policy of scorched earth – for nothing, as it turned out. Salah ad-Din went on to bring most of Syria under his control and break the back of the Crusader kingdoms in Palestine, symbolised by his capture of Jerusalem. It was Salah ad-Din's idea to erect a defensive wall enclosing Cairo and Fustat together, and he established the Citadel that still dominates the city.

His dynasty met its end in 1250 when the Mamluks, a Turkish slave-soldier class, took the reins of power. To them are owed a great many of the monuments remaining in what today is called Islamic Cairo. Their rule was colourful and often bloody. There was no real system of succession, and every change of power usually involved an orgy of blood-letting.

Mamluk rule lasted until the arrival of the Ottoman Turks who incorporated Egypt into their empire in 1517. Cairo's days as a great imperial centre were at an end.

The growing influence of the French and British in the 19th century, despite continued nominal Ottoman rule, left its imprint in the part of Cairo that lies between the Nile and Islamic Cairo, and on the island of Zamalek. Mohammed Ali, the Albanian trooper who became the virtual sovereign of Egypt, left behind him the great mosque, in a gaudy Turkish style, that still dominates the Citadel.

Cairo was the headquarters of British operations during WWI, and Common-wealth troops brought a colourful, if not terribly reputable, dimension to Cairo life while on leave in the war years. Already in the early years of the century, Cairo was attracting increasing numbers of Egyptians from elsewhere in the country, but the pace of growth picked up rapidly after WWII. The most spectacular recent event in the lives of Cairenes, and one that demonstrated again how far Egypt has still to come, was the earthquake that hit the city in October 1992. More than 500 people died, 800 buildings were flattened and many of the city's monu-ments were also damaged. Another large quake in November 1995 sent tremors of fear through the city but, thankfully, no-one in the capital was killed.

ORIENTATION

Finding your way through the chaos is, remarkably, not as complicated as you may first think, and Cairo is a great city for walking around because it's not too spread out. Midan Tahrir is the centre of Cairo. From there, north-east to Midan Talaat Harb and Ezbekiya Gardens, you will find most of Cairo's western-style shops and many of the budget hotels.

Farther east are some of Cairo's poorer districts, the market and medieval neigh-bourhoods of Al-Muski and Darb al-Ahmar and, south of the latter, the ancient Citadel. All these areas are collectively known as Islamic Cairo. To the east and south of here are the northern and southern Cities of the Dead, vast necropolises inhabited by both the living and the dead. Continuing farther north-east towards the airport you will enter Heliopolis, also called Masr al-Gedida or New Cairo.

North of Midan Tahrir are the neighbourhoods of Bulaq and Shubra. In the 1800s, under Mohammed Ali, Bulaq became Cairo's industrial centre. Today, it's one of Cairo's most densely populated areas and the industrialisation has spread northward to Shubra. Much of the recent Islamic unrest has its source in this area. Ramses station, the city's main railway terminus, is at the junction of the two districts.

West of Midan Tahrir, sitting on a large island in the middle of the Nile River, is the residential suburb of Gezira, home of Cairo's elite, including diplomats and one of Egypt's foremost soccer teams. On the northern end of Gezira is Zamalek, with its embassies and modern apartment buildings. Connecting these two areas is the Gezira Club, a large private sports club.

Across the river from Gezira, on the Nile's west bank, are the districts of (from south to north): Giza, which stretches to the edge of the desert; Doqqi (often written Dokki), which has the rest of Cairo University and the zoo; Agouza; Mohandiseen, which was originally conceived by President Gamal Abdel Nasser as a district of engineers; and Imbaba. Until recently, the latter was home to Cairo's famous camel market, which is now sited at Birqash, about 35 km north-west of the city.

Heading south from Midan Tahrir along Sharia Qasr al-Eini, you come to Garden City, an area of embassies and expensive residences. The convoluted street pattern was designed by the British early this century to allow a quick, defensible escape from their embassy.

From Garden City, bridges cross the Nile to Roda Island, home of the Manyal Palace, the Nilometer, the Meridien Hotel, and Cairo University's Faculty of Medicine.

Old Cairo encompasses the sprawl of suburbs from Sayyida Zeinab south to a small area known as Coptic Cairo, about three km south of Garden City. Eight km farther on is the district of Maadi, home to wealthier citizens and several thousand expatriates.

That's Cairo.

Maps

Some of the Egypt maps described in the Facts for the Visitor chapter also include detailed maps of Cairo.

The Society for the Preservation of the Architectural Resources of Egypt (SPARE) has put out a series of maps covering Islamic Cairo – for more details see that section.

INFORMATION
Registration

All foreigners are required to register with the police within seven days of their arrival. The registration is done at Midan Tahrir in the Mogamma (see Central Cairo map), an extraordinarily ugly 14 storey building housing 18,000 bureaucrats from 14 ministries and 65 other government departments. A visit to this government behemoth can be an adventure and a frustrating lesson in Egyptian bureaucracy.

You can go yourself to register, which is usually a simple procedure. However, most hotels, even the cheap ones, will do it for you, sometimes for a small fee (E£2)

The registration office is on the 1st floor – take the stairs to the right after entering then, at the top of the stairs, turn a sharp left and follow this corridor to the end where you'll find a long row of numbered windows. Windows 48 to 50 (off to the left) deal with registration. You fill in a small form and they stamp your passport. The whole process takes about a minute. As with all the other offices in the Mogamma, these windows are open daily except Friday from 8 am to 2 pm. Outside these hours you can register at the little booth marked 'Registration' on the 1st floor at the top of the stairs. This booth is open daily from 2 to 4 pm, and from 7 to 9 pm (winter) and 8 to 10 pm (summer). These hours are, however, apt to change, especially during Ramadan.

Visa Extensions

This is also done in the Mogamma, although

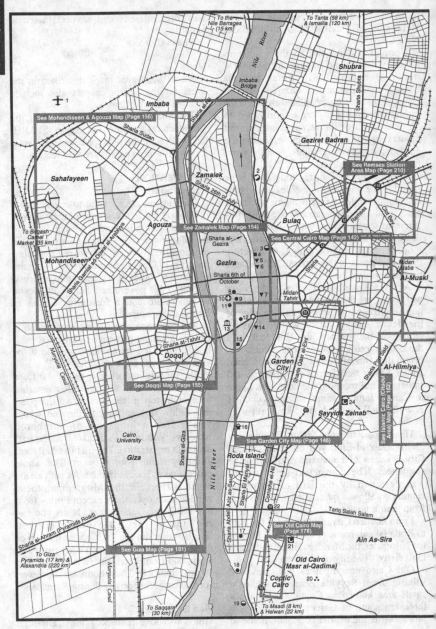

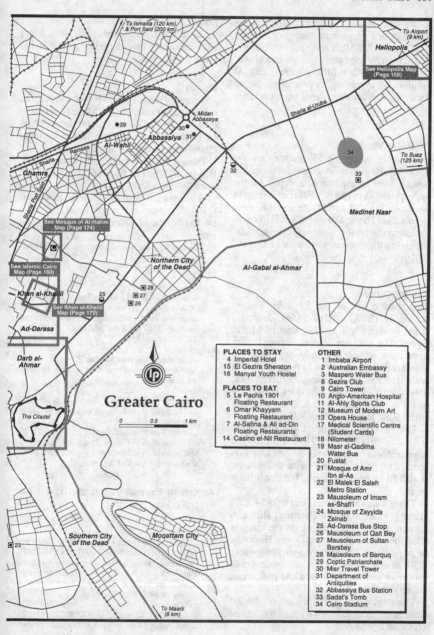

To Ismailia (120 km)
& Port Said (200 km)

To Airport
(8 km)

Heliopolis

See Heliopolis Map
(Page 158)

Midan
Abbassiya

Sharia al-Uruba

•29

30

Abbassiya

31•

Al-Wahli

34

To Suez
(125 km)

Sharia Ramses

33

Ghamra

32

Sharia Port Said

Medinet Nasr

See Mosque of Al-Hakim
Map (Page 174)

C

Northern City
of the Dead

Al-Gabal al-Ahmar

See Islamic Cairo
Map (Page 160)

28

Khan al-Khalili

25

27

26

See Khan al-Khalili
Map (Page 170)

Ad-Darasa

Darb al-
Ahmar

The Citadel

Greater Cairo

0   0.5   1 km

PLACES TO STAY
4 Imperial Hotel
15 El Gezira Sheraton
16 Manyal Youth Hostel

PLACES TO EAT
5 Le Pacha 1901
   Floating Restaurant
6 Omar Khayyam
   Floating Restaurant
7 Al-Safina & Ali ad-Din
   Floating Restaurants
14 Casino el-Nil Restaurant

OTHER
1 Imbaba Airport
2 Australian Embassy
3 Maspero Water Bus
8 Gezira Club
9 Cairo Tower
10 Anglo-American Hospital
11 Al-Ahly Sports Club
12 Museum of Modern Art
13 Opera House
17 Medical Scientific Centre
   (Student Cards)
18 Nilometer
19 Masr al-Qadima
   Water Bus
20 Fustat
21 Mosque of Amr
   Ibn al-As
22 El Malek El Saleh
   Metro Station
23 Mausoleum of Imam
   as-Shafi'i
24 Mosque of Zayyida
   Zeinab
25 Ad-Darasa Bus Stop
26 Mausoleum of Qait Bey
27 Mausoleum of Sultan
   Barsbey
28 Mausoleum of Barquq
29 Coptic Patriarchate
30 Misr Travel Tower
31 Department of
   Antiquities
32 Abbassiya Bus Station
33 Sadat's Tomb
34 Cairo Stadium

23

Southern City
of the Dead

Moqattam City

To Maadi
(8 km)

it can take longer than registration. A six month extension, called a 'tourism residence visa' costs E£12.10; a one year extension is E£38.10. You need one passport-size photo. Go to window 42 to fill in a form (E£8). At window 24 everything is processed, and at window 28 you pick up your passport, after paying the balance.

Re-Entry Visas
Once again, go to the Mogamma (see the previous Registration entry for opening hours). Start at window 42 and pay for the appropriate form (65 pt). Fill it in and go to windows 16 or 17. It will take about an hour to process. The re-entry visa's validity will extend to the limit of your visa or extension. Single/multiple re-entry visas cost E£10.10/ 13.10.

Tourist Offices
The head office of the Egyptian Tourist Authority (ETA) (☎ 391-3454), 5 Sharia Adly, is about half a block west of Midan Opera. The staff are helpful, although they have their off days. If they can't find the answers to your questions in their sparse but colourful tourist brochures or notebooks, they will call someone who does know. The office is open daily from 8.30 am to 8 pm (from 9 am to 5 pm during Ramadan).

Cairo international airport's new Terminal II has a tourist office (☎ 291-4255/2223) just after customs control; so does the older Terminal I (☎ 667475). The office at Terminal II should be open 24 hours, but don't bank on it.

There's also a tourist office (☎ 385-0259) at the pyramids; it's on Pyramids Rd (also known as Sharia al-Haram), on the left just after the junction with the Desert Highway to Alexandria. It's usually open daily from 8.30 am to 5 pm. There are other small offices at the Manyal Palace and in Ramses railway station.

The tourist police (☎ 126) are on the 1st floor in the alley just to the left of the tourist office on Sharia Adly.

Foreign Embassies
A list of foreign embassies in Cairo, along with consulates elsewhere in Egypt, is in the Facts for the Visitor chapter.

Money
For general details about banks and foreign exchange bureaus, see the Money section in the Facts for the Visitor chapter. Information on banking hours is given in the Business Hours section in the same chapter.

Banque Misr exchange offices in the Nile Hilton and inside Shepheard's Hotel are open 24 hours a day.

A growing number of exchange bureaus is springing up around Cairo. Horus Exchange (☎ 761799) at 11 Sharia Alfi Bey has good rates.

Money can be wired through the following banks in Cairo:

Barclays International
    Banque du Caire, 12 Midan Yusuf, Garden City (☎ 354-9415); personal banking services are available, but the office specialises in corporate banking. Mail must be addressed to PO Box 2325, Cairo.
Lloyds Bank
    44 Sharia Mohammed Mazhar, Zamalek (☎ 341-8366); personal and corporate banking facilities are available.
Citibank
    4 Sharia Ahmed Pasha, Garden City (☎ 355-1873); open from 8.30 am to 2 pm Sunday to Thursday.
Misr America International Bank
    12 Sharia Nadi el-Sayyid, Doqqi (☎ 361-6613); this is the head office of an Egyptian bank affiliated with the Bank of America.

American Express American Express has several offices in Cairo:

Central Cairo
    15 Sharia Qasr el-Nil, between Midan Tahrir and Midan Talaat Harb (☎ 574-7991; fax 574-7947); open daily from 8.30 am to 4.30 pm (during Ramadan from 9 am to 3.30 pm) and on Friday from 9 am to 3 pm. The client letter service is closed on Friday and Saturday.
Central Cairo
    Nile Hilton, Corniche el-Nil (☎ 578-5001/2); open from 8.30 am to 5 pm daily except Friday.

Zamalek
    Cairo Marriott (☎ 340-6855)
Giza
    Nile Tower, 21 Sharia al-Giza (☎ 570-3411)
Maadi
    Hotel Pullman Maadi Towers, Rd 18 (☎ 370-7817)
Heliopolis
    72 Sharia Omar Ibn el-Khattab (☎ 418-2144)
Cairo International Airport
    (☎ 417-6577); assistance only, no foreign exchange.

Thomas Cook Thomas Cook has a handful of offices in Cairo open daily from 8 am to 5 pm:

Central Cairo
    17 Sharia Mohammed Bassiuni (☎ 574-3955; fax 762750)
Maadi
    88 Rd 9, Station Square (☎ 351-1438; fax 350-2651)
Mohandiseen
    Shop 10, Sharia 26th of July (☎ 346-7187; fax 303-4530)
Heliopolis
    Heliopolis Club, Sharia al-Mirghani (☎ 677239)
Cairo International Airport
    (☎ 291-4255 ext 2128; fax 291-6378); foreign exchange counters are open 24 hours in both the arrival and departure halls.

Post

Cairo's GPO, on Midan Ataba, is open from 7 am to 7 pm, supposedly seven days a week (be wary on Fridays and public holidays). The poste restante is through the last door down the side street to the right of the main entrance, opposite the EMS fast mail office, and is open from 8 am to 6 pm (Fridays and holidays from 10 am until noon). Mail is held for three weeks.

There are also post office branches at Cairo international airport Terminal II (in the departure hall), on Midan Falaki (see Central Cairo map), in the grounds of the Egyptian Museum, and at Ramses station. There are also branches on Sharia Shagarat ad-Durr and Sharia al-Brazil in Zamalek.

To send a package abroad you must go to the Post Traffic Centre at Midan Ramses. It is open daily except Friday from 8.30 am to 3 pm. Set aside half an hour for this process

and bring your passport. You'll need to go to the first big room to the left on the 2nd floor. At the counter get form No 13 (E£5), have the parcel weighed and pay for it. Probably customs will have a look at it – for details on these formalities see the Post & Communication section in the Facts for the Visitor chapter. After it has been inspected, someone will wrap it for you (E£1.50 per metre of paper used plus E£1.60 for sealing).

Fast mail can be sent through: EMS (☎ 393-9796), opposite the GPO's poste restante (open from 8 am to 7 pm daily except Friday); DHL (☎ 355-7301), 20 Sharia Gamal ad-Din Abu al-Mahasin, Garden City; Federal Express (☎ 357-1300), 1079 Corniche el-Nil, Garden City; and TNT Skypak (☎ 348-8204), at 33 Sharia Doqqi, Doqqi. Most of them have several offices.

Telephone

There are several telephone offices around Cairo, and most have a few card phones. In central Cairo there are offices on the north side of Midan Tahrir, near the tourist information office in Sharia Adly, on Sharia Alfi Bey, and on Sharia Mohammed Mahmud in the Telecommunications building. In Zamalek there's an office on Sharia 26th of July, near the Zamalek Bridge. These main telephone offices are open 24 hours a day while branch offices, such as the one just off Sharia Ramses, are open from 8 am to 10 pm. There are also other branch offices in Heliopolis, Doqqi and Giza.

The business centre in the Nile Hilton on Midan Tahrir has a bank of pay phones for which they sell E£1 tokens.

For information on rates, making collect calls and telephones in general, see the Post & Communications section of the Facts for the Visitor chapter.

Fax & Telex

Faxes can be sent to/from the telephone offices on Sharia Adly (fax 393-3909 – the fax office is to the right of the main office and up the stairs), on Midan Tahrir (fax 578-0979) and also on Sharia Alfi Bey (fax 589-7662). You can also send and receive

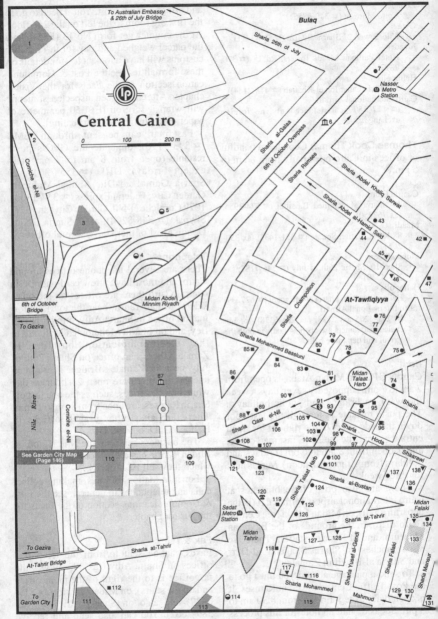

Central Cairo

0   100   200 m

Bulaq

Sharia 26th of July

To Australian Embassy
& 26th of July bridge

Nasser
Metro
Station

7

6

Sharia al-Qalaa

6th of October Overpass

Sharia Ramses

Sharia Abdel Khaliq Sarwat

Sharia Abdel al-Hamid Said

43

44

42

45

46

47

At-Tawfiqiyya

76

77

75

Sharia Champollion

Sharia Mohammed Bassiuni

85

84

83

81

82

80

79

78

86

Midan
Talaat
Harb

74

Sharia

90

88   89

Sharia Qasr el-Nil

91   92

93

94   95

96

Sharia

Hoda

Shaarawi

105

104

103

102

98

99

97

106

108

107

100

101

137

138

136

Midan Abdel
Minnim Riyadh

6th of October
Bridge

To Gezira

Nile River

Comiche el-Nil

87

110

109

See Garden City Map
(Page 146)

122

121   123

120

119

118

117   116

112

111

To Garden City

113

114

115

Midan
Tahrir

Sadat
Metro
Station

124

125

126

127   128

Sharia at-Tahrir

Sharia Talaat Harb

Sharia al-Bustan

Sharia Yusef al-Gendi

Sharia Falaki

Midan
Falaki

135

134

133

Sharia Mansur

129   130

131

Sharia Mohammed
Mahmud

Comiche el-Nil

To Gezira

At-Tahrir Bridge

Sharia at-Tahrir

5

3

4

2

1

CAIRO

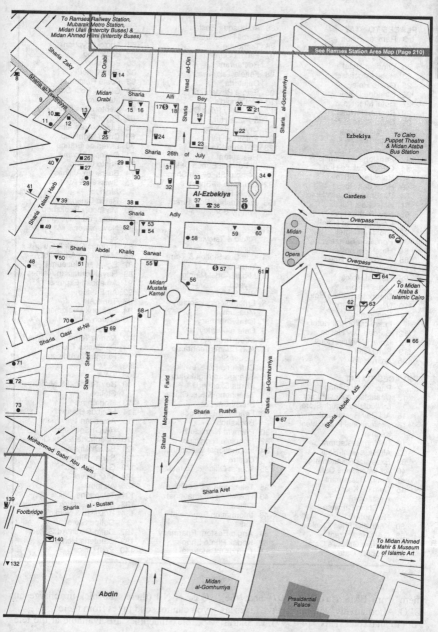

To Ramses Railway Station,
Mubarak Metro Station,
Midan Ulali (Intercity Buses) &
Midan Ahmed Hilmi (Intercity Buses)

See Ramses Station Area Map (Page 210)

Sharia Zaky

Sh Orabi

Sharia al-Tawfikiya

Sharia Imad ad-Din

Sharia al-Gomhurriya

Midan Orabi

Sharia Alfi Bey

Ezbekiya

To Cairo Puppet Theatre & Midan Ataba Bus Station

Sharia 26th of July

Sharia Talaat Harb

Al-Ezbekiya

Gardens

Sharia Adly

Overpass

Sharia Abdel Khaliq Sarwat

Midan Opera

Midan Mustafa Kamel

Overpass

Sharia Qasr el-Nil

To Midan Ataba & Islamic Cairo

Sharia Sherif

Sharia Mohammed Farid

Sharia Rushdi

Sharia al-Gomhurriya

Sharia Abdel Aziz

Mohammed Sabri Abu Alam

Sharia Aref

Footbridge

Sharia al - Bustan

To Midan Ahmed Mahir & Museum of Islamic Art

Abdin

Midan al-Gomhurriya

Presidential Palace

PLACES TO STAY

3 Ramses Hilton
12 Tawfikia, Safary & Sultan Hotels
20 Windsor Hotel
23 Hotel Nitocrisse
25 Grand Hotel
26 Claridge Hotel
27 Hotel Minerva
29 Scarabee Hotel
31 Cairo Khan Hotel
33 Pension Roma
37 Hotel Tee
38 Hotel Select
42 Pensione de Famille
44 Odeon Palace Hotel
47 Hotel Beau Site
49 Hotel des Roses
54 Panorama Palace Hotel
61 Hotel Petit Palais
66 New Riche Hotel
72 Cosmopolitan Hotel
77 Gresham Hotel
80 Pensione Suisse
84 Hotel Viennoise
85 Anglo-Swiss Hotel
95 Tulip Hotel
99 Golden Hotel
103 Lotus Hotel
107 Cleopatra Palace Hotel
110 Nile Hilton
111 Semiramis InterContinental Hotel
112 Garden City House
118 Ismailia House Hotel
119 Sun Hotel
136 Amin Hotel

PLACES TO EAT

2 Paprika Restaurant
13 Casablanca Restaurant & Nicolakis Liquor Store
16 Alfi Bey Restaurant
18 International Public Meal Kushari
19 Peking Restaurant
22 Ali Hassan al-Hatti
39 Excelsior Restaurant
40 À l'Américaine Café
41 Amira Restaurant
45 Coin de Kebab Restaurant
46 Fu Shing Chinese Restaurant
50 Kentucky Fried Chicken
53 GAD Restaurant
59 Garden Groppi's Cafe
81 Groppi's Cafe

88 Arabesque Restaurant
90 Caroll Restaurant
96 Teahouse
97 Felfela Garden Restaurant
98 Felfela Takeaway & Cafeteria
105 Estoril Restaurant
116 McDonald's
117 Kentucky Fried Chicken & Pizza Hut
125 Crystal Bakery
127 Fatatri at-Tahrir
128 El-Tahrir Kushari Restaurant
129 El Fornaia Etman Bakery
130 24-hour Sandwich Shop
132 Cafeteria el-Shaab & Fiteer Place
135 Lux Kushari Restaurant
138 Wimpy Bar

OTHER

1 Radio & Television Building
4 City Bus Station & Tram Terminal
5 Midan Abdel Minnim Riyadh Bus Station
6 Entomological Society Museum
7 Isaaf Pharmacy
8 Cafe el-Agatey
9 Souq Tawfiqiyya
10 Ash-Shams Teahouse
11 Liquor Store
14 Cafeteria Port Tewfik
15 Shahrazad Night Club
17 Horus Exchange
21 Telephone & Fax Office
24 Pussy Cat Bar
28 Lehnert & Landrock Bookshop
30 Palmyra Nightclub
32 Honolulu Nightclub
34 International Vaccination Centre
35 Tourist Office & Tourist Police
36 Telephone & Fax Office
43 Hostelling International Office
48 Information Service of India
51 Anglo-Eastern Pharmacy
52 Kodak Photo Shop
55 Cap d'Or Cafeteria

56 Turkish Airlines
57 Banque Misr
58 Anglo-Egyptian Bookshop
60 EgyptAir
62 EMS Office
63 Poste Restante
64 GPO & Post Office Museum
65 Hebton Bus Company
67 Egypt Free Shop
68 Libyan Arab Airlines
69 Disco Nightclub
70 Livres de France
71 Olympic Airways
73 Photo Centre
74 Bulgarian Airlines
75 Swissair & Austrian Airlines
76 Radio Cinema
78 Madbouly Bookshop
79 Atelier du Caire Gallery
82 Newspaper & Magazine Stand
83 Thomas Cook & Gulf Air
86 Mashrabia Art Gallery
87 Egyptian Museum
89 Royal Jordanian Airlines
91 American Express
92 Air France
93 Tunis Air
94 Shorouk Bookshop
100 Czech Airlines
101 EgyptAir
102 Norma Tours
104 De Castro Tours & Hungarian Airlines
106 KLM
108 TWA
109 Bus Terminal & Minibus Station
113 Mogamma
114 Minibus Station
115 American University (AUC) Bookstore
120 Telephone & Fax Office
121 British Airways
122 Sudan Airways
123 Goethe Institut
124 Misr Travel
126 Air India
131 Telephone Office
133 Souq Mansur
134 Brazilian & Yemini Coffee Store
137 Cairo-Berlin Art Gallery
139 Cafeteria Horea
140 Post Office

them from EMS (fax 393-4807) near the GPO. Alternatively, you can receive faxes at American Express (fax 574-7997), 15 Sharia Qasr el-Nil (there's no pick-up charge but you cannot send faxes from there).

Telex machines are available at the telephone offices on Sharia Adly and Sharia Alfi Bey.

Travel Agencies

The area around Midan Tahrir is teeming with travel agencies. Although it is no London bucket shop scene, you should hunt around, but don't expect huge differences or amazing deals.

Fairly efficient is De Castro Tours (☎ 574-3144), at 12 Sharia Talaat Harb. It offers a wide range of flights, many with considerable student discounts. Just down the road at No 10 is Norma Tours (☎ 760007), which touts itself as being a cheap air-fare specialist.

Avoid Metro Travel and Wonder Travel, as well as the touts from these agencies who hang around Midan Talaat Harb.

The official Egyptian government travel agency, Misr Travel (☎ 393-0010; fax 392-4440), has its head office at 1 Sharia Talaat Harb, but it handles mainly administrative matters. For general information or bus tickets go to the office (☎ 393-0168) at 7 Sharia Talaat Harb.

Bookshops

Cairo has a good selection of bookshops. If you've got the time, it's worth shopping around as prices can vary considerably. Many bookshops are closed Saturday afternoon and all day Sunday.

One of the best English-language bookshops in Egypt is the Anglo-Egyptian Bookshop (☎ 391-4337) at 165 Sharia Mohammed Farid. However, finding a particular item among books piled from the floor to the ceiling can be a bit of a chore.

For those who speak English, the American University in Cairo (AUC) Bookstore (☎ 357-5377), inside the university entrance on Sharia Mohammed Mahmud, carries an excellent selection of books in English as well as Lonely Planet titles, periodicals and newspapers from Europe and the USA, and a few maps. It's open Sunday to Thursday from 8.30 am to 4 pm; Saturday from 10 am to 3 pm. It's closed on Friday and in August. There is also a much smaller branch (☎ 339-7045) at the relatively new AUC College at 16 Sharia Mohammed Sakeb, Zamalek.

If these fail to satisfy, the next stop might be Lehnert & Landrock (☎ 393-5324), 44 Sharia Sherif. It boasts a good selection of books on Egypt in English, French and German and maps and novels too; it's open from 9.30 am to 2 pm and 4 to 7.30 pm but closed Saturday afternoon and Sunday.

If you're looking for somewhere open on Sunday, try Shorouk (☎ 391-2480) on Midan Talaat Harb and at 3 Sharia al-Bursa al-Gedida, across from Olympic Airways. It has a reasonable range of books, mainly in English and French, with a good travel section. In front, there are several major news magazines and newspapers.

Also on Midan Talaat Harb and also open on Sunday is Madbouly (or Madbouli) bookshop (☎ 347-7410).

The nearby L'Orientaliste (☎ 575-3418), 15 Sharia Qasr el-Nil, is one of only a handful of bookshops in the world specialising in Egyptology. It has an excellent collection of antiquarian books and prints of 19th century Egypt. It is open daily, except Sunday, from 10 am to 7.30 pm.

If it's books in French you're after, head straight for the Livres de France (☎ 393-5512) at 36 Sharia Qasr el-Nil.

There are quite a few other bookshops around town and in most of the big hotels, but none match the ones already listed.

Newsstands

On Midan Talaat Harb (in front of Groppi's cafe) is one of the better newspaper and magazine stands in Cairo. It carries the most recent editions of major newspapers and magazines from around the world and most of the English-language Cairo publications, as well as a selection of second-hand books. Also good for a wide range of newspapers and magazines is the newsstand on Sharia Mohammed Mahmud, opposite the entrance to the AUC, and the one near Simmonds Coffee Shop on Sharia 26th of July in Zamalek.

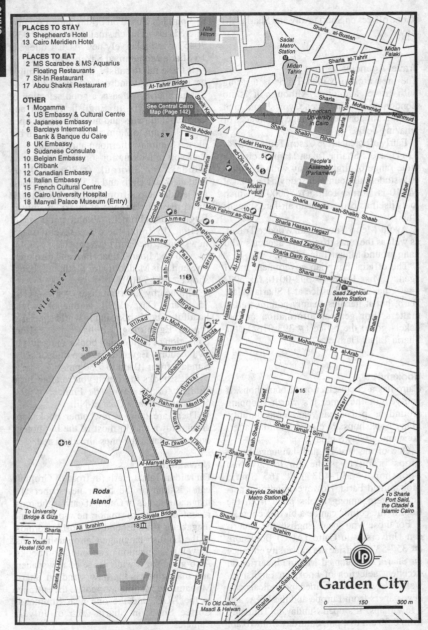

PLACES TO STAY
3 Shepheard's Hotel
13 Cairo Meridien Hotel

PLACES TO EAT
2 MS Scarabee & MS Aquarius
  Floating Restaurants
7 Sit-In Restaurant
17 Abou Shakra Restaurant

OTHER
1 Mogamma
4 US Embassy & Cultural Centre
5 Japanese Embassy
6 Barclays International
  Bank & Banque du Caire
8 UK Embassy
9 Sudanese Consulate
10 Belgian Embassy
11 Citibank
14 Canadian Embassy
14 Italian Embassy
15 French Cultural Centre
16 Cairo University Hospital
18 Manyal Palace Museum (Entry)

See Central Cairo
Map (Page 142)

Nile Hilton

Sadat Metro Station

Midan Tahrir

Sharia al-Bustan

Midan Falaki

Sharia at-Tahrir

Sharia al-Gendi

At-Tahrir Bridge

Sharia Yusef Mohammed Mahmud

Sheikh Kamel

Sharia

Sharia Abdel

Kader Hamza

American University in Cairo

Sharia Sheikh Rihan

ad-Din Salah

People's Assembly (Parliament)

Sharia Latin America

Midan Yusuf

Moh Fahmy as-Said

Sharia Maglis ash-Sheikh Shaab

Falaki Mansur Nubar

Ahmed Raghed

Ahmed

Gamal ad-Din ash-Shennawi

Kamel

Itlihad

Aisha

Shulla

Taymouria

Dar as

Ghandy

Abu al

Birgas

al-Muhamiyin

Pasha

Saray al-Kubra

Mahasin

Hassan Murad

al-Hars

al-Eini

Qasr

Sharia Hassan Hegazi

Sharia Saad Zaghloul

Sharia Darih Saad

Sharia Ismail Abaza

Saad Zaghloul Metro Station

Sharia Mohammed Izz al-Arab

Walda (Salamlek)

Abdel Rahman Manlahmy

Kamel

al-Hadiqa

Ad- Diwan

Sharia

as-Sukkar

Ali Yusef

Sharia ash-Sheikh Sirri

al-Masri

al-Khalig

Comiche el-Nil

Ahmed

Raghed

Nile River

Fontana Bridge

13

Al-Manyal Bridge

16

Roda Island

To University Bridge & Giza

To Youth Hostel (50 m)

Sharia Al-Manyal

Ali Ibrahim

As-Sayala Bridge

18

Comiche el-Nil

Sharia Qasr al-Eini

Ali

Ibrahim

Sharia

Sayyida Zeinab Metro Station

Sharia Ismail Sirri

Sharia Mawardi

17

15

To Sharia Port Said, the Citadel & Islamic Cairo

as-Saad al-Barran

To Old Cairo, Maadi & Helwan

Garden City

0   150   300 m

Midan Yusuf

Coniche el-Nil

Libraries

The best public library is the new and very grand Great Cairo Library (☎ 341-2280), 15 Sharia Mohammed Mazhar, Zamalek. It's open daily except Monday from 9 am to 7 pm. Otherwise, many cultural centres (see further in this section) have libraries which are open to the public.

Campuses

For details about the American University in Cairo (AUC) and some Egyptian universities, see the Courses section in the Facts for the Visitor chapter.

Cultural Centres

There are many cultural centres in Cairo sponsored by other countries – for a full list see *Egypt Today*. Most run libraries, show films and stage various lectures, exhibitions and performances. They are great places to catch up on the latest news from home or to watch a free movie or video. Bring your passport along as many require some ID before they'll allow you to enter. Among the countries with centres here are:

France

    1 Madrassat al-Huquq al-Fransiyya, Mounira (☎ 355-3725). This newly renovated centre is at the southern end of Sharia Falaki, just east of Garden City. It's open Sunday to Thursday from 9 am to 9 pm.

    27 Sharia Sabri Abu Alam, Midan Ismailia, Heliopolis (☎ 414-4824)

    Both centres regularly put on films, lectures and exhibitions, have libraries open to the public (call to check hours, as they are all over the place) and get news and views from the French-speaking world via the satellite TV station TV-5. The centre at Mounira also runs French and Arabic language courses.

Germany

    Goethe Institut, 5 Sharia al-Bustan (☎ 575-9877). Not far from Midan Tahrir, this centre presents seminars and lectures in German on Egyptology and other topics. There are also performances by visiting music groups and special art exhibits and film screenings. The library has rather erratic hours, so phone first.

India

    Information Service of India, 23 Sharia Talaat Harb (☎ 392-5243). If you don't have Lonely Planet's *India – travel survival kit*, this is the next best source of information on India.

Italy

    Istituto Italiano di Cultura, 3 Sharia ash-Sheikh Marsafy, Zamalek (☎ 340-8791). The centre puts on films and organises lectures and has a library.

Japan

    2nd floor, 2 Sharia Abdel Kader Hamza, Garden City (☎ 355-3962). This centre is open from 10 am to 3.30 pm Sunday to Thursday.

Netherlands

    Netherlands Institute of Archaeology & Arabic Studies, 1 Sharia Mahmoud Azmy, Zamalek (☎ 340-0076). The institute usually has lectures every Thursday evening, except in summer.

UK

    British Council, 192 Sharia el-Nil, Agouza (☎ 345-3281). In a villa near the circus grounds, the Council has a library which carries most major daily and weekly newspapers and has more than 35,000 books and 90 periodicals. The reading rooms are open daily, except Sunday, from 9 am to 1.50 pm and from 3 to 8 pm; Friday and Saturday from 9 am to 3 pm. Library membership costs E£40, or you can pay E£25 to read only. Alternatively, nonmembers can browse for 20 minutes *only* free of charge. The Council offers an extensive range of classes in English and Arabic, and occasionally puts on films and plays.

USA

    5 Sharia Latin America, Garden City (☎ 354-9601). Part of the embassy complex, this cultural centre has a library with more than 200 periodicals and 10,000 books, and is where you can watch *Worldnet's MacNeil/Lehrer News Hour* Monday to Friday from noon and the CBS *Evening News* Monday to Friday from 1 to 1.30 pm. The reading rooms are open from 10 am to 7 pm on Monday and Wednesday, and from 10 am to 4 pm the rest of the week; closed on Saturday and US and Egyptian holidays. Admission to the reading rooms is free.

Film & Photography

Central Cairo and suburbs like Zamalek, Heliopolis and Maadi are dotted with places that will process film, however, the quality is not always great.

One place which is recommended – both for quality and price – is the Photo Centre (☎ 392-0031) at 3 Sharia Mahrani. It's on the 1st floor of an apartment building in a backstreet off Sharia Sherif. Colour prints cost E£2 for one hour film processing plus 50 pt for each print. Slide processing costs E£10 and takes only three hours.

Alternatively, the Kodak shop on Sharia Adly is also recommended, or there's an Agfa outlet at 22 Sharia Hassan Sabri in Zamalek.

There are numerous places to have passport photos done. The cheapest option is to ask one of the photographers in front of the Mogamma. They will use an antique box camera to copy your passport photo or other photo and make four copies (B&W only and often a bit out of focus) for E£4. It's worth buying the photos even if you don't need them just to watch the photographer mastering his equipment, closing little hatches on the box and exposing the film.

For colour shots done quickly, your cheapest bet is the instant photo booth (E£6 for four photos) near the ticket windows in Sadat metro station under Midan Tahrir. Studio Express on the ground floor of the Mogamma building is expensive.

Medical Services

Hospitals There are several hospitals in Cairo with more modern facilities than most of Egypt's other hospitals: Cairo Medical Centre (☎ 258-0566) in Heliopolis; Anglo-American Hospital (☎ 340-6162), next to the Cairo Tower in Zamalek; Misr International Hospital (☎ 360-8261), next to the Indiana Hotel in Doqqi; and As-Salam International Hospital (☎ 363-8050), Corniche el-Nil, Maadi. The latter has another branch (☎ 302-9091) at 3 Sharia Syria, Mohandiseen. Both the Doqqi and Maadi hospitals have 24 hour facilities.

Doctors & Dentists It's best to inquire at your embassy for the latest list of recommended doctors and dentists.

There are International Association for Medical Assistance to Travellers (IAMAT) centres at:

Central Cairo
13 Sharia Wakf al-Kharboutly (☎ 284-1375/6/8/9, 243-4653); coordinator Dr Nabil Ayad al-Masry

Maadi
87 Rd 9 (☎ 350-3105, 351-0230); coordinator Dr Sherif Doss
Heliopolis
1 Midan Roxy (☎ 258-2729); coordinator Dr Amin Iskander Fakry

It might also be worth contacting SOS Assistance, especially if you are considering a long stay in Egypt. This organisation can be contacted care of Cairoscan (☎ 360-0965), 35 Sharia Suleiman Abaza, Mohandiseen. Its policy offers full medical cover in case of emergency, including a flight out to the country of your choice under the SOS MEDEVAC scheme. Contact SOS Assistance for more information.

Pharmacies There's no shortage of pharmacies in Cairo, and almost anything can be obtained without a prescription. Pharmacies that operate day and night include Isaaf (☎ 743369) on the corner of Sharia Ramses and Sharia 26th of July, central Cairo, and El-Ezaby (☎ 418-0838) at 1 Sharia Ahmed Tayseer, Heliopolis.

In the city centre, the Anglo-Eastern Pharmacy on the corner of Sharia Abdel Khaliq Sarwat and Sharia Sherif is open from 10 am to 3 pm and 6.30 to 10 pm; closed Friday. In Zamalek, the pharmacy (☎ 341-6424) at 3 Sharia Shagarat ad-Durr is open daily from 10 am to 9 pm.

Vaccinations The International Vaccination Centre is in the former Hotel Continental on Sharia al-Gomhurriya facing the Ezbekiya Gardens; it's at the back of the lobby on the right side. Vaccinations against cholera and yellow fever are available from the centre for E£1.50 each, and you are given the standard yellow International Certificate of Vaccination card free. If you are getting a yellow fever vaccination, keep in mind that protection doesn't become effective until 10 days after vaccination. The centre is open daily from 10 am to 1 pm and 6 to 7 pm (closed Friday evening). It's advisable to bring your own needles.

Emergency Some important numbers in Cairo are:

Ambulance
 Cairo Ambulance Service (☎ 123 or 770123/230); possibly slow
 Giza (☎ 720385)
 Heliopolis (☎ 244-4327)
 Maadi (☎ 350-2873)
Police
 Central (☎ 13)
 Emergency (☎ 122 or 900112)
 Tourist Police (☎ 126)
Fire
 All districts (☎ 125 or 391-0115)

Dangers & Annoyances

Theft can be a problem in Cairo – see the Dangers & Annoyances section in the Facts for the Visitor chapter for more details.

CENTRAL CAIRO

Many travellers begin their Egyptian experience in the vicinity of Midan Tahrir and Sharia Talaat Harb. It's the bustling, noisy centre of Cairo where you'll find an amazing variety of shops as well as most of the budget hotels and eating places, banks, travel agencies and cinemas. Central Cairo also has a number of museums, art galleries, markets, gardens and scenic views of the Nile.

Egyptian Museum

This museum is in a huge building a little north-west of Midan Tahrir. Also called the Museum of Egyptian Antiquities, it should not be missed. In fact, it's a good idea to visit this place twice – at the beginning of your visit to familiarise yourself with Egypt's ancient history, and at the end to understand better all you have seen.

More than 100,000 relics and antiquities from almost every period of ancient Egyptian history are housed in the museum. This vast collection was first gathered under one roof in 1858 by Auguste Mariette, a French archaeologist who excavated the temples of Edfu, Dendara, Deir al-Bahri, Amun (at Karnak in Luxor) and a few others. The place is virtually bursting at the seams, and it's hardly the last word in modern museum techniques.

The exhibits are arranged chronologically from the Old Kingdom to the Roman Empire. Each room could easily be a museum in its own right; if you spent only one minute at each exhibit it would take more than nine months to see everything. Guidebooks are available to help you deal with this fascinating but overwhelming labyrinth.

A Guide to the Egyptian Museum, a 300 page list of the museum's artefacts, is available at the museum's ticket window or the gift shop for E£10. It's organised by catalogue number rather than by room, with very little description on each item. The *Blue Guide* is a costlier alternative at E£125 but it describes the museum room by room in excellent detail. *The Egyptian Museum Cairo – Official Catalogue* is slightly cheaper (E£100) and is still a good reference source. There are two other alternatives that more or less fill the gap. *Egyptian Museum Cairo*, by Dr Edouard Lambelet, is published in English, French and German, and has a fairly extensive and generously illustrated description of the main objects of interest, identified by room and catalogue numbers. It sells for E£30. A less ordered version of the same thing is put out by the French publishers Hachette and is called *The Egypt of the Pharaohs at the Cairo Museum*, by Jean-Pierre Corteggiani (E£80).

Admission to the museum is E£10, or E£5 for students. Access to the recently reopened Royal Mummy Room costs an additional E£60 (E£30 for students); tickets for this must be bought on the 1st floor at the entrance to the room. The museum is open daily from 9 am to 5 pm but closes on Friday between noon and 2 pm (summer) and 11.30 am and 1.30 pm (winter). If you're visiting on Friday morning, take note that you can't get back in with the same ticket in the afternoon. Room 3, which displays the gold mask and coffins of Tutankhamun, the Royal Mummy Room and room 53 all close at 4.15 pm. Permission to use cameras (without flash) costs E£10; otherwise cameras must be left at the entrance. Use of a video camera costs E£100. There are official guides who will take you around for about E£40 per hour.

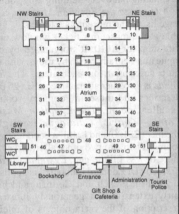

Egyptian Museum

Ground Floor

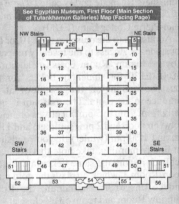

First Floor

See Egyptian Museum, First Floor (Main Section of Tutankhamun Galleries) Map (Facing Page)

Exhibit Highlights

Tutankhamun

Without doubt, the exhibit that outshines everything else in the museum is the treasure of the young and comparatively insignificant New Kingdom Pharaoh Tutankhamun.

The tomb and treasures of this king, who ruled for only nine years during the 14th century BC, were discovered in 1922 by English archaeologist Howard Carter. Its well-hidden location in the Valley of the Kings, below the much grander but ransacked tomb of Ramses VI, had prevented tomb robbers and, later, archaeologists from finding it any earlier. The incredible contents of his rather modest tomb can only make one wonder about the fabulous wealth looted from the tombs of Pharaohs far greater than Tutankhamun.

The king's decaying mummified body, the outer of three mummiform coffins and the huge stone sarcophagus are all that remain in his tomb. The rest of his funerary treasures, about 1700 items, are spread throughout 12 rooms on the 1st floor of the museum. The rooms and the best relics are:

Rooms 3 & 4 Gold is the glittering attraction of these rooms, which feature an astounding collection of jewellery, including the 143 amulets and pieces of jewellery found among the wrappings on the king's body, and a pair of gold sandals which were on the feet of the mummy. The two innermost coffins of Tutankhamun's tomb, one of inlaid gold foil and the other of solid gold, are in room 3. However, the centrepiece of this room is Tutankhamun's legendary and exquisite mask of beaten gold inlaid with lapis lazuli and other gems.

Up until a few years ago, room 4 also displayed much of Tutankhamun's treasures. There are still bits and pieces in this room, but the highlight now is a magnificent Roman-era crown made of gold which was discovered in 1989 around Qasr ad-Dush, at the southern end of Kharga Oasis.

Rooms 7 & 8 The gilded wooden shrines that fitted inside each other and held the gold sarcophagus of Tutankhamun at their centre are in these rooms.

Room 9 The attraction of this room is the chest filled with four alabaster Canopic jars, each shaped as a goddess, which once contained the viscera of the young Pharaoh.

Room 10 King Tutankhamun's bed befits a Pharaoh; it is covered with sheet gold, with string stretched across a frame that represents Hathor. The elongated cows wearing sun discs between their horns were used as the supports. This bed is accompanied by two less costly beds (in room 9) featuring hippos and lions.

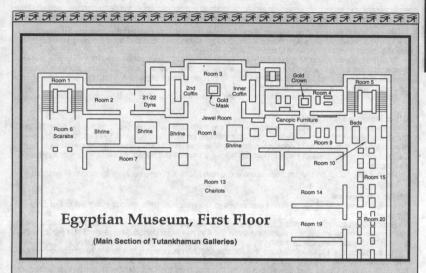

Egyptian Museum, First Floor

(Main Section of Tutankhamun Galleries)

Room 15 Beautifully rigged model ships, to be used by the Pharaoh on his voyage through the afterworld, are found in this room.

Room 20 Here you can see some exquisite alabaster jars and one chalice in particular, in which a small light has been inserted to demonstrate the delicacy of its translucent artwork.

Room 24 Here you will see the originals of the papyrus paintings that you find in bazaars throughout Cairo. More can be seen in room 5, in the stairwell leading up to the Tutankhamun exhibits.

Room 30 A gilded bronze trumpet is the feature of this room; it was once 'played' in 1939.

Room 35 The most interesting item in this room is Tutankhamun's wooden throne. Covered with sheet gold, silver, gems and glass, the wooden throne has winged cobras and lions' heads on the arms and the back; it is decorated with the famous scene of Tutankhamun's queen placing her hand on his shoulder. Here, too, is a beautifully carved wooden clothes chest.

Rooms 40 & 45 Exhibits in these rooms include a board game (room 45, case 189) with ivory playing pieces that resembles checkers or draughts, and the statue of Anubis, the dog who was the god of mummification, found in Tutankhamun's tomb.

Akhenaten
For those interested in the Pharaoh who set up Ancient Egypt's first and last monotheistic faith, room 3 on the ground floor contains statuary and artefacts from the time of this unusual predecessor to Tutankhamun.

Royal Mummy Room
After being hidden for 15 years behind closed doors, a selection of Egypt's ancient rulers is again on display for the public to view. Opened in 1995, the Royal Mummy Room (No 56 on the 1st floor) houses the bodies of 11 kings and queens from the 18th to 21st dynasties who ruled Egypt between 1552 and 1069 BC. They include Ramses II, his father Seti I, Tuthmosis II and Queen Meret Amun (wife of Amenhotep I and one of the daughters of Ramses II).

In 1981, the room housing the royal mummies (27 in total) was closed to the public as *(continued)*

President Sadat thought it disrespectful to the dead (he had just berated the Iranians for displaying the charred bodies of eight Americans killed during the hostage crisis). The remaining 16 mummies are still under lock and key in that room (No 52).

The mummies moved to room 56 now lie in individual glass showcases (kept at a constant temperature of 22˚C) in a sombre, dimly lit environment reminiscent of a tomb. Talking above a hushed whisper is not permitted and, for this reason, tour guides are not allowed in, making it one of the most peaceful havens in the whole museum.

For more information on the mummies, there's a booklet on sale at the ticket counter for E£3.

Other Mummies & Coffins
A rather dismal alternative to the royal remains are the mummies in room 53, on the 1st floor. Before the rise of Pharaonic dynasties in Egypt, animal cults proliferated. A few of the results can be seen here in the dusty mummies of dogs, cats, rams and jackals. Better are the two new showcases in room 54 (close to the entrance of room 53) which house a mummified falcon, fish, cat, ibis, monkey and a tiny crocodile.

Rooms 46 and 47 on the 1st floor contain the royal coffins of several New Kingdom Pharaohs.

Statues & Palettes
There are thousands of statues and statuettes in the museum from almost every period of ancient Egyptian history.

Room 47 on the 1st floor is lined with sarcophagi and statues. Check out the centre exhibit cases, which have several interesting statuettes from the Old Kingdom period. These include a hunchback, a dwarf, and figures engaged in everyday activities such as plucking birds, kneading dough and baking.

Room 42 on the 1st floor contains the Palette of Narmer, possibly the oldest record of a political event and one of the most significant items in this room. It describes, in a series of pictures and symbols, the unification of Upper and Lower Egypt for the first time by King Narmer. Narmer was probably another name for Menes, the founder of the 1st dynasty.

Solar Barques
Solar barques were wooden boats placed in or around the tombs of Pharaohs. They were symbolically important as vessels for transporting the Pharaoh's soul over the sea of death beneath the earth. Two of these barques are on the ground floor in room 43, just inside the entrance. Both are from the 12th dynasty (1990 to 1780 BC); one comes from the Pyramid of Senusert III in Dahshur and the other from the Colossus of Senusert III at Karnak in Luxor.

Graeco-Roman Artefacts
Apart from a reasonable collection of statuary, the Graeco-Roman period in Egypt is perhaps most curiously represented by a collection of portraits in room 14 (1st floor), most of them found at Karanis in Al-Faiyum Oasis, dating from 60 to 230 AD. A collection of Graeco-Roman era coins is located in room 4 on the ground floor. ■

Tutankhamun owes his fame in modern times to the discovery of his tomb in 1922. This was found, remarkably, with its contents undisturbed. Tutankhamun is depicted here with his wife, Ankhesenamon, in the famous relief that decorates his throne, that can be viewed in Room 35.

Entomological Society Museum

This museum, at 14 Sharia Ramses, houses an excellent and well-preserved collection of the birds and insects of Egypt. It's open daily except Thursday and Friday from 10.30 am to 1 pm and 6 to 9 pm.

Post Office Museum

The Post Office Museum is on the 1st floor of the GPO on Midan Ataba. There are collections of old stamps and displays of the history of Egypt's postal service. It's open daily except Friday from 9 am to 1 pm.

Cairo Puppet Theatre

Also on Midan Ataba, this theatre presents colourful puppet shows. Although the presentations are in Arabic they are still worth seeing, as most of the actions are self-explanatory. Just behind it is a theatre for modern experimental works in Arabic.

Egyptian National Railways Museum

A sign outside the main entrance to Ramses station leads you to the museum at one end of the station. This well-organised museum displays the history of railways and railway-related architecture in Egypt. On the ground floor are locomotives once used by Egypt's 19th century rulers.

A beautifully preserved locomotive built in 1862 for Princess Eugénie on the occasion of the opening of the Suez Canal still has its original upholstery and oil lamps. The museum is open daily except Monday from 8 am to 1 pm. Admission is E£1.50, but E£3 on Fridays and holidays.

Art Galleries

Hidden in nooks and crannies throughout Cairo are a few small art galleries where contemporary local and foreign artists and sculptors exhibit their works. *Al-Ahram* and *Egypt Today* list most of these galleries, many of which are closed during the summer. The better central ones include:

Mashrabia
    8 Sharia Champollion (☎ 303-5382); open Saturday to Thursday from 5 to 9 pm.

Atelier du Caire
    2 Sharia Karim el-Dawlas, just off Sharia Mohammed Bassiuni (☎ 574-6730); open from 10 am to 1.30 pm and 6.30 to 9.30 pm.
Cairo-Berlin Art Gallery
    17 Sharia Yusef al-Gendi, just north of Sharia al-Bustan (☎ 393-1764)

WESTERN CAIRO

There is a number of worthwhile sites in the suburbs of Gezira and Zamalek, on the island immediately west of central Cairo, and in Doqqi and Agouza on the Nile's west bank.

Gezira & Zamalek

Opera House Just over At-Tahrir Bridge in Gezira is the Opera House, a US$30 million arts complex that includes a museum, library, art gallery and music halls with modern technical equipment and superb acoustics. The complex was built using traditional Islamic designs, visible in both the geometric layout of the courtyards and the styles of the windows and doors. There's always something happening here – for more details see the Entertainment section later in this chapter.

Museum of Modern Art This museum (☎ 342-0592), housed in an impressive building in the grounds of the Opera House, will give you an interesting insight into contemporary culture and changing life in modern Egypt. Exhibitions by foreign artists are also held here. The museum is open daily except Monday from 10 am to 1 pm and 5 to 9.30 pm. Admission is E£10, or E£5 for students.

Moukhtar Museum At the time of writing, this museum was in search of a new home and, subsequently, was closed. Moukhtar (1891 to 1934) was the sculptor laureate of Egypt, and the museum's collection contains most of his major works. Check with the tourist office for its new location.

Cairo Tower One of the best places for a panoramic view of Cairo is the 185m-high Cairo Tower in Gezira (see Greater Cairo

CAIRO

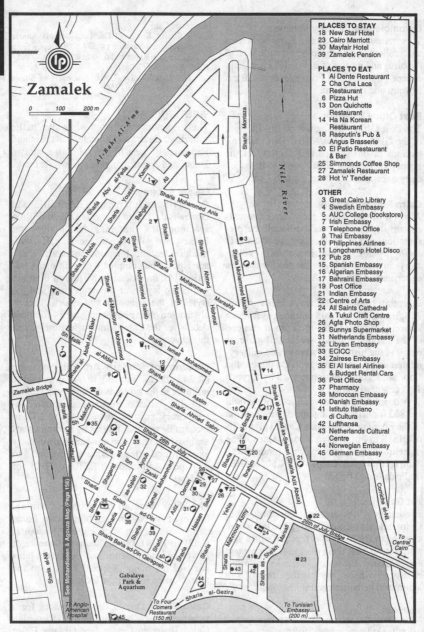

Zamalek

0   100   200 m

PLACES TO STAY
18 New Star Hotel
23 Cairo Marriott
30 Mayfair Hotel
39 Zamalek Pension

PLACES TO EAT
1   Al Dente Restaurant
2   Cha Cha Laca
    Restaurant
6   Pizza Hut
13 Don Quichotte
    Restaurant
14 Ha Na Korean
    Restaurant
18 Rasputin's Pub &
    Angus Brasserie
20 El Patio Restaurant
    & Bar
25 Simmonds Coffee Shop
27 Zamalek Restaurant
28 Hot 'n' Tender

OTHER
3   Great Cairo Library
4   Swedish Embassy
5   AUC College (bookstore)
7   Irish Embassy
8   Telephone Office
9   Thai Embassy
10 Philippines Airlines
11 Longchamp Hotel Disco
12 Pub 28
15 Spanish Embassy
16 Algerian Embassy
17 Bahraini Embassy
19 Post Office
21 Indian Embassy
22 Centre of Arts
24 All Saints Cathedral
    & Tukul Craft Centre
26 Agfa Photo Shop
29 Sunnys Supermarket
31 Netherlands Embassy
32 Libyan Embassy
33 ECICC
34 Zairese Embassy
35 El Al Israel Airlines
    & Budget Rental Cars
36 Post Office
37 Pharmacy
38 Moroccan Embassy
40 Danish Embassy
41 Istituto Italiano
    di Cultura
42 Lufthansa
43 Netherlands Cultural
    Centre
44 Norwegian Embassy
45 German Embassy

map). Built in 1961, this structure is, after the pyramids, the city's most famous landmark. Early morning, when you can usually see the pyramids at Giza, or late afternoon are the ideal times for taking photographs. There's an expensive revolving restaurant on top as well as a cheaper cafeteria. The entrance fee for the tower, if you're going to the top, is E£10 (plus E£10 for a video). Hours for the viewing area are 9 am to midnight, daily. You might find a bit of a queue at dusk.

Gabalaya Park & Aquarium Gabalaya

Park, between Sharia Om Kolthum and Sharia Hassan Sabri in Zamalek, includes an aquarium where fish inhabit tunnels that resemble bomb shelters. Even if fish don't interest you, the park is still worth a visit for the respite it offers from the chaos of Cairo. It's open from 9 am to 3.30 pm daily and entry costs 50 pt.

Centre of Arts Just north of the 26th of July Bridge in Zamalek is this tiny haven of modern art. There are works from Egypt and Europe, but there's not all that much to it.

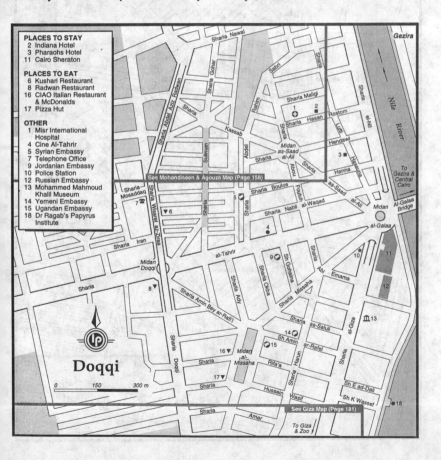

PLACES TO STAY
2 Indiana Hotel
3 Pharaohs Hotel
11 Cairo Sheraton

PLACES TO EAT
6 Kushari Restaurant
8 Radwan Restaurant
16 CIAO Italian Restaurant & McDonalds
17 Pizza Hut

OTHER
1 Misr International Hospital
4 Cine Al-Tahrir
5 Syrian Embassy
7 Telephone Office
9 Jordanian Embassy
10 Police Station
12 Russian Embassy
13 Mohammed Mahmoud Khalil Museum
14 Yemeni Embassy
15 Ugandan Embassy
18 Dr Ragab's Papyrus Institute

Doqqi

0   150   300 m

See Mohandiseen & Agouza Map (Page 156)

See Giza Map (Page 181)

CAIRO

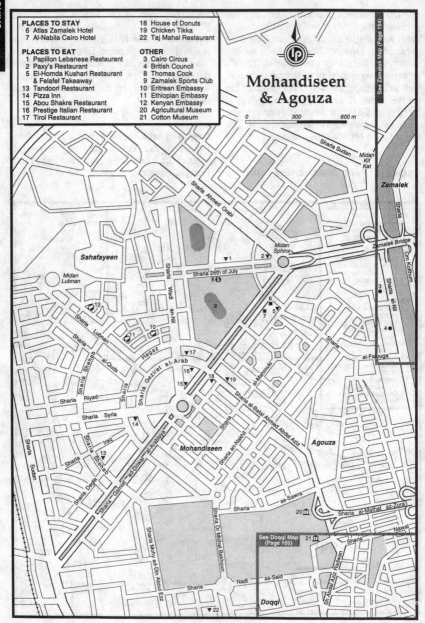

PLACES TO STAY
6 Atlas Zamalek Hotel
7 Al-Nabila Cairo Hotel

PLACES TO EAT
1 Papillon Lebanese Restaurant
2 Paxy's Restaurant
5 El-Homda Kushari Restaurant
  & Felafel Takeaway
13 Tandoori Restaurant
14 Pizza Inn
15 Abou Shakra Restaurant
16 Prestige Italian Restaurant
17 Tirol Restaurant

18 House of Donuts
19 Chicken Tikka
22 Taj Mahal Restaurant

OTHER
3 Cairo Circus
4 British Council
8 Thomas Cook
9 Zamalek Sports Club
10 Eritrean Embassy
11 Ethiopian Embassy
12 Kenyan Embassy
20 Agricultural Museum
21 Cotton Museum

See Zamalek Map (Page 154)

Mohandiseen
& Agouza

0   300   600 m

Sharia Sudan

Midan
Kit
Kat

Zamalek

Sharia Ahmed Orabi

Midan
Sphinx

Zamalek Bridge

Om Kolthum

Sharia el-Nil

Sahafayeen

Sharia 26th of July

Midan
Lubnan

Sharia Lubnan

Wadi an-Nil

al-Faluuga

al-Quds

Hegaz

Sharia Geziret al-Arab

Sharia Shehab

Sharia Riyad

Sharia Syria

Sharia Iraq

Sharia Degla

Sharia Sudan

Sharia Gamal Abd-Dowal al-Arabiya

Sharia Mohy ad-Din Abdul Ezz

Sharia Dr Michel Bakhoun

Mohandiseen

Sharia an-Nakhil

Sharia al-Batal Ahmed Abdel Aziz

al-Mavrouki

Agouza

as-Sawra

Sharia al-Mathat az-Zoral

Nawal

See Doqqi Map
(Page 155)

Nadi

as-Said

Doqqi

Sh Abdel Aziz Radwan

20

21

The centre (☎ 340-8211) is open daily except Friday from 10 am to 1 pm and 5 to 7 pm; admission is free.

Doqqi & Agouza
Mohammed Mahmoud Khalil Museum
This museum (☎ 336-2379) was recently moved to a superbly restored three storey villa on Sharia al-Giza next to the Russian embassy, on the border of Doqqi and Giza. The building used to be the home of Mohammed Mahmoud Khalil, a noted politician during the 1940s, and was later taken over as the official residence of the President of Egypt. The museum claims to have the Middle East's finest collection of 19th century European art and houses sculptures by Rodin, a rich selection of French works by the likes of Gauguin, Monet and Pissaro, as well as contemporary paintings by Egyptian artists. It is open daily except Monday from 9.30 am to 6 pm; admission is a whopping E£25, or E£5 for students.

Dr Ragab's Papyrus Institute Dr Ragab's original Papyrus Institute is on the river south of the Mohammed Mahmoud Khalil Museum in Doqqi. Here you can see some displays on the ancient art of papyrus writing and painting, as well as buy some of the doctor's work. It's open from 9 am to 9 pm.

Agricultural & Cotton Museums This complex (☎ 360-8682) is off Sharia Wisarat az-Ziraa, at the foot of the overpass on Sharia 6th of October, roughly on the border of Doqqi and Agouza. The Agricultural Museum contains lots of stuffed animals and exhibits that show life in Egyptian villages. The Cotton Museum has displays of the history of cotton production in Egypt. Both are open from 9 am to 2 pm, except on Monday, and admission is a mere 10 pt.

Cairo Circus This small big top is at the foot of Zamalek Bridge, off Sharia 26th of July in Agouza, before the British Council. There rarely seems to be anything going on, but check with the tourist office or *Egypt Today* to see if there are performances.

HELIOPOLIS
Early this century, Baron Edouard Empain, a Belgian industrialist, was responsible for creating the chic north-eastern suburb of Heliopolis (known to the Egyptians by the less fanciful name of Masr al-Gedida – New Cairo). The baron's aim was to make a garden city isolated from the squalor of Cairo which would attract the elite of Europe. Construction began in 1906, and within a few years Heliopolis had spawned large Christian, Jewish and Islamic communities. In the 1950s, however, the tide turned, and many foreigners moved out as overcrowding in Cairo caught up with this not-so-distant neighbour.

These days Heliopolis is home to much of Cairo's prosperous middle class. Rows of apartment buildings littered with satellite TV dishes now outnumber the graceful, old villas built during the baron's time. Terrace bars, restaurants, shops and nightclubs also proliferate. But despite all this, the area still has an urbane air, with spacious boulevards winding around the presidential palace, and some remarkable architecture (including elegant, Moorish facades along Sharia al-Ahram and tear-drop turrets on Sharia Ibrahim Laqqany).

Heliopolis can be easily reached by bus or tram from central Cairo. For details, see the Getting Around section later in this chapter.

Qasr al-Baron
The 'Baron's Palace' is certainly one of the weirder monuments to European fantasies about the Orient. Designed like an Asian temple – the last thing you'd expect to see in Egypt – it was the *pièce de résistance* of his work and Baron Empain's family's former residence. Now disused, it lies on Sharia al-Uruba – you can see it off to the left coming in from the airport.

Basilica
Heliopolis' basilica was designed by Belgian architect Alexander Marcel in 1913 as a miniature version of Istanbul's famous Aya Sofia. Although it has none of the grandeur of the church which inspired it, it's still worth

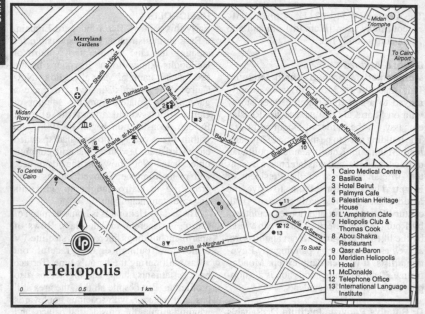

Heliopolis

1 Cairo Medical Centre
2 Basilica
3 Hotel Beirut
4 Palmyra Cafe
5 Palestinian Heritage House
6 L'Amphitrion Cafe
7 Heliopolis Club & Thomas Cook
8 Abou Shakra Restaurant
9 Qasr al-Baron
10 Meridien Heliopolis Hotel
11 McDonalds
12 Telephone Office
13 International Language Institute

a visit if you happen to be up the northern end of Sharia al-Ahram, Heliopolis' premier shopping street. If not, the Nouzha (red line) tram will take you right past it. Baron Empain and his family are buried in the crypt.

Palestinian Heritage House

Occupying the ground floor of an apartment building at 5 Sharia Damascus, the Palestinian Heritage House (☎ 258-0318) was established in 1984 by Khadeja Arafat, Yasser Arafat's sister-in-law, as a centre where exiled Palestinian women could make and sell crafts. It's now a modest showcase of Palestinian history and culture as well as traditional and contemporary art, with century-old bridal gowns from Gaza and Galilee exhibited alongside richly embroidered shawls woven by women in a workshop situated out the back. The house is open daily from 8.30 am to 3 pm (until 1 pm on Thursday); admission is free.

October War Panorama & Sadat's Tomb

About two km south-west of Qasr al-Baron, farther in towards the city in the suburb of Medinet Nasr, is the October War Panorama. Coming in from the airport, it's off to the left on Sharia al-Uruba. Built with help from North Korean artists, this memorial to the 1973 'victory' over Israelis occupying the Sinai is quite an extraordinary propaganda effort.

Inside the cylindrical building at the centre, you climb two flights of stairs to a revolving dais which carries the audience around a three-dimensional mural depicting the breaching of the Bar Lev line on the Suez Canal by Egyptian forces and the initial retreats by the Israelis. A stirring commentary recounts the heroic victories but is short on detail on the successful Israeli counterattacks that pushed the Egyptians back before both sides accepted a UN-brokered ceasefire. The Sinai was eventually 'liberated' – but by negotiation six years later.

Ancient Egyptian Cosmogonies

Ancient Egypt produced at least four great cult centres: Heliopolis, Hermopolis, Memphis and Thebes. Of the four, we know most about the Heliopolitan cult. All, however, centred on a belief that the world arose from chaos or primordial waters and that moral and political order as well as royal power stemmed from a creator god.

According to the Heliopolitan cosmogonies, Aten (who eventually became regarded as the sun-god Ra) created himself and a hill to stand on. He then created other gods, including Shu and Tefnut who produced Geb and Nut who, in turn, created Isis, Osiris, Nephthys and Seth. This 'family' was referred to as the divine ennead (nine).

Memphis was established as a capital around 3000 BC after the unification of Upper and Lower Egypt by Menes. In the Memphite cosmogonies, Ptah was credited with creating the world and the divine ennead of Heliopolis nearby was regarded as merely a manifestation of him. As a creator god, he established moral and political order as well as royal power.

The Hermopolitan cosmogonies centred on an ogdoad, a group of eight gods (in fact, four male deities with female consorts). There are several variants of this creation myth. One states that the world began as a cosmic egg laid by a celestial goose (the Great Cackler, although sometimes an Ibis is credited with laying the egg) which broke the world's silence. From this egg hatched the bird of light and creator of the world (Ra). Another variant tells of how the divine child Ra sprang from a lotus.

The ruling god of Thebes was Amun, who incorporated aspects of other creator gods. Amun was said to have created himself as well as both men and gods. ■

It's closed on Tuesday. Admission is E£8 and performances, usually with an Arabic commentary, begin at 9.30 and 11 am and 6 pm. Groups can request a performance with an English commentary.

Nearby is the tomb of President Sadat who was assassinated by a member of a radical Islamic group during a military parade in 1981.

ISLAMIC CAIRO

Islamic Cairo (a more appropriate name would be Medieval Cairo, given that the area is no more nor less Islamic than any other part of Egypt, but this appears to be the convention) is replete with medieval mosques, apartment buildings and the greatest density of people in the country – and probably the Middle East.

An unhappy feature, even today, is the evidence of the extent to which the whole area was shaken by the 1992 earthquake. Few buildings of historical significance escaped damage. Before climbing any minarets, it would be as well to try to ascertain how badly they were hit.

It is easy to get lost in this district. In the back alleyways and streets of neighbourhoods such as Darb al-Ahmar you'll suddenly find yourself back in the Cairo of six or seven centuries ago; in a time when donkeys and camels transported people and goods, buildings were like shaky wooden pyramids, and exotic foods were hawked from pavement stalls. Be prepared for this passage to the past because it hits all your senses.

Splendid mosques and imposing buildings still loom over narrow, crowded streets and bustling squares; the sweet, pungent aromas of tumeric, basil and cumin drift from open barrels, mix with the offensive odours of livestock and grab at your nose like invisible fingers; and people go about their daily business as they have done, it seems, forever. This could be the medieval Cairo of Ibn Tulun or Salah ad-Din, except that the age-old aromas now mingle with petrol fumes as donkeys compete with cars for space, and an awful lot of poverty offsets the grandeur of the architecture throughout what was once the intellectual and cultural centre of the Arab world.

Your tour can begin anywhere in the area, but the following describes two different walking tours. They are by no means an exhaustive guide to all the monuments, but rather a selection of the more important ones.

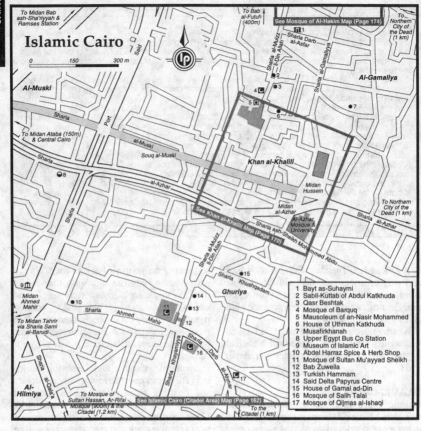

Islamic Cairo

To Midan Bab ash-Sha'riyyah & Ramses Station

To Bab al-Futuh (400m)

See Mosque of Al-Hakim Map (Page 174)

To Northern City of the Dead (1 km)

0   150   300 m

Al-Muski

Sharia al-Muizz li-Din Allah

Sharia Darb al-Asfar

Sharia al-Gamaliyya

Al-Gamaliya

Said

Port

Sharia

al-Muski

Souq al-Muski

Khan al-Khalili

To Midan Ataba (150m) & Central Cairo

Sharia

al-Azhar

Sharia

Midan Hussein

To Northern City of the Dead (1 km)

Midan al-Azhar

Al-Azhar Mosque & University

Sharia

al-Azhar

See Khan al-Khalili Map (Page 170)

Sharia ash-Sheikh Mohammed Abdu

Sharia al-Muizz li-Din Allah

Sharia Khushqadam

Ghuriya

Midan Ahmed Mahir

Sharia

Ahmed   Mahir

Sharia Khayamiyya

Darb al-Ahmar

To Midan Tahrir via Sharia Sami al-Barudi

Al-Hilmiya

Sharia al-Qala'a

To Mosque of Sultan Hassan, Ar-Rifai Mosque (900m) & the Citadel (1.2 km)

See Islamic Cairo (Citadel Area) Map (Page 162)

To the Citadel (1 km)

1 Bayt as-Suhaymi
2 Sabil-Kuttab of Abdul Katkhuda
3 Qasr Beshtak
4 Mosque of Barquq
5 Mausoleum of an-Nasir Mohammed
6 House of Uthman Katkhuda
7 Musafirkhanah
8 Upper Egypt Bus Co Station
9 Museum of Islamic Art
10 Abdel Harraz Spice & Herb Shop
11 Mosque of Sultan Mu'ayyad Sheikh
12 Bab Zuweila
13 Turkish Hammam
14 Said Delta Papyrus Centre
15 House of Gamal ad-Din
16 Mosque of Salih Talai
17 Mosque of Qijmas al-Ishaqi

A closer examination of the more than 150 buildings of historical interest in the area would involve weeks, if not months, of exploring a labyrinth of nooks and crannies.

You may therefore want to buy a more specialised guide. *A Practical Guide to Islamic Monuments in Cairo*, by Parker & Sabin, is packed with detailed explanations and maps of the monuments in Islamic Cairo. The Society for the Preservation of the Architectural Resources of Egypt (SPARE) has put out a series of maps covering the area. Dedicated shoppers might want to pick up Ola Seif's *Khan al-Khalili*, a mapped guide

to every stall in the bazaar. All these publications are available from the AUC Bookstore.

Appropriate dress is necessary for visiting this part of Cairo – legs and shoulders should be decently covered and in some buildings women will need to don a scarf. That said, there are a few places where the pressure of receiving bus loads of day-trippers has resulted in cloaks being handed out to those who are inadequately clad.

As you begin your exploration of this part of Cairo, carry lots of small change for baksheesh. You'll need it for tipping guards and

KRISTIE BURNS

KRISTIE BURNS

KRISTIE BURNS

Top: Smoking shisha pipes outside a local cafe in Old Cairo.
Bottom Left: A Tamr hindi juice vendor washes a glass, ready for his next customer.
Bottom Right: Tables set for the break-fast during Ramadan, Cairo.

LEANNE LOGAN

LEANNE LOGAN

The contrast between old and new, modern and traditional, and east and west are more pronounced in Cairo than perhaps any other city of the world: the city's skyline and landscaped river banks (top) place it firmly in the present, while views over the northern City of the Dead (bottom) reveal a world of the past.

SCOTT WAYNE

CHRIS BEALL

GLENN BEANLAND

Top: The Mosque of Al-Hakim houses the oldest surviving minarets in Cairo.
Left: A minaret casts a shadow across Cairo's City of the Dead.
Right: Enclosed within the Citadel is the imposing Mosque of Mohammed Ali, built in imperial Turkish style.

KRISTIE BURNS

KRISTIE BURNS

KRISTIE BURNS

DAMIEN SIMONIS

Top Left: Handcrafting drums for a local festival, Khan al-Khalili, Cairo.
Top Right: Weaving a rug on a large wooden loom in a village school, near Cairo.
Bottom Left: Sorting through old books and magazines for recycling.
Bottom Right: Ornate building facade and street lamp – part of the charm of Old Cairo.

caretakers, who will expect baksheesh if you ask to see something special, such as a minaret. Also note that any given opening times should be interpreted as only a rough guide, as caretakers are as apt to close early as they are to open late, depending on their mood. Additionally, most mosques are closed to visitors during prayer times.

Walking Tour 1

The first walking tour begins at Midan Salah ad-Din at the foot of the Citadel, in front of the mosques of Sultan Hassan and Ar-Rifa'i. Lots of buses go there from different parts of Cairo – for details, see Getting to/from the Citadel later in this section.

There are several interesting monuments to visit in the area, apart from the Citadel. Around it you can visit the Mosque of Sultan Hassan, Ar-Rifa'i Mosque, an open-air market, Ibn Tulun Mosque, Gayer-Anderson House, the Mausoleum of Shagarat ad-Durr and the Mausoleum of Imam ash-Shafi'i. It's pointless giving a time limit for a tour like this as everyone takes things at their own pace. However, you'll need to allow at least a day to cover all of the sights mentioned below.

Mosque of Sultan Hassan With the Citadel behind you, this mosque is to the left of Sharia al-Qala'a. It was built between 1356 and 1363 AD, during the time of Mamluk rule, with stones that historians believe were taken from one of the Great Pyramids of Giza. Originally the mosque was a *madrassa*, or theological school, and each of the four *iwans*, or vaulted halls, surrounding the central court served as classrooms for each main school of Sunni Islam. The interior is typically devoid of decoration to make it easier for worshippers to concentrate on prayers. Long chains which once held oil lamps still hang from the ceiling of each iwan. Behind the iwans is the mausoleum. The southernmost of the two minarets is the second highest in Cairo, after that of the new Al-Fath Mosque near Ramses station. Try to visit this place in the morning when the sun lights up the mausoleum portion of the

mosque; the effect is quite eerie. The mosque is open daily from 8 am to 5 pm (6 pm in summer). Entrance is E£12.

Ar-Rifa'i Mosque Just across Sharia al-Qala'a from the Mosque of Sultan Hassan is this 19th century imitation of a Mamluk-style mosque. The dowager princess Khushyar, mother of the khedive Ismail, had the mosque built in 1869 to serve as a tomb for herself, her descendants and future khedives. Members of modern Egypt's royal family, including King Farouk, are buried here – as is the Shah of Iran, whose casket was paraded through the streets of Cairo from Abdin Palace to the mosque in 1980, with President Sadat, the shah's family and Richard Nixon leading the cortege. Hours and tickets are the same as for the Mosque of Sultan Hassan. For a little baksheesh, you can see the tombs of Egypt's royals and the shah.

After visiting these two mosques, walk south-west down Sharia ash-Sheikhun and Sharia as-Salibah away from the Citadel to the Ibn Tulun Mosque. Keep your eyes open along the way. You will pass a 15th century *sabil-kuttab* (public fountain-cum-Qur'anic school) – this one named after Sultan Qait Bey. Just before it is a prison – the sight of faces and hands pressed up against the bars of prison trucks is enough to make you not want to transgress any law here! You then pass between the **Mosque of Sheikhu** on the right and, opposite it, the **Khanqah of Sheikhu.** Both were built by a Mamluk army commander in 1349 and 1355, respectively. Just off on the right is the 19th century **Sabil-Kuttab of Um Abbas**, which houses the Centre for Art & Life. The centre, once serving as a small museum on the island of Roda, now seems only to house bureaucrats. You pass another small 15th century mosque before arriving at the huge Ibn Tulun Mosque. Turn left and the entrance is on your right.

Ibn Tulun Mosque This is one of the largest mosques in the world. Ibn Tulun was sent to rule Cairo in the 9th century by the Abbassid

To Islamic Museum (400m)
See Islamic Cairo Map (Page 160)
To Bab Zuweila (700m) & Khan al-Khalili
To Bab Zuweila (700m) & Khan al-Khalili
To Northern City of the Dead (500m) & Heliopolis (6km)

Darb al-Ahmar

Souq as-Silah

Islamic Cairo (Citadel Area)

0   200   400 m

Al-Hilmiya

1 Maridani Mosque
2 Hammam Bashtak
3 Mosque of Aqsunqur
4 Mosque of Sultan Hassan
5 Ar-Rifa'i Mosque
6 Mosque of Sheikhu
7 Khanqah of Sheikhu
8 Ibn Tulun Mosque
9 Gayer-Anderson House
10 Mausoleum of Shagarat ad-Durr
11 Al-Gawhara Palace & Museum
12 Joseph's Well
13 Bab al-Muqattam
14 Mosque of An-Nasir
15 Mosque of Mohammed Ali
16 Clocktower
17 National Police Museum
18 Entrance to Citadel
19 Military National Museum
20 Bab al-Qullah
21 Archaeological Garden
22 Carriage Museum
23 Seized Museum

Midan Salah ad-Din
Sharia as-Salibah

Sharia Tulun

To Mausoleum of Imam as-Shafi'i (1.5 km) & Southern City of the Dead

caliph of Baghdad. He had the mosque built in 876, with an inner courtyard large enough for most of his army and their horses. The 13th century fountain in the centre continues to provide water for washing before prayers.

After wandering around the massive courtyard, you should climb the spiral minaret. The views of the Citadel to the east and Cairo in general are magnificent and in the morning you can usually see the Great Pyramids of Giza. Opening hours for the mosque and the minaret are from 8 am to 6 pm; admission to both is E£6, plus baksheesh for slippers to put over your shoes in the mosque – if you don't want to just take your own off, that is.

Gayer-Anderson House This museum is immediately adjacent to the Ibn Tulun Mosque, and you can reach it from the outer court of the mosque, to the left of the main entrance.

The house is also called Bayt al-Kretlya (House of the Cretan Woman). It is actually two houses, both dating from the 16th century, named after a British major, John Gayer-Anderson, who occupied and restored it between 1935 and 1942. In 1942 he bequeathed the house and exotic furnishings to Egypt for use as a museum. Each room of the museum has a different exotic theme – the Persian Room, the Chinese Room, the Queen Anne Room, the Mohammed Ali Pasha Turkish Room and the Harem Room of Amina Bint Salem al-Gazzar.

Most of the rooms have windows with intricately carved wooden *mashrabiyyah* screens, which enabled the women of the harem to discreetly observe the goings-on of any male visitors without being seen themselves. There are also some fine mosaics here. Hours are 8 am to 4 pm daily but it closes from noon to 1 pm on Friday. Admission is E£8, or E£4 for students. Those with a camera/video must pay another E£10/25.

When you leave Gayer-Anderson House turn right on the street parallel to the Ibn Tulun Mosque and walk to Sharia Tulun. Turn left and walk the short distance to the intersection with Sharia al-Khalifa, then turn right. After about 250m you will come to the Mausoleum of Shagarat ad-Durr on the left.

Mausoleum of Shagarat ad-Durr Built in 1250, this is a small simple tomb which has Byzantine glass mosaics gracing the prayer niche. The most interesting thing, however, is the story of the woman whose remains are entombed here (see the boxed story on Shagarat ad-Durr).

Sharia al-Khalifa becomes Sharia al-Ashraf, and you continue walking down this street into a district called the Southern Cemetery which is, in fact, the beginning of Cairo's southern City of the Dead, a vast Muslim necropolis stretching all the way to the suburb of Maadi, about five km south.

Mausoleum of Imam ash-Shafi'i This mausoleum is two km south of Midan Salah ad-Din, in the Southern Cemetery. To get there, walk south from the Citadel along Sharia Mabarrat Mustafa Kamel to Tariq Salah Salem. Turn right and then left off the square into Sharia al-Qadiriyyah, which becomes Sharia Imam ash-Shafi'i. The mausoleum is a little over one km farther on.

You can also take bus No 405 from Midan Salah ad-Din, get off before it turns left towards the Moqattam Hills, and walk the remaining distance down Sharia Imam ash-Shafi'i. You can't miss the building, as it has a large red, blue and gold dome topped by a bronze boat.

Imam ash-Shafi'i, a descendant of an uncle of the Prophet, was the founder of the Shafi'ite sect, one of the four major schools of Sunni Islam. Regarded as one of the great Muslim saints, he died in 820 and his mausoleum – the largest Islamic tomb in Egypt

---

Shagarat ad-Durr

Shagarat ad-Durr was a slave from a nomadic tribe who managed, albeit briefly, to become the only female Muslim sovereign in history. She secured this position fairly easily and in the process instigated Mamluk rule, which was to last for the next 200 years; however, she came to a very nasty end.

Salih Ayyub, the last ruler of the Ayyubid dynasty, married Shagarat ad-Durr at a time when the soldiers of the 7th Crusade had taken control of Damietta in the Nile Delta. Knowing that Ayyub was sick and dying, the Crusaders were prepared to wait out his death and attack Cairo when the government collapsed. So when he died in 1249, Shagarat ad-Durr hid his corpse and for three months managed to pretend that he was still alive and passing on orders to his generals through her. She waited for her son to come back from Mesopotamia and take control, but when he did return he proved to be a weak ruler, so she had him killed.

She then declared herself Sultana of Egypt and ruled for 80 days – the only woman to rule over Muslims until Queen Victoria. But the Abbassid caliph of Baghdad refused to recognise her position, so she married a Mamluk, the leader of her slave warriors, and ruled through him. When he decided that he needed an extra wife, Shagarat ad-Durr had him killed and threw his second wife into prison. When the Mamluk warriors discovered Shagarat ad-Durr's part in the assassination, she offered to marry their new leader but was imprisoned instead. She was eventually turned over to her husband's second wife who, along with several other women, beat Shagarat ad-Durr to death with wooden clogs. They hung her body from the side of the Citadel as food for the dogs. What was left of her was salvaged and entombed. ■

– is the centre of a great annual *moulid*, or birthday festival, held in his honour.

In the 12th century Salah ad-Din founded the first madrassa on the same site to counter the influence of the Shi'ite Muslim sect of the Fatimid dynasty he had overthrown. It became a centre of Shafi'ite missionary work. Today most Muslims in Cairo are Shafi'ite. Shafi'ite Sunni Islam is also predominant in Malaysia and East Africa.

The Citadel A spectacular medieval fortress of crenellated walls and towers perched on a hill above Midan Salah ad-Din, the Citadel was home to most of those who ruled Egypt during a period of about 700 years, from the 12th to the 19th century.

Today the Citadel is a complex of three mosques and an assortment of museums plus a cafe or two. From Midan Salah ad-Din, walk east along Sharia Sikkat al-Maghar. The road leading to the entrance goes off to the right, about 100m past the intersection with Sharia Bab al-Wazir. You can also enter from Tariq Salah Salem, on the south side through Bab al-Muqattam.

Salah ad-Din began building the Citadel in 1176 to fortify the city against the Crusaders, and over the centuries it has been modified and enlarged with the palaces and buildings of subsequent rulers and governments.

Mohammed Ali, one of the last rulers to reside in the Citadel, actually levelled most of the buildings of the Mamluk period to build his own mosque and palace. And it was in a narrow rock-hewn passage near one of the Citadel's front gates that he sealed his control over Egypt with the massacre of the Mamluks.

On 1 March 1811 he treated the Mamluk leaders to a day of feasting and revelry, at the end of which they were escorted from the Citadel through a narrow lane. Mohammed Ali's troops sealed both ends of the passage, trapping all 470 dinner guests. Only one managed to escape; the rest were massacred from the wall above.

19th century artistic impression of the Citadel, home to the rulers of Egypt for about 700 years.

The Citadel is open daily from 8 am to 5 pm (winter) and 6 pm (summer), but the museums close at 4.30 pm. Admission is E£20. The main sights include:

Mosque of Mohammed Ali Also known as the Alabaster Mosque, this mosque and mausoleum was built by Mohammed Ali between 1830 and 1848. His gilt tomb is on the right as you enter. Although the interior is vast, it is badly decorated. The clock in the central court has never worked; it was given to Mohammed Ali by King Louis-Philippe of France in return for a Pharaonic obelisk from Luxor that still stands in the Place de la Concorde in Paris. The most spectacular features of the mosque are outside: its huge dome and half-domes and tall, slim minarets are very impressive.

Should you happen to turn up here inappropriately dressed (it's amazing how many people do), the mosque custodians will give you a flowing green robe to wear over your clothes. Try to refrain from tucking it up into your shorts as some tourists do!

Mosque of An-Nasir Built in 1318 by Sultan An-Nasir Mohammed, this mosque once featured marble panels on the floor and walls until the Ottoman ruler Selim I instructed his troops to strip the mosque of its marble. There's an admission fee of E£6.

Al-Gawhara Palace & Museum This palace was built in 1814 by Mohammed Ali, but after the 1952 Revolution it was used as a museum for the jewels of the khedives. In 1972 thieves attempted to make off with that valuable collection, and in doing so set part of the palace on fire. Today the museum contains a diorama of palace life.

National Police Museum This museum has an interesting collection of exhibits covering such subjects as 'the police struggle' and 'police in Islamic and Pharaonic times'. There is also an Assassination Room, where descriptions and photographs tell the stories of some of the nation's most sensational murders, including that of Sir Lee Stack and

the attempted assassination of President Nasser. However, Sadat, assassinated by Islamic radicals, fails to get a mention.

At the entrance to the police museum complex is the **Prison Museum**, consisting of two rows of stone cells with models of prisoners 'through the ages'. It's hardly riveting stuff, though the custodian tries to bring it to life by locking visitors in a cell and waiting for baksheesh before letting them out.

Northern Enclosure There is a handful of sights worth seeing in the Citadel's northern enclosure. The entrance to the enclosure, Bab al-Qullah, faces the north-east side of the Mosque of An-Nasir.

The **Military National Museum** contains exhibits detailing Egypt's military history, from Pharaonic times through the Graeco-Roman and Islamic periods to the present, as well as an extensive display on Egypt's modern conflicts with Israel. There's a E£1 photography fee.

Those with a yearning to dress up like royalty can try the **photo studio** near the military museum where you'll be decked out like a sultan and photographed (E£15).

From here, follow the road east to the **Carriage Museum** which contains a small but interesting collection of 19th century horse-drawn carriages and painted wooden horses.

Nearby, the new **Seized Museum** (signposted in Arabic only) houses sarcophagi, mummies, jewellery, Coptic icons, guns and a whole lot of other antiquities confiscated, some as recently as 1990, from smugglers.

The **archaeological garden** is neither a garden nor a museum, but it does have a collection of statues and pieces of monuments spread out among the park benches.

Joseph's Well A tower stands over Joseph's (or Yusef's) Well, which is on the south side of the Mosque of An-Nasir (but inaccessible at the time of writing). It is also called the Well of the Snail because of the spiral staircase leading 88m down a shaft to the level of the Nile. Yusef was one of Salah ad-Din's names. The well was named after him (not the biblical Joseph) because it was built in the 1180s by Crusaders who were imprisoned by him in the Citadel. The prisoners were attempting to escape, or at least ensure a secure water supply in the event of a siege.

Views Two viewing points on the western side of the Citadel offer fantastic panoramas of Cairo. One is round the back of the Mosque of Mohammed Ali, the other is in the grounds of the National Police Museum. From the edge of these parapets you'll see all of Islamic Cairo beneath you while, in the distance, rise the tall buildings of central Cairo and, sometimes, the Great Pyramids of Giza.

Getting to/from the Citadel There are several buses to various parts of the city from the small bus station next to Midan Salah ad-Din, or you can pick up one of the numerous other passing buses or minibuses. Bus No /174 from Midan Ramses passes the Citadel as does bus No /173 which starts and terminates at Midan Falaki. Bus No 905 operates between the Citadel and the pyramids. The No 404 from Midan Ataba passes the Citadel and goes on to Midan Tahrir. Bus Nos 57 and 951 go to Midan Ataba; the No 54 minibus goes to Midan Tahrir.

For more details on buses to the Citadel and Midan Salah ad-Din, see the Getting Around section later in this chapter.

You can now either catch one of the buses or a taxi out of here or continue to the next part of the walking tour.

From the Citadel to Al-Azhar This part of the walking tour takes you through one of Cairo's oldest and poorest districts. It is called Darb al-Ahmar, which means 'red road'.

An alternative to starting your exploration at the Citadel would be to do the tour in reverse, beginning at the Al-Azhar Mosque. The following section, which is written as if you are starting at the Citadel, describes some of the main sights.

Leave the Citadel by the main entrance

and go downhill along Sharia Sikkat al-Maghar, then take the first right into Sharia el-Mahgar which later becomes Sharia Bab al-Wazir (the Street of the Gate of the Vizier). About 400m up the street on the east side there is a unique mosque – the Mosque of Aqsunqur.

Mosque of Aqsunqur Also called the Blue Mosque, this was built in 1347 and then rebuilt in 1652 by a Turkish governor, Ibrahim Agha, who added the blue tiles on the walls. Agha imported the decorated tiles from Damascus, but apart from making the mosque unique in Egypt they do little for the aesthetics of the place.

Behind the mosque you can see part of Salah ad-Din's city walls, which run from north to south and have largely been covered with rubbish and tumbledown buildings.

Admission to the mosque costs E£6. It is open from about 9 am to 5 pm (6 pm in summer).

Maridani Mosque Continue walking up Sharia Bab al-Wazir another 350m as it becomes Sharia at-Tabbanah. The Maridani Mosque will be on your left. Built in 1339, the mosque is one of the oldest buildings in the area.

Several styles of architecture were used in its construction: eight granite columns were taken from a Pharaonic monument; the arches were made from Roman, Christian and Islamic designs; and the Ottomans added a fountain and wooden housing. There are several other decorative details inside. The lack of visitors, the trees in the courtyard and the detailed wood panelling make for a peaceful spot to stop. There is no official entry ticket, but someone will probably expect baksheesh.

Hammam Bashtak Before pursuing this walk north, you may want to double back a bit down Souq as-Silah to the only baths in Cairo open to women. The place is not in the least inviting, but it's the only choice women have. For E£15, you can have a massage and bath daily from 11 am to 5 pm (*hareem –*

women only). From 8 pm until 10 am the following day it opens to men. Men pay E£10.

Mosque of Qijmas al-Ishaqi The beautiful little Mosque of Qijmas al-Ishaqi is about 200m north of Maridani Mosque on Sharia Darb al-Ahmar (the continuation of Sharia at-Tabbanah). Qijmas was master of the sultan's horses and took charge of the annual pilgrimage to Mecca. His mosque is one of the best examples of architecture from the 15th century Burgi Mamluk period.

The plain exterior of the building is quite deceiving, as inside there are beautiful stained-glass windows, inlaid marble floors and stucco walls. The floor under the prayer mats in the eastern iwan is a fantastic marble mosaic.

Mosque of Salih Talai This small but intriguing building, 150m farther up on the left, is one of the best examples of the Fatimid style of architecture, with strangely shaped arches, classical columns and wooden beams. Ask the guard to show you up to the roof, as the views of the surrounding neighbourhood are great. The guard will expect some baksheesh.

Sharia Khayamiyya This is the Street of the Tentmakers, which intersects Sharia Darb al-Ahmar at the Mosque of Salih Talai. About 400m farther south, it becomes Sharia as-Surugiyyah, the Street of the Saddlemakers. Part of this thoroughfare is a wooden arcade that has stood for several centuries. Medieval apartments with mashrabiyyah screens on the windows jut out over the street. The tentmakers here make the appliqué panels used throughout Egypt on the ceremonial tents that are set up for funerals, wakes, weddings, holidays and other celebrations. This is also the best place to buy hand-sewn cushion covers and wall hangings.

Bab Zuweila Of the original 60 gates of the medieval city of Cairo, Bab Zuweila, built in 1092, is one of only three that remain. The other two, Bab an-Nasr and Bab al-Futuh, were built at about the same time, and even as recently as the late 19th century were used to close off the city. Bab Zuweila, the southern gate, was also often the site of public executions. The last Mamluk sultan, Tumanbay, was hanged here three times – he survived the first two attempts! You can climb up to the top of the gate through the adjoining Mosque of Sultan Mu'ayyad Sheikh.

Mosque of Sultan Mu'ayyad Sheikh This was built between 1416 and 1420 by the Burgi Mamluk Mu'ayyad Sheikh, a freed Circassian slave who eventually rose through the ranks of the Mamluks to become sultan of Egypt. Mu'ayyad had a drinking problem before becoming sultan, and his fellow Mamluks considered beatings and incarceration just therapy for such a weakness. Mu'ayyad was imprisoned on this site and vowed that one day he would replace the prison with a mosque. Although it's not a terribly impressive building there is a magnificent view of Cairo from its minaret, which is on top of Bab Zuweila, not the mosque.

If you climb the minaret, be careful on both the first set of stairs, where the wooden railing is very shaky, and on the second set, which is steep and very dark in parts. The guard will insist on giving you a tour and showing you the entrance to the minaret. This is not necessary, but be careful if you refuse his offers of assistance or don't give him baksheesh, you may find the door locked when you want to get back out.

The entrance fee is E£3 (E£1.50 for students) plus baksheesh.

Turkish Hammam In front of the Mosque of Sultan Mu'ayyad Sheikh there is a small door which leads to an old Turkish bathhouse (men only) which was closed at the time of writing. There is no sign – just head for the blue-tiled entrance.

Said Delta Papyrus Centre A little farther up on the same side of the street is one of the best places to buy your papyrus souvenirs, the Said Delta Papyrus Centre (☎ 512-0747). Said learnt his craft from the famed Dr Ragab, and some of his work is stunning. The shop is up on the 3rd floor. On the ground floor is a huge shoe shop. Most people who come here are led by someone, who Said claims gets a 40% commission. At any rate, the posted prices appear to be negotiable.

Abdel Harraz Spice & Herb Shop If you follow Sharia Ahmed Mahir west from Bab Zuweila you'll pass a variety of shops selling striped cotton and canvas before coming to this well-known spice shop which sells every imaginable herb, spice and exotic concoction. It's on the right side, one block before the Museum of Islamic Art.

Museum of Islamic Art With the treasures of the Pharaohs being the main objective of most tourists to Cairo, this museum, which has one of the world's finest collections of Islamic art, is rarely crowded. The museum, established in 1881, is on the north side of Midan Ahmed Mahir.

Some exhibits are arranged chronologically to show the influence of various eras, such as the Fatimid, Ayyubid or Mamluk periods, on Islamic art in Egypt; others are in special displays dealing with a particular subject. The latter include collections of textiles, glassware, calligraphy, tapestries and pottery from throughout the Islamic world.

The intricate woodwork in the collection of mashrabiyyah window screens is among the best you will see in Egypt. There is also one room of inlaid metalwork, another with a collection of superb Oriental carpets, an exhibit of medieval weapons and suits of armour, and a collection of magnificent illuminated books and ancient Qur'anic manuscripts.

The museum has been undergoing renovation and some sections may still be temporarily closed. Judging by the sign at the entry, this must have caused some public irritation in the past, as visitors are now reminded that 'your visit is up to you'. The

museum is open daily from 9 am to 4 pm but is closed on Friday from 11.30 am to 1.30 pm. Admission is E£8, or E£4 for students. Labelling is in Arabic, English and occasionally in French. There is a shady cafeteria in the grounds.

Back to the City Centre This is the end of the first walking tour through Islamic Cairo. You can return to Midan Tahrir by walking the 1.5 km west along Sharia Sami al-Barudi and its continuations, or north to Midan Ataba along Sharia al-Qala'a.

Walking Tour 2
The second walking tour around Islamic Cairo begins at the Al-Azhar Mosque and University. Once again, you'll need to set aside at least a day to cover all the sights on this tour.

Al-Azhar & Khan al-Khalili The first set of things to see is south of Al-Azhar Mosque, back towards Bab Zuweila.

Al-Azhar Mosque & University The oldest university in the world, and one of the first mosques, Al-Azhar was built in 970 AD for the study of Qur'anic law and doctrine.

There are more than 80,000 Islamic manuscripts in its libraries. While the basic curriculum in theology has changed very little since the time of the Mamluks, the university has expanded to cover subjects such as medicine and physics as well as foreign languages.

Courses in Islamic theology sometimes last as long as 15 years, and the traditional Socratic method of teaching with one tutor and a small group of students is still practised. Over 4000 students from all over the Islamic world receive free board and tuition and live all year on mats around the courtyard of the mosque. On the eastern side there is also a Chapel of the Blind, which accommodates blind students. Like many other buildings throughout the area, the university was badly shaken by the earthquake in 1992.

The university is open daily from about 9 am to 7 pm except on Friday, when it is closed from 11 am to 1 pm. This seems to be fairly flexible, and it seems quite possible to get in as late as 10 pm. Admission is E£12, and for a little extra the guard will show you up the minaret for a great view of the complex. Women must cover their heads with scarves.

Wakala of Al-Ghouri This ancient caravanserai, at 3 Sharia ash-Sheikh Mohammed Abdu, just around the corner from the Al-Azhar Mosque, is excellently preserved and now serves as a cultural centre. It was built in 1505 as a merchants' hotel. The merchants would sleep in rooms above where their animals were stabled, and business would be carried out in the courtyard around the fountain.

The courtyard now serves as a theatre and concert hall. The rooms have been converted into student ateliers; one houses a small permanent exhibition of peasant and Bedouin crafts, and workshops for teaching traditional crafts are held there. The *wakala* is open from 9 am to 8 pm daily except during Ramadan, when it's open from 9 to 11 am and 2 to 4 pm. The entrance fee is E£6.

Madrassa & Mausoleum of Al-Ghouri Opposite each other, at the intersection of Sharia al-Muizz li-Din Allah and Sharia al-Azhar, are two of the last great Mamluk structures built before the Ottomans took control of Egypt. Al-Ghouri, the penultimate Mamluk sultan, went all out to ensure that he left his architectural mark on the city. During his 16 years of rule he managed, quite well, to perpetuate the Mamluks' reputation for being thieves, murderers and tyrants. His madrassa, though elegant and peaceful, was apparently partly built from materials extorted or just simply stolen from other buildings.

Al-Ghouri, who was killed in a battle against the Turks near Aleppo in Syria when he was well into his 70s, is not entombed in his mausoleum. The body which is there is that of his successor, the almost-lucky Sultan Tumanbay, who was hanged three times

from Bab Zuweila before the rope held together long enough to kill him.

The madrassa and mosque complex, on the north-west corner, was badly jolted by the 1992 earthquake. The mausoleum is fronted by a sabil-kuttab and now serves as a youth and cultural centre. Inside the library is a beautifully carved dome. You can also see an enchanting display of the *raqs ash-sharqi*, or Sufi dancing, performed here every Wednesday and Saturday night (for details see the Entertainment section later in this chapter). The two buildings were once connected by awnings over the market street in-between and known collectively as the Ghouriyya.

House of Gamal ad-Din This restored upper class 16th century merchant's house is at 6 Sharia Khushqadam, which runs east off Sharia al-Muizz li-Din Allah, just south of Sharia al-Azhar. Enter through the mammoth wooden door and continue into the courtyard through the foyer, where horses used to be tied up, then call out for the guard, who will show you around. Don't miss the beautiful mashrabiyyah and stained-glass windows of the 'business room'. The house is open from 9 am to 5 pm, and admission is E£3, or E£1.50 for students.

Khan al-Khalili To reach this famous bazaar, return to Sharia al-Muizz li-Din Allah, turn right and walk north past the Madrassa of Al-Ghouri, then continue along Sharia al-Muizz li-Din Allah to Sharia al-Muski (also called Sharia Gahwar).

The Khan is one of the largest bazaars in the Middle East, if not the world. It stretches from Sharia al-Muski, between Sharia Port Said and Midan Hussein, up Sharia al-Muizz li-Din Allah and Sharia al-Gamaliyya, to the Mosque of Al-Hakim.

The bazaar began as a caravanserai built in 1382 by Garkas al-Khalili, who was Sultan Barquq's master of horses. When the Ottomans gained control of Egypt, the caravanserai changed from a fairly simple inn where caravans rested and a little trade was carried out to a fully fledged Turkish bazaar which attracted traders and customers from throughout the world.

Today the Khan is an immense conglomeration of markets and shops (many of which are closed on Sunday). As you wander through the labyrinth of narrow streets you'll find artisans building, dyeing, carving and sewing, as well as shop after shop selling all manner of things from woodwork, glassware, leather goods, perfumes and fabrics to souvenirs and Pharaonic curiosities.

Some parts of the Khan are tourist traps where anxious and aggressive shopkeepers try to get as much of your money as they can. These people are some of the greatest salespeople and smooth talkers you will ever meet. Almost anything can be bought in the Khan, and if one merchant doesn't have what you're looking for, then he'll find somebody who does. And remember, bargaining is the rule here.

After you've finished roaming through the bazaar, stop for refreshments at the famous Fishawi's teahouse, one of Cairo's oldest such establishments, a few steps off Midan Hussein.

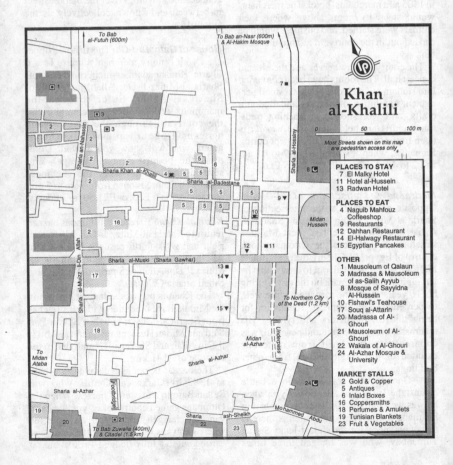

Khan al-Khalili

Most Streets shown on this map are pedestrian access only

PLACES TO STAY
7 El Malky Hotel
11 Hotel al-Hussein
13 Radwan Hotel

PLACES TO EAT
4 Naguib Mahfouz Coffeeshop
9 Restaurants
12 Dahhan Restaurant
14 El-Halwagy Restaurant
15 Egyptian Pancakes

OTHER
1 Mausoleum of Qalaun
3 Madrassa & Mausoleum of as-Salih Ayyub
8 Mosque of Sayyidna Al-Hussein
10 Fishawi's Teahouse
17 Souq al-Attarin
20 Madrassa of Al-Ghouri
21 Mausoleum of Al-Ghouri
22 Wakala of Al-Ghouri
24 Al-Azhar Mosque & University

MARKET STALLS
2 Gold & Copper
5 Antiques
6 Inlaid Boxes
16 Coppersmiths
18 Perfumes & Amulets
19 Tunisian Blankets
23 Fruit & Vegetables

To Bab al-Futuh (600m)
To Bab an-Nasr (600m) & Al-Hakim Mosque
Sharia an-Nahassin
Sharia Khan al-Khalili
Sharia al-Badestane
Sharia al-Hossiny
Midan Hussein
Sharia al-Muizz li-Din Allah
Sharia al-Muski (Sharia Gawhar)
To Northern City of the Dead (1.2 km)
Midan al-Azhar
Underpass
To Midan Ataba
Sharia al-Azhar
Sharia al-Azhar
Sharia ash-Sheikh
Mohammed Abdu
To Bab Zuwella (400m) & Citadel (1.5 km)

Should you want to head back to Midan Tahrir from here, get minibus No 77 or bus No 815.

From Al-Azhar to Bab an-Nasr The second set of sights takes you from the mosque to Bab an-Nasr.

Mosque of Sayyidna Al-Hussein On the northern side of Midan Hussein is one of the most sacred places of Muslim worship in Cairo (see the Sayyidna Al-Hussein boxed story for more details).

The mosque is supposedly only open to Muslims, and this seems to be the case for groups. Modestly dressed foreigners in ones and twos seem to have little trouble getting in outside prayer times. The best times to visit are during the moulid of Al-Hussein in the month of Rabei at-Tani or during Ramadan, when the breaking of the fast each evening is a major event. On both occasions, the square in front of the mosque comes alive with festive celebrations.

Souq al-Muski This bazaar stretches on both sides of Sharia al-Muski between Midan Hussein and Sharia Port Said, one block in and parallel to Sharia al-Azhar. Almost always jammed with a moving mass of people, this souq is where the locals shop for things like bolts of colourful cloth, plastic furniture, toys, spices and food. Although less exotic than Khan al-Khalili, it's still interesting to wander through.

Souq al-Attarin A true delight for all the senses is the Souq al-Attarin, or spice bazaar, where dried and crushed flowers and fruit add their aromas to those of saffron, cinnamon, ginger, pepper, cloves, and other exotic or easily recognisable spices. The bazaar is just off Sharia al-Muizz li-Din Allah, south of Sharia al-Muski.

Sharia al-Muizz li-Din Allah This street is the thoroughfare which runs all the way from Bab Zuweila to Bab al-Futuh. The section north of Khan al-Khalili is also known as Sharia an-Nahassin (Street of the Coppersmiths). During the times of the Fatimids and Mamluks, Sharia al-Muizz li-Din Allah was the major avenue through the heart of Cairo, and it was along this street that parades of

---

Sayyidna Al-Hussein

The Mosque of Sayyidna Al-Hussein is revered as the final resting place of the head of Al-Hussein, grandson of the Prophet. The area of Islamic Cairo from here north to the city gates is known as Al-Gamaliyya. In 1153, almost 500 years after his death, Al-Hussein's head was brought to Cairo in a green silk bag and placed in the Fatimid mosque that preceded this more modern 19th century structure, which was completed in 1878.

The powerful Omayyad family of Mecca, who were supported by the Prophet's favourite wife, had assumed control of the caliphate after Mohammed had died without naming a successor. As Islam began to spread and gain more power in the world, the tribal tensions over the rights of succession to the position of the Apostle of God also grew. Ali, who was the husband of Mohammed's daughter Fatima, put himself forward as the natural successor, claiming the right by marriage. When he was passed over he took up arms against the Omayyads, but was assassinated. His son, Al-Hussein, a blood relative of the Prophet, then led a revolt but was killed in battle.

Their deaths resulted in the schism which still exists in Islam today. The followers of Al-Hussein and Ali became the Shi'ites, or partisans of Ali, who refuse to acknowledge as caliph anyone but descendants of Mohammed, believing only someone of the Prophet's blood has the divine right to succession. However the Sunnis (followers of the Sunna, or 'the way') still have the power and the majority, and have banned any descendants of Mohammed from the caliphate for all time.

Despite being the mausoleum of a Shi'ite martyr, the shrine of Al-Hussein is one of the main congregational mosques in Cairo. Even the president of Sunni Egypt prays there on special religious holidays. ■

pilgrims marched on their return from Mecca. It is still easy to imagine how life may have been here several centuries ago. If you're into buying a *shisha* (waterpipe), head for this street.

Madrassa & Mausoleum of as-Salih Ayyub

The madrassa is just off Sharia al-Muizz li-Din Allah, on a small alley on the right about 125m north of Sharia al-Muski. The entrance is marked by an arch but there is not much left to see. The mausoleum can be entered by going back to Sharia al-Muizz li-Din Allah and turning right. The door, below the dome on your right, will probably be locked, but there will be someone around who can find the keeper, for the usual bit of baksheesh.

The madrassa and mausoleum were built in the 13th century by the last sultan of Salah ad-Din's Ayyubid dynasty. As-Salih Ayyub died before his complex was finished, so it was completed by his wife, Shagarat ad-Durr, who became one of Egypt's few female rulers (see the boxed story on Shagarat ad-Durr earlier in this chapter). During the following Mamluk period the complex became Cairo's central court. Executions were conveniently carried out just outside the doors, on Sharia al-Muizz li-Din Allah.

Mausoleum of Qalaun

There is a hospital, madrassa and mausoleum in this late 13th century complex opposite the Mausoleum of as-Salih Ayyub, however, at the time of writing the whole place was closed for renovation. Qalaun, one of the most successful Mamluk sultans and also one of the longest lived (1220 to 1290), founded a dynasty which lasted nearly a century.

A *maristan*, or hospital and psychiatric institution, has stood on this site for more than 700 years, but a modern facility has been built within the boundaries of the original. Sultans like Qalaun built the facilities that enabled enlightened care for the sick and insane. Hospitals and separate clinics were established, and even delicate surgery such as the removal of cataracts was performed here.

The interior of the mausoleum is beautifully decorated, especially near the entrance, and once your eyes become accustomed to the soft rainbow effect of sunlight through the stained-glass windows the tomb seems to be much larger than it is. Mashrabiyyah screens, inlaid stone and carved stucco add to the overall feeling of peace and tranquility that pervades the entire Qalaun complex. The entry fee is E£6.

Hammam as-Sultan Qalaun

Just off to the side from the hospital part of the Qalaun complex is a men-only hammam, also known as Hammam an-Nahassin, open from 9 am to 7 pm. A bath and massage costs you E£25, and you are bound to be invited to participate in 'extracurricular activities'.

Mausoleum of an-Nasir Mohammed

Except for the facade, doorway and courtyard, there is very little left of this 14th century tomb. It is just north of the Mausoleum of Qalaun, in Sharia al-Muizz li-Din Allah. It was one of several public works projects undertaken by Qalaun's son, an-Nasir Mohammed, who also built the Mosque of an-Nasir in the Citadel and the aqueduct from the Nile. His 40 year reign marked the pinnacle of Egyptian culture and prosperity under the Mamluks.

The Gothic doorway was taken from a church in Acre, which is in present-day Israel, when an-Nasir and his Mamluk army ended Crusader domination there in 1290. Not many people visit the mausoleum; an-Nasir is actually buried in his father's tomb next door. Opposite is a Turkish-era sabil.

House of Uthman Katkhuda

Katkhuda was an 18th century city official who built his house from a 14th century palace. His house is opposite the tomb of Qalaun, on a small street which runs east from Sharia al-Muizz li-Din Allah. The doorway is about halfway down on the left side and you either knock or go upstairs and ask for someone to show you around.

Despite Katkhuda's renovations the house is still a fine example of Mamluk domestic architecture, and what's left of the decor of the spacious interior shows the influences of both the 14th and 18th centuries.

Mosque of Barquq This mosque is just north of the Mausoleum of an-Nasir Moham-med, in Sharia al-Muizz li-Din Allah. Barquq, the first Burgi Mamluk sultan, came to power like most of the Mamluks through a series of plots and murders. His beautifully restored mosque, with its black and white marble entrance way and silver-inlaid bronze door, was built in 1386 as a madrassa.

The colourful ceiling over part of the inner courtyard is supported by four Pharaonic columns made of porphyry quarried from near the Red Sea coast. Barquq's daughter is buried in the splendid domed tomb chamber while the sultan himself rests in his mauso-leum in the northern City of the Dead. Admission is E£3, half for students. For the usual consideration, you can go up to the top of the minaret, but you may want to think twice as it was visibly damaged during the 1992 earthquake.

Hammam as-Sultan This seems a slightly better bathhouse than the one just down the road. It's open 24 hours a day and also costs E£15. The entrance is marked by an old sign engraved in stone. The doorway is directly opposite a shop signposted 'Saad al-Khawanky', just north of the Mosque of Barquq.

Qasr Beshtak Only a small part of this splendid 14th century palace remains. It's on Sharia al-Muizz li-Din Allah, just north of the Mosque of Barquq on the east side (though the entry is round the back on a side street), and was built on the foundations of an earlier Fatimid palace. The Emir Beshtak was a very wealthy man who was married to the daughter of Sultan an-Nasir. When he built this palace in 1334 it had five storeys, each with running water. Climb up on to the roof for a beautiful view south along Sharia al-Muizz li-Din Allah.

Sabil-Kuttab of Abdul Katkhuda Also on Sharia al-Muizz li-Din Allah, where the street forks, is a sabil-kuttab built in 1744 by Uthman Katkhuda's son, Abdul. The porches of the kuttab overhang the street on both sides of the fork. The kuttab is still used as a local school. The remains of the great sabil are underneath (note the exquisite Turkish ceramic work inside the fountain) and behind the kuttab is a 14th century apartment building.

Bayt as-Suhaymi This superb merchant's house, built in the 16th and 17th centuries, is one of Cairo's greatest houses, however, at the time of writing it was closed for much needed restoration. To find it, turn right on Sharia Darb al-Asfar, which runs east off Sharia al-Muizz li-Din Allah. It's at No 19, on the left. Mashrabiyyah screens, lattice windows, beautiful tiling and arched galler-ies abound, and overall it has a peaceful and elegant atmosphere that invites you to linger as long as possible.

Bab al-Futuh One of the original 60 gates of medieval Cairo, Bab al-Futuh (the Gate of Conquests) is at the end of Sharia al-Muizz li-Din Allah. Built in 1087, thousands of pilgrims have passed through it upon their return from Mecca. Of the three remaining gates of Cairo, Bab al-Futuh has the most interesting interior. Wide stone stairs lead to a large room with a high ceiling. Various additions and alterations have been made to the gate, including some by Napoleon, which also explains the names carved into the stone of two of the wall's towers, the Tour Junot and the Tour Perrault.

There are narrow slits, just wide enough for arrows, cut in the sides of the room, and along the tunnel which leads to Bab an-Nasr. Soldiers were once housed in this tunnel while awaiting their next battle.

There's a wonderful view of the Fatimid wall, Bab an-Nasr, and the minarets of the Mosque of Al-Hakim. You can walk along the wall linking the two gates with the roof and one of the minarets of the mosque. Admission is E£6. The caretaker usually sits in the teahouse opposite the gate.

CAIRO

Mosque of Al-Hakim The haunting mosque of the ruthless and paranoid Al-Hakim (see the boxed story on Al-Hakim, following) has rarely been used as a place of worship. Completed in 1010, it has been used as a prison for Crusaders, as one of Salah ad-Din's stables, and as a warehouse by Napoleon. The building has been largely repaired by members of the Ismaili sect of Shi'ite Islam, who claim the Fatimids as their religious ancestors and the Aga Khan as their spiritual leader. Admission is E£6.

At this point, it may be convenient for some to return to Midan Hussein. If so, it might be an idea to follow Sharia al-Gamaliyya down from Bab an-Nasr. While not the enchanting excursion into Medieval Cairo that is Sharia al-Muizz li-Din Allah, it is a bustling hive of activity, with a smattering of remnants of Cairo's crowded past.

Bab an-Nasr Still attached to Bab al-Futuh by a tunnel inside the old wall, this is the Gate of Victory. Look for the hole over the entrance. Boiling oil was poured through this aperture to discourage unwelcome visitors from entering the city. Wandering through the passageways between the gates is quite an eerie experience. Climb the stairs to the roof and the minaret of the adjoining Mosque of Al-Hakim. Outside the gate and walls you can see part of the northern City of the Dead, with its tombs stretching for several km across the horizon.

Musafirkhanah As you're heading back to al-Azhar on the way down Sharia al-Gamaliyya, of particular interest is this Ottoman palace, whose name loosely translates to 'travellers' caravanserai'. Although restoration, which began in 1986, was set back by the 1992 earthquake, this lavish guesthouse is a gem. It's a little south of the Mosque of Baybars II in a side street called Darb at-Tablawi (if you come from Al-Azhar, it's pretty clearly signposted) and was built between 1779 and 1788 by a wealthy merchant from Al-Faiyum, Mahmoud Muharram. It was later bought by Ibrahim, the son and short-lived successor of Egypt's

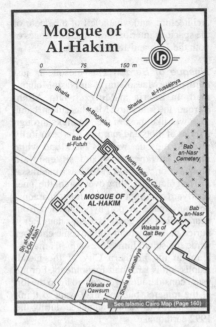

independent-minded 19th century ruler, Mohammed Ali. A later successor, Ismail, was born here.

The central attraction is what is claimed to be the biggest mashrabiyyah in the world, jutting out from the *haramlik* (women's quarters) above a courtyard and garden where the royal family enjoyed plenty of dancing and festivities – so the women of the house could watch, but not join in the fun. The male equivalent of the haramlik, the *selamlik*, is the first main room in the building to the left when you enter. You can also see a couple of private bath and sauna rooms – the coloured glass in the roof is original, as is most of the exquisite, carved mahogany used in the ceilings and the stained glass. This place is often overlooked, but well worth a detour. Admission is E£6 and opening hours are flexible.

City of the Dead
The City of the Dead, or Northern Cemetery,

is a vast Mamluk necropolis inhabited by hundreds of thousands of Cairenes, both dead and alive. The dead are still buried there in tombs which date from the 12th century, while the living exist in what amounts to little more than a huge shanty town among the impressive marble tombs of Mamluk sultans and nobles.

On Friday and holidays visitors flock here to picnic and pay their respects to the dead. Sometimes you can see an entire Egyptian family feasting on top of a tomb. When wandering around this area, you often have to remind yourself that you are indeed in a cemetery.

The City of the Dead begins outside and to the right of Bab an-Nasr and Bab al-Futuh, and stretches away to the north and also around to the east – it's actually the eastern part most people want to visit. As you leave Bab an-Nasr turn right down Sharia Galal and walk about half a km east; cross Sharia Mansuriyya and dogleg to your left and right before continuing down to the multilane highway, Tariq Salah Salem. When you cross this, you're in the cemetery. Head in and turn right at the first main tomb you see – the Mausoleum of Barquq is then a couple of hundred metres down to the right and left. Ask anyone for Barquq if you feel lost.

Mausoleum of Barquq You will be able to see the minarets of this mausoleum, 1.5 km from Bab an-Nasr, long before you cross into the City of the Dead. From the outside the effect of its domes is reduced by the surrounding architecture but the interior of these high vaulted structures is quite splendid. The building was completed in 1411 and the tomb chambers contain the bodies of Barquq, who was moved from his mosque, his sons and the women of the family. Don't miss the beautiful marble *minbar*, or pulpit. For a little baksheesh the caretaker will take you up the northern minaret; there is a magnificent view of the necropolis. It's open from 8 am to 5 pm; admission is E£6.

Mosque & Mausoleum of Sultan Barsbey
The interior of the decorated dome and the mosaics on the floor and minbar are the highlights of this edifice, which was completed in 1432. It is 50m down the road from the Tomb of Barquq and contains several other tombs, including one of Amir Ganibak al-Ashrafi, whom Barsbey bought as a boy. He stayed loyal to his master, even joining him for a stint in jail, and was rewarded later when Barsbey became sultan by being made an emir. Keep an eye open for the wooden minbar in the mosque, which is the first building you enter. Look for the guard or have one of the children in the area find him;

𓂋𓂋𓂋𓂋𓂋𓂋𓂋𓂋𓂋𓂋𓂋𓂋𓂋𓂋

Al-Hakim

Al-Hakim was the third of the Fatimid caliphs, who ruled with absolute political, religious and military authority. His name means 'he who rules at the command of God', which was something he professed to do, with complete disregard for anyone but himself, so that he's ranked close to the infamous Caligula in the dreadful treatment of his subjects.

At the age of 15, Al-Hakim murdered his tutor. He then decided he didn't like his advisers any more so he murdered them too. He loved the night and took to riding after dark on Moon, his pet mule, so it became illegal and punishable by death to work during the day and sleep at night.

Al-Hakim also hated merchants who cheated their customers, and women. He tried to impose a 24 hour curfew on them, and when that didn't work he imposed a ban on the manufacture of women's shoes. He figured that without shoes women would not want to plod through the manure and open sewers on the streets. He also restricted the free movement of Jews and Christians, and incited riots which resulted in huge sections of the city being burnt.

On one of his nightly jaunts on Moon, he headed into the Moqattam Hills, where he often went looking for portents from the stars, and was never seen again. Some believe he was murdered by his sister, whom it is said he planned to marry. The Copts believe he had a visitation from Christ, while others, later to become the Druse, believed he was a divine incarnation. Although the Druse still exist in Lebanon, Syria, Jordan and Israel, very little is known of their beliefs and practices, as it is blasphemous for the Druse to reveal their people's secrets to outsiders. ■

𓂋𓂋𓂋𓂋𓂋𓂋𓂋𓂋𓂋𓂋𓂋𓂋𓂋𓂋

he'll let you in for E£1 of baksheesh –
although he'll probably start higher and
insist it's for a 'ticket'. It's generally open
from 9 am to 5 pm.

Mausoleum of Qait Bey Completed in 1474
and rated as one of the greatest buildings in
Cairo, Qait Bey's tomb is also featured on
the E£1 note. The exquisite dome and the
finely tapered minaret, with its three intricately decorated tiers (you can climb to the
second level), stand out among the mausoleums in the area. The splendid, refined
interior is equally beautiful.

Sultan Qait Bey, a prolific builder, was the
last Mamluk leader with any real power in
Egypt. He ruled for 28 years and, though he
was as ruthless as the Mamluk sultans before
him, he had a reputation for fairness. He also
had a great love of beautiful architecture.
The tomb contains the cenotaphs of Qait Bey
and his two sisters, as well as two stones
which supposedly bear the footprints of the
Prophet. Admission is E£3 (E£1.50 for students).

Back to the City Centre From the Mausoleum of Qait Bey you could walk back to
Midan Hussein (about 1.5 km). Cross Tariq
Salah Salem and head for the Ad-Darasa bus
stop (use the footbridge over the highway as
a landmark). From here just continue down
the highway until you come to the turn-off
on the right which leads down the hill to
Islamic Cairo. Or you can get bus No 65,
which will take you to Midan Ataba via
Midan Hussein, and then on to Midan
Ramses. To Midan Tahrir, you can get
minibus No 77 or bus No 905 (the latter
continues on to the pyramids).

If you're heading up to Heliopolis, the
easiest way from the mausoleum is to take
the tram to Midan Triomphe from the station
next to the Ad-Darasa bus stop.

RODA ISLAND
Roda Island is south of Gezira. In the 13th
century, Sultan as-Salih Ayyub built an
immense fortress here for his army of
Mamluks. The fortress had barracks,

palaces, mosques and more than 50 towers.
Various sultans used the facilities until the
18th century, by which time other, stronger
fortresses in Egypt had replaced this one.
Today the island is home to an eclectic palace
built in the early 20th century, the Nilometer,
a couple of pleasant riverside restaurants and
several thousand Cairene apartment dwell-
ers.

Manyal Palace Museum
The Manyal Palace Museum is on your left
after you take Sharia Ali Ibrahim across the
canal to Roda Island. (See the Garden City
map.)

It was built in the early part of this century
as a residence for Prince Mohammed Ali
Tawfiq. The government converted it into a
museum in 1955. Apparently the prince
couldn't decide which architectural style he
preferred for the palace, so each of the five
main buildings is different. Indeed, the first
of them, known now as the Reception Palace
(which you enter on your right just inside the
main entrance – you have to buy a ticket first
at a booth farther inside the grounds), is itself
a combination of several. The ceramics and
some of the ceiling woodwork is exquisite.
The styles include Persian, Syrian, Moorish
and Ottoman.

After you enter the palace grounds, walk
along the path on the right to the **Mosque of
Mohammed Ali** and the **hunting museum**
of the royal family. The hunting museum was
added to the complex in 1962 to house King
Farouk's huge collection of stuffed animal
trophies. This is not a place for animal lovers.

Return to the path leading from the palace
entrance and follow it to the other buildings.

Residence Palace Each room is ornately
decorated with hand-painted geometric
shapes – a traditional design in Islamic art.
Several of the doors are inlaid with carved
pieces of ivory, and the windows feature
intricate mashrabiyyah screens.

The largest building contains Mohammed
Ali's fascinating collection of manuscripts,
clothing, silver objects, furniture, writing
implements and other items dating from

medieval times to the 19th century. A self-appointed guide likes to show you around this part of the museum, object by object. If you don't want his services let him know.

The palace is open daily from 9 am to 4 pm, and admission is E£5, or E£2.50 for students. Photography permits are E£10; video shooting costs E£150.

Nilometer

This interesting ancient monument is on the southern tip of Roda Island (see the Greater Cairo map). Built in the 9th century to measure the rise and fall of the Nile, it helped predict the state of the annual harvest. If the Nile rose to 16 cubits, approximately equal to the length of a forearm, this would hold great promise for the crops, and the people would celebrate.

The conical dome was added when the Nilometer was restored in the 19th century. The measuring device, a graduated column, is well below the level of the Nile in a paved area at the bottom of a flight of steps. The admission fee is E£6. Access is down the east side of the island.

OLD CAIRO

Broadly speaking, Old Cairo incorporates the whole area south of Garden City and Sayyida Zeinab down to the quarter known to foreigners as Coptic Cairo. Most people visiting this area head straight to the latter, from where you can explore sights farther north-east such as the Mosque of Amr Ibn al-Aas and the ancient Fustat site.

This is a very traditional part of Cairo and appropriate dress is essential. Visitors of either sex wearing shorts or having bare shoulders will not be allowed into churches or mosques. And, unlike in a few places in Islamic Cairo where cloaks are handed out to those who carelessly rock up in little more than beach attire, here there are no such concessions.

Coptic Cairo

Originally a Roman fortress town called Babylon, this part of Cairo was of great importance to the early Christians. Egypt was one of the first countries to embrace the new Christian faith in the 1st century AD. The fortress was built about 900 years before the Fatimids founded Cairo, on a then-strategic point on the Nile. The river has since shifted its course about 400m west.

The development of Coptic Christianity, and the monastic tradition it adopted after Paul of Thebes chose a life of solitude in the Egyptian desert, greatly influenced early European Christianity. But for Egypt the Christian period was merely one of transition from Pharaonic times to the Islamic era. During the several centuries that Christianity did predominate in Egypt, this town, only five km south of where the Muslims would later build their city, became quite a metropolis. It was considered a holy place not only by the Copts but by the Jews and later the Muslims who lived in the area. At one time there were 20 churches and a synagogue there. The Christian monuments that have survived the centuries are still very important to the Copts. There are also several mosques in the area, and Cairo's small Jewish population still worships at the ancient synagogue.

Many visitors find Coptic Cairo to be a haven of serenity, especially after experiencing Islamic and central Cairo. You can sip a coffee under a shady tree at the teahouse at the junction with the road to Fustat, or simply meander around the quarter's cobbled alleys and shaded courtyards.

Fortress of Babylon The main remaining part of the fortress, built in 98 AD by Emperor Trajan, is a tower that was part of the waterside Roman battlements. The tower originally overlooked an important port on the Nile before the river shifted course, and excavations directly below the tower have revealed part of the ancient quay, several metres below street level.

Coptic Museum The fortress' tower now marks the entrance to the tranquil courtyards and lush, verdant gardens of the Coptic Museum. The museum building is paved with mosaics and decorated with elegant mashrabiyyah screens from old Coptic houses. Its exhibits cover Egypt's Christian era from 300 to 1000 AD, demonstrating the Pharaonic, Graeco-Roman and Islamic influences on the artistic development of the Copts. It is the world's finest collection of Coptic religious and secular art. The icons and textiles on the 1st floor are particularly interesting, and there are also splendid examples of stonework, manuscripts, woodwork, metalwork, glass, paintings and pottery. Explanations are in French and English.

The 1992 earthquake badly damaged the south side of the museum, which takes in some excavated remains of the old fortress. That part of the museum is closed for repairs.

The museum is open from 9 am to 4 pm from Sunday to Thursday, and from 9 to noon and 1 to 4 pm on Friday. Admission is E£8, or E£4 for students; the camera fee is E£10 (videos are not allowed).

Al-Muallaqa Church Dubbed the Hanging Church, this is one of the oldest Christian places of worship in Egypt. It was built on top of one of the old fortress gatehouses with its nave suspended over the passage. Dedicated to the Virgin Mary and properly known as Sitt Mariam, or St Mary, it is also one of Cairo's most beautiful churches.

Just inside the entrance, through a doorway in the walls just south of the Coptic Museum, there is an interesting 10th century icon of the Virgin and Child. The inner courtyard is adorned with icons and the interior of the church, renovated many times over the centuries, is quite beautiful. In the centre, standing on 13 slender pillars that represent Christ and his disciples, is a fine pulpit which is used only on Palm Sunday every year. One of the pillars is darker than the rest, symbolising Judas.

There is no admission fee because the church is still in use. Coptic Mass is held on Friday from 8 to 11 am and on Sunday from 7 to 10 am. The ancient liturgical Coptic language is still used in most of the services.

Monastery & Church of St George This church is one of the few remaining circular

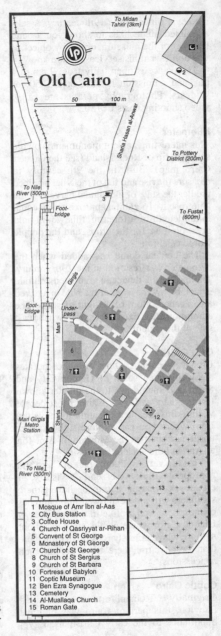

Old Cairo

0   50   100 m

To Midan Tahrir (3km)
To Pottery District (200m)
To Nile River (500m)
To Fustat (600m)
Sharia Hasan al-Anwar
Footbridge
Girgis
Mari
Footbridge
Underpass
Sharia
Mari Girgis Metro Station
To Nile River (300m)

1 Mosque of Amr Ibn al-Aas
2 City Bus Station
3 Coffee House
4 Church of Qasriyyat ar-Rihan
5 Convent of St George
6 Monastery of St George
7 Church of St George
8 Church of St Sergius
9 Church of St Barbara
10 Fortress of Babylon
11 Coptic Museum
12 Ben Ezra Synagogue
13 Cemetery
14 Al-Muallaqa Church
15 Roman Gate

ones left in the Middle East. The interior is a bit gutted from past fires, but the stained-glass windows are bright and colourful. The monastery next door is closed to the public, but it can sometimes be entered if you ask permission at the church or monastery.

Convent of St George This is an especially interesting place to visit because of a rather strange ritual that is practised here. To get there take the underground passage about 25m north of the Monastery of St George, on the right. On the other side you'll see a wooden door to your left leading to the court-yard of the Convent of St George.

On the left side is a chapel. Remove your shoes before entering. Inside is a beautiful, wooden door, almost eight metres high, behind which is a small room still used for the chain-wrapping ritual. The chains are symbolic of the persecution of St George during the Roman occupation. Visitors wishing to be blessed are welcome to be wrapped – a nun oversees the procedure and says the requisite prayers while standing next to an icon more than 1000 years old.

Church of St Sergius To get to St Sergius, also called Abu Serga, leave the Convent of St George by the same door you entered, turn left and walk down the lane to the end. Pass under the low archway on the right and enter the church on the left side.

This is supposedly the oldest church in Egypt, built on one of the places where the Holy Family rested after fleeing from King Herod. Every year, on 1 June, a special mass is held here to commemorate the event. At the turn of the century this little church, which dates from the 10th century, was the most important pilgrimage spot in Old Cairo for visiting Christian tourists. There are 24 marble columns lining the central court, and a series of 12th century icons above an ico-nostasis (a partition screen bearing icons) depicting the 12 apostles. It's open from 9 am to 4 pm.

Church of St Barbara Farther down the alley is the Church of St Barbara, which is

similar to the Church of St Sergius. It is dedicated to the saint, who was beaten to death by her father for trying to convert him to Christianity and was restored during the Fatimid era. St Barbara's relics supposedly rest in a small chapel to the left of the nave, and the remains of St Catherine, after whom the famous monastery in the Sinai was named, are also said to rest here.

Should you wish to wander around Coptic Cairo's large cemetery, you can enter it from near here – it's up the stairs through the iron gate at the end of the lane next to St Barbara's Church.

Ben Ezra Synagogue This synagogue, one of the oldest in Egypt, is a few metres south of the Church of St Barbara. Turn left when leaving the church and enter the first gate on your left, marked by a Star of David. Although there is no rabbi, and services are rarely held, it is used by the 40 or so Jewish families that reside in the area.

Set in a shady garden, it was built on the site of a 4th century Christian church, which the Copts had to sell in the 9th century to enable them to pay taxes to Ibn Tulun for the construction of his mosque. The synagogue, named after a 12th century Rabbi of Jerusa-lem, Abraham ben Ezra, was severely damaged by Arabs after the 1967 war with Israel, but it has been almost completely renovated.

There are also many legends about the synagogue. It is said that the temple of the prophet Jeremiah once stood on the same spot and that Jeremiah is actually buried under a miracle rock in the grounds. There is also a spring which is supposed to mark the place where the Pharaoh's daughter found Moses in the reeds, and where Mary drew water to wash Jesus.

Getting There & Away Coptic Cairo is 5.5 km south of central Cairo. To get there you can take either a bus, a taxi – ask for Masr al-Qadima – or the metro (get off at Mari Girgis station, which is above ground); the metro only costs 30 pt from Midan Tahrir and is by far the easiest way to get there.

Several buses run past Midan Tahrir on their way to the terminus by the Mosque of Amr – Nos 135 and 814 among them. Bus Nos 444 and 412 run along the Corniche to Midan Tahrir, and No /134 heads up to Midan Ramses.

The slow way, but perhaps more pleasant if you have the time, is to get a water bus (every 15 minutes) from near the Radio & Television building, just north of the Nile Hilton. Ask for the Masr al-Qadima water bus and make sure it's going all the way to the terminus, as many only do a few stops. It takes about 50 minutes and costs 25 pt (the last one back to Maspero from Coptic Cairo leaves at 4.15 pm). From the landing head straight in from the river and veer left. You'll soon see the metro station, and there's a bridge over the tracks just to the north of it.

Fustat

This was where Cairo first rose as a city. To get there from Coptic Cairo, head north along Sharia Mari Girgis, take the first road to the right, follow it for about 400m and then go left along a short lane to the Fustat site.

The site has been excavated by an archaeological team from the American University in Cairo. Although the remains are scanty, you can make out traces of alleyways, houses, wells and water-pipe systems surrounded by a low wall. Part of the original wall of Cairo has also been restored here. It costs E£6 to visit the site.

Fustat started out in about 640 AD as a tent city, a garrison town for the conquering Muslim army. It became the first Islamic capital in Egypt and for three centuries it continued to grow and prosper. At the height of its glory, before the conquering Fatimids founded the neighbouring city of Cairo in 969 AD, Fustat had a water supply, sewerage and sanitation facilities far superior to anything that was known in Europe before the 18th century.

The city was destroyed and abandoned in 1168 to prevent it falling into the hands of the invading Crusader, King Amalric of Jerusalem.

Mosque of Amr Ibn al-Aas

This mosque is a few blocks north of the Fortress of Babylon but it isn't all that interesting. The original mosque, of which nothing remains, was the first place of Muslim worship built in Egypt. It was constructed in 642 AD by the victorious invader Amr, the general who is said to have founded Fustat on the site where he had pitched his tent. However, according to Coptic history books, the mosque was built over the ruins of a Coptic church. There couldn't have been much left of those ruins, as the first structure is said to have been made of palm branches and leaves. The site witnessed a series of replacements as the mosque was rebuilt and extended several times under the Omayyad and Abbassid dynasties. The core of the present mosque structure probably dates back to 827, although much of the mosque has been restored quite recently. Admission is E£6.

Pottery District

Behind the mosque, nestled beneath smouldering mounds that are actually workshop roofs and kilns, is a community of potters. You can wander around and watch them make and fire pottery vessels and utensils.

GIZA

The Giza district begins on the west bank of the Nile opposite Roda Island, and stretches 18 km westward to the Great Pyramids. Most of the things of interest are either near the Nile or at the western end of Pyramids Rd.

Information

As you follow the road up, you'll pass the tourist office off to the left, where you can check on the official rates for horse and camel rides (about E£12 per hour, or E£36 per person for the ride to Saqqara). However, it's not uncommon for prices to be higher or lower. The tourist office is open daily from 8.30 am to 5 pm. If anyone around here starts steering you into the unmistakable stench of a stable, backtrack fast – ignore all the jabbering about them being able to get you into the pyramids area without a ticket.

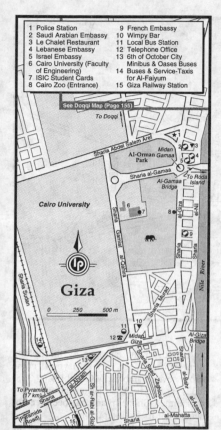

The other entrance to the pyramids is by the Sphinx; the ticket office there is near the Cheops Pavilion. Most people seem to exit this way. The road down to it is off to the left (facing west), just before the turn-off for the Desert Highway.

Should you need them, the tourist police have a small office near the entrance to the Pyramid of Cheops.

There's an admission fee of E£20 for the site and the same again to enter the Great Pyramid of Cheops. Tickets must be bought at the entrance to the site. Admission to the Solar Barque Museum is yet another E£10

(plus E£10/100 for cameras/videos); tickets are sold at the museum itself. The pyramids are open from 8.30 am to 4 pm, but the site itself is open from about 7 am to 7.30 pm. The Solar Barque Museum is open from 9 am to 4 pm (5 pm in summer). The best times to visit are at sunrise, sunset and night. During the day it can get very hot and crowded, and the hazy sky makes it difficult to take good photographs.

Pyramids Road

The road to the pyramids was built in the 1860s so that Empress Eugénie could travel the 11 km from Cairo in her carriage. The road was another in a long list of public works projects initiated by Khedive Ismail. However, it wasn't paved until US President Jimmy Carter visited the pyramids. The khedive also had a palace (now the Cairo Marriott) built for the empress, so that she would have a place to stay while attending the ceremonies for the opening of the Suez Canal.

Pyramids Rd is also known as Sharia al-Ahram, but invariably called Sharia al-Haram by the locals (*haram* means pyramid; *ahram* is the plural, which nobody ever seems to say or even fully understand). It starts near Midan Giza, about 500m south of Cairo Zoo.

Great Pyramids of Giza

The ancient Greeks considered the Great Pyramids to be one of the Seven Wonders of the World. They are Egypt's most visited monuments, and among the world's greatest tourist attractions. For centuries the Great Pyramids of Giza have intrigued and puzzled visitors and, even in the 20th century, it is difficult to stand before them and not be overwhelmed. For 4½ millennia, surviving the rise and fall of great dynasties and outlasting Egypt's many conquerors, they have shared the desert plateau of Giza with other monuments: smaller attendant pyramids, some for royal wives; rows of mastabas, the tombs of 4th and 5th dynasty princes and nobles; and the imposing figure of the Sphinx.

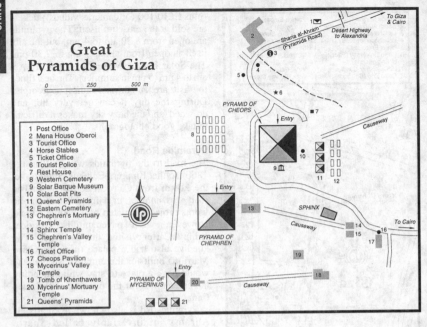

Great Pyramids of Giza

0   250   500 m

1 Post Office
2 Mena House Oberoi
3 Tourist Office
4 Horse Stables
5 Ticket Office
6 Tourist Police
7 Rest House
8 Western Cemetery
9 Solar Barque Museum
10 Solar Boat Pits
11 Queens' Pyramids
12 Eastern Cemetery
13 Chephren's Mortuary Temple
14 Sphinx Temple
15 Chephren's Valley Temple
16 Ticket Office
17 Cheops Pavilion
18 Mycerinus' Valley Temple
19 Tomb of Khenthawes
20 Mycerinus' Mortuary Temple
21 Queens' Pyramids

Getting Around Every visit to the Great Pyramids includes a stroll, or sometimes a run, through a veritable obstacle course of hustlers, souvenir shops, alabaster factories, papyrus museums and self-appointed, and usually unwanted, guides. A common tactic they employ is to pretend, with all the pompous officious bombast they can muster, to be employees demanding to see your tickets – don't give them to these people whatever you do – the real ticket inspectors near the ticket booth are a much friendlier, more laid-back bunch, because they don't want anything from you. Above all, try not to despair; escape from this maddening onslaught is possible.

The best strategy is just to ignore them, although this is not always easy. An alternative is to hire a horse or camel and gallop, glide, or jolt through the desert around the pyramids. There are stables near the tourist office on Pyramids Rd but the animals here are often not in very good condition. If you

head south of the entrance by the Sphinx (turn right on your way out) you'll come across several stables. MG stables (☎ 358-3832) on Sharia Abu el-Houl is owned by Mohammed Ghoneim and has been recommended for its well-kept horses.

You can also try approaching one of the many camel and horse owners around the pyramids. Some people would suggest avoiding these people altogether. If you are burning to get on one of these critters and do not have the time to explore the stables south of the Sphinx, bargain fiercely and be sure of what you have agreed on. Stories abound of people getting on to their mounts and being led around for all sorts of unwanted extras and then being charged accordingly. Not a few people have found themselves paying ridiculous amounts of money to be let *off* camels. *Don't* hand your camera over to these people for that shot of you on the camel or there's a good chance you'll have to pay to get your camera back! A horse or camel should not cost more than E£12 an hour. If, at the end of your ride, you find yourself in an unresolvable dispute, enlist the aid of the tourist police. Women should take care, as the animal owners are not beyond trying to exploit a position of power.

The best time to go for a ride is at sunset, ending at the Cheops Pavilion just as the sound & light show illuminates the pyramids and the Sphinx.

Great Pyramid of Cheops This great pyramid, the oldest at Giza and the largest in Egypt, stood 146.5m high when it was completed around 2600 BC. After 46 centuries its height has been reduced by only nine metres. Approximately 2½ million limestone blocks, weighing around six million tonnes, were used in the construction. It supposedly took 10 years to build the causeway and the massive earth ramps used as a form of scaffolding, and 20 years to raise the pyramid itself. The job was done by a highly skilled corps of masons, mathematicians, surveyors and stonecutters as well as about 100,000 slaves who carried out the back-breaking task of moving and laying the stones. The blocks had to be exactly placed to prevent excess pressure building up on any one point and causing the collapse of the whole structure.

Although there is not much to see inside the pyramid, the experience of climbing through such an ancient structure is unforgettable. The entrance, on the north face, leads to a descending passage which ends in an unfinished tomb (usually closed) about 100m along and 30m below the pyramid. About 20m from the entrance, however, there is an ascending passage, 1.3m high and one metre wide, which continues for about 40m before opening into the Great Gallery, which is 47m long and 8.5m high. There is also a smaller horizontal passage leading into the so-called Queen's Chamber.

As you ascend the Great Gallery to the King's Chamber at the top notice how precisely the blocks were fitted together. Unlike the rest of the pyramid, the main tomb chamber, which is just over five metres wide

and 10m long, was built of red granite blocks. The roof, which weighs more than 400 tonnes, consists of nine huge slabs of granite, above which are another four slabs separated by gaps designed to distribute the enormous weight away from the chamber. There is plenty of air in this room, as it was built so that fresh air flowed in from two shafts on the north and south walls. Entry costs E£20.

Climbing the outside of the Great Pyramid was, for centuries, a popular adventure despite the fact that every year a few people fell to their death. Scaling the pyramid is now forbidden. Don't be tempted by 'guides' who may want to show you the way; there is a strong school of thought that suggests it does nothing for the pyramids themselves.

On the eastern side of the pyramid are the Queens' Pyramids, three small structures about 20m high, which resemble little more than pyramid-shaped piles of rubble. They were the tombs of Cheops' wives and sisters.

Solar Barque Museum Along the eastern and southern sides of the Pyramid of Cheops are five long pits which once contained the Pharaoh's boats. These solar barques may have been used to bring the mummy of the dead Pharaoh across the Nile to the valley temple, from where it was brought up the causeway and placed in the tomb chamber. The boats were then buried around the pyramid to provide transport for the king in the next world.

One of these ancient wooden vessels, possibly the oldest boat in existence, was unearthed in 1954. It was restored and a glass museum built over it to protect it from damage from the elements. For the same reason, visitors to the museum must don protective footwear in order to keep sand out.

The barque is 43m long and eight metres high and sits in a five-metre-deep pit. Entry costs E£10 (plus E£10/100 for cameras/videos); tickets are sold at the museum entrance.

Pyramid of Chephren South-west of the Great Pyramid, and with almost the same

Pyramid of Cheops

Height: 137.2 (Originally: 146.5m)

Relieving Chamber
Ventilation Shaft
Ventilation Shaft
Great Gallery
King's Chamber
Original Entrance
Present Entrance
Queen's Chamber
Old Tomb Chamber

Pyramid of Chephren

Height: 136.5m (Originally: 143.5m)

Original Entrance
Present Entrance
Burial Chamber (Sarcophagus)

Pyramid of Mycerinus

Height: 62m (Originally: 66.5m)

Entrance
Tomb Chamber

The Great Pyramids of Giza

Imhotep's architectural genius changed the face of Egypt. Less than 100 years after his tribute to Zoser in Saqqara, there arose from the sands of Giza the perfection of the Great Pyramid of Cheops. (For more information on Egypt's pyramids and Imhotep, see the Pyramids section in Pharaonic Egypt.)

The mortuary complexes of Cheops, Chephren and Mycerinus, who were father, son and grandson, included the following: a pyramid, which was the Pharaoh's tomb as well as a repository for all his household goods, clothes and treasure; a funerary temple on the east side of the pyramid; pits for the storage of the Pharaoh's solar barques, which were his means of transport in the afterlife; a valley temple on the banks of the Nile; and a causeway from the river to the pyramid.

The entrance passageways face north towards the Pole Star, as do those in all 80 royal pyramids found in Egypt; the tomb chambers inside face west, towards the Kingdom of the Dead; and the mortuary temples outside face east, towards the rising sun.

The tops of the pyramids were originally separate granite rock structures known as the pyramidion. Up until recently, archaeologists believed pyramidions were coated in gold but inscriptions discovered in the newly opened Pyramid of Sahu Ra at Abu Sir near Saqqara state platinum was used instead.

The pyramids and temples at Giza were built from stone quarried locally and from the Moqattam Hills. Napoleon estimated that there would be enough stones in the three main pyramids at Giza alone to build a wall, three metres high, all around France. ∎

dimensions, is the Pyramid of Chephren. At first it seems larger than his father's, because it stands on higher ground and its peak still has part of the original limestone casing which once covered the whole structure. It is 136.5m high (originally 143.5m).

The chambers and passageways are less elaborate than those in the Great Pyramid, but are almost as claustrophobic. The entrance leads down into a passage and then across to the burial chamber, which still con-

tains the large granite sarcophagus of Chephren.

Among the most interesting features of this pyramid are the substantial remains of Chephren's mortuary temple outside to the east. Several rooms can be visited, and the causeway, which originally provided access from the Nile to the tomb, still leads from the main temple to the valley temple.

Pyramid of Mycerinus At a height of 62m

(originally 66.5m), this is the smallest of the three pyramids. Extensive damage was done to the exterior by a 16th century caliph who wanted to demolish all the pyramids.

Inside, a hall descends from the entrance into a passageway, which in turn leads into a small chamber and a group of rooms. There is nothing particularly noteworthy about the interior, but at the very least you can have the adventure of exploring a seldom-visited site.

Outside are the excavated remains of Mycerinus' mortuary temple and, farther east, the ruins of his valley temple, still lying beneath the sand.

The Sphinx Legends and superstitions abound about this relic of antiquity, and the mystery surrounding its long-forgotten purpose is almost as intriguing as the sight of the structure itself. Known in Arabic as Abu al-Hol (Father of Terror), the feline man was called the Sphinx by the ancient Greeks because it resembled the mythical winged monster with a woman's head and lion's body who proposed a riddle to the Thebans and killed all unable to guess the answer.

Carved almost entirely from one huge piece of limestone leftover from the carving of the stones for Cheops' pyramid, the Sphinx is about 50m long and 22m high. It is not known when it was carved but one theory is that it was Chephren who thought of shaping the rock into a lion's body with a god's face, wearing the royal headdress of Egypt. Another theory is that it is the likeness of Chephren himself that has been staring out over the desert sands for so many centuries.

One legend about the Sphinx is associated with the fact that it was engulfed and hidden by sand for several hundred years. The sun-god Ra appeared to the man who was to become Tuthmosis IV and promised him the crown of Egypt if he would free his image, the Sphinx, from the sand. The stelae (stone tablets) found between the paws of the Sphinx recorded this first known restoration.

During the period of the Ottoman Empire the Turks used the Sphinx for target practice, and its nose and beard, which are now in the British Museum, fell off. Negotiations are under way to have them returned. A team of US and Egyptian archaeologists is restoring parts of the Sphinx.

Tomb of Khenthawes This rarely visited but imposing structure, opposite the Great Pyramid and north of Mycerinus' causeway, is the tomb of the daughter of Pharaoh Mycerinus. Khenthawes became queen of Userkaf and founder of the 5th dynasty. The tomb is a rectangular building cut into a small hill. You can go down a corridor at the back of the chapel room to the burial chambers, but the descent is a bit hazardous.

Cemeteries Private cemeteries with several rows of tombs are organised around the pyramids in a grid pattern. Most of the tombs are closed to the public, but those of Qar, Idu and Queen Mersyankh III, in the eastern cemetery, are accessible, although it's sometimes difficult to find the guard who has the keys.

The Tomb of Iasen, in the western cemetery, contains interesting inscriptions and wall paintings which show life and work during the Old Kingdom.

Sound & Light Show The Sphinx takes the role of the narrator in this sound & light show, which is designed with the tourist in mind but definitely worth seeing. The booming narrative that accompanies the colourful illumination of the pyramids and Sphinx is an entertaining way to learn a little of Egypt's ancient history.

There are two or three shows each evening in English, French, German, Japanese, Italian, Spanish or Arabic. Show times are 6.30, 7.30 and 8.30 pm in winter and one hour later in summer. At the time of writing, the schedule was as follows:

Day	Show 1	Show 2	Show 3
Monday	English	French	–
Tuesday	English	Italian	French
Wednesday	English	French	–
Thursday	Japanese	English	Arabic
Friday	English	French	–
Saturday	English	Spanish	–
Sunday	Japanese	French	German

There is open-air seating on the terrace of the Cheops Pavilion, near the Sphinx and facing Chephren's valley temple. Admission costs E£30 (half for students). During the Ramadan period performance times can be different. If you are unsure, call ☎ 385-2880, 385-7320, or the tourist office.

Ride to Saqqara If you're after adventure you could rent a camel or horse for the ride across the desert to Saqqara. This trip is not really for inexperienced riders. By the end of the day you will have spent about six to seven hours atop a horse or camel and a few more hours roaming around the sites at Saqqara.

The trip takes about three hours each way, and costs anywhere between E£30 to E£50 for a horse and E£30 to E£70 for a camel, depending on how desperate the owners are and how good you can bargain. Don't forget that a camel can carry two people.

Kerdassa
Many of the scarves, *galabiyyas* (men's robes), rugs and weavings sold in the bazaars and shops of Cairo are made in this touristic village near Giza. There is one main market street along which you'll find all of the above as well as a hideous collection of stuffed animals such as gazelles, jackals and rabbits. In fact, Kerdassa is almost as well known for its illegal trade in Egyptian wildlife as it is for crafts. The Egyptian Environmental Affairs Agency periodically raids the bazaar to try and halt this disgusting trade, but clandestine activities still seem to be going on in the backstreets.

The camel trail across the Western Desert to Libya begins in Kerdassa. If you're looking for an incredibly challenging adventure join a caravan here – but it's definitely only for the experienced!

To get to Kerdassa, head down Pyramids Rd towards the pyramids, turn right at the Maryutia Canal, and follow the road for about five km to the village. The minibus from Midan Tahrir to the pyramids begins and ends its trips at the junction of the canal and Pyramids Rd, and a local microbus does the stretch along the canal for 25 pt. You can

also get bus No 116 from Midan Giza all the way to Kerdassa; the trip takes 20 minutes and costs 25 pt.

Wissa Wassef Art Centre
This tranquil art centre is next to the Motel Salma in Harrania, on the Saqqara Rd, about four km south of Pyramids Rd . It specialises in woollen and cotton tapestries, as well as batiks and ceramics, and features a museum, workshops and sales gallery.

The centre is the creation of Ramses Wissa Wassef. Believing that the imagination of children was unintentionally suppressed by teachers and parents, Ramses Wissa Wassef founded a tapestry school in 1942 to allow young children to create freely. He ran it until his death in 1974 when the centre's management was taken over by his widow, Sophie Habib Gorgy.

Over the years, two 'generations' of weavers have grown up with the school. Some of the original artists, now in their 40s and 50s, are still creating, as is the second wave of younger weavers. A lot of the tapestries are representational, depicting rural scenes, folklore, flora and fauna; others are pure imagination. Some superb pieces are showcased in the domed museum at the rear of the complex. If you want to know more about the centre, pick up the book *Threads of Life – a Journey through Creativity* when you're there.

The centre is open daily from 10 am to 6 pm (summer) and from 9.30 am to 5 pm (winter); admission is free. If you particularly want to see tapestries being woven, don't come on Friday when the workshops are closed. To get there, take a microbus for Abu Sir down the Saqqara Rd from Pyramids Rd. It's the same stop as for the Motel Salma.

There's a multitude of other carpet and tapestry workshops along this road. Children as young as five are slaving away at looms in some of these hot sheds.

Cairo Zoo & Al-Orman Park
The zoo is near Cairo University, between Sharia Gamiat al-Qahira (Cairo University St) and Sharia al-Giza. Though a popular

excursion for local families and couples, especially on Fridays and Saturdays, it can hardly be described as a pleasant place. Some of the animals, particularly the lions, bears and elephants, are living in the most shocking environments. The zoo is open from 9.30 am to 6 pm and admission costs 10 pt.

If it's open space and greenery you're after rather than the heartbreaking sight of wild animals being kept in dismal and prison-like confinement, you'd be better off across the road from the zoo in the small but well-kept Al-Orman Park.

Dr Ragab's Pharaonic Village
This floating excursion into a world of people dressed up as ancient Egyptians is only for those with money to burn. It's about 20 minutes walk south of Al-Giza Bridge in Giza. For E£40 (students E£20), you can float down the 'canal of mythology' and try to imagine you've been thrown back a millennium or two. It's open from 9 am to 5 pm in winter, and until 10 pm in summer.

Getting There & Away
For a mere 25 pt you can have the bone-crushing experience of riding bus No 904 or 905 (which pass by Midan Tahrir) almost all the way to the pyramids. They will drop you at or near the turn-off to the Desert Rd to Alexandria, just short of the Hotel Mena House Oberoi on Pyramids Rd. From Ramses station you can take bus No 804 and from Midan Giza bus No 3. You can also get bus No 913 from Midan Tahrir to the Sphinx entrance. Buses are much easier to take in the other direction, from the pyramids to central Cairo, because they start off empty; get a seat near the front so you'll be able to get out more easily.

A much more practical and comfortable alternative is to take a minibus. They leave from the bus station in front of the Nile Hilton on Midan Tahrir; the fare to the pyramids is 35 pt and the trip takes about 30 minutes. Look for No 83 or the men standing next to minibuses and shouting 'haram, haram', which means 'pyramid, pyramid'.

There are also privately run microbuses from the Hilton station. They are far more frequent and cost you 50 pt. You can also get one from Midan Giza for 25 pt.

Another way to get through Giza and out to the pyramids is to take a taxi, which should cost about E£10, although you may have to bargain with the driver to get this price. Ask locals for the latest estimate.

Alternatively you can get here on a tour – for details see the Organised Tours section later in this chapter.

Some of the public transport may leave you at Saqqara Rd, so you will have to either walk the rest of the way to the pyramids – about 15 minutes away – or flag down one of the many passing minibuses which will drop you at the junction of the Desert Rd to Alexandria. The pyramids are just up the hill from here.

LANGUAGE COURSES
For information on the most recognised organisations offering Arabic lessons in Cairo, namely the AUC, British Council and International Language Institute (ILI), refer to Courses in the Facts for the Visitor chapter. Arabic lessons are also offered by some cultural centres. The French Cultural Centre offers various courses of quite a high standard through its Département de l'Étude d'Arab du Caire (☎ 355-9517) in Garden City.

The Goethe Institut (☎ 575-9877), 5 Sharia al-Bustan, also offers relatively inexpensive Arabic lessons, but generally concentrates on not overly demanding courses in colloquial Egyptian Arabic.

The Egyptian Centre for International Cultural Cooperation (ECICC) (☎ 341-5419), 11 Sharia Shagarat ad-Durr, Zamalek, offers courses in classical Arabic. Intensive courses (96 hours over 12 weeks) cost US$220 and regular courses (48 hours over the same period) US$110. Contact Mrs Abla Ghoneim any day between 10 am and 1 pm.

Check the magazine *Egypt Today* for a list of other organisations that offer Arabic courses, but be wary of quality and cost.

FELUCCA RIDES

Feluccas are the ancient broadsail boats seen everywhere up and down the Nile. Taking a felucca ride while you're in Egypt is an absolute must; there's no better way to see the Nile, especially at sunset. If you don't have the time or inclination to spend a couple of days on one between Luxor and Aswan, the next best thing is to hire one in Cairo and take a leisurely cruise for a few hours. It costs about E£10 per hour to hire a felucca (along with its captain). This rate is, of course, subject to haggling and could be higher or lower depending on your negotiating (or arguing) skills. Feluccas congregate at several quays along the river, but one of the most popular departure points is in Garden City, opposite the Meridien Hotel. Others are along the south-east end of Gezira just north of At-Tahrir Bridge, and in Maadi.

DIVE CLUBS

The Cairo Divers Group (☎ & fax 570-3242) organises monthly diving trips, rents equipment, offers interesting discounts and has plenty of information on the dive sites. The club meets on the first Monday of each month at the Semiramis InterContinental Hotel. The annual membership fee for divers is E£50.

The Maadi Divers is another group. They organise trips and sell and rent equipment as well. Membership is E£50 – call Magdy al-Araby (☎ 353-7144) for details.

Diving equipment is available at Scubatec (☎ 418-0118), at 9 Sharia Dr Hassan Aflaton, Heliopolis, and Scuba Plus (☎ 574-7988), 1st floor, World Trade Centre, 1191 Corniche el-Nil, Bulaq.

HORSE RIDING

Certainly popular with some expatriates, a horse ride out by the pyramids, especially in the evening, can be a great way to fully escape the clamour of Cairo and vent some pent-up aggro. For details, see Getting Around in the earlier Giza section.

HAMMAMS

There are several old Turkish baths functioning in Islamic Cairo. These are mostly men-only institutions working virtually round the clock, and some are definitely no-go areas for people not interested in more than just a scrub down and massage. If you'd like to try your luck, see the Islamic Cairo section for the location and details of some individual bathhouses. It has to be said, however, that if you have the opportunity to try out bathhouses in Damascus or Aleppo (in Syria) or Istanbul (in Turkey), do so. The Cairo hammams tend to be dingy and not overly inviting places.

SWIMMING

Finding a place to go for a swim is not easy in Cairo. There are a few private clubs about, but generally membership is required. The Heliopolis Club, for example, has an Olympic-size pool, as well as squash courts, and a gym which is open to outsiders for a E£10 fee.

You could also try some of the five star hotels, which charge anywhere from E£25 to E£160 – the former being the price for the pool on the sun deck of the floating Imperial Hotel at Gezira, the latter being the charge for two (including the use of a cabin) at the Nile Hilton. The Meridien asks E£39.

One place expatriates use a bit is the Atlas Zamalek Hotel in Mohandiseen, near Midan Sphinx. Entry to the pool costs E£23. Cheaper still is the Fontana Hotel on Midan Ramses which asks just E£10.

ORGANISED TOURS

Some of the budget hotels in central Cairo arrange tours to various places around the city such as the Giza and Saqqara pyramids and Memphis. The price is usually about E£20 and includes transport only – there's no guide and admission fees are extra. The stories about these trips have often been negative, so forewarned is forearmed. The Select and Panorama Palace hotels (see Places to Stay – bottom end) are two of the many places offering trips.

Better still, arrange to go with Salah Mohammed Abdel Hafiez (☎ 298-0650). This genial chap runs a full day excursion to the places mentioned earlier, as well as to the Wissa Wassef Art Centre at Harrania, for E£18 (once again, lunch and admission prices are extra). If you're staying at one of the city centre hotels, he'll pick you up at around 9 am. You'll need to arrange the tour at least one day in advance – leave a message on the answering machine if he's not there.

A third option is to go through a travel agency like Misr Travel. It does daily sightseeing tours in winter, less often in summer. Half-day tours to the pyramids, Sphinx and Citadel cost US$30; the full day trip for US$40 also includes Memphis, Saqqara and lunch. American Express offers a variety of tours (usually three hours) for US$20 taking in such destinations as the Egyptian Museum and Coptic Cairo, the pyramids, Islamic Cairo or Saqqara.

Tours to the Birqash camel market are organised by the Sun Hotel (☎ 578-1786) at 2 Sharia Talaat Harb (for more details see the Around Cairo chapter).

SPECIAL EVENTS
Cairo International Film Festival
Held in late November/early December every year, this 14 day festival is a veritable feast of modern (although not always the latest) cinema, and most of it is uncensored. Although the censors retain the right to reject films outright (or to chop the odd scene), they are more lenient than usual for the occasion.

The films are shown in many cinemas; the *Egyptian Gazette* usually carries details. The screenings are generally more expensive than usual cinema performances, and often it is necessary to buy tickets in advance.

Arab Music Festival
If you happen to be in Cairo in early November and are interested in classical, traditional and orchestral Arabic music, try to catch part of this 10 day festival held at the Opera House. Started in 1992, this annual festival brings together some of the best musicians from 14 Arab countries. Programmes are usually in Arabic only but the tourist office should have details.

PLACES TO STAY
Cairo offers visitors the full spectrum of accommodation, from the big international five star chains to flee-ridden dives. The more expensive hotels usually quote prices in US dollars. In most cases, however, there is no problem paying in E£.

There's a plethora of inexpensive hotels and pensions, concentrated mainly in the busy city centre area. Prices for these places can be deceiving, because they aren't always accurate indicators of the hotel's quality and because prices can sometimes be negotiated. So consider the room rates given for budget and mid-range accommodation as estimates; although they were obtained directly from the hotels, travellers have reported paying different prices for the same accommodation.

The suburb of Zamalek is a great place to stay if you prefer a leafy, relatively peaceful area. It's not that far from the centre of town, and has most of the facilities you may need nearby (phone, post and banks).

Almost all the world's major hotel chains have hotels – either around central Cairo, near the pyramids or in Heliopolis to the north-east. Their prices, standards and amenities are usually on a par with their hotels in other countries. A few of the more expensive hotels are interesting to visit and pleasant places in which to seek refuge from the chaos and cacophony of Cairo's streets.

Unless otherwise indicated, the prices quoted for bottom-end and mid-range hotels include breakfast and taxes.

Places to Stay – bottom end
Camping The *Motel Salma* (☎ 384-9152; fax 385-1010) is next to the Wissa Wassef Art Centre at Harrania south of Giza. It is owned by an Egyptian who goes by the nickname Sid. Camping costs E£7 per person with your own tent or campervan, or you can get a two/four person cabin for E£30/40, or E£50 with your own shower. There are cold and hot showers and the toilets are fairly clean. The restaurant is way over the top. Breakfast costs E£6 (E£10 if you want an omelette!), soft drinks are

E£1.50, Stella beer is E£7 and main meals about E£20. Some overland tour companies occasionally use this camping ground, which has views of the pyramids from the back area. If you have your own vehicle and/or tent, it might just be worth it for the views (the cabins are claustrophobic and stuffy), otherwise not.

To get there, take a microbus for Abu Sir down the Saqqara Rd from Pyramids Rd. It's about four km in; ask the driver about the best place to alight. Be prepared for a mosquito attack at sunset.

Hostels The *Manyal Youth Hostel* (☎ 364-0729; fax 984107), 135 Sharia Abdel Aziz as-Saud on Roda Island, is one of the cheapest options in Cairo. It's in reasonable nick with clean toilets, although the beds are nothing great. Dorm rooms sleep six people each; there are no rooms for couples or families. Mosquitoes and cats are plentiful enough to ensure constant companionship of a sort. Breakfast is included. It's a 30 minute walk from Midan Tahrir, and costs E£8.60 for members, or E£12.10 for nonmembers.

From Midan Tahrir, take minibus No 82 (Nile Hilton terminal), get off at the Al-Gamaa Bridge and head about 100m down the riverside street.

Hotels – Central Cairo There is a handful of hotels in Cairo which undercut the youth hostel. Two of them are right next to each other on the 3rd floor of a building on Sharia al-Tawfiqiyya, the area's colourful market street. The *Tawfikia Hotel* (☎ 755514) has dorm beds for E£6 and hot water. For E£1 more, you can get a bed in the *Safary Hotel* next door. This place is well known by Japanese travellers. In the same building on the 1st floor is the friendly, popular *Sultan Hotel* (☎ 772258). It has simple dorms (E£7 for a bed) and a communal kitchen and bathroom, but it's all somewhat cramped.

The *Pensione de Famille* (☎ 574-5630) in Sharia Abdel Khaliq Sarwat is in a building that should have been condemned years ago. The beds are a little lumpy, but at E£8/11 for a single/double room (excluding breakfast),

you can't go too far wrong. There's a grotty kitchen if you're desperate to cook something.

The *Hotel Select* (☎ 393-3707), 8th floor, 19 Sharia Adly, is next to the heavily guarded synagogue. The rate is a simple E£10 per person in a clean, share room – although you may end up with only a fairly well-used mattress on the floor.

The *Golden Hotel* (☎ 392-2659), 3rd floor, 13 Sharia Talaat Harb, was once something of an institution among travellers, but it has deteriorated over the years and is now overpriced and not recommended.

The *Hotel Beau Site* (☎ 392-9916), 5th floor, 27 Sharia Talaat Harb, is actually down a small passage just off Sharia Talaat Harb. Reports about this hotel are mixed. A few travellers have said it is an interesting place to stay, and more than one 'star' has been discovered here by Cairene advertising agents on the hunt for foreign faces for local TV commercials. The big rooms, most with a minuscule balcony, are OK, but tend to be dark and dusty. At E£15/25, it's not totally unreasonable. The elevator, however, can be temperamental.

Two of the city's most popular backpackers' haunts are down by Midan Tahrir. One is the new *Sun Hotel* (☎ 578-1786) at 2 Sharia Talaat Harb; it's on the 9th floor and has an up-only elevator. It has decently sized singles/doubles with big comfortable beds for E£25/40, or E£15 per person in a four bed room. The clean, communal bathrooms have hot water and there's a lounge room with satellite TV and a small spotless kitchen. This place arranges a tour to the Birqash camel market every Friday (for details see the Around Cairo chapter).

The other is the relatively new *Ismailia House Hotel* (☎ 356-3122) at No 1 Midan Tahrir. It's on the 8th floor (the elevator will take you up *and* down) and is immensely popular with travellers. The bright, white-washed rooms are clean and the linen is regularly changed. There's also satellite TV in the lounge and, perhaps best of all, several bathrooms, all with electric water heaters ensuring hot showers. The rooms vary in quality, and have little or no furniture. Singles, a few of which are pretty dingy, cost E£20. Doubles without/with private bathroom are E£40/45 and are the best value. A bed in a share room (a double with two extra rickety beds crammed in) costs E£12 to E£15, depending on the room. You can sleep in the hall for E£10. If you end up with one of the better rooms, it's very good value, and it's hard to argue with the location. Most of the rooms have balconies – the view over Midan Tahrir is intoxicating.

The same people have also totally renovated the *Hotel Petit Palais* (☎ 391-1863), at 45 Sharia Abdel Khaliq Sarwat. It is done out in similar style and has comparable prices. The bathrooms are spotless and, unlike at the Ismailia, each room has hot water in the sink.

The *Tulip Hotel* (☎ 393-9433, fax 361-1995) on the 3rd floor, 3 Midan Talaat Harb, is right on the midan, but it is not as good value as it once was. Rooms, with and without bathrooms, go from E£20 to E£40. The ones with balconies are lighter and cooler than the inside rooms, and all of them have a fan and a bit more furniture than those at the Ismailia.

The *Gresham Hotel* (☎ 575-9043), 3rd floor, 20 Sharia Talaat Harb, hasn't changed its room rates in years and is now pretty good value. Single rooms cost E£25, or E£35 with private bath and air-con. Doubles without/with bath go for E£40/45 and are all air-conditioned. If you stay more than three nights, there's a 5% discount. The hotel has a cosy bar which should have reopened by now.

The *Hotel des Roses* (☎ 393-8022), 4th floor, 33 Sharia Talaat Harb, has gone a little overboard with prices. A single/double without bath is E£31/45; with bath E£42/65. The views of Cairo are great from the rooms on the top floor along the balcony.

The *Anglo-Swiss Hotel* (☎ 575-1497), 6th floor, 14 Sharia Champollion, is generally clean and comfortable and, for the price, a reasonable deal. In the mornings, a team of workers cleans and polishes the floors and furniture. It costs E£25 for a big single, E£20 for a poky one, and E£32/42 for doubles/

triples. There is hot water from 10 pm to midnight in winter only, and the elevator is known to break down.

The 6th-floor *Pensione Suisse* (☎ 574-6639), in Sharia Mohammed Bassiuni, just west of Midan Talaat Harb, has a collection of grotty single/double/triple rooms for E£15/25/50, all without shower or fan. According to one traveller, this place has a 'major wildlife problem'.

The *Hotel Viennoise* (☎ 574-3153; fax 575-3136), 11 Sharia Mohammed Bassiuni, is not representative of anything related to the beautiful city of Vienna. Big, dusty rooms without bath go for E£25, or E£35 with bath and hot water. Some of the rooms are indeed huge and have balconies.

The *Panorama Palace Hotel* (☎ 392-9127), 20B Sharia Adly, is in an alley by the Kodak shop. Like so many Cairo hotels in this range, it is a little on the musty side but the rooms are acceptable. Prices range from E£15 for a bed in a share room to E£40 for a double with bathroom.

The *Pension Roma* (☎ 391-1088), 169 Sharia Mohammed Farid, near the junction with Sharia Adly, is tucked away in a side alley. All the rooms have shiny hardwood floors and beautiful antique furniture. Single/double/triple rooms without a bath are E£20/38/50. A room with four beds can be had for E£66. It is best to make reservations here, especially during the high season, because a few adventure travel companies have discovered it. Even so, some travellers reckon it's overrated.

A place forgotten by all and sundry is *Hotel Tee* (☎ 391-1002), 4th floor, 13 Sharia Adly, near the telephone office. It has small rooms for E£25/35/40 with showers, hot water and dirty carpets. Even towels and toilet paper are provided. Doubles and triples without bath are E£5 cheaper.

Hidden in an alley off Sharia 26th of July, just across the road from À l'Américaine Café, is the entrance to the 6th floor *Hotel Minerva* (☎ 392-0600). It has big clean rooms and cold showers that are cleaned every day. Single/double rooms are E£16/28; doubles with bath E£32.

The nearby *Claridge Hotel* (☎ 393-7776), near the corner of Sharia Talaat Harb and Sharia 26th of July (on the 2nd floor, but actually at least four flights up), seems to have lifted its game. Most of the (not so well-maintained) rooms have attractive balconies and there's a pleasant cafeteria in the corridor. Singles/doubles/triples without shower start at E£25/35/45, or E£30/45/51 with bath.

In the alley leading to the Palmyra nightclub, just off Sharia 26th of July, is the 7th floor *Scarabee Hotel* (☎ 393-9434). It's remarkable mainly for its king-size beds. Rooms go for E£37/47.

Nearby, on the corner of Sharia Mohammed Farid and Sharia 26th of July, is the *Hotel Nitocrisse* (☎ 391-5166). Big singles/doubles without fans are E£19/35. The hotel in general is reasonably clean and quiet.

The *Amin Hotel* (☎ 393-3813), 38 Midan Falaki, Bab al-Louk, has big and fully carpeted rooms all with fans and some with bathrooms. The shared bathrooms tend to get somewhat messy. Single rooms without/with bathroom cost E£23/29; doubles cost E£30/34.

Hotels – Around Midan Ramses The *Everest Hotel* (☎ 574-2707) on Midan Ramses is in the tallest building opposite Ramses station. Its 80 rooms are on the 14th, 15th and 16th floors; the reception desk and cafeteria are on the 15th floor. The rooms go for E£12/17 and are cheap, dusty and don't have baths. The low prices, its proximity to the railway station and the fantastic views from the balcony once made this a popular place, but the deteriorating conditions have begun to discourage people from staying. One bit of graffiti seen here sums it up well: 'Don't mind the bedbugs in this room, we were visited by the rat!'

The shabby *Luna Park* (☎ 918626), 65 Sharia al-Gomhurriya, between Midan Ramses and Midan Opera, is a quiet place with a somewhat sombre atmosphere. Rooms are supplied with soap, towels, toilet paper and a sink with hot and cold water. A

small cafe and bar are attached to the hotel. Singles/doubles are E£18/27.

Hotels – Zamalek There are two places worth investigating here, not far to the south of Sharia 26th of July. The great thing about both is that they get you out of the hassle of central Cairo without really taking you that far away.

The *Mayfair Hotel* (☎ 340-7315), 1st floor, 9 Sharia Aziz Osman, has rooms without bath for E£20/24, or air-con doubles with bath for E£60 (E£45 if only one person). There are also a few triples starting from around E£50. All prices include breakfast, and favourable rates may be offered to those who show this book. The showers are hot, but the standard Egyptian bed (nice and hard) is a slight drawback. It's a very tranquil and friendly place, and has deck chairs and a shady terrace.

Two blocks south and then a little way west along Sharia Salah ad-Din is the *Zamalek Pension* (☎ 340-9318). It's really heading into the middle range of places with clean, comfortable singles/doubles for E£35/70, but the prices are reasonable for what you get.

Places to Stay – middle
Central Cairo The *Garden City House* (☎ 354-4969), 23 Sharia Kamal ad-Din Salah, is opposite the Semiramis InterContinental Hotel. Look for the small sign outside the 3rd floor and the bronze plaque at the front of the building. This hotel was, for a long time, a favourite among Egyptologists and Middle East scholars, but it's now more popular with young students from the AUC. It's a bit dusty, and some travellers have reported it not worth the money; others still love it. Singles/doubles range from E£43/72 without bath to E£54/87 with. The price includes breakfast and either lunch or dinner, whether you want it or not. Better rooms can be found for lower rates at other hotels, but you can't beat this hotel's location.

The *Lotus Hotel* (☎ 575-0966; fax 575-4720), 12 Sharia Talaat Harb opposite Felfela Cafeteria, is one of the best hotels in

Top: In Cairo, eclectic city of contrasts, the sun sets over a church's steeple and the domes of a mosque.
Left: Detail of the ornate mashrabiyyah found inside the Sultan Barsbey Mosque, Cairo.
Right: A small mosque nestled in Cairo's crowded Sayyida Zeinab quarter.

GREG ELMS

KRISTIE BURNS

CHRIS BEALL

Left: City of the Dead, Giza, with the Pyramid of Mycerinus in the background.
Right: The proximity of Giza's pyramids to the bustle of Cairo takes many visitors by surprise.
Bottom: Abounding in legends and superstition, the Sphinx remains shrouded in mystery.

KRISTIE BURNS

GLENN BEANLAND

PAUL STEEL

Hailed as one of the Seven Wonders of the World by the ancient Greeks, the Great Pyramids of Giza have survived the rise and fall of numerous dynasties and outlasted Egypt's many conquerors for 4½ millennia. These ancient monuments have intrigued and puzzled visitors for centuries, and are perhaps most spectacular at sunrise and sunset.

Egypt's Camels

The one-humped dromedary, or Arabian camel, has made a unique contribution to the people and history of desert lands. These lovable creatures were domesticated thousands of years ago by frankincense traders who trained them to travel the ancient spice routes across Arabian deserts. For the Bedouins, camels were the primary source of transport, milk, meat, shade, wool and hides. These days camels are valued more as nostalgic images of desert lands.

That camels are so inextricably associated with the desert is hardly surprising – they are perhaps more suited to desert conditions than any other creature. Camels can go without food and water for five to seven days without impairing their normal functions. They do not pant, and perspire little as a result of a unique ability to raise their body temperature tolerance as much as 6°C. When food is scarce they are able to draw energy from the fatty tissue that makes up their hump. (Contrary to popular belief, water is not stored in the hump but in the bloodstream – a result of the creature's unique metabolism.) Two rows of long eyelashes protect their eyes from the desert sands while thick eyebrows shield them from the relentless sun.

The marked absence of camels in the artwork of Pharaonic tombs suggested to many historians that camels were introduced to Egypt by the Romans. Scientists, however, claim that ancestors of the modern camel originated in North America at least 40 million years ago, and wandered across the Alaskan 'land bridge' to Asia approximately one million years ago, eventually making their way to Africa.

Top: Smiling after a sunrise ride around the pyramids, Giza.
Left: On show at the camel market at Birqash, outside Cairo.
Right: The branded beast, shaved and tatooed by camel traders.

this price range. The elevator to the reception desk (7th floor) is reached through an arcade which almost faces Sharia Hoda Shaarawi. The rooms are clean, comfortable and have air-con and large balconies. You'll pay E£35/65 for a single without/with a bath; doubles are E£65/85. There are also some triples. There's a restaurant, bar and a quasi-sun deck on the top floor. The hotel seems to have particular favour with European tour groups.

The *Cosmopolitan Hotel* (☎ 392-3663; fax 393-3531) is in Sharia Ibn Taalab, just off Sharia Qasr el-Nil. It is an upper-middle range hotel that's quite popular with various tour groups, so getting a room here can sometimes be difficult. It has beautifully plush old rooms with dark lacquered furniture, central air-con and tiled bathrooms with tubs. Some rooms have balconies and there's a wonderful old open elevator. Singles/doubles cost US$40/50 and despite the hotel's very central location it's surprisingly quiet. It's one of those places with lots of the fast-disappearing 'old world charm'.

The *Odeon Palace Hotel* (☎ 776637; fax 767971), 6 Sharia Abdel al-Hamid Said, is about 1½ blocks north-west of Sharia Talaat Harb. It is an upper-middle range hotel, but lacks the old Victorian character of the Cosmopolitan. The rooms have a mini-fridge, TV, telephone and air-con and go for US$113/142. Breakfast is E£10 extra. All credit cards are accepted here.

The *Grand Hotel* (☎ 575-7509; fax 575-7593), 17 Sharia 26th of July, has clean and comfortable rooms with Art Deco style furniture. You'll find a wide variety of singles and doubles, with and without bathrooms and air-con, starting from E£112/145.

The *Cleopatra Palace Hotel* (☎ 575-9900; fax 575-9807), just back from Midan Tahrir on Sharia al-Bustan, has had some pretty scathing reports. If you don't like toenails and pubic hair in your bed, this is not the place to stay. Maybe it's not as bad as all that, but the rooms are indeed pretty shabby. Singles/doubles cost US$63/81.

The *New Riche Hotel* (☎ 390-0145; fax 390-6390), 47 Sharia Abdel Aziz, near Midan Ataba and the GPO, has air-con singles/doubles with shower for E£52/70. The staff at the front desk are not overly welcoming.

The *Windsor Hotel* (☎ 591-5277; fax 921621), 19 Sharia Alfi Bey, was once a great place with lots of class and comfort, but it has deteriorated. The Windsor has an interesting history. During the time of the Ottoman Empire it was the private bathhouse of the Turkish leaders; it was used to house Russian engineers during the construction of the Aswan Dam; and it was set on fire during the 1952 Revolution because it was the British Officers' Club. More recently, the British comedian Michael Palin stayed here when making his BBC *Around the World in 80 Days* series. There's a wide variety of rooms, with and without bath or shower, with prices ranging from about E£72 for a single with shower to E£137 for a 'luxury' double.

Around Midan Ramses Secreted in a quiet backstreet off Sharia Imad ad-Din (just behind the Karim Cinema) is one of the best value-for-money options in this range. The *Happyton Hotel* (☎ 928671; fax 928600), 10 Sharia Aly el-Kassar, is a relaxed place with a small, open-air rooftop bar and a restaurant. It's popular with both foreigners and Egyptians and has singles/doubles with air-con for E£40/52. There are also triples. Some of the rooms are a tad small, but most are OK and towels, soap and toilet paper are provided. It's handy to both central Cairo and Ramses station.

The three star *Fontana Hotel* (☎ 922321; fax 922145), just off Midan Ramses, is hardly in an inviting location, but the views from the clean rooms are impressive. There's even a swimming pool and disco on the 8th floor. Singles/doubles go for E£57/84.

The two star *Capsis Palace Hotel* (☎ 575-4219), 117 Sharia Ramses, is conveniently situated near the railway station and intercity bus terminals (Midan Ulali and Midan Ahmed Helmi) but the rooms are small and a bit much at E£52/80.

Islamic Cairo On Midan Hussein the *Hotel*

CAIRO

al-Hussein (☎ 591-8089) is right in the thick of things in the Khan al-Khalili bazaar. The rooms are clean and the restaurant on the roof has a fantastic view of medieval Cairo. Singles/doubles with bath and views over the midan cost E£50/60. Smaller rooms without bath or view are E£30/40. Air-con, a telephone, mini-fridge and hot water are included, but a TV or fan is extra.

Diagonally opposite is the *Radwan Hotel* (☎ 590-1311). It has quite OK rooms without such hot views for E£31/42 with breakfast and bath. Be aware that in either of these places you're almost sure to be woken by the early calls to prayer.

If you'd prefer to be more out of the bazaar, try the accommodating *El Malky Hotel* (☎ 589-1093) at 4 Sharia al-Hossiny (just north of the Mosque of Sayyidna Al-Hussein) which has air-con rooms with TV for E£40/60.

Zamalek Given the competition, the *New Star Hotel* (☎ 340-0928; fax 341-1321), Sharia Yehia Ibrahim, might be worth the extra dollars. This three star place has single/double/triple suites for US$30/35/45. The rooms have kitchenettes, sparkling bathrooms, air-con, colour TV, reception rooms and very clean bedrooms. There are a few other middle to upper-middle level hotels scattered around Zamalek.

Doqqi The *Indiana Hotel* (☎ 335-4503; fax 360-7947), at 16 Sharia Hasan Rostom, has clean, comfortable rooms for US$46/58, some with TV and refrigerator. Ask for one at the front, as the rooms at the back are pretty poky. It has a small pool, restaurant and a bar.

The *Pharaohs Hotel* (☎ 361-0871; fax 361-0874), 12 Sharia Lutfi Hassuna, is one of the lower end hotels in this bracket. The rooms are a tad dark but reasonably priced at E£35/47 and the hotel is quiet and well located.

Mohandiseen The *Atlas Zamalek Hotel* (☎ 346-6569; fax 347-6958), 20 Sharia Gamiat ad-Dowal al-Arabiyya, has rooms

for E£73/91 including taxes but not breakfast. Better value is the *Al-Nabila Cairo Hotel* (☎ 347-5661; fax 303-0302), on the same road at No 6, which offers rooms at E£70/90 including breakfast. This place is often used by European tour groups and has a pool and bar.

Heliopolis There are plenty of four and five star hotels – such as the Mövenpick, Meridien and Baron – in Heliopolis and on the road out towards the airport. If you want to be relatively close to the airport but don't wish to spend top dollars you could try the three star *Hotel Beirut* (☎ 662347; fax 669422), 43 Sharia Baghdad, where singles/doubles cost US$61/79. There are a few other cheaper hotels in Heliopolis as well.

Places to Stay – top end
The prices given below are generally exclusive of breakfast and taxes.

Central Cairo The *Nile Hilton* (☎ 578-0444; fax 578-0475), on the Corniche el-Nil, is one of the focal points of Cairo. It has terrific river views and is very centrally located, backing on to Midan Tahrir. It is one of the most popular hotels with westerners, but don't expect it to be up to the standard of Hiltons in other countries. It was one of Egypt's first five star hotels and the rooms are large and clean although the plumbing is unreliable. Prices for the better singles/doubles are about US$165/200.

Just north of the Nile Hilton, and also right by the river, is the newer *Ramses Hilton* (☎ 574-4400; fax 575-7152), 1115 Corniche el-Nil. Rooms range from US$140 for a standard single to US$2030 for a three bed suite.

Head along the Corniche el-Nil, south of the Nile Hilton, and you'll come to the palatial *Semiramis InterContinental Hotel* (☎ 355-7171; fax 356-3020). It's right on the Nile and the rooms and amenities here are exactly what you would expect from the lines of Mercedes and Rolls-Royces parked outside. Singles/doubles with views of the Nile are US$155/175, while rooms looking over the city are US$20 cheaper. Suites range from US$300 to US$1000.

A cheaper alternative to the big names is the relatively new *Cairo Khan Hotel* (☎ 392-2015; fax 390-6799) on the corner of Sharia 26th of July and Sharia Mohammed Farid. Comfortable but smallish singles/doubles with the usual facilities cost US$52/65, but they seem keen to do deals. The suites (US$110) come with kitchenettes.

Garden City The five star *Shepheard's Hotel* (☎ 355-3800; fax 355-7284), on Corniche el-Nil just south of the Semiramis InterContinental Hotel, was renovated several years ago and has all but lost its British Empire atmosphere, which in any case was a bit artificial, since the original, burnt down during the 1952 Revolution, was in fact located in Midan Opera. After its destruction, the new version was built on the Nile in 1957. Founded in 1841 by an Englishman, Samuel Shepheard, it was one of the first European-style tourist hotels in Cairo. During the British occupation of Egypt, the original hotel and its rooftop terrace bar were favourites with British military officers and administrators. Singles/doubles/triples fronting the Nile go for US$138/162/192, while those at the back cost US$109/126/156. There's a buffet breakfast for E£28.

Zamalek The *Cairo Marriott* (☎ 340-8888; fax 340-6667) is on Sharia al-Gezira, just south of the 26th of July Bridge. It is in a palace built in 1869 by Khedive Ismail to accommodate Empress Eugénie during the opening of the Suez Canal. The hotel, with 1250 rooms, is 19th century elegance at its best: polished marble floors, engraved brass lamps and ornately carved mashrabiyyah screens. Have a Stella beer in the garden next to the swimming pool. Single/double rooms are US$145/165.

Roda Island, Gezira & Doqqi The *Cairo Meridien* (☎ 362-1717; fax 362-1927), Corniche el-Nil, Roda Island, is right on the river, and the views are magnificent. Spa-

cious single/double rooms with all facilities are US$165/185.

The views from the Cairo Meridien are matched only by those from the *El Gezira Sheraton* (☎ 341-1333) at the southern end of Gezira. Singles/doubles start at US$90/96. It's cheaper than the *Cairo Sheraton* (☎ 348-8600; fax 348-9051), across the river in Doqqi, which has rooms from US$125/150.

Cairo's only floating hotel is the new five star *Imperial* (☎ 341-4290; fax 341-4541), moored opposite the Gezira Club in Gezira. This relatively new cruise boat has 38 rooms priced from US$87/112 including taxes.

Giza There are plenty of top-range hotels near the pyramids. Most of the five star places are along the Desert Highway to Alexandria, while the four star jobs tend to stretch along Pyramids Rd back towards central Cairo. The closest hotel to the pyramids is the *Mena House Oberoi* (☎ 383-3444; fax 383-7777). It's one of the grand old hotels of the world, with an abundance of elegance and opulent Oriental decor. It has played an important role in Middle East history as a base for the British in WWII and the site of peace negotiations between Egypt and Israel. Prices start at US$112/140.

PLACES TO EAT
Like much in Cairo, dining can be a sensory sensation. There are market stalls where you can find exotic or plain food and where it's easy to have a very filling meal for less than E£5. On the more expensive side there are plenty of restaurants serving European dishes and places where you can get western-style fast food.

Cheap Eats
North of Midan Talaat Harb The *International Public Meal Kushari*, on the corner of Sharia Imad ad-Din and Sharia Alfi Bey, is a great kushari joint. The woodchip floor, eager waiters and large servings (E£1.25) all seem to add to the flavour of this authentic little place.

The *Casablanca*, opposite the Grand

Hotel on Sharia Talaat Harb, does an excellent meat or cheese fiteer (pizza) – the latter is a good vegetarian dish if you can eat egg – for E£6. Next door is one of those seemingly rare, little milk-produce shops where you can buy pots of yoghurt or a cheese sandwich.

Ali Hassan al-Hatti just south of the Windsor Hotel is one of those Cairo gems – a relic with chandeliers, tall mirrors, high ceilings, and waiters who may well have been employed 40 years ago. Their speciality is moza – roast lamb on rice – a meal of which costs about E£15. Alternatively, a meal for two of chicken, side dishes and molokhiyya will come to about E£30.

Similarly priced is the *Alfi Bey Restaurant* on Sharia Alfi Bey, a relaxing 1940s style place with meat and chicken meals for around E£15 or a plate of spaghetti bolognaise for less than E£4.

Excelsior, on the corner of Sharia Talaat Harb and Sharia Adly, is popular with the cinema crowds, though it's somewhat big and bland. Again, the main dishes are around the E£15 mark but many of the meat dishes are overcooked. They serve great ice creams for E£3.50 to E£5.

Directly across the road from the Excelsior is the *Amira*, a 24 hour eatery where film extras are sometimes recruited. You can get a delicious lentil soup for E£1.50 or a number of other small dishes for a couple of pounds. The main meals like kebab and kofta come to around E£6 to E£7.50, and beer is served.

The *Coin de Kebab* (or Kebab Corner) is about one block off Sharia Talaat Harb, near the Odeon Palace Hotel. You can get excellent kebab and tahina here. On Sharia Adly, *GAD* serves fairly cheap, decent meals in its rather unappetising setting.

If you wander into the arcades linking Sharia Adly and Sharia 26th of July near the EgyptAir office, you'll find some great sweet and ice-cream shops.

South of Midan Talaat Harb The *Felfela Garden* (☎ 392-2751), 15 Sharia Hoda Shaarawi, is one of the better all-round restaurants in Cairo, although its enormous popularity with foreigners means there are quite a few dishes you could get elsewhere for less. This is the original Felfela Restaurant, founded in 1963 by Madame Amina Zaghloul as a small vegetarian restaurant serving mostly fuul and ta'amiyya. A vegetarian, she started the restaurant because she was dismayed by the lack of clean, inexpensive vegetarian restaurants in Cairo. To earn a four star government tourism rating, she eventually had to add various meat and poultry dishes such as pigeon and kofta. Your dinner of fuul, ta'amiyya, tahina, and tea can cost as little as E£10, especially if you come with a small group and share a selection of dishes. You can also get beer here. The Felfela chain is spreading, and you can find it along Pyramids Rd, on Roda Island and in Maadi.

The *Felfela Cafeteria*, just around the corner from the main restaurant, is a tiny stand-up or takeaway joint which serves excellent ta'amiyya, shawarma, kofta and fuul sandwiches, from 40 pt to E£1.25. Buy a ticket from the overworked cashier at the entrance before battling the throng inside.

Da Mario at the Nile Hilton serves good small pizzas and various Italian dishes such as spaghetti carbonara. It's moderately priced, but really heading out of the budget range, with pizzas from E£11. It's open from noon to 2 am.

At 166 Sharia at-Tahrir is the 24 hour *Fatatri at-Tahrir*, an excellent place for a sweet or savoury fiteer – E£6 for small ones, E£8 for medium and E£10 for large.

Farther east along Sharia at-Tahrir are two equally good kushari places, the *El-Tahrir* and *Lux*. A big serve of the stuff costs from E£1 to E£2.

The block of Sharia Mansur that stretches from Midan Falaki to Sharia Mohammed Mahmoud has a wonderful variety of cheap eats possibilities and is a great place to introduce yourself to Egyptian food. There's everything from sandwich places to fiteer restaurants, juice stands, bakeries, fuul and ta'amiyya stands and kushari restaurants. Or you can get fuller meals of chicken, kebab or kofta for E£3 to E£4.

One of the better places is *Cafeteria el-Shaab*, about halfway along Sharia Mansur. You can get a serve of makarone and potato stew for E£2. The fatatri next door does a superb fiteer for E£3. When you've finished eating, there are several local teahouses along Sharia Mansur where you can relax over a coffee and shisha and observe the antics in and around the market.

If you're just after a plain old sandwich, head round the corner from Sharia Mansur to the 24 hour sandwich shop on Sharia Mohammed Mahmud. Sandwiches of basturma, cheese and olives or egg cost about E£1.50.

A few doors along on Sharia Mohammed Mahmud (towards Midan Tahrir) is *El Fornaia Etman* bakery. At any time of the day or night, Cairenes come here to load up with small loaves of French bread, aysh baladi, and date and sesame cookies. There's another bakery, the *Crystal Bakery*, on Sharia Talaat Harb near Midan Tahrir.

The *Sit-In Restaurant* (☎ 535-4341) on Sharia Latin America in Garden City serves everything from shrimps at E£25 to hot dogs and sandwiches for between E£3 to E£5. It's at No 1 (look for the big Donald Duck sign across from the British embassy) and is open daily until 10 pm.

Around Midan Ramses One of the best places for a cheap meal in Cairo is *El-Tabie El-Domiati* at 31 Sharia Orabi. The portions are large, the service fast and friendly, the setting clean, and the food is excellent. It's predominantly vegetarian and has a wonderful salad bar where you can choose from about 15 prepared salads and a variety of pickles – a large platter costs just E£3. Other specialities include musaga, ta'amiyya and a very tasty lentil soup (don't be put off by the classic misspelt menu which promotes lentils as 'a type of Egyption legune which we lick and cook very well'). A filling meal for two here can come to as little as E£6 to E£8.

Islamic Cairo *Al-Hussein Restaurant*, right in Khan al-Khalili near Midan Hussein, is a rooftop restaurant in the hotel of the same name. The views of the Citadel and surrounding area are great and compensate somewhat for the lousy food. During Ramadan this is one of the most popular places in the area. Not surprisingly, there's no alcohol.

There are a couple of places on the square by the Mosque of Sayyidna Al-Hussein. They serve a tasty half kg of mixed meats, salad and soft drinks for two for E£30 – a bit pricey, but the food tastes good.

In the next street, which runs off Sharia al-Muski, there's a popular teahouse and *Egyptian Pancakes*, which has excellent pancakes. Here too you'll find the 24 hour *El-Halwagy* (☎ 591-7055), an excellent ta'amiyya, fuul and salad place (E£10 for a meal for two) which has been around for nearly a century. You can dine at sidewalk tables or secrete yourself upstairs where one of the tables has a veiled view over the bazaar below.

The *Dahhan* on Sharia al-Muski is popular with Egyptians. A big plate of moza with salad, tahina and a soft drink costs about E£14.

Zamalek Cheap dining is not one of Zamalek's fortes but there are a couple of possibilities. *Al Dente* (☎ 340-9117), at 26 Sharia Bahgat Ali Isa, is a tiny new Italian place frequented by students from the nearby AUC College and young expats. You'll be looking at between E£6 and E£10 for a pasta meal of average proportion. There's no alcohol.

The *Zamalek Restaurant* is a cheap little kebab house on Sharia 26th of July.

Roda Island Just 100m south of the youth hostel is another of the expanding chain of *Felfela* restaurants. The food is more or less the same as in the other places, and the riverside location is perfect for a relaxing beer. There are one or two other places in a similar vein as you continue down the same street.

Doqqi & Mohandiseen This is not really budget territory, but if you happen to be on Sharia Doqqi you could try the *Radwan* restaurant just near Midan Doqqi. This quite pleasant little place serves the usual sort of food, but at decent prices. Across the road and north of Sharia at-Tahrir is a good kushari joint.

In Mohandiseen, there's a place on the corner behind the Atlas Zamalek Hotel which sells heavenly felafel. Alternatively, the nearby *El-Homda* has good kushari, as well as a snooker table on the 1st floor.

Restaurants

Alcohol is served in some restaurants in Cairo and not at others, and there doesn't seem to be any obvious rule on this.

Central Cairo *Fu Shing* (☎ 575-6184), 28 Sharia Talaat Harb, is actually in a lane; look for the sign on the main street. It is one of Cairo's few Chinese restaurants and it has a menu in English. For about E£25 you can get a full meal that could include chop suey, shark fin soup and various fried noodle dishes. For those worried about authenticity, they work out your bill on an abacus.

The *Valley of the Kings Restaurant* (☎ 575-7509), on the 1st floor of the Grand Hotel, 17 Sharia 26th of July, has a great view over the busy streets below and an exotic-looking fountain in the centre. The food is quite good – meals cost from about E£25.

The *Caroll Restaurant* (☎ 746434), 12 Sharia Qasr el-Nil, is a popular place for European and Egyptian food. It does a wide range of meat and fish dishes for E£25 plus. Some of the pastas are very good and considerably cheaper. The service is friendly and the place has a pleasing atmosphere with just a touch of class.

Across the road is *Estoril*; the address is 12 Sharia Talaat Harb, although it's actually in a lane next to the American Express office. Meals are a combination of French and Middle Eastern cuisine and cost E£19 to E£30. Dishes include grilled beef, veal cutlets, roasted chicken and prawns. On the

cheaper side, try the cannelloni for E£7.60; it's very good.

The *Taverne du Champs de Mars*, on the ground floor of the Nile Hilton, is a great old-fashioned Belgian bar that's OK for lunch, dinner or a snack.

Arabesque, 6 Sharia Qasr el-Nil, between Midan Talaat Harb and Midan Tahrir, is the only restaurant in Egypt which doubles as an art gallery. The gallery is small, but sometimes there are interesting works displayed. The food is mediocre at best and seems quite overpriced (main meals E£25 to E£30) for what you get.

Paprika (☎ 749744), 1129 Corniche el-Nil, just south of the Radio & Television building, serves various European dishes, including pizza. It's open from noon to midnight. Radio and TV personalities like to hang out here.

The *Peking* (☎ 591-2381), 14 Sharia al-Ezbekiya, off Sharia Imad ad-Din, serves Cantonese meals for about E£30. It's not bad, although some of the dishes seem to have been 'Egyptianised' in one way or another. It has other restaurants in Maadi, Mohandiseen and Heliopolis.

The *Kowloon* (☎ 575-9831) in the Cleopatra Palace Hotel, Sharia al-Bustan, is a popular Korean and Chinese restaurant that serves dinner from 7.30 to 10 pm. Meals cost about E£30.

Garden City At *Abou Shakra* (☎ 364-8811), 69 Sharia Qasr al-Eini (about 1.5 km south of Midan Tahrir), you will find some of the best kofta and kebab in Cairo. The guy who opened the place in 1947, Ahmed Abu (or Abou) Shakra, was known as the 'King of Kebab'. He has since expanded to open restaurants in Mohandiseen and Heliopolis.

To get there from Midan Tahrir, walk or take any of the buses heading south for Manyal Bridge and beyond and get off when they turn right. A half-order is plenty of food for one person. The prices are moderate to high – a kg of kebab costs E£34. One speciality, pigeon stuffed with rice and served with chips, costs E£13. There are several salads and a cheaper takeaway service. There are a few cheap eating places and teahouses just around here.

Zamalek Zamalek is generally not the cheapest part of town for anything, but there are some good places to track down, especially in the streets north of Sharia 26th of July.

The *Cha Cha Laca* (☎ 341-3870), 22 Sharia Taha Hussein, in the President Hotel complex, is a Mexican restaurant with main dishes around E£24. You can also get cheaper fare such as tacos for between E£8 to E£12. Alcohol is served.

The *Angus Brasserie* (☎ 340-0928), in the New Star Hotel building, Sharia Yehia Ibrahim, claims to be 'the only typical Argentinian steakhouse in Egypt' and has steaks from E£25.

El Patio, at 5 Sharia as-Sayed al-Bakry, is an intimate but casual little air-conditioned restaurant with reasonable pasta dishes at around E£14, plus good desserts and cold beers. There's also a bar upstairs.

The *Ha Na* Korean restaurant serves high-quality food in generous helpings. For E£20 per person you will get an authentic and satisfying meal that would cost four times as much in a place like London. Alcohol is available.

Don Quichotte (☎ 341-5496) at 9 Sharia Ahmed Hishmat is a small, rather formal, seafood restaurant with mains ranging between E£30 and E£65. There's a decent drinks menu but everything, including a local Stella beer, is pricey.

South of Sharia 26th of July is the *Four Corners* (☎ 341-2961, 340-7510), 3rd floor, 4 Sharia Hassan Sabri, which is actually four restaurants in one. One is a classic French restaurant called *Justine* that serves typical haute cuisine; another is *La Piazza*, which has an international menu with Italian pasta specialities; the third is *Matchpoint*, a dark, windowless bar (accessible to couples only) with American sports videos and music; and the fourth is a Chinese restaurant, *Chin Chin*.

Mohandiseen There's an extensive selection of middle to upper-class restaurants in Mohandiseen, though the suburb itself lacks flavour.

The *Tandoori* (☎ 348-6301) at 11 Sharia Shehab, just off Sharia Gamiat ad-Dowal al-Arabiyya, serves tandoori chicken, kema (a curry of minced lamb with potatoes and peas) and jhinga (curried prawns cooked in a special sauce). A meal costs about E£30 per person. No alcohol is served.

Papillon (☎ 347-1672) is a popular Lebanese restaurant on Sharia 26th of July. It has a wide range of Oriental dishes, some of them a pleasing variation on Egyptian cuisine. Try the kofta khoshkhash (E£22), which is the usual minced meat cooked on skewers but in this case served on a very tasty tomato sauce base, or fattah (E£18), a yoghurt and chicken combination.

Prestige (☎ 347-0383) at 43 Sharia Geziret al-Arab is, as its name indicates, one of Cairo's chic restaurants. Actually, it's two restaurants in one: a dapper, romantic (when the lights and rock music are turned down) pizzeria on one side; a full Italian restaurant with cloth serviettes and candles on the other. Beer is served inside only. The Italian restaurant is more expensive than the pizzeria, but at E£20 and up for a main course is still reasonable by international standards.

For a culinary leap north, you could head a few doors up to No 38 for the Alpine atmosphere of the *Tirol Restaurant* (☎ 344-9725), where an array of dishes seems to have the stamp of approval from Cairo's Austrian community. It's not cheap, though – reckon on about E£30 for a main.

The *Taj Mahal* (☎ 348-4881) is at 15 Midan Ibn Afaan, just across Sharia Ibn al-Waleed from the Singaporean embassy. It is one of the best restaurants in Cairo. You'll walk away feeling stuffed and satisfied with the tandoori chicken, papadums, curried vegetables and other typically Indian foods. An average meal costs about E£40.

You'll find a decent Korean and Chinese restaurant called *Paxy's* (☎ 347-3928) in the basement of the Amoun Hotel on Midan Sphinx. A good meal from an extensive menu will cost you about E£30 to E£40 a head.

One of the popular *Abou Shakra* (☎ 344-2299) restaurants is at 17 Sharia Gamiat ad-Dowal al-Arabiyya (see the earlier Garden City restaurant section for details of this expanding chain).

Gezira & Doqqi Just south of At-Tahrir Bridge, across from the Opera House, is an outrageously priced 'singing restaurant' called the *Casino el-Nil*. The food is nothing special and the singing you could live without. Rather, go outside and down the stairs. You can sit right by the river away from the traffic noise and the Stella costs a fairly standard E£6.

If you happen to be down around Midan al-Missaha in Doqqi and looking for somewhere to eat you could try the *CIAO Restaurant* (☎ 335-2482) at No 10 on the midan. It has an enjoyable atmosphere and serves pizzas from E£7 to E£20, as well as pasta and meat dishes.

Heliopolis This chic suburb is a popular getaway for well-to-do Cairenes who are looking for good dining and nightlife. One of the best restaurants here is Swissair's *Le Chantilly* (☎ 669026) at 11 Sharia Baghdad.

For something a little less pricey you could try the brand-new *Abou Shakra* (☎ 417-9557) at 82 Sharia al-Mirghani (see the previous Garden City section for details).

Giza Swissair has two restaurants in the Nasr building on Sharia el-Nil just north of the Al-Gamaa Bridge. *Le Chalet* is a quaint restaurant/bar which stays open until 1 am and serves European-style snacks and delicious cakes in a pseudo-Swiss coffee shop atmosphere. Upstairs is the chic *Le Château* (☎ 348-6270) where steak or fish main courses start at around E£42.

There are several options along Maryutia Canal, a canal which leads off to your right (as you head towards the pyramids) from Pyramids Rd, and ends near the village of Kerdassa. However, there are not many bridges spanning the canal, so if you're at a restaurant on one side of the canal and prefer to be at another on the other bank you'll have to walk back to Pyramids Rd or get one of the service taxis (of the microbus variety) that run up and down each side of the canal.

Andrea's Chicken & Fish Restaurant (☎ 851133) and *La Rose* are both about one km from Pyramids Rd on the left bank (when heading towards Kerdassa). Andrea's is usually a bit overrun by tour groups, making La Rose the quieter, more preferable option.

The *Felfela Village* (☎ 383-0574) is several hundred metres down the road, on the right bank. If you're after a packaged Middle Eastern atmosphere with everything that is supposedly exotic, then this is the place. This restaurant and circus has everything – dancing horses, camel rides, acrobats, snake charmers, and a playground and small zoo for the kids – and is very popular with Egyptians. Massive amounts of traditional Egyptian food are served. About 100m past Felfela Village is *The Farm*.

The *Restaurant el Dar* (☎ 385-2289) is on Saqqara Rd, about six km from the junction with Pyramids Rd (a couple of km past the Motel Salma). This place too is aimed at groups rather than individuals. Expect to pay about E£15 for a meal of fish or chicken.

There are few options close to the pyramids. At the Cheops Pavilion directly in front of the Sphinx is the *Sphinx House* restaurant/cafe. It has a shaded terrace with unobstructed views of the Sphinx but, as you'd expect with such a prime position, everything is over the top. A beer alone costs E£9.

Halfway between the bus stop and the Sphinx entrance to the pyramids is a small place called the *China Restaurant*. Clustered around it are a few of the usual stands selling ta'amiyya and the like.

Close to the turn-off for the Desert Highway from Pyramids Rd is an overpriced fish restaurant called *Christo* (☎ 383-3582) where you can eat upstairs with a view of the pyramids or dine in the garden below. It has set menus ranging from E£25 to E£42.

All the big hotels around Giza and out along the Desert Highway to Alexandria have various restaurants catering to most tastes, if not most budgets. The *Moghul*

Room Indian restaurant at the Mena House Oberoi Hotel is an expensive place but popular with expatriates for a special treat.

Floating Restaurants

A series of floating restaurants is moored up near the Gezira Club in Gezira. Some of them are elaborate monsters while others look ready to be scuttled.

Heading north from At-Tahrir Bridge, the first one you meet is the *Al-Safina* (☎ 341-0430), where a main meal of chicken or seafood will cost about E£20/45.

Next door is a much more modest place with an open-air cafe on the top deck. It's called *Ali ad-Din*. An average dish here will cost around E£8, although cheaper snack fare is also served. There's no alcohol.

Next up, past the Casino al-Nahr and the 6th of October Bridge, is the *Omar Khayyam Restaurant*. It occupies a decrepit houseboat and has one of those hilariously misspelt menus, offering 'chipsy or bon freete' (aka chips) for E£1.

Le Pacha 1901 (☎ 340-6730) is the last of the Gezira crowd, and is relatively new and ritzy. This huge vessel has nine restaurants, stained glass windows and arabesque decor. It's popular with foreign tour groups.

The MS *Scarabee* and its more modern and luxurious stablemate, the MS *Aquarius* (☎ 354-3198), are usually moored alongside Corniche el-Nil, next to Shepheard's Hotel. The MS *Scarabee* has three cruises each day – at 2.30 pm for a 1½ hour lunch cruise that costs E£48; at 6 pm for a E£21 sunset cruise; and at 8 pm for a two hour voyage including a buffet dinner, belly dancing and band for E£65. All prices are excluding drinks. At the time of writing, the MS *Aquarius* was in dry dock but, once back on the water, it should be offering similar but more expensive services. It's advisable to book ahead.

Breakfast

Almost all the major hotels offer all-you-can-eat breakfast buffets, some of which are fairly good deals, if you are sick of the budget hotel food.

The *Nile Hilton* has two types of breakfast buffet, both served in the Ibis Cafe from 5 to 11 am. There's an open buffet for E£27 or the all-you-can-eat hot and cold buffet for E£35. The latter is a wonderful treat, particularly after a long, dusty tour around Egypt. If you plan to eat here at any time other than breakfast, you must spend a minimum of E£10.50 (which wouldn't be difficult given the prices).

Shepheard's Hotel offers a breakfast buffet from 6 to 11 am for E£28.

The *Cairo Meridien* buffet, from 7 to 10.30 am, costs E£29 plus taxes. The views of the Nile from the dining room are incredible, the chocolate croissants are great, and there are free newspapers in French or English.

The *Hotel Mena House Oberoi* is a wonderful place to have breakfast before touring the pyramids. At E£19 its continental breakfast is skimpy, but the special breakfast buffets are not bad at E£34.

Cafes

Groppi's, on Midan Talaat Harb, used to be one of the most popular places in Cairo for sipping coffee, munching on baqlawa and watching a unique assortment of people troop in and out. However, the management changed and it's not quite like it used to be. There is also a *Garden Groppi's* on Sharia Adly, opposite the tourist office, but the atmosphere is a bit sterile.

The *À l'Américaine Café* on the corner of Sharia Talaat Harb and Sharia 26th of July has lousy food and is shabbier than Groppi's.

The cafe on the 18th floor of the *Everest Hotel* on Midan Ramses is good for a Pepsi or coffee while watching the melting pot below.

In Islamic Cairo, the *Naguib Mahfouz Coffeeshop*, smack in the middle of Khan al-Khalili, caters predominantly to tourists and has fine decor and expensive treats.

The closest thing you'll find to a real Italian cafe this side of the Mediterranean is the little *Simmonds Coffee Shop* on Sharia 26th of July in Zamalek. The owner, Mohammed Eid, known locally as Am Arabi, has been serving cappuccinos and pastries (E£1.70) to an eclectic clientele, including artists, diplomats and travellers, for more than 40 years.

Two other cafes with a vaguely European feel are *L'Amphitrion* and *Palmyra*, both on Sharia Al-Ahram in Heliopolis. The tiled spacious terraces of both of these cafes are perfect for people-watching while sipping a cold beer, and light meals are available (though only the Palmyra has an English menu). Given a touch-up and a few more chairs, these cafes wouldn't be out of place in Brussels or Paris. The Nouzha-line tram stops near both.

Fast Food

Major western fast-food chains have mushroomed in Cairo. Most have outlets in the city centre (particularly along Sharia Mohammed Mahmoud opposite the AUC) as well as in the suburbs and on the road to the pyramids. If you haven't got the energy to go out and find one – not an uncommon situation in the madness of Cairo – most will do home delivery. They include:

Chicken Tikka – Sharia al-Batal Ahmed Abdel Aziz in Mohandiseen.

Hot 'n' Tender – in an alley just around the corner from Sunnys supermarket in Zamalek (☎ 340-2655); it has takeaway pizzas from E£7.50 or Japanese cuisine for about E£18.

House of Donuts – on Sharia al-Batal Ahmed Abdel Aziz, Mohandiseen; offers a range of donuts every bit as good as anything you'll find in the west – at a price.

Kentucky Fried Chicken – branches in the city centre opposite the AUC and on Sharia Abdel Khaliq Sarwat, in Maadi, Heliopolis and Mohandiseen.

McDonald's – branches on Sharia Talaat Harb and Sharia Mohammed Mahmud, as well as one on Sharia al-Mirghani in Heliopolis, to mention but a few.

Pizza Hut – all-you-can-eat salad bar (E£4) which offers travellers a cheap alternative to eating ta'amiyya and fuul everyday. There are Huts in Doqqi, Heliopolis, Zamalek, Giza, Maadi and along Pyramids Rd, as well as one on Sharia Mohammed Mahmoud across from the AUC.

Pizza Inn – restaurants at 10 Sharia Syria in Mohandiseen, 13 Sharia al-Khalifa al-Mamoun in Heliopolis and along Pyramids Rd.

Wimpy – serves the Egyptian version of British hamburgers; you'll find branches, among other places, on Sharia Hoda Shaarawi near Midan Falaki and on Sharia Mohammed Mahmoud, on Sharia Taha Hussein in Zamalek and on Sharia Murad near Midan Giza in Giza.

Self-Catering

A great place to introduce yourself to Egyptian shopping strategies is *Souq Mansur*, which occupies a converted warehouse off Sharia Mansur in central Cairo. This market does not cater at all for tourists, and is a real sensory experience. Each stall and shop specialises in something different like eggs, fruit, spices or flowers. Watch out for the huge hunks of meat that the meat men hang on high hooks. You probably won't see them until something wet and red drips on you. Most prices are posted, but it's not uncommon to bargain. Go early in the morning before the stench of old meat and live chickens, turkeys, ducks and rabbits gets too strong.

For a second sensory thrill head to the *Brazilian & Yemini Coffee Store* just around the corner from Souq Mansur on Sharia at-Tahrir. Coffee is ground fresh here every day and the smell, for some people anyway, is intoxicating.

Another colourful central market, this time for fruit and vegetables only, is the *Souq Tawfiqiyya* along Sharia al-Tawfiqiyya just west of Midan Orabi. Decoratively arranged stalls operate here until late at night, though prices are sometimes pepped up.

If it's just a good old supermarket you're in need of, head to *Sunnys* on Sharia Aziz Osman in Zamalek. This place is something of an institution among expats for the wide range of goodies it stocks. It also has a community noticeboard advertising flats for rent, language tutors, missing pets and the like. Sunnys has another store in Mohandiseen.

Takeaway alcohol supplies can be bought at Sunnys, as well as from the occasional liquor stores dotted round the city. One such central place is *Nicolakis*, next to the Casablanca Restaurant on Sharia Talaat Harb. There's another one just round the corner on Sharia 26th of July (near the alley leading to Ash-Shams). A third is situated on Sharia

Imad ad-Din near the International Public Meal Kushari joint. Sunnys charges E£3.25 for a local Stella and has foreign beers such as Stella Artois and Holstein for about E£4 per 330 ml can.

ENTERTAINMENT

Western-style discos, movie houses with English-language movies and nightclubs with floor shows abound in Cairo. With bucks to burn you can head to the casinos at many of the five star hotels. If, on the other hand, you've already blown the budget, there are thousands of teahouses where you can while away the hours over a game of backgammon and a cheap cup of *shay* (tea).

Cinemas

Cairo's movie houses generally charge between E£4.50 and E£10, except during the Cairo International Film Festival (for details see the earlier Special Events section) when prices are pepped up. Many of the city's cultural centres (listed earlier in this chapter) also screen films. *Al-Ahram* newspaper carries listings for some of the better cinemas, which include:

Cairo Sheraton Hotel – Doqqi (☎ 360-6081)
Cine Al-Tahrir – 122 Sharia al-Tahrir in Doqqi (☎ 335-4726); this is one of Cairo's better movie houses.
Karim I & II – Sharia Imad ad-Din (a street thick with cinemas) (☎ 924830)
Normandy – 31 Sharia Akrani, Heliopolis (☎ 258-0254)
Radio Cinema – spanking new cinema on Sharia Talaat Harb boasting air-con, stereo sound and a ban on smoking and talking.
Cinema Ramses Hilton – Corniche el-Nil (☎ 574-7436)

Discos

Discos vary greatly in quality, and entrance prices generally start at around E£15. Some places impose a minimum charge which sometimes includes a drink or two. Most are closed by 3 am.

Jackie's at the Nile Hilton is interesting if you can get in. It's a private, couples-only club where, in dark corners at candle-lit tables, Egyptian couples momentarily forget

their conservatism and get a bit cosy. Outside on the street, such displays of affection are scorned. There's a minimum charge of E£25; Thursday, Friday and Saturday nights are the most popular.

The *Tamango Disco* in the Atlas Zamalek Hotel in Mohandiseen is another popular couples-only place. Tables often have to be reserved, but it is possible to get in without booking ahead. It costs E£40 for men and E£1.25 women (which includes a drink), and the crowd is an interesting mix of westerners and trendy, wealthy Egyptians.

A much less exclusive place is the *Longchamp Hotel Disco*, next to the Cypriot embassy, in Zamalek. The E£15 minimum charge includes a beer and soft drink. It's on nightly from 9 pm and is known to be a bit of a meat market.

There's a string of discos and nightclubs along Pyramids Rd, most of them pretty expensive and tacky. You could try the *Vendome Blow Up Disco* or the *Palma*, within a km of each other about 10 minutes drive from the pyramids back towards town. *Africana* also on Pyramids Rd is the place for some African sounds.

Up in Heliopolis, the disco in the basement of the *Hotel ·Beirut* at 43 Sharia Baghdad is frequented by expats and locals and has a E£10 minimum charge (including one soft drink). The decor is nothing exceptional, but even on a quiet Sunday afternoon you can find couples moving to the blaring music here.

Nightclubs

There are two categories of nightclub. The ones usually patronised by foreigners are generally fairly expensive and often include a lavish feast, folkloric dance performances, belly dancers and Arabic music. Expect to spend at least E£20 just to watch the show. All the major hotels have floor shows, as do many of the overpriced clubs along Pyramids Rd. Note that cover charges and other costs usually have taxes tossed on top at the end. The action generally starts at about 11 pm and can roll on until 5 am. Drinks cost about E£11/6 for a beer/soft drink.

Even more interesting are the little places catering mainly to Egyptians – although it has to be said these can be tacky, even sleazy. They all have their good and bad nights – sometimes they're full, on other occasions hardly anyone seems to be there.

The *Palmyra*, off Sharia 26th of July, is run by someone who has come to be known as Madame Monocle because, well, she really does get about the place holding up said monocle in order to keep an eye on proceedings. This place has the full Arab music contingent, belly dancers from about 1 to 4 am and occasionally other acts like acrobats. There is an entry charge of E£3. Around the Palmyra are a couple of other similar nightclubs, one of them called the *Miami*.

Another similar but smaller and tackier place on Sharia Qasr el-Nil is simply called *Disco*. It's on the 9th floor, and has introduced an appalling and obligatory E£40 meal on top of its cover charge.

Just down from the Cairo Khan Hotel on Sharia Mohammed Farid is an even sleazier place – the *Honolulu* – half the time there's only an awful 'disco' going on there. The cover charge of E£40 includes two beers.

You might want to pop into the *Shahrazad Night Club* – a belly-dancing and drinking hole above the Alfi Bey Restaurant, but it's not as entertaining as the Palmyra. Entry costs only E£2.50 and the decor, in sort, resembles an old opera hall.

Classical Music, Theatre & Dance

The Cairo Opera House (☎ 342-0598) in Gezira is the city's premier performing arts venue. Well-known international troupes sometimes perform here for prices that would be unheard of in the west. Some of the recitals by local companies, such as the Cairo Opera Ballet Company and Cairo Orchestra, are quite reasonable too. Check *Egypt Today* and *Al-Ahram* for the latest details, or go down and pick up a programme. Jacket and tie are required, but less well dressed travellers have been known to borrow them from staff.

There are often music recitals and plays of varying quality at the Ewart Hall and Wallace Theatre, both in the AUC. Entry is often free or next to it. Check out the notice boards around the campus or inquire at the AUC's public relations office (building No 4) on Sharia Sheikh Rihan.

Traditional Music & Dance

On Wednesday and Saturday nights from 9 pm (9.30 pm in winter) you can treat yourself to a display of raqs ash-sharqi, or Sufi dancing. It's performed by the Al-Tannoura Egyptian Heritage Dance Troupe in the Madrassa of Al-Ghouri in Islamic Cairo. The troupe does the dancing as a cultural performance, although it is supposed to be a form of ecstatic mystical dance (Sufis are adherents of a Muslim mystical order which emphasises dancing as a direct personal experience of God). The troupe has toured overseas, and their colourful performances are extremely popular. Admission is free and it's advisable to come early, especially in winter, as the small auditorium can get quite crowded.

Alternatively, you may be lucky enough to witness a *zikr*, or Sufi ceremony and dancing, at one of the Sufi mosques around Islamic Cairo and the City of the Dead. There tend to be more from October to April, as this seems to be when the bulk of moulids (annual celebrations of a Muslim or Christian holy person) take place. For details on moulids, see the Moulid Celebrations boxed story in the Religion section of the Facts about the Country chapter.

Pubs & Bars

Zamalek is a good hunting ground for bars and live music. *Rasputin's Pub* above Angus Brasserie in Sharia Yehia Ibrahim in Zamalek has live blues, jazz or rock music on Monday, Wednesday, Friday and Saturday. The *El Patio* restaurant at 5 Sharia as-Sayed al Bakry in Zamalek has an upstairs bar where live rock is played on Wednesday and Friday from 10 pm to 1 am. The minimum charge of E£10 includes a beer or two soft drinks.

If it's just a typical pub scene you're

missing, then try *Pub 28* just off Sharia Hassan Assim in Zamalek. This pseudo-British pub has a mixed crowd and pricey (E£7) local Stellas, and you can get a meal here too for about E£22. It closes at 2 am.

In central Cairo, the *Odeon Palace Hotel* off Sharia Talaat Harb has a small terrace bar that usually stays open 24 hours; the minimum charge is E£7 (or E£10 after 10 pm).

The Windsor Hotel has a particularly atmospheric drinking spot called the *Barrel Lounge*. A lot of locals use it and solo women travellers should feel quite comfortable here. Talk to Mahmoud, the 1955 Mr Egypt who still boasts rock-hard biceps and a particular liking for being in group photos with patrons – ask to see his photos.

The *Gresham* and *Lotus* hotels, both in Sharia Talaat Harb, each have a cosy bar. Places like this are generally open until about 1 am.

In the big hotels, there are places to avoid and others that are quite reasonable. You can sit in the garden bar of the *Cairo Marriott* and sip a Stella for normal prices, but *Harry's Pub* has a E£25 minimum charge. The 36th floor *Window of the World* bar in the Ramses Hilton offers superb views of the city, especially at sunset, but the minimum charge of E£35 and 'no jeans' policy deters many (as they're no doubt designed to do). In the *Cairo Sheraton* in Doqqi you can drink with no minimum charge but a local Stella will set you back E£8.50.

The Cairo Meridien's *La Pergola* is a breezy terrace at the end of the promontory with wide views over the Nile. It's a wonderful spot to unwind. The minimum charge fluctuates from E£12 (from 11 am to 6 pm) to E£24 (6 pm to 1 am).

The entire interior of the *Taverne du Champs de Mars* at the Nile Hilton was transported from Belgium and reassembled. It's a warm place for a drink, and the E£10.50 minimum charge is not too onerous. Stellas cost E£7.50 and the flow of peanuts is endless.

For those looking for the authentic Egyptian pub scene at the bottom rung, there's a string of out-of-sight places where foreigners are a surprising and rare addition to the clientele. They are mostly simple drinking establishments and don't go out of their way to advertise themselves. Some double as brothels or tacky pick-up joints. One such bar is on the Corniche el-Nil, by the 26th of July Bridge. Another is the *Pussy Cat*, in an alley around the corner from the Alfi Bey Restaurant. It's modern and sterile and definitely nasty.

Cafeterias
Many local bars actually call themselves 'cafeterias', though the only food in sight are the plates of beans and salad you're given to munch on while you drink. A typical representative of this spit-and-sawdust species is the nameless little Stella *bar* on the corner of Sharia Talaat Harb and Sharia Hoda Shaarawi near the Felfela restaurant. Look for the sign 'Cafeteria' above the door. It has been doing business for more than 30 years. Women may not feel at home here, especially if they have to go to the loo – it must be the smallest *pissoir* in the world.

The *Cap d'Or Cafeteria* on Sharia Abdel Khaliq Sarwat is another typical lively *baladi* bar or you could head for the *Cafeteria Port Tawfik* on Midan Orabi.

One of the better ones in central Cairo is *Cafeteria Horea* on Midan Falaki. It's a huge airy place with enormous window panes and is great for people-watching or for sharing a few cold Stellas over a leisurely game of backgammon.

The more you look, the more of these places you'll turn up – half the fun is in discovering them. Another area to look in is just east of Midan Opera. Happy hunting.

Coffee & Tea Houses
Of the thousands of coffee and tea houses dotted around Cairo, one of the oldest is the famous *Fishawi's* a few steps off Midan Hussein in Khan al-Khalili. With its gilded mirrors, wooden benches and smoke-stained walls, it's a colourful place where you can chat with the locals, or just sit and soak up

some real atmosphere. People have been doing just that here for more than 200 years.

Another authentic place is the colourful *Ash-Shams*. This traditional teahouse is hidden from the crowds in a side lane between Sharia 26th of July and Sharia al-Tawfiqiyya at the northern end of Sharia Talaat Harb. Waiters hustle back and forth carrying water pipes and glasses of tea while in the background there's a constant clatter of domino tiles and backgammon pieces.

A nearby alternative to Ash-Shams is the *Cafe el-Agatey*, down the last alley on your left at the western end of Sharia al-Tawfiqiyya. It has a smoky Arabian room and a rooftop terrace and is a meeting place for actors, journalists and musicians.

If you're just in need of a break from the bustle of Sharia Talaat Harb, head to the little *teahouse* at the end of the alley next to (the now defunct) Café Riche. The mint tea here is very good, and there are tables set up under a few shady trees.

THINGS TO BUY

The Things to Buy section in the Facts for the Visitor chapter outlines many of Egypt's shopping possibilities. If it's available anywhere in Egypt it will be found in Cairo.

For regular, run-of-the-mill tourist souvenirs the sprawling Khan al-Khalili bazaar is definitely the place to head for. The confusing maze of alleys is packed with shops but unfortunately a great deal of it is simply tourist junk.

A good place to buy sturdy baskets, handwoven fabrics and screenprinted items like tablecloths and cushion covers is the Tukul Craft Centre (☎ 341-8391), in the basement of the All Saints Cathedral behind the Marriott Hotel. 'Tukul' means 'small house' in one of the languages of southern Sudan, and everything sold in this modest little shop is made by displaced Sudanese. The prices aren't cheap but the quality is excellent.

The Egyptian Museum has a great series of posters for sale including a fine one of Tutankhamun's tomb. They're available from the shops just inside the museum entrance but you'll often find them cheaper

at other outlets, such as the Lehnert & Landrock bookshop on Sharia Sherif.

In addition to the usual postcards and the like, some bookshops sell some very attractive prints of drawings done in Cairo and Egypt by several 19th century artists and draughtsmen.

GETTING THERE & AWAY
Air

EgyptAir has a number of offices around town including a big barn-like office on Midan Opera (open daily from 8 am to 8 pm) and another office on Sharia Talaat Harb (open the same hours). For international airfare details, see the Getting There & Away chapter; for domestic flights, see the Getting Around chapter.

There are a lot of travel agencies clustered around Midan Tahrir. For details on a few of these, see the Travel Agencies section earlier in this chapter. It is possible to pay for airline tickets with a credit card, but not all airlines and agents accept them.

You can call Cairo airport for flight information (☎ 291-4255). The addresses of some airlines which are represented in Cairo include:

Air France
    2 Midan Talaat Harb (☎ 575-8899)
Air India
    1 Sharia Talaat Harb (☎ 393-4864/73/75)
Air Sinai
    Nile Hilton (☎ 760948/772949)
Alitalia
    Nile Hilton (☎ 574-3488/574-0984)
Austrian Airlines
    22 Sharia Qasr el-Nil (☎ 392-1522)
British Airways
    1 Sharia al-Bustan (☎ 578-0743)
Bulgarian Airlines
    13 Sharia Qasr el-Nil (☎ 393-1211); entrance is on Sharia Mohammed Sabri Abu Alam
Czech Airlines
    9 Sharia Talaat Harb (☎ 393-0395)
EgyptAir
    Nile Hilton (☎ 765200)
    Midan Opera (☎ 391-4501)
    6 Sharia Adly (☎ 390-0999)
    9 Sharia Talaat Harb (☎ 393-2836)
    22 Sharia Ibrahim Laqqany, Heliopolis (☎ 290-8453)
    Cairo International Airport (☎ 244-1460)

El Al Israel Airlines
5 Sharia Makrizy, Zamalek (☎ 341-1620)
Ethiopian Airlines
Nile Hilton (☎ 574-0603)
Gulf Air
21 Sharia Mahmoud Bassiuni (☎ 574-3336)
Hungarian Airlines (Malev)
12 Sharia Talaat Harb (☎ 764251)
Japan Airlines (JAL)
Nile Hilton (☎ 574-7233)
KLM (Royal Dutch Airlines)
11 Sharia Qasr el-Nil (☎ 574-7004)
Kenya Airways
Nile Hilton (☎ 762494)
Libyan Arab Airlines
37 Sharia Qasr el-Nil (☎ 392-4595)
Lufthansa
6 Sharia el-Sheikh el-Marsafi, Zamalek (☎ 342-0471)
Olympic Airways
23 Sharia Qasr el-Nil (☎ 393-1459/1318)
Philippines Airlines
17 Sharia Ismail Mohammed, Zamalek (☎ 341-9409)
Royal Jordanian Airlines
6 Sharia Qasr el-Nil (☎ 575-0875)
Singapore Airlines
Nile Hilton (☎ 578-0321)
Sudan Airways
1 Sharia al-Bustan (☎ 578-7398)
Swissair
22 Sharia Qasr el-Nil (☎ 393-7955)
Trans World Airlines (TWA)
1 Sharia Qasr el-Nil (☎ 574-9904)
Tunis Air
14 Sharia Talaat Harb (☎ 575-3420)
Turkish Airlines
3 Midan Mustafa Kamal (☎ 390-8960/1)

Bus

Cairo has five long-distance bus stations. The main one is on Midan Abdel Minnim Riyadh (near the Ramses Hilton along Sharia al-Galaa in central Cairo). There is also a station on Midan Ulali (near Midan Ramses). Other stations include the Ahmed Hilmi bus station (behind Ramses railway station), the Upper Egypt Bus Company station at 45 Sharia al-Azhar (a few blocks east of Midan Ataba) and Abbassiya station (a block from Midan Abbassiya), which is commonly known as the Sinai Terminal.

From Midan Abdel Minnim Riyadh, luxury buses leave to Alexandria, the Delta, Marsa Matruh, Hurghada, Sharm el-Sheikh,

Luxor and Aswan. It's also the departure point for ordinary buses to the Cairo satellite towns of the 6th of October and 10th of Ramadan cities. Also from here you can book tickets to destinations as far afield as Tunis, Istanbul, Damascus, Amman and cities throughout Saudi Arabia and the Gulf. None of these are direct services, but involve transfers to national carriers.

Alexandria & the Mediterranean Coast

Superjet's mega-comfy buses will whisk you from Midan Abdel Minnim Riyadh to Midan Saad Zaghloul in Alexandria (E£19 to E£28, about 2½ hours). There are departures every half an hour, starting at 5 am and finishing at 9 or 10 pm. Superjet also has a daily bus to Marsa Matruh (E£35, five hours) plus, in summer only, two extra services at 7 and 8 am.

West Delta Bus Company buses also depart from Midan Abdel Minnim Riyadh. It has two types of services running to Alexandria; luxury buses (with video, air-con and toilet) cost E£15 and take about 2¾ hours while ordinary buses cost E£8 to E£10 (depending on how clapped out they are) and take longer. Buses leave at 5.30, 6, 6.30 and 7 am and then hourly until midnight. They all pass by the international airport. There's a daily West Delta Bus Company bus to Marsa Matruh (E£30, five hours) at 8.45 am which operates year-round. In summer, there are six extra luxury buses to Marsa Matruh (E£35); five in the morning (the first one is at 7.15 am) and one in the afternoon. In addition there's a no-frills bus at 8.30 am for E£18.

The Nile Delta, Suez Canal & Red Sea

The East Delta Bus Co's white and yellow-green striped buses leave from Midan Ulali near Midan Ramses for Mansura (E£6 to E£7, every 30 minutes, 2½ hours) and Damietta (E£9 to E£10.50, hourly, 3½ hours). They run from 6 am to 6.30 pm. Tickets can be bought from the Delta zone booth. From the Canal zone booth around the corner, there are buses to Port Said (E£10 to E£16, hourly, three hours), Ismailia (E£5, every 45 minutes, 2½ hours) and also to Suez (E£5, every 30 minutes, 1½ to two hours).

Superjet buses depart from Midan Abdel Minnim Riyadh. It has nine daily services to Port Said (E£15, three hours). The first leaves at 6 am, the last at 4 pm, and it stops to pick up passengers in Heliopolis on the way.

To get to Tanta (E£5.50) and some other smaller destinations along the route, you must take a Middle Delta Bus Company bus from Midan Abdel Minnim Riyadh.

The Upper Egypt Bus Company runs luxury buses from Midan Abdel Minnim Riyadh to Hurghada (E£30 to E£40, six hours) at 9 am, noon, 3, 10.30, 11 and 11.30 pm and midnight. The 10.30 pm bus goes on to Al-Quseir (E£42, 11 hours). The Upper Egypt Bus Co's ordinary buses to Red Sea coast destinations depart from the Ahmed Hilmi bus station, behind Ramses station. The five services to Hurghada (E£25 to E£30) leave at 9 am, noon, 3, 10.30 and 11 pm and have air-con and video. The 9 am and 3 pm services go on to Port Safaga (E£25 to E£40). There's a bus for Al-Quseir (E£30) at 7 am and 10 pm.

Superjet also has a bus to Hurghada (E£40 to E£45), departing from Midan Abdel Minnim Riyadh.

Upper Egypt The Upper Egypt Bus Company has luxury buses from Midan Adbel Minnim Riyadh to Luxor (E£40, 10 to 11 hours) at 9.15 pm and Aswan (E£50, 12 hours) at 5 pm. The Upper Egypt Bus Co's ordinary buses (cheap no-frills green buses) leave from the Ahmed Hilmi station and go to destinations such as Beni Suef (E£4.50), Al-Minya (E£8 to E£11, four hours), Asyut (E£10 to E£15, six to seven hours), Luxor and Aswan. Buses to destinations such as Al-Minya and Asyut run every half to one hour from about 6 am to 6 pm.

Superjet has a bus to Qena (E£25), departing from Midan Abdel Minnim Riyadh.

Sinai Nearly all East Delta Company buses to the Sinai leave from Abbassiya station (commonly known as the Sinai terminal), a

block from Midan Abbassiya. These buses are considerably more expensive than those in the rest of the country. They run to Sharm el-Sheikh (seven hours) at 7 and 10 am, 2, 4, 9.30 and 9.45 pm. The exception is the 5 pm bus to Sharm el-Sheikh which leaves from Midan Ulali. The 7 am and 4 and 9.45 pm buses go on to Dahab (nine hours), and all buses stop at a few places such as El-Tor. The 9 am bus to Nuweiba (nine hours) goes via St Catherine's (7½ hours), and the 7 and 9 pm one goes on to Taba. Ticket prices (it is irritating to note that foreigners pay E£10 to E£20 more than Egyptians) vary. The daytime buses to Sharm el-Sheikh cost E£30 or E£40 (with the exception of the 4 pm bus which costs E£26), while the two late-night services are E£50. To Dahab it cost E£31 to E£45. The day bus to Nuweiba costs E£40 (E£40 also to St Catherine's) and the night buses E£55 (E£10 extra to go all the way to Taba).

The buses to Al-Arish and Rafah leave from Midan Ulali but also pick up at the Sinai terminal. There are buses to Al-Arish (five hours) at 7.30 and 8.30 am and noon for E£35, and one at 4 pm for E£25. To Rafah (E£35, six hours) buses leave at 7.30 and 8.30 am.

Superjet has a nightly service to Sharm el-Sheikh (E£50) which leaves at 11 pm from its terminal on Midan Abdel Minnim Riyadh.

Note that it is generally cheaper to travel first to Suez and pick up other transport from there. See the Suez Getting There & Away section.

The Western Oases Buses travel daily to the Western Desert oases in the New Valley (or Al-Wadi al-Gedid) from a small Upper Egypt Bus Company station at 45 Sharia al-Azhar, a few blocks east of Midan Ataba – look out for the small white on green sign. All buses stop near Midan Giza – at the 6th of October City minibus stop where the overpass forks and Pyramids Rd begins – to take on additional passengers. However if you want to be sure of a place it's best to reserve tickets 24 hours in advance and catch the bus from the main terminal.

There are no direct buses from here to Siwa – to get there you must first get a bus to Alexandria or Marsa Matruh, and then another from there.

To Bahariyya (Bawiti) there are buses at 8 am (E£10) and noon (E£12) from Saturday to Thursday; on Friday there's one service only at 9 am which costs E£10. Usually these buses do not have air-con. The trip takes about six hours (take some food and water, as sometimes the oasis buses don't stop anywhere useful for breaks).

To Farafra (E£25, 10 to 11 hours) there is only one option – the 8 am service to Bahariyya which continues on to Farafra. At the time of writing, this service was under threat of being reduced to three times a week so check the present situation. The road linking Bahariyya and Farafra is still partly unpaved which makes this leg of the journey long and dusty.

To Dakhla (Mut) there are three daily buses via Asyut and Al-Kharga. All of these buses have air-con (if it works); the pricier ones have video also. They leave at 7 am and 5 and 7 pm and cost E£26/35/37 respectively. The trip takes about 12 to 14 hours. The evening services are supposedly direct and do not stop in Asyut itself (though you could get off at the desert road turn-off).

To Al-Kharga (nine hours) there are two buses a day via Asyut. The first leaves at 10 am and costs E£21; the second departs at 8 pm and costs E£32 with air-con and video. The three buses to Dakhla also go via Al-Kharga but, according to the Upper Egypt Bus Company, they are direct buses for Dakhla and do not pick up or set down passengers in Al-Kharga. Check to be sure of the latest schedules. Even if you do take one of these buses to Kharga, you'll probably be made to pay the full Dakhla fare.

Al-Faiyum Buses for Al-Faiyum (E£3, two hours) leave from the Ahmed Hilmi station and a separate station in the vicinity of Midan Giza. For the latter, continue past the minibus stop until you reach Sharia Sudan.

The bus lot is on the other side of the railway line.

Israel & the Palestinian Territories For details on buses to Tel Aviv and Jerusalem, see the Land section in the Getting There & Away chapter.

Jordan & the Gulf It is possible to book a combined bus-ferry ticket from Cairo through to Aqaba in Jordan at Midan Ulali or Midan Abdel Minnim Riyadh stations, but the bus for the Cairo-Nuweiba leg leaves from the Sinai terminal at Midan Abbassiya. The bus costs US$23 and the ferry is E£40.20. Note that tickets bought in Jordan coming the other way are cheaper.

To Saudi Arabia and other Gulf destinations, tickets must be bought at the Sinai terminal itself. The one-way trip to Riyadh is E£210; the fare to Kuwait is E£380.

Libya The East Delta Bus Company runs a daily service to Benghazi from Midan Ulali (you can also book the ticket at the Midan Abdel Minnim Riyadh office). One-way tickets cost E£100. The bus leaves at 9 am and takes about 20 hours. On Monday and Thursday the bus continues for another 16 hours to Tripoli. That ticket costs E£180. Make sure you have a visa.

Superjet runs a bus to Benghazi (E£100) and Tripoli (E£200) which departs at 7.30 am from Midan Abdel Minnim Riyadh.

Cheaper tickets are available with the Hebton bus company at 305 Sharia Shubra, Midan al-Khalifawi, Shubra, or at its office on Midan Ataba. Its bus costs E£80 to Benghazi and departs at around 8 pm daily.

Train
Ramses station, on Midan Ramses, is Cairo's main railway station. Everything and everyone seems to be moving all at once, and at first it can be a bit confusing trying to buy tickets from the right window. There is a tourist office with tourist police just inside the main entrance on the left; it is open from 8 am to 8 pm. Note also that among the phones, farther inside on the left, are a few

card phones. In a secondary entrance to the right is a small post office and, next to it, the left-luggage area (marked 'cloak room') which is open 24 hours every day and the service costs E£1 per piece. The electronic departure indicators are in Arabic only.

For general details about the types of trains and tickets that are available, students discounts and so on, see the Train section in the Getting Around chapter.

Wagons-Lits The wagon-lit office (☎ 574-9474; fax 574-9074) is in a separate building south of the car park on the left side of the

main building; it's open from 9 am to 4 pm (Friday until 2 pm). Follow the blue on yellow signs which read 'Res. Office'. The spacious office is on the 1st floor. This is the only kind of sleeper available to foreigners and there is now only one train a day which travels to Luxor and Aswan. For either destination it costs E£451 one way in 1st class, or E£293 in 2nd class (E£540 return), and includes all meals. There is no student reduction. If you want to do both, you have to use the Luxor to Aswan leg within 72 hours. In the high season (from about October to April) it is best to book two or three days in

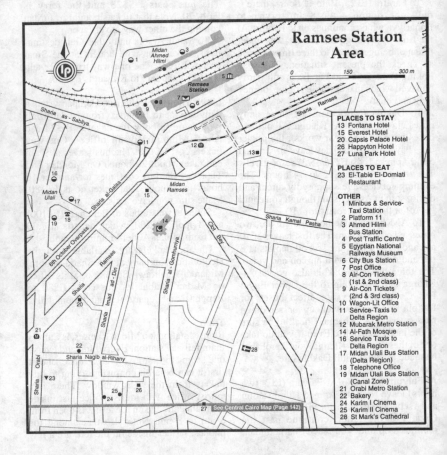

Ramses Station Area

0   150   300 m

PLACES TO STAY
13 Fontana Hotel
15 Everest Hotel
20 Capsis Palace Hotel
26 Happyton Hotel
27 Luna Park Hotel

PLACES TO EAT
23 El-Tabie El-Domiati
   Restaurant

OTHER
1 Minibus & Service-
   Taxi Station
2 Platform 11
3 Ahmed Hilmi
   Bus Station
4 Post Traffic Centre
5 Egyptian National
   Railways Museum
6 City Bus Station
7 Post Office
8 Air-Con Tickets
   (1st & 2nd class)
9 Air-Con Tickets
   (2nd & 3rd class)
10 Wagon-Lit Office
11 Service-Taxis to
   Delta Region
12 Mubarak Metro Station
14 Al-Fath Mosque
16 Service Taxis to
   Delta Region
17 Midan Ulali Bus Station
   (Delta Region)
18 Telephone Office
19 Midan Ulali Bus Station
   (Canal Zone)
21 Orabi Metro Station
22 Bakery
24 Karim I Cinema
25 Karim II Cinema
28 St Mark's Cathedral

advance. From Cairo, the train leaves at 7.45 pm and arrives at Luxor about 5 am and at Aswan at 11 am. The return train leaves Aswan at 3 pm and Luxor at 8.30 pm and arrives in Cairo at 6 am.

Tickets for this train can also be booked at the wagon-lit office at Shepheard's Hotel on Corniche el-Nil.

2nd Class Ordinary & 3rd Class Tickets in these classes for southern destinations are available from platform 11; for all other destinations they can be bought at the row of windows next to the wagon-lit office, between the car park and platform eight.

Some examples of 3rd/2nd class fares from Cairo include:

Alexandria	E£2.50/5.50
Al-Minya	E£2.90/6.50
Damietta	E£2.40/5.40
Ismailia	E£1.80/4.20
Mansura	E£1.70/3.70
Port Said	E£3.00/5.50
Suez	E£1.05/2.60
Zagazig	E£1.00/3.20

Southern Destinations The overnight trains to Luxor and Aswan are the ones most commonly taken by foreigners. They are among the best trains in Egypt. Even for sit-up tickets you'll need to book at least a day, and probably two days, in advance.

There are five express overnight trains from Cairo to Luxor and Aswan. However, foreigners are only allowed to travel on three of them – No 84 (the wagon-lit train) and Nos 980 and 996. The latter two make hardly any stops outside Luxor and Aswan and leave at 7.30 and 10 pm, respectively. Where stops are made, they can last for up to 45 minutes. Heading north, the respective trains are No 85 (wagon-lit) and Nos 981 and 997.

First class, 2nd and 3rd class seat tickets for destinations south of Cairo are bought along platform 11. There are eight windows and each one deals with specific trains. The destinations and train numbers are written up in Arabic on the windows, although the

system does not seem to be rigorously applied.

The 1st/2nd class air-con fare from Cairo to Luxor (about 10 hours) is E£48/28 and the student fare is E£28/22. These fares are excluding meals. The trip to Aswan (about 15 hours) is E£60/34 in 1st/2nd class. Fares can vary a little depending on whether or not you're on one of the faster trains (about E£3 to E£4 more for the faster ones).

A lot of people have reported an odd, and slightly suspicious, practice. Sometimes passengers have been told they cannot buy tickets all the way to Aswan, but that they must pay for as far as, say, Edfu, and worry about the rest later. They then find themselves paying rather a lot for another ticket on the train to complete the journey. It all seems a bit mysterious, and it's difficult to see who gets what out of it.

Another scam to watch out for is being told that 2nd class tickets on the trains to Luxor or Aswan are sold out. Several travellers have reported buying tickets in 1st class after being told this, only to find that there were plenty of seats available in 2nd class. If this happens, you could either try to get an Egyptian friend to buy the ticket for you or take pot luck that the train really isn't full and simply buy a ticket once you're actually on board (you'll have to pay a small fee of E£3 if you do this).

Northern Destinations For 1st and 2nd class air-con tickets to Alexandria, Marsa Matruh and the Nile Delta, head for the windows directly in front of you when come in the main entrance, past the tourist office and the telephones. For 2nd class ordinary tickets, walk past the 1st class ticket windows outside and across to the next office.

The best trains running between Cairo and Alexandria are the Turbos. They make only one stop, at Sidi Gaber station in Alexandria, and take two hours. Second class in this train is about as good as 1st class in most others. You can't mistake the train – it looks a little like the French TGV (although it's not quite as fast!). Turbo Nos 905, 917 and 927 leave

Cairo respectively at 9 am and 2 and 7 pm. It is more expensive than other trains and the student discount is not very high. Tickets for 1st/2nd class air-con cost E£22/17.

Other direct trains leave at 9 am and 3, 6 and 10.30 pm. They're the same price as the Turbos and take roughly the same time.

Other trains, known as the 'French-line' services, take at least 2¾ hours (often longer) and cost E£20/12 in 1st/2nd class. They call at Benha, Tanta (E£9/6) and Damanhur on the way and leave at 6, 8.30 and 11 am, noon (this train stops in Tanta only) and 2.10, 4, 5, 8 (does not stop in Tanta) and 9.30 pm.

Eastern Destinations Four trains make the trip from Cairo to Port Said (four hours), stopping en route at Zagazig, Ismailia and Qantara. They leave at 6.20 and 11.30 am and 2.30 and 6.30 pm. There are six other trains for Ismailia (three hours). Those making the fewest stops leave at 5.35 and 8.45 am. The 2nd class air-con fare to Port Said is E£14 and to Ismailia it's E£8.

Six slow trains leave for Suez from 'Ain Shams station, in the east of the city. This is particularly awkward for most people, so stick to the buses and service taxis.

Service Taxi

Cairo's service taxis depart from various places around the city. By Ramses station, they stretch around from the Midan Ulali bus station up to the railway station. They depart for Mansura, Qantara, Damietta (Ras al-Bar), Alexandria (E£8 to E£10), Suez (E£5), Ismailia (E£5), Port Said (E£8), Al-Arish (E£12, five hours) and Rafah (E£15, six hours). Fares are determined by the distance travelled, so keep an eye out for what others pay to get the set price.

Service taxis for Alexandria also leave from in front of Ramses station and the Nile Hilton. Taxis for destinations in and around Al-Faiyum (E£4) leave from the Al-Faiyum bus stop near Midan Giza. Note that sometimes 'service taxis' are in fact microbuses (private minibuses).

The service-taxi station at Midan Ahmed

Hilmi covers the Delta area. There are regular departures for Mansura (E£8), Tanta (E£5), Zagazig (E£4) and other destinations.

GETTING AROUND

Getting around Cairo can be a confusing and frustrating experience, but several modes of transport are available. Buses are the most common form of transport for the majority of Cairenes, but minibuses are equally popular, less crowded, and increasingly prevalent. Taxis are everywhere at any time of the day or night. There's a partially underground metro train service between Helwan and Al-Marg, near Heliopolis, and there's also a water bus that travels the Nile from Maadi to Qanater, north of Cairo. Several tram lines (confusingly, Cairenes also call trams 'metros') run in north-eastern parts of the city. Private donkey carts and *hantours* (horse-drawn carriages) continue to weave through the streets and alleyways, along with an occasional camel laden with goods for the market.

The Airport

The great majority of visitors to Egypt come through Cairo airport. You will be hassled no end to take a taxi or limousine for inflated prices – if you accept, triple check what they think you have agreed to pay, as there is an irritating tendency to nod at what you say and hit you with an out-of-the-world fare later on. Despite claims that the 'official' taxi fare to central Cairo is E£28, ruthless bargaining can get them down to between E£10 and E£15; using the meter (which few will agree to do) it should cost about E£6! Ignore pleas about petrol being expensive and other such ploys. It seems that the closer you are to the arrival hall, the higher the taxi fare. Keep your cool, walk away to the bus stops and let them come to you with their offers.

Don't believe anyone who tells you that there is no bus to the city centre. In fact there are quite a few buses and minibuses to various points in Cairo from the older Terminal I, and several pass first by the newer Terminal II.

At Terminal II buses stop on the ground

level between the arrival and departure halls. They serve as a shuttle to Terminal I, where buses stop in front of the obelisk across the parking lot from the main building. Here you have a wider choice of buses and minibuses into the city centre (25 to 50 pt). There are at least hourly buses to Midan Tahrir (No 422) for 25 pt, to Midan Giza (No 949) via Midan Ramses and Tahrir, and to Midan Ataba (No 948). Bus No 400 (25 pt) and minibus No 27 (50 pt) depart frequently round the clock. The journey to Midan Tahrir will take at least an hour; longer if it's peak hour.

Going to the airport, you can take the same bus (No 400) from the city bus terminal on Midan Abdel Minnim Riyadh in central Cairo (just north of the Egyptian Museum), or minibus No 27 from the stands in front of the Nile Hilton.

It is possible to get a bus to destinations beyond Cairo directly from the airport. Superjet has frequent buses to Alexandria en route from Midan Abdel Minnim Riyadh passing by Terminals I and II. Buses leaving before 4 pm cost E£24, those afterwards E£30. The last service leaves at 8.45 pm. The Upper Egypt, the East Delta and the West Delta bus companies have booths at Terminal I with occasional departures for destinations all over the country.

There are a few limousine taxi services that operate between both terminals and various destinations in Cairo. Bank Nasser Limousine (☎ 506-1348) will take passengers to central Cairo for E£45. To Alexandria they charge an outrageous E£350. The more luxurious Limousine Misr (☎ 285-6721) charges E£65 to or from central Cairo. These services have counters at the arrival lounges.

Bus & Minibus

If you're really planning on squeezing in and out of Cairo's crowded buses, you may want to try to get your hands on the booklet that lists all the city's bus and minibus routes. It is sold at some newsstands and is called the *Daleel an-Naql al-Aam*. It's in Arabic only, and is not always easy to get a hold of, but could make life easier for the dedicated supporter of public transport.

Riding a bus in Cairo requires more than just the slippery eel-like qualities necessary for claiming your space. Route numbers are usually indicated in Arabic numerals (sometimes in English also) on small signs behind the windscreen and on painted signs on the side of the bus. You have to be able to recognise the numerals quickly, because the buses hardly stop. They roll into the station, sometimes already full, and a few seconds later roll out the other side, seemingly with even more passengers and less space. If there are lots of people waiting for the bus, the strategy for boarding (through the rear door) is to push, shove and grunt. Watch your wallets and money pouches because it is during this crunch that a lot of things tend to disappear. Once you're on the bus, try to squeeze your way up towards the front door, which is the exit. At some point during the trip, a man will somehow manage to squeeze his way right down the bus to sell you your ticket, which is usually 25 pt.

Cairo's main bus terminal (for local buses only) is directly in front of the Nile Hilton on Midan Tahrir. From here, minibuses and buses leave for Islamic Cairo, Heliopolis, Shubra, Bulaq, Zamalek, Agouza and Mohandiseen. This is also where the minibus station is. A minibus is easily recognised by its smaller size (roughly half the size of a bus) and orange and white stripes (sometimes a black and red one). Minibuses run to Giza and the pyramids, the Citadel, the City of the Dead, Maadi and places like Doqqi and Mohandiseen in the west of the city. Taking a minibus is one of the best ways to travel. It costs only 25 to 50 pt (depending on your destination) for a seat. Passengers are not allowed to stand and crowd each other (this rule is frequently overlooked), and each minibus leaves as soon as every seat is taken.

Although the area in front of the Nile Hilton is the main terminal, many buses passing through Midan Tahrir from other parts of the city don't actually stop here. Instead, a lot of buses heading out to Zamalek, Doqqi and beyond slow down (and sometimes even stop!) to set down and pick up passengers as they pass between the Nile Hilton and the Mogamma on Sharia at-Tahrir. Others stop in front of the Mogamma building before heading off down Sharia Qasr al-Eini to Manyal and Roda Island, crossing the river and heading out towards Giza, the pyramids and other destinations. Some buses heading towards Islamic Cairo stop on Sharia at-Tahrir and then also on Midan Falaki.

There are other local bus terminals worth noting. On Midan Abdel Minnim Riyadh, underneath the 6th of October Bridge off Sharia Ramses just north of the Egyptian Museum, is a terminal for some buses bound for Abbassiya and the airport. Midan Ataba, which is just east of the Ezbekiya Gardens, has plenty of buses going out to the Citadel, and some heading from there on to Midan Tahrir, Manyal and Giza. There is a smaller terminal (City Bus Station) in front of Ramses station (see the Ramses Station map) although if you're just trying to get into the centre of town, you're better off taking the metro.

The local bus station at Giza has buses going to the pyramids, the airport and the Citadel. Next to it is a microbus stand, where you can catch a microbus to the pyramids for 25 pt.

Following is a list of some of the bus numbers and their destinations. One word of caution, though. Sometimes bus route numbers change (usually the high numbers indicate new numbers) without any other change taking place. Cairenes say this is little more than a ruse to put up fares – new route number, higher fare. Note that some buses servicing the airport terminals occasionally have fares higher than the 25 pt fare. Some numbers in the following list have an oblique stroke in front of them, corresponding to the numbers appearing on the buses which have a stroke through them.

Note that some of the information in the schedule that follows overlaps for ease of use from various bus stations and sites in the city. Some information covered here also appears in the relevant Getting There & Away sections.

To/From Midan Tahrir – Nile Hilton terminal

No 422	Midan Tahrir – Midan Roxy – airport terminals I & II
Minibus No 27	Midan Tahrir – Abbassiya – Heliopolis – airport terminals I & II
Minibus Nos 30 & 32	Midan Tahrir – Abbassiya (Sinai bus terminal)
Minibus No 2	Midan Tahrir – Midan Ahmed Hilmi – Shubra
Minibus No 38	Midan Tahrir – Sharia Port Said – Al-Amiriyya
Minibus No 54	Midan Tahrir – Sayyida Zeinab – Citadel
Minibus No 83	Midan Tahrir – pyramids
Minibus No 52	Midan Tahrir – Maadi
No 16	Midan Tahrir – Galaa Bridge – Agouza
No 99	Midan Tahrir – Agouza – Sharia Sudan – Midan Lubnan
No 815	Midan Tahrir – Sharia Port Said – Mosque of Al-Azhar & Khan al-Khalili
Minibus No 77	Midan Tahrir – Sharia Port Said – Mosque of Al-Azhar & Khan al-Khalili
No 913	Midan Tahrir – Sphinx (Abu al-Hol)

To/From Midan Abdel Minnim Riyadh

No 400	Midan Abdel Minnim Riyadh – Midan Roxy – Heliopolis – airport Terminal I
No 300	Midan Abdel Minnim Riyadh – Abbassiya – 'Ain Shams
Minibus No 35	Midan Abdel Minnim Riyadh – Abbassiya
Minibus No 24	Midan Abdel Minnim Riyadh – Midan Roxy

To/From Midan Ataba

No /99	Midan Ataba – Sharia Ahmed Orabi – Midan Lubnan
No 904	Ad-Darasa (City of the Dead) – Midan Ataba – Midan Tahrir (Mogamma) – pyramids
No 404	Midan Ataba – Citadel – Midan Tahrir (Nile Hilton)
No 951	Midan Ataba – Citadel
No 57	Midan Ataba – Citadel
No 65	Midan Ataba – Midan Hussein (Khan al-Khalili) – Ad-Darasa
No 48	Midan Ataba – Zamalek
No 930	Midan Ataba – Qanater
No 948	Midan Ataba – airport

| Minibus No 84 | Midan Ataba – zoo |
| | – Midan Giza |

To/From Ramses Station

No 812	Ramses station – Midan Giza
No 804	Ramses station – Midan Tahrir – Giza pyramids
No /174	Ramses station – Citadel
No 210	Ramses station – Qanater
Minibus No 63	Ramses station – Al-Azhar
No 65	Ramses station – Midan Ataba – Midan Hussein (Khan al-Khalili) – Ad-Darasa (City of the Dead)
Minibus No 72	Ramses station – Sharia Sudan – Midan Lubnan

To/From Midan Giza

No 3	Midan Giza – pyramids
No 812	Midan Giza – Ramses station
No 116	Midan Giza – Kerdassa
No 929	Midan Giza – Midan Tahrir
No 949	Midan Giza – Midan Ramses – airport terminals I & II

To/From Zamalek

No 13	Midan Falaki (near Bab al-Louk) – Midan Tahrir – Zamalek – Sharia Abu al-Feda
Minibus No 48	Midan Ataba – Zamalek
Minibus No 49	Midan Falaki – Midan Tahrir – Gezira – Zamalek
Minibus No 47	Midan Ramses – Zamalek

To/From the Pyramids

No 904	Ad-Darasa (City of the Dead) – Midan Ataba – Midan Tahrir – pyramids
No 905	Citadel – Midan Tahrir – Qasr al-Eini – Manyal – pyramids
No 3	Midan Giza – pyramids
No 804	Ramses station – Citadel – Midan Tahrir – Manyal – pyramids
Minibus No 82	Midan Tahrir (Nile Hilton) – Manyal – Giza – pyramids
Minibus No 83	Midan Tahrir (Nile Hilton) – Doqqi – pyramids

To/From the Citadel

No /173	Midan Falaki – Citadel
No /174	Ramses station – Citadel
No 905	Citadel – Manyal – Giza – pyramids
No 404	Midan Ataba – Citadel – Midan Tahrir (Nile Hilton)
No 951	Midan Ataba – Citadel
No 57	Midan Ataba – Citadel
Minibus No 54	Midan Tahrir – Citadel

To/From Abbassiya

No 800	Abbassiya – Ramses station – Giza
Minibus No 48	Abbassiya – Midan Ataba
No 922	Abbassiya – Maadi
No /400	Abbassiya – Midan Abdel Minnim Riyadh

Other Routes

| No 913 | Sphinx (Abu al-Hol) – Midan Tahrir – Shubra |
| Minibus No 77 | Ad-Darasa (City of the Dead) – Midan Hussein (Khan al- Khalili) – Midan Tahrir – Doqqi – Bulaq ad-Dakrur |

Microbus

Increasingly, Cairenes are using private microbuses (as opposed to the public minibuses) to get around. Destinations are unmarked in any language, so they are hard to use, except for those travelling to the pyramids from in front of the Nile Hilton for 50 pt. If you do want to catch one while about town, it's best to position yourself at a large intersection at the start of the road you want to go along. When a microbus passes, yell out your destination; if it's going in the right direction, the driver will stop.

Metro

Cairo's metro system is a single line of 33 stations that stretches for 43 km from the southern suburb of Helwan to Al-Marg, near Heliopolis. The five stations in central Cairo are the only ones underground. Stations are easily identified by signs with a big red 'M' in a blue star. The Greater Cairo and Central Cairo maps show entrances to the main metro stations.

Construction has started on a second metro line between Shubra el-Kheima and Giza. The city centre section of it should be operating by 1998. It is planned to reach Giza by the year 2000.

The metro is fast, inexpensive and usually not too crowded. It costs 30 pt to ride up to nine stops; 50 pt for up to 16 stops; 70 pt for up to 22 stops; E£1 for up to 28 stops; and

E£1.20 to ride the length of the line. If you're going to be in Cairo for a long time and using the metro on a regular basis, it might be worth inquiring about weekly or monthly passes. The service starts at about 5 am and closes around 11.30 pm.

Men should note, to save themselves red faces, that the first carriage (as well as the second in peak hours) is reserved for women only.

Tram

Most of Cairo's trams (known to Cairenes, confusingly for outsiders, as 'metros') have been phased out. Three of the original lines still run in the north-east of town, coming from Nouzha, Mirghani and Abdel Aziz Fahmy and merging at Midan Roxy in Heliopolis. From here they all follow the same line down to Midan Ramses and onto the terminus at Midan Abdel Minnim Riyadh behind the Egyptian Museum.

There are several other lines such as one from Mataraya north-west of Heliopolis which runs along Sharia Port Said next to the Islamic Museum en route to its terminus at Sayyida Zeinab, and another from Midan Triomphe in Heliopolis to Ad-Darasa next to the northern City of the Dead.

The trams are as cheap, and often as crowded, as the buses. It costs 25 pt from Midan Ramses to Midan Roxy and takes 20 to 30 minutes depending on whether it's peak hour or not. Tram stations are not signposted in English, so you'll have to ask someone where to get off. The Heliopolis trams are supposed to have colour-coded direction boards – Nouzha (red), Mirghani (green) and Abdel Aziz Fahmy (yellow) – but these are often not displayed.

Car

If you're crazy enough to want to battle the traffic in Cairo, there are several car rental agencies in the city, including the 'big three' – Avis, Hertz and Budget. Their rates and terms vary and change, so shop around. For a rough guide to prices and a few road rules, see the Car & Motorcycle section in the Getting Around chapter.

Avis
   16 Sharia Ma'mal as-Sukkar, Garden City (☎ 354-7400; fax 356-2464)
   Cairo Meridien Hotel (☎ 989400)
   Nile Hilton (☎ 766432)
   Cairo airport (☎ 291-4266)
   Heliopolis Sheraton (☎ 291-0223)
   Meridien Heliopolis (☎ 290-5055)
   Alexandria – Cecil Hotel (☎ 483-7173 ext 706)
   Sharm el-Sheikh (☎ 600979)
Budget Rent-a-Car
   5 Sharia al-Makrizi, Zamalek (head office) (☎ 340-0070; fax 341-3790)
   Marriott Hotel (☎ 340-8888)
   Cairo airport (☎ 291-4288)
Europcar
   In the Max building on Sharia Lebanon, Heliopolis (☎ 347-4712; fax 303-6123)
   Cairo airport (☎ 2914255 ext 2212)
   Sharm el-Sheikh (☎ 600686)
   Nuweiba (☎ 520320)
   Taba (☎ 379222)
   Hurghada (☎ 443660)
Hertz
   195 Sharia 26th of July, Mohandiseen (☎ 347-4172; fax 344-6627)
   Ramses Hilton (☎ 574-4400)
   Semiramis InterContinental (☎ 354-3239)
   Cairo airport (☎ 291-4288 ext 2430)
   Sharm el-Sheikh (☎ 600459)
J Car
   33 Sharia Misaha, Doqqi (☎ 704175; fax 360-3255)
   Cairo airport (☎ 2914255 ext 2340)
Max Rent Cars
   27 Sharia Lubnan, Mohandiseen (☎ 347-4712/3); reasonably priced but only rents cars with unlimited km when bookings are made from overseas.
Thrifty
   1 Sharia al-Entesar, Heliopolis (☎ & fax 266-3313)
   Cairo airport (☎ 291-4288 ext 2620)

Taxi

A taxi is one of the most convenient ways to get around Cairo. Flag fall is 60 pt, and fares should be no more than E£3 for a cross-town ride of up to about 30 minutes (short hops are less), although you'll often have to fight not to be charged much more. The best way to check the latest fares is to ask a local.

If possible, don't set the price unless the ride is especially long, such as from central Cairo to the airport (E£15 to E£20) or the pyramids (about E£10). Wait until you arrive at your destination, get out of the car, pay the driver through the window, and walk away. If the driver throws a tantrum on the spot, yells for more money and pursues you, it's possible you really have underpaid him.

For more information on the different sorts of taxis and how to flag them down, see the Getting Around chapter.

Hantour

These horse-drawn carriages and their insistent drivers hang around on the Corniche near Shepheard's Hotel. If you're going to Luxor or Aswan, or even towns in the Delta where hantours are still used as local trans-

port, wait until then to have a ride. There's nothing pleasant about getting a face full of exhaust fumes as you battle Cairo's congested thoroughfares.

Water Bus

Two water buses leave from the Maspero landing in front of the big, round Radio & Television building (see Central Cairo map) and go north as far as the Nile barrages and Qanater. One stops en route at Imbaba while other water buses go south and stop near Cairo University, Roda Island, Giza, Old Cairo and Maadi. The fare costs from only 10 to 25 pt.

Around Cairo

The region around Cairo offers some of Egypt's most interesting attractions, including the ancient tombs and pyramids of Saqqara, the Birqash camel market, historic towns of the Delta region, Al-Faiyum – one of the world's largest oases – and the medieval monasteries of Wadi Natrun. Most of the destinations described in this chapter can be visited on day trips from Cairo, but others, such as Al-Faiyum, are better visited on overnight trips.

MEMPHIS

Memphis, once the glorious Old Kingdom capital of Egypt, has almost completely vanished. It is believed that the city was founded around 3100 BC, probably by King Menes, when Upper and Lower Egypt were first united. It had many splendid palaces and gardens, and was one of the most renowned and populous cities of the ancient world. Like most Egyptian cities with any degree of importance, Memphis also had its own deity, the all-powerful creator-god Ptah, who formed the world with words from his tongue and heart.

Even as late as the 5th century BC, long after Thebes had taken over as capital of Egypt, Memphis was described by the Greek historian Herodotus as a 'prosperous city and cosmopolitan centre'. Its enduring importance, even then, was reflected in the size of its cemetery on the west bank of the Nile, an area replete with royal pyramids, private tombs and sacred animal necropolises. This city of the dead, centred at Saqqara, covers 30 km along the edge of the desert, from Dahshur to Giza.

Centuries of annual floods have inundated the city with Nile mud, while other ancient buildings and monuments have long since been ploughed over and cultivated by the fellahin. Today there are few signs of the grandeur of Memphis: in fact, it's extremely difficult to imagine that a city once stood where there is now only a small museum and

some statues in a garden. The partly open-air museum contains a colossal limestone statue of Ramses II, similar to the one which stands at the centre of Midan Ramses in Cairo. This one, however, is lying down and is a lot more neglected and damaged.

In the garden there are more statues of Ramses II, an eight-tonne alabaster sphinx, the sarcophagus of Amenhotep and the alabaster beds on which the sacred Apis bulls were mummified before being placed in the Serapeum at Saqqara. Admission is E£7 and half for students plus E£5/25 for a camera/video. It's open from 8 am to 5 pm. There is an extraordinarily overpriced cafeteria across the road where you could swear they are growing the oranges prior to making you a fruit juice.

Getting There & Away

Train Memphis is 24 km south of Cairo and three km from Saqqara. The cheapest way to get there from Cairo is to take a 3rd class train from Ramses station to Al-Manashy, and get off at Al-Badrashein village; the trip takes about two hours (that's right – two hours to go 24 km!) and costs 35 pt. From the village, you can either walk for about half an hour, catch a Saqqara microbus for 25 pt or take a taxi.

Metro, Boat & Microbus Rather than catch the slow train, you could just as easily go via Helwan on the metro, get a microbus (don't believe it if you're told there are none) from the station to the boat landing (ask for the *markib lil-Badrashein* – 15 pt). Get a boat across the Nile to Al-Badrashein and then another microbus from there. This way, however, will still take you a good 1½ hours to get to Memphis.

Note that the reverse procedure may be a little tricky, as there does not always seem to be any transport waiting at the boat landing on the Helwan side of the Nile. If this is the case, take a microbus from Al-Badrashein to

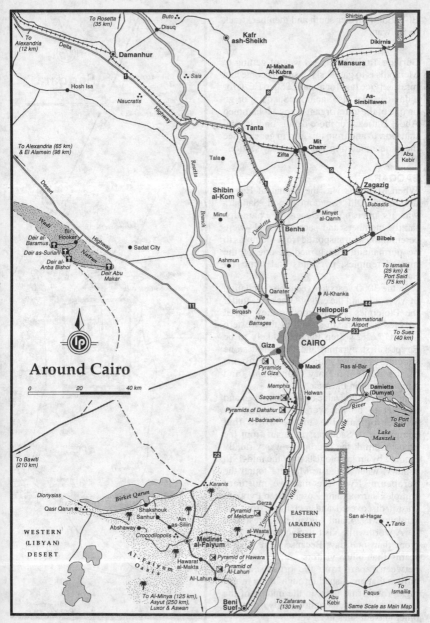

AROUND CAIRO

Around Cairo

0   20   40 km

To Rosetta
(35 km)
Buto
Disuq
Kafr
ash-Sheikh
Shirbin
See Inset
Dikirnis
To
Alexandria
(12 km)
Delta
Damanhur
Al-Mahalla
Al-Kubra
Mansura
Hosh Isa
Sais
As-
Simbillawen
Naucratis
Highway
Tanta
Mit
Ghamr
Abu
Kebir
To Alexandria (65 km)
& El Alamein (98 km)
Tala
Zifta
Zagazig
Rosetta
Shibin
al-Kom
Branch
Bubastis
Wadi
Minuf
Minyet
al-Qamh
Desert
Bir
Hooker
Natrun
Damietta
Benha
Bilbeis
Deir al-
Baramus
Highway
Deir as-Suriani
Sadat City
Branch
Deir al-
Anba Bishoi
Deir Abu
Makar
Ashmun
To Ismailia
(25 km) &
Port Said
(75 km)
Qanater
Al-Khanka
Heliopolis
44
Birqash
Nile
Barrages
Cairo International
Airport
33
To Suez
(40 km)
Giza
CAIRO
Pyramids
of Giza
Maadi
Ras al-Bar
Memphis
Damietta
(Dumyat)
Saqqara
Helwan
River
Pyramids of Dahshur
Al-Badrashein
Nile
To Port
Said
Lake
Manzela
To Bawiti
(210 km)
22
Karanis
Joins Main Map
Birket Qarun
Dionysias
Shakshouk
Gerza
San al-Hagar
Qasr Qarun
Sanhur
Pyramid
of Meidum
Yousef
EASTERN
(ARABIAN)
DESERT
Tanis
Ain
as-Silin
WESTERN
(LIBYAN)
DESERT
Abshaway
Crocodilopolis
Medinet
al-Faiyum
al-Wasta
Bahr
Al-Faiyum
Oasis
Hawarat
al-Makta
Pyramid of Hawara
Pyramid
of Al-Lahun
To
Ismailia
Abu
Kebir
Faqus
Al-Lahun
Same Scale as Main Map
To Al-Minya (125 km),
Asyut (250 km),
Luxor & Aswan
Beni
Suef
To Zafarana
(130 km)

El-Tabbim further south and then backtrack to Helwan.

Service Taxi The easiest way of getting to Memphis is to gather six or seven people and hire a service taxi for about E£60 to E£70 for a day trip that also includes Saqqara, or go on one of the tours organised by Mohammed Abdel Hafiez. For more details on this, and transport to and from this area in general, see the Saqqara Getting There & Away section.

SAQQARA

When Memphis was the capital of Egypt, during the Old Kingdom period, Saqqara was its necropolis. Deceased Pharaohs, family members and sacred animals were ceremoniously transported from Memphis to be permanently enshrined in one of the myriad temples, pyramids and tombs at Saqqara.

In the 3000 years between the foundation of Memphis and the end of Greek rule under the Ptolemies, the necropolis grew till it covered a seven km stretch of the Western Desert. Zoser's Step Pyramid, likely to be Egypt's first pyramid and the oldest stone structure of its size in the world, was just one of the many funerary monuments and temples built in the area.

In terms of the value of what has been and has yet to be uncovered, there are few archaeological sites in the world that compare with Saqqara; yet, apart from the Step Pyramid, the necropolis was virtually ignored by archaeologists until the mid-19th century, when Auguste Mariette found the Serapeum. Even the massive mortuary complex surrounding Zoser's Step Pyramid wasn't discovered and reclaimed from the sand until 1924, and it is still being restored.

A worthwhile visit to Saqqara will take more than one day. Because of its size it seems that other visitors are few and far between, apart from the organised tour groups that are rushed through in the mornings. You'll find here, in the middle of the desert, a peaceful quality rarely found at other ancient sites in Egypt.

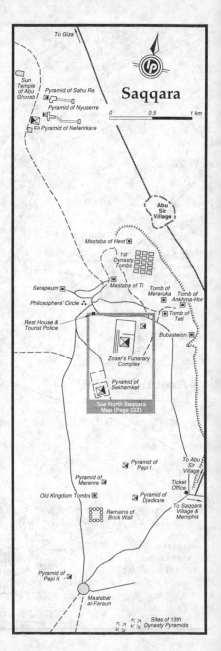

Saqqara

Orientation & Information

The main places of interest are in North Saqqara. Other sites are scattered further north, such as the pyramids of Abu Sir, and to the south, at South Saqqara. Most travellers start their visit in North Saqqara (Zoser's Step Pyramid area) and, if they are up to it, continue by taxi, donkey or camel to Abu Sir and/or South Saqqara. It's imperative to have some form of transport to get around here as the tombs and sites are spread over a vast distance and walking is not feasible. Make sure you bring some water as it gets very hot. Before setting off, ask first at the ticket office, which is at the base of the plateau of North Saqqara, about which monuments are open.

Most of the pyramids and tombs at Saqqara can be 'officially' visited between 7.30 am and 4 pm (5 pm in summer). The guards start locking the monument doors at about 3.30 pm, although some have been known to lock up even earlier – with tourists inside – in order to extract some baksheesh. The admission fee for all North Saqqara sights is E£20, or E£10 for students. There is a E£5 fee for using a camera, collected only at the entrance to Zoser's Step Pyramid.

Step Pyramid

When it was constructed by Imhotep, the Pharaoh's chief architect, in the 27th century BC, the Step Pyramid of King Zoser was the largest stone structure ever built. It is still the most noticeable feature of Saqqara. Imhotep's brilliant use of stone, and his daring break with the tradition of building royal tombs as underground rooms with the occasional mud-brick mastaba (the flat tomb superstructure common at the time), was the inspiration for Egypt's future architectural achievements.

The pyramid began as a simple mastaba, but Imhotep added to it five times. With each level of stone he gained confidence in his use of the new medium and mastered the techniques required to move, place and secure the huge blocks. This first pyramid rose to over 62m, in six steps, before it was sheathed in fine limestone.

The Step Pyramid dominates Zoser's mortuary complex, which is 544m long and 277m wide and was once surrounded by a magnificent bastioned and panelled limestone wall. Part of the enclosure wall survives, to a height of over 4.5m, and a section near the south-eastern corner has been restored, with stones found in the desert, to its original 10m elevation. In the enclosure wall, the many false doors which were carved and painted to resemble real wood with hinges and sockets allowed the Pharaoh's *ka*, or attendant spirit, to come and go at will.

For the living there is only one entrance, on the south-eastern corner, via a vestibule and along a colonnaded corridor into the broad hypostyle hall. The 40 pillars in the corridor are the original 'bundle columns', ribbed to resemble a bundle of palm or papyrus stems. The walls have been restored, but the protective ceiling is modern concrete. The roof of the hypostyle hall is supported by four impressive bundle columns and there's a large, false, half-open ka door. Here you will be accosted by a bevy of 'guides' eager to show you around.

The hall leads into the Great South Court, a huge open area flanking the south side of the pyramid, with a rebuilt section of wall featuring a frieze of cobras. The cobra, or uraeus, was a symbol of Egyptian royalty, a fire-spitting agent of destruction and protector of the king. A rearing cobra, its hood inflated, always formed part of a Pharaoh's headdress.

Near the frieze is a shaft that plunges 28m to the floor of Zoser's Southern Tomb, which is similar in decoration to the main tomb beneath the Step Pyramid. Originally, it probably stored the Canopic jars containing the Pharaoh's preserved internal organs.

In the centre of the Great South Court are two stone altars representing the thrones of Upper and Lower Egypt. During the 30th year of a Pharaoh's reign it was traditional for him to renew his rule by re-enacting his coronation. In a ritual called the Heb-Sed Race, he would sit first on one throne and then on the other to symbolise the unification

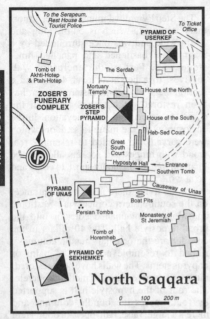

AROUND CAIRO

To the Serapeum,
Rest House &
Tourist Police

To Ticket
Office

PYRAMID OF
USERKEF

Tomb of
Akhti-Hotep
& Ptah-Hotep

The Serdab

ZOSER'S
FUNERARY
COMPLEX

Mortuary
Temple

House of the North

ZOSER'S
STEP
PYRAMID

House of the South

Heb-Sed Court

Great
South
Court

Hypostyle Hall

Entrance
Southern Tomb

PYRAMID
OF UNAS

Causeway of Unas

Boat Pits

Persian Tombs

Monastery of
St Jeremiah

Tomb of
Horemheb

PYRAMID OF
SEKHEMKET

North Saqqara

0   100   200 m

the pyramid is the Pyramid of Userkef, now little more than a mound of rubble.

The serdab, a stone structure right in front of the pyramid, contains a slightly tilted wooden box with two holes drilled into its north face. Look through these and you'll have the eerie experience of coming face to face with Zoser himself. Inside is a life-size, lifelike painted statue of the long-dead king, gazing stonily out towards the stars. Although it's only a copy (the original is in the Egyptian Museum), it is still quite haunting. Serdabs were designed so that the Pharaoh's ka could communicate with the outside world. The original entrance to the Step Pyramid is directly behind the serdab, but is closed to the public.

Pyramid & Causeway of Unas

What appears to be a big mound of rubble to the south-west of Zoser's tomb is actually the Pyramid of Unas, the last Pharaoh of the 5th dynasty. This is one of the easiest pyramids to visit at Saqqara, which means if there's a tour group in the area it will probably be crowded. However, at the time of writing, it was closed for restoration. The entrance is on the north face along a 1.4m-high passage.

Only 350 years after the inspired creation of the Step Pyramid, and after the perfection of the Great Pyramids of Giza, this unassuming pile of loose blocks and dirt was built. In fact, despite the tomb's exterior, it marked the beginning of a trend in design. Until Unas' time (24th century BC), pyramid interiors had been unadorned – so while the outside of his tomb looks more like Zoser's than Cheops', the inside is of immense historical importance.

In 1881, Thomas Cook & Sons sponsored the excavation of the tomb by Gaston Maspero, who found the walls covered in hieroglyphs. Carved into the huge slabs of white alabaster, these so-called Pyramid Texts are the earliest known examples of decorative writing in a Pharaonic tomb chamber. The texts record the rituals, prayers and hymns that accompanied the Pharaoh's burial to enable the release of his ka, and list

of Egypt. He would also, during the five-day jubilee, present all the provincial priests with gifts, obliging them to recognise his supremacy over their local gods. The jubilee would actually have been held in Memphis, while these altars in the Great South Court perpetuated in stone the cosmic regeneration of the Pharaoh's power and ka.

On the eastern side of the pyramid are two 'houses' representing the shrines of Upper and Lower Egypt, which symbolise the unity of the country. The House of the South, which is faced with proto-Doric columns, features the oldest known examples of tourist graffiti. The vandalism of visiting 12th century BC Theban scribes, who scrawled their admiration for Zoser on the wall in a cursive style of hieroglyphs, is now protected under a piece of transparent plastic just inside the entrance. The House of the North is similar to its southern counterpart, except that sculpted papyrus flowers grace the capitals of its columns. To the north of

the articles, like food and clothing, necessary for his existence in the afterlife.

Part of the one km causeway, which ran from the east side of the Pyramid of Unas, has been restored. On either side of it more than 200 mastabas have been excavated and there are several well-preserved tombs, some of which can normally be visited. The beautiful tomb of the 5th dynasty princess Idut, who was probably a daughter of Unas, is next to the southern wall of Zoser's complex. On the walls of its 10 chambers are colourful scenes of oxen, gazelle, ibex, hippopotamuses and other animals. The Mastaba of Queen Nebet and the Mastaba of Mehu are also beautifully decorated; and the Tomb of Nebkau-Her, which may be closed, is worth visiting if you can gain access.

Egyptologists debate whether the huge, sculpted boat pits, made of stone and located south of the causeway, actually held the royal barges which took the Pharaoh on his journey to the afterlife, or whether they merely represented these solar boats. Nothing was found when the 40m-long crescent-shaped trenches were excavated.

Persian Tombs

The tombs of three Persian noblemen, just south of the Pyramid of Unas, are some of the deepest subterranean burial chambers in Egypt. The entrance is covered by a small inconspicuous wooden hut, to which a guard in the area has the key. If you don't have your own torch he will lead you the 25m down the winding staircase to the vaulted tombs of Psamtik, Zenhebu and Pelese. According to the ancient wall drawings, which are colourful and fantastic, Zenhebu was a famous Persian admiral and Psamtik was chief physician of the Pharaoh's court. The tombs were built to prevent grave robbers from stealing the contents. It didn't work: it was thieves who cut the spiral entrance passage.

Monastery of St Jeremiah

The half-buried remains of this 5th century AD monastery are up the hill from the Causeway of Unas and south-east of the boat pits. There's not much left of the structure

because it was ransacked by invading Arabs in 950 AD, and more recently the Egyptian Antiquities Department took all the wall paintings and carvings to the Coptic Museum in Cairo.

Pyramid of Sekhemket

The unfinished Pyramid of Sekhemket is a short distance to the west of the ruined monastery. It was abandoned before completion, for unknown reasons, when it was only three metres high. There's an unused alabaster sarcophagus in one of the underground passageways, but no-one is permitted to enter this pile of rubble because of the danger of a cave in.

Tomb of Akhti-Hotep & Ptah-Hotep

Akhti-Hotep and Ptah-Hotep, who were father and son officials during the reign of Djedkare (a 5th dynasty Pharaoh), designed their own tomb complex, which consists of two burial chambers, a chapel and a hall of pillars. The Hotep duo were judges, overseers of the priests of the pyramids, and chiefs of the granary and treasury. The reliefs in their chambers are some of the best at Saqqara and depict everyday life during the 5th dynasty. You'll see: Akhti-Hotep in the marshes building boats, fighting enemies and crossing rivers; a splendid scene of wild animals with Ptah-Hotep and other hunters in hot pursuit; people playing games, collecting food and eating; and Ptah-Hotep having a manicure while being entertained by musicians. The dual tomb is south of the main road, between the Step Pyramid and the rest house.

Philosophers' Circle

Down the slope, to the north-west of the rest house, are several statues of Greek philosophers and poets, arranged in a circle beneath a protective roof. From left to right, the statues are Plato (standing), Heraclitus (seated), Thales (standing), Protagoras (seated), Homer (seated), Hesiod (seated), Demetrius of Phalerum (standing against a bust of Serapis) and Pindar. The circle was set up, during the Ptolemaic period, at the eastern end of a long avenue of sphinxes running from the temple, where a live Apis bull was worshipped, to the Serapeum, where the bulls of this strange animal cult were buried.

Serapeum

The sacred Apis bulls were by far the most important of the cult animals entombed at Saqqara. The Apis, it was believed, was an incarnation of Ptah, the god of Memphis, and was the calf of a cow struck by lightning from heaven. Once divinely impregnated, the cow would never again give birth and her calf was kept in the Temple of Ptah and worshipped as a god. The Apis was always portrayed as black, with a distinctive white diamond on its forehead, a sun disc between its horns, the image of an eagle on its back and a scarab on its tongue. When it died, the bull was mummified, then carried on an alabaster bed to the subterranean galleries of the Serapeum at Saqqara, and placed in a huge sarcophagus.

The Apis catacombs date from the 13th century BC, when Ramses II began the first gallery, which reached a length of 68m. In the 7th century BC Psammetichus I cut a new gallery, which was extended by the Ptolemies to a length of 198m, and used till around 30 BC. Twenty-five Apis were embalmed and stabled in perpetuity here in monolithic granite coffins weighing up to 70 tonnes each. Only one mummified bull, now in the Cairo Agricultural Museum, was found when the Serapeum was excavated.

Until 1851, the existence of the sacred Apis tombs was known only from classical references. Having found a half-buried sphinx at Saqqara, and following the description given by the Greek historian Strabo in 24 BC, the French archaeologist Auguste Mariette began digging, and uncovered the avenue of sphinxes leading to the Serapeum. His great discovery sparked the extensive and continuing excavation of Saqqara. In 1856 Mariette wrote that he'd been so profoundly struck with astonishment on first gaining access to the Apis vaults, five years before, that the feeling was still fresh in his mind. Only one chamber, walled up during the reign of Ramses II, had escaped the notice of tomb robbers. Finding it intact, Mariette wrote:

> The finger marks of the Egyptian who had inserted the last stone in the wall built to conceal the doorway were still recognisable on the lime. There were also the marks of naked feet imprinted on the sand which lay in one corner of the tomb chamber. Everything was in its original condition in this tomb where the embalmed remains of the bull had lain undisturbed for 37 centuries.

The Serapeum is near the rest house, on the main road, west of the Philosophers' Circle. It's very likely you'll experience the same feeling as Mariette, for this place is definitely weird and gets stranger still as you wander along galleries lit only by tiny lanterns that cast a murky light over the vaults and the enormous, macabre black sarcophagi they contain. The largest sarcophagus, at the end of the main gallery, was carved from a single piece of black granite and is covered in hieroglyphs.

Mastaba of Ti

This tomb, or mastaba, is one of the main sources of knowledge about life in Egypt towards the end of the Old Kingdom. Ti, an important court official who served under three Pharaohs, collected titles like his kings collected slaves. He was Lord of Secrets, Superintendent of Works, Overseer of the Pyramids of Abu Sir, Counsellor to the Pharaoh and even Royal Hairdresser. He married a woman of royal blood and the inscriptions on the walls of his tomb reveal that his children were rated as royalty. One of the best reliefs depicts Ti standing regally on a boat sailing through papyrus marshes, while others show men and women at various jobs like ploughing, ship-building, reaping grain and feeding cranes. The tomb, discovered by Mariette in 1865, is a few hundred metres to the north-east of the Philosophers' Circle.

Tombs of Teti, Mereruka & Ankhma-Hor

The avenue of sphinxes excavated by Mari-

Top: In his construction of the Step Pyramid at Saqqara, Imhotep is credited with creating the inspiration for Egypt's future architectural achievements.
Bottom: Reliefs in the Mastaba of Ti reveal much about life in the Old Kingdom, Saqqara.

DAMIEN SIMONIS

ROB VAN DRIESUM

BETHUNE CARMICHAEL

GEERT COLE

BETHUNE CARMICHAEL

BETHUNE CARMICHAEL

Top: Careta, Marsa Matruh; heavy duty biker, Cairo; temple guard, Karnak.
Left: Exquisite facade of a leather shop in Khan al-Khalili.
Middle Right: Hitching a ride, Cairo.
Bottom Right: Cairo minus the hustle and bustle.

ette in the 1850s has again been engulfed by desert sands, but it once extended as far east as the Tomb of Teti. To get to this somewhat weathered tomb now, you must follow the road from the rest house, heading a little to the north once you've passed the Step Pyramid. The interior is often closed to the public but is worth seeing if you can get in.

Nearby is the Tomb of Mereruka, which has 31 rooms, many with magnificent wall inscriptions. Egyptologists have learned a great deal about the wildlife of ancient Egypt from these drawings. As you enter the tomb, notice on one of the walls the large-mouthed, sharp-tusked hippopotamuses.

The Tomb of Ankhma-Hor, a little further east, contains some very interesting scenes depicting 6th dynasty surgical operations, including toe surgery and a circumcision.

Mummified Animals
Excavations in this area have also uncovered several temples, however, they may be closed to the public. They include the Anubieion, sacred to the jackal-headed Anubis, god of embalming and the dead, which has a gallery for dogs; the Bubasteion, sacred to the cat-goddess Bastet, which is filled with mummified cats; as well as other galleries with thousands of mummified birds and monkeys.

Abu Sir
The three pyramids of Abu Sir, at the edge of the desert, surrounded by a sea of sand dunes, formed part of a 5th dynasty necropolis. There were originally 14 pyramids at Abu Sir. Those that remain are mostly just mounds of rubble and are closed. The exception is the Pyramid of Sahu Ra, which opened to the public for the first time in mid-1996.

Pyramid of Sahu Ra This is the most complete and the northernmost of the group. The entrance is only half a metre high – you have to crawl along for about two metres through Pharaonic dust and spider webs to get into the Pharaoh's tomb. The remains of Sahu Ra's mortuary temple still stand nearby.

From his pyramid, on a clear day, you can see as many as 10 pyramids stretching out before you to the horizon.

Pyramid of Neferirkare Neferirkare's tomb is one of the best in the area and stands 45m high. It now resembles Zoser's Step Pyramid but, like the Giza pyramids, originally had an outer casing of stone.

Pyramid of Nyuserre Though the most dilapidated of the three, the Pyramid of Nyuserre has a causeway that runs to what's left of Nyuserre's mortuary temple to the south-east.

Other Monuments
North of the temple there are several interesting monuments, including several mastabas and the Tomb of Ptahshepses, who was a court official and relative of King Nyuserre. If you happen to be going to Abu Sir by camel, horse or donkey across the desert from Giza, then stop off at the 5th dynasty Sun Temple of Abu Ghorab. It was built by King Nyuserre in honour of the sun-god Ra. The huge altar is made from five big blocks of alabaster and once served as the base of a large solar obelisk. Very few travellers ever make it this far off the beaten track.

Mastabat al-Faraun
The oldest structure in the South Saqqara area is the unusual mortuary complex of the 4th dynasty king Shepseskaf, believed to be a son of Mycerinus. Shepseskaf's tomb is neither a mastaba nor a pyramid. The Mastabat al-Faraun, or 'Pharaoh's bench', is an enormous stone structure resembling a sarcophagus topped with a rounded lid. The complex once covered 700 sq metres and the interior consists of long passageways and a burial chamber. It is possible to enter the tomb if you can find a guard.

Southern Pyramids
The pyramids of the 6th dynasty Pharaohs Pepi I, Merenre and Pepi II, who made the move to South Saqqara, have been cleared of

sand and feature some interesting hiero-glyphic texts. The crumbling southernmost pyramids, built of sun-dried bricks, belong to 13th dynasty Pharaohs.

Pyramid of Pepi II A little north of the Mastabat al-Faraun is the pyramid of this 6th dynasty Pharaoh, who allegedly ruled for 94 years. Pepi II's tomb contains some fine hieroglyphs. The ruins of his mortuary temple, which was once connected to the pyramid by a causeway, can also be explored. Nearby, to the west, are the remains of the pyramids of Queen Apuit and Queen Neith.

Pyramid of Djedkare North of what's left of Pepi II's valley temple is the Tomb of Djedkare, a 5th dynasty Pharaoh. Known as Ahram ash-Shawaf, or 'pyramid of the sentinel', it stands 25m high and can be entered through a tunnel on the north side.

Organised Tours

For details on organised tours to this area – there's a good, inexpensive one arranged by Salah Mohammed Abdel Hafiez – see the Organised Tours section in the Cairo chapter.

Getting There & Away

Saqqara is about 25 km south-west of Cairo and about three km north-west of Memphis. Although it is possible to get within 1½ km of the Saqqara ticket office using public transport, this is a very time consuming business and, once there, you'll be stuck for getting around unless you try to hitch a ride up onto the plateau and then haggle for a camel or donkey. The site is really best combined with a visit to Memphis and the whole lot covered in a taxi. You'll have to arrange this option in Cairo as there are no taxis hanging around the site.

If you're coming from Cairo or Giza, and are determined to do it on your own, you have several options.

Train Refer to the Memphis Getting There & Away section for details on the train. The train from Cairo to the village of Al-Badrash-ein also goes to Dahshur; a taxi from either to North Saqqara should cost about E£5. You can arrange a microbus from Memphis, to the turn-off to the Saqqara site on the Giza-Memphis road, from where it's about a 1.5 km walk to the Saqqara ticket office. There is usually a bit of traffic along the Giza-Memphis road.

From Al-Badrashein, by the way, there are (sometimes) direct microbuses to Giza.

Bus One of the cheapest ways of getting to Saqqara without going via Memphis is to take a bus or minibus (25 to 50 pt) to the Pyramids Rd (see the Giza section in the Cairo chapter) and get off at the Maryutia Canal (Saqqara Rd) stop. From the canal, you can get a microbus to the turn-off to the Saqqara site (don't ask for Saqqara village as you'll end up in the wrong place), from where you'll probably have to walk the last 1½ km to the ticket office. Once at the ticket office, you'll have to try and hitch.

Taxi This is one of the best ways to get to and around the Saqqara site. A taxi from central Cairo will cost about E£70 shared among a maximum of seven people. However, make sure you know what you want to see and stipulate how long you want to be out – it's not unknown for taxi drivers to simply skip the main sights (like the Step Pyramid!) and dump unsuspecting visitors at a few of the lesser monuments before whisking you back to Cairo. Also, if you're going to be out for the day, don't let the taxi driver decide where you're going to have lunch or you'll pay through the nose at his brother's restaurant.

Camel The most adventurous (although physically strenuous) option is to hire a camel, donkey or horse and cross the desert from the Great Pyramids of Giza to Saqqara. This takes about six to seven hours for a round trip so make sure you're prepared for it. Unless you're accustomed to it, that amount of time spent in a saddle will make sitting down rather difficult for a few days. Also keep in mind that you won't have much time left to explore Saqqara unless you start off very early and make it one very long day.

Animals can be hired from the stables near the Hotel Mena House and the Giza pyramids. See also Getting Around in the Giza section of the Cairo chapter for more details.

Getting Around

It is not feasible to explore Saqqara on foot and, as there are no taxis near the ticket office, you're only option for getting around, if you do arrive independently, is to attempt to hitch or to hire a camel, horse or donkey at North Saqqara. They can be hired at the rest house near the Serapeum. A trip around North Saqqara should cost, after bargaining, E£4 for a camel or horse, but don't be surprised if it's more as the handlers are well aware that you're in need of the extra legs and that you have little bargaining power.

The only taxis you'll find around here are those coming from Cairo and they're usually already full.

DAHSHUR

Up until mid-1996, Dahshur was off limits to most foreigners as it was considered a military zone. However, the military's decision to relinquish the area means that it is now open to visitors.

This southern extension of the necropolis of Memphis is a field of royal tombs, about 3½ km long, just west of the village of Dahshur. It's visible in the distance from Saqqara.

The Bent and Red pyramids were both built by Pharaoh Sneferu, the father of Cheops and founder of the 4th dynasty. Why Sneferu had two pyramids, and possibly a third at Meidum, is a mystery that has not been altogether solved by Egyptologists. If the purpose of a pyramid was to be a container for the Pharaoh's ka, then why would one Pharaoh with one ka need more than one tomb?

The other two dilapidated pyramids at Dahshur, which belong to 12th dynasty Pharaohs Amenemhet III and Sesostris III, are less interesting and really only for those with pyramid fever. Around all the pyramids there are also the customary tombs of the members of the royal families, court officials and priests.

Bent Pyramid

This is the most conspicuous of the four pyramids at Dahshur. Although its rather strange shape seems to suggest otherwise, this tomb and the Pyramid of Meidum, also built (or at least completed) by Sneferu, demonstrate the design transition from step pyramid to true pyramid.

For some reason though, just a little over half way up its 105m height, the angle of its exterior was reduced from 52 to 43.5°, giving it its distinctive blunt shape. The reason for the change in design is not known, but perhaps it was believed the initial angle was too steep to be stable. If it was considered unsafe it could explain why Sneferu built another tomb only two km away, the so-called Red Pyramid, which rises at a constant angle of 43.5°.

Most of the Bent Pyramid's outer casing is still intact and it is unique in having two entrances. Nearby are the remains of the mortuary temple and further north are the ruins of Sneferu's valley temple, which yielded some interesting reliefs.

Getting There & Away

See the Saqqara Getting There & Away section for details. You can get a microbus to Dahshur along the Giza-Memphis road.

HELWAN

Helwan, an industrial suburb of some 40,000 people, is about 25 km south of Cairo. At one time this was probably quite a pleasant place, but as a factory city it grew quickly and is now probably the most polluted area in Egypt. There are, however, a few unique things that are almost worth seeing.

Japanese Gardens

Strange as it may seem, Helwan is home to the only Japanese gardens in the Middle East. Although most of the grounds are scruffy and overgrown with weeds, and the once-grand duck ponds now have more squawking human bathers than quacking ducks, it is still obvious that this was once a magnificent place. It's worth seeing if only to check out the row of red Buddhas – probably one of the last things you expect to see in Egypt. To get to the gardens, head east (left as you exit the railway station) for about 500m – the gardens are at the end of the street. Admission is 50 pt and, believe it or not, they want another 50 pt for photography.

Wax Museum

Helwan's Wax Museum, which depicts Egypt's history from Ramses II to Nasser in not awfully lifelike tableaus, was closed at the time of writing. Previously, its displays included the death of Cleopatra, Roman soldiers stabbing Christians with spears, a man being hanged, scenes of peasant life and Nasser's leadership of the 1952 Revolution. Fans whir at the feet of the figures to keep them cool, although most of them look as if they've already melted once and been remoulded. To get to the wax museum, get off the metro one stop before the end of the line, at 'Ain Helwan. The museum is just outside to your left. You could also walk from the Helwan station – it's about 20 minutes north – just follow the tracks.

Getting There & Away

The easiest way to get to Helwan from Cairo is to take the metro from any of the central Cairo stations to Helwan, which is the end of the line (70 pt). There are trains every five minutes or so, and it takes about 40 minutes.

Getting Around

If you don't feel like walking around Helwan you can take a *hantour*, or horse-drawn carriage, from the metro station to both the Japanese Gardens and the museum.

AL-FAIYUM OASIS

About 100 km south-west of Cairo is Al-Faiyum, Egypt's largest oasis. The region of Al-Faiyum is about 70 km wide and 60 km long, including the lake known as Birket Qarun. Home to more than two million people, it is an intricately irrigated and extremely fertile basin watered by the Nile via hundreds of capillary canals.

The region was once filled by Birket Qarun, which is fed by the Bahr Yusef, or 'river of Joseph', a tributary that leaves the Nile at Dairut between Al-Minya and Mallawi. The lake, which lies 45m below sea level, now occupies only about one fifth of Al-Faiyum.

The Pharaohs of the 12th dynasty reduced the flow of water into the lake and reclaimed the land for cultivation by regulating the annual flooding of the Nile. The oasis became a favourite vacation spot for Pharaohs of the 13th dynasty, and many fine palaces were built. The Greeks later called the area Crocodilopolis, because they believed the crocodiles in Birket Qarun were sacred. A temple was built in honour of Sobek, the crocodile-headed god, and during Ptolemaic and Roman times pilgrims came from all over the ancient world to feed the sacred beasts. Al-Faiyum has been called the garden of Egypt: lush fields of vegetables and sugar cane, and groves of citrus fruits, nuts and olives produce abundant harvests; the lake, canals and vegetation support an amazing variety of bird life (some of which is unfortunately hunted by groups of tourists); and the customs, living conditions and agricultural practices in the mud-brick villages throughout the oasis have changed very little over the centuries.

All this tradition and fertility, however, surrounds the rather grimy Medinet al-Faiyum, or 'town of the Faiyum', which sadly is a microcosm of everything that is bad about Cairo: horn-happy drivers, choking fumes and dust, crowded streets and a population of more than 400,000.

Orientation

The canal acts as the city's main artery; most of the commercial activities take place around it and the further you wander away from the canal, the quieter things become. The bus and taxi stations, unfortunately, are all a bit of a hike from the centre.

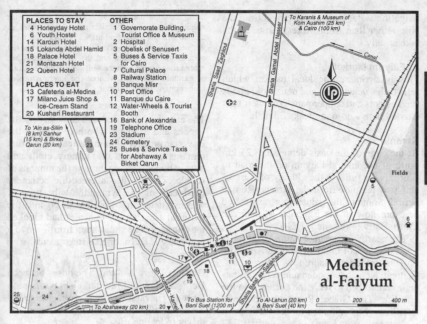

PLACES TO STAY
4 Honeyday Hotel
6 Youth Hostel
14 Karoun Hotel
15 Lokanda Abdel Hamid
18 Palace Hotel
21 Montazah Hotel
22 Queen Hotel

PLACES TO EAT
13 Cafeteria al-Medina
17 Milano Juice Shop & Ice-Cream Stand
20 Kushari Restaurant

OTHER
1 Governorate Building, Tourist Office & Museum
2 Hospital
3 Obelisk of Senusert
5 Buses & Service Taxis for Cairo
7 Cultural Palace
8 Railway Station
9 Banque Misr
10 Post Office
11 Banque du Caire
12 Water-Wheels & Tourist Booth
16 Bank of Alexandria
19 Telephone Office
23 Stadium
24 Cemetery
25 Buses & Service Taxis for Abshaway & Birket Qarun

Medinet al-Faiyum

Information

Tourist Office At the rear of the governorate building in Medinet al-Faiyum, there is a tourist office (☎ 342313) which is open daily except Friday from 8 am to 2 pm. There's also a booth (☎ 325211) by the water wheels in the centre of town, which is open daily from 8 am to 5 pm. Other branches are at 'Ain as-Siliin and about half way along the road between Beni Suef and Medinet al-Faiyum.

Money Close by one another across the canal from the tourist office are the Banque Misr, the Banque du Caire and, on the same side as the tourist office, the Bank of Alexandria. All keep the usual hours. You can't get cash advances on credit cards.

Post & Communications A 24 hour phone and telegraph office is also located by the canal. There's a post office on Sharia an-

Nasr, open from 8 am to 2 pm and closed on Friday.

Obelisk of Senusert

Arriving from Cairo you'll see this 13m high obelisk dominating a roundabout to the north-east of town. It's supposedly the only one in Egypt with a rounded top, and also features a cleft in which a golden statue of Ra was placed reflecting the sunrays in the four directions of the wind.

Museum

In the governorate building is a museum with a variety of interesting displays on the history and fauna of the oasis, and on its future as a tourist destination.

Water Wheels

Four functioning models of the actual water wheels still in use around Al-Faiyum (in total, there are about 200 dotted around the oasis) can be seen opposite the tourist office.

Irrigation water has to be obtained from the Nile rather than from Birket Qarun, as the lake is salty.

Al-Faiyum Market
This is an interesting local market which sells fruits, vegetables, and household goods such as pots and copper pans. You won't get hassled here – no-one speaks English.

Karanis
At the edge of the oasis depression, 25 km north of Medinet al-Faiyum on the road to Cairo, is the ruins of the old city of Karanis and two temples from the Graeco-Roman period. Some of the painted portraits found here are now in the Egyptian Museum in Cairo. Entry to the site is E£16.

The nearby Museum of Kom Aushim has good displays of Old and Middle Kingdom objects including sacred wooden boats, Canopic jars, and wooden and ceramic statuettes entombed to serve the deceased in the afterlife. The Graeco-Roman period, and later history, is exhibited on the 1st floor. It is open daily from 8 am to 4 pm; entry is E£3 (half price for students).

Getting There & Away There's a bus (50 pt) to Karanis at 7 am and 2.30 pm, or simply take one of the Cairo-bound buses.

Pyramid of Hawara & Labyrinth
About 12 km south-east of Medinet al-Faiyum, off the road to Beni Suef, is the dilapidated 58m mud-brick Pyramid of Hawara, also known as the Pyramid of Amenemhet III (12th Dynasty). His once vast mortuary complex is now nothing but mounds of rubble, and even his temple, which had quite a reputation in ancient times, has suffered at the hands of stone robbers. Herodotus said the temple (300m by 250m) was a 3000 room labyrinth that surpassed even the pyramids; while Strabo claimed it had as many rooms as there were provinces, so that all the Pharaoh's subjects could be represented by their local officials in the offering of sacrifices. In 24 BC, Strabo wrote:

there are long and numerous covered ways, with winding passages communicating with each other, so that no stranger could find his way in or out of them without a guide. The roofs of these dwellings consist of a single stone each, and the covered ways are roofed in the same manner with single slabs of stone of extraordinary size, without the intermixture of timber or any other material.

The area was also used as a cemetery by the Greeks and Romans, who here adopted the Egyptian practice of mummification. All that remains are pieces of mummy cloth and human bones sticking through the mounds of rubble. There's also a crocodile cemetery north-east of the pyramid. At the time of writing, it was not possible to go into the pyramid as rising groundwater had blocked the entrance. The site is open from 7 am to 5 pm; entry is E£16, or E£8 for students.

Getting There & Away The buses between Beni Suef and Medinet al-Faiyum pass through Hawarat al-Makta, from where it's a short walk to the pyramid. Just ask the driver to let you off.

Pyramid of Al-Lahun
About 10 km south-east of Hawara, on the Nile side of the narrow fertile passage through the desert that connects Al-Faiyum to the river, are the ruins of a small mud-brick pyramid. Once cased in limestone, it was built by Senusert II back in the Middle Kingdom period around 1885 BC. This is definitely off the beaten track. Although there's not much of it left, you can climb to the top for a great view of the surrounding area. The people in the neighbouring village will probably be so surprised to see you that they'll invite you to tour their fields and houses. The hitch is the entry price – E£16 and half for students.

Getting There & Away You can hitch from Beni Suef or Medinet al-Faiyum, or take the local bus between the two cities, to the village of Al-Lahun. From there it's about two km north.

'Ain as-Siliin

The spring waters and gardens here, about eight km north-west of Medinet al-Faiyum around a branch of Bahr Yusef, merit an excursion if only to see their location amidst a lovely lush valley. The spring water itself is sweet to taste and is said to help in the prevention of arteriosclerosis because of the traces of titanium found in it. One of the springs recently dried up, supposedly due to the earthquake of 1992. There are a few cafes, restaurants and little stores for water, biscuits and the like. Farmers from the adjacent gardens sell their seasonal produce along the walkway. It costs 25 pt to get in.

Getting There & Away From Medinet al-Faiyum, get a Sanhur service taxi or a bus (hourly) from the station in the west of the town (50 pt) and tell the driver where you want to get off.

Birket Qarun

This is another pleasant enough spot where there is really nothing to do, except sit at one of the beach-side cafes or hire a boat for a trip out on the lake for about E£5 an hour.

There's a 'beach' ticket (50 pt) on Friday and public holidays.

Getting There & Away To get here, take a Sanhur to Shakshouk pick-up (E£1). When you see the lake and Auberge du Lac, you've arrived; get off wherever you choose. It's easy enough to get another pick-up going either way along the south bank road.

Qasr Qarun

The ruins of the ancient town of Dionysus, once the starting point for caravans to Bahariyya Oasis in the Western Desert, are just near the village of Qasr Qarun at the western end of Birket Qarun.

The Ptolemaic temple is just off to the left of the road shortly before the village, and was erected to the god of Al-Faiyum, Sobek, in the fourth century before Christ. It was partly restored in 1956. You can ask to go down to the underground chambers and climb up to the top for a view of the desert, the sparse remains of Ptolemaic and Roman settlements and the oasis. Entry is E£8 (half for students).

Getting There & Away Getting out here is a bit of an ordeal, considering the relatively small distances involved. From Medinet al-Faiyum, take a service taxi or pick-up to the town of Abshaway (55 pt; one hour) and from there another the 40 km on to Qasr Qarun (E£1.20, another hour). There are also some pick-ups plying the road along the south side of the lake to Qasr Qarun, but they are few and far between.

Places to Stay

Camping You can pitch a tent in the grounds of the Museum of Kom Aushim at Karanis for E£4.

It is also possible to camp at the lake; get a permit from the tourist police. Bring mosquito repellent, as the nasty little critters get a bit thick sometimes. Also prepare your nose for the slightly offensive smell of the lake; it is possible to get used to it.

Hostels The *Youth Hostel* (☎ 323682), down by the Cairo bus station, almost two km from the centre, costs E£3 for members and E£5 without for a bed in a room of six. The building looks like it has been bombed out.

Hotels – Medinet al-Faiyum The cheapest (and stinkiest) accommodation is the fairly horrible *Karoun Hotel*, opposite the Cafeteria al-Medina. It has doubles for E£3 but it is far from recommended.

Trying hard to meet the same grimy standards is the *Lokanda Abdel Hamid* (just 'Hotel' in English), around the corner facing the canal. Doubles cost E£5; triples cost E£9. They do have hot water.

The quiet *Montazah Hotel* (☎ 328662), almost a km north of the centre, has fairly good singles/doubles with bath and fan for E£30/35 without breakfast.

Also in the same area is the *Queen Hotel* (☎ 326819) with basic rooms for E£33/ 55;

with air-con, TV and fridge E£53/75. Breakfast is included.

The *Palace Hotel* (☎ 321222) is keeping its standards up by providing soap and towel. It has good, clean singles/doubles (including breakfast) without bath for E£20/35, and with bath for E£30/45. The showers are a little temperamental.

The *Honeyday Hotel* (☎ 341205; fax 340105) has good rooms for E£40/60, including breakfast. It has also a bar, coffee shop and restaurant.

Hotels – 'Ain as-Siliin The *Hotel-Chalet 'Ain as-Siliin* (☎ 522113) is pleasantly located amidst the greenery near the springs. Its simple rooms are quite big and boast some sort of a terrace. They cost E£38 and breakfast is included.

Hotels – Birket Qarun Arriving at the lake, the place you'll pass first is the four-star *Auberge du Lac* (☎ 700002; fax 700730). World leaders met at the original hotel on this site after WWI to decide on the borders of the Middle East. It later served as King Farouk's private hunting lodge. These days it is often taken over by hunting groups targeting ducks and geese. Lodging and food isn't cheap, but you could have a Stella beer in the Churchill Bar or splurge on a big lunch (E£45). Singles/doubles are E£233/287; breakfast is another E£10.

Further to the west is the *Oasis Motel* (☎ 701565) near Kibr Melguf, one of the rare bays dotted around the lake. It offers a row of unattractive, weather-beaten rooms for E£30/50 a single/double.

Another 500m further west is the *Panorama Shakshouk Hotel* (☎ 701746; fax 701757), a three star joint with rooms for E£100/125, including breakfast; or E£160/220 for half board. They have a swimming pool built out over the lake.

Places to Eat
Aside from the standard fuul and ta'amiyya and kushari stands (there's a good one in Sharia Mustapha Kamel, not far in from Sharia al-Hurriya), there's the *Cafeteria al-*

Medina in Medinet al-Faiyum, built around the water wheels, which serves shish kebab and a few other meat and chicken dishes. It charges a pricey E£20 for a generous but unoriginal meal and it also has beer. The *Milano* juice shop serves good juices, and the neighbouring ice-cream stand doesn't do a bad job either. On Sharia Mustafa Kamel is a good kushari place.

There are several restaurants at 'Ain as-Siliin.

At the lake many restaurants are only open during high season. The big hotels here all have restaurants, and the cafeteria at the Kom Aushim museum can whip you up something too.

Things to Buy
Throughout Al-Faiyum, especially at 'Ain as-Siliin, you will see lots of colourful basketware and rugs. The baskets come in all shapes and sizes and cost as little as E£1 for the simplest ones. The rugs are made in cooperatives in and around Medinet al-Faiyum. If you're interested in visiting the cooperatives, ask at the tourist booth for locations. One of them sells its wares through the Exhibition of Families of Ain as-Siliin, at the springs itself, which is open daily except Wednesday from 8 am to 2 pm.

Getting There & Away
Bus Buses leave regularly from the station in the east of town for the Ahmed Hilmi station behind Ramses railway station in Cairo. The bus costs E£3 and takes about two hours. It stops in Giza just after Midan Giza under the flyover. Buses can get pretty full in the high season, so, coming from Cairo, you're better off getting on at Ahmed Hilmi.

From a separate station in the west of the town, buses leave regularly for Beni Suef (E£1, one hour). For Al-Minya (E£4.25) there are buses at 7.30 am and 2.30 pm.

Train For the 2nd/3rd class train buff, there are five daily departures to Cairo for E£3/1.50, leaving at 4.40, 7.30 and 11.30 am, and 2.50 and 7.50 pm. Its progress must be so slow as to be barely perceptible – it takes more than four hours. From Cairo trains depart at 5 and 9.10 am, and 1.20, 4.40 and 9.30 pm.

Service Taxi Service taxis leave from the bus stations. To Giza, in Cairo, they cost E£4; to Beni Suef E£1.50.

Getting Around

For details of how to get to the various sights around the oasis, see the respective entries. Note that departures of these buses are pretty unreliable. Around Medinet al-Faiyum itself, there are green and white minibuses covering all areas of town, between the western and eastern bus stations and the centre of town *(wust al-balad)*, for 25 pt.

PYRAMID OF MEIDUM

Standing beyond the vegetation belt, about 32 km north-east of Medinet al-Faiyum and 45 km north of Beni Suef, is the ruin of the first true pyramid attempted by the ancient Egyptians. The Pyramid of Meidum is impressive, although it looks more like a stone tower than a pyramid, rising abruptly as it does from a large hill of rubble. This is one case, however, where the apparent state of disrepair was not caused by time or centuries of stone robbers, but was actually the result of one instantaneous accident. The pyramid began as an eight-stepped structure; the steps were then filled in and the outer casing was added, forming the first true pyramid shell. However, there were serious design flaws and sometime after completion (possibly as late as the time of the Ptolemaic rulers in the last centuries before Christ's birth) the pyramid's own weight caused the sides to collapse, leaving just the core that still stands today.

The pyramid was started by King Huni, but completed by his son Sneferu, the founder of the 4th dynasty. Sneferu's architects obviously learnt from the mistakes that eventually led to the disaster of Meidum, as he also built the more successful Bent and Red pyramids at Dahshur, and his son Cheops built one of the Great Pyramids at Giza.

Entrance to the site is E£16 (half for students). Ask the guard at the nearby house to unlock the entrance of the pyramid for you. You can follow the steps down 75m to the empty underground burial chamber.

Getting There & Away

It is actually much easier to get to the pyramid from Beni Suef, about 45 km to the south, than from Medinet al-Faiyum. Get a pick-up from Beni Suef to Al-Wasta for 75 pt (45 minutes). From there take another to Meidum village (35 pt), from where you'll have to walk a couple of km – unless you can get a ride.

Alternatively, you could get one of the service taxis or buses running between Beni Suef and Cairo and ask to get off at the Meidum turn-off, from where you still have about six km to go. The reverse of this is probably the easiest way to get back to Beni Suef (or to Cairo for that matter) – just flag down a service taxi or hitch a ride.

BIRQASH CAMEL MARKET

Egypt's largest camel market – or Souq al-Gamaal – is held at Birqash, about 35 km north-west of Cairo. Up until 1995, this famous market was located among rundown tenements and overcrowded streets in Imbaba, one of Cairo's western suburbs. But a burgeoning population has made land, even on the city's periphery, a valuable commodity – too precious to be the home of camels – and so one of Cairo's age-old institutions was relocated to an area deemed more suitable for camel trading on the edge of the Western Desert.

The market is an easy half-day trip from Cairo but, like all of Egypt's animal markets, it's not for animal lovers or the faint-hearted. Hundreds of camels are sold here every day, most having been brought up the 40 Days Road from western Sudan to just north of Abu Simbel by camel herders. From here, they're hobbled and crammed into trucks for the 24 hour journey to Birqash. By the time they arrive, many are emaciated while others are fit only for the knackery. Traders stand no nonsense and camels that get out of line are beaten relentlessly; the sound of bawling beasts is sickening.

In addition to those from Sudan, there are camels from various parts of Egypt (including Sinai, the west and the south) and sometimes as far away as Somalia. They are traded for other livestock such as goats, sheep and horses or sold for farm work and for slaughter – yes, your kofta is probably camel meat. If you're interested in buying a camel, smaller ones cost about E£1500 while the bigger beasts are E£3000. The market is most lively on Friday and Monday mornings, from about 6 to 9 am. As the day wears on, the bargaining activity subsides and by early afternoon it becomes quite subdued.

For a long time a question mark has hung over whether or not there is an official entrance fee for tourists to the market, but the practice has established itself and you are issued with a ticket saying, in Arabic, 'Government souq'. Admission is E£2.

Getting There & Away

There are several options for getting to and from Birqash. The cheapest way involves getting yourself to the site of the old camel market at Imbaba, from where microbuses filled with galabiyya-clad traders and potential buyers shuttle back and forth to Birqash. To get to the old camel market take bus No 99 from Midan Tahrir (next to the Nile Hilton), or minibus No 72 from Ramses station, to Midan Lubnan (in Sahafayeen) and then catch a microbus from there. It's much easier to simply take a taxi from central Cairo all the way to the old site – ask for Imbaba airport (Imbaba matar) as it's the closest landmark. Expect to pay about E£3 to E£5 for this ride. Microbuses to Birqash (E£1) leave from a cafe (look for the sign 'Modern Cairo House') opposite the old souq site (which has become, for the time being, a garbage dump-cum-playground).

From Imbaba, the road winds through fields dotted with date palms, dusty villages and orange orchids before climbing the desert escarpment to the market. In all, it's a 45 minute taste of rural Egypt. Microbuses from Birqash back to Imbaba leave when full

so, depending on the time of the day, you may have to wait an hour or so.

Alternatively, on Friday only, the Sun Hotel (☎ 578-1786) at 2 Sharia Talaat Harb organises a minibus tour to the souq, leaving from the hotel at 7 am and returning at about noon. The charge is E£20 per person (minimum five people); you must book a day or two in advance.

The final option is to hire a taxi to take you all the way there and back. Depending on your bargaining skills, you'll be looking at around E£60; make sure to negotiate waiting time.

WADI NATRUN

Wadi Natrun is a partly cultivated valley, about 100 km north-west of Cairo, that was important to the Egyptians long before the Copts took refuge there. The natron used in the mummification process came from the large deposits of sodium carbonate left when the valley's salt lakes dried up every summer. Those deposits are now used on a larger scale by the chemical industry.

A visit to the monasteries of Wadi Natrun should explain the endurance of the ancient Coptic Christian sect. It is the desert, in a sense, that is the protector of the Coptic faith, for it was there that thousands of Christians retreated to escape Roman persecution in the 4th century AD. They lived in caves, or built monasteries, and developed the monastic tradition that was later adopted by European Christians.

St Makarios retreated with his pupils in Wadi Natrun in 330 AD, and soon there were more than 50 monasteries. These originally isolated, unprotected communities were fortified after destructive raids in 817 AD by Arabs who were on their way to conquer North Africa. The focal point of the monasteries was the church, around which were built a well, storerooms, a dining hall, kitchen, bakery and the monks' cells. The whole complex was surrounded by walls about 12m high and two metres thick, and guarded by the keep – a tower which also served as an internal fort during sieges.

While only four of the monasteries survived the Romans, the Bedouin raids and the coming of Islam, the religious life they all protected is thriving. The Coptic pope is still chosen from among the Wadi Natrun monks, and monasticism is experiencing a revival, with younger Copts again donning hooded robes to live within these ancient walls in the desert.

As a general rule, you can visit all of the monasteries excepting Deir Abu Makar (Makarios). If you wish to stay overnight, you need to call the monasteries' Cairo residences for permission: Deir al-Anba Bishoi (☎ 591-4448); Deir as-Suriani (☎ 929658); Deir al-Baramus (☎ 922775); Deir Abu Makar (☎ 770614). The Patriarchate Secretariat (☎ 285-7889), next to St Mark's Church, 222 Sharia Ramses, Abbassiya does not usually issue permission; nor does the Patriarchate in Alexandria which is on Sharia al-Kineesa al-Kobtiyya (Coptic Church St), one block behind Sharia an-Nabi Daniel. Women may not be allowed to stay overnight in some of the monasteries and if men wish to do so they need written permission from one of the above residences. You can visit the monasteries as a side trip en route between Cairo and Alexandria or as a day tour from either city.

You can generally get a simple meal of fuul or the like at the monasteries. It costs nothing, but a small donation wouldn't hurt.

Deir al-Anba Bishoi
St Bishoi founded two monasteries in Wadi Natrun, this one (which bears his name) and the nearby Deir as-Suriani. Deir al-Anba Bishoi – a great place to watch a desert sunset – contains the saint's body, which is said to be perfectly preserved under a red cloth, and the remains of Paul of Tamweh, who made quite a name for himself by committing suicide seven times. The monks there claim that it is not uncommon for St Bishoi to perform miracles for true believers.

Deir as-Suriani
Deir as-Suriani, or the 'monastery of the Syrians', is named after a wealthy Syrian who founded it in the 8th century, and after

the many Syrian monks who subsequently came to live here; it's about 500m north-west of Deir al-Anba Bishoi. In the 17th century the monastery, and its valuable manuscript collection, was taken over by the Copts. There are several domed churches in the gardens and courtyards of this tranquil monastery. Ask the monks to show you St Bishoi's private cell where he stood for nights on end with his hair attached to a chain dangling from the ceiling. It was during one of these marathon prayer vigils that Christ is said to have appeared and allowed Bishoi to wash His feet and then drink the water.

Deir Abu Makar (Makarios)
This monastery is nearly 20 km south-east of Deir al-Anba Bishoi and was founded around the hermit's cell where St Makarios spent his last 20 or so years. Although structurally it has suffered worst at the hands of raiding Bedouins, it is perhaps the most renowned of the four monasteries, as over the centuries most of the Coptic popes have been selected from among its monks. It is the last resting place of many of those popes and also contains the remains of the '49 Martyrs', a group of monks killed by Bedouins in 444 AD. It is also the most secluded of the monasteries, and permission even to visit must be organised in advance.

Deir al-Baramus
Deir al-Baramus was the most isolated of the Wadi Natrun monasteries until recently when a good road was built between it and Deir al-Anba Bishoi to the south-east. Despite this, it still has an isolated feel, and is probably the best monastery to stay at, as it's a little less austere than the others. The special feature of St John's church here is a superb iconostasis of inlaid ivory.

Getting There & Away
From Midan Abdel Minnim Riyadh in Cairo, near the Ramses Hilton, you can get a West Delta Bus Co bus to Wadi Natrun for E£3 every hour from 6.30 am. From there you have to negotiate for a taxi.

If you have your own vehicle and you're

coming from Cairo, take Pyramids Rd (Sharia al-Ahram) through Giza and turn onto the Desert Highway just before the Hotel Mena House. At about 95 km from Cairo (just after the rest house) turn left into the wadi, go through the village of Bir Hooker and continue on, following the signs indicating the monasteries. The first one is Deir al-Anba Bishoi. Deir as-Suriani is about half a km to the north-west, Deir Abu Makar is 20 km via a paved road to the south-east, and Deir al-Baramus is off to the north-west.

THE NILE DELTA

If you have the time, it's well worth the effort to explore the lush, fan-shaped Delta of Egypt between Cairo and Alexandria. This is where the Nile divides in half to flow north into the sea at the Mediterranean ports of Damietta and Rosetta (Rashid). The Delta is also laced with several smaller tributaries and is reputedly one of the most fertile and, not surprisingly, most cultivated regions in the world.

The Delta region played just as important a part in the early history of the country as did Upper Egypt, although few archaeological remains record this. While the desert and dryness of the south helped preserve the Pharaonic sites, the amazing fertility of the Delta region had the opposite effect. Over the centuries, when the ancient cities, temples and palaces of the Delta were left to ruin, they were literally ploughed into oblivion by the fellahin. The attraction of this area, then, is the chance of coming across communities rarely visited by foreigners, where you can gain a little insight into the Egyptian peasant farmer's way of life.

Service taxis and buses crisscross the region from town to town, but if you really want to explore off the beaten track and wander through this incredibly green countryside you'll have to hire a car. If you do so you'll need to pay extra attention when you're on the road as it's a heavily populated area and accidents are common. Theoretically, you're not supposed to leave the main roads, but in the unlikely event of you being hassled by the police you can always say you're lost.

Nile Barrages (Qanater)

The Nile Barrages and the city of Qanater (which simply means barrages) lie 16 km north of Cairo where the Nile splits into the eastern Damietta branch and the western Rosetta branch. The barrages, begun in the early 19th century, were successfully completed several decades later. The series of basins and locks, on both main branches of the Nile and two side canals, ensured the vital large-scale regulation of the Nile into the Delta region, and led to a great increase in cotton production.

The Damietta Barrage consists of 71 sluices stretching 521m across the river; the Rosetta Barrage is 438m long with 61 sluices. Between the two is a one-km-wide area filled with beautiful gardens and cafes. It's a superb place to rent a bicycle or a felucca and take a relaxing tour.

The town of Qanater, at the fork of the river, is officially the start of the Delta region.

Getting There & Away To get to the barrages from Cairo you can take a river bus for 50 pt from the water-taxi station in front of the Radio & Television building (Maspero station), just north of the Ramses Hilton. The trip takes about two hours. A faster but less relaxing way to get there is by taking bus No 930 from Midan Ataba bus station or No 950 from Ahmed Hilmi bus station behind Ramses railway station.

Zagazig

Just outside this town, founded in the 19th century, are the ruins of Bubastis, one of the most ancient cities in Egypt. There's not much to see in Zagazig itself, but as it's only 80 km north-east of Cairo it's an easy day trip to the ruins (though there's also a hotel or two in town should you want to stay overnight). The train heading for Port Said from Cairo takes about 1½ hours to Zagazig and a service taxi (E£4) from Midan Ahmed Hilmi in Cairo takes about one hour. There are buses to Zagazig from Cairo, Alexandria, Ismailia and Port Said (E£5.50), and even two services from Sharm el-Sheikh in Sinai.

Bubastis The great deity of the ancient city of Bubastis was the elegant cat-goddess Bastet. Festivals held in her honour are said to have attracted more than 700,000 revellers, who would sing, dance, feast, consume great quantities of wine and offer sacrifices to the goddess. The architectural gem of Bubastis was the Temple of Bastet, sited between two canals, surrounded by trees and encircled by the city, which was built at a higher level to look down on it. The temple was begun by Cheops and Chephren during the 4th dynasty, and Pharaohs of the 6th, 12th, 18th, 19th and 22nd dynasties made their additions over about 17 centuries. Herodotus wrote:

Although other Egyptian cities were carried to a great height, in my opinion the greatest mounds were thrown up about the city of Bubastis, in which is a Temple of Bastet well worthy of mention; for though other temples may be larger and more costly, none is more pleasing to look at than this.

The temple is now just a pile of rubble, and the most interesting site at Bubastis is the cat cemetery 200m down the road. The series of underground galleries, where many bronze statues of cats were found, is perfect for a bit of exploration.

Tanis

Just outside the village of San al-Hagar, 70 km north-east of Zagazig, are the ruins of ancient Tanis, which many believe to be the Biblical city where the Hebrews were persecuted by the Egyptians before fleeing through the Red Sea in search of the Promised Land. It was certainly of great importance to a succession of powerful Pharaohs, all of whom left their mark through the extraordinary buildings or statues they commissioned, and for several centuries Tanis was one of the largest cities in the Delta.

Tanis covers about four sq km, only part

The Tanis sphinx was among artefacts uncovered at the excavations at Tanis, thought to be placed there by the Ramessids.

of which has been excavated. The monuments uncovered date from as early as the 6th dynasty reign of Pepi I, around 2330 BC, through to the time of the Ptolemies in the 1st century BC. The excavation of the city so far has revealed sacred lakes, the foundations of many temples, a royal necropolis and a multitude of statues and carvings.

Although it's less impressive than other archaeological sites in the country, the Egyptian government has been promoting Tanis as a tourist destination for the past few years.

Tanta

Tanta, the largest city in the Delta, is 90 km from Cairo and 110 km from Alexandria. There's nothing much of interest there, although it is a centre for Sufism, a form of Islamic mysticism. A mosque in Tanta is dedicated to Sayyid Ahmed al-Badawi, a Moroccan Sufi, who fought the Crusaders from there in the 13th century and then went on to assist in the defeat of Louis IX at Damietta. The moulid held in his honour follows the October cotton harvest and is one of the biggest such events in Egypt, drawing crowds of one to two million.

In this area of the western Delta, although there are no actual structural remains, are the sites of three ancient cities. North-west of Tanta, on the east bank of the Nile, is **Sais**, Egypt's 26th dynasty capital. Sacred to Neith, the goddess of war and hunting and protector of embalmed bodies, Sais dates back to the start of Egyptian history and once had palaces, temples and royal tombs.

West of Tanta, more then half way along the road to Damanhur, is the site of **Naucratis**, an ancient city where the Greeks were allowed to settle and trade during the 7th century BC. The city of **Buto**, north-east of Damanhur and north-west of Tanta, was the cult centre of Edjo, the cobra-goddess of Lower Egypt, always represented on a Pharaoh's crown as a uraeus.

Places to Stay The *Hotel Arafa* (☎ 336952; fax 331800) is one of the best hotels in town. It has single/double rooms for E£83/113, including breakfast and taxes. It's one (big) block from the railway station – turn to the right as you exit.

Should you want something cheaper, try the basic *Hotel Bab el-Salam* (☎ 333520) on Sharia Saka el-Gideda, one block from Hotel Arafa (it's on the left as you head towards the big mosque). It's signposted in Arabic only, so look for the orange building with green shutters. It has doubles for E£12.

Getting There & Away From Cairo, service taxis from near the Midan Ahmed Hilmi bus station cost E£5. Middle Delta Bus Co buses from Midan Abdel Minnim Riyadh in Cairo cost E£5.50. There are buses and service taxis from Alexandria too. Nearly all Alexandria to Cairo trains (except the Turbos and one or two others) stop in Tanta.

Mansura

At the centre of Egypt's cotton industry is Mansura, one of the most important cities in the Delta. The best thing about a visit to Mansura is the chance to taste the city's delicacy – buffalo milk ice cream. Should you want to stay, there is the odd hotel.

Mansura is known as the 'city of victory' for the part it played in Egypt's early Islamic history. In 1249, the Egyptians retreated from the coast and set up camp at Mansura after the Crusader forces, under Louis IX of France, had captured the Mediterranean port of Damietta. When the Crusaders decided to make their push inland, they charged straight through the Muslim camp, only to be cut down on the other side of Mansura by 10,000 Mamluk warriors. Louis himself was captured and ransomed for the return of Damietta.

Getting There & Away There are regular train connections with Cairo, and a service taxi from Midan Ahmed Hilmi costs E£8. The East Delta Co bus from Midan Ulali costs about E£7 and takes 2½ hours. Buses shuttle regularly between Mansura and Port Said (E£4) and there are services taxis to Ismailia (E£5.50).

Damietta (Dumyat)

Once a prosperous Arab trading port, Damietta's fortunes suffered greatly with the construction of the Suez Canal and the subsequent development of Port Said. During the Middle Ages, its strategic position on the north coast of Egypt, at the mouth of the Nile, meant it was regularly being threatened by foreign armies. Over the centuries it was taken by the Germans, English and French, and defended by, among others, Salah ad-Din and Mohammed Ali. When it wasn't being attacked by marauding Crusaders, Damietta (Dumyat to the locals) was doing a roaring trade in coffee, linen, oil and dates, and was a port of call for ships from all over the known world.

Besides a few old Delta-style mansions, there's not much to see, but it is the easiest place from which to go on to Ras al-Bar, about 12 km to the north, or to do a spot of bird-watching on Lake Manzela. Should you want to stay, try the *El Manshy Hotel* (☎ 323308) at 5 Sharia Nokrashy, which has singles/doubles from E£20/27.

There are East Delta Co buses from Midan Ulali in Cairo every hour from 6 am to 6.30 pm for around E£10. Regular buses to Port Said take about an hour and cost E£2.75.

Ras al-Bar

The small town of Ras al-Bar, north of Damietta, is at the point where the eastern branch of the Nile meets the sea, 170 km north-east of Cairo. It is a pleasant beach resort, and if you're planning on staying anywhere in the Delta region this would be the best choice.

The town is actually spread over both banks of the Nile. The majority of the local people live on the eastern side. The bulk of the hotels, restaurants and so on are on the western side, which is actually a tongue of land, with the Nile on one side and the Mediterranean on the other. Little motor ferries connect the two halves, weaving in-between the flocks of sky-blue fishing trawlers.

Information The post and telephone offices are on Sharia Mahmoud Talaat, a couple of blocks north-east of the big mosque where buses and microbuses from Damietta terminate.

Places to Stay & Eat Ras al-Bar is crawling with hotels and private villas, but outside the summer season most of them are closed. Most of the streets are numbered rather than named, and the easiest thing to do is wander along the Nile-side road and duck into the side streets wherever you see a hotel that might look OK. The *Families Hotel*, a block north of Sharia Mahmoud Talaat, costs E£12 a night. Further up, on the road next to the Nile, the *Dar al-Abyad Hotel* (the name, as with many of the smaller places, is in Arabic only), costs E£17 for a double.

Other OK hotels a bit higher up the price scale are the *Marine an-Nil* (☎ 528006) and the *Marine Ras al-Bar* (☎ 528728), both on Sharia Mahmoud Talaat, and the *Hotel Mobasher* (☎ 527097), which is closer to the point where the Nile spills into the sea.

There are numerous restaurants – many of them called *casinos* – along the Nile, and on the point is one called *High Garden*. As you work your way back along the Mediterranean side, there are a couple of other restaurants, one with a sometimes-full seawater pool. Along the beach you can hire parasols and deckchairs.

For cheaper eats, look in the area around the big mosque – here you'll find the *Greece Restaurant* and *King Fish* plus ta'amiyya stands and teahouses.

Getting There & Away East Delta Co buses run regularly from Cairo or Port Said to Damietta, and from there you can get a bus for 50 pt. Microbuses also cost 50 pt, and are fine for the trip from Damietta to Ras al-Bar but, on the return journey, they tend to drop you about two km from the main bus station in Damietta. In summer there are supposed to be regular buses direct from Cairo, for which you need to book ahead.

Gamasa, Baltim & Al-Burg
There are other quiet little beach resorts to the west of Ras al-Bar. The closest is Gamasa; Baltim and Al-Burg are on the eastern edge of Lake Burullus, roughly halfway between Ras al-Bar and Rosetta.

There are three listed hotels in Gamasa. The three star *Amoun Hotel* (☎ 760660) in the souq area has singles/doubles for US$36/45. The two star *Beau Rivage Hotel* (☎ 760268) has rooms for E£25/30 or you could try the one star *Hannoville Hotel* (☎ 760750) at E£16/18.

In Baltim you have just two options; both are one star places charging E£8/10.50 a night for singles/doubles. They are the *Baltim Beach Hotel* (☎ 501541) and the *Cleopatra Touristic Hotel*.

The Nile Valley – Beni Suef to Qus

He who rides the sea of the Nile must have sails woven of patience.

Egyptian proverb

The ancient Greek traveller and writer Herodotus described Egypt as 'the gift of the Nile'; the ancient Egyptians likened their land to a lotus – the Delta being the flower, the oasis of Al-Faiyum the bud and the river and its valley the stem. Whichever way you look at it, Egypt is the Nile. The river is the lifeblood of the country and the fertile Nile Valley is its heart. And whether you journey down the valley by felucca, train, bus or plane you'll discover that even an outsider cannot ignore the power of the Nile and the hold it has always had over Egyptian life.

Rain seldom falls in the Nile Valley, so the verdant stretch of land, ranging from a couple of metres to a few km wide on either

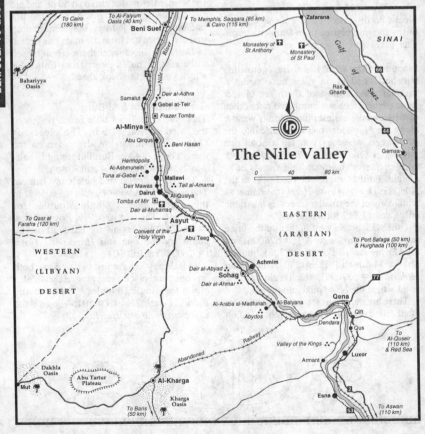

240

side of the river, is rendered fertile only by the winding Nile as it makes its way through the barren desert. The countryside is dotted with thousands of simple villages where people toil, day in day out, using tools and machinery modelled on designs thousands of years old. Even the region's large towns and cities, like Al-Minya, Asyut, Luxor and Aswan, are in some ways merely modernised extensions of these villages.

Travelling south from Cairo you pass through a world where ancient and medieval monuments almost seem to be part of the present. From Saqqara to Luxor, while you marvel at the remarkable history of the Pharaonic tombs and their builders, you'll realise that the daily labour and recreation of the fellahin in the 20th century differs very little from the images depicted in the wall paintings of the ancient monuments. The colourful scenes of Egyptians building, hunting, fighting, feasting, harvesting and fishing more than 2500 years ago are repeated daily on the banks of the Nile and in the valley's fertile fields.

BENI SUEF

Beni Suef is a provincial capital 120 km

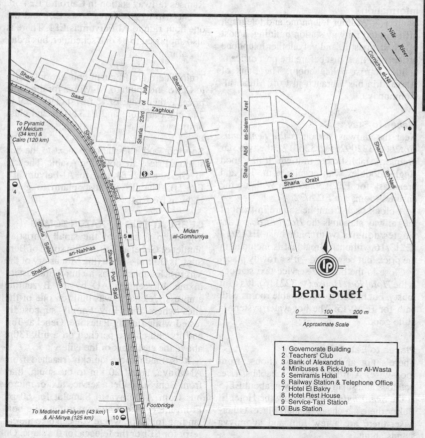

Beni Suef

0   100   200 m

Approximate Scale

1 Governorate Building
2 Teachers' Club
3 Bank of Alexandria
4 Minibuses & Pick-Ups for Al-Wasta
5 Semiramis Hotel
6 Railway Station & Telephone Office
7 Hotel El Bakry
8 Hotel Rest House
9 Service-Taxi Station
10 Bus Station

south of Cairo. Even with a population of about 150,000 and a few multistorey buildings it isn't a big town, but is typical of the large Egyptian country towns that are basically overgrown farming villages. There are more donkey carts and *hantours* in the streets than cars and buses. While there's nothing of particular interest in Beni Suef itself, it is a good base for visiting Al-Faiyum Oasis, and probably the best point from which to visit the Pyramid of Meidum. (See the Around Cairo chapter for details on Al-Faiyum Oasis and the Pyramid of Meidum.)

Information
There is a 24 hour telephone and telegraph office in the railway station building, a post office just past it, and yet another telephone office after that. Just before the post office is a little tourist police booth. The Bank of Alexandria has a branch just off Midan al-Gomhurriya.

Places to Stay
Near the railway station is the *Semiramis Hotel* (☎ 322092; fax 326017), the two star premier establishment in town. It has good singles/doubles with ensuite bath, TV and breakfast for E£29.50/39.50. Without the ensuite, rooms are E£24/32.

A block back from the square in front of the railway station is the *Hotel El Bakry*. Its singles/doubles with bath cost E£15/17 (E£13/16 without). Breakfast is included in the price, but be warned – it's a rowdy place.

Close to the bus and service-taxi stations is the *Hotel Rest House* (☎ 322116). It's a bit musty, but has pretty reasonable rooms with bath for E£10/15. The hot water system is quite good.

Places to Eat
There's not an awful lot to choose from food-wise. A filling meal of kebabs, rice, potatoes and salad will cost you about E£15 at the *Semiramis Hotel*. Below the Hotel El Bakry there's a cheap kushari place. Otherwise, there are a few fuul and ta'amiyya stands about.

Getting There & Away
Beni Suef is a departure point for the trek across the desert to the Monastery of St Anthony, which is about 150 km east, near the Gulf of Suez (see the Monastery of St Anthony in the Suez Canal and the Red Sea Coast chapter for details). It might be difficult to hire a service taxi in Beni Suef for the whole trip. But you might be able to get close taking the Zafarana bus.

Bus The bus station is along the main road, south of town. Buses run from about 6 am to 6 pm to Ahmed Hilmi bus station behind Ramses railway station in Cairo for E£4.50.

The trip to Al-Minya costs E£4 and the one hour ride to Al-Faiyum is E£1. There is also supposed to be one scheduled bus a day to Zafarana.

Train There are frequent connections north to Cairo and south to Al-Minya for the same prices either way: E£13 in 1st class; E£9 in 2nd class air-con; and E£3.50 in 2nd class ordinary.

Service Taxi The station is next to the bus station. Prices are posted in Arabic. The trip to Giza costs E£4 and to Al-Faiyum it's E£1.50. The drivers also claim to go to Helwan for E£4.

GEBEL AT-TEIR & FRAZER TOMBS
The main feature of the small Christian hamlet of Gebel at-Teir, 93 km south of Beni Suef, is **Deir al-Adhra** (the Monastery of the Virgin). Established as a church/monastery in the 4th century AD by the Byzantine empress Helena, it was built on one of the sites where the Holy Family supposedly rested while fleeing Palestine. Gebel at-Teir and its church are perched on a hill 130m above the east bank of the Nile.

It is much more quickly reached from Al-Minya, about 20 km to the south, than from Beni Suef. Get a service taxi or microbus from Al-Minya to Samalut for 60 pt. From there, take a pick-up to the Nile boat landing for 25 pt, where you can take the car ferry for E£1 or the felucca for the same. On the other side is a pick-up going to Deir al-Adhra, but you may find yourself paying about E£1 to get it moving, as there are not always a lot of passengers going that way. When you arrive, ask for the *kineesa*, or church, and someone will appear with the keys and give you a short tour. There are some interesting 400 year-old icons inside.

About five km south of Gebel at-Teir are the Frazer Tombs which date back to the 5th and 6th dynasties. These Old Kingdom tombs are hewn into the desert cliff on the east bank of the Nile and overlook the plain and fields. The four tombs are very simple, containing eroded statues and carved hieroglyphs but no colourful scenes. If you're attracted to places where other tourists rarely go, these are for you.

To get there from Al-Minya, take a pick-up (25 pt) from the bridge 500m south-east of town. It will head north along the east bank road until a turn-off at two white pillars. From the turn-off, you must walk to the cliffs (a short cut through the fields – along the path starting at the pump house – will halve the distance).

AL-MINYA

They call it the 'Bride of Upper Egypt' (Arous as-Sa'id), as Al-Minya more or less marks the divide between Upper and Lower Egypt. A semi-industrial provincial capital 247 km south of Cairo, it is a centre for sugar processing and the manufacture of soap and perfume. It has a population of about 500,000. There are several hotels, which make this a convenient place to base yourself for day trips to the Pharaonic tombs and temples of Beni Hasan, Tuna al-Gebel and Hermopolis.

Information

Visa Extensions Should you need to extend your visa, the passport office is on the 2nd floor of the post office.

Tourist Office There's a tourist information office (☎ 320150) in the governorate building. Its branch in the railway station (☎ 342044) is certainly as good and it is open

24 hours a day. There's a tourist office kiosk down by the dock for Nile cruisers but it only opens when a flotel arrives.

Money The Banque Misr branch on Midan as-Sa'a actually does Visa card cash advances – it takes some time though. There are a couple of other banks for cash and travellers' cheque transactions.

Post & Communications The post office is open daily except Friday from 8 am to 2 pm. The telephone office is in the railway station and sells phone cards.

Things to See

There's not much to see or do in town. The tree-lined Corniche along the Nile is a pleasant place for a picnic or a ride in a hantour.

There is a large Muslim and Christian cemetery about seven km south-east of town, on the east bank near the ferry landing. It's called **Zawiyet al-Mayyiteen** (Corner of the Dead). The cemetery consists of several hundred mud-brick mausolea stretching for four km from the road to the hills. It is said to be one of the largest cemeteries in the world.

Places to Stay

Camping It's possible to pitch a tent on the east bank of the Nile in the public gardens near the bridge, about 1.5 km from the railway station; check with the tourist office to make sure it's still OK.

Hotels The cheapest place in town must be the *Majestic Hotel* (☎ 324212) on Sharia al-Gomhurriya. A three bed room costs E£6.60 but there's little to attract you to this dusty, depressing place.

The *Palace Hotel* (☎ 324071/21) is just up the road on Midan Tahrir (Palace). Even if you don't want to stay there, walk in for the decorative experience; high-ceilinged rooms and a big, airy central lobby. Rooms are E£10.50/7.50 with/without bath. The rooms with bathrooms are by all measures quite a good deal.

Along the road a bit further is the *Amoun*

Hotel (not signposted). For E£12 you can have a comfy bed in a room to yourself with hot water. Breakfast is E£3.

The *Hotel Seety* (☎ 323930), 71 Sharia Saad Zaghloul, is half a block south of the railway station. It looks an old building from the outside, but several of the rooms are clean, comfortable and airy, and are quite cheap at E£8/10 without bath and E£10/14 with bath. The best part is a central living room full of antique furniture and an out-of-tune piano.

The *Savoy Hotel* (☎ 323270) is directly opposite the railway station. With its big hall and high, painted ceilings it exudes some old grandeur. The large, though decrepit, rooms cost E£20/30/36 with bathroom, or E£15/25/30 without.

The *Ibn Khassib Hotel* (☎ 324535) at 5 Sharia Raghib is in an ageing building on a side street near the railway station. It has 12 doubles and six singles, all with high ceilings and Victorian-style furniture. Bathrooms/showers are crammed together. Singles/doubles with breakfast, dinner, air-con and bath are a bit pricey at E£50/60. Without bath

PLACES TO STAY
3 Touristic Lotus Hotel
5 El Zahra Hotel
7 Dahabia Houseboat
8 Beach Hotel
9 Akhnaton Hotel
10 Amoun Hotel
11 Palace Hotel
12 Majestic Hotel
14 Savoy Hotel
17 Ibn Khassib Hotel
18 Hotel Seety

PLACES TO EAT
2 Cafeteria Aly Baba
13 Savoy Cafe (Coffee House)
15 El Sadhi Restaurant

OTHER
1 Tourist Office & Governorate Building
4 Banque du Caire
6 Post Office
16 Railway Station, Tourist Office & Telephone Office
19 Minibuses & Service Taxis (for Samalut)
20 Hospital
21 Mosque
22 Banque Misr
23 Service Taxis (for Cairo, Mallawi & Asyut)
24 Bus Station

Al-Minya

0   100   200 m

or dinner, they come down to E£34.25/ 43.75. There's a restaurant and bar.

The *Beach Hotel* (☎ 322307) is a clean, pleasant place down near the river. At E£27/50 for a single/double without bath, it's OK.

The nearby *Akhnaton Hotel* (☎ 325917/8; fax 326996), on the Corniche, has 42 clean, carpeted rooms with air-con on the 3rd and 4th floors, some with great views of the Nile. Get one of these rooms and in terms of value for money, this is the best place to stay. Singles/doubles are E£26/34 without breakfast, and a few pounds extra with air-con.

The Coptic Evangelical Organisation runs an old houseboat, called the *Dahabia* (☎ 325596), with four cosy rooms for E£30/ 55, including breakfast. The deck becomes some sort of a cafeteria during the day.

The *Touristic Lotus Hotel* (☎ 324541; fax 324576) is at 1 Sharia Port Said, about a 10 minute walk north of the railway station. It's popular with German groups and pretty reasonable. Singles/doubles, all with air-con and TV, cost E£35/48.50, including breakfast.

Around the corner is the *El Zahra Hotel*. It's a basic cheapie at E£10 a person. Breakfast costs E£3.

About a km north of town is the *Nefertiti & Aton* (☎ 331515; fax 326467), a four star hotel that has rooms facing the Nile for US$51/61, not including taxes. It has three restaurants and two bars.

Places to Eat

The *Cafeteria Aly Baba – Patisserie*, on the Corniche just north of Sharia Port Said, serves a satisfying meal of the usual favourites – kebabs or another meat dish, salad, tahina and a soft drink for about E£10. This is also a good place for a morning cup of coffee and a pastry.

The restaurant and cafeteria on top of the *Lotus Hotel* serve simple filling meals for E£15 (if you don't mind vegetables in a pool of oil). The views of the Nile and surrounding fields are nice. Another place with good views is the restaurant at the top of the *Akhnaton Hotel*.

The *El Sadhi*, to the right of the Savoy Hotel, has a menu similar to the other places, with good meals for around E£12.

The restaurant at the *Ibn Khassib Hotel* gives you a good feed for E£10. This will get you chicken, potato stew, rice with bits of kidney and liver in it (not as bad as it sounds), salad, baba ghanoug and an orange at the end for dessert. A local Stella beer here is E£5.

There are a lot of smaller places and the usual cheap felafel stands scattered around Midan al-Mahatta, Midan Tahrir and along the market street stretching south off the

BENI SUEF TO QUS

Troubles in the Nile Valley

Al-Minya has a big Christian population and is part of the belt of towns (including Mallawi, Dairut, Asyut and Sohag) where clashes between Christians and Muslims (usually said to be fundamentalists) have taken place since the early 1990s – although feuding of the sort has long been a part of the territory.

If you haven't already felt the tension caused by this sectarian violence and the occasional pot shots taken at tourists in the area, you may begin to here. The high profile of troops and military police, the constant checkpoints along the highway up and down the Nile, and the anxious assertions by officials and others that there are no problems and that tourists are well liked combine to give a slight feel for the kind of troubles most visitors, thankfully, never have any direct experience.

Even so, the violence is continuing, and very few tourists have spent much time in any of these towns or the ancient sites dotted between them in recent years. If you do happen to stay along this stretch, it's likely the local police will be onto you as soon as your presence in town is known. They'll then insist on an armed escort to the ancient sites, particularly Tuna al-Gebel, the monasteries near Sohag, and Abydos. It probably pays to agree with their assertions that the 'police are good' and that the troubles are over. How safe you'll actually feel under their escort is moot. The fact that the security forces have been in the thick of many of the shoot outs may make you feel like a sitting duck. ■

latter. The *Savoy Cafe* is not a bad place for a cup of tea and a game of backgammon.

Getting There & Away

Bus The bus station is near the Cairo and Asyut service-taxi row. There are hourly buses to Cairo (E£8 to E£11, four hours) from 5 am to 4 pm. You can book ahead or try your luck on the day. The ticket office only seems to be open in the morning.

Buses depart for Beni Suef (E£4) every 20 to 40 minutes; the last one leaves at 4 pm.

Buses to Asyut (E£3.50, two to three hours) leave every half an hour from 6 am to 5 pm both ways.

On Sunday, Monday and Wednesday mornings there's a bus to Hurghada (E£24).

In summer there is a morning bus right through to Alexandria (E£15).

Train The trip from Cairo (four hours) costs E£23 in 1st class or E£14/6.50 in 2nd class with/without air-con.

Trains heading south depart fairly frequently, with the fastest trains leaving Al-Minya between about 11 pm and 1 am. Fares (1st class/2nd with air-con/2nd without) from Al-Minya are: Asyut E£13/8/3.40; Sohag E£21/13/5.80; Qena E£31/19/9; Luxor E£34/21/10; and Aswan E£45/27/13.20.

Service Taxi From Cairo, service taxis take three to four hours to Al-Minya and cost E£8. From Al-Minya, they still have departures as late as 8 pm. There are also service taxis to Asyut (E£4.50, two hours) and Mallawi (E£1). The depot is about a five minute walk from the railway station (just past the bridge). Microbuses also do the Mallawi run.

BENI HASAN

Beni Hasan is a necropolis on the east bank of the Nile about 20 km south of Al-Minya. More than 30 distinctive Middle Kingdom tombs of varying sizes are carved into a limestone cliff. Only a few of them are accessible.

The Beni Hasan necropolis is open from 7 am to 5 pm, but you should get there by 3 pm at the latest. It's a good idea to start earlier because it can get quite hot here towards the end of the day. Admission is E£12 (half for students). You are expected to give the guard a bit of baksheesh for unlocking the tombs, although that's his job anyway. Photography used to be prohibited inside the tombs; now you can take pictures without flash if you pay E£5 – per tomb!

There are various tombs at Beni Hasan, the best of which (and the only ones open to the public) are described below.

Tomb of Kheti (No 17)

Kheti was a governor of the nome, or district, of Oryx during Egypt's 11th dynasty (about 2000 BC). Wall scenes in his tomb show daily life in the Middle Kingdom.

Tomb of Baqet (No 15)

Baqet was the father of Kheti. His tomb has some interesting wall paintings: wrestlers doing more than just wrestling with each other, gazelles doing the same, and a hunt for unicorns and winged monsters.

Tomb of Khnumhotep (No 3)

This is a beautiful tomb. Khnumhotep served as a governor under Amenemhet III (about 1820 BC). The walls show colourful scenes of Khnumhotep's family life, and above the door are some interesting scenes of acrobats.

Tomb of Amenemhet (No 2)

This has the unusual addition of a false door facing west. The dead are supposed to enter the underworld only from the west. Amenemhet was a nomarch, or governor, and commander in chief of the Oryx nome.

Getting There & Away

From Al-Minya, take the Mallawi service taxi or microbus, which costs E£1, and get the driver to let you off at Abu Qirqus. Alternatively, walk past the bus station and overpass, cross the railway tracks and veer left until you find another microbus station, and take the Abu Qirqus microbus (50 pt). It takes about half an hour. Once there, walk across the Ibrahimiya Canal and railway tracks and on for about 200m. There you take a pick-up (25 pt) to the river (it's quite a long walk).

At the river you'll find an office, where boat tickets cost E£6 (if less than six people). The price drops to E£2 if there are six or more. This is for the round trip, and includes the little microbus service at the other side that takes you part of the way to the tombs. There's a great view of the Nile from the tombs further up the slope. Watch out for the baksheesh kids from the nearby village. Walking towards the village is asking to be mobbed by them.

MALLAWI

Mallawi is 48 km south of Al-Minya. There is not much in town, except for a museum and one hotel. It's a convenient departure point for the ancient sights of Hermopolis, Tuna al-Gebel and Tell al-Amarna but, once again, few tourists have stayed here in recent times (see the Troubles in the Nile Valley boxed story in the Al-Minya section).

Archaeological Museum

The small museum in town houses a collection of artefacts from Tuna al-Gebel and Hermopolis. It is open daily except Wednesday from 9 am to 4 pm (Friday until noon); entry is E£6.

Places to Stay & Eat

There is only one – the *Semiramis Hotel* (☎ 652955) on the west bank of the Ibrahimiya Canal, just north of the railway station. The rooms aren't bad, but the bathrooms are a bit grimy. They charge E£5.50/9 for a single/double. You can get a meal in the hotel's restaurant, which is probably the best bet in the town.

Getting There & Away

All buses to or from Al-Minya and Asyut stop here. A service taxi from Al-Minya costs E£1; from Asyut it's E£2 for the one hour trip.

HERMOPOLIS

Little remains of this ancient city, eight km

north of Mallawi, that was once the centre for the cult of Thoth, the ibis-headed god of wisdom, healing and writing. At the time of writing, Hermopolis was closed – the tourist office in either Asyut or Al-Minya should know if it has reopened.

The Greeks associated Thoth with their own Hermes – hence the city's Hellenic name – but in ancient times the city was known as Khmunu. Khmun was one of the eight all-powerful deities of the primordial chaos that preceded creation, and this city was believed to be sited where the sun first rose over the earth. The Arabic name for the present-day village, and the area surrounding the ruined city of Hermopolis, is Al-Ashmunein – a derivation of Khmun.

Apart from a few Middle and New Kingdom remains, the only real monument at Hermopolis is a ruined Roman agora and its early Christian basilica – the largest of its type still standing in Egypt. There is a small museum near two large sandstone statues of Thoth unearthed in the area.

Getting There & Away

To get to Hermopolis from Mallawi, take a local microbus or service taxi to the village of Al-Ashmunein (25 pt); the turn-off to the site is one km from the main road. From the junction you can either walk the short distance to Hermopolis or coax your driver to go a bit further. Hitching around the area shouldn't be a problem, as the sight of a foreigner walking down the road is bound to attract quite a lot of attention.

TUNA AL-GEBEL

Tuna al-Gebel is seven km west of Hermopolis. The site is open from 7 am to 5 pm and admission costs E£12 (half for students). The very few tourists who come here these days are usually escorted by police from Mallawi or Al-Minya. It gets very hot here, even in winter, so bring plenty of water, a hat and sun screen if you plan to trek across the desert to the sights.

Apart from bordering on Akhetaten, the Pharaoh Akhenaten's short-lived capital, Tuna al-Gebel was also the necropolis of

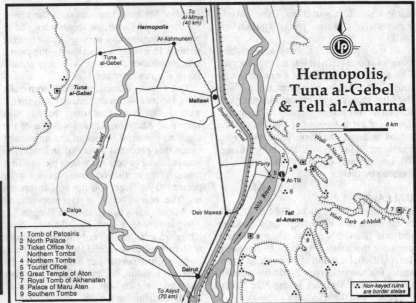

To
Al-Minya
(40 km)

Hermopolis

Al-Ashmunein

Tuna
al-Gebel

Tuna
al-Gebel

Mallawi

Hermopolis,
Tuna al-Gebel
& Tell al-Amarna

0   4   8 km

Wadi al-Nachla

Bahr Yusef

Ferry

At-Till

Dalga

Deir Mawas

Tell
al-Amarna

Wadi Darb al-Melek

Ibrahimiya Canal

Nile River

Dairut

To Asyut
(70 km)

```
1  Tomb of Petosiris
2  North Palace
3  Ticket Office for
   Northern Tombs
4  Northern Tombs
5  Tourist Office
6  Great Temple of Aton
7  Royal Tomb of Akhenaten
8  Palace of Maru Aten
9  Southern Tombs
```

Non-keyed ruins
are border stelae

Hermopolis. The area's oldest monument is one of the six stelae that marked the boundary of Akhetaten – in this case the western perimeter of the city's farmlands and associated villages. The stele, a rock-hewn shrine and some statues show Akhenaten and Nefertiti in various poses.

To the south of the stele, which is about five km past the village of Tuna al-Gebel, are the catacombs and tombs of the residents and sacred animals of Hermopolis. A German team has been working at Tuna al-Gebel since 1979.

The most interesting things to see there are the dark catacomb galleries once filled with thousands of mummified baboons, ibises and ibis eggs – baboons and ibises were sacred to Thoth. Most of the animals have been destroyed by robbers, and in fact only one of the baboons was found fully intact by archaeologists. Most of the mummification was done in the Ptolemaic and Roman periods. The subterranean cemetery extends

for at least three km, but Egyptologists suspect it may stretch all the way to Hermopolis. You definitely need a torch if you're going to explore the galleries.

Tomb of Petosiris

This is an interesting Ptolemaic tomb chapel; a sign directs the way. Petosiris was a high priest of Thoth; his family tomb, in the design of a temple, is entered through a columned vestibule. The tomb paintings show a mixture of two cultures: although they depict typical Egyptian farming scenes, the figures are wearing Greek dress.

Mummy of Isadora

In a small building behind the Tomb of Petosiris is the extremely well-preserved mummy of a woman who drowned in the Nile in about 150 AD. Isadora's teeth, hair and fingernails are clearly visible. You'll need to give the guard a bit of baksheesh to see her, though.

Well

The *sakiya*, or well, is next to a water wheel that once brought water up from its depths. The well was the sole source of water for the priests, workers and sacred baboons of Tuna al-Gebel. For a bit more baksheesh the guard will unlock the door and let you walk down to the bottom of the well. Watch out for the bats!

Getting There & Away

There's a fair amount of traffic between the Hermopolis junction and the village, so it should be fairly easy to hitch. If you're with the police, they take you there and back.

TELL AL-AMARNA

The scant remains of this once-glorious city, 12 km south-west of Mallawi, may be a little disappointing when compared to its fascinating, albeit brief, moment in history.

In the 14th century BC, the rebellious Pharaoh Akhenaten and Queen Nefertiti abandoned the gods, temples and priests of Karnak at Thebes to establish a new city, untarnished by other gods. There they and their followers, through their worship of Aten, god of the sun disc, developed what many scholars believe was the first known form of monotheism.

The city, in the area now known as Tell al-Amarna, was built on the east bank of the Nile on a beautiful, yet solitary, crescent-shaped plain, extending about 12 km from north to south. Except for the side bounded by the river, the palaces, temples and residences of the city were surrounded by high cliffs, broken here and there by wadis. The royal couple named their city Akhetaten (Horizon of the Sun Disc), and it served as the capital of Egypt for about 14 years.

It was abandoned for all time shortly after Akhenaten's death, when the priests of Karnak managed to regain their religious control. They desecrated the temples of Aten and generally did their best to obliterate all record of the heretic Pharaoh's objectionable new religion. Polytheism again predominated throughout the land as the Karnak priests persuaded Akhenaten's son-in-law

and successor Tutankaten, or Tutankhamun as he became known, to re-establish the cult of Amun at Thebes. Akhetaten fell into ruin, and the stones of its palaces and temples were used for buildings in Hermopolis and other cities.

The Tell al-Amarna necropolis comprises two groups of cliff tombs, one at each end of the city, which feature colourful wall paintings of life during the Aten revolution. Akhenaten's royal tomb is in a ravine about 13 km up Wadi Darb al-Melek, the valley that divides the north and south sections of the cliffs. Admission is E£16. He was not buried there, however, and no other tomb bearing his name has ever been found.

Due to the city's sudden demise, many of the tombs were never finished and very few were actually used.

Orientation & Information

The site is open from 7 am to 4 pm in winter; 5 pm in summer. On arriving at the west bank ferry landing, there's a good chance you'll be met by Mohammed Abdel Wahed, a friendly young guy and one of the few people around here who speaks English. Should you be in need of food, he'll probably be able to arrange something with a local family. He may also be able to help you make head or tail of the extremely confusing admission price system in effect here.

To start with, you have three options to cross the Nile – the local passenger launch (25 pt), the car ferry (50 pt) or the blue tourist boat (E£4 return for one or two people; E£1 each for three or more). Tickets for the latter are bought from the tourist office on the east bank – you cross the river before paying for your ticket.

Once you've crossed the river, you'll be led to the so-called tourist office just up from the tourist-boat landing where everyone must pay E£1 to enter the site. What you pay from here on depends on how many of you there are, which sites you wish to visit, and what mode of transport you used to cross the river. All payments are made to the staff at the tourist office except the admission fee to the north tombs which must be paid near the site.

For one or two people, you'll be looking at E£8 for a two hour bus tour around the northern tombs and the palace; for three or more people you each pay E£3.75. On arrival at the northern tombs, everyone must pay a E£14 (E£7 for students) entry fee.

Those wishing to take a bus tour to the southern tombs and the Great Temple of Aten must pay E£23 (shared among one to six people), or E£3.75 each for groups of more than six. It takes about 30 minutes to drive to the south tombs and you can supposedly stay as long as you want. To the Royal Tomb of Akhenaten it costs E£35 for the bus (one to six people) or E£5 each when there are more than six people.

The northern tombs are about three km from the boat landing At-Till, the southern ones about eight km away. Other remains of temples and private or administrative buildings are scattered about a wide area.

Tombs

In all, there are 25 tombs cut into the base of the cliffs, numbered from one to six in the north, and seven to 25 in the south. Those worth visiting are described below.

Tomb of Huya (No 1) Huya was the superintendent of Akhenaten's royal harem. The Pharaoh and his family are depicted just inside the entrance on the right.

Tomb of Mery-Re II (No 2) Together with tomb No 1, this is the most distant of the northern tombs and guides are often keen to skip them unless you really insist on visiting. The tomb has just been restored.

Tomb of Ahmose (No 3) Ahmose was one of the king's versatile fan-bearers; his statue is at the back of the tomb.

Tomb of Merirye (No 4) Merirye was the high priest of Aten. The tomb paintings show the Pharaoh riding around town in his chariot and visiting the Temple of Aten.

Tomb of Panehse (No 6) Panehse was vizier of Lower Egypt and a servant of Aten. Most of the scenes in this tomb show Akhenaten and his family attending ceremonies at the Sun Temple.

Tomb of Mahu (No 9) This southern tomb is one of the best preserved, and the wall paintings provide interesting details of Mahu's duties as Akhenaten's chief of police.

Tomb of Ay (No 25) This is the finest tomb at Tell al-Amarna. The wall paintings show street and palace scenes, and one depicts Akhenaten and Nefertiti presenting Ay and his wife with golden collars.

Getting There & Away

To get to Tell al-Amarna from Mallawi, take a service taxi or a covered pick-up from the south depot (25 pt) to the ferry crossing at At-Till. From Asyut, it's easiest to take a service taxi to Mallawi (E£2.50) and then backtrack using one of the pick-ups previously mentioned.

Alternatively, coming from Asyut, you can get off at a little bridge on the main road a few km north of Deir Mawas and then walk, or try to hitch, the four km from the bridge to the ferry crossing. However, you'll find most of the pick-ups coming from Mallawi will be full. Don't bother trying to get to At-Till directly from Deir Mawas as few vehicles take this route. A special taxi will get you there for E£5.

When leaving, you may find you have to pay E£5 for a pick-up from the west bank ferry landing back to either Mallawi or Deir Mawas as not many vehicles head in those directions after about 3 pm.

DAIRUT

Dairut is about 10 km south of Deir Mawas, but there is not a lot of interest to most travellers here. It has a large Christian population and over the years has been the scene of numerous bloody clashes between them and Muslims. Several travellers have been attacked here, and it may be wiser, at least as long as the violence continues, to keep away.

AL-QUSIYA

About eight km south-west of the small rural town of Al-Qusiya, 35 km south of Mallawi, is the Coptic complex of Deir al-Muharraq. Seven km further west, on an escarpment at the edge of the desert, lie the Tombs of Mir. There are no hotels in Al-Qusiya, but there's a large guesthouse just outside the pseudo-medieval crenellated walls of Deir al-Muharraq and the monks sometimes allow groups of travellers to stay there (but not usually individuals). In any event, both sites can be visited in an easy day trip from Mallawi or Asyut providing you have your own wheels.

Deir al-Muharraq

The 100 or so monks who reside in Deir al-Muharraq (the Burnt Monastery) claim that Mary and Jesus inhabited a cave on this site for six months and 10 days after fleeing from Herod into Egypt – their longest stay at any of the numerous places they are said to have rested during that flight. For 10 days every year (usually 18-28 June), thousands of pilgrims attend feasts to celebrate the consecration of the Church of Al-Adhra (Church of the Virgin) which was built over the cave. Coptic Christians believe Al-Adhra to be one of the first churches in the world.

Monks clad in black robes and embroidered head scarves will show you the cave, its large stone altar and a special pillar which stands in front over an ancient water well. The religious significance of this place, they say, is given in the Old Testament; remember to remove your shoes before entering.

In that day there will be an altar to the Lord in the midst of the land of Egypt, and a pillar to the Lord at its border. It will be a sign and a witness to the Lord of Host in the land of Egypt; when they cry to the Lord because of oppressors he will send them a saviour, and will defend and deliver them. And the Lord will make himself known to the Egyptians; and the Egyptians will know the Lord in that day and worship with sacrifice and burnt offering, and they will make vows to the Lord and perform them. (Isaiah 19:19)

Next to Al-Adhra is a square tower, a 5th century structure built for the monks to use as added protection in case of attack. It has four floors, an old sundial on an outer wall, and a church inside.

The Church of St George (also known as Mari Girgis), built in 1880, is behind Al-Adhra and is decorated with paintings of the 12 apostles and other religious scenes. Again, be sure to take off your shoes.

Guided tours usually finish with a brief visit to the new church built in 1940 and the nearby gift shop, and sometimes with a cool drink in the monastery's reception room. Donations are appreciated. Within the complex there is also a college for young monks.

Tombs of Mir

The necropolis of the governors of Cusae, or the Tombs of Mir as they're also known, were dug into the barren escarpment during the Old and Middle Kingdoms. Nine of the tombs here are decorated and open to the public; six others were never finished and remain unexcavated. Egyptian archaeologists together with Australian students work here each season, however, very few tourists pass this way.

Tomb No 1 and the adjoining tomb No 2 are inscribed with 720 Pharaonic deities but, during early Christian times, the Copts used the tombs as cells and many faces and names of the gods were destroyed. In tomb No 4 you can still see the original grid drawn on the wall to assist the artist in designing the layout of the tomb art. Tomb No 3 features a cow giving birth.

Admission to the tombs is E£16 (E£8 for students) and there's a hefty E£10 camera fee per tomb, or E£150 for video.

Getting There & Away

The Asyut to Al-Minya bus will drop you at Al-Qusiya (E£1.25, about 50 minutes from Asyut); otherwise, you could take a service taxi from either Asyut or Mallawi. From there, you may be able to get a local microbus to the monastery, or the military police, worried about your welfare, may take you there themselves.

Few vehicles from Al-Qusiya go out to the

BENI SUEF TO QUS

Tombs of Mir, so you'll have to hire a taxi to take you there. Ideally, you could combine this with a visit to the monastery.

ASYUT

Asyut, settled during Pharaonic times on a broad fertile plain bordering the west bank of the Nile, is 375 km south of Cairo. It's the largest town in Upper Egypt and the region's chief agricultural centre, dealing in camels, cotton and grain. There is also a small carpet-making industry.

It has been an important trading town since ancient times and was once head of the great caravan route to the Western Desert oases and across the Sahara. For several centuries, the camel caravans that travelled up the 40 Day Road from Darfur province in Sudan ended their trip in Asyut, and as recently as 150 years ago the town boasted the largest slave market in Egypt.

Asyut was once the capital of the 13th nome and cult centre of the wolf-god Wepwawet, the avenger of Osiris (god of the dead). In the 4th century AD Christianity became the dominant religion and today there are often confrontations in the city between the Copts and Muslim funda-mentalists. The military and police presence in and around the city of Asyut can take the visitor by surprise. There are checkpoints all over town and various important points are covered by troops with machine guns squat-ting by sandbag emplacements. You will almost certainly have the military on your back when you arrive – remember that they see themselves as doing a job to protect you, so this is not the time to lose your cool. Generally, you'll be left to your own devices, but the simple presence of so many people under arms can be a trifle off-putting.

Asyut is still a major departure point for trips to the Western oases, or the New Valley as the region is now known.

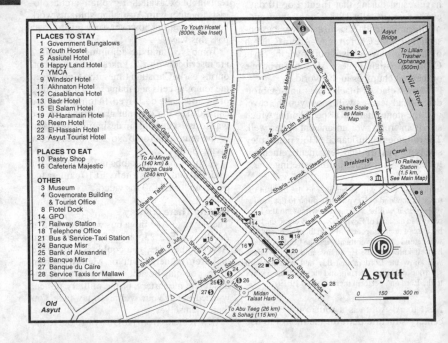

PLACES TO STAY
1 Government Bungalows
2 Youth Hostel
5 Assiutel Hotel
6 Happy Land Hotel
7 YMCA
9 Windsor Hotel
11 Akhnaton Hotel
12 Casablanca Hotel
13 Badr Hotel
15 El Salam Hotel
19 Al-Haramain Hotel
20 Reem Hotel
22 El-Hassain Hotel
23 Asyut Tourist Hotel

PLACES TO EAT
10 Pastry Shop
16 Cafeteria Majestic

OTHER
3 Museum
4 Governorate Building & Tourist Office
8 Flotel Dock
14 GPO
17 Railway Station
18 Telephone Office
21 Bus & Service-Taxi Station
24 Banque Misr
25 Bank of Alexandria
26 Banque Misr
27 Banque du Caire
28 Service Taxis for Mallawi

Asyut

0   150   300 m

Information
Tourist Office There is a tourist office (☎ 310010) on Sharia ath-Thawra on the 1st floor of the governorate building. The staff is very friendly and willing to help, and has recently produced a good brochure and map of the town. The office is open daily except Friday from 8.30 am to 2 pm. On the ground floor there's a showroom of local souvenirs, most of which are for sale. The tourist office also has a new branch office at the recently opened flotel dock.

Money There's a cluster of banks on Midan Talaat Harb. Banque Misr, which does Visa and MasterCard cash advances, has two branches and the Bank of Alexandria, good for changing Eurocheques, has one. Just up the road is the Banque du Caire.

Post & Communications The new GPO is opposite Badr Hotel behind the railway station. The telephone office is to the right of the entrance of the railway station.

Museum
There is a small museum of Pharaonic, Coptic and Islamic artefacts in what used to be the American College on Sharia al-Gomhurriya. The museum, which includes a mummy display and is housed in a building called the Taggart Library, was renovated in 1986, but you'll need to find someone to dig out the key. The school is now the As-Salam secondary school, and the grounds are worth a quick look. There are plans to build a new museum but it probably won't materialise for a few years.

Geziret al-Moz
'Banana Island' is in the Nile at the end of Sharia Salah Salem. The island's lush tropical forest is a pleasant place to picnic. You'll have to bargain with a felucca captain for the ride across.

Asyut Barrage
At the northern edge of town, this barrage was built across the Nile in the late 19th century, under British supervision, to regulate the flow of water into the Ibrahimiya Canal and assist in the irrigation of the valley as far north as Beni Suef. It's an impressive structure, but you're not allowed to walk on or around it. Photographing it would be unwise.

Lillian Trasher Orphanage
Born in Jacksonville, Florida, in the USA, Lillian Trasher came to Egypt in 1910 at the age of 23 in search of some useful work to do. The following year she founded an orphanage in Asyut, which has since grown to be the biggest and most well known of its type in Egypt. Some 650 children live there now. Trasher never left, but died in her adopted country in 1961. The orphanage is something of a symbol of Christian charity in a city with a heavy concentration of Copts and a history of sectarian fighting between the Copts and the Muslims. The orphanage welcomes interested visitors, and won't say no to a donation.

Getting There & Away The orphanage is on the east bank of the Nile, about 200m to the right after you've crossed the barrage. Microbuses run near it from the centre of town for 15 pt; a taxi will cost E£1. Ask for the *malga Trasher*.

Places to Stay – bottom end
The *Youth Hostel* (☎ 324846) is at Lux Houses, 503 Sharia al-Walidiyya (the entry is off the side street). It costs E£4 for a bed in a crowded dorm of eight. The staff don't seem too fussed about membership cards.

The *YMCA* (☎ 323218), about 500m down Sharia Salah ad-Din al-Ayoubi, deservedly gets rave reviews from many people. There are two sections, the old and new buildings. Reception is on the 3rd floor of the new building. A bed in the old dorm section costs E£6. The new building has singles/doubles with air-con, TV, mini-fridge and private bath for E£25/35. The furnishings in some of the rooms are a bit melodramatic, but it's all spotless and there's hot water and a big garden.

A cheap place, overlooking the bus

BENI SUEF TO QUS

station, is the *El-Hussain Hotel* which has basic doubles for E£10.

The *Asyut Tourist Hotel* (☎ 322615) used to be a reasonable cheap deal, but the owners are not keen on foreign guests.

The *Al-Haramain Hotel* (☎ 320426) on Sharia Salah Salem, around the corner from the Badr Hotel, has 18 beds in clean, carpeted rooms on two floors in a quiet apartment building. It is, however, often full. Singles/doubles are E£10/20, and the water is hot. The beds are of the usual rock-hard variety though.

The *Windsor Hotel* (☎ 322973), which has double rooms with bath for E£12, is noisy, but not a bad spot to stay for the money involved.

Moving up the scale, the *Akhnaton Hotel* (☎ 337723; fax 331600) has pretty reasonable rooms with clean linen, TV, hot water and soap in the bathrooms at E£28/35 for singles/doubles. Some rooms are small so ask to see one first. Continental/English breakfast is E£6/8.25 extra.

The *Reem Hotel* (☎ 311421; fax 311424), on Sharia Nahda next to the railway tracks, is a medium-priced place with singles for E£37 and doubles for E£56, including taxes, TV and breakfast. It's OK, if a little overpriced. The rooms overlooking the railway are very noisy.

The *El Salam* (☎ 332256), off Sharia Talaat Harb has singles/doubles with bath for E£29.50/41.20. Air-con costs E£5 more. TVs and breakfasts are extra, and all up it's not that stunning for the price.

Places to Stay – middle & top end

Immediately north of the barrage is a line of five new government-run *bungalows* with river-front views and a small but well tended garden. The air-con bungalows have refrigerators, a kitchen, bathroom, hot water and TV. They were due to open in early 1996; inquire at the tourist office if you're interested.

The *Casablanca Hotel* (☎ 337662; fax 336662) does not have the greatest location, but it is pretty good. Clean singles/doubles cost E£55/70 with breakfast. The bathrooms have toilet paper, soap and towels.

Down by the Nile is the four storey *Happy Land Hotel* (☎ 320444; fax 320444). Rooms with breakfast cost E£40/60; air-con and TV are extra. It's not such a great deal, as the place is a bit gloomy, the elevator is temperamental and little English is spoken, but it does have a bar.

Not far away is the *Assiutel Hotel* (☎ 312121; fax 312122), with very comfortable rooms and amenities costing E£114/129. It's a bit overpriced, as you don't really get anything much that isn't at the Happy Land, however, it's a more pleasant hotel. Breakfast is E£7.50 extra and there's a restaurant and bar.

Back in the centre of town, the deluxe *Badr Hotel* (☎ 329811; fax 322820) is a western-style hotel and an expatriate hangout. A single/double room costs E£81/89. There's a restaurant and bar.

Places to Eat

The *Cafeteria Majestic*, opposite the railway station, serves good cheap meals of rice, salad and potatoes, among other things, from about E£7, and felafel sandwiches for 30 pt. It's a lively place with a good atmosphere.

All the bigger hotels have their own restaurants. At the cheaper end of the scale, the air-con restaurant at *Akhnaton Hotel* does an escalope for E£10.50 – with real chips – as well as good pizza (E£6.50) and soup. Beer is also served. There are a few of the usual fuul and ta'amiyya stands scattered around and you can get pastries and ice cream from the shop near the Casablanca Hotel.

Getting There & Away

Asyut is a major hub for all forms of transport.

Bus Buses leave for Asyut and the Western Desert oases from a small station at 45 Sharia al-Azhar, near Midan Ataba in Cairo. Buses to Asyut only leave Cairo from Ahmed Hilmi station, behind Ramses railway station. For more details see the Cairo Getting There & Away section.

From Asyut buses depart for Cairo (E£10 to E£15, six to seven hours) at 12.30, 7, 8, 10 and 11 am, at noon and at 2, 3, 5, 7, 10, 11 pm and midnight.

There are buses to Alexandria (E£20, 10 hours) regularly departing between 7 am and 7 pm.

Buses depart for Al-Minya (E£3.50, two to three hours) every two hours from 6 am to 5 pm. There are no bookings – you just grab a seat.

At 8 am there's a bus for Esna and Luxor (E£10). Buses for Qena (E£7) leave at 7 and 9 am, and 1, 2 and 5 pm. A bus for Hurghada (Al-Ghardaka, E£16) leaves at 9 am.

There's a departure for Sohag (E£2.75, 1½ hours) about every half an hour from 6 am to 5 pm.

If you are heading out to the oases, there are buses to Kharga (E£6 to E£7, four hours) at 7 and 8 am, and 1, 3, 5 and 10 pm.

Train Trains arrive and depart for destinations north and south of Asyut frequently. There are about 20 trains throughout the day to Cairo and Al-Minya, and about half that number to Luxor. The 1st and 2nd class fares to Cairo are E£31 and E£19 (E£21/14 for students). The quicker trains take five to seven hours.

The same fares to Al-Minya (two to three hours) are E£13/8 (E£9/6 for students). To Luxor (four to six hours) it costs E£29/19 (E£20/14). There are regular trains to the next main centre down the line, Sohag, and the fast train costs E£10/6 (student E£6/5). The normal train can take hours, stopping at every possible one-donkey village.

Service Taxi Service taxis gather around the bus station. There are services to Cairo (E£15), Al-Minya (E£4.50, two hours) and to Kharga (E£8). Microbuses and service taxis to Mallawi (E£2) leave from the big lot near the mosque.

AROUND ASYUT
Convent of the Holy Virgin
About 10 km south-west of Asyut in an area known as Dirunka, this convent was built near a cave, which Coptic Christians believe the Holy Family sought refuge in during their flight into Egypt. Some 50 or so nuns and monks live at the convent, which is built into a cliff about 120m above the valley, and one of the monks will happily show you around. During the Moulid of the Virgin (7-22 August), tens of thousands of pilgrims descend on the place and there are daily parades with portraits of Mary and Jesus carried around.

Groups and individuals are welcome to stay in the rest house just outside the main gate, but food is not available. A dorm bed costs E£3, or E£5 per bed in one of the smaller rooms. The convent is open from 6 am to 6 pm.

In November 1994, the village of Dirunka was the site of Egypt's worst disaster since the 1992 earthquake. More than 500 people were killed when lightning struck fuel storage tanks during heavy storms, igniting a fire storm. Blazing fuel raged unchecked through the flooded village for hours before emergency crews arrived.

SOHAG
The city of Sohag, 115 km south of Asyut, is the administrative centre for the governorate of the same name and one of the major Coptic Christian areas of Upper Egypt. The only real reason to go there, however, is to see the White and Red monasteries just outside Sohag, and to visit the town of Achmin across the river. On Monday morning there is also an animal market, known as the *souq el-itnayn*, held on Midan Abdel Minnim Riyadh.

Sohag is also not too bad as a base for a trip to Abydos, although Al-Balyana is more convenient.

There is less of a police presence on the streets here than in Asyut but, even so, the police take their job of protecting the few tourists who do pass through very seriously. If they know you're in town they will insist on escorting you everywhere and you'll probably be banned from leaving your hotel after dark.

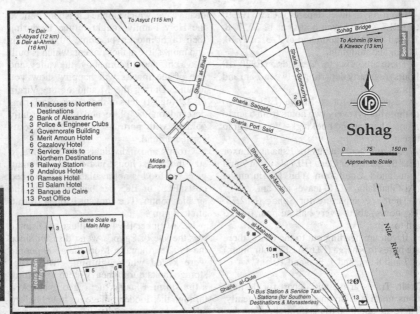

Map legend:

1 Minibuses to Northern Destinations
2 Bank of Alexandria
3 Police & Engineer Clubs
4 Governorate Building
5 Merit Amoun Hotel
6 Cazalovy Hotel
7 Service Taxis to Northern Destinations
8 Railway Station
9 Andalous Hotel
10 Ramses Hotel
11 El Salam Hotel
12 Banque du Caire
13 Post Office

Information

There's no tourist office. You can get a few out-of-date pamphlets from the governorate building but it will take hours.

You can change cash or travellers' cheques at the Bank of Alexandria or the Banque du Caire, both on Sharia al-Gomhurriya.

The post office is a little way down the road from the Banque du Caire along the Nile.

White Monastery

Deir al-Abyad was built in 400 AD by the Coptic saint Shenouda, with chunks of white limestone from a Pharaonic temple. The White Monastery, as it is called, once supported a community of 2000 monks; today there are just four. Its fortress walls still stand, but most of the interior is in ruins, though you can see the several types of arches used in its construction. The monas-

tery is 12 km north-west of Sohag and is open from 8 am to 8 pm.

Red Monastery

Deir al-Ahmar, the Red Monastery, is four km from Deir al-Abyad and is hidden at the rear of a village so you'll need to ask directions. It was founded by Bishoi, a thief who converted to Christianity. He built this and two monasteries in Wadi Natrun and eventually became a Coptic saint. There are two chapels on the grounds, Santa Maria Chapel and the St Bishoi Chapel. Be sure to see the remains of a 10th century fresco in a frame on a side altar – it contains a 1000 year-old icon. There are interesting though fading frescoes on the walls, unusual pillars and old wooden peg locks on the doors.

Getting There & Away Unless you're visiting sometime during the first two weeks of July, when you can catch a bus to the monasteries for about E£1 with thousands of

LEANNE LOGAN

BETHUNE CARMICHAEL

GEERT COLE

Left: Achmin's statue of Queen Meret Amun was unearthed accidentally in 1982.
Right: The southern wall of Dendara's splendid Temple of Hathor, depicting Cleopatra with her son Ptolemy XVI (Caesarian).
Bottom: The Tombs of Mir were dug into the barren escarpment near Al-Qusiya.

BETHUNE CARMICHAEL

DAMIEN SIMONIS

GREG ELMS

GLENN BEANLAND

Top: The Great Hypostyle Hall at Karnak resembles an awesome forest of towering pillar
Left: All that remains of the Temple of Amenophis III are the famous Colossi of Memnon.
Right: The colossal statue of Ramses II lies scattered among the ruins of the Ramesseum

other pilgrims, your only option seems to be to take a taxi, which should cost about E£10 to both monasteries and back. There are supposed to be service taxis from a lot about 300m from Midan Abdel Minnim Riyadh, although there's not much traffic heading out that way.

Achmin

The town of Achmin, on the east bank of the Nile, is well known for its unique woven carpets and wall hangings and, more recently, the discovery of the statue of Meret Amun. A microbus from Sohag takes 15 minutes and costs 20 pt.

Statue of Queen Meret Amun This is the tallest statue of an ancient queen to have been discovered in Egypt and is Achmin's main sight. Meret Amun (Beloved of the God Amun) was one of the daughters of Ramses II and wife of Amenhotep. She was also a priestess of the Temple of Min, which was dedicated to a local deity and god of fertility. Little is left of the temple itself, and the statue of Meret Amun now stands in a huge excavation pit among the houses in the middle of town. Accidentally unearthed in 1982 during excavations to build a new school, it was not until recently that the statue was raised and the site was opened to the public. Admission costs E£10 (half for students) and the site is open daily from 9 am to 5 pm. As the statue is so tall, you can get a good view of it without even entering the site.

Weaving Factories Opposite the statue of Meret Amun is a tiny post office and, across the road from this, a small weaving factory. It's the house with the green door – just knock to be led through to the showroom where you can buy silk and cotton hand-woven textiles straight from the bolt or packets of ready-made tablecloths and serviettes. Ask to see the men and boys who make the products at work – you'll hear the 25 looms clattering away before you even climb the stairs.

With your own vehicle, you may also want to visit the weavers at Kawsor, 13 km east of Sohag at the base of the escarpment. This huge new industrial estate has about 80 bungalows where women make and sell textiles. As an example of the prices, you'd be looking at about E£60 for a bedspread.

Places to Stay

There is a *Youth Hostel* at 5 Sharia Port Said, but it's not keen on accepting foreigners.

Directly opposite the railway station is the basic *Andalous Hotel* (☎ 324328). Singles/doubles with shared bathrooms are E£7/10, or E£9/14 with private facilities. Breakfast is not included in the price. It's quite adequate and the water is hot.

A little way down the same street is the *Ramses Hotel*, which has very basic rooms at E£5 a bed. The rooms are acceptable for the price.

The *El Salam Hotel* (☎ 333317) is next door and is outrageously priced for what it is. Basic singles/doubles without bath cost E£15/20, or E£20/40 with bath.

The two best places in town are both on the east bank. The *Merit Amoun Hotel* (☎ 601985; fax 603222) is a big place with a fanciful three star rating, and with an overgrown garden out the back. Singles/doubles are E£70/88 including breakfast and taxes. It has a restaurant of sorts. The hotel is 100m on the right after you cross the Nile.

About 100m further down the road and also on the right is the *Cazalovy Hotel* (☎ 601185). It offers the best value in town, with rooms for E£27/36, or E£33/46 with air-con. Soap and towels are provided and breakfast is included.

Places to Eat

As well as the usual fruit and vegetable stands, there are also a few fuul and ta'amiyya places near the railway station. If you follow the street south of the railway station (left as you walk out the entrance) to a big square, and cross this, there is an OK kebab restaurant where a plate of kebab will cost you E£5.

There are restaurants in the *Cazalovy* and *Merit Amoun* hotels; the former is probably the better of the two. Meals may also be available at the police and engineer clubs, about 300m north of the bridge on the east bank.

Getting There & Away

Bus The main bus station is around the corner from the big square south of the railway station. It is near the city prison and service-taxi station for southern destinations. There are seven buses a day for Cairo (E£17). The first leaves at 5 am and the last at 10 pm. There is a bus to Aswan (E£13) via Luxor (E£6.50) at 6 am. If you miss this one, get a bus or service taxi to Qena where there are many services a day. Buses to Asyut (E£2.75, 1½ to two hours) depart every 30 to 40 minutes. The bus takes about an hour to Al-Balyana (for Abydos) and costs E£1.50, leaving every 30 minutes.

Train Trains north and south stop fairly frequently at Sohag. The 1st/2nd class fare to Asyut is E£10/6. The train to Al-Balyana generally makes a lot of stops (E£1.50 in 3rd class ordinary).

Service Taxi There are several service-taxi stations in Sohag. The one for Asyut (E£3.50) and other northern destinations, including Cairo (E£20), is north of the railway station on Midan Europa. Service taxis for Qena (E£5, 1½ hours) and Nag Hammadi leave from the southern depot, which is on the main road south, just after a canal. From Qena another taxi to Luxor costs E£2. There are also stations for local taxis to the monasteries and to Achmin – on some of these local routes wonderful vintage cars are used as service taxis.

AL-BALYANA

The only reason to go to this town is to visit the village of Al-Araba al-Madfunah, 10 km away. There you'll find the necropolis of Abydos and the magnificent Temple of Seti. If you're coming from Sohag or Al-Balyana, you'll probably be escorted to and from Abydos by police.

Should you need to change money, there's a tiny Banque Misr kiosk at the entrance to Abydos but don't rely on it being open.

Abydos

The temples at Abydos served several dynasties of Egyptians and its huge necropolis was, for a long time, *the* place to be buried. Excavations indicate that it was a burial place of the last pre-dynastic kings, before 3100 BC. Seti I and Ramses II built the most important temples of the complex in the 13th century BC; and Abydos was still important during Roman times.

The centre of the walled town of Abydos was a mound called **Kom as-Sultan**; nearby was the all-important **Temple of Osiris**, of which little remains. Abydos maintained its importance for so many centuries because of the cult of Osiris, god of the dead.

The area was a natural shrine for the worship of this ruler of the netherworld because, according to mythology, it was here that the head of Osiris was buried after his brother Seth had murdered him, cut his body into several pieces, and scattered the bits all over Egypt. Osiris' wife and sister, the goddess Isis, searched for and found all the pieces and put him back together again, building temples wherever she found the dissected parts. Osiris and Isis then begat Horus, the falcon-god, who killed his uncle Seth. The temple at Abydos was the most important of the shrines to Osiris and became a place of pilgrimage. Most Egyptians would have made the journey there at least once in their lifetime.

Abydos is open from 7 am to 5 pm daily. The admission fee for both temples is E£12, or E£6 for students. Bring a torch.

At the time of writing, the section northwest of the sacred lakes was closed to the public.

Should you want more information, there's a booklet on sale at the Osiris Park shop for E£10. There's also *Abydos – The Holy City in Ancient Egypt* by Dorothy Eady. Better known to some as Omm Sety, Dorothy Eady was an English woman who believed she was a temple priestess and lover of Sety I. For 35 years, until her death in 1981, she

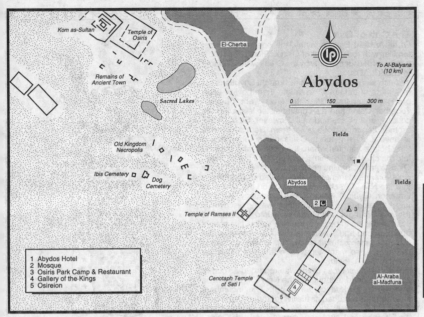

1 Abydos Hotel
2 Mosque
3 Osiris Park Camp & Restaurant
4 Gallery of the Kings
5 Osireion

BENI SUEF TO QUS

lived at Abydos. *The Search of Omm Sety* by Jonathan Cott is a biography of her life there.

Cenotaph Temple of Seti I The first structure you'll see at Abydos is one of Egypt's most complete temples. A cenotaph temple was a secondary mortuary temple dedicated to one or more gods and honouring the deified, deceased Pharaoh who built it. Pharaoh Seti's splendid temple honours seven gods: Osiris, Isis, Horus, Amun, Ra-Harakhty, Ptah and Seti I himself. The Osiris Sanctuary was especially important; it opens into an area extending the width of the temple, with two halls and two sets of three chapels dedicated to Osiris, Isis and Horus.

As you roam through Seti's dark halls and sanctuaries a definite air of mystery, an almost tangible impression of ancient pomp and circumstance, surrounds you. The colourful hieroglyphs on the walls, describing the rituals that were carried out there, make it easy to imagine the ceremonies honouring

the death and rebirth of Osiris and the great processions of cult worshippers that passed in and out of the temple.

It's possible to enter the Osireion, directly behind the main temple, but only if you wade through ankle-deep water. It is sited lower than the main temple and, since the rise of the water table, it has been permanently underwater. Here you'll find excerpts from the *Book of the Dead* and the *Book of Gates*, and images of Horus holding a scale in front of Osiris.

In a corridor known as the Gallery of the Kings, to the left of the sanctuaries, a list of Egypt's Pharaohs up to Seti I was found. Though not complete, the 76 cartouches – oblong figures containing each king's name – greatly assisted archaeologists in unravelling Egypt's long history from Menes onwards.

Temple of Ramses II North-west of Seti's

The Cult of Osiris

Of all Ancient Egypt's myths, the one we are most familiar with today is that of Osiris. This is because it was recorded for posterity by the Greek writer Plutarch in about 1 AD.

According to Plutarch, Osiris brought Egyptians out of a state of barbarity. He taught them how to grow crops and ensured that the laws were obeyed. Together Osiris and his consort/sister Isis ruled the country, and all seemed well. However, Seth, Osiris' brother, began to plot against them. Seth's plan was to have a chest made to Osiris' measurements and then hold a banquet where the person who could fit into the chest could claim it as a prize. At the banquet, Osiris climbed into the chest and, as he did so, Seth's collaborators slammed it shut, sealed it and flung it into the Nile. The chest washed up on the shores of Lebanon (Byblos) where it was eventually found by Isis and returned to Egypt. Seth, however, discovered the chest first, hacked Osiris' body into 14 parts and scattered them throughout the Nile Valley. Isis sought out each part and, when she discovered one, held a burial ceremony at that place. This is why, according to Plutarch, so many temples in the Nile Valley lay claim to Osiris' tomb.

From earliest times Osiris was regarded as god or king of the dead (although in the New Kingdom he is referred to as lord of the living). The incumbent Pharaoh was regarded as the living Horus (Osiris' son, and credited with avenging his father's death). When the Pharaoh died, his name was prefaced with 'Osiris', the implication being that he would take his place on Osiris' throne from where he could give orders to the living. ∎

Osiris is typically depicted holding the crook and flail which represent kingship.

temple his son Ramses II built another temple dedicated to Osiris – and himself. The roof of the Temple of Ramses II has collapsed, and only a quarter of the huge statues and pillars remain, but the hieroglyphs on the walls are interesting. You have to get the guard to unlock the gate. The local villagers will let him know that a *khawagah* (an uncomplimentary term for 'foreigner') wants to get into the temple.

Cemetery The extensive cemetery between Kom as-Sultan and Seti's temple includes buried dogs, falcons and ibises as well as the cenotaphs or actual graves of those ancient Egyptians who wanted to lie forever in the company of Osiris, however there's not much to see these days.

Places to Stay & Eat

If you really have to stay in Al-Balyana, there's the *Wadi Melouk Hotel*, which looks as if it has suffered greatly from its position right next to the railway tracks. A very basic double costs E£5, and there is only cold water. There is a cafe below the hotel and a few basic food stands around the town.

Right in front of Abydos is the *Osiris Park Restaurant & Camp* (☎ 812200), where a row of four tents, each with two beds on a grass floor, has been set up; a bed costs E£5. You can pitch your own tent for E£3 per person, and the showers (cold) are clean. Horus, the owner, is friendly and helpful.

The only other option is the *Abydos Hotel* (☎ 812102), 200m before Osiris Park, which has simple, but pricey rooms for E£30/50.

Eating and drinking is an expensive business around here. You can be hit for E£5 just for an omelette at Osiris Park, and the standard 25 pt tea somehow seems to cost E£2. Beers, however, are reasonably priced at E£6.

At the time of writing, plans were underway to build a spiritual healing centre, to be called *Isis Village*, behind Osiris Park. It will have 22 self-contained double chalets plus a small museum dedicated to Omm Sety.

Getting There & Away
Al-Balyana is serviced by buses, trains and service taxis. The respective stations are conveniently close to each other.

Bus There are hourly buses to Luxor (E£5) as well as frequent services to Qena (E£4). There are buses between Al-Balyana and Sohag (E£1.50) about every half an hour from 6 am to 5 pm. The buses to Sohag or Qena tend to do a circuit around the town before actually hitting the road.

Train The 2nd class fare to Luxor/ Qena is E£4.10/2.50; 2nd class with air-con is E£14/6. To Sohag, fares are E£1.50/4.70.

Service Taxi A service taxi to Sohag costs E£1.50, or E£5.50 to Asyut. Service taxis (75 pt) and microbuses (30 pt) both go to the temple complex from Al-Balyana.

QENA
Qena, a provincial capital 91 km east of Al-Balyana and 62 km north of Luxor, is at the intersection of the main Nile road and the road across the desert to the Red Sea towns of Port Safaga and Hurghada.

Unless you're on your way to or from the Red Sea and don't have a through connection, the only reason to stop in Qena is to visit the spectacular temple complex at Dendara,

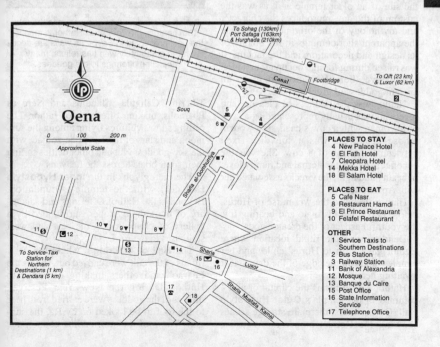

Qena

0   100   200 m
Approximate Scale

To Sohag (130km)
Port Safaga (163km)
& Hurghada (210km)

To Qift (23 km)
& Luxor (62 km)

Canal
Footbridge

Souq

Sharia al-Gomhuriyya

Sharia Luxor

Sharia Mustafa Kamel

To Service-Taxi
Station for
Northern
Destinations (1 km)
& Dendara (5 km)

PLACES TO STAY
4   New Palace Hotel
6   El Fath Hotel
7   Cleopatra Hotel
14 Mekka Hotel
18 El Salam Hotel

PLACES TO EAT
5   Cafe Nasr
8   Restaurant Hamdi
9   El Prince Restaurant
10 Felafel Restaurant

OTHER
1   Service Taxis to
    Southern Destinations
2   Bus Station
3   Railway Station
11 Bank of Alexandria
12 Mosque
13 Banque du Caire
15 Post Office
16 State Information
    Service
17 Telephone Office

just outside the town. There are two service-taxi stations quite a long way apart from one another, one for northern destinations and places across the Nile, the other for southern destinations. If you need money, there is a Bank of Alexandria and a Banque du Caire in town.

Dendara

Although it indicates the decline of a purely Egyptian style of art, the wonderfully preserved complex at Dendara is a sight to behold. Complete with a massive stone roof, dark chambers, underground passages and towering columns inscribed with hieroglyphs, the main Temple of Hathor is almost intact.

While the Dendara necropolis includes Early Dynastic tombs and evidence that Cheops and later Pharaohs built there, the temple complex, as it stands today, was built by the Ptolemies and the Romans. Its very design, however, suggests that it was built on the site of an older temple and, as was the custom of the day, reproduces the character and mythology of the original. So, despite the apparent shortcomings in the quality of its design and decoration, and the fact that it was raised during foreign occupation, it is an impressive, beautiful monument to an ancient goddess of great renown.

Hathor was the goddess of pleasure and love; she was usually represented as a cow, or a woman with a cow's head, or a woman whose headdress was a sun disc fixed between the horns of a cow. She was the beneficent deity of maternal and family love, of beauty and light; the Greeks associated her with Aphrodite.

Hathor was also the wet nurse of Horus, before becoming his mate and bearing Ihy, the youthful aspect of the creator-gods.

Dendara was the ritual location where Hathor gave birth to Horus' child, and her temple stands on the edge of the desert as if awaiting her return.

Hathor's head forms the capital of all 24 columns in the temple's **Outer Hypostyle Hall**. On the walls, there are strange scenes showing the Roman emperors Augustus,

Buried by sand until its excavation in the mid-19th century, the Temple of Hathor is among the best preserved in Egypt. Its walls are decorated elaborately with bas reliefs, many depicting offerings to the goddess.

Tiberius, Caligula, Claudius and Nero as Pharaohs, making offerings to Hathor. The ceiling shows vultures flying among the sun, moon and stars of the Egyptian zodiac, with the sky-goddess Nut and other deities sailing their solar boats across the heavens.

The hieroglyphs in the **Inner Hypostyle Hall** deal with the temple's foundation. Beyond is the Hall of Offerings and sanctuary of the temple proper, surrounded by a gallery of **chapels** and the east and west staircases to the roof.

The **Hall of Offerings**, where the daily rituals of the cult were carried out, shows the Pharaoh and others making offerings to Hathor. During the New Year Festival, images of the goddess were carried from here to the roof to be looked on by Ra, the sun-god. Views of the surrounding countryside

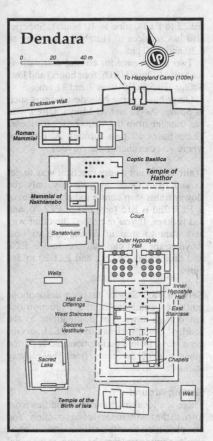

The reliefs on the exterior of the temple's south wall show various Roman emperors such as Nero and Caesarian – son of Julius and Cleopatra – and the great Egyptian queen herself making offerings to the head of Hathor.

Behind the main temple is the smaller **Temple of the Birth of Isis** built by Emperor Augustus. North of the main temple, the second structure on your left is a **Roman mammisi**, or birth house, which is dedicated to Hathor and her son Ihy.

A 5th century **Coptic basilica** is squeezed in-between the mammisi, the court of Hathor's temple and another birth house. The birth house was begun by Nakhtanebo, a 30th dynasty Pharaoh, and completed by the Ptolemies.

The Dendara complex is open from 7 am to 6 pm and admission is E£12, or E£6 for students. There are several souvenir stalls, public toilets, a phone, an ambulance base and a cafe where you can get an expensive bottle of soft drink (E£1). There is also a hotel (see Places to Stay).

Getting There & Away Dendara is four km west of Qena on the other side of the Nile. From Qena you can take a local microbus to the northern service-taxi station for 25 pt, and from there another microbus (also 25 pt) along the main road. It drops you at the turn-off (just after a new railway bridge), from where you have about a 20 minute walk to the temple. Hantours will take you to Dendara for about E£4. To get back to Qena, it is usually no problem to hitch with one of the locals or, more likely, pick up a passing service taxi. They will ask for all sorts of ridiculous amounts when you get there. E£1 should be the limit for getting you to the centre of town.

Places to Stay

You can stay by the temple itself at the *Happyland Camp*. It is basically a hotel with fairly expensive beds – E£25 per person. Camping is possible in its messy garden for E£10. You're better off staying in Luxor, really, and doing a day trip from there.

from the roof are magnificent. The graffiti on the edge of the temple were left by Napoleon's commander Desaix, and other French soldiers, in 1799.

The **sanctuary** was usually kept bolted and only the Pharaoh, or priests acting on his behalf, could enter. Reliefs on the walls show the special rituals of the Pharaoh entering the sanctuary to show his adoration for the goddess.

From the chapel behind the sanctuary Hathor would embark each New Year on her annual journey to Edfu, where she would lie in blissful union with Horus.

If you are determined to stay in Qena, the *New Palace Hotel* (☎ 322509) is just behind the Mobil petrol station, over the road from the railway station. Singles/doubles cost E£12/20 and rooms come with bath and fan. Some have balconies.

The *Mekka Hotel* (☎ 322909) is a dump with beds for E£4.

There are a few other cheap dives along Sharia al-Gomhurriya, like the *El Fath Hotel*, which charges E£8/12 (its facade is better than the very basic rooms); and the *Cleopatra*, which is mostly full (E£4 per person).

The *El Salam Hotel* (☎ 322495) behind the telephone office is supposedly always full.

Places to Eat

Cafe Nasr has backgammon and good cheap food such as spinach, tahina, salad and tea for E£2.50.

Restaurant Hamdi serves full meals of chicken and vegetables for E£6 and almost next door is a very decent ta'amiyya place. The *El Prince* is similar.

Along the main street there are also several kushari, kofta and ta'amiyya places.

Things to Buy

Pottery, particularly water jugs, is the speciality in Qena; but, bear in mind that it's probably difficult to carry pottery around in your backpack.

Getting There & Away

Bus The bus station is in front of the railway station. However, buses not originating or terminating here pass along the main road and drop (and might pick up) passengers at the bridge over the canal.

There are two Superjet buses to Cairo (E£25) at 8.30 am and 7 pm.

Eleven buses go to Aswan (E£8.50) from 6.30 am to 7.45 pm, and most stop in Luxor (E£1.50 to E£2). A few other buses only go as far as Edfu or Luxor.

There are nine buses to Hurghada (E£8, three hours) and six of them go on to Suez (E£22 to E£38, nine to 10 hours). Superjet also has services to Hurghada and Suez at 4.30 and 8.30 pm

Two buses leave for coastal destinations such as Al-Quseir (E£6, four hours) and Port Safaga (E£5 to E£10) at 7 and 11 am.

Other buses serve Nile destinations such as Sohag, Asyut and Al-Minya. Often, you can transfer from the Cairo buses for these. These buses all pass through Al-Balyana, where you can change for Abydos.

Train This is not a very practical way to get to and from Qena, as generally only the slower trains stop here. First class to Luxor is E£7, 2nd is E£5 (air-con) or E£2.70, and 3rd is 80 pt. If you're headed the other way and want to stop in Al-Balyana to visit Abydos, the 2nd class air-con fare is E£6, 2nd ordinary is E£2.50, and E£1.20 in 3rd class.

Service Taxi Service taxis to destinations north of Qena leave from a T-junction one km outside town. For destinations to the south of Qena, such as Luxor (E£2), service taxis leave from a taxi station that is on the other side of the canal from the railway station.

Getting Around

There is a local microbus that shuttles from town to the northern service-taxi station. You can pick it up near the railway station or, if you're coming up from the south, at the canal bridge near the southern service-taxi station. It costs 25 pt. The microbus from the north service-taxi station to Dendara costs 25 pt as well.

Hantours will take you to Dendara for about E£4.

QIFT

In Graeco-Roman times Qift was a major trading town on the Arabia-India trade route and an important starting point for expeditions to the Red Sea and the Sinai. The town lost its importance as a trading centre from the 10th century onwards. The harvest and fertility-god Min, who was also the patron deity of desert travellers, was considered the protector of Qift. There is nothing that can't really be missed in this town.

QUS

During medieval times this was the most important Islamic city in Egypt, after Cairo.

Founded in 1083, it served as a port and transit point for goods coming and going between the Nile and Al-Quseir on the Red Sea. Today, the town is the site of a US$246 million Egyptian-German paper mill project that converts bagasse – the waste product of sugar cane refining – into paper products.

The Nile Valley – Luxor

The sheer grandeur of Luxor's monumental architecture, and its excellent state of preservation, have made this village-city one of Egypt's greatest tourist attractions. Built on and around the 4000 year old site of ancient Thebes, Luxor is an extraordinary mixture of exotic history and modern commercialism.

Here the fellahin work the fields as they have done since time immemorial; mundane daily business is carried on as if there weren't hordes of foreigners walking the streets; modern hotels are full of westerners; the souqs are full of fake antiquities made just for the tourists; and modern Egyptians make a fine living out of the legacy of their ancestors.

It is one of the world's greatest open-air museums, a time capsule of a glorious long-gone era. Yet at the same time this overgrown village, with a population of about 120,000, thrives and bustles with life.

Its attraction for tourists is by no means a recent phenomenon: travellers have been visiting Thebes for centuries, marvelling at the splendid temples of Luxor, Karnak, Ramses II and Hatshepsut. As far back as Graeco-Roman times visitors would wait in the desert to hear the mysterious voice of Memnon emanating from the colossal statues of Amenophis III; and in the past hundred years or so, since archaeology became a respectable science, curious travellers have been following the footsteps of the excavators into the famous tombs of the Valley of the Kings.

What most visitors today know as Luxor is actually three separate areas: the city of Luxor itself, the village of Karnak a couple of km to the north-east, and the monuments and necropolis of ancient Thebes on the west bank of the Nile.

Along the river, feluccas and antiquated barges compete for space with the posh hotel ships of the Hilton and Sheraton, and the many other 'flotels' plying the Nile from Cairo to Aswan.

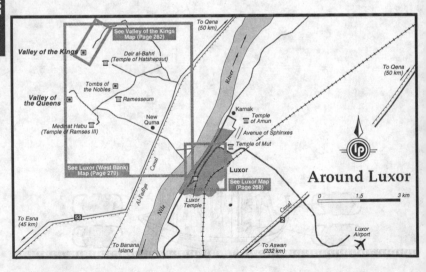

Around Luxor

With such a huge proportion of the town's economy derived from tourism, Luxor has been heavily hit by Egypt's severe downturn in tourism in recent years.

Behind the tourist facade, the dirt streets are crowded with mud-brick tenements, pocked with mud puddles and filled with ordinary, friendly people. Unfortunately, the friendliness has developed a predictable commercial edge, and travellers in Luxor complain increasingly of the almost incessant hassle from vendors, street hawkers and felucca middlemen. In the steamy summer months, when business is slack, it can be enough to tip a temper already frazzled by the heat. In winter, it's easier to bear in mind that they are just trying to make a living.

HISTORY

Following the collapse of centralised power at the end of the Old Kingdom period, the small village of Thebes, under the 11th and 12th dynasty Pharaohs, emerged as the main power in Upper Egypt. Rising against the northern capital of Heracleopolis, Thebes reunited the country under its political, religious and administrative control and ushered in the Middle Kingdom period. The strength of its government also enabled it to re-establish control after a second period of decline; liberate the country from foreign rule; and bring in the New Kingdom dynasties.

At the height of its glory and opulence, from 1570 to 1090 BC, all the New Kingdom Pharaohs (with the exception of Akhenaten who moved to Tell al-Amarna) made Thebes their permanent residence; the city had a population of nearly one million and the architectural activity was astounding.

Because so many kings left their mark at Thebes it can quickly become very confusing trying to keep track of who built what temples or tombs and when they did so. For detailed information on the history of Thebes, see the reference books listed in the Facts for the Visitor chapter.

Over the ages, Thebes has been known by many names. To the ancient Egyptians, it was called Waset (the City), while the Greeks (332 to 30 BC) called it the City of 100 Gates.

The Romans knew it as Diospolis Magna (Great City of God) and the Arabs called it El Kosur (the Palaces).

ORIENTATION

There are only three main thoroughfares in Luxor, so it's easy to find your way around – as long as you don't ask for street names. Some streets have signs, some have names but no signs and some seem to have no names at all. If you ask the locals what the name of a particular street is they're quite likely to make one up on the spot, which is why nearly every map of Luxor is different. So, it's best to ask directions to a specific location rather than to the street or road it's on. The three main roads are Sharia al-Mahatta, Sharia al-Karnak and the Corniche. Another road you may want to know if you're looking for cheap accommodation is Sharia Television, around which are clustered many, although by no means all, of the cheap hotels.

Sharia al-Mahatta – the street directly in front of the railway station – runs perpendicular to the Nile all the way to the gardens of Luxor Temple. Sharia al-Karnak (or Sharia Maabad al-Karnak, 'Karnak Temple Street') runs one block in from, and parallel to, the river, from Luxor Temple to Karnak Temple. To confuse matters Sharia al-Karnak, where it meets Sharia al-Mahatta, is also known as Sharia al-Markaz; to the south, around the temple to the river, it's known as Sharia al-Lokanda. The Corniche is known variously as Sharia al-Bahr, Sharia Bahr el-Nil or simply the Corniche.

INFORMATION
Visa Extensions

The passport office (☎ 380885) is almost opposite the Isis Hotel, south of the town centre. It's open Saturday to Thursday from 8 am to 2 pm (and also from 5 to 9 pm for registration only). Some people swear it's much easier to get a visa extension here than in the Mogamma building in Cairo. You'll need a photo and E£12.

Tourist Offices

The tourist police and tourist office are in the

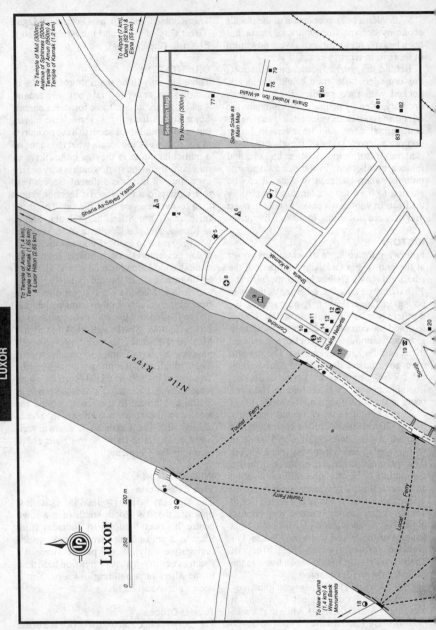

LUXOR

Luxor

Nile River

To Temple of Mut (300m);
Avenue of Sphinxes (500m);
Temple of Amun (950m) &
Temple of Karnak (1.2 km)

To Airport (7 km);
Qena (62 km) &
Esna (55 km)

To Temple of Amun (1.4 km);
Temple of Karnak (1.65 km)
& Luxor Hilton (2.65 km)

Sharia As-Sayed Yasouf

Sharia al-Karnak

Corniche

Sharia Nefertiti

Sharia Khaled Ibn el-Walid

See Main Map

To Novotel (300m)

Same Scale as
Main Map

Souqs

Tourist Ferry

Local Ferry

Tourist Ferry

To New Qurna
(1.4 km) &
West Bank
Monuments

500 m

250

0

N

PLACES TO STAY

3 Rezeiky Camp
4 Pola Hotel
5 Youth Hostel
6 YMCA Camping Ground
10 Merryland Hotel
11 Windsor Hotel
13 Philippe Hotel
14 Nile Hotel
16 Mercure ETAP Hotel
20 Emilio Hotel
21 Mina Palace Hotel
25 Venus Hotel
26 Pyramids Hotel
27 Nobles Hotel
28 St Catherine Hotel
29 Sphinx Hotel
30 El-Shazly Hotel
31 Nefertiti Hotel
36 Horus Hotel
41 Hotel El Salam
43 Saint Mina Hotel
44 Negem el-Din Pension
47 New Karnak Hotel
49 Anglo Hotel
50 Akhnaton Hotel
51 Arabesque Hotel
52 Luxor Wena Hotel
54 New Winter Palace
55 Old Winter Palace
59 Mubarak Hotel
60 Salah ad-Din Hotel
62 Oasis Hotel
63 Grand Hotel
64 New Nour Hotel
65 Atlas Hotel
66 Princess Pension
67 Everest Hotel
68 Santa Maria Hotel
69 Shady Hotel
70 Pension Roma
71 Fontana Hotel
73 Titi Hotel
74 Moon Valley Hotel
75 Happy Land Hotel
76 Novotel
77 Club Med Belladona Resort
78 St Joseph Hotel
79 Flobater Hotel
82 Gaddis Hotel
83 Isis Hotel

PLACES TO EAT

24 El Dar Restaurant
32 Amoun & El Hossein Restaurants
37 Abu Negem el-Din
39 Abu Ashraf
40 Mensa Restaurant
46 New Karnak Restaurant & Salt & Bread Cafeteria
48 Twinky's Patisserie
57 Fiteer Restaurant & El Dabaawy Restaurant
58 Sayyida Zeinab Kushari Restaurant
61 Restaurant Abu Hager
72 Mish Mish Restaurant

OTHER

1 Ticket Office
2 Taxis to West Bank Monuments
7 Service-Taxi Station
8 Hospital
9 Luxor Museum
12 Banque Misr
15 Bank of Alexandria
17 Dr Ragab's Papyrus Museum
18 Taxis & Donkeys to West Bank Monuments
19 Telephone Office
22 Brooke Hospital for Animals
23 Police Station
33 Entrance to Luxor Temple
34 Luxor Temple
35 Bus Station
38 GPO
42 Pharmacy La Confiance
45 Railway Station & Post/ Telephone Offices
53 Tourist Bazaar (Tourist Office & Tourist Police)
55 Thomas Cook, EgyptAir, American Express, Misr Travel & A A Gaddis Bookshop
56 National Bank of Egypt
80 Kings Head Pub
81 Passport Office

LUXOR

Labels on map: Sharia Youssef Hassan; Sharia; Sharia al-Souq; Sharia as-Souq; Midan al-Mahatta; Sharia al-Mahatta; Sharia Abdel Moniem al-Adasi; Farid; Sharia Mohammed; Ahmed Orabi; Midan Salah ad-Din; Sharia Television; Avenue of Sphinxes; Sharia al-Karnak; Corniche (Sharia al-Bahr); Local Ferry; Tourist Ferry; Car Ferry; See Inset

Tourist Bazaar on the Corniche, next to the new Winter Palace Hotel. The tourist office is open daily from 8 am to 8 pm and the staff can fill you in on what the official prices for various services should be, as well as the most recent schedule and prices of the sound & light show at Karnak Temple. Travellers can leave messages on a notice board next to the main information counter. There is another tourist office at the railway station which is supposedly open the same hours, although it hardly ever seems to be staffed, and another one at the airport which is open daily from 8 am to 8 pm.

The new 'visitors' centre' on the Corniche opposite the Mina Palace Hotel is closed; apparently it's destined to be turned into a museum.

Money

The Bank of Alexandria has a branch on the Corniche, a little way up from the ETAP Hotel. Banque Misr is on Sharia Nefertiti, around the corner from the ETAP, and the National Bank of Egypt is down on the Corniche near the old Winter Palace. Banks are usually open from 8.30 am to 2 pm and again for a few hours from 5 or 6 pm. In addition, the big hotels have various bank branches, and there is an exchange booth open quite long hours on the Corniche in front of the Tourist Bazaar.

The American Express office (☎ 372862) is at the old Winter Palace Hotel and operates from 8 am to 7 pm, although the hours seem flexible. All the usual services are available.

There's also a Thomas Cook exchange office and travel agent (☎ 372196; fax 376502) across from American Express; it's open daily from 8 am to 8 pm.

Post & Communications

The GPO is on Sharia al-Mahatta and there's a branch office in the Tourist Bazaar.

The central telephone office is on Sharia al-Karnak and is open 24 hours; there's another branch below the resplendent entrance of the old Winter Palace Hotel (open from 8 am to 10 pm) and a third at the railway station (open from 8 am to 8 pm).

Bookshops

Aboudi's Bookshop, in the Tourist Bazaar near the tourist information office, has a very good selection of books, guidebooks, maps and postcards. A few doors down towards the old Winter Palace Hotel is AA Gaddis, where you can also find books and even aerogrammes embellished with mug shots of Tutankhamun. It also has pop-up cardboard models of Pharaonic temples. The bookshop in the ETAP Hotel has a good selection of guidebooks and books on Egypt but its prices tend to be slightly higher.

A limited range of second-hand novels is sometimes for sale in the foyer of the Emilio Hotel.

Medical Services

There's a hospital (☎ 372025) across the road from the Luxor Museum.

THINGS TO SEE – EAST BANK
Luxor Museum

This great little air-conditioned museum on the Corniche, about halfway between the Luxor and Karnak temples, has a small but well-chosen collection of relics from the Theban temples and necropolis. The displays, which include pottery, jewellery, furniture, statues and stelae, were arranged by the Brooklyn Museum of New York.

To the right just after you enter is a well-preserved cow-goddess head from King Tutankhamun's tomb. The showpiece of the 1st floor is exhibit No 61, a finely carved statuette of Tuthmosis III that dates from at least 1436 BC.

The most interesting exhibit is the Wall of Akhenaten on the 2nd floor, which is actually a set of 283 sandstone blocks found within the ninth pylon of the Karnak Temple. The reliefs show the rebel Pharaoh and his queen, Nefertiti, making offerings to Aten.

Also on the 2nd floor, check out King Tutankhamun's well-preserved funerary boats and the box of animal-headed Canopic jars that once contained the internal organs of the priest of the god Montu.

Immediately on your right after entering the museum is the entrance to a relatively new hall which contains 16 of the 24 statues that were uncovered in Luxor Temple in 1989. Some of them, such as that of Amenhotep III, are exquisite pieces of art.

The museum is open daily from 9 am to 1 pm, and 4 to 9 pm (winter) or 5 to 10 pm (summer). Entry costs E£15 (E£8 for students); the last tickets are sold 30 minutes before closing time. The right to take photos costs E£10 (no flash or tripod allowed), while video costs E£100.

Luxor Temple

Amun, one of the gods of creation, was the most important god of Thebes and head of the local triad of deities. As Amun-Ra, the fusion of Amun and the sun-god Ra, he was also a state deity worshipped in many parts of the country. Once a year from his Great Temple at Karnak the images of Amun and the other two gods in the local triad – Amun's wife, the war-goddess Mut, and their son, the moon-god Khons – would journey down the Nile to Luxor Temple for the Opet Festival, a celebration held during the flood season.

Built by the New Kingdom Pharaoh Amenophis III, on the site of an older sanctuary dedicated to the Theban triad, Luxor Temple is a strikingly graceful piece of architecture on the banks of the Nile. Amenophis rededicated the massive temple as Amun's sacred 'harem of the south', and retained what was left of the original sanctuary built by Tuthmosis III and Hatshepsut 100 years earlier.

The Luxor Temple was added to over the centuries by Tutankhamun, Ramses II, Nectanebo, Alexander the Great and various Romans. At one point the Arabs built a mosque in one of the interior courts, and there was also once a village within the temple walls. Excavation work has been going on since 1885, and has included removing the village and clearing the forecourt and first pylon of debris, and exposing part of the avenue of sphinxes leading to Karnak.

Fronting the entrance to the temple is the enormous **first pylon**, about 24m high, in front of which are some colossal statues of

Six imposing statues of Ramses II once guarded the entrance to Luxor Temple, however, only three of the original structures remain.

Ramses II and a pink granite obelisk. There were originally six statues, four seated and two standing, but only two of the seated figures and the westernmost standing one remain. The **obelisk**, too, was one of a pair; its towering counterpart now stands in the Place de la Concorde in Paris.

Behind the pylon, which is decorated with Ramses' victorious exploits in battle, is another of his additions to the main complex. The **Great Court of Ramses II** is surrounded by a double row of columns with lotus-bud capitals, more reliefs of his deeds of derring-do and several huge statues. In the western corner of the court is the original Middle Kingdom **Temple of the Theban Triad** and south of that is the 13th century AD **Mosque of Abu al-Haggag**, dedicated to a local sheikh and holy man.

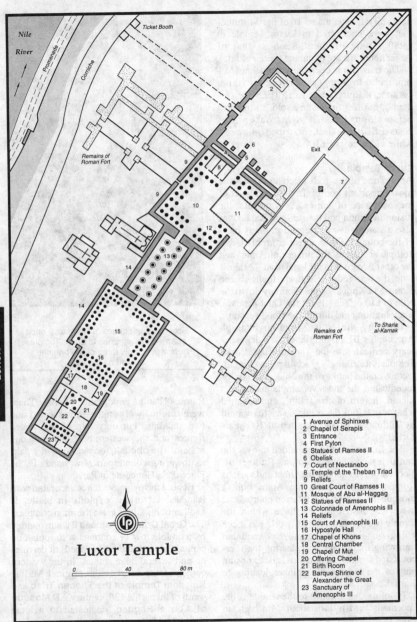

LUXOR

Luxor Temple

0   40   80 m

1 Avenue of Sphinxes
2 Chapel of Serapis
3 Entrance
4 First Pylon
5 Statues of Ramses II
6 Obelisk
7 Court of Nectanebo
8 Temple of the Theban Triad
9 Reliefs
10 Great Court of Ramses II
11 Mosque of Abu al-Haggag
12 Statues of Ramses II
13 Colonnade of Amenophis III
14 Reliefs
15 Court of Amenophis III
16 Hypostyle Hall
17 Chapel of Khons
18 Central Chamber
19 Chapel of Mut
20 Offering Chapel
21 Birth Room
22 Barque Shrine of
   Alexander the Great
23 Sanctuary of
   Amenophis III

Beyond the court, 14 papyrus columns form the **Colonnade of Amenophis III**. The walls behind the splendid columns were decorated during the reign of the young Pharaoh Tutankhamun and celebrate the return to Theban orthodoxy. The Opet Festival is depicted in great detail, with the king, the nobility and the common people joining the triumphal procession of Amun, Mut and Khons from Karnak.

The colonnade takes you into the **Court of Amenophis III**. This was once enclosed on three sides by double rows of towering columns, of which the best preserved, with their architraves extant, are those on the east and west sides.

The **hypostyle hall**, on the south side of the court, is the first inner room of the temple proper and features four rows of eight columns each.

Beyond are the main rooms of the **Temple of Amun**, the central chamber of which was once stuccoed over by the Romans and used as a cult sanctuary. Through this chamber, on either side of which are chapels dedicated to Mut and Khons, is an **Offering Chapel** with four columns.

The interesting inscriptions in the birth room, to the eastern side of the chapel, show scenes of how mortal Amenophis claimed divine status by coming up with the notion that Amun had visited his mother Mutemuia in the 'guise' of his father Tuthmosis IV, with the result that he, Amenophis III, was actually the god's son.

Alexander the Great rebuilt the **Barque Shrine**, beyond the Offering Chapel, adding to it reliefs of himself being presented to Amun. The **Sanctuary of Amenophis III** is the last chamber on the central axis of the temple.

The Luxor Temple is open daily from 6 am to 9 pm (winter) and 10 pm (summer). Entry costs E£20 (E£10 for students) by day and E£10 (E£5 for students) by night. Taking photographs is free. The best time to visit is in the evening, when the temperature is lower and the temple is lit up, creating an eerie spectacle beside the shimmering black of the Nile.

Temples of Karnak

The Amun Temple Enclosure (sometimes referred to as the Precinct of Amun) is the central enclosure of the numerous temples that make up the enormous Karnak complex; it was the main place of worship of the Theban triad. Its ancient name was Ipet-Isut (the Most Perfect of Places).

Although the original sanctuary of the Great Temple of Amun was built during the Middle Kingdom period, when the Theban Pharaohs first came to prominence, the rest of the temples, pylons, courts, columns and reliefs were the work of New Kingdom rulers.

Karnak was built, added to, dismantled, restored, enlarged and decorated over a period of nearly 1500 years. During the height of Theban power and prosperity it was the most important temple in all Egypt.

The complex can be divided into three distinct areas: the Amun Temple Enclosure, which is the largest enclosure; the Mut Temple Enclosure, on the south side, which was once linked to the main temple by an avenue of ram-headed sphinxes; and the Montu Temple Enclosure, to the north, which honoured the original local god of Thebes.

A canal once connected the Amun and Montu enclosures with the Nile, providing access for the sacred boats in the journey to the Luxor Temple during the Opet Festival. A paved avenue of human-headed sphinxes also once linked Karnak, from Euergetes' Gate on the south side of the Mut Temple Enclosure, with Luxor Temple. Only a small section of this sacred way, where it leaves the Great Temple of Amun and enters the forecourt of his Southern Harem, has been excavated. The rest of the three km avenue lies beneath the city and paved roads of modern Luxor.

The Karnak site measures about 1.5 km by 0.8 km, which is large enough to hold about 10 cathedrals, and the first pylon, at the entrance, is twice the size of the one at Luxor Temple. The further into the complex you venture the further back in time you go.

The oldest parts of the complex are the

LUXOR

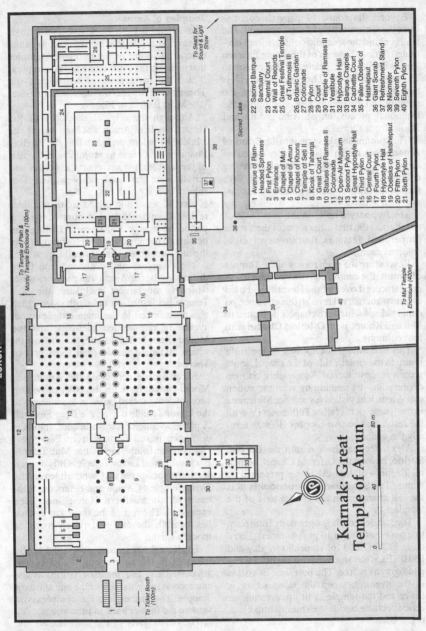

To Seats for
Sound & Light
Show

Sacred Lake

22 Sacred Barque Sanctuary
23 Central Court
24 Wall of Records
25 Great Festival Temple of Tuthmosis III
26 Botanic Garden
27 Colonnade
28 Pylon
29 Court
30 Temple of Ramses III
31 Vestibule
32 Hypostyle Hall
33 Barque Chapels
34 Cachette Court
35 Fallen Obelisk of Hatshepsut
36 Giant Scarab
37 Refreshment Stand
38 Nilometer
39 Seventh Pylon
40 Eighth Pylon

1 Avenue of Ram-Headed Sphinxes
2 First Pylon
3 Entrance
4 Chapel of Mut
5 Chapel of Amun
6 Chapel of Khons
7 Temple of Seti II
8 Kiosk of Taharqa
9 Great Court
10 Statues of Ramses II
11 Colonnade
12 Open-Air Museum
13 Second Pylon
14 Great Hypostyle Hall
15 Third Pylon
16 Central Court
17 Fourth Pylon
18 Hypostyle Hall
19 Obelisks of Hatshepsut
20 Fifth Pylon
21 Sixth Pylon

To Temple of Ptah &
Montu Temple Enclosure (100m)

To Mut Temple
Enclosure (400m)

To Ticket Booth
(100m)

LUXOR

**Karnak: Great
Temple of Amun**

0   40   80 m

White Pavilion of Sesostris I and the 12th dynasty foundations of what became the most sacred part of the Great Temple of Amun, the Sacred Barque Sanctuary and Central Court of Amun (behind the sixth pylon). The limestone fragments of the demolished pavilion, or chapel, were recovered from the foundations of the third pylon, built five centuries after Sesostris' reign, and expertly reconstructed in the open-air museum to the north of the Great Court.

The major additions to the complex were constructed by Pharaohs of the 18th to 20th dynasties, between 1570 and 1090 BC. The Pharaohs of the later dynasties extended and rebuilt the complex, and the Ptolemies and early Christians also left their mark on it.

You'll need to visit Karnak at least twice to fully appreciate the size and magnificence of the complex. A return visit in the evening for the sound & light show would complete the picture. The refreshment stand shown on the map is expensive in the extreme. A cup of Coca-Cola costs E£2.50.

General admission to the temples of Karnak is between 6 am and 5.30 (winter) and 6.30 pm (summer), and tickets cost E£20, or E£10 for students. Photography is free.

Amun Temple Enclosure – main axis
From the entrance you pass down the processional avenue of ram-headed sphinxes, which once led to the Nile, to the massive **first pylon**. You used to be able to climb the stairs on your left to the top of the pylon's north tower, from where there is an amazing view of Karnak and the surrounding country. The stairs were closed off when a tourist fell backwards to the ground and died.

You emerge from the first pylon into the **Great Court**, the largest single area of the Karnak complex. To the left is the **Temple of Seti II**, dedicated to the Theban triad. The three small chapels held the sacred barques of Amun, Mut and Khons during the lead-up to the Opet Festival.

The north and south walls of the court are lined with columns with papyrus-bud capitals. The south wall is intersected by the

Temple of Ramses III, which was built before the court. Obligatory scenes of the Pharaoh as glorious conqueror adorn the pylon of this 60 metre long temple which also features an open court, a vestibule with four columns, a hypostyle hall of eight columns and three barque chapels.

In the centre of the Great Court is the one remaining column of the Kiosk of Taharqa. A 25th dynasty Ethiopian Pharaoh, Taharqa built his open-sided pavilion of 10 columns, each rising 21m and topped with papyrus-form capitals.

The **second pylon** was originally built by Horemheb, an 18th dynasty general who headed a military dictatorship and became the last Pharaoh of his dynasty. Ramses I and II added their names and deeds to the pylon above that of Horemheb. Ramses II also raised two colossal pink granite statues of himself on either side of the entrance.

Beyond the second pylon is the awesome **Great Hypostyle Hall**. It was begun by Amenophis III while he was also building Luxor Temple, continued by Seti I and finished by Ramses II. Covering an area of 6000 sq metres (which is large enough to contain Notre Dame Cathedral), the hall is an unforgettable forest of towering stone pillars. It is impossible to get an overall idea of this court; there is nothing to do but stand and stare up at the dizzying spectacle. You'll notice that the papyrus-form capitals seem to sway and jostle each other for space.

Between the **third pylon**, built by Amenophis III, and the **fourth pylon**, raised by Tuthmosis I, is a narrow court. Tuthmosis I and III raised two pairs of obelisks in front of the fourth pylon, which was, during their reign, the entrance to the temple proper. Only one of the four is still standing, but parts of the others lie in the court.

Beyond the fourth pylon is the oldest preserved part of the complex, its 14 columns suggesting that it was originally a small hypostyle hall. It was constructed by Tuthmosis III in his attempt to eradicate or hide all signs of the reign of his stepmother, Queen Hatshepsut. (See the section on Deir al-Bahri later in this chapter.) In this hall,

LUXOR

around the two magnificent **Obelisks of Hatshepsut**, the vengeful king built a 25m-high sandstone structure. The upper shaft of one of the obelisks, which Hatshepsut raised to the glory of her 'father' Amun, lies on the ground by the Sacred Lake; the other obelisk still stands, reclaimed from the sandstone, in front of the fifth pylon. It is the tallest obelisk in Egypt, standing 29.2m high, and was originally covered in electrum (a commonly used alloy of gold and silver) from its pyramidal peak to halfway down the shaft.

The **fifth pylon** was constructed by Tuthmosis I, with little space between it and the now ruined sixth pylon (built at a later date). The latter, the smallest pylon at Karnak, was raised by his son Tuthmosis II (Hatshepsut's husband and half-brother). In the small vestibule beyond the sixth pylon are two pink granite columns on which the emblems of Egypt are carved in high relief: the lily of Upper Egypt on the north pillar and the papyrus flower of Lower Egypt on the south pillar. Nearby are two huge statues of Amun and his female counterpart Amunet, which date from the reign of Tutankhamun.

Also among the ruins of this area around the temple's original Central Court are a **Sacred Barque Sanctuary** and at least two well-preserved walls.

Hatshepsut's wall and its colourful reliefs survived the years well because once again Tuthmosis III chose to cover her structure with one of his own rather than destroy it once and for all.

Although the king was no match for his powerful though peace-loving stepmother, he made up for Hatshepsut's domination of him during his teenage years by setting out, almost immediately after her death, to conquer the known world. His reputation as a great hero and empire builder was justly deserved, as portrayed in the relief work on what is known as the **Wall of Records**. Though unrelenting in his bid for power, he had a penchant for being fairly just in his treatment of the people he conquered. This wall was a running tally of the organised tribute he exacted in honour of Amun from his subjugated lands.

East of the foundations of the original Temple of Amun stands the **Great Festival Temple of Tuthmosis III**. It contains several fine reliefs of plants and animals in the so-called Botanic Garden. Twenty of the temple's many columns are unique in Egypt in that they are larger at their peak than their base.

Between the Great Festival Temple and the eastern gate of the enclosure are the ruins of two other structures – a portico built by Taharqa and a smaller temple that was built by Tuthmosis III. The world's largest obelisk once stood on the base in front of this temple. The so-called **Lateran Obelisk**, which was 32.2m high, was removed from Karnak in 357 AD on the orders of the Roman Emperor Constantine. Although it was bound for Constantinople, it ended up in the Circus Maximus in Rome and finally, in the 1580s, was re-erected in the Piazza San Giovanni in Laterano, Rome.

Against the northern enclosure wall of the precinct of Amun is the cult **Temple of Ptah**, started by Tuthmosis III and finished by the Ptolemies. Access to the inner chambers is through a series of five doorways which lead you to two of the temple's original statues. The headless figure of Ptah, the creator-god of Memphis, is in the middle chapel behind a locked door – the custodian will unlock it for the usual remittance. To his left is the eerily beautiful, bare-breasted and lioness-headed, black granite statue of his goddess-wife Sekhmet (the Spreader of Terror).

Montu Temple Enclosure A usually locked gate on the wall near the Temple of Ptah (Amun Temple Enclosure) leads to the Montu Temple Enclosure. Montu, the falcon-headed warrior-god, was the original deity of Thebes. The main temple was built by Amenophis III and modified by others. The complex is very dilapidated.

Amun Temple Enclosure – southern axis The secondary axis of the Amun Temple Enclosure runs south from the third and fourth pylons. It is basically a processional way, bounded on the east and west sides by walls, and sectioned off by a number of pylons which create a series of courts. Just before you get to the **seventh pylon**, built by Tuthmosis III, is the **Cachette Court**, so named because of the thousands of stone and bronze statues discovered there during excavation work in 1903. Seven of the statues, of Middle Kingdom Pharaohs, stand in front of the pylon. Nearby are the remains of two colossal statues of Tuthmosis III.

The well-preserved **eighth pylon**, built by Queen Hatshepsut, is the oldest part of the north-south axis of the temple. Four of the original six colossi are still standing, the most complete being the one of Amenophis I.

The **ninth** and **tenth pylons** were built by Horemheb, who used some of the stones of a demolished temple that had been built to the east by Akhenaten (before he decamped to Tell al-Amarna).

To the east of the seventh and eighth pylons is the **Sacred Lake**, where the priests of Amun would purify themselves before performing ceremonies in the temple. On the north-west side of the lake is the top half of Hatshepsut's fallen obelisk, and a huge stone statue of a scarab beetle dedicated by Amenophis III to Aten, the disc of the rising sun. Tour guides tell visitors to walk around the scarab – once for good luck, three times for marriage and seven times for a first child.

There are the ruins of about 20 other chapels within the main enclosure of the southern axis. In a fairly good state of repair in the south-west corner is the **Temple of Khons**, god of the moon and time, and son of Amun and Mut. The pylon faces Euergetes' Gate and the avenue of sphinxes leading to Luxor Temple, and provides access to a small hypostyle hall and ruined sanctuary. The temple was started by Ramses III, and added to by other Ramessids, Ptolemies and also Herihor. Herihor, like Horemheb, had pushed his way up through the ranks of the army to claim power, declaring himself not only Pharaoh but high priest of Amun as well.

Nearby is the small, finely decorated Temple of Opet, dedicated to the hippopotamus-goddess Opet, mother of Osiris.

Mut Temple Enclosure From the tenth pylon an avenue of sphinxes leads to the partly excavated southern enclosure – the precinct of Mut. The badly ruined Temple of Mut was built by Amenophis III and consists of a sanctuary, a hypostyle hall and two courts. The Temple of Ramses III stands south-west of the lake, which partly surrounds the main temple. Throughout the area are granite statues of Sekhmet, with her leonine head crowned by a solar disc. At one time, more than 500 of these statues stood here.

Open-Air Museum Just before the second pylon, off to the left, is an open-air museum, which contains a collection of statuary found throughout the temple complex. A separate ticket is required for the museum, which closes at 5.30 pm. Entry is E£10 (half for students).

Sound & Light Show Karnak Temple's sound & light show easily rivals the one at the Great Pyramids of Giza. The 90 minute show recounts the history of Thebes and the lives of the many Pharaohs who built sanctuaries, courts, statues or obelisks in honour of Amun. The show starts at the avenue of ram-headed sphinxes, passes through the first pylon to the Great Court and on through the Great Hypostyle Hall to the grandstand at the Sacred Lake for the show's finale.

There are usually three and sometimes four performances a night in either English, French, German, Japanese, Italian, Spanish or Arabic. The show costs E£33 (there is no student discount). The sessions start at 6.15, 7.30, 8.45 and 10 pm; about one hour later in summer. The following language schedule was correct at the time of writing, however, check it at the tourist office:

Day	Show 1	Show 2	Show 3	Show 4
Monday	English	French	Spanish	–
Tuesday	Italian	Japanese	English	–
Wednesday	German	English	French	–
Thursday	Arabic	English	French	Italian
Friday	Italian	English	French	Spanish
Saturday	Japanese	English	German	–
Sunday	·German	English	French	Italian

Getting There & Away To get to Karnak you can take a microbus from Luxor station or from behind Luxor Temple for 25 pt or hire a *hantour* (horse-drawn carriage) for around E£3. Give the driver baksheesh if you want him to wait. It's a quick bicycle ride to the temple or you can easily walk.

Brooke Hospital for Animals

Although not really a tourist sight, the hospital, part of a worldwide UK network of clinics aiming to provide at least minimum care for animals, especially those put to work, is interesting. It's up the road from the Mina Palace Hotel, and has been operating in Luxor for more than three decades (although the original hospital was on a different site). You might like to visit and see what they do for the horses which used to pull the hantours through the streets of Luxor – they have a notice board of dos and don'ts on treatment of horses, including not tipping drivers for pushing the animals into going too fast. It's open daily from 8 am to 1.30 pm, and 4 to 6 pm (winter) or 6 to 8 pm (summer).

If you are particularly interested in its work, it also has clinics in Cairo, Alexandria, Edfu and Aswan.

THINGS TO SEE – WEST BANK

The west bank of Luxor was the necropolis of ancient Thebes, a vast City of the Dead where magnificent temples were raised to honour the cults of Pharaohs entombed in the nearby cliffs, and where queens, royal children, nobles, priests, artisans and even workers built tombs which ranged, in the quality of their design and decor, from the spectacular to the ordinary.

During the New Kingdom, the necropolis also supported a large living population. In an attempt to protect the valuable tombs from robbers, the artisans, labourers, temple priests and guards lived permanently in the City of the Dead, their lives devoted to its construction and maintenance. They perfected the techniques of tomb building, decoration and concealment, and passed the secrets down through their own families.

The desire for secrecy greatly affected tomb design. Instead of a single mortuary monument like a pyramid, which was both a venue to worship the immortal Pharaoh and the resting place of his mummified remains, the New Kingdom Theban rulers commissioned their funerary monuments in pairs.

Magnificent mortuary temples were built on the plains, where the illusion of the Pharaoh's immortality could be perpetuated by the devotions of his priests and subjects, while the king's body and worldly wealth were laid in splendidly decorated secret tombs excavated in the hills. The prime location for the latter was an isolated canyon to the north-west, surrounded on three sides by high rugged cliffs.

However, even though there was only one way into the Valley of the Kings and the tombs were well hidden, very few escaped the vandalism of the grave robbers.

From the canal junction it is three km to the Valley of the Queens, seven km to the Valley of the Kings, and two km straight ahead to the student ticket office, past the Colossi of Memnon.

Information

What to Bring Bring a torch (flashlight) and, more importantly, your own water because although drinks are available at some sites, they can be relatively expensive. At the rest house just outside the Valley of the Kings, for instance, meals and drinks (including bottled water) are overpriced.

Lastly, bring plenty of small change for baksheesh. The tomb and temple guards will often try to pretend to show you something hidden or mysterious. Apparently, they want you to think that whenever they are whispering in their best tomb, temple and tourist English they are telling or showing you something special. (See the boxed story Tips on Tipping: Mastering the Payment of Baksheesh, in the Facts for the Visitor chapter.)

The best way to avoid these guys is to tag along with a group in each tomb or temple. Unfortunately, that also diminishes the aura of mystery surrounding solitary visits to these ancient sites.

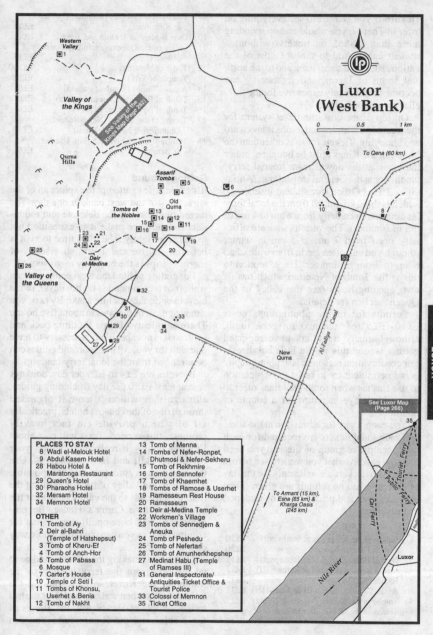

Luxor (West Bank)

0   0.5   1 km

To Qena (60 km)

Al-Fadliya Canal

New Qurna

New Qurna

To Armant (15 km),
Esna (65 km) &
Kharga Oasis
(245 km)

Nile River

Luxor

Tourist Ferry
Public Ferry
Car Ferry

See Luxor Map
(Page 268)

Western Valley

Valley of the Kings

See Valley of the Kings Map (Page 282)

Qurna Hills

Assarif Tombs

Old Qurna

Tombs of the Nobles

Deir al-Medina

Valley of the Queens

LUXOR

PLACES TO STAY
- 8 Wadi el-Melouk Hotel
- 9 Abdul Kasem Hotel
- 28 Habou Hotel & Maratonga Restaurant
- 29 Queen's Hotel
- 30 Pharaohs Hotel
- 32 Mersam Hotel
- 34 Memnon Hotel

OTHER
- 1 Tomb of Ay
- 2 Deir al-Bahri (Temple of Hatshepsut)
- 3 Tomb of Kheru-Ef
- 4 Tomb of Anch-Hor
- 5 Tomb of Pabasa
- 6 Mosque
- 7 Carter's House
- 10 Temple of Seti I
- 11 Tombs of Khonsu, Userhet & Benia
- 12 Tomb of Nakht

- 13 Tomb of Menna
- 14 Tombs of Nefer-Ronpet, Dhutmosi & Nefer-Sekheru
- 15 Tomb of Rekhmire
- 16 Tomb of Sennofer
- 17 Tomb of Khaemhet
- 18 Tombs of Ramose & Userhet
- 19 Ramesseum Rest House
- 20 Ramesseum
- 21 Deir al-Medina Temple
- 22 Workmen's Village
- 23 Tombs of Sennedjem & Aneuka
- 24 Tomb of Peshedu
- 25 Tomb of Nefertari
- 26 Tomb of Amunherkhepshep
- 27 Medinat Habu (Temple of Ramses III)
- 31 General Inspectorate/ Antiquities Ticket Office & Tourist Police
- 33 Colossi of Memnon
- 35 Ticket Office

Tickets If you wanted to see everything on offer in Thebes, you would end up spending more than US$65 on tickets (without a student card). Add to that the cost of the various sites on the east bank and to the north and south of Luxor, and sightseeing can become prohibitively expensive for the traveller on a tight budget.

On top of the cost, the ticket system for the west bank temples and tombs is awkward and annoying. Tickets for sites other than the Valley of the Kings must be bought at either the kiosk at the downstream 'tourist ferry' landing or at the General Inspectorate/Antiquities Ticket Office (for student discounts), which is three km inland from the local ferry landing and open daily from 6 am to 4 pm (5 pm in summer). The various sites are officially open from 7 am to 5 pm in winter (though you can often get in from 6 am), and 6 am to 7 pm in summer. The exception to this is the Tomb of Nefertari which has its own opening hours (see the Valley of the Queens section for details).

Permits for taking photographs costs E£10 (E£5 for students) for *each* tomb, although many travellers have reported getting around this with a little baksheesh. For conservation reasons, flash photography is not permitted; try to resist the temptation to use flashes when tomb guardians offer to turn a blind eye in return for a couple of pounds.

You cannot pay for admission at the sites, and individual tickets are required for each tomb, temple or group of sites, so you need to know exactly what you want to see before you set off. Tickets are valid only for the day of purchase and no refunds are given. They are numbered and priced (half for students) as follows:

1	Valley of the Kings (three tombs only)	E£20
2	Tomb of Tutankhamun	E£20
3	Deir al-Bahri (Temple of Hatshepsut)	E£12
4	Medinat Habu (Temple of Ramses III)	E£12
5	Ramesseum	E£12
6	Assasif Tombs (Kheru-Ef & Anch-Hor)	E£12
7	Tombs of the Nobles (Menna & Nakht)	E£12
8	Tombs of the Nobles (Sennofer & Rekhmire)	E£12
9	Tombs of the Nobles (Ramose, Userhet & Khaemhet)	E£12
10	Deir al-Medina Temple and Tombs	E£12
11	Valley of the Queens (excluding Tomb of Nefertari)	E£12
12	Tomb of Nefertari	E£100
13	Temple of Seti I	E£12
14	Assasif Tombs (Tomb of Pabasa)	E£6
15	Tomb of Peshedu (Deir al-Medina)	E£6
16	Tomb of Ay (Western Valley)	E£6
17	Tombs of the Nobles (Nefer-Ronpet, Dhutmosi & Nefer-Sekheru)	E£10
18	Tombs of the Nobles (Khonsu, Userhet & Benia)	E£6

Getting Around

It's unrealistic to attempt to explore all of the attractions of the west bank in one day. The incredible heat and the desolate and mountainous landscape make it an expedition not to be taken lightly. The ideal time to visit is between sunrise and 1 pm, so a series of morning trips is the best way to go about it.

For getting around the west bank, you can walk (not recommended on hot days), rent a bicycle or donkey, or hire a taxi. By taxi, you can visit most of the sites in about five hours. There are plenty of taxis shuttling back and forth so it is not absolutely necessary to have one wait for you. All transport and guides can be arranged from the local ferry landing.

Bicycles are E£4 to E£6 per day, donkeys cost at least E£10 per day (including guide), although they will cost more if organised through one of the cheaper hotels, practically all of which provide (in fact heavily promote) this service. Taxis will cost about E£8 per hour – it really depends on your bargaining skill and how business is. Use these prices as a guideline only. It is possible to cycle to the Valley of the Kings along the road which leads to the valley from near the intersection near Carter's House. Be prepared for a half-hour uphill slog – great for coming back as you can coast the whole way down.

One way of making the circuit could be to take a taxi from the ferry landing to the Valley of the Kings. After exploring the tombs you can then walk up and over the hill to the Temple of Hatshepsut, the Tombs of the Nobles and the Ramesseum. You can then catch another taxi to the Valley of the Queens and the Temple of Ramses III, or even continue on foot. However, it should be noted that walking across the mountain between the Valley of the Kings and the Temple of Hatshepsut is now officially discouraged, as some tourists have fallen making the crossing.

Temple of Seti I

Seti I, the father of Ramses II, expanded the Egyptian Empire to include Cyprus and parts of Mesopotamia. His imposing mortuary temple, dedicated to Amun, was an inspiring place of worship for his own cult and also served as a treasure house for some of the spoils of his military ventures.

Although the first two pylons and courts are in ruins, the temple itself is in reasonable repair and the surviving reliefs, in the hypostyle hall, chapels and sanctuary, are superbly executed and some of the finest examples of New Kingdom art. This temple, just off Sharia Wadi al-Melouk (the road to the Valley of the Kings), is seldom visited by tourists, so is well worth the effort. However, at the time of writing, it was closed.

Carter's House

On a barren hill, where the road from Deir al-Bahri to the Valley of the Kings meets the road from Seti's temple, there is a domed house where Howard Carter lived during his search for the tomb of Tutankhamun.

Valley of the Kings

Once called the Gates of the Kings or the Place of Truth, the canyon now known as the Valley of the Kings is at once a place of death – for nothing grows on its steep, scorching cliffs – and a majestic domain befitting the mighty kings who once lay there in great stone sarcophagi, awaiting immortality.

The isolated valley, behind Deir al-Bahri, is dominated by the natural pyramid-shaped mountain peak of Al-Qurn (the Horn). The valley consists of two branches, the east and west valleys, the former containing most of the royal burial sites.

All the tombs (except the newly discov-

ered Tomb of the Sons of Ramses II) followed a similar design, deviating only because of structural difficulties or the length of time spent on their construction. The longer the reign of the Pharaoh, the larger and more magnificent his tomb. Two groups of workers and artisans would live, in alternating shifts, in the valley itself for the duration of the work, which usually took many years.

The tombs were designed to resemble the underworld, with a long, inclined rock-hewn corridor descending into either an antechamber or a series of sometimes pillared halls, and ending in the burial chamber. Once the tomb was cut its decoration was started; this dealt almost exclusively with the afterlife and the Pharaoh's existence in it.

The colourful paintings and reliefs are extracts from ancient theological compositions, or 'books', and were incorporated in the tomb to assist the Pharaoh into the next life. Texts were taken from the *Book of Amduat* – 'the book of him who is in the netherworld'; the *Book of Gates*, which charted the king's course through the underworld; and the *Book of the Litany of Ra*, believed to be the words spoken by Ra, the sun-god, on his own journey through the caverns of death.

The worshippers of Amun or Amun-Ra (the fusion of the two deities and king of the gods) believed that the Valley of the Kings was traversed each night by Ra, and it was the aim of those who had been buried that day to secure passage on his sacred barque.

To do this, they had to be well equipped with a knowledge of the magic texts (hence the tomb decorations) before they could enter the boat of the god. Once aboard, they were brought to the kingdom of Osiris, god of the dead, where they were judged. Those kings who passed the ordeal would then board a second sacred barque for the journey to the east, where, having overcome the powers of darkness and death, they would live again, immortal in the company of Amun-Ra.

Tuthmosis I was the first Pharaoh to have his tomb cut into the barren cliffs of the

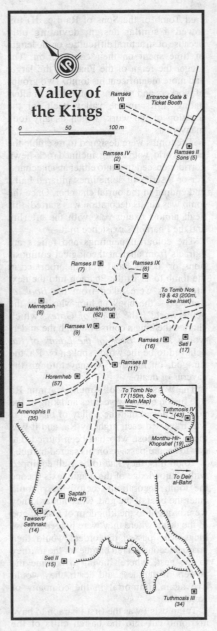

Valley of the Kings

0   50   100 m

Ramses VII

Entrance Gate & Ticket Booth

Ramses IV (2)

Ramses II Sons (5)

Ramses II (7)

Ramses IX (6)

To Tomb Nos 19 & 43 (200m, See Inset)

Merneptah (8)

Tutankhamun (62)

Ramses VI (9)

Ramses I (16)

Seti I (17)

Ramses III (11)

Horemheb (57)

To Tomb No 17 (150m, See Main Map)

Amenophis II (35)

Tuthmosis IV (43)

Monthu-Hir-Khopshef (19)

To Deir al-Bahri

Saptah (No 47)

Tawsert/ Sethnakt (14)

Seti II (15)

Cliffs

Tuthmosis III (34)

LUXOR

Valley of the Kings (around 1495 BC) and, in all, more than 60 tombs have been excavated in the valley, although not all belong to Pharaohs.

Each tomb is numbered in order of discovery but not all are open to the public and there are often some tombs closed for renovation work. It's worth having your own torch to illuminate badly lit areas. Sometimes the guards have the endearing habit of switching off the lights if you won't give them baksheesh – and they wait till you're halfway in to leave you in the dark.

The road into the Valley of the Kings is a gradual, dry, hot climb, so be prepared if you are riding a bicycle. There is a rest house before the entrance to the valley where you can buy mineral water, soft drinks and meals. It's expensive and usually crowded.

If you want to avoid the inevitable crowds that tour buses bring to the tombs, head for the tombs outside the immediate area of the entrance. There are many to choose from, but among the better ones are the tombs of Ramses VI (No 9), Queen Tawsert/Sethnakt (No 14), Tuthmosis III (No 34) and Saptah (No 47).

You cannot buy tickets for the tombs at the entrance to the valley itself (see the Tickets section, earlier in this chapter). Note that any one ticket is for three tombs only. If you want to visit more, you'll have to buy more tickets (and if you wanted to visit, say, four tombs, you'd still have to buy two tickets). The Tomb of Tutankhamun has been deemed worth a ticket on its own (E£20).

Tomb of Ramses IV (No 2) This is the second tomb on the right as you enter the Valley of the Kings. Its whereabouts was known even by the Ptolemies, as is evident from the graffiti dating back to 278 BC which can be seen on the walls. Only recently opened to the public, it's not one of the finest tombs – many of the paintings in the burial chamber have deteriorated, although the painting of the goddess Nut, stretched across the blue ceiling, is still in good condition.

Tomb of Ramses IX (No 6) This tomb consists of a long, sloping corridor, a large antechamber decorated with animals, serpents and demons, then a pillared hall and short hallway before the burial chamber. The goddess Nut is the feature of the ceiling painting; she is surrounded by sacred barques full of stars. Just before the staircase down to the burial chamber are the cartouche symbols of Ramses IX.

Tomb of Ramses II (No 7) This tomb, the burial place of Egypt's longest reigning Pharaoh, is being excavated by French archaeologists. It's expected to be opened to the public in about the year 2000.

Tomb of Merneptah (No 8) Reliefs of Isis, the wife of Osiris and divine mourner of the dead, and Nepthys, the sister of Isis and guardian of coffins, adorn the entrance to this tomb. Merneptah was the son of Ramses II and the Pharaoh mentioned in the biblical book *Exodus*. The walls of the steep corridor, which descends 80m to his burial chamber, are decorated with texts from the *Book of Gates*.

Tomb of Ramses VI (No 9) The early excavation of this tomb forestalled the discovery of Tutankhamun's tomb below it. Originally built for Ramses V but usurped by his successor, who saved time and money by appropriating the site, this tomb extends 83m into the mountain. The passageway is decorated with scenes from the *Book of the Dead* and the *Book of the Caverns* and the complete text of the *Book of Gates*.

Ramses VI's smashed sarcophagus lies in the pillared burial chamber at the end of the corridor. The burial chamber has a beautiful and unusual ceiling that details the *Book of Day & Night* and features the goddess Nut twice, stretched across the morning and evening sky. At the time of writing, it was temporarily closed for restoration.

Tomb of Ramses III (No 11) The burial chamber of this tomb, which is one of the largest in the valley, remains unexcavated and is closed to the public.

There is, however, plenty to see in the three passageways and 10 side chambers in the first part of the tomb. Also known as the Tomb of the Harpers, because of the painting of two musicians playing to the gods in a room off the second passage, it is interesting because the colouring of its sunken reliefs is still quite vivid. The side chambers are decorated with pictures of their former contents, while other walls depict daily happenings in Egyptian life.

Tomb of Queen Tawsert/Sethnakt (No 14) Queen Tawsert was the wife of Seti II. Her tomb was later taken over by Sethnakt after he had trouble building his own tomb. The tomb is decorated with well-preserved paintings showing scenes from the *Book of the Dead*, the *Book of Gates* and the ceremony of the Opening of the Mouth. Sethnakt's granite sarcophagus is in the tomb.

Tomb of Seti II (15) Adjacent to Queen Tawsert's tomb is that of her husband, Seti II. The tomb entrance starts with some fine reliefs but it was abruptly abandoned before completion. During the excavation of Tutankhamun's tomb it was used by Howard Carter for preliminary storage and restoration work on the finds. Today the mummy of an unknown person can be seen in the tomb.

Tomb of Ramses I (No 16) Although the tomb next to Seti's belongs to the founder of the 19th dynasty, it is a very simple affair because Ramses I only ruled for a couple of years.

The tomb, which has the shortest entrance corridor of all the royal resting places in the valley, has a single, almost square, burial chamber, containing the king's open pink-granite sarcophagus. The chamber is the only part of the tomb that is decorated; it features the Pharaoh in the presence of deities such as Osiris, Ptah, Anubis and Maat set on a blue-purple background.

LUXOR

Tomb of Seti I (No 17) The longest, deepest, most splendid and best preserved tomb in the Valley of the Kings is the burial site of Seti I, which plunges over a hundred metres down into the hillside. The detail of the enchanting, finely executed reliefs rivals even the renowned decorations in his Cenotaph Temple at Abydos.

Three long passages, intersected by decorated chambers, culminate in the large, two-part burial chamber. Colourful scenes include Seti appearing before Ra-Harakhty (god of the morning sun) beneath a ceiling of flying vultures and texts from the *Litany of Ra*.

In the first chamber Seti is shown in the presence of deities and in another passage the walls feature the Opening of the Mouth ritual which ensured that the mummy's organs were functioning.

The first section of the burial chamber is a pillared hall decorated with texts from the *Book of Gates*, while the second part, which contained Seti's magnificent alabaster sarcophagus, features texts from the *Amduat* and an astronomical ceiling.

Unfortunately, at the time of writing, this tomb was closed for restoration. There is talk that it will reopen in late 1996.

Tomb of Monthu-Hir-Khopshef (No 19) The Tomb of Ramses IX's son, whose name translates as 'the Arm of Montu is Strong', is one of several newly opened tombs in the valley. Located high up in the valley's eastern wall, its entrance corridor is adorned with life-sized reliefs of various gods, including Anubis and Horus, receiving offerings from the young prince.

Tomb of Ay (No 23) This newly opened tomb is in the western valley, next to the main eastern branch. It is accessed by a rough dirt road (leading off from the car park at the Valley of the Kings) which winds for a long way up a desolate valley past sheer rock cliffs. The well-hidden tomb dates from the 18th dynasty and is noted for its paintings of scenes depicting daily life in ancient Egypt

– hunting, gathering reeds and so on. One wall features twelve baboons.

Before making your way up to this tomb, ask at the ticket office to ensure that it's open. Those on bikes should note that it is not feasible to cycle up here unless you happen to have a good mountain bike.

Tomb of Tuthmosis III (No 34) Hidden in the hills between high limestone cliffs and reached only via a steep staircase that crosses an even steeper ravine, this tomb demonstrates the lengths to which the ancient Pharaohs went to thwart the cunning of the ancient thieves.

Tuthmosis III was one of the first to build his tomb in the Valley of the Kings. As secrecy was his utmost concern, he chose the most inaccessible spot and designed his burial place with a series of passages at haphazard angles and a deep shaft to mislead or catch potential robbers – all to no avail, of course.

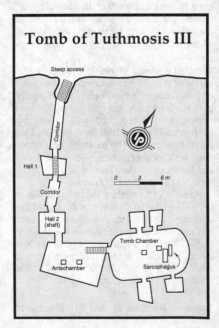

Tomb of Tuthmosis III

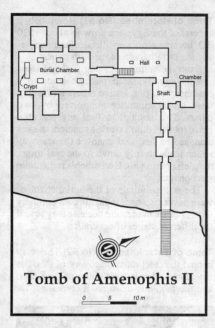

Tomb of Amenophis II

0   5   10 m

thieves did manage to make off with everything of value, they did no damage to the interior and left the king himself undisturbed.

When the huge tomb was excavated, by the French in 1898, a total of 13 mummies were found, including that of Amenophis lying *in situ* in his sarcophagus, a garland of flowers still around his neck. Nine of the other mummies, hidden there by priests, were also of royal blood, including those of Tuthmosis IV, Seti II, Amenophis III and his wife Queen Tiy.

A word of warning: this tomb can sometimes be exceedingly hot and humid; drink lots of water. At the time of writing, this tomb was closed but should reopen by late 1996.

Tomb of Tuthmosis IV (No 43) Only recently opened to the public, this is one of the largest and deepest tombs constructed during the 18th dynasty. It's above the Tomb

The shaft, now traversed by a narrow gangway, leads to an antechamber supported by two pillars, the walls of which are adorned with a list of over 700 gods and demigods.

The burial chamber, which is oval-shaped like a cartouche, is decorated in a fairly restrained manner. The roof is supported by two pillars, between which is the king's empty, red sandstone sarcophagus; his mummy was found at Deir al-Bahri.

Tomb of Amenophis II (No 35) One of the deepest structures in the valley, this tomb has more than 90 steps that take you down to a modern gangway built over a deep pit designed to protect the inner, lower chambers from thieves.

Stars cover the entire ceiling in the huge burial chamber and the walls feature, as if on a giant painted scroll, the entire text of the *Book of Amduat*. This was indeed the final resting place of Amenophis II, for although

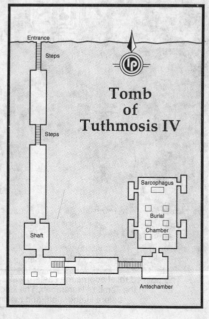

Tomb of Tuthmosis IV

of Monthu-Hir-Khopshef and accessed by a separate path (though the guardians will probably show you a short cut up the hill). Two long flights of steps lead down and around to the burial chamber where there's an enormous sarcophagus covered in hieroglyphs. Most of the walls in this tomb were never finished. However there are two, well-preserved painted sections where various gods, such as Osiris and Hathor, are shown presenting the Pharaoh with the key of life.

Tomb of Saptah (No 47) This colourful tomb is also one of those recently opened to the public and, according to some, it's one of the finest in the valley. The entry corridor is lined with hieroglyphs while the azure ceiling is decorated with vultures. Notice the sun disc above your head as you enter. Pieces of the funerary furniture found in this tomb now grace the Metropolitan Museum of Art in New York. Saptah's mummy was one of those found in the Tomb of Amenophis II.

Tomb of Horemheb (No 57) Horemheb, a general of the Egyptian army in about 1320 BC, became a military dictator and eventually the last Pharaoh of the 18th dynasty.

From the entrance a steep flight of steps and an equally steep passage leads to a chamber with fine festive reliefs and then a false burial chamber supported by two pillars. This attempt to fool any potential grave robbers didn't work, as ancient thieves managed to find and uncover the stairway which leads steeply down to the real tomb; they left nothing but Horemheb's red granite sarcophagus.

The wall paintings of the burial chamber were never finished, indicating an untimely death, but are interesting because they reveal the different stages of decoration.

Tomb of Tutankhamun (No 62) The story behind the celebrated discovery of this, the most famous tomb in the Valley of the Kings, and the fabulous treasures it contained, far

This painted relief adorns the eastern wall of the chamber preceding the sarcophagus in the Tomb of Horemheb. The king is depicted standing in adoration before Hathor (left) and making offerings to Horus (right).

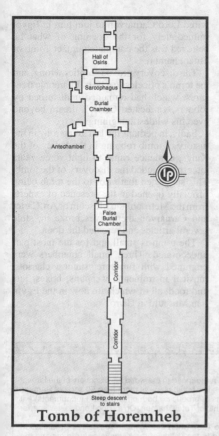

Hall of
Osiris

Sarcophagus

Burial
Chamber

Antechamber

False
Burial
Chamber

Corridor

Corridor

Steep descent
to stairs

Tomb of Horemheb

For years archaeologists believed that if, in fact, Tutankhamun was buried in the valley, his tomb would contain little of interest. The nephew of Akhenaten, he was merely a puppet Pharaoh of the priests of Amun, supporting their counter-revolution against the parvenus of the late rebel king's desertion from Thebes.

During his brief reign Tutankhamun was seen to re-embrace the cult of Amun, restoring its popularity with the people, and then he died, young, with no great battles or buildings to his credit.

The English Egyptologist Howard Carter, however, believed he would find the young Pharaoh buried among his ancestors with his treasures intact. He slaved away for six seasons in the valley, excavating thousands

LUXOR

Part of Tutankhamun's famous gold coffin, inlaid with enamel and semiprecious stones. Its complete height measures 185 cm, and it is displayed in the Egyptian Museum, Cairo.

outshines its actual appearance, making it dubious whether or not it warrants the E£20 charged for entry (half for students). It may, in any case, be closed for restoration by the time you read this.

Tutankhamun's tomb is neither large nor impressive and bears all the signs of a rather hasty completion and inglorious burial. The extraordinary contents of this rather modest tomb built for a fairly insignificant boy-king, however, can only make you guess at the immense wealth that must have been laid to rest with the likes of the powerful Seti I or Ramses II.

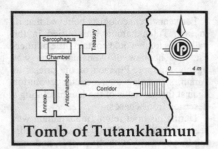

Tomb of Tutankhamun

and thousands of tonnes of sand and rubble from possible sites, until even his wealthy patron, Lord Carnarvon, tired of the obsession.

With his funding about to be cut off Carter made one last attempt at the only unexplored area that was left – a site covered by workers' huts just under the already excavated Tomb of Ramses VI.

On 4 November 1922 he uncovered steps and then a door, its seals untouched, and wired Lord Carnarvon to join him in Egypt immediately for the opening of what he believed was the completely intact Tomb of Tutankhamun.

The discovery proved sceptics wrong, and the tomb's priceless cache of Pharaonic treasures, which had remained undisturbed by robbers, vindicated Carter's dream beyond even his wildest imaginings.

Sadly, in perhaps the last great irony in the history of tomb robbing in the Valley of the Kings, evidence came to light some years later that clouded the discovery of the tomb. This suggested that prior to the tomb being officially opened in the presence of experts from the Metropolitan Museum of Art, Carter and Carnarvon themselves broke in, stole several articles and resealed the door.

The tomb is small and for the most part undecorated. Three small chambers were crammed with furniture, statues, chariots, musical instruments, weapons, boxes, jars and food, all of which are now in the Egyptian Museum in Cairo.

The Tomb of the Sons of Ramses II

In May 1995, American archaeologist Kent Weeks announced to the world his discovery of the largest tomb ever to be unearthed in Egypt. Believed to be the burial place of more than 50 sons of Ramses II – one of Egypt's most prolific Pharaohs (in terms of producing both offspring and monuments) – it was immediately hailed as the greatest find since that of Tutankhamun. Or, as one London newspaper succinctly put it: 'The Mummy of all Tombs'.

The story of the tomb's discovery dates back to 1987 when the Egyptian Antiquities Organisation announced plans to level a hillside at the entrance to the Valley of the Kings in order to expand the paved car park. Weeks was familiar with the area and knew that there was a tomb entrance hidden somewhere in the hill. Indeed, Howard Carter had uncovered it earlier this century and, believing it to be insignificant, used it as a dump while clearing the debris out of Tutankhamun's tomb.

A year later, after moving mountains of rubble, Weeks finally located the entrance – adjacent to that of Ramses II. Together with his wife and a small team of workers, he then set about clearing the entrance chambers. Remnants of pottery, fragments of sarcophagi and, more importantly, wall decorations led Weeks to believe it was the tomb of the sons of Ramses II.

However, it wasn't until 1995 that the then 56 year old archaeologist unearthed a doorway leading to a long corridor flanked by dozens of rooms. Weeks was dumbfounded by the size, plan and proportion, realising at once that no other tomb in Egypt had such a design. The actual burial chambers, he believes, are on a second level accessed by stairs. Exactly how many sons are buried here, however, is still unknown.

Weeks estimates it will take between five and 10 years to study the tomb. Electricity must be installed, climate controls set in place to protect the decorations, and precarious areas reinforced. As for visitors...they'll have to wait at least a decade before being allowed into tomb No 5 in the Valley of the Kings. ■

Preserving the Tomb of Nefertari

Since the Tomb of Nefertari was discovered in 1904 by Italian archaeologist, Ernesto Schiaparelli, Egyptian and foreign archaeologists have pondered the best way to restore and preserve it. It wasn't until 1986 that the Egyptian Antiquities Organisation, together with the Getty Conservation Institute in the USA, embarked on a programme to safeguard this magnificent tomb.

During the years since its discovery, the tomb paintings had suffered due to dehydration of the plaster and a build-up of salt crystals under the paintings, causing the images to flake off the limestone walls. With minimal intervention and ensuring the reversibility of materials used, the paintings were cleaned and adhesion between the plaster and rock reinforced. No colours were added to the paintings. The restoration work, estimated to cost about US$6 million, took five years, after which the tomb was prepared for visitors: devices to monitor the temperature, humidity and salt levels were installed, and wooden floors to keep dust at bay were laid. As breathing can raise humidity levels which in turn can activate salt crystallisation, a limit of 150 visitors per day was set. However, even this figure has been subject to controversy, with some archaeologists believing only two people per day should be allowed to view Egypt's finest tomb.

LEANNE LOGAN

LEANNE LOGAN

Restored reliefs in Egypt's finest tomb.

Top & Left: At the Temple of Horus in Edfu you'll find hieroglyphs inscribed along the Passage of Victory (top), and columns adorned with fine carvings (left).

Right: Hymns to the ram-god Khnum and the descriptions of annual sacred festival of Esna are recorded on the columns of the Temple of Khnum.

The second coffin of gilded wood, the solid gold mummy case and the magnificent funerary mask, found on the king's body, are also in Cairo. The outermost coffin of gilded wood containing the decaying, mummified body of Tutankhamun, still lies within the carved granite sarcophagus in the burial chamber of his tomb, the walls of which are decorated with texts from the *Book of the Dead*.

Walk to Deir al-Bahri

From the tombs of Seti I and Ramses I you can continue south-east and hike over the hills to Deir al-Bahri (or vice versa of course). The walk takes about 45 minutes through an amazing lunar-type landscape.

From the top, there are various views of the Temple of Hatshepsut in the amphitheatre setting of Deir al-Bahri below and excellent views across the plain towards the Nile.

In summer you should start this hike as early as possible, partly to catch the changing colours of the barren hills as the sun rises, but also because it gets mighty hot there later in the day. If you tire on the ascent there are donkeys available to carry you to the top!

If you plan to visit the sites, however, you will need tickets, which can only be obtained when the ticket offices open. There's also a much longer trail from the Valley of the Kings to the Valley of the Queens via Deir al-Medina.

Alternatively, if you're just hankering for a view, you can scramble up the hill from the Valley of the Kings to the viewpoint overlooking Deir al-Bahri (a climb of about 15 minutes or, as one traveller put it, '...less if salespeople are in pursuit') then return back to the valley.

Deir al-Bahri (Temple of Hatshepsut)

Rising out of the desert plain, in a series of terraces, the Mortuary Temple of Queen Hatshepsut merges with the sheer limestone cliffs of the eastern face of the Theban Mountain as if nature herself had built this extraordinary monument.

The partly rock-cut, partly freestanding structure is one of the finest monuments of ancient Egypt, although its original appearance, surrounded by myrrh trees, garden beds and approached by a grand sphinx-lined causeway, must have been even more spectacular.

Discovered in the mid-19th century by Auguste Mariette, it wasn't completely excavated till 1896 and is still being restored. Unfortunately, over the centuries the temple has been vandalised. Akhenaten removed all references to Amun, before taking his court off to Tell al-Amarna; and the early Christians who took it over as a monastery (hence the name Deir al-Bahri, or Monastery of the North), also defaced the pagan reliefs.

The worst damage, however, was done out of pure spite by Hatshepsut's successor, Tuthmosis III, who developed a fairly strong hatred of the queen in the 20 years he waited to ascend the throne of Egypt. Within weeks of her death he had obliterated or covered her

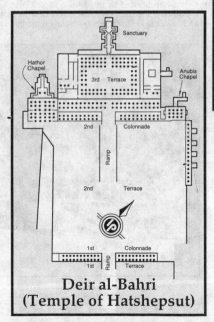

Deir al-Bahri (Temple of Hatshepsut)

LUXOR

name or image wherever he found it. Even in her own mortuary temple, where he and Hatshepsut were always represented together, as co-rulers, he hacked out her likeness, leaving only his own.

The temple's 37 metre wide causeway leads on to the three huge terraced courts, each approached by ramps and separated by colonnades. The renowned delicate relief work of the lower terrace features scenes of birds being caught in nets, and the transport from the Aswan quarries to Thebes of a pair of obelisks commissioned by Hatshepsut.

The central court contains the best pre-

Hatshepsut

Following the death of Tuthmosis I in 1495 BC, a great controversy arose, between the late Pharaoh's daughter Hatshepsut and his grandson Tuthmosis III, over the rights of succession. The struggle for ultimate control was eventually won by the formidable Hatshepsut. As well as being only the third queen ever to rule ancient Egypt, Hatshepsut declared herself Pharaoh – which made her the first woman ever to reign as king.

Hatshepsut had married her father's son, her own half-brother Tuthmosis II, and she held many titles, including 'Pharaoh's wife and daughter' and of course 'queen'. She failed, however, to bear any sons, so it was Tuthmosis III, the son of one of the king's concubines, who became heir presumptive.

Following the death of her sibling/husband, Hatshepsut became regent to the new Pharaoh Tuthmosis III, but such was her power that the young boy had little chance of ruling in his own right.

Despite the backing of the army, Tuthmosis was never a match for his aunt/stepmother/co-ruler, and Hatshepsut eventually overshadowed him enough to proclaim herself absolute monarch as both queen and king. She still, however, had to win over the priesthood and this she managed by claiming divine birth (as most Pharaohs did), by assuming the dress and manner of a man and by having herself depicted wearing the traditional Pharaonic beard in reliefs.

Hatshepsut ruled for 20 years, and for Egypt it was a time of peace and internal growth. It is not known how she died – whether it was of natural causes or something more sinister. Almost as soon as Tuthmosis III finally took his place on the throne he led his country into war with Palestine. ■

Partly rock-cut, partly freestanding, Deir al-Bahri (the Temple of Hatshepsut) built by 'King' Hatshepsut and dedicated to her father, Tuthmosis I, is considered a work of architectural genius.

served reliefs. There Queen Hatshepsut recorded her divine birth and told the story of an expedition to the Land of Punt to collect myrrh trees needed for the precious myrrh incense used in temple ceremonies. There are also two chapels at either end of the colonnade. At the northern end the colourful reliefs in the Chapel of Anubis show the co-rulers, Hatshepsut and Tuthmosis III (with the queen's image again disfigured by her nephew), in the presence of Anubis, the god of embalming, Ra-Harakhty, the falcon-headed sun-god, and his wife Hathor. In the Chapel of Hathor you can see (if you have a torch) an untouched figure of Hatshepsut worshipping the cow-headed goddess.

Although the third terrace is out of bounds while a Polish-Egyptian team works on its restoration, you can see the pink granite doorway leading into the Sanctuary of Amun, which is hewn out of the cliff.

In 1876 the greatest mummy find in history was made just north of the Temple of Hatshepsut. After many antiquities began showing up in the marketplace the authorities realised someone had found, and was plundering, an unknown tomb. After investigations they discovered a massive shaft at the foot of the cliffs containing the mummies of 40 Pharaohs, queens and nobles.

It seems that the New Kingdom priests realised that the bodies of their kings would never be safe from violation in their own tombs, no matter what precautions were taken against grave robbers, so they moved them to this communal grave. The mummies included those of Amenophis I, Tuthmosis II and III, Seti I and Ramses I and III.

You can hike over the mountain to the Valley of the Kings from here (see Valley of the Kings section). It should take about 45 minutes, but be prepared for a strenuous trek on hot days. Take plenty of water. The view of Deir al-Bahri from above is spectacular. Note that climbing over the mountain is officially frowned upon.

Assasif Tombs

This group of tombs, situated between Deir al-Bahri and the Tombs of the Nobles, dates

back to the 18th dynasty and is under excavation by archaeologists. Of the many tombs here, several may be open to the public including Kheru-Ef, Anch-Hor and Pabasa. Like the Tombs of the Nobles further south, the artwork here concentrates on everyday life, with scenes depicting such things as fishing and hunting, viticulture and bee keeping, rather than more noble themes.

Tombs of the Nobles

The tombs in this area are some of the best, though least visited, attractions on the west bank. Nestled in the foothills and among the houses of the old village of Qurna (Sheikh Abd al-Qurna) are at least 400 tombs that date from the 6th dynasty to the Graeco-Roman period. The tomb chapels in the area date from the 18th to the 20th dynasties.

Of the hundred or so tombs that have something of interest, 13 are highly recommended. They have been numbered and divided into five groups, each requiring a separate ticket (for details see the earlier ticket information section). It's possible some of the tombs may be closed; the ticket office people will know.

There are no signs indicating the tombs, so you'll need to ask the locals or look out for the modern stone walls built around the entrances to some of the tombs. If you're on your own, most of the guardians here will give you a guided tour whether you want it or not.

Tombs of Khonsu, Userhet & Benia (Nos 31, 51 & 343) This trio of small tombs is one of two groups that has recently opened to the public. Khonsu was an adviser to Tuthmosis III. Scenes inside his colourful tomb include a boat carrying the dead to Abydos and, before the final shrine, Khonsu offering incense to Osiris and Anubis. The ceiling is adorned with birds and eggs.

The Tomb of Benia, just behind that of Khonsu, is more colourful than its neighbour. Benia was a child of the royal nursery during the 18th dynasty. At the end of the tomb, there's a *ka* statue (substitute body) of Benia flanked by his parents. Statues such as

A Roman impression of a painted relief found in the Tomb of Nakht that portrays Nakht hunting and fishing in the marshes of the Nile Valley, accompanied by his family.

these are typical of tombs in this area, but the faces of this trio have been destroyed.

The Tomb of Userhet (not to be confused with Userhet No 56) was closed at the time of writing.

Tombs of Menna & Nakht (Nos 52 & 69) Situated close to Khonsu, Userhet and Benia, the wall paintings in the tombs of Menna and Nakht (which may be closed to the public) emphasise rural life in the 18th dynasty. Menna was an estate inspector and Nakht was an astronomer of Amun. Their finely detailed tombs show scenes of farming, hunting, fishing and feasting. The Tomb of Nakht has a small museum area in its first chamber. Although this tomb is so small that only a handful of visitors can squeeze in, the walls have some of the best known examples of Egyptian tomb paintings, including familiar scenes like the three musicians that grace a million T-shirts, posters, postcards and papyrus paintings.

Tombs of Ramose, Userhet & Khaemhet (Nos 55, 56 & 57) The Tomb Chapel of Ramose, who was a governor of Thebes during the reigns of Amenophis III and Akhenaten, is a fascinating tomb. It's one of the few monuments dating from that time, when the cult power of the priests of Karnak was usurped by the new monotheistic worship of Aten. Exquisite paintings and low reliefs grace the walls, showing scenes from the reigns of both kings and the transition between the two forms of religious worship. The reliefs of Ramose, his wife and other relatives are extraordinarily lifelike and clearly show their affectionate relationships.

LUXOR

Inner Hall

Burial Chambers under Inner Hall

Hall

Court

Tomb of Ramose

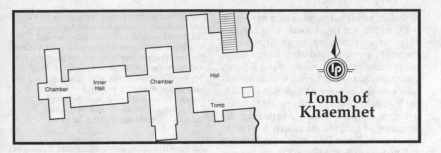

Tomb of Khaemhet

The tomb was never actually finished because Ramose deserted Thebes to follow the rebel Pharaoh Akhenaten to his new city at Tell al-Amarna.

The Tomb of Userhet, who was one of Amenophis II's royal scribes, is right next to Ramose's. Its most distinctive features are the wall paintings depicting daily life in ancient Egypt. Userhet is shown presenting gifts to Amenophis II; there's a barber busy

This delicate artwork found in the Tomb of Ramose reflects a transition in style towards a more naturalistic representation that evolved under Akhenaten.

cutting hair on another wall; and there are men making wine, and hunting gazelles from a chariot.

The third tomb belongs to Khaemhet, who was Amenophis III's royal inspector of the granaries and court scribe. Scenes on the walls show Khaemhet offering sacrifices; the Pharaoh depicted as a sphinx; the funeral ritual of Osiris; and images of daily country life and official business.

Tombs of Sennofer & Rekhmire (Nos 96 & 100) Prince Sennofer of Thebes worked for Amenophis II as a supervisor of the gardens of the Temple of Amun. The most interesting parts of his tomb are deep underground in the main chamber. The ceiling there is covered with clear paintings of grapes and vines, while most of the scenes on the surrounding walls and columns depict Sennofer with his sister. The guard usually has a kerosene lamp, but bring a torch just in case.

The Tomb of Rekhmire, a governor during the reigns of Tuthmosis III and Amenophis II, is one of the best preserved in the area. In the first chamber, to the extreme left, are scenes of Rekhmire receiving gifts from foreign lands. The panther and giraffe are gifts from Nubia; the elephant, horses and chariot come from Syria; and the expensive vases come from Crete and the Aegean Islands.

Tombs of Nefer-Ronpet, Dhutmosi & Nefer-Sekheru (Nos 178, 295 & 296) This trio of tombs is not far from Khonsu, Userhet

LUXOR

& Benia, and is surrounded by a new stone wall, so it's not too difficult to recognise. Like the neighbouring group, it is newly opened to the public and the paintings inside are protected by glass panels. Nefer-Ronpet, commonly known as Kenro, was an official scribe of the treasury. Discovered in 1915, the highlight of this brightly painted tomb is a scene showing Kenro overseeing the weighing of gold at the treasury. Next door, the Tomb of Nefer-Sekheru is equally rich in yellow hues and, like Kenro's tomb, features a ceiling painted with a riot of geometric designs. From this long tomb, a small passage leads into the Tomb of Dhutmosi which is in poor condition.

The Ramesseum

The Ramesseum is yet another monument raised by Ramses II to the ultimate glory of himself. The massive temple was built to impress his priests, his subjects, his successors and of course the gods, so that he, the great warrior king, could live forever. Many of his other works were rather crudely constructed but in this, his mortuary temple, he demanded perfection in the workmanship so that it would stand as an eternal testimony to his greatness.

Sadly, the Ramesseum, which was dedicated to Amun, is mostly in ruins. This fact no doubt disappoints Ramses II more than it does modern-day visitors to the site. He dared all those who questioned his greatness in future centuries to gaze on the magnificence of his monuments in order to understand his power over life and death. How the mighty fall!

The scattered remains of the colossal statue of the king and the ruins of his temple prompted the English poet Shelley to cut this presumptuous Pharaoh down to size by using the undeniable fact of Ramses' mortality to ridicule his aspirations to immortality.

In the early 19th century Shelley wrote 'Ozymandias':

I met a traveller from an antique land
Who said: Two vast and trunkless legs of stone
Stand in the desert...Near them, on the sand,

Half sunk, a shattered visage lies, whose frown,
And wrinkled lip, and sneer of cold command,
Tell that its sculptor well those passions read
Which yet survive, stamped on these lifeless things,
The hand that mocked them, and the heart that fed:
And on the pedestal these words appear:
'My name is Ozymandias, king of kings:
Look on my works, ye Mighty, and despair!'
Nothing beside remains. Round the decay
Of that colossal wreck, boundless and bare
The lone and level sands stretch far away.

Although a little more elaborate than other temples, the fairly orthodox layout of the Ramesseum, with its two courts, hypostyle hall, sanctuary, accompanying chambers and storerooms, is uncommon in that the usual rectangular floor plan was altered to incorporate an older, smaller temple – that of Ramses' mother, Tuya, which is off to one side.

The **first** and **second pylons** measure more than 60m across and feature reliefs of Ramses' military exploits. Through them are the ruins of the huge **First Court**, including the double colonnade that fronted the royal palace.

Near the western stairs is part of the **Colossus of Ramses II**, the Ozymandias of Shelley's poem, lying somewhat forlornly on the ground. When it stood, it was 17.5m tall. The head of another granite statue of Ramses, one of a pair, lies in the **Second Court**. Twenty-nine of the original 48 columns of the **Great Hypostyle Hall** are still standing. In the smaller hall behind it, the roof, which features astronomical hieroglyphs, is still in place.

There is a rest house/restaurant next to the temple which is called, not surprisingly, the *Ramesseum Rest House*. It is owned by Sayed Hussain, whose father was a friend of Howard Carter. The rest house is a great place to relax and have a cool drink or something to eat, though at E£3 for a coffee or Coke, it's not cheap. Beers, however, are reasonably priced. You can leave your bike here while exploring the surroundings.

Deir al-Medina

One km off the road to the Valley of the

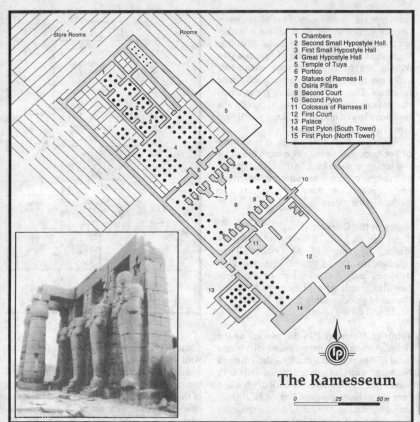

1 Chambers
2 Second Small Hypostyle Hall
3 First Small Hypostyle Hall
4 Great Hypostyle Hall
5 Temple of Tuya
6 Portico
7 Statues of Ramses II
8 Osiris Pillars
9 Second Court
10 Second Pylon
11 Colossus of Ramses II
12 First Court
13 Palace
14 First Pylon (South Tower)
15 First Pylon (North Tower)

The Ramesseum

0   25   50 m

LUXOR

Queens and up a short, steep paved road is Deir al-Medina (Monastery of the Town). It is named after a temple here that was occupied by early Christian monks. Near the temple is a ruined settlement known as the Workmen's Village, for it was here that many of the workers and artists who created the royal tombs lived and were buried.

Temple The small Ptolemaic temple of Deir al-Medina is just north of the Workmen's Village, along a rocky track. The temple was built between 221 and 116 BC by Philopator, Philometor and Euergetes II. It was dedi-

cated to Hathor, the goddess of pleasure and love, and to Maat, the goddess of truth and the personification of cosmic order.

Workmen's Village Archaeologists have been excavating this settlement for most of this century and at least 70 houses have been uncovered. Three tombs in the village's terraced necropolis are now open to the public.

The beautifully adorned **Tomb of Sennedjem (No 1)** belonged to a 19th dynasty servant who worked in the so-called Place of Truth – the Valley of the Kings. The tomb has only one chamber, but the wall paintings are magnificent. One of the most famous scenes shows a cat killing a snake; it's above the doorway to the burial chamber. Right next to it is the **Tomb of Aneuka (No 359)**, a 20th dynasty tomb that contains two small chambers and some equally exquisite paintings. Due to the popularity and small size of both these tombs, only 10 people at a time are allowed inside; it's likely you'll find yourself in a sizeable queue.

While you wait, take a look at the **Tomb of Peshedu** just up the slope from the other two tombs. It dates back to the 19th dynasty. Most of the other tombs in the area belonged to the servants, overseers and labourers who worked in the valley.

Valley of the Queens

There are at least 75 tombs in Biban al-Harim, the Valley of the Queens. They belonged to queens of the 19th and 20th dynasties and other members of the royal families, including princesses and the Ramessid princes. Only tombs Nos 43, 44, 52, 55 and 66 are open.

Tomb of Nefertari (No 66) Hailed as the finest tomb in the Theban necropolis – and in all of Egypt for that matter – the Tomb of Nefertari was first opened to the public in November 1995 and has been solidly booked ever since. Entry costs E£200, or E£100 for students, making it by far the most expensive monument in the whole country.

Nefertari was one of the five wives of Ramses II, the New Kingdom Pharaoh known for his colossal monuments of self-celebration. However, the tomb he created for his favourite queen is a shrine to her beauty and, without doubt, an exquisite labour of love. Every inch of the walls in the tomb's three chambers and connecting corridors is adorned with colourful scenes of Nefertari in the company of the gods and with associated text from the *Book of the Dead* nearby. Invariably 'the most beautiful of them', as Nefertari was known, is depicted wearing a divinely transparent white gown and a golden headdress featuring two long feathers extending from the back of a

Tomb of Nefertari

vulture. The ceiling of the tomb is festooned with golden stars.

Some of the best scenes in the tomb are in the side room off to your right at the bottom of the first set of stairs. In one panel here, the queen is shown with her arms outstretched next to the mummiform body of Osiris. At the top of the second staircase, which leads to the burial chamber, is another of the tomb's highlights – Nefertari offering two bowls of milk to Hathor, the goddess of pleasure and love.

Like most of the tombs in the Valley of the Kings, this one had been plundered by the time it was discovered by archaeologists. Only a few fragments of the queen's pink granite sarcophagus remained.

In order to preserve the tomb's exquisite artwork, ticket sales are limited to 150 each day. A maximum of 10 people are allowed in at any one time, and photography is strictly prohibited. You may be required to wear shoe covers and nose masks. The tomb is open daily from 8.30 am to noon and 1 to 4 pm in winter, and 7.30 am to noon and 1 to 5 pm in summer.

Tomb of Amunherkhepshep (No 55) Until the opening of Nefertari's tomb, the Tomb of Amunherkhepshep was the valley's showpiece. Now thoroughly overshadowed, it is still a worthwhile option for those who can't afford, or who miss out on, tickets to Nefertari.

Amun was the son of Ramses III and was nine years old when he died. The scenes on the tomb walls show his father grooming him to be Pharaoh by introducing him to various gods. Amun's mother was pregnant at the time of his death and in her grief she aborted the child and entombed it with Amun. A five month old mummified foetus was discovered there. Wall paintings also show Ramses leading his son to Anubis, the jackal-headed god of the dead, who then takes the young Prince Amun down to the entrance of the Passage of the Dead.

Medinat Habu
The temple complex of Medinat Habu was one of the first places in Thebes to be closely associated with the local god Amun. Hatshepsut, Tuthmosis III and Ramses III constructed the main buildings of the complex – which is second only to the Temples of Karnak in size and complexity – but Medinat Habu was added to and altered by a succession of rulers right through to the Ptolemies. At its height there were temples, workshops, storage rooms, administrative buildings and accommodation for the priests and officials. It was the centre of the economic life of Thebes for several centuries and was still inhabited as late as the 9th century AD.

The original **Temple of Amun**, built by Hatshepsut and Tuthmosis III, was later completely overshadowed by the enormous **Mortuary Temple of Ramses III**, which is the dominant feature of Medinat Habu.

Ramses III was inspired in the construction of his shrine by the Ramesseum of his father. His own temple and the smaller one

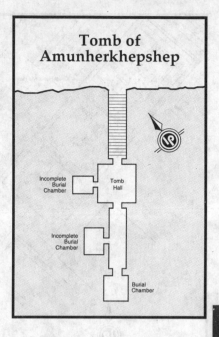

dedicated to Amun are both enclosed within the massive outer walls of the complex.

Also just inside, to the left of the gate, are the **Tomb Chapels of the Divine Adorers**, which were built for the principal priestesses of Amun. Outside the eastern gate, one of only two entrances, was a landing quay for a canal which once connected Medinat Habu with the Nile.

The well-preserved **first pylon** marks the front of the temple proper. Ramses III is portrayed in its reliefs as the victor in several wars. To the left of the **First Court** are the remains of the Pharaoh's palace; the three rooms at the rear were for the royal harem. There is a window between the First Court and the palace known as the **Window of Appearances**, which allowed the king to show himself to his subjects.

The reliefs of the **second pylon** feature Ramses III presenting prisoners of war to Amun and his vulture-goddess wife, Mut. Colonnades and reliefs surround the **Second**

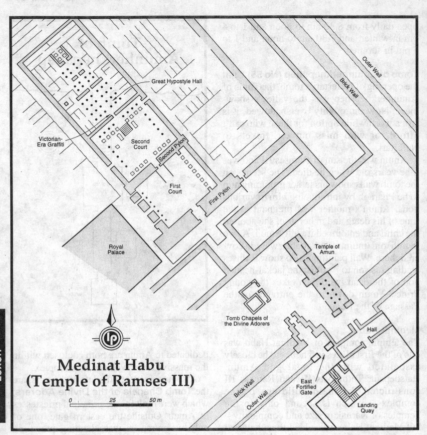

**Medinat Habu
(Temple of Ramses III)**

0   25   50 m

(map labels:) Great Hypostyle Hall · Victorian-Era Graffiti · Second Court · Second Pylon · First Court · First Pylon · Royal Palace · Tomb Chapels of the Divine Adorers · Temple of Amun · Hall · East Fortified Gate · Landing Quay · Brick Wall · Outer Wall

Court, depicting various religious ceremonies.

Medinat Habu is off the road on your right as you return from the Valley of the Queens. After you have finished wandering around the complex treat yourself to a cold Stella beer at the Habou Hotel opposite.

Colossi of Memnon

The massive pair of statues known as the Colossi of Memnon are all that remain of the temple of the hedonistic Amenophis III. Rising about 18m from the plain, the enthroned, faceless statues of Amenophis have kept a lonely vigil on the changing landscape around them, surviving the rising floodwaters of the Nile which gradually, through annual inundation, destroyed the temple buildings behind them.

Over the centuries, the crumbling rubble of what was believed to have been one of the most splendid of the Theban temples was ploughed into the fertile soil. A stele, now in the Egyptian Museum, describes the temple as being built from 'white sandstone, with gold throughout, a floor covered with silver, and doors covered with electrum'.

The colossi were among the great tourist attractions of Egypt during Graeco-Roman times because the Greeks believed they were actually statues of the legendary Memnon, a king of Ethiopia and son of the dawn-goddess Eos, who was slain by Achilles during the Trojan War.

It was the northern statue that attracted most of the attention because at sunrise it would emit a haunting, musical sound that the Greeks believed was the voice of Memnon greeting his mother each day. Eos in turn would weep tears of dew for the untimely death of her beautiful son.

Actually, the phenomenon of the famous vocal statue was probably produced by the combined effect of a simple change in temperature and the fact that the upper part of the colossus was severely damaged by an earthquake in about 30 BC. As the heat of the morning sun baked the dew-soaked stone, sand particles would break off and resonate inside the cracks in the structure. Certainly, after a well-meaning Roman governor repaired the statue some time in the 2nd century AD, Memnon's plaintive greeting to his mother was heard no more.

The colossi are just off the road, west of New Qurna – you won't miss them.

Amenophis III had quite a reputation for high and fast living. The ruins of his amazing palace are about one km south of Medinat Habu. The royal residence featured a lake, a banquet hall, private state rooms for Amenophis, a separate residence for his beloved queen Tiy, and quarters for court officials, servants, guests and of course the Pharaoh's extensive harem, which numbered over 300. Although the palace is badly ruined, the remains are quite substantial.

ACTIVITIES
Felucca Rides
The best thing to do in Luxor in the late afternoon or early evening is to relax aboard a felucca. Local feluccas cruise the river throughout the day and cost around E£3 per person per hour or E£10 per boat per hour. In the low season, you may be able to do even better.

An enjoyable outing is the trip upriver to Banana Island. The tiny isle, dotted with palms, is about five km from Luxor and the trip takes two to three hours. Plan it in such a way that you're on your way back in time to watch a brilliant Nile sunset from the boat.

Ballooning
Two companies – Hod Hod Suleiman and Ballons Over Egypt – offer early-morning or late-afternoon balloon flights over Luxor. It costs about US$200 for the flight plus breakfast or a sundowner buffet afterwards. If you have that kind of money for an hour of hot air, contact the top-end hotels or any of the travel agencies displaying signs.

Donkey & Camel Rides
Almost all the smaller hotels organise donkey treks around the west bank. These trips, which start at about 7 am (sometimes 5 am) and finish about lunch time, cost a minimum of about E£20 per person, and may be more expensive. The hotels push these trips pretty hard, and although a lot of travellers have reported being pleased with them, you can probably organise it more cheaply yourself with some hard bargaining when you cross the river.

If you just want to loll about on the back of a camel and take in the sights of the Nile, go see the boys at the local ferry dock on the west bank. Their asking price is E£25 for an hour. Some of the bigger hotels offer camel trips, which include visits to nearby villages for a cup of tea.

Swimming
Many of the bigger hotels and even some at the budget end have swimming pools. The Windsor, Emilio and Arabesque hotels and the Rezeiky Camp all charge E£7 for the use of their pools. The St Joseph and Flobater hotels, next to each other on the way out to the Sheraton, ask E£10 per person, as do the Shady and Wena Luxor hotels. The Novotel and Club Med charge E£15. The Winter Palace, Isis and Mercure ETAP hotels all charge E£20, however, in winter, when the Winter Palace is fully booked, only guests

can use the pool. The Green Palace Restaurant, near the YMCA camp, charges E£15 to use its small pool, or E£35 including lunch.

ORGANISED TOURS

Misr Travel (☎ 380951), Thomas Cook and other travel agencies around the Winter Palace will organise half and full-day tours to the west bank in air-conditioned buses. In summer this might be worth considering, as there are hefty reductions. Otherwise, it's generally an expensive option at around E£85/120 for a half/full-day trip.

The Novotel organises full-day cruises once or twice weekly to Dendara or Esna for E£150 including lunch, guide and admission.

SPECIAL EVENTS

Luxor's premier tourist event is the **Opet Festival**, a modern-day recreation of the ancient festival in which images of the local deities – Amun, Mut and Khon – were paraded from the Karnak Temple by boat upriver to Luxor Temple. Traditionally held during the inundation season, it's now celebrated on 4 November – the day that the tomb of Tutankhamun was discovered – in order to bring it into line with Luxor's main tourist season. Check with the tourist office for the time of the parade, and whether there's any folkloric dancing on afterwards.

The town's biggest traditional festival is the Moulid of Abou el-Haggag. Held in honour of Luxor's patron sheikh, it takes place around the Mosque of Abou el-Haggag, the town's oldest mosque, overlooking Luxor Temple. It's a five day event and starts two weeks before the beginning of Ramadan; the climax is a procession of boats on the last day.

Now in its 10th year, the **International Rowing Festival**, is a colourful three day event to watch out for in mid-December.

PLACES TO STAY

Perhaps more than at any tourist destination in Egypt, the cost of accommodation in Luxor fluctuates seasonally. There is no hard-and-fast rule on how much rates might increase in winter, or drop in summer. Some hotels halve their charges in the low season,

others barely alter them at all. Where only one rate is given, it is the low-season rate.

Due to the slump in tourism, many places have not raised their prices much in recent years, although this could change.

Places to Stay – bottom end

Luxor is full of 'bottom end' places to stay, though a few of them have had a tough time staying afloat during the last couple of years. Most of them are concentrated on or around the main streets south-west of the railway station, and some – especially the newer ones – offer a higher standard for your money than you get in much of the rest of the country.

Many hotels boast both roof gardens and washing machines. Roof gardens vary from rooftop restaurants to concrete platforms with chunks of cement and swirls of twisted iron all over the place. This is sometimes the breakfast area. Most hotels offer breakfast – which almost universally means bread, (butter), jam, cheese and maybe an egg, and a cup of tea or coffee. Unless stated otherwise, the prices below include breakfast.

Another common feature is the notice board. The quality of these varies considerably – some have a lot of useful information, others are more of a token effort.

Try to avoid the squawking hotel touts who pounce on travellers as they get off the train (and take a 25 to 40% cut, which goes on to the traveller's hotel bill).

Warning Female travellers should exercise extreme caution when looking for a place to stay in Luxor. Several have reported being sexually assaulted after being given spiked drinks by hotel staff.

Camping The *YMCA* (☎ 372425) camping ground, on Sharia al-Karnak, costs E£3 per night, including the use of its 20 showers. This place was once popular with overland travel groups, but it has lost business to the more expensive Rezeiky Camp, further up the road towards the temple.

The *Rezeiky Camp* (☎ 381334; fax 381400) charges E£10 per person to pitch a tent, for which you get access to the dinky swimming pool and showers. A bed in the small mud bungalows costs an exorbitant E£15. The camp also has large, clean, air-conditioned rooms for E£30/50 but, again, you're paying for the privilege of having the pool on your doorstep. There's a large garden with a restaurant and bar (E£6 for a beer).

Hostels The *Youth Hostel* (☎ 372139) is in a street just off Sharia al-Karnak. Rooms are clean and have at least three beds, but the showers tend to get swampy and stinky, so wear thongs (flip-flops). With a membership card the charge is E£6.10; E£7.10 without. Breakfast is E£2 extra. It is a little out of the hustle and bustle but close to the service-taxi station.

Hotels – South of Sharia al-Mahatta The first hotel you'll see as you leave the railway station is the *New Karnak Hotel* on the left side of the square. This hotel was once a favourite among travellers – more for its convenient location than anything else – but at the time of writing it was closed for renovations.

One often overlooked, and just to the south of the New Karnak, is the *Anglo Hotel* (☎ 381679). It costs E£10/15 for a single/double room with breakfast and shared bathroom. It's clean and the management is friendly. A double with private bath is E£20.

Sharia Abdel al-Moneim al-Adasi (also known as Manches St) leads away from the railway station to Sharia Mohammed Farid and then on to Sharia Television. Around these two streets teems a growing family of little budget pensions and hotels. You'll see the signs to some as you reach Sharia Mohammed Farid, which is about three minutes walk from the railway station.

The *Oasis Hotel* (☎ 381699) on Sharia Mohammed Farid has spacious double rooms and more poky singles. Quite a few travellers stay here, and their reports have invariably been good (though the breakfast is skimpy). Some rooms have their own bath but all rooms have fans and comfortable beds. The bathrooms are clean, and there's

plenty of hot water. Singles/doubles cost E£6.50/13, or E£8/16 with air-con.

Two streets past the Oasis then down a dead-end alley off to the right is the *Grand Hotel* (☎ 374186) – it's signposted. Newly renovated and, for the time being at any rate, very clean, it has a small rooftop terrace with great views, and decent shared bathrooms with hot water. Double rooms with fans and a bit of furniture go for E£5. The owner, a local schoolteacher, is friendly, despite what you may think after reading the sign at reception: 'I always kill people for money but because you are my friend I killed you for nothing.' Don't take it to heart – the rooms are in fact excellent value and there's a washing machine, and bikes for hire for E£4 per day.

The *New Nour* backs on to the Grand Hotel but is accessed via an alley leading off from Sharia Abdel al-Moneim. It's basic but clean; there is hot water, a roof terrace and the rooms have fans. It has had good reports from a few travellers however at E£6/12/15 for singles/doubles/triples, plus E£2 for breakfast, it's overpriced.

Heading towards the Nile on Sharia Mohammed Farid is the *Akhnaton Hotel* (☎ 373979), which looks fancier on the outside than most other hotels and pensions around here, but has quite modest, cramped rooms. The bathrooms could be cleaner and the rooms lighter, but carpet in the hallways and rooms, overhead fans and hot water somewhat compensate for the negatives. Singles without/with bath cost E£8/10; doubles are E£13/15.

Back on Sharia Abdel al-Moneim, if you head down another block you'll arrive at the intersection with Sharia Ahmed Orabi. The next main street running more or less parallel to it is Sharia Television. Between and around these two streets hotels abound, most of them budget places.

The *Salah ad-Din* and *Mubarak* hotels are fairly crummy and, with all the other alternatives around, can be avoided.

If you turn left into Sharia Ahmed Orabi and then right into the second dusty laneway, you'll find the *Atlas Hotel* (☎ 373514). At

E£6 a person (plus E£2 for breakfast) for a room with bath, this is not a bad place and with 40 rooms it's rarely full.

Continue down this lane, turn right and take the next two lefts, and you'll find one of the better deals in Luxor – providing you can bargain well. The relatively new *Fontana Hotel* (☎ 380663) is popular with backpackers. The owner asks E£10/15 for a room with shared facilities, or E£20 for a double with air-con and private bathroom. However he has been known to come down to E£5 for rooms with shared baths, as well as to raise his prices for the unwary – so sharpen your haggling skills. In general, the rooms are clean but those with air-con (and no window) tend to be musty. The eight new rooms on the top floor share just one bathroom, so it can be a bit of a scramble in the morning. There's a kitchen (of sorts), rooftop terrace and washing machine for guests to use.

The nearby *Princess Pension* (☎ 373997) charges E£5 per person for a room with private bath. If you don't mind a saggy bed, it's definitely good value considering you get breakfast and the use of a washing machine. Some people have reported being unhappy with the trips (eg donkey treks) organised from here.

In a deadend lane running off Sharia Television is the *Everest Hotel* (☎ 370017). The renovated rooms are OK and come with air-con or fan and attached bathrooms (even toilet paper is provided!), but at E£15/20 the rooms are possibly a tad overpriced.

If none of these appeal and you find your way out of the rabbit warren, there are more on the west side of Sharia Television. The main disadvantage is that you are getting further away from the transport and the centre of town here.

The closest is the 2nd-floor *Pension Roma* in a lane opposite the old garage on Sharia Television. Run by a friendly Egyptian guy and his English wife, it's small, homey and OK value at E£5 for a poky double with shared facilities, though some of the beds are a bit saggy.

A block further south is the *Titi Hotel* (☎ 376094) which asks E£10 a person. The prices go up in winter and are subject to bargaining in summer. The bathrooms are outside, but clean.

Keep going down this street; west of Pension Roma is the *Moon Valley Hotel* (☎ 377510) on your right. This place is relatively new and charges E£10 per person. The rooms are modern and comfortable, and come with air-con or fan plus private shower and toilet.

Another street down is the *Happy Land* (☎ 371828) run by Mr Ibrahim. The cheapest rooms are E£5 a person, including breakfast, which is served on the unfinished 3rd floor. A good single with private bath costs E£10. It's about a 10 to 15 minute walk from the railway station. Alternatively, take a minibus from the railway station to one stop south of the Novotel on the Corniche – get off when you see the Hamees Gallery over on your left. The hotel is in the lane to the left of the gallery.

Hotels – North of Sharia al-Mahatta The *Hotel El Salam* (☎ 372517), in a lane just off Sharia al-Mahatta, is a deservedly popular haunt for the impecunious. At E£5/10, the prices are reasonable and include use of a washing machine. The rooms have fans. If you have a double with bath, the charge is E£15. Perhaps its most appealing feature is the pleasant, shaded rooftop terrace.

The *Saint Mina Hotel* (☎ 386568) is a very good deal if you've got a little extra to pay. The 20 room hotel is relatively new, and although the rooms are small, they are modern and clean with air-con or fans. A single with bath is E£30, but singles/doubles without bath go for E£20/35. It's as good a place as some of the middle-range joints asking double or more.

Just north of the railway station, virtually on the train tracks, is the *Negem el-Din Pension*. This place has hot water, awful mattresses and wonderful views of the neighbour's chicken coop – all for an outrageous E£15. Breakfast is not available.

Down in a side street by the souqs near Luxor Temple is the deteriorating *Nefertiti Hotel*. It asks E£10/20 for singles/doubles in rooms with uncomfortable beds, no fans and a noisy location.

Sharia Youssef Hassan is another hotel street. The first along here (as you come from the railway station) is *El-Shazly Hotel* (☎ 731264). It has had a facelift in recent times and now sports some colourful murals. Unfortunately, the beds are still saggy and the air-con noisy. Rooms with bath cost E£10/14.

The *Sphinx Hotel* (☎ 372830) has singles/doubles for E£10/20 which may or may not include breakfast depending on how well you can haggle. The rooms have clean, private baths and the staff are friendly.

The *Nobles Hotel* (☎ 372823) is not quite as good, but is not a terrible deal either, at E£12/20 with a fan. Breakfast is not included. If you want air-con, a double costs E£30.

Across the road, the *Venus* (☎ 382625) has 25 reasonable rooms with bath. Singles/doubles cost E£10/20 and the hotel has a restaurant and bar. This is not a bad choice at all. The food is good too and there's a 6th floor terrace where you can down a cold Stella for E£6.

Almost opposite the Venus is the *Pyramids Hotel* (☎ 373243). A bed here costs E£15/17 without bath, or E£27/35 with. Breakfast and taxes are not included. The location is good, there's hot water and the rooms have air-con, however, it's a bit overpriced unless you can bargain the price down (which many travellers have successfully done).

Hotels – West Bank On the west bank there is only a handful of bottom-end places to stay. The *Memnon Hotel* is across the road from the Colossi of Memnon and is basically a pit. Wild camels would not drag most right-minded people to stay here. And they want E£10/20!

Opposite the Medinat Habu temple complex is the *Habou Hotel* (sometimes spelt 'Habu'). It has dark, dingy and rather overpriced rooms (compared with what is available in Luxor). Singles/doubles cost E£10/20 in summer, and a bit more in winter.

You're really paying for the great location overlooking Medinat Habu. It's a pleasant spot to have a beer (E£6).

Even more expensive is the *Maratonga Restaurant* just across the road. It's not really geared for overnight visitors, having just two rooms which are rented out to the occasional passer-by. The asking price is a ridiculous E£20 per person.

The rooms at the nearby *Queen's Hotel* (☎ 384835) are slightly better than those at the Habou Hotel, but the view is not the best. However, the roof restaurant has a good panorama.

The *Mersam Hotel* (☎ 382403), also known as the *Ali Abd el-Rasul Hotel* or the *Sheik Ali Hotel*, is set back from the road, opposite the antiquities office. Rooms in the main building are somewhat better than the primitive mud-wall rooms in an adjacent building. Singles/doubles with an 'English' breakfast cost E£25/30, though prices double in winter. The tranquil shady garden out the back has views over the fields and cold drinks are served (no beer). This hotel was once home to Sheikh Ali Abdul Rasul, a cantankerous old guy with a bone-cracking handshake and an aggressive sense of hospitality that kept you riveted to your seat, whether you liked it or not. Sheikh Ali actually helped discover the Tomb of Seti I and if you've read Richard Critchfield's book *Shahatt*, then you'll know about this guy already. His son has now taken over the hotel.

The *Abdul Kasem Hotel* (☎ 310319) is near the Temple of Seti I on Sharia Wadi al-Melouk. It has singles/doubles for E£20/30 and is one of the best lower budget places on the west bank. There's a great view from the roof. The owners, the Kasem family, also have an alabaster factory attached to the hotel and rent bicycles for E£5 a day.

The *Wadi el-Melouk Hotel* (☎ 382798), on the east side of Al-Fadlya canal, is a little run-down and overpriced. Rooms have balconies but no fans, and cost E£18/30. Bargaining with the old man who runs it might be possible.

Places to Stay – middle

Many mid-range places have dropped their prices substantially in the last few years following the decline in tourism. If visitors start returning, prices will no doubt increase again.

East Bank About three km north of the town centre, opposite the Hilton, is the new five storey *Karnak Hotel* (☎ 374155). If you want to be out of the bustle of Luxor, this is a great place to be. It has a garden plus a clean pool and has received rave reviews from some travellers. Prices in winter go down to about E£40/50, including taxes, however in summer you'll be looking at four times this price. Breakfast is E£15 extra.

Heading back into town, the *Pola Hotel* (☎ 380551; fax 380552), just off Sharia al-Karnak opposite the Rezeiky Camp, has wonderful views from the roof, plus a pool, bar and restaurant. Pleasant rooms go for E£170/237.

The *Windsor Hotel* (☎ 375547; fax 373447) is in a small alley just off Sharia Nefertiti. It's a good 120 room hotel, although some of the rooms are a little shoddy and others are decidedly gloomy and dark. Most are fully carpeted and have wallpaper, modern tiled bathrooms, TV and air-con. It's popular with European tour groups and singles/doubles cost E£60/80. This place's particular boast, aside from pretty good rooms and the rooftop bar, is the pool complex, which comes with a jacuzzi, sauna and solarium.

Just across the way is the *Merryland Hotel* (☎ 371746). Its 32 rooms are more modest than those of the Windsor, but with TV, phone, air-con, bath and balcony, E£40/60 for singles/doubles is very reasonable. It too offers a bar on the roof.

The *Philippe Hotel* (☎ 373604; fax 380050) is on Sharia Nefertiti, between the Corniche and Sharia al-Karnak. It's an upper middle range hotel with clean, carpeted rooms. All the rooms have powerful air-con, TV, mini-fridge and bathrooms with bathtubs, and there are some rooms with balconies. There's a pleasant roof garden with a small bar and pool. Including breakfast a single/double costs E£50/70, however, the rates jump up significantly in winter. Reservations are recommended.

Next door to the Philippe is the sombre *Nile Hotel* (☎ 382859; fax 382859), which has 50 double rooms of varying quality. Most of them have balconies, powerful air-con and bathrooms with bathtubs, and all have TV and phone. Singles/doubles cost about E£45/55 in summer and E£60/70 in winter, altogether a much better deal than next door.

The *Emilio Hotel* (☎ 373570; fax 370000) at the northern end of Sharia Youssef Hassan is a very good upper middle range hotel. It has 48 rooms, all with bathrooms (hot water can be sporadic), air-con, TV, mini-fridge and a hotel video channel; some rooms have Nile views. The astroturf roof terrace has plenty of shade, reclining chairs and a popular pool. Singles/doubles cost E£100/135, including taxes and breakfast. Reservations are essential here in winter, because it is often taken over by travel groups.

The *Mina Palace Hotel* (☎ 372074) is on the Corniche north of Luxor Temple. It is popular with German groups and has singles/doubles with air-con and private bathrooms for E£65/88. Ask for a corner room with two balconies – one looking towards Luxor Temple and the other over the Nile. Beers are available in the somewhat noisy street front terrace.

The two star *St Catherine Hotel* (☎ & fax 372684), 2 Sharia Youssef Hassan, is sometimes spelled 'Catreen' or 'Cathrine'. It has little to recommend it except the price. It's opposite a mosque, the staff are generally unfriendly and some of the rooms are small. It has halved its prices in recent years – a double room for two costs E£30; for one person E£20. There is a rooftop bar.

On Sharia al-Karnak, about a block north of Sharia al-Mahatta, you'll see the *Horus Hotel* (☎ 372165; fax 373447). Rooms are clean and comfortable, with air-con and relatively new bathrooms. The asking price is E£35/45 which is not a bad deal, and the hotel is nicely placed near the souqs and Luxor Temple. A few of the rooms face a mosque, which could mean waking up with the early morning call to prayer.

The *Arabesque Hotel* (☎ 371299; fax 372193) on Sharia Mohammed Farid, not far from the GPO, has modern, air-con rooms with very small beds for E£130/160. The roof garden has good views over Luxor Temple and the Nile, and there's a pool, but the rooms suffer a little from street noise. It's OK in summer when the rates are reduced by 15% but is otherwise way overpriced.

Down on Sharia Television, there are two middle-range places offering comfortable rooms with all the necessary mod cons. When business is slow, both are prepared to discuss discounts. The *Shady Hotel* (☎ 381262; fax 374859) is the larger and more expensive of the two. It charges E£100/128 for rooms on the street side, E£10 extra for the quieter pool side. Taxes are extra. Doubles drop to about E£84 in winter. Across the street, the much cheaper *Santa Maria Hotel* (☎ 380430) offers singles/doubles for E£50/70.

A couple of relatively new three star hotels are situated past the Club Med on Sharia Khaled Ibn el-Walid. The *St Joseph Hotel* (☎ 381707; fax 381727) costs about E£94/120 for a single/double with TV, air-con, phone and bath. There is also a pool and bar. Next door, the rather oddly named *Flobater Hotel* (☎ 374223; fax 370618) is similarly priced. It has a token pool and a pleasant roof garden.

Further along Sharia Khaled Ibn el-Walid opposite the Isis Hotel is the spanking new and very kitsch *Gaddis Hotel* (☎ 382838; fax 382837). Rooms start at E£170/223, and it has three restaurants, a bar and pool.

West Bank *Pharaohs Hotel* (☎ 310702) is the only middle-range place to stay on the west bank. It's near the antiquities office and has 14 rooms, most with air-con or strong overhead fans, wallpaper and tiled floors. Three of the rooms have private bathrooms. There's a small restaurant and bright flower garden in front. The restaurant is popular with a few tour groups and is especially renowned for its sun-baked bread.

Single/double rooms with fan cost E£30/40, or E£60/70 with air-con.

Places to Stay – top end

Despite the tourist slump in recent years, top-end hotels are continuing to mushroom in Luxor. At the time of writing, Marriott and Sonesta hotels were under construction along Sharia Khaled Ibn el-Walid, Luxor's premier resort strip, and the Edrestut Hotel, near the centre of town, was all but finished.

The hotels in this price range start at about US$50 for a single and generally have all the usual attributes of the big international hotels. Where not otherwise specified, the rates do not include breakfast or taxes of up to 26%. Some of the top-end options include (listed alphabetically):

Club Med Belladona Resort (☎ 384000; fax 380879) on Sharia Khaled Ibn el-Walid is a four star resort charging US$63/85 for singles/doubles including taxes and breakfast. Half and full board are available.

Hilton Hotel (☎ 374933; fax 376571) is one km north of Karnak Temple and has rooms ranging from US$65/85 to US$140/168. Buses are on hand to shuttle guests into the centre of town.

Isis Hotel (☎ 372750; fax 372923) on Sharia Khaled Ibn el-Walid has a lush garden setting with manicured hedges and two pools. Singles/doubles at this five star hotel range from US$64/73 to US$170/350.

Luxor Wena Hotel (☎ 380018; fax 380017) is a dilapidated four star place on Sharia al-Karnak near Luxor Temple. Rooms go for US$48/60 in winter, or US$30/35 in summer. There's a swimming pool and a variety of restaurants.

Mercure ETAP Hotel (☎ 580944; fax 384912) is a four star place on the Corniche with two categories of rooms. Those overlooking the Nile cost US$85/113 in winter (including breakfast and taxes) while rooms facing the garden are US$74/94. In summer, prices are reduced by 10 to 15%.

Mövenpick Hotel Jolie Ville (☎ 374855; fax 374936) is on Crocodile Island, four km south of town. It's a five star Swiss-managed place with a swimming pool, tennis courts and sailboats. There are 320 modern, well-appointed rooms set out in bungalow style amidst tropical gardens. Singles/doubles range from US$80/100 to US$160/205. The hotel motorboat shuttles guests to and from the centre of town.

LUXOR

Winter Palace & New Winter Palace (☎ 380422; fax 374087) stand side by side on the Corniche, but the new section is not nearly as interesting and romantic as the old, which was built to attract the aristocracy of Europe. Rooms in the old section cost US$130/140 with a Nile/garden view, while deluxe rooms start at US$150/160. In the new wing, prices start at US$75/85. There's a swimming pool, table-tennis tables and a tennis court.

PLACES TO EAT

Near the railway station, the *New Karnak Restaurant* and the *Salt & Bread Cafeteria* next door serve cheap meals for about E£4. The latter offers many entrees, including kebab, pigeon and chicken; the former has rather small portions of chicken or other meat. Its menu includes six kinds of omelette – one wonders how different they can be. Don't get your hopes up about the ice cream – it's just a teeny bucket of vanilla whipped out of the freezer.

The *Mensa Restaurant*, on Sharia al-Mahatta, has basic food that's slightly overpriced. Dishes include chicken, pigeon stuffed with rice, sandwiches, and chicken with French fries and mixed vegetables. You can have almost a full meal for about E£8.50.

Across the road, *Abu Ashraf* is a no-frills, open-air diner with bowls of soup for E£1, a plate of rice, potatoes and salad for E£3, and a variety of cheap meat dishes. The music here is loud.

There are a few juice stands at the Luxor Temple end of Sharia al-Mahatta. This street also has a number of good sandwich stands and other cheap eats possibilities.

A little more expensive is *El Hossein* on Sharia al-Karnak. Most main dishes cost E£7 to E£10 before service is added on. The fish in a tomato and basil sauce is very tasty, and the pizzas are acceptable, if smallish, for E£7. The soups are sometimes good, sometimes watery. Next door is the *Amoun Restaurant* which serves oriental kebab, chicken, fish and various rice and vegetable dishes for similar prices. These are two of the town's most popular eating houses for tourists.

Up the road from the El Hossein is the small and busy local hang-out, the *Abu Negem el-Din*, where half a chicken will cost you E£5, and a plate of makarone E£2. Try the tagen, a kind of stew, with or without meat, in a clay casserole pot.

There is a huddle of small eateries and cafes in the lanes around Sharia al-Mahatta between the Amoun and the police station, where the food is cheap and the atmosphere busy. One of them, the tiny *El Dar Restaurant*, is up on the 1st floor of a building in a laneway off Sharia al-Karnak. The portions tend to be a bit small, but you can get a beer here for E£6.

At the northern end of Sharia Television is another cluster of small diners, a juice stand and a very good, no-name, open-air *fiteer restaurant*. It's sandwiched between a teahouse and the El Dabaawy Restaurant – just look for the flashing 'Pizza' sign.

A little further along Sharia Television is *Sayyida Zeinab*, one of Luxor's best kushari joints. The prices are written in English, so there's no attempt to rip tourists off and the portions are large.

Further up Sharia Television, near the Titi Hotel, is the *Mish Mish* restaurant. Try the Mish Mish salad – a mixed platter with hoummos and cold meats, enough to constitute a light meal, for E£6. A version of pizza is also available.

The *Marhaba Restaurant* is an Oriental-style dining room on the roof of the Tourist Bazaar building on Sharia al-Karnak, near Luxor Temple. This place commands great views of the river, but the food is rather expensive (main courses average E£20) and no better than you'll find in a lot of other places.

The air-conditioned *Restaurant Abu Hager* on Sharia Abdel al-Moneim al-Adasi serves shish kebab and kofta for E£6.50 and soups for E£1.50.

A new and very trendy travellers' hang-out is the *Kings Head Pub* on Sharia Khaled Ibn el-Walid near the passport office. This place is England through and through – from the dart board and billiard table to the western music and counter meals. The only difference with pubs in England is that it's open 24 hours. It's a laid-back place to spend an afternoon catching up on foreign newspapers or tucking into toasted sandwiches and chips. On the whole, the food prices are a little inflated but then you're paying for the imported atmosphere. After all, where else in Luxor can you get a E£15 roast beef and yorkshire pudding lunch-time special on a Sunday? Beers are reasonably priced and there's a huge array of cocktails (E£12 each) and spirits.

Most of the middle-range hotels have their own restaurants, generally rooftop jobs of varying quality.

The Mercure ETAP Hotel has the *Champollion* snack bar, where you can get pizza, cakes and beer. The *Winter Palace* serves reasonable buffet meals throughout the day should you feel like splashing out. Breakfast costs E£35, lunch costs E£52 and dinner is E£60, not including taxes.

If, after all this, you're hunting around for sweets or ice cream, you could pop into *Twinky's*, around the corner from the New Karnak Hotel.

Those in search of a few takeaway beers can try the hole-in-the-wall shop opposite the Pharmacie La Confiance on Sharia al-Mahatta.

ENTERTAINMENT

A night out in Luxor is limited to the shows, discos and bars at the big hotels or, for those missing the mother country, the new *Kings Head Pub* (see the previous Places to Eat section for details).

The *Mövenpick Hotel Jolie Ville* presents a quite extravagant floor show. You are dressed up in a galabiyya, taken for a felucca ride at sunset, introduced to 'peasants', and then fed and entertained in a tent by the Nile.

The *Isis* and *Winter Palace* hotels have folkloric and belly dance performances as well as discos. In the low season, the belly dancing is usually held only three or four nights a week, so check with the hotels beforehand.

At the *Mercure ETAP Hotel*, non-guests must pay a minimum charge of E£20 to get into the Sabil disco. This covers you for the belly dancer at 11.30 pm too.

THINGS TO BUY

Pretty much the whole range of standard Egyptian souvenirs can be bought in Luxor, although the variety is not nearly as great as in Cairo. One exception is alabaster. You will notice a plethora of alabaster shops on the west bank. The alabaster is mined about 80 km north-west of the Valley of the Kings, and some of the handmade cups, vases and other articles make sturdy and original souvenirs. If you're interested in buying alabaster objects, this is probably the place to do it.

There's also one of Dr Ragab's papyrus museums on the Corniche, if you are interested in buying reasonably well made, but expensive, papyrus.

GETTING THERE & AWAY
Air

The EgyptAir (☎ 380580) office is on the Corniche, next to American Express. Egypt-Air flies daily between Cairo, Luxor and Aswan. A one-way ticket to Luxor from Cairo costs E£361. There are frequent daily departures. There are also daily flights from Luxor to Aswan (E£163) and two flights per week to Sharm el-Sheikh (E£412). In the high season, there are several flights a day to Abu Simbel (E£718 return) via Aswan and one flight a week to Hurghada (E£163).

EgyptAir also has direct flights from Luxor to Europe. Flights to London (E£2863) and Zürich (E£2475) operate year-round; to Frankfurt (E£2644) and Paris (E£2644) they operate in winter only.

Bus

The bus station is behind Luxor Temple on Sharia al-Karnak (the garage on Sharia Television is not an official pick-up point).

From Cairo, the Upper Egypt Bus Company has luxury services departing from Midan Abdel Minnim Riyadh and cheaper buses from Midan Ahmed Hilmi (see the Getting There & Away section in the Cairo chapter for more details).

From Luxor, there are two departures to Cairo: at 4.30 pm (E£34) and 7 pm (E£40). The trip takes 10 to 11 hours.

Buses leave for Aswan (E£5.50 to E£6.50,

four to five hours) about every hour from 6 am to 3.30 pm. These include through buses from Qena and Hurghada, so there may not always be seats. The same buses go to Esna (E£2) and Edfu (E£4).

To Hurghada, the first bus is at about 6.30 am and costs E£8 (five hours). The 2.30 pm may be full as it comes up from Aswan; it costs E£16. The 4 pm bus costs E£11; the 7 pm bus is the deluxe service, costing E£31. The 2.30 and 4 pm buses to Hurghada usually go on to Suez; tickets for Suez cost E£24 or E£31, depending on whether or not the bus has air-con.

There are 10 buses to Qena from 6 am to 7 pm that cost from E£1.50 to E£2.

Train

The railway station at Luxor has a post office, card phones, left-luggage, telex and telegraph facilities and an often-closed tourist information office.

For tickets, the 3rd-class window is on your left when facing the tracks; other tickets are sold at windows on the right.

If you want a sleeper to Cairo, you can only travel on the wagon-lit train. Berths have to be booked two or three days in advance (the ticket window (☎ 581577) for these is open only between 9 am and 2 pm and 5.30 and 8.30 pm) and cost E£451/293 one way in 1st/2nd class (from Aswan or from Luxor!). The train leaves Luxor at about 8.30 pm and reaches Cairo at 6 am. First and 2nd-class sitting fares to Cairo are E£48/28 for the 11.30 am train, and E£51/31 for the slightly faster 11.30 pm service. Student discounts are available on both these services but not on the wagon-lit train.

First and 2nd-class tickets to Aswan (four hours) cost E£20/12 on the 6.30 am train, and E£22/14 on the 4.30 pm service. Heading in the other direction, fares to Al-Minya are E£34/21 on the 11.30 am train, and E£3 more for the 11.30 pm train.

Service Taxi

The service-taxi station is on a street off Sharia al-Karnak, a couple of blocks inland from the Luxor Museum.

Regular destinations include Aswan (E£7.50, 3½ hours), Esna (E£2, 45 minutes), Edfu (E£5, two hours), Kom Ombo (E£6.50, 2½ hours), Qus (E£1.25), Qena (E£2) and Nag Hammadi (E£4).

The drivers are always ready to bargain for special trips down the Nile to Aswan, stopping at the sights on the way – reckon on about E£100 for the car.

Those planning a trip from Luxor to the New Valley oasis of Kharga via the new direct road will probably be able to hire a 'special' taxi (maximum seven people) for about E£300.

Cruise Ship

About 200 flotels and cruise boats ply the Nile all year round, and many of them just do the Luxor to Aswan stretch (or the other way around) as part of a package deal.

In times of plenty, you'd need hundreds of pounds (and in the case of some boats, dollars) for one of these trips and bookings well in advance – sometimes months – are required. However, the dearth of tourists in recent years has seen prices for these cruises plummet. At the time of writing, Thomas Cook and some of the other travel agencies around the old Winter Palace were offering cruises for between US$40 and US$75 per person per night in a double cabin, including meals and sightseeing. On top of that, only a day's notice was required. Prices are on the rise again, but if you're interested in this type of splurge it could still be worthwhile asking around.

Felucca

You can get a felucca from here to Aswan – there's no shortage of captains and touts offering you rides, but the trip upstream can be hopelessly slow. If the wind dies, with the current against you, you can end up going backwards. For this very reason you may have trouble finding other people to join you. The great majority of travellers do the trip the other way, downstream from Aswan towards Luxor – for more details see Getting There & Away in the Aswan section of the Nile Valley – Esna to Abu Simbel chapter.

GETTING AROUND

The Airport

Luxor airport is seven km east of town and the official price for a taxi is E£10.

Motorcycle

A few hotels have started renting out motorcycles for about E£40 to E£60 a day. If you are interested, hunt around a bit and check the condition of the bikes carefully.

Bicycle

Luxor is bursting with bicycle rental shops, and you'll get as many offers to rent one as to buy papyrus. Depending on the quality of the bike, how good business is and the determination of your bargaining, they can cost from E£4 to E£10 a day. You are often asked to leave your passport or student identification card.

Many hotels, including top-end abodes like the Isis and Gaddis as well as many of the cheap joints, will also rent bicycles and it's possible to rent children's bicycles if you inquire. Bicycles can also be rented on the west bank, near the local ferry landing, but the choice of bicycle is better in the town itself and the prices over here are sometimes inflated.

Hantour

For about E£4 per hour you can get around town by horse and carriage. Rates are, of course, subject to haggling, squabbling and, sometimes, screaming!

Felucca

There are, of course, a multitude of feluccas to take you on short trips or day tours from Luxor. They leave from various points all along the river. See the Felucca Rides section earlier in this chapter for more information.

Ferry

A total of five ferries cross the Nile from east to west, two for tourists and three for locals, at least one of which also carries vehicles. The distinction used to be important, as the local ferry used to cost everyone only 10 pt. That's all changed, as the Luxor town

Sharing a ferry ride with the locals across the Nile, from Luxor to the west bank, is all part of the Egyptian experience.

LUXOR

council has decided that foreigners can pay E£2.50 regardless of which ferry they get on. Large signs by the local ferry dock make this quite clear. If you are taking a bicycle across, or want a service taxi or to bargain on donkeys, bicycles and the like, you'll have to get one of the local ferries. It is a little galling to have to pay 25 times what the locals are paying though. The local boats leave from in front of the Mina Palace Hotel, Luxor Temple and the Winter Palace (car ferry). A shuttle sometimes runs from the local ferry dock to the antiquities office (25 pt), where you can buy student and full-price tickets for the west bank sights.

The tourist boats drop you off at the tourist landing, where you can buy full-price tickets to the sights. It's about one km north of the local ferry dock. If you don't have a bicycle and want to haggle for a taxi on the other side, you may as well get this boat. The tourist ferry landings are in front of the ETAP and the Winter Palace hotels. You must pay for the return trip in advance.

AROUND LUXOR

An increasingly popular side trip from Luxor is a visit to the supposedly typical village of **Armant**, on the west bank slightly south of Thebes. It is one of the biggest villages between Luxor and Esna. To get there, take the local ferry from the east side and a service taxi from the landing. Alternatively, you could take an Esna-bound service taxi along the east bank and get out (Armant lies on both banks). Most Luxorians can't understand why tourists would want to go. Why Armant? No particular reason, except perhaps its relative proximity to Luxor and the fact that it's a little bigger than other villages in the area.

The Nile Valley – Esna to Abu Simbel

Following the death of Alexander the Great, his huge empire was divided between his Macedonian generals. For 300 years the Greek-speaking Ptolemies ruled Egypt in the guise of Pharaohs, respecting the traditions and religion of the Egyptians and setting an example to the Romans who succeeded them.

Their centre of power tied them to Alexandria and the coast but they also pushed their way south, extending Graeco-Roman power into Nubia through their politically sensible policy of assimilation rather than subjugation.

In Upper Egypt they raised temples in honour of the local gods, building them in grand Pharaonic style to appease the priesthood and earn the trust of the people. Somehow, though, these archaic imitations lost something in the translation; in many ways they were stilted, unimaginative edifices lacking the artistic brilliance that marked the truly Egyptian constructions they copied.

In southern Upper Egypt, south of Luxor, the major Graeco-Roman works were a series of riverside temples at Esna, Edfu, Kom Ombo and Philae, admirable as much for their location as their actual artistic or architectural merit.

Beyond Edfu the ribbon of cultivation on the east bank gives way to the Eastern (Arabian) Desert. At Silsileh, 145 km south of Luxor, the Nile passes through a gorge, once thought to mark a cataract. In this area, there are Early Dynastic and New Kingdom ruins, including Elephantine and Abu Simbel; there's also the city of Aswan, the great High Dam and Lake Nasser, which mark the end of Egypt proper, for beyond them lie the forbidding, infertile desert lands of Nubia and the border with Sudan.

ESNA

The Graeco-Roman Temple of Khnum is the main attraction of Esna, a small, busy farming town on the west bank of the Nile, 54 km south of Luxor. The post office and a branch of the Bank of Alexandria are on the street that leads to the Nile from the canal. On Saturday, there's an animal market here too. The tourist police are in the bazaar near the temple.

Temple of Khnum
All that actually remains of the temple is the

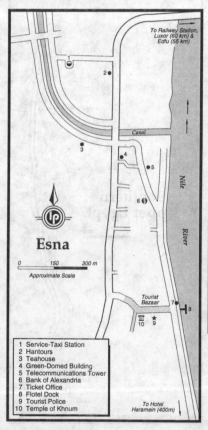

Esna

0	150	300 m

Approximate Scale

1 Service-Taxi Station
2 Hantours
3 Teahouse
4 Green-Domed Building
5 Telecommunications Tower
6 Bank of Alexandria
7 Ticket Office
8 Flotel Dock
9 Tourist Police
10 Temple of Khnum

To Railway Station, Luxor (60 km) & Edfu (55 km)

Canal

Nile

River

Tourist Bazaar

To Hotel Haramein (400m)

311

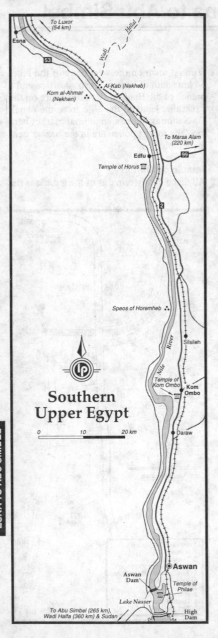

Southern Upper Egypt

To Luxor (54 km)

Esna

Wadi

Hellal

53

Al-Kab (Nekheb)

Kom al-Ahmar (Nekhen)

To Marsa Alam (220 km)

Edfu

Temple of Horus

99

2

Speos of Horemheb

Nile River

Silsileh

Temple of Kom Ombo

Kom Ombo

Daraw

0   10   20 km

Aswan

Aswan Dam

Temple of Philae

Lake Nasser

To Abu Simbel (265 km), Wadi Halfa (360 km) & Sudan

High Dam

well-preserved Great Hypostyle Hall built during the reign of the Roman Emperor Claudius. This sits, rather incongruously, in its huge excavation pit among the houses and narrow alleyways in the middle of town.

Dedicated to Khnum, the ram-headed creator-god who fashioned humankind on his potter's wheel using Nile clay, the temple was begun by Ptolemy VI and built over the ruins of earlier temples. The hall, as it stands today, was built later; it was excavated from the silt that had accumulated through centuries of annual Nile floods and is about nine metres below the modern street level.

The intact roof of the hall is supported by 24 columns decorated with a series of texts recording hymns to Khnum and relating the annual sacred festivals of Esna. The texts also refer to other temples in the area and one from the same era has in fact been excavated at Kom Mer, 12 km south of Esna. The west wall of the Roman-built hall is also the only remaining part of the original Ptolemaic temple and features reliefs of Ptolemy VI, Philometor and Euergetes II.

The ticket booth is on the river itself, about one km upriver from the main bridge across the Nile. You buy your ticket and follow the tourist bazaar through to the temple. The original quay, once connected to the temple by a processional way, is still in use. The temple is open from 6 am to 5.30 pm (an hour longer in summer) and admission costs E£8, or E£4 for students.

Places to Stay & Eat

About 800m south of the temple and then 100m inland, via another covered bazaar, is Esna's only accommodation option, the basic *Hotel Haramein*. Esna is an easy day trip from Luxor, so there is little need to stay here anyway.

There are a few of the usual food stands around for a cheap snack, although you should watch out for the odd rip-off in the small tourist bazaar. Basic food and drinks are available at the service-taxi station, and there's a teahouse that's good for some small talk with the locals along the canal.

Getting There & Away

Trains are a pain, because the station is on the east bank of the Nile. There are frequent buses and service taxis from Luxor. The bus costs E£2, but stops a lot on the way; in Esna, the bus stop is just by the little canal bridge.

The service taxi (sometimes in the form of a microbus) is the quickest alternative, taking 45 minutes from Luxor and costing E£2. The service-taxi station is next to the canal, however, arrivals are generally dropped on the main thoroughfare into town along which *hantour* drivers congregate in the hope of picking up a fare. They ask E£2 each way for the five to 10 minute ride to the temple.

Should you prefer to walk from the service-taxi drop-off point, head straight (south) down the main road, cross a small bridge over the canal and continue for 50m until you come to a small green-domed building on your left. Turn left after the building and follow this lane for 100m until you get to a telecommunications tower. Turn right and simply continue along this road, which eventually meets up with the Nile, for about 800m. You'll see the ticket office next to the mooring for the Nile cruisers. The temple is 50m inland, up through the tourist bazaar.

Sometimes you can arrange for felucca trips from Aswan to finish here.

AL-KAB & KOM AL-AHMAR

Between Esna and Edfu are the scattered ruins of two settlements dating from Pre-dynastic to Late Dynastic times. The earliest remains in the area, now known as Al-Kab, on the east bank of the Nile, are about 6000 years old. Much of what is visible, however, dates from later than that, when the ancient settlement of Nekheb was capital of the nome. The local deity was the vulture-goddess Nekhbet. Not only was she regarded as the greatest of the Upper Egyptian goddesses but, along with Edjo, the cobra-goddess of Lower Egypt, she was also guardian of the Pharaohs and one of the deities associated with royal and divine births.

The town of Nekheb was enclosed by massive mud-brick walls and still contains the remains of a Roman temple, a sacred lake and cemeteries, and the ruins of the main Temple of Nekhbet with its several pylons, hypostyle hall and *mammisi* (birth house). The temple was probably begun before 2700 BC but was enlarged considerably by numerous Pharaohs of the 18th to 30th dynasties including Tuthmosis III, Amenophis II and the Ramessids.

A few km east of the town enclosure are three desert temples. At the entrance to Wadi Hellal is the rock-hewn Ptolemaic Sanctuary of Sheshmetet. To the south-east of that is a chapel built during the reign of Ramses II, restored under the Ptolemies and dedicated to a number of deities. About 3.5 km from Nekheb is the Temple of Hathor and Nekhbet; it was built by Tuthmosis IV and Amenophis III. North of Nekheb are a number of rock-cut tombs with fine reliefs.

On the opposite side of the river, the remains of the ancient town of Nekhen, which predated Nekheb as capital of the nome, stretch for about three km along the edge of the desert. Now known as Kom al-Ahmar (the Red Mound), the area features the ruins of Predynastic settlements and cemeteries and in the nearby wadis there are several Middle and New Kingdom tombs. The local god was Nekheny, a falcon with two long plumes on his head, who was later associated with Horus.

Al-Kab and Kom al-Ahmar are 26 km south of Esna, and north of Edfu.

EDFU

The largest and most completely preserved Pharaonic, albeit Greek-built, temple in Egypt is the extraordinary Temple of Horus at Edfu. One of the last great Egyptian attempts at monument building on a grand scale, the structure dominates this west bank riverside town, 53 km south of Esna. The town and temple were established on a rise above the broad river valley around them, and so escaped the annual Nile inundation that contributed to the ruination of so many

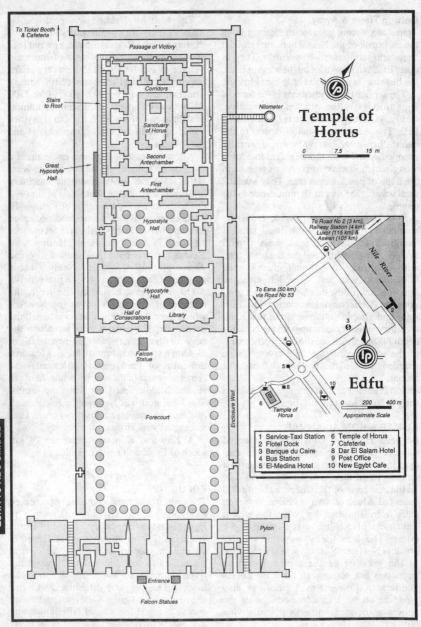

Temple of Horus

0 — 7.5 — 15 m

To Ticket Booth & Cafeteria

Passage of Victory

Corridors

Stairs to Roof

Sanctuary of Horus

Nilometer

Second Antechamber

Great Hypostyle Hall

First Antechamber

Hypostyle Hall

Hypostyle Hall

Hall of Consecrations

Library

Falcon Statue

Forecourt

Enclosure Wall

Pylon

Entrance

Falcon Statues

Edfu

0 — 200 — 400 m
Approximate Scale

To Road No 2 (3 km), Railway Station (4 km), Luxor (115 km) & Aswan (105 km)

Nile River

To Esna (50 km) via Road No 53

1 Service-Taxi Station	6 Temple of Horus
2 Flotel Dock	7 Cafeteria
3 Banque du Caire	8 Dar El Salam Hotel
4 Bus Station	9 Post Office
5 El-Medina Hotel	10 New Egybt Cafe

other buildings of antiquity. Edfu, a sugar and pottery centre, is also a very friendly place.

Just before you get to the temple you cross a square that appears to be the nerve centre of town. Approaching the square, the post office is along the first street off to the left. The bus station is about 100m in along the street to the right. The service-taxi station is at the entrance to town, next to the bridge over the Nile.

Temple of Horus

Construction of this huge complex began under Ptolemy III Euergetes I in 237 BC and was completed nearly 200 years later during the reign of Ptolemy XIII (the father of Cleopatra) in the 1st century BC. In conception and design it follows the traditions of authentic Pharaonic architecture, with the same general plan, scale and ornamentation, right down to the 'Egyptian' attire worn by the Greek kings depicted in the temple's reliefs. Though it is much newer than the temples of Karnak, Luxor and Abydos, its excellent state of preservation fills in a lot of historical gaps because it is, in effect, a 2000

🕊 🕊 🕊 🕊 🕊 🕊 🕊 🕊 🕊 🕊 🕊 🕊 🕊 🕊

Ancient Rites at Edfu

Dedicated to Horus, the falcon-headed son of Osiris, who avenged his father's murder by slaying his uncle Seth, the temple was built on the site where, according to legend, the two gods met in deadly combat. Ancient festivals at Edfu celebrated the divine birth of Horus and the living king (as all Pharaohs were believed to be incarnations of the falcon-god), as well as the victory of Horus over Seth and the yearly conjugal visit of the goddess Hathor.

Another ritual was the annual recoronation of the Pharaoh to symbolise his oneness with Horus. During the proceedings, a live falcon was taken from the sacred aviary, crowned in the central court and placed in an inner chamber, where it 'reigned' in the dark for a year as the living symbol of Horus. As with the image of Hathor at Dendara, an image of Horus was taken each year to the roof of the temple for a rejuvenating sun bath. ■

🕊 🕊 🕊 🕊 🕊 🕊 🕊 🕊 🕊 🕊 🕊 🕊 🕊 🕊

---

year old replica of an architectural style that was already archaic during Ptolemaic times.

Being a copy it lacks artistic spontaneity. Where the Greek influence does penetrate, however, it produces a strangely graceful effect, which is most obvious in the fine line of the columns.

Excavation of the temple from beneath sand, rubble and part of the village of Edfu, which had been built on its roof, was started by Auguste Mariette in the mid-19th century. The entrance to the temple is through a massive 36m-high pylon guarded by two huge and splendid granite falcons and decorated with colossal reliefs of Pharaoh Ptolemy XIII pulling the hair of his enemies while Horus and Hathor look on. Beyond the pylon is a court surrounded on three sides by a colonnade of 32 columns covered in reliefs.

Before you enter the temple proper, through the 12 enormous columns of the first of two hypostyle halls, check out the areas on either side. On your left is the **Hall of Consecrations** where, according to the wall inscriptions, Horus poured sacred water on the king; on your right is the so-called **Library**, which features a list of books and a relief of Seshat, the goddess of writing. On either side of the second hall are doorways leading into the narrow **Passage of Victory**, which runs between the temple and its massive protective enclosure walls.

Once through the magnificent **Great Hypostyle Hall** there are two **antechambers**, the first of which has a staircase of 242 steps leading up to the rooftop and a fantastic view of the Nile and surrounding fields. You may have to pay the guard a bit of baksheesh if you want to go up because the stairs are usually closed.

The second chamber, which is beautifully decorated with a variety of scenes, leads to the **Sanctuary of Horus**, where the live falcon, the god and his wife reigned and received offerings. Around the sanctuary, there are a number of smaller chambers with fine reliefs and, off the Passage of Victory, a staircase leads down and passes under the outer wall of the temple to a Nilometer.

The Temple of Horus is open from 7 am

to 4 pm in winter and 6 am to 6 pm in summer. Admission is E£20, or E£10 for students.

Places to Stay & Eat

The *El-Medina Hotel* (☎ 701326) in the centre of town costs E£10/15 a night for simple rooms without/with bathroom. Though a very basic hotel, several travellers have sung its praises. The manager apparently loves a bit of song and dance, and for a pound or two will sing your favourite Christmas songs!

Another option is the *Dar El Salam Hotel*, further down the road towards the temple. It has similar rooms, but charges E£15 for single occupancy. The hot water is unreliable, but the rooms have fans and are OK. The couple of other hotels dotted around town are best avoided.

Apart from the expensive cafeteria in the temple grounds, there are a few kebab places on the square, as well as the *New Egybt* (sic) cafe opposite the post office which serves watery soup, tasty beans and spinach and roast chicken. At all these eateries you should ask how much prices are first. One fly-blown place charged E£14 for a plate of greasy kebab that was more fat than meat.

Getting There & Away

Trains, buses and service taxis stop frequently in Edfu. However, the railway station is on the east bank of the Nile, about four km from town. Buses travelling between Luxor and Aswan sometimes only stop on this side too – a real pain. Leaving is not so bad, as you can at least *take* a bus from the station in town. The fare is E£4 to Luxor or E£2.50 to Aswan.

Service taxis are again the best option. From Esna, the trip takes about an hour and costs E£2, direct taxis from Luxor (E£5) take about two hours, and from Aswan (E£3.50) they take 1½ hours. They will drop you at the station just over the bridge on the west bank; from here you can get a covered pickup to the temple.

If you've had enough of the Nile, tombs and temples, you can exit east and head

straight for Marsa Alam on the Red Sea. The daily bus servicing this route originates in Aswan and passes Edfu at about 8 to 8.30 am. However, it does not usually stop at the bus station in town. Instead, it pulls up for half an hour at a cafe on the east bank of the river at the start of the desert road. It takes three hours to Marsa Alam and costs E£7. This bus actually goes on to Bir Shalatayn (E£12, eight hours) on the disputed administrative boundary with Sudan, but you need a military permit to travel south of Marsa Alam.

Feluccas will also stop at Edfu on their way north from Aswan. Very patient travellers who prefer to travel against the current can get a felucca heading south.

SILSILEH

At Silsileh, about 42 km south of Edfu, the Nile narrows considerably to pass between steep sandstone cliffs which are cluttered with ancient rock stelae and graffiti. Known in Pharaonic times as Khenu (Place of Rowing), the gorge also marks the change from limestone to sandstone in the bedrock of Egypt. The local Silsileh quarries were worked by thousands of men throughout the New Kingdom and Graeco-Roman periods to provide the sandstone used in temple building.

On the west bank of the river is the Speos of Horemheb, a rock-hewn chapel dedicated to Pharaoh Horemheb and seven deities, including the local god Sobek.

KOM OMBO

The fertile, irrigated sugar cane and corn fields around Kom Ombo, 65 km south of Edfu, support not only the original community of fellahin but also a large population of Nubians displaced from their own lands by the encroaching waters of Lake Nasser. It's a pleasant little place easily accessible en route between Aswan and Luxor but possibly best visited on a day trip from Aswan, which is 40 km to the south.

In ancient times Kom Ombo was strategically important as a trading town on the great caravan route from Nubia, and was the meeting place of the routes from the gold mines of the Eastern Desert and the Red Sea. During the Ptolemaic period it served as the capital of the Ombite nome, and elephants were brought up from Africa to Kom Ombo to train with the armies to defend the region. The main attraction these days, however, is the unique riverside Temple of Kom Ombo, about four km from the centre of town.

Temple of Kom Ombo

The Temple of Kom Ombo or, more precisely, the dual Temple of Sobek and Haroeris, stands on a promontory at a bend in the Nile, where in ancient times sacred crocodiles basked in the sun on the river bank. Although substantially ruined by the changing tides of the river and by later builders who used many of its stones for new buildings, Kom Ombo is, nevertheless, a stunning sight.

It is also unusual in that, architecturally, everything is doubled and perfectly symmetrical along the main axis of the temple. There are twin entrances, twin courts, twin colonnades, twin hypostyle halls, twin sanctuaries and, in keeping with the dual nature of the temple, there was probably a twin priesthood.

The left side of the temple was dedicated to Haroeris, or Horus the Elder, the falcon-headed sky-god; the right half was dedicated to Sobek, the local crocodile-headed god, who was also worshipped in Al-Faiyum.

The Graeco-Roman structure faces the Nile. The entrance pylon, the outer enclosure wall and part of the court, all built by Augustus after 30 BC, have been either mostly destroyed by pilfering stonemasons or eroded by the river. The temple proper was actually begun by Ptolemy VI Philometor in the early 2nd century BC; Ptolemy XIII (also known as Neos Dionysos) built the outer and inner hypostyle halls; and subsequent Ptolemies and Romans contributed to the relief decoration.

South of the main temple is the **Roman Chapel of Hathor**, dedicated to the wife of Horus, which is used to store a collection of mummified crocodiles dug up from a nearby sacred animal cemetery. Four of the collection are on display.

The temple is open from 8 am to 4 pm; admission costs E£20 and half for students.

Places to Stay & Eat

The *Cleopatra Hotel* (☎ 500325) next to the local pick-up station is the best option in town. It's basic but quite adequate at E£9.50/16 for singles/doubles and E£21/22 for triples/quadruples. The rooms have fans and the shared facilities are spotless. There's hot water, and towels are provided; breakfast is not.

The only alternative is the rather grimy *Radwan Hotel* just south of the service-taxi station on the main road. A bed here costs E£3 but the hotel is reluctant to take foreigners.

The *El-Noba Restaurant*, on the main road a little way north of the service-taxi station, is the only sit-down eatery in this part of town. It's cheap and relatively clean, and serves chicken, rice and vegetables. Otherwise, there are the usual ta'amiyya and kebab stands.

Snacks can be had at the two cafeterias situated on the bank of the Nile between the temple and the boat landing. Of the two, the *Cafeteria Venus* has the best atmosphere, serving burgers, kofta and beers in a pleasant garden setting.

Getting There & Away

A service taxi or minibus from Aswan to the town of Kom Ombo takes between 45 minutes and one hour, and costs E£1.50. Trains and buses also frequently stop in the town; trains are slower, and both trains and buses are much less frequent than service taxis.

As you approach Kom Ombo from Aswan, you can ask the driver to drop you off at the road leading to the temple – look for the 'tembel' sign. From here it's about a two km walk or hitch. If you are heading back to Aswan, it shouldn't be hard to get a lift or flag down a passing service taxi or microbus once on the highway.

Otherwise, to get to the temple from Kom

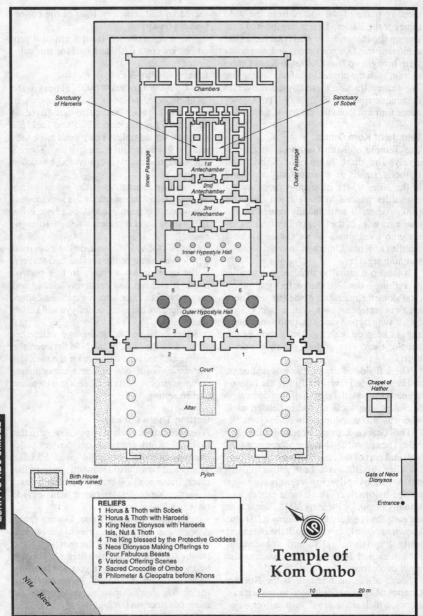

Sanctuary of Haroeris

Sanctuary of Sobek

Chambers

Inner Passage

Outer Passage

1st Antechamber

2nd Antechamber

3rd Antechamber

Inner Hypostyle Hall

7

8   6

Outer Hypostyle Hall

3   4   5

2   1

Court

Altar

Chapel of Hathor

Birth House (mostly ruined)

Pylon

Gate of Neos Dionysos

Entrance ●

RELIEFS
1 Horus & Thoth with Sobek
2 Horus & Thoth with Haroeris
3 King Neos Dionysos with Haroeris Isis, Nut & Thoth
4 The King blessed by the Protective Goddess
5 Neos Dionysos Making Offerings to Four Fabulous Beasts
6 Various Offering Scenes
7 Sacred Crocodile of Ombo
8 Philometer & Cleopatra before Khons

Temple of Kom Ombo

0   10   20 m

Nile River

ESNA TO ABU SIMBEL

Ombo, take a covered pick-up (25 pt) to the boat landing on the Nile about 800m north of the temple, then walk the remainder. Pick-ups to the boat landing leave from opposite the Cleopatra Hotel.

A private taxi between the town and temple should cost about E£7 return. Feluccas travelling between Aswan and Luxor often stop at the temple itself.

Should you want to head to the Red Sea from here, the daily bus from Aswan to Marsa Alam calls in at about 7 am.

DARAW

The main reason to stop in this small village eight km south of Kom Ombo is to see the Tuesday camel market (Souq al-Gamaal). Camels are brought up in caravans from Sudan along the 40 Days Road to just north of Abu Simbel, from where they're trucked to Daraw. Merchants from Cairo come here to buy camels for the camel market at Birqash, about 35 km north-west of the capital. From Birqash, the camels are sold and shipped all over North Africa and the Middle East.

Getting There & Away

The service taxis and minibuses running between Aswan and Kom Ombo stop in Daraw (if passengers indicate they want to get off). The fare is E£1.50 – the same as for the whole stretch.

Aswan

Over the centuries Aswan, Egypt's southern-most city, has been a garrison town and frontier city, the gateway to Africa and the now inundated land of Nubia, a prosperous marketplace at the crossroads of the ancient caravan routes and, more recently, a popular winter resort.

In ancient times the area was known as Sunt; the Ptolemaic town of Syene stood to the south-west of the present city; and the Copts called the place Souan, which means

'trade', from which the Arabic 'Aswan' is derived.

The main town and temple area of Sunt was actually on the southern end of the island called Yebu (meaning both 'elephant' and 'ivory'), which the Greeks later renamed Elephantine Island. A natural fortress, protected by the turbulent river, Aswan was then capital of the first Upper Egyptian nome and a base for military expeditions into Nubia, Sudan and Ethiopia. From those foreign parts, right up into Islamic times, the city was visited by the great caravans of camels and elephants laden with slaves, gold, ivory, spices, cloth and other exotic wares.

Pharaonic and Ptolemaic leaders took their turn through history to guard the southern reaches of Egypt from the customary routes of invasion; their fleets patrolled the river as far as the Second Nile Cataract at Wadi Halfa and their troops penetrated several hundred km into Sudan. Aswan was also, to a certain extent, the Siberia of the Roman Empire, one of those far-flung garrisons where troublesome generals were sent to protect the interests of the emperor while staying out of the Forum.

The modern town of Aswan, which is the perfect place for a break from the rigours of travelling in Egypt, lies on the east bank of the Nile opposite Elephantine Island. The town is at the northern end of the First Nile Cataract, one of six rocky outcrops (the remaining five are all in Sudan) situated between Aswan and Khartoum.

Although its ancient temples and ruins are not as outstanding as others in the country, Aswan does have a few things to offer the traveller, one of which is the town's superb location on the river. The Nile is magically beautiful here as it flows down from the dams and around the giant granite boulders and palm-studded islands that protrude from the cascading rapids of the First Nile Cataract. The Corniche is one of the most attractive of the Nile boulevards.

So, while you can visit Pharaonic, Graeco-Roman, Coptic, Islamic and modern monuments, a good museum, superb botanical gardens, the massive High Dam, Lake

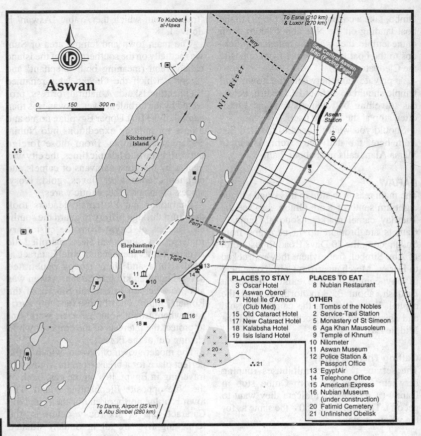

Aswan

0   150   300 m

To Kubbet al-Hawa

To Esna (210 km) & Luxor (270 km)

Ferry

Nile River

See Central Aswan Map (Facing Page)

Aswan Station

Kitchener's Island

Ferry

Elephantine Island

Ferry

To Dams, Airport (25 km) & Abu Simbel (280 km)

PLACES TO STAY	PLACES TO EAT
3 Oscar Hotel	8 Nubian Restaurant
4 Aswan Oberoi	
7 Hôtel Île d'Amoun	**OTHER**
(Club Med)	1 Tombs of the Nobles
15 Old Cataract Hotel	2 Service-Taxi Station
17 New Cataract Hotel	5 Monastery of St Simeon
18 Kalabsha Hotel	6 Aga Khan Mausoleum
19 Isis Island Hotel	9 Temple of Khnum
	10 Nilometer
	11 Aswan Museum
	12 Police Station &
	Passport Office
	13 EgyptAir
	14 Telephone Office
	15 American Express
	16 Nubian Museum
	(under construction)
	20 Fatimid Cemetery
	21 Unfinished Obelisk

Nasser and one of the most fascinating souqs outside Cairo, by far the best thing to do in Aswan is sit by the Nile and watch the feluccas gliding by at sunset.

The best time to visit Aswan is in winter, when the days are warm and dry, with an average temperature of about 26°C. In summer, the temperatures are around 38°C to 45°C and it's too hot to do anything other than just sit by a fan and swat flies or flop into a swimming pool.

Orientation

It's quite easy to find your way around

Aswan because there are only three main avenues and most of the city is along the Nile or parallel to it. The railway station is at the northern end of town, only three blocks east of the river and its boulevard, the Corniche el-Nil.

The street which runs from north to south in front of the station is Sharia as-Souq (also occasionally signposted as Sharia Saad Zaghloul), Aswan's splendid market street, where the souqs overflow with colourful, tempting and aromatic wares and where merchants and traders from all over the region jostle and bargain with each other. Running

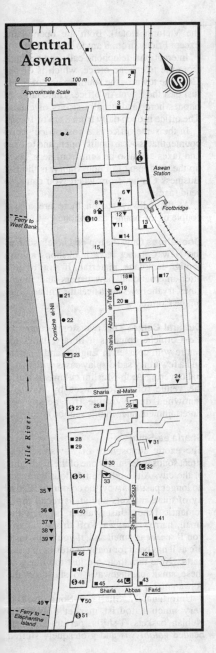

Central Aswan

0   50   100 m
Approximate Scale

Aswan Station

Footbridge

Ferry to West Bank

Corniche el-Nil

Sharia Abtal at-Tahrir

Sharia al-Matar

Nile River

Sharia as-Souq

Sharia Abbas Farid

Ferry to Elephantine Island

PLACES TO STAY
- 1 New Abu Simbel Hotel
- 2 Mena Hotel
- 3 Rosewan & El-Saffa Hotels
- 7 Marwa Hotel
- 9 Youth Hostel
- 13 Noorhan Hotel
- 14 El-Amin Hotel
- 15 Ramses Hotel
- 17 Bob Marley Hotel
- 18 Cleopatra Hotel
- 20 Nubian Oasis Hotel
- 21 Abu Simbel Hotel
- 25 Aswan Palace Hotel
- 26 Happi Hotel
- 28 El-Salam Hotel
- 29 Hathor Hotel
- 30 Victoria Hotel
- 40 Horus Hotel
- 41 Molla Hotel
- 42 Hotel al-Oraby
- 43 Abou Shelib Hotel
- 45 El Amir Hotel
- 46 Memnon Hotel
- 47 Philae Hotel

PLACES TO EAT
- 6 Restaurant Derwash
- 8 El Dar Restaurant
- 11 Esraa (Kofta Place)
- 12 El Nasr Pizza Place
- 16 Medina Restaurant
- 24 El Masry Restaurant
- 31 Al Sayed Nafesa Restaurant
- 35 Saladin Restaurant
- 37 Aswan Moon Restaurant
- 38 Emy Restaurant
- 39 Monalisa Restaurant
- 49 Panorama & El-Shati Restaurants
- 50 Restaurant el-Nil

OTHER
- 4 Governorate Building
- 5 Tourist Office
- 10 Tourist Office & Nile Valley Navigation Office
- 19 Bus Station
- 22 Cultural Centre
- 23 GPO
- 27 Banque Misr
- 32 Mosque
- 33 Post Office (Poste Restante)
- 34 Bank of Alexandria
- 36 Dr Ragab Papyrus Museum
- 44 Mosque
- 48 Banque du Caire
- 51 Thomas Cook

ESNA TO ABU SIMBEL

parallel to it is Sharia Abtal at-Tahrir where you'll find the Youth Hostel and a few hotels. Most of Aswan's government buildings, banks, travel agencies, restaurants and top hotels are on the Corniche, and from there you can see the rock tombs on the west bank, as well as Elephantine Island.

Information

Visa Extensions The passport office is on the Corniche and is open Saturday to Thursday from 8.30 am to 1 pm and 6 to 8 pm.

Tourist Office There are two tourist offices – one (☎ 312811) is next to the railway station and the other (☎ 323297) on a side street, one block in from the Corniche. The staff at both, who are very friendly and helpful, will assist in booking accommodation and can give you official prices for taxis and felucca trips, but lower prices are usually obtainable with some haggling.

Both offices are open Saturday to Thursday from 8.30 am to 2 pm and again from 6 to 8 pm; Friday opening hours are from 10 am to 2 pm, and 6 to 8 pm.

Money The main banks have their branches on the Corniche. Banque Misr and the Banque du Caire will issue cash advances on Visa and MasterCard. The Bank of Alexandria accepts Eurocheques. Banque Misr also has a foreign-exchange booth (open daily from 8 am to 3 pm and from 5 to 8 pm) next to its main building.

The American Express office (☎ 322909) is in the Old Cataract Hotel and is open daily from 8.30 am to 6 pm. If you happen to be heading south, this is the last American Express office where you can cash personal cheques and buy travellers' cheques until you get to Nairobi.

The Aswan branch of Thomas Cook (☎ 304011; fax 306209) is on the Corniche and is open daily from 9 am to 5 pm.

Post & Communications The GPO is also on the Corniche, next to the municipal swimming pool. However, poste restante must be collected from the smaller post office on the corner of Sharia Abtal at-Tahrir and Sharia Salah ad-Din (go around the back, opposite the Victoria Hotel). Both are open daily, except Friday, from 8 am to 2 pm.

International telephone calls can be made from the telephone office, which is on the Corniche towards the southern end of town, just past the EgyptAir office. There are card phones here (and usually stocks of cards). The office is open daily from 8 am to 10 pm.

In the same office is a post office stamp counter that is occasionally open, and telexes and faxes can also be sent from here. Back up the road, next to Photo Sabry, is the BC Business Centre, from where you can also send faxes.

At the railway station there are also a couple of the orange card phones.

Bookshops Only the top-end hotels such as the New Cataract have bookshops selling foreign-language material. If you're just after international newspapers and magazines, try the newsstand near the Philae Hotel on the Corniche.

Cultural Centre This two storey centre on the Corniche contains a library, language centre with courses in English and French, and a few fairly sad display cases with material covering Arab-Muslim culture. It's also the venue for performances by Aswan's renowned dance troupe (for details see Entertainment later in this section).

Sharia as-Souq

The exotic atmosphere of Aswan's backstreet souqs is definitely one of the highlights of the city. Although the fabulous caravans no longer pass this way, the colour and activity of these markets and stalls recall those romantic times. Just wander through the small, narrow alleyways off this street and you'll see, hear, smell and, if you want, taste life as it has been for many centuries in these parts. (Note that there are just too many of these small passageways to show on the Aswan map.)

Unfortunately, Sharia as-Souq itself is very much a tourist market nowadays. Nubian baskets, T-shirts, perfume, spices, beaded *galabiyyas* and grotesquely stuffed crocodiles and desert creatures are all for sale. The traders here tend not to be as persistent as those in Luxor.

Fresh and live produce, such as fruit and vegetables and chickens or pigeons, are traded in the street running between the Aswan Palace and Happi hotels.

Nubian Museum

This museum is planned to be a showcase of Nubian art and architecture, however, at the time of writing, it was still under construction. The tourist office will know if it has opened. It is on the road to the Aswan Dam, due east of the New Cataract Hotel. It's a 10 to 15 minute walk from the EgyptAir office.

Fatimid Cemetery

Opposite the Nubian Museum is a collection of low stone buildings with domed roofs topped by crescents. Some of these early Islamic tombs also feature figures of local holy people, or the more widely revered Sayyida Zeinab, granddaughter of the Prophet.

Unfinished Obelisks

There are two unfinished obelisks in the vicinity of Aswan.

The closest, and most visited, is about 1.5 km from town and opposite the Fatimid Cemetery. This huge discarded obelisk lies on the edge of the northern granite quarries, which supplied the ancient Egyptians with most of the hard stone used in pyramids and temples. Three sides of the shaft, which measures nearly 42m long, were completed except for the inscriptions and it would have been the largest single piece of stone ever handled if a flaw had not appeared in the granite. So it lies there, where the disappointed stonemasons abandoned it, still partly attached to the parent rock and with no indication of what it was intended for.

Entry to the site costs E£20, or E£10 for students. No service taxis run past the site, but you can get one to the junction on Sharia Kisr al-Haggar and then walk (about 10 minutes). Private taxis will charge about E£2. Most people simply visit the obelisk at

the end of an organised day trip to Abu Simbel.

The other unfinished obelisk – this time complete with hieroglyphs – is in the desert west of the Monastery of Saint Simeon. You'll need a guide, preferably on camel back, to find it.

Elephantine Island

Perhaps elephants once roamed the banks of the Nile here. They certainly passed through in the great caravans or with various armies, but it is more likely that Aswan's longest inhabited area was named Yebu after the numerous giant grey granite boulders, in the river around the island, which resemble a herd of elephants bathing.

Apart from being Egypt's frontier town, where the island officials were known as 'Keepers of the Gate of the South', Elephantine also produced most of the Pharaohs of the 5th dynasty. It was also the centre of the cult of the ram-headed Khnum, creator of humankind and god of the cataracts who controlled the Nile's water level, and his companion goddesses Satis (his wife) and Anukis (his daughter).

Excavation of the ancient town, which began at the start of this century, is still being carried out by a German team and the jumbled remains of the fortress and three temples are visible. There's also a small 3rd dynasty step pyramid; a tiny chapel reconstructed from the Temple of Kalabsha, which is just south of the High Dam; and, taking up much of the northern end of the island, the deluxe and incongruous Aswan Oberoi Hotel which has its own private ferry and a three metre fence around it to keep the tourists in, and away from the local Nubians. Another five star hotel is being built next to the Oberoi on the island's northern tip.

The inhabitants of the three colourful Nubian villages on the east side of Elephantine are friendly and the alleyways are worth exploring.

Aswan Museum At the south-eastern end of the island, overlooking the ruins of the original town and situated next to an attractive flower and spice garden, this modest little museum houses a collection of antiquities discovered in Aswan and Nubia. Most of the Nubian artefacts were found and rescued before the construction of the old Aswan Dam. The weapons, pottery, utensils, statues, encased mummies and sarcophagi date from Predynastic to late Roman times and everything is labelled in Arabic and English. The sarcophagus and mummy of a sacred ram, the animal associated with Khnum, are in a room by themselves to the right of the main entrance, while four mummies can be seen in the left of the museum.

The building itself dates back to 1898 and was a rest house for Sir William Willcocks, the architect of the Aswan Dam. The museum is open Sunday to Thursday from 9 to 11.30 am, and 1 to 5 pm (Friday in the morning only); in summer it opens and closes an hour later. Admission is E£5 (E£2.50 for students); there's a E£15 camera fee. You'll probably be shepherded around the well-tended gardens, for some baksheesh of course.

Nilometer Heavenly portents and priestly prophecies aside, the only sure indication in ancient times of the likelihood of a bountiful harvest was that given by the Nilometer. Descending to the water's edge from beneath a sycamore tree near the museum, the shaft of the ancient Nilometer measured the height of the Nile. Although it dates from Pharaonic times, and bears inscriptions and cartouches from the reigns of Amenophis III and Psammetichus II, it was rebuilt by the Romans, and restored last century.

When the Nilometer recorded that the level of the river was high it would mean that the approaching annual flood would be heavy and therefore sufficient for the irrigation vital to a good harvest. It also affected the taxation system, for the higher the river, the better the crop season and the more prosperous the fellahin and merchants – and therefore the higher the taxes.

You can enter the Nilometer from the river or down steps from near the Aswan Museum or just view it from a felucca on the water.

Temple of Khnum Among the ruins of the ancient town are the remains of a large temple built by Nectanebo, a 4th century BC Pharaoh, and dedicated to Khnum, the patron of Elephantine and the god who created humankind on his potter's wheel. At the gateway to the temple Ptolemy XI Alexander II, who ruled around 80 BC, is shown worshipping the ram-god. A team of German archaeologists has been excavating and restoring the temple; at the time of writing it was closed to the public.

Nearby are the remains of a small portion of the **Temple of Satis**, dedicated to Khnum's goddess daughter. The **Temple of Heqaib**, an interesting stone shrine honouring a prince of the nome, is also close by. A 6th dynasty official, Heqaib was deified after his death and remained a cult figure for many centuries. A small Ptolemaic temple discovered on the tip of the island has been restored.

Getting There & Away To get to Elephantine Island you can take a felucca or rowboat for 25 pt from either the landing opposite the telephone office or the one across from Thomas Cook.

Kitchener's Island

One of the most delightful places in Aswan, this island to the west of Elephantine was given to Lord Horatio Kitchener in the 1890s when he was consul-general of Egypt and commander of the Egyptian army. Indulging his passion for beautiful flowers, Kitchener turned the entire island into a botanic garden, importing plants from the Far East, India and other parts of Africa. The only ugly part of the island is the area with caged animals, including monkeys. The gardens are perfect for a peaceful stroll except on Friday when the island is invaded by picnic crowds with ghetto blasters. The cafeteria at the southern end of the island is invariably closed. Entry is E£5 and there is no student reduction.

Getting There & Away There are no ferry services to Kitchener's Island but it's easy enough to hire a felucca for a return trip or incorporate the gardens on a river tour. The price for a felucca is negotiable and starts to come down quickly if you first show that you are interested and then begin to walk away. You would be doing well to get a felucca for an hour for less than E£5, and often you'll be looking at something closer to E£10. The official price for a two hour tour taking in stops at Kitchener's and Elephantine islands and the Mausoleum of the Aga Khan is E£20 for the whole boat.

Dr Ragab Papyrus Museum

Dr Ragab is well known throughout Egypt for mass producing high-quality papyrus paintings. His Aswan papyrus museum/shop is actually a barge moored to the shore. Beautiful papyrus paintings of various sizes hang from the walls and are displayed in glass cases.

Mausoleum of the Aga Khan

Aswan was the favourite wintering place of Mohammed Shah Aga Khan, the 48th imam, or leader, of the Ismaili sect of Islam. When he died in 1957 his wife, the Begum, oversaw the construction of his domed granite and sandstone mausoleum, which is part of the way up the hill on the west bank opposite Elephantine Island.

Modelled on the Fatimid tombs of Cairo, the interior, which incorporates a small mosque, is more impressive than the exterior. The sarcophagus, of Carrara marble, is inscribed with texts from the Qur'an and stands in a vaulted chamber in the interior courtyard. Part of the sarcophagus has been reserved for the Begum.

Now in her 90s, the Begum still lives for some of the year in the white villa (below the mausoleum) which used to be their winter retreat. Every day she places a red rose on his sarcophagus; a ritual that is carried on in summer by her gardener.

The tomb is open Tuesday to Sunday from 8 am to 4 pm and admission is free (the guards are not supposed to accept baksheesh). Remember to dress modestly and to remove your shoes.

The felucca dock, just below the mausoleum, doubles as a mini souq, with hordes of traders selling all sorts of souvenir stuff. Negotiating a ride on a felucca or rowboat to Elephantine Island can be a bit laborious. There's not much competition, so you're looking at about E£4 one way.

Monastery of St Simeon

Deir Amba Samaan is a 6th century monastery which, although unused for more than 700 years, is one of the best preserved of the original Christian strongholds in Egypt. It is not known who St Simeon was, exactly, but his monastery survived until the monks were driven out or murdered by Arabs in the 14th century.

Surrounded by desert sands, except for a glimpse of the fertile belt around Aswan in the distance, the monastery bears more resemblance to a fortress than a religious sanctuary. It once provided accommodation for about 300 resident monks plus a further 100 or so pilgrims. Built on two levels, the lower of stone and the upper of mud brick, it was surrounded by 10m-high walls and contained a church, stores, bakeries, offices, a kitchen, dormitories, stables and workshops.

The monastery is open from 9 am to 5 pm; admission costs E£6 (half for students).

Getting There & Away There is a paved pathway to the monastery from the Mausoleum of Aga Khan, which is, however, inaccessible when the mausoleum is closed (unless you're prepared to scale the wall). Camels and their owners also hang around the mausoleum in the hope of snaring people to ride up to the monastery.

It is quite possible to scramble up the desert track to the monastery (about 25 minutes) from the felucca dock if the mausoleum is closed.

Alternatively, you can ride a camel or donkey from the Tombs of the Nobles or Kubbet al-Hawa.

Tombs of the Nobles

The high cliffs opposite Aswan, a little north of Kitchener's Island, are honeycombed with the tombs of the princes, governors, 'Keepers of the Gate of the South' and other dignitaries of ancient Yebu. They date from the Old and Middle kingdoms and although most of them are in a sorry state of repair, there are a few worth visiting.

To get to the west bank tombs, you can either take the ferry from a landing in front of the tourist office (when the river is low ferries leave from in front of the Abu Simbel Hotel) for 50 pt or include them on a felucca tour of the river. Admission to the tombs is E£12, or E£6 for students. Hours are 8 am to 4 pm (winter) and 5 pm (summer).

Tombs of Mekhu & Sabni (Nos 25 & 26)

These tombs are of roughly around 6th dynasty construction. The reliefs in No 26 record a tale of tragedy and triumph. Mekhu, one of the 'Keepers of the Gate', was murdered on an expedition into Africa, so his son Sabni led the army into Nubia to punish the tribe responsible. Sabni recovered his father's body and sent a messenger to the Pharaoh in Memphis to inform him that the enemy had been taught a lesson. On his return to Aswan he was met by priests, professional mourners and some of the royal embalmers, all sent by the Pharaoh himself to show the importance that was attached to the keepers of the kingdom's southern frontier.

Tomb of Prince Sarenput II (No 31)

Dating from the 12th dynasty, this is one of the best preserved tombs. There are statues of the prince and wall paintings depicting Sarenput and his son hunting and fishing.

Tomb of Prince Sarenput I (No 36)

This tomb also dates from the 12th dynasty but it's older than No 31. On the rear wall of a columned court, to the left of the door, the prince is shown being followed by his dogs and sandal-bearer, and there are other scenes of his three sons and of women bearing flowers.

Tomb of Heqaib (No 35)

The Tomb of Heqaib, the deified official whose temple stood on Elephantine, has a columned facade and some fine reliefs showing fighting bulls and hunting scenes.

Kubbet al-Hawa

Also on the west bank is Kubbet al-Hawa, a small tomb constructed for a local sheikh at the top of the hill. If you climb up to it, you'll be rewarded with fantastic views of the Nile and the surrounding area.

Felucca Rides

As you will quickly discover if you spend any time near the Nile, feluccas are the traditional canvas-sailed boats of the Nile. They have probably changed little in centuries. A visit to Aswan wouldn't be complete without at least an hour's ride on a felucca between the islands in the Nile. One of the most scenic sections of the river is around the southern end of Elephantine Island. Here too, in front of the Old Cataract Hotel, you'll probably encounter a troop of young boys furiously hand-paddling their minuscule self-made boats in pursuit of larger vessels in order to score some baksheesh from passers-by.

For advice about hiring a felucca, see Getting There & Away later in this section.

Swimming

Aswan is a hot place, and sometimes a swim seems just the way to escape the worst of it. Short of joining the local kids and jumping into the Nile to cool off (this, by the way, is not recommended), there are a few hotels with swimming pools open to the public, generally from 9 am to sunset. The cheapest by far is the small pool at the Cleopatra Hotel which costs E£8. The Oberoi and Isis Island hotels have pools which non-guests can use for E£21; entry to the New Cataract Hotel's Olympic-size pool is E£35. The municipal pool next to the GPO does not admit tourists.

Organised Tours

For details on tours to Abu Simbel, see the Getting There & Away information under Abu Simbel at the end of this chapter.

Special Events

Aswan's only 'festival' is Aswan Dam Day

on 15 January. It's nothing to get excited about, consisting of little more than a civic parade in front of the governorate building on the Corniche.

Places to Stay

As in Luxor, prices for accommodation vary greatly with the season. The high season officially extends from October to April, however, its zenith is December and January when many Egyptians come here in groups. In the low season, and even right up until early November, you'll have no trouble finding a room, and haggling is part of the game. All the prices below are low-season rates, so expect prices to be higher if you're here in winter.

Arriving by train, you'll invariably be met by a handful of hotel touts each postulating the best deal in town and often claiming to be the owner of a particular place. Unless you want to be hassled by them for the rest of your stay in Aswan, it's best to give these guys a wide berth and find your own place to stay.

Places to Stay – bottom end

The hotel rates given in this section include breakfast, unless otherwise specified. Don't expect much – usually it's just coffee or tea, two pieces of bread or rolls, an egg, jam and butter.

Camping There's an official camping ground next to the Unfinished Obelisk, which is a 20 to 25 minute walk from the area around EgyptAir. Facilities are basic (cold showers only) but there are grassy spaces for setting up tents and a few trees to provide shade. Bright lamps and guards keep the place secure, but the former can make it difficult to sleep. It costs E£3 per person plus E£5/2 for a car/motorbike.

Hostels The *Youth Hostel* (☎ 322235) is on Sharia Abtal at-Tahrir, not far from the railway station. At E£8 for a bed in a share double or triple, it's not a bad deal (though breakfast is not included). The rooms have fans, the showers and toilets are clean and

the place generally empty. They make a point of keeping foreigners separate from locals.

Hotels – North of Aswan Station The 27 room *Rosewan Hotel* (☎ 324497) has been popular with low-budget travellers for quite a few years but the rooms are now a bit overpriced. It has clean, simple, rather small singles/doubles with shower/toilet combinations for E£16/26, or E£14/25 without shower. All rooms have fans and tiled floors, and, according to some disgruntled travellers, bugs.

The next-door *Hotel El-Saffa* (☎ 322173) is starting to show its age but is OK at E£5/10 for rooms with sinks and balconies. A few rooms also have showers with hot water. The price does not include breakfast.

A few blocks north is the *Mena Hotel* (☎ 324388). Its carpeted rooms have air-con, TVs, phones, showers, toilets and small balconies. A few rooms have either poor air-con or just fans. Singles are E£15, doubles (with the choice of one large bed or two singles) cost E£25. The best deal in the hotel is a comfy suite with two bedrooms and a 'salon' that can sleep five people for E£35. There's a colourful, 6th floor roof garden with cushioned chairs which is ideal for an evening beer (E£5). To get to the Mena, follow the street that runs parallel to the railway line for about four minutes. Despite being away from the centre of town, it is often full in high season.

Hotels – South of Aswan Station The *Marwa Hotel* is entered from an alley off Sharia Abtal at-Tahrir, directly across the street from the Youth Hostel. The rooms are simple and a little cramped, but at E£4 a person in a share room of three or four beds, it is fairly popular. Each room has a fan and there's hot water in the communal showers. Breakfast is E£1 extra.

The *El-Amin Hotel* (☎ 322298, 314189) is an inexpensive hotel (not to be confused with the dark, uninviting El-Eman Hotel two blocks south) that lists itself as being on Sharia Abtal at-Tahrir, but is actually on a side street just across from the Ramses Hotel.

A few rooms are somewhat dusty and the toilet/shower combinations are rather small, but there are fans and it's not a bad deal at E£8/12.

Not far from the tourist office on the Corniche is the 66 room *Abu Simbel Hotel* (☎ 322888, 322327). It used to be a middle-range place but the hotel is so decrepit that it is now a definite bottom ender. Double rooms with shower cost E£28 for one or two people. The view of the Nile from the tiny balcony of each room is fantastic, and for some people makes up for the filthy bathrooms and generally shabby state.

The *Nubian Oasis Hotel* (☎ 312126/123), just off Sharia as-Souq, is one of Aswan's most popular travellers' haunts. It has good clean rooms for E£8 per person with bath, or E£6 without. There's a large lounge area and a roof garden where Stellas cost E£5.

On the eastern side of Sharia as-Souq there are two budget options. The *Noorhan Hotel* has had mixed reviews from a number of travellers and is not all that special. The *Bob Marley Hotel*, one block east of the Medina restaurant, is one of the cheapest options around. For E£5 per person you get a reasonable double room with fan and balcony. The newer rooms with air-con cost a bit more. Make sure you ask for a room with a lock that's working.

In the midst of the souq is the *Aswan Palace Hotel* (☎ 313664). It's no palace though and, at E£8/12 for noisy singles/doubles (breakfast is not available), it's also no great deal.

Two blocks south, opposite the small post office, is the *Victoria Hotel*. This old timer boasts rickety wooden balconies, iron bed frames and a wonderful sweeping staircase, though few foreigners ever seem to stay here. Large rooms cost E£7/10 (without breakfast) and the shared facilities are clean.

At the southern end of Sharia as-Souq is the one star *Abou Shelib Hotel* (☎ 323051). The hotel is next to a mosque. Rooms are clean and simple, with fans and/or air-con, and toilet/shower combinations (big bathrooms in some). Singles/doubles are E£16/20, but you may be able to negotiate,

depending on the size of the rooms and whether or not they have showers.

One block away, on a quiet side street just off the souq, is the relatively new *Hotel al-Oraby* (☎ & fax 317578). Its central location is an advantage for exploring the souq and the Corniche, the staff are friendly, the rooms are modern and comfortable, and the communal bathrooms are clean (though prone to flooding). Some rooms have big balconies. The cost is E£7 per person in a room with fan; air-con is a few pounds more. It's a 15 to 20 minute walk from the railway station and is definitely one of the better options in this range.

The nearby *Molla Hotel* (☎ 326540) has similar, but less comfortable, rooms for E£15/20. Each room has a sink and there are hot showers just off the hall.

Places to Stay – middle

The *Ramses Hotel* (☎ 324000; fax 315701) on Sharia Abtal at-Tahrir, is a good deal and, according to some travellers, is the best value hotel in Aswan. Singles/doubles with showers, toilets, air-con, colour TV, mini-refrigerators and Nile views cost about E£35/55. This hotel is popular with tour groups from all over Europe.

The *Happi Hotel* (☎ 314115) is also on Sharia Abtal at-Tahrir, a few blocks down from the Ramses Hotel, and is particularly popular with German groups. It has 64 clean rooms with spotless bathrooms for E£32/40. The rooms have fans and some also have balconies, TV and double beds. There is one suite containing three bedrooms and a kitchenette. The owner also runs the Cleopatra Hotel, which explains why guests can use the Cleopatra's pool for free.

Further away from the Nile is the *Oscar Hotel* (☎ 323851, fax 306066), which has become something of a travellers' favourite. Rooms cost E£25/35. Some have balconies, and some even have working bedside reading lights! There's a rooftop terrace where beers (E£5) are available.

Several blocks north of the railway station is the 34 room *New Abu Simbel Hotel* (☎ 312143). At E£25/35, the screened rooms, all with private bathroom and air-con, are good value. It's out of the centre, but the management is friendly, towels and toilet paper are provided and there's a pleasant garden where you can cool off with a beer.

On the Corniche is the *El-Salam Hotel* (☎ 322651, 323649), which can be considered a fair deal for the price. Singles/doubles cost E£27/35 with air-con, or E£22/30 without. Most rooms have fans, private bathrooms and views of the Nile, as does the 2nd floor restaurant. The manager, Mahmoud Hussein, is a genial bloke.

Next to the El-Salam Hotel is the 36 room *Hathor Hotel* (☎ 314580), which has rooms crammed in next to toilets for E£30. Singles/doubles with air-con are E£20/40, but some of them are tiny. There's an inexpensive restaurant in the lobby.

Somewhat better is the 4th floor *Horus Hotel*, also on the Corniche. Singles/doubles with air-con and bath are E£30/40. Without bath they are E£5 cheaper. The 40 rooms are large and comfortable, and you should try to get one with Nile views. There is a rooftop bar and restaurant. A few travellers have complained about the hard-sell tactics used by some staff here to push felucca trips.

The *Philae Hotel* (☎ 312090), also on the Corniche, is altogether a bit rundown and gloomy. At E£25/40 it's not a brilliant deal, and the owners seem to be aware of this, as a bit of bargaining can bring the price down.

Also along the Corniche, there are two new places worth mentioning. The 34 room *Memnon Hotel* (☎ 322650) is above the National Bank of Egypt (but can only be entered through the back alley). The reception is on the 2nd floor. Double rooms with private bath and views over the alley/Nile cost E£25/35; singles are E£5 cheaper. All the rooms have air-con and very comfortable beds.

The other new place, *El Amir Hotel* (☎ 314735), is one street back from the Corniche on Sharia Abbas Farid. It's popular with Egyptians and offers 28 rooms with all the essentials such as thick mattresses, bathroom slippers, TV, air-con and phones. It's next to a mosque, and somewhat overpriced

– singles/doubles cost E£70/90; the eight suites are E£115.

Another place in the top end of this category is the *Cleopatra Hotel* (☎ 314003; fax 314002). It's on Sharia as-Souq not far from the railway station, and is well situated for exploring the old market area. With singles/doubles for about E£74/95, it's out of the range of most budget travellers. All 109 rooms are clean and comfortable with air-con, private bathroom and telephone, and there's a pool.

Places to Stay – top end

The *Old Cataract Hotel* (☎ 316002, fax 316011) is an impressive Moorish-style building surrounded by gardens on a rise above the river, with splendid views of the Nile and across the southern tip of Elephantine Island to the Mausoleum of the Aga Khan. Doubles here cost US$110/120 for a standard room with a garden/Nile view, or US$150 for a deluxe room with a Nile view, plus 23% in taxes and service charges. Suites range from US$300 to US$700. There is no discount for single occupancy. The hotel is worth visiting just to partake of a cool Stella or a cocktail on the verandah, however, a minimum charge of E£15 is imposed. The hotel's exterior was used in the movie of Agatha Christie's *Death on the Nile*, in part because Christie once did some of her writing here.

Everything about the Old Cataract bespeaks turn-of-the-century elegance, from its finely bevelled glass elevator to its large, well-furnished rooms. Both standard and 'deluxe' rooms are equally super – high ceilings, hardwood floors, Oriental carpets, antique furniture. You can get a buffet breakfast for E£20.

The *New Cataract Hotel* (☎ 316000; fax 316011) is a high-rise lump next door. Single/double rooms with a garden view are US$65/80; with a Nile view they cost US$75/90. This hotel has none of the style of the Old Cataract though its setting is also sublime and it has a big pool.

The nearby four star *Kalabsha Hotel* (☎ 322666; fax 325974) is another classy affair, with an excellent view of the First Nile Cataract. Singles/doubles are US$27/33 at the back and US$39/50 at the front, plus the usual taxes. Guests can use the swimming pool at the New Cataract Hotel for free.

The *Aswan Oberoi* (☎ 314666; fax 313538) is the blot on the horizon that rises from Elephantine Island. It has two hotel launches that ferry guests and visitors from the east bank. The views from the tower are, of course, magnificent and the gardens are a pleasant place to just hang around and watch the feluccas, or to have a dip in the pool. Rooms here, however, start at US$75/106 (without breakfast or taxes) and head up to about US$300.

The four star Isis Hotel between the Corniche and the Nile is closed. However, the same people have recently opened a 400 room monstrosity, the *Isis Island* (☎ 317400; fax 317405), on one of the islands south of Elephantine. A lot of controversy surrounded the construction of this place as it was built within a few metres of a group of islands which are home to the only original Nile vegetation remaining in Egypt and which have been designated a protected area. An extremely ostentatious launch ferries guests (and outsiders wanting to use the pool) from in front of the EgyptAir office.

The salmon-toned *Hôtel Île d'Amoun* (☎ 313800; fax 317190) is on a neighbouring islet. It's operated by Club Med, which took over the original building years ago and transformed it into an idyllic little garden paradise. Rooms (including taxes but not breakfast) cost US$47/61. Modest motor boats there leave from in front of EgyptAir.

Places to Eat

Along Sharia as-Souq is a veritable smorgasbord of small restaurants and cafes in the midst of the lively atmosphere of the souqs. There are also plenty of cafes by the railway station. The *Restaurant Derwash* on the south side of the Aswan Station Square has been recommended by some travellers. A block from the station is *Samah*, a little ta'amiyya stall. Down a side street, a bit further, is *El Nasr* which has pizza (or 'betza'

as they prefer to spell it), as well as fried fish and chicken.

Next to the Youth Hostel is an OK place called the *El Dar*, which does a nice, if smallish, vegetable soup. Alternatively you could try *Esraa*, a tiny kofta place just down the road.

The *Medina Restaurant* on Sharia as-Souq, across from the Cleopatra Hotel, is recommended for its kofta and kebab deals, and is often patronised by travellers. They also do a vegetarian meal for E£4.50, which includes a cola.

The *El Masry Restaurant* on Sharia al-Matar is not too expensive for a meaty meal; expect to pay around E£16. Opposite is a cheaper place where a full dinner will set you back E£6.

The *Al Sayed Nafesa*, tucked away in a side alley in the heart of the souq, is a good-value place serving kofta for E£5, soup for E£1, and a meal of rice, salad, vegetables and bread for E£2.50.

There are three places on the Corniche where you can sit out on a barge in the river and get decent food and beers. Of the trio, the *Aswan Moon Restaurant* remains the most popular among foreigners and Egyptians. Main courses go for about E£12 and a beer is E£6. It serves generous soups and pizzas (E£10), but the salads tend to be small. The atmosphere is particularly laid-back and the service is excellent (albeit a bit slow).

Next door is a two storey boat belonging to the *Emy Restaurant*. It prepares especially nice fruit cocktail drinks, as well as serving the usual selection of meals (some of which are a bit too greasy). The view from the top deck at sunset is bliss, and the beers are the cheapest in town. Everyone under about 40 seems to benefit from the advertised 20% 'student discount', though you may have to show a student card.

The third barge is owned by the *Saladin Restaurant* and while it's pleasant enough for a drink, the food is nothing to rave about. It's less popular than the other two and rarely full.

The tiny *Restaurant el-Nil* is on the Corniche a few doors along from Thomas Cook.

A full meal with fish (carp from Lake Nasser), chicken or meat with rice, vegetables, salad, tahina and bread should cost about E£9.

The restaurant at the nearby *Abou Shelib Hotel* will give clients a free meal if, as their sign states, 'our food is not good'. Now how's that for a consolation prize!

On the Nile side of the Corniche there are several other restaurants floating on pontoons on the river, all offering a similar range of dishes at virtually the same prices. They include the *Monalisa Restaurant*, the *Panorama* and the *El-Shati*.

Those intending to splurge at the restaurant at the *Old Cataract Hotel* should note that while the decor is delightful, the French cuisine is average and the Egyptian woman crooning away on old Frank Sinatra classics is decidedly off-putting. The Nubian musicians and dancers who come on later, however, liven things up.

Alternatively, you can partake in a buffet dinner at either the *Kalabsha* (E£32) or *Aswan Oberoi* (E£55) hotels.

The new *Nubian Restaurant* on Essa Island, opposite the Old Cataract Hotel, serves meals for about E£30; obviously you're paying for the exclusive setting.

Entertainment

Aswan's world-famous folkloric dance troupe performs at the cultural centre (☎ 313390) on the Corniche between October and February nightly (except Friday) from 9.30 to 11.30 pm. Admission is E£10. The centre also presents traditional Upper Egyptian and Nubian music performances and exhibits the instruments used in them. Whether or not there are any performances during Ramadan seems to be a matter of whim.

Otherwise, strolling along the Corniche, watching the moon rise from a rooftop terrace, and having a beer at one of the floating restaurants is about all that most travellers get up to in Aswan at night. The top-end hotels all have discos and nightclubs; one of the most popular is the *King Ramses Disco* at the Ramses Hotel. It goes from about 10 pm to 2 am, and has no minimum charge.

Getting There & Away

Air The EgyptAir office (☎ 315000) is at the southern end of the Corniche. There are daily flights from Cairo to Aswan (E£497 one way, 1¾ hours). The one-way hop to Luxor is E£163; to Hurghada via Luxor it's E£323.

The return flight from Aswan to Abu Simbel costs E£439 and includes bus transfers between the airport and the temple site. For information on other routes within Egypt refer to the EgyptAir Domestic Flights Table in the Getting Around chapter.

Bus The bus station is in the middle of town on Sharia Abtal at-Tahrir.

A direct bus for Cairo (12 hours) leaves at 3.30 pm and costs E£50. The bus leaving an hour later costs E£10 less. They both supposedly have air-con, video and toilet, so what the difference is anybody's guess.

There are two daily buses to Abu Simbel (E£26 return). One leaves at 8 am and arrives back at about 5.30 pm; the other is a night service departing at 5 pm. You should book in advance. Take note – neither of these buses has air-con.

There are hourly buses to Kom Ombo (E£1.25, one hour), Edfu (E£2.50, two hours), Esna (E£4.50, three hours) and Luxor (E£5.50 to E£6.50, four to five hours).

The green buses are cheaper and less reliable than the green-and-yellow buses.

There are two buses going right through to Hurghada (Al-Ghardaka, seven hours). The first leaves at 8 am and costs E£16; the second departs at 3.30 pm and costs E£30. Both these buses go onto Suez (E£26 or E£32), but that's a long 15 hour haul. The bus to Marsa Alam (E£10.50, five hours), also on the Red Sea coast, departs at 6.15 am and continues all the way south to Bir Shalatayn (E£18).

Train There's a handful of trains running daily between Cairo and Aswan, however, only three of them can be used by foreigners.

The most expensive is the wagon-lit train

(No 85) which costs E£293 one way (2nd class) to Cairo (which is the same fare as from Luxor) and departs at 3 pm. See the Cairo Getting There & Away section for more details on this train.

Express train Nos 981 and 997 to Cairo leave at 5.45 am and 6.30 pm. The 1st/2nd class fare is E£60/34; student discounts are available. These trains have air-con and a restaurant. The trip to Cairo is scheduled to take about 15 hours but has been known to take more than 20. Reservations are needed for all these trains. If you don't want to dine on the train, make sure you ask for a ticket without meals otherwise they'll automatically issue meal tickets.

Tickets for the train to Luxor (four hours) cost E£20/12 in 1st/2nd class on the afternoon service, and a few pounds more on the morning train.

Service Taxi The service-taxi station is across the train tracks on the east side of town. Just off Sharia as-Souq, one block south of the railway station, is an overpass over the tracks. Climb the overpass and walk to the end of the street on the other side (about 10 minutes). Turn right and walk about half a km to the service-taxi station. Alternatively, just follow the tracks south until the tunnel: the service-taxi station is on the other side of the railway line. Service taxis (which are sometimes actually microbuses) depart regularly for Luxor (E£7.50, 3½ hours), Edfu (E£3.50, 1½ hours), Kom Ombo (E£1.50, one hour) and Daraw (E£1.50, 30 minutes).

Car & Motorbike The road south of Abu Simbel into Sudan is closed. In the past it was possible to take your vehicle across Lake Nasser, although travellers who did so had to hire a boat (at a cost of about E£5000 in 1993) especially for the effort. This is not a recommendation as, even with a 4WD, the going is very tough, and petrol scarce.

Cruise Ship For information about cruise ships between Aswan and Luxor, see the

Getting There & Away section in the Luxor chapter.

For details about the new five star cruiser, the MS *Eugénie*, which sails between Aswan High Dam and Abu Simbel, see the Organised Tours section in the Getting Around chapter at the start of the book, or inquire at some of the travel agents in town.

Felucca The most popular felucca trip is a three day (two night) trip from Aswan to Edfu. From there, you take a service taxi to Luxor for about E£5. Another alternative is a one or two night trip to Kom Ombo, returning by service taxi to Aswan or continuing onto destinations further south. The only problem with the latter is that you may have to walk about two km from the Nile to the main road, but it's usually easy to hitch a ride. The last option is three nights, four days to Esna, returning by service taxi to Luxor. The felucca captains are quite adamant about not continuing on to Luxor, and often will refuse to go on to Esna (and sometimes even to Edfu), even after having agreed to do so. The reasons are simple enough. The trip back upstream can take much longer, and that means lost opportunities to take out more passengers – ideally, they would do short trips down the river and turn their boats around quickly back to Aswan to get more passengers.

Officially, feluccas can carry a minimum of six passengers and a maximum of eight, for the following prices: E£25 to Kom Ombo, E£45 to Edfu, and E£50 to Esna. On top of this you must add E£5 for police registration and the cost of food supplies. As usual, the official prices are generally inflated, and often more than six get on to the one boat. More than eight on the bigger ones is about the limit – it can get pretty cramped.

Finding a felucca is easy – as soon as you approach the Corniche, you will be swamped with offers. However, finding a good captain can be a problem, especially if you are a single woman or a group of women. On overnight trips, a few women travellers have reported sailing with felucca captains who had groping hands and exhibitionist tendencies.

Any of the low and middle-range hotels are good sources for assembling a group for this type of trip. Leaving messages at the tourist office is also a good move. In fact, the staff at both these offices are keen to recommend good captains to travellers (though some of the felucca crews have caught onto this and it's not unusual for boys at the dock to tell you that the particular captain you're looking for has died).

When dealing with a felucca captain, be sure about a few things. Firstly, that he has what appears to be a decent, functioning boat, with some blankets and cooking implements, and something comfortable to sit on. Establish whether the price includes food and, if so, go with him to the market to do the shopping to see just what you are getting. Otherwise, set a price without food and do your own shopping. If you get a good captain, you'll probably be better off doing it with him – he'll have a good idea of the supplies needed and is less likely to pay extortionate prices for the supplies.

Agree on the number of passengers before you go and don't let him talk you into taking 'a few others on board later downriver', otherwise you'll find yourselves sharing limited supplies of food, water and space.

Don't hand over your passports. Often captains, or more likely middlemen, like to take them so that they have a couple of passengers in the bag. They then scour around for other people. With your passport in his hands, you commit yourself to him until he finds other people or gives up, all of which can be quite inconvenient. It's advisable to accompany the captain to the police when organising permission too.

Take plenty of bottled water for the trip; otherwise the captain will dip into the Nile for cooking and drinking water.

Bring a sleeping bag – it can get bitterly cold at night, and the supply of blankets on board won't be enough. Insect repellent is a good idea, but you can probably do without mosquito nets – it's a bit difficult to rig them up anyway! A hat is essential.

And, lastly, if you camp overnight on an island or beach, take your rubbish with you when you leave. As one traveller put it after encountering piles of plastic bottles and beer cans left by previous travellers: 'I'm not old or fussy or picky – I just enjoy sitting on a clean beach, not on a garbage dump'.

Once you're off, sit back and enjoy a rare side of Egypt – quiet. No hawkers, no car horns, just the Nile lapping against the side of your boat. Often the captain will take you to visit his family in a village along the way, or drop in on other villages. As you sail down, you'll see the life of the river and the people who depend on it going on much as it has for millennia.

Boat to Sudan Boat services along Lake Nasser to Wadi Halfa in Sudan were stopped in late 1994 and it's anyone's guess when they will resume. The best place to ask about this is the Nile Valley Navigation Office (☎ 322348), next to the tourist office, one street in from the Corniche. This used to be the place to buy tickets, and the office is open from 9 am to 1.30 pm. The following information has been included in the event the service recommences.

Boat traffic has become extremely erratic over the years and it is worth keeping an eye out for activity at the Nile Valley Navigation Office. Crowds of Sudanese could indicate an imminent departure. The golden rule is, if they tell you one day that there isn't another boat for two weeks, pop in again a day or two later and see what their latest story is – it's bound to be different.

Depending on whether you get the 10 year old Egyptian boat or one of the much older steamers, the trip south can take as few as 14 hours or as many as 24.

You can go 1st or 2nd class, which in early 1994 cost E£135.35/85.75. On the Egyptian boat at least, 1st class means bunks in small cabins – if you want them. The most pleasant place to be (on what is almost always an extremely crowded journey) is outside on deck – a small area by the wheelhouse is generally set aside for foreigners, or if you're feeling more sociable you can mix it with the

Sudanese elsewhere on the deck. The seating below is crowded, stuffy and uncomfortable – you can hardly breathe let alone sleep. The fare includes a meal – fuul in 2nd class or meat and rice in 1st. If you've gone 2nd class, you can still buy a 1st class meal for E£2. Tea and soft drinks are also available on board. Bring some food yourself too.

The trip is fairly relaxing, and if you're lucky you'll sail past Abu Simbel in daylight.

As a foreigner, you should be ushered through the various customs and passport hurdles at Aswan. You may need E£2 as an exit tax from Egypt. Some of the Sudanese immigration formalities are carried out on the boat – they will ask for your yellow fever certificate. The boat departs from near the High Dam.

Getting Around

The Airport The airport is 25 km south-west of town and the taxi fare is about E£20.

Taxi A taxi tour that includes the Philae Temple, the High Dam and the unfinished obelisk near the Fatimid Cemetery costs around E£25 for five to six people.

Bicycle There are a few places at the railway station end of Sharia as-Souq where you can hire bicycles for about E£4 a day. Try around the Marwa and Ramses hotels.

Boat A ferry shuttles across the Nile to just below the Tombs of the Nobles on the west bank. It departs either from near the tourist office or opposite the Abu Simbel Hotel, depending on the level of the water. The fare is 50 pt each way. Note that the boat is divided into two sections – women up front, men in the back.

Felucca Apart from a few buses, taxis and horse-drawn carriages, feluccas are the most common form of transport to the attractions around Aswan. The official government price for hiring a felucca capable of seating one to 10 people is E£10 per hour, but with a bit of bargaining you should be able to hire a boat for five or six hours for a reasonable

price. A shorter three or four hour tour costs about E£25 to E£30, but prices vary widely according to the effectiveness of your bargaining and the time of year – if they're having a bad season, they may be willing to take people out for less than they would normally find acceptable.

Officially at least, a two hour jaunt taking in Kitchener's Island and the Mausoleum of the Aga Khan should cost no more than E£20. You'll need an extra hour to see Elephantine Island as well. A three hour trip down to Sehel Island is E£30.

Around Aswan

THE ASWAN DAM

When the British constructed the Aswan Dam above the First Nile Cataract at the turn of the century it was the largest of its kind in the world. The growing population of Egypt had made it imperative to put more land under cultivation and the only way to achieve this was to regulate the flow of the Nile. Measuring 2441m across, the dam was built between 1898 and 1902 almost entirely of local Aswan granite.

Although its height had to be raised twice to meet the demand, it not only greatly increased the area of cultivable land but also provided the country with most of its hydro-electric power. Now completely surpassed in function, and as a tourist attraction, by the High Dam six km upstream, it is still worth a brief visit, as the area around the First Nile Cataract below it is extremely fertile and picturesque. All trips to Abu Simbel include a drive across this dam.

SEHEL ISLAND

Sehel, the large island north of the old Aswan Dam, was sacred to the goddess Anukis and her husband Khnum. As a destination for an extended felucca trip on this part of the Nile, Sehel Island is a good choice, although there isn't much to see apart from a friendly Nubian village and a great many rock

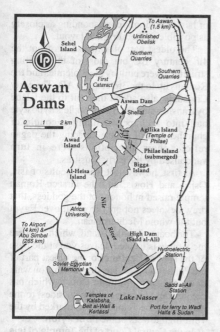

most legendary tourist attractions. Even when it seemed that they were destined to be lost forever beneath the rising waters of the Nile, travellers still came, taking to rowboats to glide among the partly submerged columns and peer down through the translucent green to the wondrous sanctuaries of the mighty gods below.

From the turn of this century, Philae and its temples became swamped for six months of every year by the high waters of the reservoir created by the construction of the old Aswan Dam. In the 1960s, when the approaching completion of the High Dam threatened to submerge the island completely and forever, the massive complex was disassembled and removed stone by stone from Philae in an incredible rescue organised by UNESCO between 1972 and 1980. The temples were reconstructed 20m higher on nearby Agilika Island, which was even landscaped to resemble the sacred isle

inscriptions, dating from Middle Kingdom to Graeco-Roman times.

One Ptolemaic inscription, on the southeastern side of the island, records the story of a seven year famine that plagued Egypt during the much earlier time of Pharaoh Zoser. It seems that Khnum, god of the cataracts, had withheld the inundation of the Nile for seven years and Zoser finally travelled to Aswan to ask the local priests why the god was punishing the Egyptians. Apparently some land belonging to Khnum's traditional estates had been confiscated; as soon as Zoser returned the land and raised a temple to Khnum on Sehel, the Nile rose to its accepted flood level.

TEMPLE OF PHILAE

The romantic and majestic aura surrounding the temple complex of Isis on the island of Philae (pronounced 'feel-i') has been luring pilgrims for thousands of years; during the 19th century the ruins were one of Egypt's

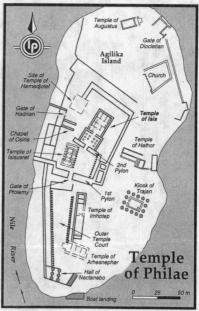

The Cult of Isis

Isis, the sister and wife of the great Osiris, was the Egyptian goddess of healing, purity and sexuality, of motherhood and women, of the promise of immortality and of nature itself. She was worshipped so passionately and her popularity was so great that she became identified with all the goddesses of the Mediterranean, finally absorbing them to become the universal mother of nature and protector of humans.

It was on Philae, during her search for the dismembered pieces of Osiris, who had been murdered by his brother Seth, that Isis supposedly found her husband's heart; hence the island became her most sacred precinct. Her cult following was so strong that she was still being worshipped long after the establishment of Christianity throughout the Roman Empire, and Philae was still the centre of the cult of Isis as late as the 6th century AD. ■

Isis, daughter of Nut and Geb, is typically represented wearing a crown of the sun disc flanked with cow's horns.

of Isis, in positions corresponding as closely as possible to their original layout.

The oldest part of Philae dates from the 4th century BC but most of the existing structures were built by the Ptolemies and the Romans up to the 3rd century AD. The early Christians also added their bit to the island by transforming the main temple's hypostyle hall into a chapel, building a couple of churches and of course defacing the pagan reliefs; their inscriptions were in turn vandalised by the early Muslims.

At first, however, it was the cults of Isis, Osiris and Horus, and the Graeco-Roman temple raised in honour of the goddess, that drew devotees not only from all over Egypt but the whole Mediterranean.

The boat to Agilika Island, which is where the temple is located, leaves you at the base of the **Hall of Nectanebo**, the oldest part of the Philae complex. Heading north, you walk down the **Outer Temple Court**, which has colonnades running along both sides, to the entrance of the Temple of Isis marked by the 18m-high towers of the **First Pylon**.

In the Central Court of the **Temple of Isis** is the mammisi (birth house) dedicated to Horus. Successive Pharaohs reinstated their legitimacy as the mortal descendants of Horus by taking part in the mammisi rituals, which celebrated the god's birth.

The **Second Pylon** provides access to the vestibule and the **Inner Sanctuary of Isis**; a staircase, on the western side, leads up to the **Osiris Chambers**, which are decorated with scenes of mourners; and everywhere there are reliefs of Isis, her husband and son, other deities and, of course, the Ptolemies and Romans who built or contributed to the temple.

On the northern tip of the island are the **Temple of Augustus** and the **Gate of Diocletian**; east of the Second Pylon is the delightful **Temple of Hathor** decorated with reliefs of musicians and Bes, the god of singing and pleasure; and south of that, the elegant, unfinished pavilion by the water's edge is the **Kiosk of Trajan**. The completed reliefs on the kiosk feature Emperor Trajan making offerings to Isis, Osiris and Horus.

The temple complex is open from 8 am to 4 pm (winter) and 7 am to 5 pm (summer), and admission is E£20, or E£10 for students. Tickets are purchased from the small office before the boat landing at Shellal.

There is a sound & light show in the evening which costs E£33 (no student discount) for the ticket and E£16 for the boat (divided between a maximum of eight people) to Agilika Island. There are usually two and sometimes three performances in English, French, German, Japanese, Italian, Spanish or Arabic. Times vary according to the season. In winter they're at 6, 7.30 and 9 pm; in summer at 8, 9.30 and 11 pm; and during Ramadan at 8.30, 10 and 11 pm. Double-check the following schedule at the tourist office:

Day	Show 1	Show 2	Show 3
Monday	Japanese	English	Italian
Tuesday	French	English	–
Wednesday	English	Spanish	–
Thursday	Japanese	French	Arabic
Friday	English	French	–
Saturday	English	French	–
Sunday	French	German	–

Getting There & Away

The boat landing for the Philae complex is at Shellal, south of the old Aswan Dam. The only easy way to get there is by taxi or organised trip (arranged by most travel agencies and major hotels in town, but possibly for more money than you may pay otherwise). The round-trip taxi fare for a group of six costs about E£30 without bargaining. It is possible, if you can get a ride to the old Aswan Dam, to walk along the water's edge to Shellal. From here, a small motorboat to the island costs E£14 (during the day) or E£16 (in the evening) divided between however many of you there are (maximum eight). If there are more than eight, each person simply pays E£1.75 for the return trip. These amounts are paid directly to the boatmen.

HIGH DAM

Egypt's contemporary example of building on a monumental scale contains 18 times the amount of material used in the Great Pyramid of Cheops. The controversial Sadd al-Ali, the High Dam, 17 km south of Aswan, is 3600m across and 111m high at its highest point. The water contained by the dam has backed up nearly 500 km, taking it well into Sudan and creating Lake Nasser, the world's largest artificial lake.

The rising level of this incredible reservoir has inundated the land of Nubia with waters as deep as 200m, forced the relocation of some 40,000 Nubians and Sudanese and washed away 45 villages along the banks of the Nile south of Aswan.

Most people get to the High Dam as part of an organised trip to Abu Simbel or other sites outside Aswan. For the privilege of driving part of the way along the dam to a small pavilion with a couple of displays detailing the dimensions and the construction of the dam, you pay E£3. If you come by foot from the railway station you'll still have to pay 50 pt.

Many visitors are disappointed by the visit, expecting views more spectacular than they actually get, so perhaps you should not hope for too much if you decide to visit. Video cameras and zoom lenses cannot be used, though no-one seems to police this policy.

On the west side of the dam, there is a stone monument honouring Soviet-Egyptian friendship and cooperation.

Places to Stay

The *Amun Village*, an expensive set of self-contained bungalows, is on the western bank of Lake Nasser, a couple of km south of the High Dam.

Getting There & Away

The cheapest way to get to the High Dam, which is 13 km south of Aswan, is to take a train (7, 8, 9.30 and 11.30 am, and 1.15 and 3 pm; 65 pt) to Sadd al-Ali station, the end of the Cairo-Aswan line. The station is near the docks for the boat to Sudan (which at the time of writing had been indefinitely suspended) and from there you can either walk

The High Dam

While the old Aswan Dam successfully regulated the flow of the Nile during the course of a year, it was realised, as early as the 1940s, that a much bigger dam was needed to counter the unpredictable annual flooding of the great river. However, it wasn't until Nasser came to power in 1952 that plans were drawn up for a new dam six km south of the British-built one.

The proposed construction created international political tension and focused worldwide attention on the antiquities that would be lost by the creation of a huge lake behind the dam. It also spelt the end of the Nubian people's homeland.

In 1956, after the USA, the UK and the World Bank suddenly refused the financial backing they had offered for the project, Nasser ordered the nationalisation of the Suez Canal as a means of raising the capital. This move precipitated the Suez Crisis in which France, the UK and Israel invaded the canal region; they were eventually restrained by the United Nations. The Soviet Union then offered the necessary funding and expertise, and work began on the High Dam in 1960 and was completed in 1971.

While the old dam simply controlled the flow of the Nile, the High Dam collects and stores water over a number of years so that a high or low annual flood can be regulated at all times. The area of Egypt's cultivable land was increased by 30%; the High Dam's hydroelectric station has doubled the country's power supply and a rise in the Sahara's water table has been recorded as far away as Algeria.

On the other hand, artificial fertilisers now have to be used because the dam hinders the flow of silt that was critical to the Nile Valley's fertility. In turn, the authorities are faced with the problem that the silt will eventually fill the lake. In recent years, the extremely high rate of evaporation from the lake, coupled with low annual floods, has reduced the water level in the reservoir forcing a reduction in the amount of water released for irrigation and power generation. The greatest fear is that should the dam ever break or be sabotaged most of Egypt would be swept into the Mediterranean.

Another consequence of the dam's construction was the fact that a great many valuable and irreplaceable ancient monuments were doomed to be drowned by the waters of Lake Nasser.

Teams from the Egyptian Department of Antiquities and archaeological missions from many countries descended on Nubia to set in motion the UNESCO-organised projects aimed at rescuing as many of the threatened treasures as possible. Necropolises were excavated, all portable artefacts and relics were removed to museums and, while some temples disappeared beneath the lake, 14 were salvaged and moved to safety.

Ten of them, including the temple complexes of Philae, Kalabsha and Abu Simbel, were dismantled stone by stone and rebuilt on higher ground in Egypt. The other four were donated to the countries which contributed to the rescue effort; they include the splendid Temple of Dendur, which has been reconstructed in a glass building in the Metropolitan Museum of Art in New York. ■

---

for a long way or try to get a service taxi to the dam.

If you're planning to take a taxi across the top of the dam, then you might also consider continuing on to the Temple of Kalabsha, which is visible from the dam on the west side of Lake Nasser. It's about three km from the western end of the dam.

KALABSHA, BEIT AL-WALI & KERTASSI

As a result of the massive UNESCO effort to rescue the doomed monuments of Nubia, these three temples were transplanted from a now submerged site about 60 km south of Aswan. The new site is on the west bank of Lake Nasser just south of the dam.

The Temple of Kalabsha was erected during the reign of Emperor Augustus, between 30 BC and 14 AD, and was dedicated to the Nubian god Mandulis. Isis and Osiris were also worshipped there and during the Christian era the temple was used as a church.

The then West German government financed the transfer and reconstruction of the 13,000 blocks of the temple, and was presented with the temple's west pylon, which is now in the Berlin Museum. During the rescue operation, evidence was found of even older structures, dating from the times of Amenophis II and Ptolemy IX.

An impressive stone causeway leads from the lake up to the first pylon of the temple, beyond which are the colonnaded court and the hypostyle hall, which has 12 columns. Inscriptions on the walls show various emperors and Pharaohs cavorting with the gods and goddesses. Just beyond the hall are three chambers, with stairs leading from one up to the roof. The view of Lake Nasser and the High Dam, across the capitals of the hall and court, is fantastic. An inner passage, between the temple and the encircling wall, leads to a well-preserved Nilometer.

The Temple of Beit al-Wali (House of the Holy Man) was rebuilt with assistance from the US government and placed just north-west of the Temple of Kalabsha. Most of Beit al-Wali, which was carved from the rocks, was built during the reign of Ramses II. On the walls of the first chamber are several interesting reliefs, including scenes of the Pharaoh's victory over the Cushites and his wars against the Libyans and Syrians. Ramses is shown pulling the hair of his enemies while women plead for mercy.

Just north of the Temple of Kalabsha are the remains of the Temple of Kertassi. Two Hathor (cow-headed) columns, a massive architrave and four columns with intricate capitals are the only pieces which were salvaged from Lake Nasser.

Kalabsha is open from 8 am to 4 pm and costs E£12 to enter (half for students). When the water level is high, you'll need a boat to get to the temple; when this happens, boatmen will offer their services for a fee.

Abu Simbel

While the fate of his colossal statue and the Ramesseum in Luxor no doubt gnaws at the spirit of Ramses II, the mere existence, in the 20th century AD, of his Great Temple at Abu Simbel must make him shake with laughter and shout 'I told you so!'.

The Abu Simbel temples were threatened with being swallowed forever beneath the rising water and silt of Lake Nasser. Their preservation, 280 km south of Aswan, must rank as the greatest achievement of the UNESCO rescue operation. And, hewn as

they were out of solid rock, the modern technology involved in cutting, moving and rebuilding the incredible temples and statues at least paralleled the skill of the ancient artisans who chiselled them out of the cliff face in the first place.

In the 1960s, as work progressed on the High Dam, UNESCO launched a worldwide appeal for the vital funding and expertise needed to salvage the Abu Simbel monuments. The response was immediately forthcoming and a variety of conservation schemes were put forward. Finally, in 1964 a cofferdam was built to hold back the already encroaching water of the new lake, while Egyptian, Italian, Swedish, German and French archaeological teams began to move the massive structure.

At a cost of about US$40 million the temples were cut up into more than 2000 huge blocks, weighing fro 10 to 40 tonnes each, and reconstructed inside a specially built mountain 210m away from the water and 65m higher than the original site. The temples were carefully oriented to face in the correct direction and the landscape of their original environment was recreated on and around the concrete, dome-shaped mountain. You can enter the dome either through a door next to the Great Temple of Ramses II or through a door across from the ticket office on the opposite side of the dome.

The project took just over four years. The temples of Abu Simbel were officially reopened in 1968, while the sacred site they had occupied for over 3000 years disappeared beneath Lake Nasser.

The Great Temple of Ramses II was dedicated to the gods Ra-Harakhty, Amun and Ptah and, of course, to the deified Pharaoh himself; while the smaller Temple of Hathor was dedicated to the cow-headed goddess of love and built in honour of Ramses' favourite wife, Queen Nefertari. They were carved out of the mountain on the west bank of the Nile between 1290 and 1224 BC. By the mid-1800s, the sandstone cliff face and temples were all but covered in sand; although they were partially cleared many times, it wasn't until the British began excavating, around

ESNA TO ABU SIMBEL

the turn of this century, that their full glory was revealed.

From the Great Temple's forecourt, a short flight of steps leads up to the terrace in front of the massive rock-cut facade, which is about 30m high and 35m wide. Guarding the entrance, the four famous colossal statues of Ramses II sit majestically, staring out across the desert as if looking through time itself. Each statue is over 20m high and is accompanied by smaller, though much larger than life-size, statues of the king's mother Queen Tuya, his wife Nefertari and some of their children.

Above the entrance to the Great Hypostyle Hall, between the central throned colossi, is the figure of the falcon-headed sun-god Ra-Harakhty. Unfortunately, the sun-god has been subjected to the trials of time and now lacks part of a leg and foot. The roof of the hall is supported by eight columns, each fronted by a 10m-high statue of Ramses; the roof is decorated with vultures representing Osiris; and the reliefs on the walls depict the Pharaoh in various battles, victorious as usual. In the next hall, the four columned vestibule, Ramses and Nefertari are shown in front of the gods and the solar barques that carry the dead to the underworld.

The innermost chamber is the Sacred Sanctuary, where the four gods of the Great Temple sit on their thrones carved in the back wall and wait for the dawn. The temple is aligned in such a way that on 22 February and 22 October every year (speculated to be the anniversaries of Ramses' coronation and birth), the first rays of the rising sun reach across the Nile, penetrate the temple, move along the hypostyle hall, through the vestibule and into the sanctuary, where they illuminate the somewhat mutilated figures of Ra-Harakhty, Ramses II and Amun. Ptah, to the left, is never illuminated. (Until the temples were moved, this phenomenon happened one day earlier.)

The other temple at the Abu Simbel complex is the rock-cut **Temple of Hathor**, which is fronted by six massive standing statues, about 10m high. Four of them represent Ramses, the other two represent his beloved wife Queen Nefertari and they are all flanked by the smaller figures of the Ramessid princes and princesses.

The six pillars of the hypostyle hall are crowned with Hathor capitals and its walls are adorned with scenes depicting: Nefertari before Hathor and Mut; the queen honouring her husband; and Ramses, yet again, being valiant and victorious. In the vestibule and adjoining chambers there are colourful scenes of the goddess and her sacred barque. In the sanctuary there is a weathered statue of a cow, the sacred symbol of Hathor, emerging from the rock.

Admission (made up of various fees) for both temples is E£20, or E£12 for students.

Places to Stay & Eat

There are two hotels at Abu Simbel. The four star *Nefertari Hotel* (☎ 316402/3; fax 316404) is about 400m from the temples in a relatively lush setting overlooking Lake Nasser. It has singles/doubles for US$60/75 and triples/suites for US$90/100, inclusive of taxes. Organised groups generally pay less. The rather small rooms have lake views, air-con, full carpeting and, in some, a mini-fridge. There's also a swimming pool. A 30% discount is often available in the summer. The restaurant stays open all year, and offers breakfast for E£11 and lunch/dinner at E£31/37. During the winter, most of the hotel's 123 rooms and suites are full, so reservations are recommended.

They will also let you camp for about E£20 – you get to use the showers, pool and mosquitoes.

The three star *Nobaleh Ramses Hotel* (☎ & fax 311660) is in the town of Abu Simbel, about 1.5 km from the temple site. The 39 singles/doubles cost US$39/74 including tax, although deals are possible. The large rooms are bright and clean, come with ensuite bath and toilet and are equipped with TV, air-con and fridge. The buffet breakfast here costs E£7.50, lunch is E£17 and dinner E£21.

The line-up of cheap cafes in town, such as the *Nubian Oasis* and *Wady el-Nil*, offers little incentive to dine there.

Getting There & Away

Until 1985, when the road between Aswan and Abu Simbel was officially opened, the only way to visit the temples was by flying in. (See the Aswan Getting There & Away section for flight details.) These days the 280 km can be covered in a variety of ways.

A bus leaves for Abu Simbel from the Aswan bus station every day at 8 am. Tickets cost E£26 return and the trip takes about 3½ hours one way; there's no air-con. The return bus leaves Abu Simbel at about 2 pm, or earlier if people wish. There's also another bus that leaves Aswan at 5 pm but taking this bus would obviously entail staying overnight at the site. You should buy your ticket for these buses at least one day in advance. If you want to cram more into one day, there are better options.

A slightly cheaper alternative would be to get a group together and hire a taxi or minibus for a tour of the temples at Philae and Kalabsha as well as the High Dam and Abu Simbel. A minibus should cost about E£25 per person (transport only). But be forewarned – a visit to Abu Simbel alone is quite enough for one day.

Many hotels in Aswan band together to arrange minibus trips to Abu Simbel. The cheapest price on offer is about E£25 for the 'short' trip, which takes in Abu Simbel and the High Dam, or E£30 for the 'long' version which also includes Philae Temple and the unfinished obelisk. Generally the trips begin between 4 and 5 am, with minibuses picking up guests from various hotels around town. They aim to get to the temple by about 8.30 am, before it gets too hot, and leave about 10 am. When you get back to Aswan depends partly on how long the driver decides to take for a shisha break at the roadside 'rest house' on the way back and how much time is spent at the High Dam. In general, those on the short trip will be back by about 2.30 pm; long haulers will be looking at about 5 pm. Admission fees are not included in the price of the trip.

Alternatively, Misr Travel organises air-con bus tours for around US$60 to the site which include lunch at the Nobaleh Ramses Hotel.

Abu Simbel is 50 km north of the Sudanese border but overland travel between Sudan and Egypt is prohibited.

ESNA TO ABU SIMBEL

The Western Oases

About 94% of Egypt is desert, lying relentlessly hot and uninhabited on both sides of the fertile Nile Valley and Nile Delta, all the way from the Mediterranean to the Sudan border. Only about 1% of the country's total population lives in this wilderness and most of them reside in the five isolated, yet thriving, oases of the Western (Libyan) Desert – Kharga, Dakhla, Farafra, Bahariyya and, way to the north-west, Siwa.

Since the 1950s, in an attempt to make use of all this spare land, the Egyptian government has been investing heavily in development projects in and around these oases. The link roads between Bahariyya and Siwa oases, and between Luxor and Kharga, are evidence of the drive to exploit this part of the country (though, as yet, very few vehicles traverse these routes). At the same time, to relieve overpopulation pressures,

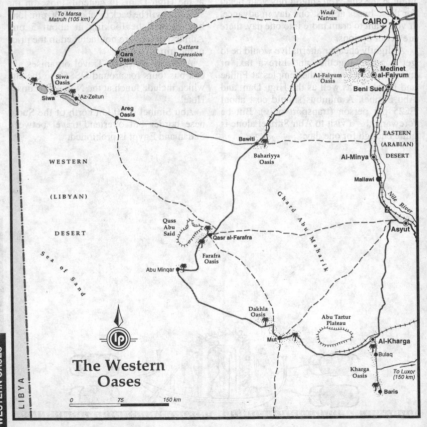

The Western Oases

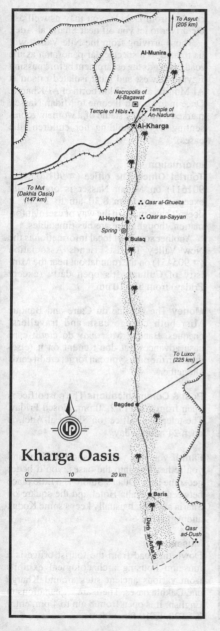

Kharga Oasis

To Asyut (205 km)

Al-Munira

Necropolis of Al-Bagawat

Temple of Hibis · Temple of An-Nadura

Al-Kharga

To Mut (Dakhla Oasis) (147 km)

Qasr al-Ghueita

Al-Haytan · Qasr as-Sayyan

Spring · Bulaq

To Luxor (225 km)

Bagded

0   10   20 km

Baris

Darb al-Arba'in

Qasr ad-Dush

landless fellahin and families from crowded towns in the Nile Valley have been encouraged to resettle in this so-called New Valley, or Al-Wadi al-Gedid, a region centred on Kharga Oasis and covering about 376,000 sq km. The first new inhabitants arrived in 1959 on 3 October – this date is now an annual public holiday throughout the New Valley.

Although the oases are attracting more and more travellers, their increased popularity has not diminished the adventure of exploring this remote region. The ideal time to visit is in late autumn or early spring, because summer temperatures can soar as high as 52°C (125°F), though humidity rarely exceeds 9%. Winter is very pleasant, but it can get very nippy (down to -2°C at times) at night.

On entering the New Valley governorate (which covers Kharga, Dakhla and Farafra oases) you must pay a one-time charge of E£4.30. The hotels or tourist office in Kharga will make you aware of this. Hang on to the receipt if you don't want to find yourself paying it more than once. Kharga and Dakhla oases are easily visited from Asyut; the oases of Farafra and Bahariyya are best visited from Cairo. There is no reason not to do a circuit right through the lot of them.

Although there is road access from Bahariyya to Siwa, there is as yet no public transport, so if you don't have your own transport, you'll be looking at a few hundred pounds to get a service taxi to take you out there on a special run. Otherwise, you have to go via Marsa Matruh.

For details about books covering the oases, see the Books section in the Facts for the Visitor chapter.

KHARGA OASIS

Kharga, the largest and most developed of the oases, lies in a desert depression about 30 km wide and 200 km long. The chief town is Al-Kharga, 233 km from Asyut; it's a boom town with a population of about 70,000 including many new inhabitants from Qena and Sohag. The present-day community of Berbers, whose ancestors were Kharga's original inhabitants, can trace their roots

THE WESTERN OASES

back to when the oasis was a way-station on the 40 Days Road caravan route between Sudan and Egypt.

Orientation

Most travellers will arrive in Al-Kharga (or Qasr Kharga), the main city and administrative centre of the governorate. It is a fairly faceless and uninteresting town, but there are a few things around it worth seeing.

The bus station is in the south-east of the town, near what's left of the old centre, and it's a fair hike to any of the hotels. If you're

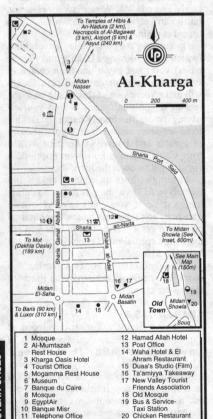

coming from Dakhla, you may as well ask the driver to let you off near Sharia al-Adel.

Those arriving from the Nile Valley will be treated to a spectacular panorama as the road descends the escarpment before passing Egypt's newest and most isolated prison at Al-Munira, about 23 km north of Al-Kharga. Once in town you'll come to Midan Nasser, marked by a large statue of a woman (representing Egypt) holding her children (the oases).

Information

Tourist Office The office (☎ 901205; fax 901611) on Midan Nasser is open daily except Friday from 8.30 am to 3 pm. It doesn't have much in the way of useful information, though there are bus timetables.

Another source of local information is the New Valley Tourist Friends Association (☎ 905451) on the roundabout near the Ministry of Culture. It's open daily (except Friday) from 5 to 10 pm.

Money The Banque du Caire and Banque Misr both change cash and travellers' cheques. Banque Misr *may* do credit card cash advances but don't count on it (elsewhere in the oases you can forget credit cards altogether).

Post & Communications The post office is open from 8 am to 2.30 pm; closed Friday. The telephone office, on Sharia al-Adel, is open 24 hours a day.

Film If you find yourself short of film, and you're heading into the oases, you'd better get some here. Duaa's Studio is a little place between the Waha Hotel and the square on Sharia al-Adel. It usually keeps some Kodak and Agfa film.

Museum

Down the road from the tourist office is a museum housing archaeological exhibits from various ancient sites around Kharga and Dakhla oases. There are explanations in English. It is open from 8 am to 4 pm; entry is E£20; E£10 for students.

Temple of Hibis
This 6th century BC structure dedicated to the god Amun was built mostly by the Persian emperor Darius I. It's two km north of town just to the left off the main road. The sandstone temple was reconstructed 25 years ago but, due to cement being used in some of the upper parts, it's now sinking under the weight of its renovations and is being eroded by rising underground water. Restoration work is still going on but there is a possibility that the temple will be relocated sometime in the future. Visitors are free to wander around the site, but you cannot enter the small temple proper.

Temple of An-Nadura
This small temple, to the north-east of the town, was built by the Roman Emperor Antonius Pius in 138 AD. You can't miss the ruins, perched on a rise off to the right of the main road, shortly before the Hibis Temple. Follow the road to the right and scramble across the desert (it's about a 10 to 15 minute walk). There's not an awful lot to see, and the guardian will hang around expecting a tip. From here you have sweeping views of the desert and oasis, and can see the Temple of Hibis before you.

Also near the temple are the ruins of a 9th century Islamic mud-brick town, most of which was built underground so the inhabitants could escape the intense desert heat. Some of the buildings are still inhabited and the locals will gladly show you around and probably even invite you to their homes for tea.

Necropolis of Al-Bagawat
One km on from the Hibis Temple, this is probably the most interesting of the three sights clustered just north of the town. Most of the several hundred mud-brick tombs in this Christian cemetery date from the 4th to the 6th centuries AD. They are traditional domed Coptic tombs, some of which have interesting wall paintings of biblical scenes. Admission is E£20 (E£10 for students). You will be dogged by someone anxious to become your guide; if you want to get inside

some of the more colourful tombs, he's your man. The site is open from 8 am to 5 pm, and an hour longer in winter.

If you're on foot, just cut across the desert when you see the necropolis to your left. By car, you'll have to drive a km or so up the road and take the paved lane back.

Temples of Al-Ghueita & As-Sayyan
Off the road through the southern stretch of the oasis down to Baris (90 km south of Al-Kharga) are a few temple remains in an advanced state of decay. About 20 km south of Al-Kharga, and a few km off to the east of the Baris road, are the remains of Qasr al-Ghueita, a temple from the 25th dynasty dedicated to the gods Amun, Mut and Khons. Another seven km further south, and about six km east of the main road, are the fairly fragmentary remains of Qasr as-Sayyan. It dates back to the Ptolemaic period, and was a temple dedicated to Amun. Given that entry to both is E£8 (half for students), they are probably not worth the effort for most people.

To get to the temples you can take a bus heading for Baris and ask the driver to let you off at the road leading to either of the temples – but you'll have a long hike to the other. If you are planning to do this, take lots of water. Tracks suitable for 4WD cars lead out to the ruins.

Places to Stay
Camping You can camp in the grounds of the Kharga Oasis Hotel for E£7 per person and use the toilet and shower inside.

Hotels The conveniently located *Waha Hotel* (☎ 900393) is a reasonable cheapie. If you're coming in from Dakhla, the bus can drop you off at the entrance. Singles/doubles without bath cost E£5.50/11, or E£12/17 with bath. The rooms have fans, the water is hot and the staff are friendly. Breakfast is an extra E£2.

There are several government rest houses in Al-Kharga. The *Mogamma*, behind the tourist office, is the best, comprising four chalets, each with two double rooms. The rooms cost E£18 per person and have refrigerators, kitchen and TV and are very clean. *Al-Mumtazah* rest house is another option but it's not nearly as good and is somewhat inconveniently located, though it's cheaper at E£9 for a bed. President Sadat stayed there for three nights in 1979 and the custodians are still raving about his visit – you'll probably be invited to see the dusty presidential suite complete with Italian furniture which has not been used since that time.

The *Hamad Allah Hotel* (☎ 900638) has 54 rooms, with and without bathrooms. Singles/doubles with bath, refrigerator, TV, breakfast and including taxes cost E£34/54, or E£51/84 with air-con. This place is popular with passing tour and overland trek groups.

The *Kharga Oasis Hotel* (☎ 901500) is the town's top-of-the-range hotel. Singles/doubles/triples without air-con cost E£55/77/103, or E£61/83/109 with air-con. Prices include breakfast and taxes. It's in a modern building at the northern end of town and has 30 rooms, each with a bathroom. It's quite good, although often seems sadly empty.

Places to Eat

The best places to eat are the hotels. At the *Hamad Allah Hotel* set lunch (E£17) and dinner (E£19) are available and there's a bar. The *Kharga Oasis Hotel* restaurant has pepped-up prices. There's no English menu, so it's best to ascertain prices before you order to save disputes when the bill arrives. There's an outdoor bar overlooking the tranquil garden.

Otherwise, try *El Ahram* at the front of the Waha Hotel which sells chicken and vegetable dishes; or there's a cheap chicken (only) place a few doors down from the bus station. There's a ta'amiyya takeaway joint on Sharia al-Adel near the roundabout, and a juice stand just opposite. With a few hours notice, the staff at the *Al-Mumtazah* rest house can prepare meals.

Getting There & Away

Air EgyptAir flies from Cairo to Al-Kharga and back again on Sunday and Wednesday;

the fare is E£399 one way. The EgyptAir office is on Sharia Gamal Abdul Nasser, just by the big mosque. The airport is five km north of town.

Bus For details about buses from Cairo, see the Getting There & Away section in the Cairo chapter.

Two buses leave Al-Kharga for Cairo, one at 6 am for E£21 and the other at 7 pm for E£32. You may be able to get on one of the three Dakhla to Cairo buses, which pass through about three hours after leaving Dakhla.

From Asyut there are six buses to Kharga; see the Asyut Getting There & Away section for more details. There are four buses from Al-Kharga to Asyut (E£6 to E£7, four hours) leaving at 6, 7, 11 am and 2 pm. Two other buses pass through Al-Kharga en route from Dakhla to Asyut.

Buses to Dakhla (E£5 to E£7, three hours) leave at 7 am and 1 pm.

Service Taxi A service taxi is a convenient way to travel to Al-Kharga from Asyut. The trip takes from three to four hours and costs E£8 per person. To Dakhla, the trip takes three hours and costs E£7.

Special Taxi At the time of writing, special taxis were about the only vehicles using the new Kharga-Luxor road (via Bulaq). You'd be looking at about E£400 for the trip (maximum seven people). There might be the odd truck going this way but hitching isn't recommended.

Getting Around

Covered pick-up trucks act as the local transport in Al-Kharga. They run up and down Sharia Gamal Abdul Nasser, as well as servicing various other routes around town.

AROUND KHARGA

Baris, 90 km south of Kharga, is the fourth town of the New Valley governorate, but there is not much of interest here. About 24 km to the south-east is Qasr ad-Dush, a sandstone temple built about the same time as the

Temple of an-Nadura in Al-Kharga. From Baris, you'll have to negotiate for a special ride out with one of the locals. Admission costs E£8/4.

There are spartan government rest houses in Baris and Bulaq. A bed in either costs E£5 but meals are not available. Check with the tourist office in Al-Kharga that they are actually open.

Getting There & Away

There are two buses a day between Al-Kharga and Baris (E£2.50), leaving Al-Kharga at 11 am and 2 pm and Baris at 6 am and 3 pm. You may be able to get a pick-up there and back for about 50 pt.

DAKHLA OASIS

Dakhla, about 189 km west of Kharga and 250 km south-east of Farafra, was created from more than 600 natural springs and ponds. The bus from Asyut and Kharga drops you off at Mut (population 13,000), the largest town in the oasis, from where you can take a service taxi to Al-Qasr, the other town of interest in the area. The bus coming from Farafra can drop you at Al-Qasr or Mut.

The oasis is home to a total of about 75,000 people and produces rice, wheat, mangoes, oranges, olives and dates as well as apricots, the latter being dried and then sold mainly during Ramadan. It has lots of sights to offer visitors and, after Siwa, is the most popular oasis with tourists.

Information

Tourist Office Omar Ahmed (☎ 941685/6) must be one of the most helpful tourist information officers in Egypt. He is a mine of knowledge about the oases and very obliging. The office is in the same building as the Government Rest House in Mut, just by the bus station, and is open from 8 am to 3 pm.

Money The Banque Misr in Mut exchanges cash and travellers' cheques only. It is open from 8 am to 3 pm and 6 to 9 pm; closed Friday.

Post & Communications The post office is behind the mosque at the bus station and is open from 8 am to 2 pm, except Friday. The 24 hour telephone office handles international traffic (but there are no card phones).

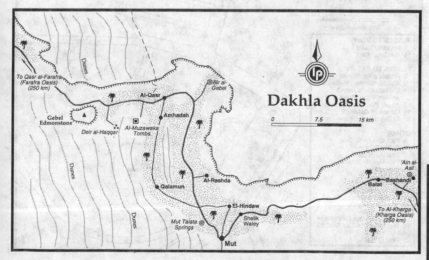

Ethnographic Museum

This museum is attached to the Dar al-Wafdeen Hotel. If you want to see displays on oasis life, ask at the tourist office to have it opened for you.

Old City of Mut

Often ignored by passing travellers, the labyrinth of mud-brick houses and winding lanes which clings to the slopes of the hill leading to the ruined citadel is worth exploring. You can climb up to the remains of the **citadel**, which used to be the town proper

(but is now used as a dump and has been taken over by goats), for views of the oasis town against the backdrop of desert cliffs and dunes. On the right of the street leading into the new town centre is a former medieval Islamic **cemetery**.

Hot Springs

There are several hot sulphur pools around the town of Mut, but the easiest to reach is the official one about three km on the road to Al-Qasr from Mut. Admission to the 1.5m deep spring, called Mut Talata (Mut Three)

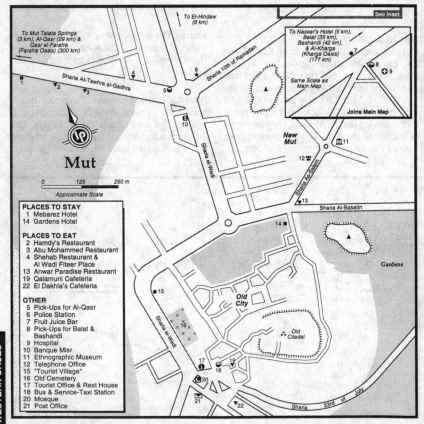

Mut

0   125   250 m

Approximate Scale

To El-Hindaw (6 km)

To Mut Talata Springs (3 km), Al-Qasr (29 km) & Qasr al-Farafra (Farafra Oasis) (300 km)

Sharia At-Tawhra al-Gadhra

Sharia 10th of Ramadan

To Nasser's Hotel (5 km), Balat (35 km), Bashandi (42 km), & Al-Kharga (Kharga Oasis) (177 km)

See Inset

Same Scale as Main Map

Joins Main Map

Sharia el-Wadi

Sharia As-Salam

New Mut

Sharia Al-Basatin

Sharia el-Wadi

Old City

Old Citadel

Gardens

Sharia 23rd of July

PLACES TO STAY
1 Mebarez Hotel
14 Gardens Hotel

PLACES TO EAT
2 Hamdy's Restaurant
3 Abu Mohammed Restaurant
4 Shehab Restaurant & Al Wadi Fiteer Place
13 Anwar Paradise Restaurant
19 Qalamuni Cafeteria
22 El Dakhla's Cafeteria

OTHER
5 Pick-Ups for Al-Qasr
6 Police Station
7 Fruit Juice Bar
8 Pick-Ups for Balat & Bashandi
9 Hospital
10 Banque Misr
11 Ethnographic Museum
12 Telephone Office
15 "Tourist Village"
16 Old Cemetery
17 Tourist Office & Rest House
18 Bus & Service-Taxi Station
20 Mosque
21 Post Office

is 50 pt, and there is a dubious rest house there. The pool's rust-coloured water may not look very inviting (and it can stain clothes) but it is very hot and relaxing. There are cold showers, but often little more than a trickle.

Sand Dunes & Camel Rides
A few km out past the bus station you can have a roll around in the sand dunes said to have been there since Roman times. They are not the most spectacular of dunes, but easy to reach for people without their own transport. Sunset camel rides out to the dunes can also be arranged – ask at Abu Mohammed Restaurant or the tourist office.

Al-Qasr
The area just north of Al-Qasr is full of lush vegetation. The town itself is a charming little place that seems to have been barely touched by the development projects in other parts of the New Valley. Some 700 people live in the town though at one time it housed 4500. It is now forbidden for newcomers to settle into the old section of Al-Qasr.

The ancient architecture of this town retains much of its medieval character – the narrow covered streets seem to hold all sorts of secrets. Their design is not an accident. They retain their cool in the hot summer months and also serve to protect, to some extent, their inhabitants from desert sandstorms. You can see quite a few entrances to old houses that go back to Ottoman and Mamluk times, some marked by *lentils* – acacia beams situated above the door and carved with the names of the carpenter, the owner of the house, the date, and a verse from the Qu'ran. There are 54 lentils in the village – the earliest dates from 924 AD but one of the finest is above the tomb of Sheikh Nasr el-Din inside the old mosque. The old mosque is marked by a mud-brick minaret which was built by the Ayyubid dynasty in the 12th century (and rebuilt in the 19th century). It has three floors and is 21m high but is not safe to climb. Also of interest is the pottery factory, madrassa, water wheel and a huge old corn mill. You can still see people

making mud bricks in the time-honoured way as well as men working an antique bellows in a tiny foundry.

There are pick-ups to Al-Qasr from near the police station in Mut for 50 pt.

Balat
About 35 km east of Mut on the road to Kharga is Balat, another town that has retained much of its medieval Islamic character. There is not much to do but wander around the alleys and imagine how little has changed here over the centuries. A pick-up from near Al-Kharga hospital costs E£1.

If you have your own vehicle you may want to explore a couple of nearby sites which date back to Pharaonic times. The el-Adaba tombs are about 200m after Balat on the road to Al-Kharga then one km into the desert. About two km south of here, still in the desert, is 'Ain al-Asil. Entry to both sites costs E£20.

Bashandi
Another so-called 'attraction' is the village of Bashandi, about three km east of Balat, then four km off the main road. A sign at the crossroads near the village announces that this is the site of a development project sponsored by an Egyptian university. In the village a more descriptive sign lists the projects: 'carpets project, girl's training centre for making and embroidering old clothes, basketmaking and dressmaking'. There has also been an attempt to make this a tourist site.

From an entirely material standpoint, everything seems to have worked. The projects are alive and well. The touristic part of the village is kept clean and tidy – no garbage on the passageways between the houses and smooth, rounded mud walls. The guardian of the local monuments gladly takes you to the village's 'Pharaonic' and 'Islamic' tombs (E£8) and, when it's open, to the carpet factory (50 pt).

Getting there from Mut is not easy if you don't have your own transport. Collective pick-ups leave from near the hospital and go to at least the crossroads (E£1). It takes about an hour to get there, as the pick-ups stop a lot on the way. Try to get a pick-up bound all the way for Bashandi; if you end up on a Teneida-bound one it'll drop you at the intersection from where you'll have to walk the four km there and, most likely, back. Don't leave your return too late or you may miss out on a ride.

Other Sights
From Mut on the road to Al-Qasr and Farafra, there are several places worth visiting if the traveller is in no hurry, although for some you'll need your own transport or have to bargain with locals.

About 25 km north of Mut there is a turn-off to the right to **Bir al-Gebel** where there is a pleasant spring about five km off the main road. A sign states that there is a rest house, but it is not operating.

About four km west of Al-Qasr, you'll find a turn-off to the left (south) to the **Al-Muzawaka tombs** which date back to Pharaonic times. From the road they are one km into the desert (signposted in Arabic only). An E£8 entrance fee applies. At the time of writing, the custodian had misplaced the key to the two main tombs (those with the brightest paintings), however, you can still wander around the flat-topped hill which is pocked with tombs. The custodian will probably delight in showing you a rough-cut tomb – just to the left of the two main tombs – which contains four adult mummies. Baksheesh is expected of course.

Seven km west of Al-Qasr, at the checkpoint on the road to Farafra, there's a signposted turn-off to **Deir al-Haqqar**. From the turn-off it's another five km to the sandstone temple which was built during the reign of Nero (45-68 AD) and has recently been restored and opened to the public (for a hefty fee of E£20 or half for students). The temple has been enclosed by a wall to help prevent wind and sand erosion, and at the entrance is a display room outlining its history and the restoration process.

Between the turn-offs to the Deir al-Haqqar and Al-Muzawaka tombs and you'll pass a controversial little village (on the left)

designed by the late Hassan Fathy. One of Egypt's best known architects, Fathy believed mud bricks and domed ceilings were two important elements of desert architecture, with the domes providing natural air-conditioning and the mud bricks keeping the house cool during the day but warm at night. The village was built to house newcomers to Dakhla from the Nile Valley, however, these same people refused to live there as the domed-shaped structures reminded them of traditional Coptic tombs. In a bid to secure their acceptance, the governor of Dakhla has now built his own domed, mud-brick home.

On a secondary road leading back to Mut, you can visit several **tombs** near the ruined village of Amhadah, dating from the 22nd century BC. About 15 km further towards Mut is the Mamluk village of **Qalamun** with a cemetery from where there is a good view of the surrounding area.

Places to Stay
Camping It's possible to camp near the dunes west of Mut or in Al-Qasr, on a desert plateau just north of town, where the night sky is a spectacular field of stars; but try not to attract too much attention. You can also camp at the Mut Talata springs for E£4 per person, however, there's room for two small tents only and the mosquitoes can be bad in the warmer months.

Rest Houses There are two rest houses in Mut. The *Government Rest House* near the bus station (in the same building as the tourist office) is pretty basic, and the question of running water problematic. But it's cheap at E£3.70 a bed. The other place is the *Dar al-Wafdeen Government Hotel* but it's reserved for officials only.

Finally, there's another *Rest House* out of town at Mut Talata springs. A bed in either a double bungalow facing the pool or in the so-called 'villa' across the road costs E£5. There is tea and a few soft drinks for sale.

Hotels The only option in Al-Qasr is the friendly *El Qasr Hotel* (☎ 940750) on the main road near the entry to the old town. It's a two storey place with a view over a small lake and Al-Qasr, and has four, big, screened rooms with narrow balconies for E£7 per person; breakfast is extra. Each room features two large beds. Shared bathrooms are clean and, contrary to the norm, have hot water only. It's run by the amiable Mohammed, who also manages the ground-floor teahouse and restaurant which serves good basic fare such as chicken, rice, fuul and salad.

The best deal in Mut itself is the *Gardens Hotel* (☎ 941577), where singles/doubles without bath or fan cost E£10/12; with bath E£12/16 (triples E£21). Breakfast is extra. The showers sometimes have piping-hot water and the rooms are reasonably comfortable, though a bit dusty. The palm-filled courtyard out the back is a peaceful spot to relax and there's a rooftop terrace (of sorts) as well. The hotel rents out bikes for E£5.

Another cheap alternative is the relatively new *Nasser's Hotel*, on the edge of Shelik Waley, a village about five km east of Mut on the road to Kharga (or 20 minutes by bicycle from Mut). It's about 400m off the main road to the left and is signposted. The young and likeable owner, Nasser, built this simple house over a period of two years. He has three rooms which guests can use for E£5 per person and is in the process of establishing a small garden. If you're interested in staying there, it's probably best to first contact Nasser at his brother Hamdy's restaurant in Mut.

If you have a bit of money to throw around, one option is the *Mebarez Hotel* (☎ 941524). It's past Hamdy's Restaurant on the road to Al-Qasr, and is popular with groups. A single/double with bath costs E£27.65/39.70 including taxes. Without bath, the rooms are E£22.90/ 33.90. There's an international phone line (but there's a 30% mark-up on normal tariffs).

A new 'tourist village' is being painstakingly built next to the old Islamic cemetery in Mut. It was the last design Hassan Fathy created before he died, and will be a three to four star establishment when it's eventually completed.

Places to Eat

There are not too many restaurants and cafes in Mut. *El Dakhla's Cafeteria* is on the square where the buses stop. It's a fair place for coffee, tea and pastries such as kounafa and basboosah but the 'food' consists uniquely of fried liver. You can do better. For example, try the *Qalamuni Cafeteria* on the same square which has a wide choice of cheap eats.

Hamdy's Restaurant is popular with travellers and serves chicken, kebab, vegetables and a few other small dishes plus excellent, freshly squeezed lime juices. It's friendly and has a small outdoor section.

The nearby *Abu Mohammed Restaurant* is the place to go for a meal that will fill you to bursting. Seemingly unending serves of soups, vegetables, rice, kebab, salads, sweets and Stella (nonalcoholic) beer emerge from a kitchen so clean it almost sparkles. It's not dirt cheap, however, so don't overorder if your budget is tight.

Down by the Gardens Hotel is the *Anwar Paradise Restaurant* which serves ta'amiyya and fuul, and is popular with the locals.

The *Gardens Hotel Restaurant* serves a range of meat dishes, rice, omelettes and salad plus a very tasty mixed vegetable dish baked and served in an earthenware pot. Prices are cheap and you can dine in the cool garden shaded by date palms. It's best to eat here in the evening when the head chef is around.

The *Mebarez Hotel Restaurant* is quite OK, but more expensive. Breakfast is E£3.50, lunch costs E£11.80 and dinner E£12.90.

Other places worth investigating are the *Shehab Restaurant* near Abu Mohammed and the *Al Wadi* next door where you can get a sweet fiteer.

There's a new fruit juice stand opposite the hospital.

Getting There & Away

Bus For details on buses from Cairo to Dakhla, see the Getting There & Away section in the Cairo chapter.

The services to Kharga Oasis (E£7) and

on to Asyut (E£15) and Cairo leave every day at 6 am and 5 pm and, sometimes, 7 pm. The respective fares to Cairo (12 to 14 hours) are E£26/35/37.

Other buses to Asyut (E£12) via Kharga (E£5) leave every day at 8.30 am and 4 pm. There is a bus to Kharga only at 2.30 pm.

There is one bus a day to and from Farafra Oasis (E£12, four to five hours) but it is worth checking the latest situation to be sure of going when you want to. There are no buses direct to Bahariyya; to get there you must first go to Farafra and then take another bus from there.

Service Taxi Service taxis leave from the bus station, and cost E£7 to Kharga and E£15 to either Farafra or Asyut. There are not a lot of them, so try in the morning.

There are also some microbuses to Farafra for E£12.

Getting Around

Bus There are buses from Mut to Al-Qasr at 7 and 10.30 am and 1 and 2 pm. There are two buses a day to Balat, at 11 am and 2 pm. Services are very unreliable so don't count on them.

Pick-Ups Most of the small towns and villages are linked by pick-up, but working out where they all go can be difficult and they can be ridiculously crowded. To Al-Qasr (50 pt) they depart from near the police station. You can take pick-ups to Balat and Bashandi from in front of the hospital for E£1. It may prove simpler on occasion to bargain for a 'special' pick-up.

Bicycle Abu Mohammed's Restaurant and the Gardens Hotel rent out a few clattering bicycles for E£5.

FARAFRA OASIS

The main town of Farafra, the smallest oasis in the Western Desert, is Qasr al-Farafra. It's named after the town's fort of which little remains. Although linked by a 300 km paved road to Mut (Dakhla) and another 185 km stretch to Bahariyya, the 2800 people of this

oasis are still quite isolated from most of the world. That is, however, starting to change as the population increases annually by about 1.8% and new constructions, in the breeze-block, four storey mould, start to take shape.

Many of the people are Bedouins and still adhere to some of the age-old traditions of their culture. The small mud-brick houses of the town all have wooden doorways with medieval peg locks, and the walls are painted with verses of the Qur'an and murals of ships and planes – references to the haj. The Bedouin women of Farafra produce beautifully embroidered dresses and shirts, although most of the work is for their own personal use and not for sale. Olives and olive oil are a speciality of the region, but the rich oasis also produces dates, figs, apricots, guavas, oranges, apples and sunflower seeds. Wheat and rice are the main crops.

There are over 100 springs and wells around the oasis, many sunk in the mid-

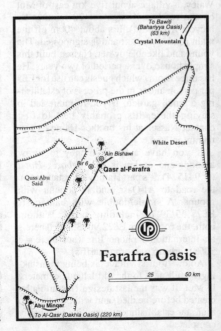

GLENN BEANLAND

GLENN BEANLAND

GEERT COLE

Left: The massive Temple of Philae was relocated, stone by stone, from Philae to Agilika Island, between 1972 and 1980.

Right: Aswan, on the fertile banks of the Nile, is Egypt's southernmost city.

Bottom: Four colossal statues of Ramses II guard the entrance to his temple at Abu Simbel.

Top: Sunrise over the mud-brick remains of the fortress enclave of Shali, Siwa.
Left: A mosque in Mut, brilliantly lit for sunset prayers, Dakhla Oasis.
Right: 'Allah' inscribed above a doorway at Bashandi, Dakhla Oasis.

1960s as part of the programme to attract outsiders to the region. The springs in town were once a favourite bathing spot among travellers, but there are plans to close them to swimmers, so they may no longer be accessible.

The calm and simplicity of this place will enchant you, especially if you're coming from Cairo or Kharga. There's precious little to do but wander around the town, the oasis and into the desert.

Information

There is no tourist office as such but Farafra's mayor is an informed chap who can be of great assistance to travellers and often extends an invitation to his chambers at the town council. The nearby post office is open from 8.30 am to 2.30 pm; closed Friday. The telephone office next door is open daily from 6 am to noon for national calls only.

There is nowhere to change money here.

Museum

This is Farafra's only 'sight', and it's well worth checking out. The museum is the showpiece of Badr, a very expressive artist who paints and sculpts not-so-subtle works of village people in everyday life. His distinctive style has won him foreign admirers, and he has had successful exhibitions throughout Europe in the early 1990s and, more recently, in Cairo. His most recent addition to the museum is a desert garden.

'Ain Bishawi

This roman spring bubbles forth on a hillock to the north-west of the rest house. It has been developed into an irrigated grove of date palms together with citrus, olives, apricots and carob trees, and is a cool haven amidst the arid landscape. Several families tend the crops here; you should seek someone out and ask permission before wandering around.

White Desert

The White Desert, or Sahra el-Beida, is an otherworldly region of blinding-white rock formations shaped by wind erosion. It's about 41 km from Qasr al-Farafra on the road

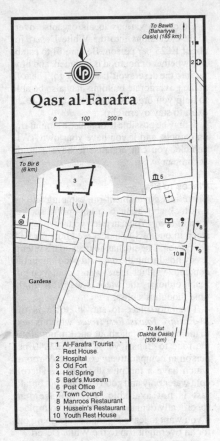

Qasr al-Farafra

0   100   200 m

To Bawiti (Bahariyya Oasis) (185 km)

To Bir 6 (6 km)

To Mut (Dakhla Oasis) (300 km)

Gardens

1 Al-Farafra Tourist Rest House
2 Hospital
3 Old Fort
4 Hot Spring
5 Badr's Museum
6 Post Office
7 Town Council
8 Manroos Restaurant
9 Hussein's Restaurant
10 Youth Rest House

to Bahariyya – look for a rough turn-off to the right (it's not signposted). Regular vehicles can drive the first km or so to the start of the formations (look out for the 'camel' and the 'hawk') but only 4WD vehicles can advance deeper into the area. The ideal time to visit is around sunrise or sunset when the colours are at their most brilliant.

You can see the desert from the bus or your car, and some travellers simply get off the bus and take themselves off into the desert – be sure to have adequate supplies, and remember that traffic either way is not very heavy.

THE WESTERN OASES

Otherwise various locals organise overnight excursions into the White Desert for about E£25 per person. Be careful to establish whether or not food is included, and how far into the desert you'll actually go. The folk at the governorate building may also be able to help you organise a car (E£80 plus E£20 extra to stay overnight).

It may be possible to organise a similar trip on camels, and if you have your own 4WD vehicle, you can organise to have a guide accompany you.

Places to Stay
There is a government-run camping site on a hillock above Bir 6, a hot spring six km west of town. You can pitch your own tent or sleep in one of 14 conical reed huts for E£5 per person. The site has no trees so it's relentlessly hot during the day, and paddling in the concrete viaduct there won't cool you off much either as the water is warm. At night time though it's bliss.

The only place to stay in town is the *Al-Farafra Tourist Rest House* which is next to the new hospital, about one km out along the road to Bahariyya. It costs E£9.40 per person in comparatively comfortable rooms which have a fan plus three beds. There's cold water only and good lighting, but breakfast is not available. The management specifically demands you pay for your place if you want to leave luggage while going out for an overnight trip to the White Desert.

The *Youth Rest House* on the same road is for Egyptians only.

Places to Eat
Only two little diners offer anything in the way of food. *Hussein's* is the larger of the pair but even here most of the pots are empty by 7 pm, so come early. Hussein offers white cheese, omelettes, molokhiyya, beans, rice and bread; on a good day you might get ta'amiyya as well. He stocks bottled water.

The nearby *Manroos Restaurant* is newer than Hussein's but has the same offerings.

Getting There & Away
For details on buses from Cairo, see the Getting There & Away section in the Cairo chapter. There is a bus from Farafra to Cairo (E£25, 10 to 11 hours) via Bahariyya (E£10, 2½ hours) every day at 6 am. However, check with the locals as, at the time of writing, there were plans afoot to reduce this service to three times a week.

For details on the bus from Bahariyya to Farafra, see the following Bahariyya section.

There is one bus a day to and from Dakhla (E£12, four to five hours). It leaves Farafra at 2 pm.

As usual, you should check the latest schedules for all these buses, or you may end up staying longer in one of the oases than you want.

A microbus to Dakhla usually leaves at about 7 am from close to Hussein's restaurant and costs about E£12. Sometimes you can hitch a ride from Farafra to Dakhla, but don't count on this.

BAHARIYYA OASIS
Bahariyya is about 330 km south-west of Cairo and 185 km from Qasr al-Farafra and is linked to both by a good paved road across the desert. There are several little villages spread throughout the oasis, but the main one, with a population of about 30,000, is Bawiti. This prosperous oasis is renowned for its dates and olives.

Bawiti has a small-town atmosphere, which you will soon feel when talking to some of the locals – take everything you are told about anyone with a pinch of salt or you'll end up embroiled in a real life Egyptian soap opera.

Information
Tourist Office The office is at the town council building opposite the police station, and is open, more or less, from 8 am to 2 pm.

Money There is a new bank, open Sunday to Thursday from 8 am to 2 pm, where you can change cash only. It's next to the post office.

Post & Communications The new post office is on the main street, in the same building as the telephone office. Interna-

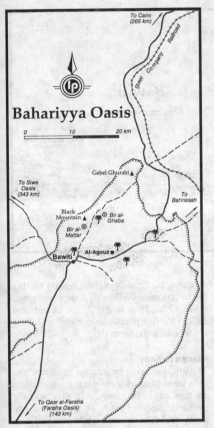

Bahariyya Oasis

0   10   20 km

To Cairo
(265 km)

Steel Company Railroad

Gebel Ghurabi ▲

To Siwa
Oasis
(343 km)

To
Bahnasah

Black
Mountain ▲   ● Bir al-
Ghaba

Bir al- ●
Mattar

Bawiti   Al-Agouz ●

To Qasr al-Farafra
(Farafra Oasis)
(143 km)

Hot & Cold Springs

The closest springs to central Bawiti are the so-called Roman springs, known as Al-Bishmu, about a 10 minute walk away. The view over the oasis gardens and the desert beyond is wonderful, but the spring is not suitable for swimming in. An equally useless place for swimming is Bir al-Muftella, about three km from the centre. It's an interesting walk out through the village, but don't go for the water alone. Take the Siwa road and keep asking. If you pass a big, white conical structure (a sheikh's tomb) on your right, you'll know you're on the right track.

The hot sulphurous spring of Bir ar-Ramla is OK if you're into scalding (45°C) baths, but you may feel a bit exposed to the donkey traffic to and fro. Women especially should think twice. It's about a three km walk from the centre of the town.

There's a spring at Ahmed's Safari Camp, if you choose to stay there but, once again, it's not big enough to bathe in.

The best spot is possibly Bir al-Ghaba, about 19 km east of Bawiti. There's nothing quite like a moonlit hot bath on the edge of the desert. The Alpenblick Hotel runs a rudimentary camping site there, so you can often arrange with them to get down there for a bath, or you may prefer to just stay in the camp for a couple of days.

At Bir al-Mattar, seven km north-east of Bawiti, cold springs pour into a viaduct and then down into a concrete pool where you can splash.

Black Mountain

The area around Bawiti is not bad territory for walking. You can't miss Black Mountain: it's a flat-top hill with the remains of a WWI British outpost on it. Head out along the road to Cairo for a while, and turn off on to the track heading to Bir al-Ghaba and the Government Rest House at Bir al-Mattar. Keep the mountain in sight and follow village tracks out to it. The walk out to it takes about 1½ hours.

White Desert

The first piece of advice is simply not to do

tional telephone lines were being installed at the time of writing.

Oasis Heritage Museum

The Oasis Heritage Museum is a smaller, newer version of the museum in Farafra, and is just over one km from the police station on the road to Cairo. Set up in a small house by a young artist called Mahmoud Eed, it features unbaked clay figurines set in scenes from traditional village life, such as men playing *siga* (a game played in the dirt with clay balls or seeds) and a man crying in agony as his injured leg is treated.

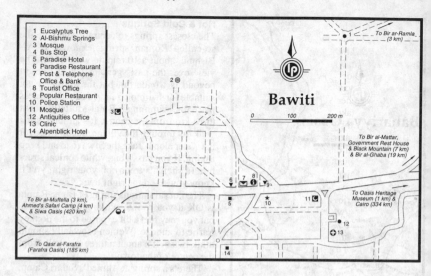

1 Eucalyptus Tree
2 Al-Bishmu Springs
3 Mosque
4 Bus Stop
5 Paradise Hotel
6 Paradise Restaurant
7 Post & Telephone
   Office & Bank
8 Tourist Office
9 Popular Restaurant
10 Police Station
11 Mosque
12 Antiquities Office
13 Clinic
14 Alpenblick Hotel

Bawiti

To Bir ar-Ramla (3 km)

To Bir al-Mattar, Government Rest House & Black Mountain (7 km) & Bir al-Ghaba (19 km)

To Bir al-Muftella (3 km), Ahmed's Safari Camp (4 km) & Siwa Oasis (420 km)

To Oasis Heritage Museum (1 km) & Cairo (334 km)

To Qasr al-Farafra (Farafra Oasis) (185 km)

the trip to the White Desert from here (as it's so expensive to arrange from Bawiti) but wait until you get to Farafra (see the previous section for details). However, if you feel you have to make an overnight trip to the desert from here, there are plenty of people trying to encourage you, occasionally even travellers themselves hoping to get a free ride for rounding up a few people.

Other Attractions

Bahariyya is not renowned for its ancient sites, although in Bawiti there are the remains of a temple and settlement dating back to the 17th dynasty. There is also a special hill, south-west of the town, known as Qarat al-Firakhi (Ridge of the Chicken Merchant). The hill features several underground galleries containing signs of bird burials. There are several ancient tombs around too. If you are interested, go to the antiquities office to get permission and help to see them.

There's a market in Bawiti on Thursdays.

Organised Tours

The tourist office can arrange (expensive) tours to various places around Bahariyya. As

an example, three days (two nights) touring the desert in a 4WD with four people will cost E£750. Trips to the White Desert cost E£350 for five people (overnight) or E£275 if you return the same day.

Places to Stay

Travellers arriving by bus are generally met by a team of hotel touts who, in an unusual attempt not to be pushy, will give you the business cards of each of their establishments and then sit back while you make up your mind; the tout from whichever place you choose will then take you there.

The *Government Rest House* is seven km out of town near Bir al-Mattar. At the time of writing it was being renovated by the Kamil Group which is planning to build a health resort out there.

The *Paradise Hotel* is a pretty dingy place in the centre of town. No-one seems to expect guests – you can wander in and find nobody around. It costs E£3.50 a bed.

Ahmed's Safari Camp, about four km west of the centre, has become a bit of a favourite among travellers and trans-Africa groups. It has a range of options (prices are per person) from cool, pleasant, domed double rooms

THE WESTERN OASES

with private bathroom for E£10 including breakfast, to rooms with shared facilities for E£5, basic reed huts at E£3 or a roof where you can sleep under the stars for E£2. Breakfast is not included in the last three options. All meals are available, as are cold beers. If you can't get a cheap enough (or free) lift and want to walk, take the Siwa fork and keep asking your way there. Alternatively you could try to rent a decrepit bike from the little shop in town but they're not too keen to do so.

More expensive is the *Alpenblick Hotel* which is a relatively attractive, two storey place with a variety of clean rooms. Large doubles without/with private bath (and hot water) cost E£35/45 including breakfast. The budget rooms are lined up in a row around the side of the main quarters and have one small double bed and an outside washbasin. They're overpriced at E£17 (breakfast is E£5 extra).

The alternative is to go out for an evening bath at Bir al-Ghaba, where the hotel has 15 huts with mattresses and nothing much else. The enclosure is watched by a warden, who will also help out with tea and firewood. It costs E£5 a night and is very peaceful.

There are one or two other places around with 'Hotel' signs up but none actually offer accommodation.

Places to Eat

Unless you make your own meals, your food will be limited to the town's two 'restaurants' and to the *Alpenblick Hotel* kitchen. Also known as *Bayoumi,* the *Popular Restaurant* serves a selection of dishes (such as a quarter chicken, rice, vegetables and a cola) for around E£8 and is also open for breakfast. The *Paradise Restaurant* serves kushari.

There are several grocery stores where you can pick up supplies for a few nights out in the desert.

Getting There & Away

Bus For details about buses from Cairo to Bahariyya, see the Getting There & Away section in the Cairo chapter. Going to Cairo, there are daily buses at 7 am (E£10) and 9 am (E£12).

Heading to Farafra (E£10), you can pick up the bus from Cairo which generally reaches Bahariyya sometime between 1 and 2 pm. This bus drops passengers off at the Popular Restaurant before continuing down the street to a new teahouse where it stops for about half an hour. It can take about 2½ hours to cover the leg to Farafra due to the unfinished state of part of the road. It makes for one dusty bus ride!

It is advisable to book, which you can only do for Cairo. The ticket office is on the 2nd floor of the building housing the telephone office. Opening hours are erratic – try from 9 am to 1 pm.

Service Taxi Supposedly, there's always a service taxi going to Sayyida Zeinab in Cairo between 3 and 4 pm, but this could be earlier or later and not every day. If and when it does go, the taxi costs E£15 per person and takes around five hours. Ask at the Popular Restaurant. A service taxi to Farafra (and they're not very frequent) will also cost E£15.

Camel Before the paved road linked Bahariyya to Cairo, camel caravans were not uncommon; the typical caravan took about 16 days. Once in a while, an intrepid foreigner organises a small caravan to make this trip. Should you be interested in following suit, ask at the tourist office or visit the family who owns the camels near Bir al-Mattar. Bahariyya's camels are kept outside Bawiti to prevent them from coming into contact with a fly which is harmful to them.

SIWA OASIS

The lush and productive Western Desert oasis of Siwa, famous throughout the country for its dates and olives, is 305 km south-west of Marsa Matruh and 550 km west of Cairo, near the Libyan border. It lies 12 m below sea level in a depression (ranging from nine to 28 km in width) which stretches for 80 km.

It is undoubtedly one of the most picturesque and idyllic places in Egypt. Against the

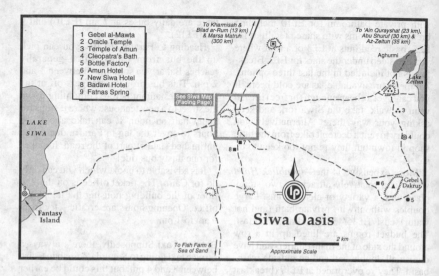

To Kharmisah &
Bilad ar-Rum (13 km)
& Marsa Matruh
(300 km)

To 'Ain Qurayshat (23 km),
Abu Shuruf (30 km) &
Az-Zeitun (35 km)

1 Gebel al-Mawta
2 Oracle Temple
3 Temple of Amun
4 Cleopatra's Bath
5 Bottle Factory
6 Amun Hotel
7 New Siwa Hotel
8 Badawi Hotel
9 Fatnas Spring

Aghurmi

Lake
Zeitun

LAKE
SIWA

See Siwa Map
(Facing Page)

Gebel
Dakrur

Fantasy
Island

Siwa Oasis

0   1   2 km

Approximate Scale

To Fish Farm &
Sea of Sand

awesome backdrop of eroded hills and a sea of sand dunes, Siwa appears like the proverbial mirage – a wealth of green date palms shading mud-brick villages which are connected by streams and springs and irrigated gardens.

Siwa lies on the old date caravan route via Qara, Qattara and Kerdassa (near Cairo) which ended at Memphis. However for centuries, apart from these desert caravans of ancient times or the occasional pilgrim who journeyed there to visit the famed Temple of Amun, few outsiders ventured to Siwa. Although Islam and Arabic did eventually reach this far into the desert, Siwa's solitary location had until recently allowed the predominantly Berber-speaking inhabitants to preserve many of their ancient traditions and customs, including their own language.

That is all changing now, and some observers feel the onslaught of the modern age and tourists will all but drown this unique place. The road linking the oasis to Marsa Matruh has now been joined by another to Bahariyya Oasis, to the south-east. Microwave stations link Siwa to the rest of the country. What started off as a trickle of travellers venturing down the new road from Marsa Matruh has turned into something of a minor avalanche. Even tour buses get down there now. Of the population of 15,000 (4000 of whom live in outlying villages), about a thousand are Egyptians, not all of whom seem all that chuffed to be here. From about September to December, a thousand or so seasonal workers come from Upper Egypt for the harvest.

The least visitors can do to help preserve Siwa's culture is to respect local sensibilities and act accordingly – do not bring alcohol to the oasis or, as the tourist office puts it, show 'displays of affection' in public. Modest dress is also appreciated. Indeed, women travellers will find themselves feeling very out of place wandering around in, for example, shorts and a T-shirt, in light of the fact that life for Siwan women is very secluded. Girls are often married by the time they're 14 after which they may speak to male members of their immediate family only. In public, women must wear a demure blue/grey shawl, known as a *tarfodit*, which totally covers their face and upper body.

There is a paved road covering the 425 km stretch between Bahariyya and Siwa, but there is no public transport link yet. Some service-taxi drivers, approached over possible prices, came up with figures like E£500! So long as this is the case, the most common access route will remain that from Marsa Matruh on the Mediterranean coast.

History

Siwa's original Berber settlers were attracted to this island of green in a desolate sea of sand many centuries ago, when they discovered several freshwater springs in the area.

The most illustrious of Siwa's early visitors was the young conqueror Alexander, who led a small party on an eight day trek through the desert in 331 BC to seek out the oracle of the Temple of Amun. Alexander's goal, which he apparently attained, was to seek confirmation that he was the son of Zeus, and also to uphold the traditional belief that, as the new Pharaoh of Egypt, he was also the son of Amun.

Apart from a Greek traveller who visited in 160 AD, the people of Siwa did not see another European until 1792. Then in WWII, the British and Italian forces chased each other in and out of Siwa and Jaghbub, 120 km west in Libya, until Rommel decided not to bother with it any more.

Information

Tourist Office The old tourist office (☎ 6130) is on the 2nd floor of the local council building. However, at the time of writing, a new purpose-built office was under construction across from the Arous el Waha Hotel. It should be finished by now, and this is where you'll probably find the very helpful and knowledgeable Mahdi Mohammed Ali Hweiti. He can arrange trips to some surrounding villages. The office is generally open daily except Friday from 8 am to 2 pm, but may be open longer hours once the new office is operating.

Money There is no bank in Siwa, so bring enough to cover your needs.

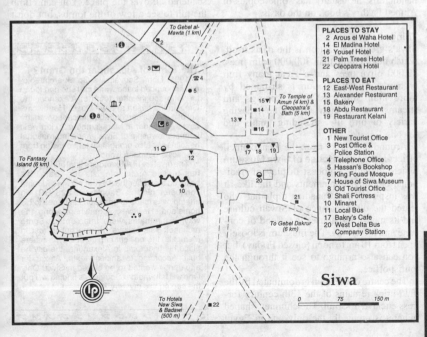

PLACES TO STAY
2 Arous el Waha Hotel
14 El Madina Hotel
16 Yousef Hotel
21 Palm Trees Hotel
22 Cleopatra Hotel

PLACES TO EAT
12 East-West Restaurant
13 Alexander Restaurant
15 Bakery
18 Abdu Restaurant
19 Restaurant Kelani

OTHER
1 New Tourist Office
3 Post Office & Police Station
4 Telephone Office
5 Hassan's Bookshop
6 King Fouad Mosque
7 House of Siwa Museum
8 Old Tourist Office
9 Shali Fortress
10 Minaret
11 Local Bus
17 Bakry's Cafe
20 West Delta Bus Company Station

To Gebel al-Mawta (1 km)

To Temple of Amun (4 km) & Cleopatra's Bath (5 km)

To Fantasy Island (6 km)

To Gebel Dakrur (6 km)

To Hotels New Siwa & Badawi (500 m)

Siwa

0   75   150 m

Post & Communications The post office is in the same building as the police opposite the Arous el Waha Hotel; it's open daily except Friday from 8 am to 2 pm. The 24 hour telephone office is nearby, but you can only make domestic calls. Should you need to phone Siwa, you must first contact the operator on ☎ (03) 934026 and then request your specific number.

Permits If you're thinking of adventuring too far off the beaten track from Siwa, you will need to get a permit. Mahdi Mohammed Ali Hweiti at the Siwa tourist office can advise you. In the past, permits invariably had to be obtained from Cairo but increasingly they are being issued (supposedly within 24 hours) from Security & Intelligence at Marsa Matruh. You'll need one photo and your passport (plus a photocopy).

Bookshop Next to the telephone exchange is Hassan's bookshop. Apart from a few handicrafts, he usually has some copies of Ahmed Fakhry's book on the oasis.

Things to See

Siwa's greatest attraction is the oasis itself, which boasts more than 300,000 palm trees, 70,000 olive trees and a great many fruit orchards. The vegetation is sustained by more than 300 freshwater springs and streams and the area attracts an amazing variety of bird life, including quails and falcons.

Around the corner from the local council offices is the small **House of Siwa Museum** which contains a modest display of traditional clothing, implements and the like. It was inspired by a Canadian diplomat who feared the disappearance of Siwan culture and its mud-brick houses in a flood of concrete and modernity. The museum is loosely open from 10 am to noon (closed Friday), but you can also arrange to see it through the tourist office.

The centre of the town is dominated by the mud-brick remains of the 13th century fortress enclave of **Shali**. The chimney-shaped minaret is reputedly the only one in Egypt where the muezzin still climbs to the top and calls the faithful to prayer without the aid of a loudspeaker.

On the hill of Aghurmi, four km east of the town of Siwa, are the ruins of the 26th dynasty **Temple of Amun**, built between 663 and 525 BC. The temple was dedicated to Amun, the ram-headed god of life, who was later associated with Egypt's sun-god, Ra, and the king of the Greek gods, Zeus. Nearby was an **oracle** supposedly used by Alexander, but there's nothing much to see now. It used to be possible to climb up the old minaret here, but it is in such an advanced state of decay that you are no longer allowed to.

Gebel al-Mawta (Mount of the Dead) is an interesting site one km north of the town. There are several tombs in the area, many of which have not yet been excavated and explored. Most of the tombs date from Ptolemaic and Roman times, and there seem to be pieces of mummies and mummy cloth scattered all over the place. You can climb the hill to see a few of the tombs, but don't

---

The Tomb of Alexander the Great?

In 1995, Liana Souvaltzi, a Greek archaeologist announced to the world that she had found the long sought after tomb of Alexander the Great in the desert at Siwa Oasis. Her discovery of a marble sarcophagus inscribed with the name Alexander at Maraki, about 20 km west from the township of Siwa, made international headlines. It also brought instant derision from sceptics around the world.

The mystery of Alexander's final burial place has teased archaeologists for years. It's believed that, after the 32 year old Macedonian conqueror died in Babylon in 323 BC, an attempt was made to transport his bones to his homeland. However, somewhere along the way, his remains were intercepted. Some archaeologists believe he was put to rest in Memphis, the ancient capital of Egypt, others place his final tomb in Alexandria, the city he built. According to ancient texts, Alexander apparently wanted to be buried in Siwa. Only time will tell whether Souvaltzi's finding will put the cap on this mystery. ◼

take photographs of the surrounding military bases. You'll need a bit of baksheesh for the guardian here, who'll only let you in from 9 am to 2 pm (until noon on Friday).

Cleopatra's Bath, also known as the Spring of Juba, pours into a stone pool, which is a popular bathing hole for the locals, but the scum floating on the surface doesn't make it very appealing. Women especially should think twice about swimming here – the ogles and sometimes worse from crowds of locals is unpleasant at best. There's little point in getting upset about it. The sight of a woman, and a foreign one even more so, jumping virtually naked (in their eyes) into a well causes the kind of stir you would get if you stripped naked in Piccadilly Circus and frolicked around.

There's a similar, more secluded and more pleasant pool on **Fantasy Island** (Fatnas), an oasis ringed by the salt Lake Siwa, which is accessible across a narrow causeway. The pool, about six km from Siwa, is in an idyllic setting amidst palm trees and lush greenery. Although a safer place for a swim than Cleopatra's Bath, women going alone should be wary. There's a custodian here who provides cups of tea and chairs, and asks E£1 for his hospitality. To get there go past the council building and take the road to the left at the first fork. Follow it around the base of Shali – at the next intersection-of-possible-confusion a sign points the way.

There are a couple of Ptolemaic tombs at **Gebel Dakrur,** about four km from town, but they are not all that interesting. Dakrur is a popular place with rheumatism sufferers. From July to September people flock here to be plopped into a bath of very hot sand for 20 minutes at a time, and then extracted and given a hot tea. Three days of this, they say, and no more rheumatism.

There are a few interesting villages to the west of the main town of Siwa. **Kharmisah** and **Bilad ar-Rum** (City of the Romans) are 15 km from the town and can be reached by local bus. They are Berber villages, and the latter has about a hundred tombs cut into the rock of the nearby hills. A few km from here is Maraki, where excavations have led some

to think that Alexander the Great was buried here (see the earlier boxed story).

To the east of Siwa are some springs. **'Ain Qurayshat** is 27 km out and **Abu Shuruf,** said by locals to be the biggest and cleanest in the oasis, is seven km further east at the next palm thicket. The clear water here is about three metres deep and spills into Lake Zeitun, another huge salt lake. The village close to Abu Shuruf keeps all the female donkeys of the oasis. Another five km brings you to **Az-Zeitun,** an abandoned mud-brick village, beaten by the sand and wind, which sits alone on the sandy plain. Hundreds of Roman-era tombs have been discovered about two km beyond Az-Zeitun and are currently under excavation, though little of interest has been found. From Az-Zeitun, another three km brings you to **'Ain Safi,** the last human vestige before the overwhelming wall of desert dunes which stretch for hundreds of km, all the way south to Kharga Oasis. Some 30 Bedouin families live at 'Ain Safi.

To visit the sights east of Siwa you'll need your own sturdy vehicle. Mahdi from the tourist office organises round trips.

About 120 km east of Siwa, near the Qattara Depression, is another oasis, **Qara,** but a permit is needed from the intelligence office at Marsa Matruh if you plan to travel this far. The oasis is home to exactly 275 Berbers. The population has remained the same since the early 1960s, with every death being compensated for by a birth. A truck goes out there about once a week; the trip along a dirt road takes about five hours.

About 13 km south of town you can visit a fish farm. This odd place is located among sand dunes in an area where oil exploration companies found only hot water and one chap decided to raise fish there – apparently they are extremely difficult to catch.

Beyond lies the **Sea of Sand,** a vast wasteland straddling Egypt and Libya, much of it quicksand. Access here is strictly forbidden – not surprising really.

Organised Tours
Mahdi from the tourist office is a great help

in coordinating trips to various sites around Siwa including the springs and village of 'Ain Safi to the east. With about six people, you'll be looking at roughly E£10 each to hire a pick-up for about four hours.

Alternatively, ask Ahmed at the Alexander Restaurant about his desert safaris by camel (E£50 per person) or 4WD (E£30 per person minimum six people). A typical full-day camel trip involves a swim or two at pools along the way, watching the sunset in the desert and returning to Siwa after dark. Lunch is E£5 extra (or you can bring your own food), and overnight safaris are also possible.

Special Events

Gebel Dakrur is the scene of an annual festival. For three days around the October full moon, thousands of Siwan men gather to celebrate friendship and togetherness, presumably burying all the hatchets that may have been taken up in the course of the previous year. Women are not allowed to attend the festivities, though young unmarried girls (up to about the age of 12) are present until sunset only. In 1995 about 200 foreigners and several hundred Egyptians also attended this festival.

Places to Stay

Siwa's march into modernity has manifested itself in the unfortunate form of hotel touts, who now meet incoming buses in a bid to snaffle all new arrivals.

Camping The tourist office recommends Gebel Dakrur as a safe area to pitch a tent, but you should inform them if you plan to set up camp out here.

Hotels The relatively new *Palm Trees Hotel*, just off the main square, is a great place to stay. It has clean rooms with fans, screened windows and small balconies and charges E£5/6 per person in a room without/with private bath. If it's full, there's a large 2nd floor terrace where you can sleep on a mattress. There's constant hot water and the bathrooms are clean. Best of all it has a shady

tranquil garden with date-palm furniture where you can relax, and there are a few good bicycles to rent.

Up until the opening of the Palm Trees Hotel, the *Yousef Hotel*, right in the town centre, attracted most of the backpacker trade. These days it's having difficulty competing, and uses bait such as a 'no Egyptians' policy to tempt foreigners. Some of the rooms here are tiny, but everything is clean, the beds are comfortable, and the showers steaming with hot water. It's E£5 a night. Next door is the oasis' long-time hotel – *El Madina*. It's E£3 a night here, but considerably more grotty and less comfortable. Both places are close to mosques.

If you head directly south of the main square you'll come to the *Cleopatra Hotel* (☎ 5716). The cheapest beds here (in a dorm) are E£5.60, but other rooms range up to about E£20.

Next up is the cheapest and scummiest place in Siwa, the *New Siwa Hotel*. It's E£2.50 a bed. A walk down past the hospital and off to the right is the *Badawi Hotel*, run by a young gent of the same name. For E£3 you get a comfortable bed and maybe a fan, however, mixed couples wanting to stay here must be able to show their marriage certificate!

Near the new tourist office is the 20 room *Arous el Waha Hotel* (☎ 6100), the most expensive place in town. It has recently been renovated but is still a little overpriced for what you get. The basic rooms *do* have bathrooms with constant hot water, fans and fairly high ceilings, helping to keep things a little cooler here than they are elsewhere. Singles/doubles with breakfast cost E£53/71, or E£36/59 without. An extra bed is E£12 and there are two suites for E£60 without breakfast. Prices include taxes.

Out at Gebel Dakrur is the *Amun Hotel*. This is generally only used by people seeking rheumatism cures at the height of summer. A bed costs E£4. There's not much in the way of food out here.

At the time of writing, an island in the salt lake north-west of town off the road to Bilad ar-Rum was being partly cleared to make room for tourist bungalows. Mahdi, at the tourist office, will probably know the state of play with this project.

Places to Eat

There's a handful of restaurants/cafes in Siwa catering to tourists and, less so, to locals. They all offer a fairly similar menu, so trial and error is probably the only way of searching out any nuances in quality.

The longest standing of them is the ever popular *Abdu Restaurant*, across the road from the Yousef Hotel. Abdu serves a whole range of traditional dishes, vegetable stews, roasted chickens (keep an eye on the resident cats – they're master thieves) and similar items. He also serves a very tasty pizza for E£4, though you might be waiting an hour or so for it.

As popular these days is the *Alexander Restaurant* opposite El Madina Hotel. The lentil soup (E£1), vegetarian shakshooka (E£2.50) and couscous (E£2.50) are excellent, and the staff are genial.

You could also try the *East-West Restaurant*, facing the mosque across the square.

Down to the left of the Restaurant Abdu is the *Restaurant Kelani* but no-one, locals

included, ever seem to eat here. There are two cafes on the square where ta'amiyya are cooked early every morning. Hot bread can be bought from the little bakery just off the square; there's a market on the square each Friday morning.

The *Arous el Waha Hotel* has its own cafeteria, and the *Palm Trees Hotel* also serves food though few people seem to take them up on this.

There are several places dotted around the square where you can have a shisha or a cup of coffee and play some backgammon. *Bakry's Cafe* (also known as the *Sohag Rest House*) next to Restaurant Abdu is one of the most popular.

Things to Buy

Several little craft shops around town compete for the tourist trade and sell replicas of old Siwan baskets, jewellery, the blue shawls worn by the local women, and pottery. Compare prices and goods at the tiny shop at the back of Palm Trees Hotel, the shop just off the main square on the road towards the Cleopatra Hotel, at Hassan's Bookshop, and the small shop next to Abdu Restaurant.

Siwan Crafts

Siwa's rich culture is easily identified these days by the abundance of traditional crafts that are still made for local use as well as for meeting the demands of tourists. Unfortunately, many older artefacts – such as jewellery, wooden chests and other family heirlooms – have become collectors' items and, over the years, have been sold to investors from around the world.

With the exception of the Nubians, Siwans adorn themselves with the biggest and most ornate jewellery to be found in Egypt. Such adornment was, and still is, a practical and secure way of investing family wealth. After all, in a community where banks did not (and still don't) exist, what safer place to store the family's worth than with women who are hidden away from the outside world? Two of the most interesting pieces of jewellery are the *aghrow* and the *adrim*. The former is a solid silver coil which is connected by a loop and hook. It's worn by young girls of marital age and announces their search for a husband. The adrim, a large silver disc, is attached to it; the whole ensemble is worn until the wedding night.

Baskets also play an integral part in Siwan society. Woven from date palm fronds by women and girls, they are traditionally utilitarian – used to store bread or collect dates – though these days they're often made simply as souvenirs for visitors. The *tarkamt*, a woven plate that features a red leather centre, is traditionally used for serving sweets, and is a popular tourist buy. Red and green are the favoured colours incorporated into basketware, and some of the more elaborate pieces are adorned with colourful silk tassels.

Wood and clay are also popularly crafted in Siwa. Local clays are mixed with straw to make pottery water jugs, drinking cups and incense burners. ■

Getting There & Away

The West Delta Bus Company station is on the main square. There is a daily bus at 6.30 am to Alexandria (E£13.50, 10 hours), stopping at Marsa Matruh (E£7, five hours) on the way. On Sunday, Tuesday and Thursday, there's a second bus to Alexandria, once again via Marsa Matruh. It departs at 10 am, is air-con and costs E£20 to Alexandria and E£10 to Marsa Matruh. You should book ahead for these services. There is an additional daily service to Marsa Matruh at 1 pm which costs E£7; no bookings are taken.

For details of getting to Siwa from Marsa Matruh and Alexandria, see the relevant Getting There & Away sections.

Although there is now a road linking the oases of Siwa and Bahariyya, there is no public transport. The first 200 km or so of this 425 km route is supposedly covered with tar but it is not actually asphalted; the remainder is dirt. Once in a blue moon, one of the trans-Africa tourist trucks heads across here. Otherwise you can hire a small truck for E£500, taking a maximum of 10 people.

To/From Libya At the time of writing it was illegal to cross into Libya and go on to the town of Al-Jaghbub, about 120 km away. There is, however, a customs house in Siwa, and a possible road linking the two towns is being surveyed. There is already a desert track, which presumably local Bedouins use – if they are allowed to make the crossing. Should it become possible to cross, there is a paved road from Al-Jaghbub to the Libyan coast.

Getting Around

There is a local bus to Kharmisah and Bilad ar-Rum once or twice a day, usually at 7 am and 2 pm, from near the King Fouad Mosque. It costs E£1 and returns shortly afterwards, so it's best to catch the morning bus and come back on the afternoon bus. Should anything happen to the afternoon bus, leaving you stranded overnight, you'll have to bunk with the locals as there's nothing in the way of accommodation or provisions in either of these places.

Bicycles are a terrific way to get around and can be rented from several sources, including the Palm Trees Hotel, the small shop near Abdu Restaurant, and Arous el Waha Hotel. The standard rate is about E£2.50/5 per half/full day.

Hiring a *careta*, a donkey-drawn cart, can be a more amusing, if less practical, way to get around.

Alexandria & the Mediterranean Coast

On the north coast of Egypt, west of where the Rosetta branch of the Nile leaves the Delta and where the desert meets the sparkling waters of the Mediterranean, is the charming, although somewhat jaded, city of Alexandria, once the shining gem of the Hellenistic world. Nearby are the Mediterranean resorts of Sidi Abdel Rahman and Marsa Matruh and the famous town of El Alamein, where the tide of the African campaign during WWII was changed in favour of the Allies. The rest of this region is sparsely populated. The road westward to the Libyan border passes along an almost deserted coast that greets the sea with craggy cliffs or smooth sandy beaches.

Alexandria

History

Having conquered Greece, the Macedonian general who became known as Alexander the Great, or Iskander al-Akbar as he's known in Arabic, set his sights on Egypt and the Persian Empire. After leading his victorious troops south to Memphis in 332 BC, Alexander followed the Nile back to the Mediterranean and chose a fishing village as the site of his capital, Alexandria.

Alexander designed the city carefully, for he envisioned it as a naval base, a great trading port, and the political and cultural centre of his empire. Although he is said to be buried there (as well as at Siwa Oasis), Alexander did not see the gift he gave the classical world, nor probably did he imagine the greatness it would achieve. Its architecture was as impressive as that of Rome or Athens, and in the last three centuries BC it attracted some of the finest artists and scholars of the time, becoming a renowned centre of scientific, philosophical and literary thought and learning.

Under the Ptolemies, who ruled Egypt

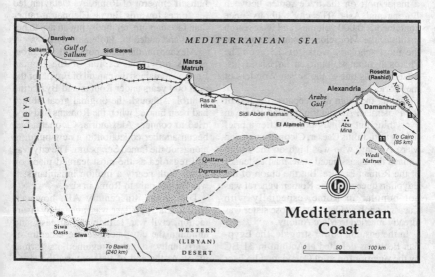

365

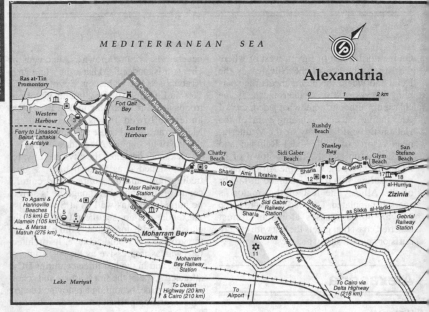

MEDITERRANEAN SEA

Alexandria

0   1   2 km

after Alexander, Alexandria developed into a major port on the trade routes between Europe and Asia. The city's library once contained 500,000 volumes, and its research institute, the Mouseion, produced some of the most scholarly works of the age. The Pharos lighthouse, built on an island just offshore, was one of the Seven Wonders of the World.

During the reign of Cleopatra, the last of the Ptolemies, Alexandria rivalled Rome in everything but military power. After a brief liaison with Julius Caesar, Cleopatra married Marc Antony, who was high on the list to replace the assassinated statesman as leader of the Roman Empire. But the union of the Egyptian queen and the Roman general was not popular in Rome, especially with Caesar's nephew Octavian, whose sister was already married to Marc Antony.

In the ensuing power struggle, the Egyptian fleet was defeated at Actium in 31 BC by the superior forces of Octavian, who later changed his name to Augustus and declared himself emperor of Rome. As Octavian led his forces towards Egypt, Cleopatra, rather than face capture, reputedly put an asp to her breast and ended the Ptolemaic dynasty.

Alexandria, the most powerful and prosperous provincial capital of the Roman Empire, remained the capital of Egypt for the next 600 years under Roman and Byzantine control. Although the original great library had been burned when the Romans had first tried to conquer Alexandria, Cleopatra had begun another collection in a new building alongside the famed Serapeum. The city was still regarded as the most learned place on earth. With nearly a million inhabitants, it was second only to Rome in size.

During the 4th century AD, however, Alexandria's populace was ravaged by insurrection, civil war, famine and disease, and although the city later became a centre of Christianity, it never regained its former glory. At the end of the century, the city's

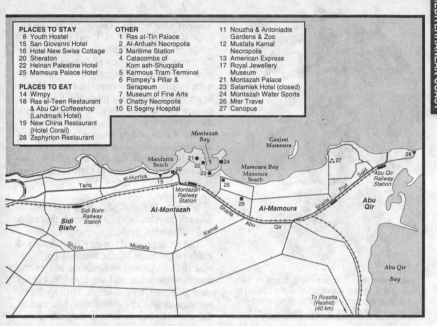

PLACES TO STAY
8 Youth Hostel
15 San Giovanni Hotel
16 Hotel New Swiss Cottage
20 Sheraton
22 Helnan Palestine Hotel
25 Mamoura Palace Hotel

PLACES TO EAT
14 Wimpy
18 Ras el-Teen Restaurant
   & Abu Qir Coffeeshop
   (Landmark Hotel)
19 New China Restaurant
   (Hotel Corail)
28 Zephyrion Restaurant

OTHER
1 Ras at-Tin Palace
2 Al-Anfushi Necropolis
3 Maritime Station
4 Catacombs of
   Kom ash-Shuqqafa
5 Karmous Tram Terminal
6 Pompey's Pillar &
   Serapeum
7 Museum of Fine Arts
8 Chatby Necropolis
10 El Seginy Hospital

11 Nouzha & Antoniadis
   Gardens & Zoo
12 Mustafa Kamal
   Necropolis
13 American Express
17 Royal Jewellery
   Museum
21 Montazah Palace
23 Salamlek Hotel (closed)
24 Montazah Water Sports
26 Misr Travel
27 Canopus

cultural importance was almost wiped out as Christianity became the official religion of the Roman Empire. Bishop Theophilus, Emperor Theodosius' right-hand man, had the Serapeum closed and partly destroyed. Later it was made into a church. All pagan temples were razed and learned institutes (including the Mouseion), along with the theatre, were closed.

The conquering Muslims abandoned Alexandria in the 7th century and established their new capital further south on the Nile. When the French arrived in the 19th century, Cairo had long since replaced Alexandria as Egypt's major city, and the latter was again little more than a fishing village with a population of 6000.

Napoleon's invasion, however, reinstated Alexandria's strategic importance, and it underwent a revival during the reign of Mohammed Ali when new docks, an arsenal, and a canal linking the city with the Nile were constructed. The stage was set for Alexandria's return as a vital Mediterranean trade centre; when the Suez Canal was completed in 1869, the city's position as a major modern port was assured.

The city also became cosmopolitan, attracting Europeans, Turks and wealthy Egyptians and providing the inspiration for Lawrence Durrell's novels known collectively as *The Alexandria Quartet*. During WWII the city was an Allied post, and part of the pivotal Battle of El Alamein was planned by Allied Intelligence from the Hotel Cecil. The revolution that brought Gamal Abdel Nasser to power in 1952 also, to an extent, struck a death knell for Alexandria's colourful European community. Probably the biggest contingent, the Greeks, began to flood out of the country, many minus the properties and belongings nationalised by the new government. The Greek community in Alexandria today numbers little more than 500 – most of them seem to run restaurants (the only thing,

Alexander the Great arrived in Egypt in 332 BC, and founded Alexandria as the capital of his growing empire. It became a centre of learning unrivalled in the ancient world.

according to one, that the government didn't nationalise).

Today Alexandria is the largest port in Egypt, a major industrial centre, and the country's unofficial summer capital, with a population of about five million. Every year the perfect Mediterranean climate, the relaxed atmosphere, and the city's reputation for the best food in the country draw thousands of holiday-makers to the waterfront cafes and beautiful beaches.

The port handles about 80% of Egypt's import and export trade; more than 5000 ships call at Alexandria annually. It is cleaner and less congested than Cairo, and although it thrives to a certain extent on the romantic reputation of its past, it is still a warm and welcoming city.

Orientation
Alexandria is a true waterfront city, nearly 20 km long from east to west and only about three km wide. The main port is on the western side of the Ras at-Tin (variously spelt Ras el Tin, Ras el Teen) promontory, while the Eastern Harbour, in front of the Corniche, is used mostly by fishing and pleasure craft. The tip of the promontory was once Pharos Island, where the famous lighthouse stood, but silting gradually formed the causeway that now connects the island with the mainland.

Sharia 26th of July sweeps from the tip of the promontory east along the beaches towards Montazah Palace. Along the way its name changes to Sharia al-Geish. These two seaside streets are referred to collectively as the Corniche.

Whereas in Cairo 'sharia' is translated as 'street', in Alexandria it's French that rules and it becomes 'rue'.

The focal point of the city is Midan Saad Zaghloul, a large square running on to the waterfront. Around the midan, and in the streets to the south and west, are the central shopping area, tourist office, airline offices, restaurants and cheaper hotels. Just east of the midan is Ramla station, the central tram depot in Midan Ramla. In fact, with the two squares so close to each other, the whole area is generally known as Ramla. Asking for Midan Saad Zaghloul is likely to get blank expressions.

Sharia an-Nabi (or Nebi) Daniel runs approximately north-south through this area, from Midan Saad Zaghloul to Midan al-Gomhurriya, which is the square in front of Masr station, the main terminal for trains to Cairo. The city's main east-west thoroughfare, Tariq al-Hurriya (*tariq* means road or avenue), intersects Sharia an-Nabi Daniel about halfway between Masr railway station and the sea.

South of the city is the Mahmudiya Canal, which links Alexandria with the Nile, and to the south-west is Lake Mariyut (or Mareotis). About 24 km east of the city centre, not far from the Montazah Palace, is the town of Abu Qir, the site of two historic battles between the French and British, and now known for its seafood restaurants.

Maps The best map of the city is published

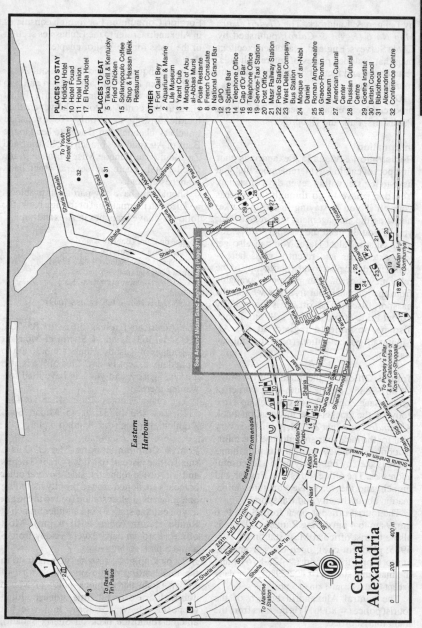

PLACES TO STAY
7 Holiday Hotel
10 Hotel Fouad
11 Hotel Union
17 El Rouda Hotel

PLACES TO EAT
5 Tikka Grill & Kentucky
   Fried Chicken
15 Sofianopoulo Coffee
   Shop & Hassan Bleik
   Restaurant

OTHER
1 Fort Qait Bey
2 Aquarium & Marine
   Life Museum
4 Yacht Club
6 Mosque of Abu
   al-Abbas Mursi
8 Poste Restante
9 French Consulate
12 National Grand Bar
13 GPO
14 Spitfire Bar
16 Telephone Office
18 Cap d'Or Bar
19 Telephone Office
20 Service-Taxi Station
21 Post Office
22 Masr Railway Station
23 Police Station
24 West Delta Company
   Bus Station
25 Mosque of an-Nabi
   Daniel
26 Roman Amphitheatre
27 Graeco-Roman
   Museum
28 American Cultural
   Center
29 Russian Cultural
   Centre
30 Goethe Institut
31 British Council
32 Bibliotheca
   Alexandrina
   Conference Centre

See Around Midan Saad Zaghloul Map (Page 371)

Eastern
Harbour

Pedestrian Promenade

Central
Alexandria

0   200   400 m

by Lehnert & Landrock. The *Clyde Leisure Map No 6 (Egypt & Cairo)*, published by Clyde Surveys, England, is another excellent map that includes places of interest, hotels, restaurants, and facts about the city and surrounding areas.

Other maps to look out for are the ones produced by Freytag & Berndt, Macmillan Publishers, Falk and Geoprojects.

Information

Registration & Visas If Alexandria is your first port of call in Egypt, remember that you have to register within seven days of arrival. You don't have to go through the process yourself if you're staying in an up-market hotel, as the management will register for you. If you do need the passport office, it's at 28 Sharia Talaat Harb. You can also get visa extensions and re-entry visas here – you'll need one photo and a photocopy of the relevant pages of your passport (available from the machines out front) as well as the passport itself. The office is open daily except Friday from 8 am to 1.30 pm. It may also be possible to register at the Al-Montazah police station (near the railway station).

Tourist Office At the main tourist office (☎ 807-9885), on the south-west corner of Midan Saad Zaghloul, you can pick up a free copy of the pocket-size information book *Alexandria by Night & Day*, published every year for the local tourism industry. The information about hotels, restaurants and things to see is sketchy but it may have a few useful addresses. The office staff speak English and French, and they can give you some information about the city and transport.

The tourist office is open from 8 am to 6 pm; 9 am to 4 pm during Ramadan. There is also a tourist office at Masr station (☎ 492-5985; platform one), open daily from 8.30 am to 6 pm; the airport (☎ 425-8764); and the maritime station (☎ 492-5986), open daily except Friday from 8 am to 3 pm.

The central Alexandria branch of the tourist police (☎ 809611) is upstairs from the main tourist office.

Foreign Consulates For foreign consulates in Alexandria, refer to the Embassies section of the Facts for the Visitor chapter.

Money Banque Misr and the Bank of Alexandria (open from 8.30 am to 2 pm and 6 to 9 pm) have branches along Sharia Talaat Harb in the centre of town, however, they handle foreign cash only. To exchange travellers' cheques you'll need to head to the Bank of Alexandria's branch at 2 Sharia Saad Zaghloul or to Banque Misr's branch in the Cecil Hotel. There are several other bank branches around.

Should you have any particular problems and need an international or foreign bank, the following have branches in Alexandria:

Banque du Caire (Bank of Cairo)
    16 Sharia Sisostris (☎ 482-5852)
    5 Sharia Salah Salem (☎ 482-1244)
Barclays International
    10 Sharia Fawatim (☎ 483-7804)
Citibank
    95 Sharia 26th of July (☎ 483-7049)

The American Express office (☎ 851708; fax 545-7363) is at 34 Sharia el-Moaskar el-Romani in Rushdy. Hours are 8.30 am to 5 pm daily except Friday. This office is also a travel agency, and you can have mail forwarded there.

The main Thomas Cook office (☎ 483-5118, fax 483-4073), at 15 Midan Saad Zaghloul, is open from 8 am to 5 pm.

Post & Communications The GPO is a small office just east of Midan Orabi. There's an EMS office round the side. Several other branches are dotted around the city including one adjacent to Masr station (round to the left as you exit the station) and another branch at Ramla station (open until 6 pm). Most offices are open daily except Friday from 8 am to 3 pm.

To pick up poste restante you must go to the mail sorting centre one block west of Midan Orabi and a block north of Midan Tahrir. It's a decrepit little stone building (opposite a new 15 storey high-rise but entered round the back on Sharia Sahafa),

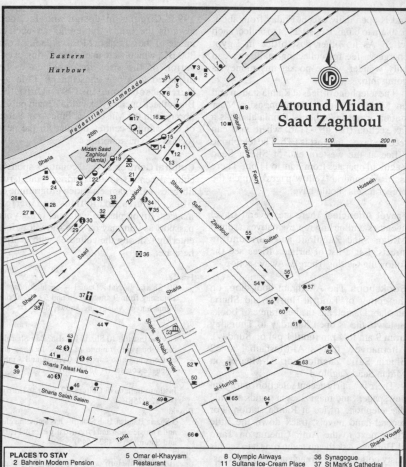

Eastern
Harbour

Around Midan
Saad Zaghloul

0   100   200 m

Midan Saad
Zaghloul
(Ramla)

PLACES TO STAY
2 Bahrein Modern Pension
4 Philip House & Bahrein Pension
9 Hotel Ailema
10 Seastar Hotel
17 Semiramis Hotel
21 Metropole Hotel
25 Cecil Hotel
26 New Hotel Welcome House
    & Pensions Gamil, Mekka
    & Normandie
27 Hotel Triomphe
28 Hotel Acropole
29 New Capry Hotel
41 Hotel Leroy
43 Pension Wiener Heim
65 Hotel Piccadilly

PLACES TO EAT
3 Darwish Restaurant
4 Denis Seafood Restaurant

5 Omar el-Khayyam
   Restaurant
6 Moustafa Darwish
   Restaurant
12 Taverna Restaurant
35 Fuul Mohammed Ahmed
   Restaurant
38 Milk Shop
44 Kentucky Fried Chicken
51 La Pizzeria
52 Chez Gaby au Ritrovo
   Restaurant
54 Lourantos Restaurant
55 Al-Ekhlass Restaurant
56 Elite Restaurant
59 Santa Lucia Restaurant
60 Cafeteria Asteria
64 Tandoor Pizza Restaurant

OTHER
1 Thomas Cook
7 EgyptAir

8 Olympic Airways
11 Sultana Ice-Cream Place
13 Baskin Robbins
   Ice-Cream Shop
14 Post, Telephone &
   Fax Office
15 Ramla Tram Station
16 Athineos Café &
   Crazy Horse Disco
18 Italian Consulate
19 Local Bus Station
20 Trianon Café
22 Superjet Bus Station
23 West Delta Company
   Bus Station
24 Menatours
30 Tourist Office
31 Al-Maaref Bookshop
32 Brazilian Coffee Store
33 Pâtisserie Délices
34 Bank of Alexandria

36 Synagogue
37 St Mark's Cathedral
39 Passport Office
40 Banque Misr
42 Banque du Caire
45 Bank of Alexandria
46 Air France
47 Lufthansa
48 KLM
49 Al-Ahram Bookshop
50 Vinous Teahouse
52 Café Royal
53 Cavafy Museum
55 Papillon Cafe
57 Cinema Metro
58 Gulf Air
61 Al-Mustaqbal Bookshop
62 Amir Cinema
63 Pastroudis Café
66 French Cultural Centre

and is open daily except Friday from about 6.30 am to 6 pm. It costs 25 pt to collect each letter. As no other post office in Egypt charges a fee for collecting mail, you can only wonder whose pocket this money is going into.

The telephone offices at Ramla station and on Midan al-Gomhurriya opposite Masr station are open 24 hours. Ramla also has a fax section (fax 483-3136) where you can receive faxes; the cost is E£6. The telephone office at the western end of Sharia Saad Zaghloul operates from 7 am to 11 pm. There is an Alexandria 'yellow pages', which the bigger hotels should have.

Travel Agencies There are several travel agencies and airline representatives around Midan Saad Zaghloul and surrounding streets. For a list of airline offices see the following Getting There & Away section.

Bookshops The Al-Ahram bookshop, on the corner of Tariq al-Hurriya and Sharia an-Nabi Daniel, has the best range of books in town and is open Saturday to Thursday from 9 am to 4 pm (until 1 pm on Sunday). Alternatively there's Al-Mustaqbal at 32 Sharia Safia Zaghloul or Al-Maaref on Midan Saad Zaghloul.

There is a fairly decent selection of foreign newspapers and magazines at stands outside the telephone office at Ramla station. For second-hand novels, track down the little kiosk next to the Amir Cinema on Tariq al-Hurriya. Ask the guy who runs it to see his dusty collection of French and English classics, stored in a mouldy alcove under the steps inside the building.

Libraries The big news on Alexandria's library scene is the construction of the Bibliotheca Alexandrina, a US$23 million project designed to revive the memory of the city's ancient library which burnt down nearly two centuries ago. Situated opposite the new conference centre, just east of the city centre, it was designed by a team of Norwegian architects and is hoped, perhaps somewhat ambitiously, to be finished by

1998. Circular in design and inclined towards the sea, it represents an ancient image of the sun disc. Mosaics dating from 300 BC, which were unearthed during excavation of the site, are expected to be displayed in a new museum on Tariq al-Hurriya sometime in 1997. Until the Bibliotheca opens, Alexandria's main public library is in the Museum of Fine Arts. Some of the cultural centres detailed in the next section also have libraries.

Cultural Centres Several countries sponsor cultural centres in Alexandria – most run libraries and organise a varied programme of films, lectures, exhibitions and performances. If you plan to visit one, bring your passport as you may have to show it before entering. Among the countries with centres here are:

France
   30 Sharia an-Nabi Daniel – open Sunday to Thursday from 9 am to noon and 5 to 7.30 pm. Films and/or videos are shown daily (☎ 492-0804).
Germany
   Goethe Institut, 10 Sharia Batalsa, Bab Sharqi – has a busy programme of films, lectures and concerts and also conducts German and Arabic language courses (☎ 483-9870)
Italy
   Instituto Italiano di Cultura, 52 Tariq al-Hurriya (☎ 482-0258)
Russia
   5 Sharia Batalsa, Bab Sharqi – has a cinema club and a music salon and is open daily except Friday and Saturday (☎ 482-5645)
Spain
   101 Tariq al-Hurriya – open from 5 to 8 pm (☎ 492-0214)
UK
   British Council, 9 Sharia Batalsa, Bab Sharqi – runs language courses, occasionally shows films and has an extensive library which is open Saturday to Thursday from 10 am to 7.30 pm (until 3 pm on Saturday). Temporary visitors can take out one day membership for E£1 (☎ 482-0199).
USA
   American Cultural Center, 3 Sharia Pharaon (behind the consulate) – shows the MacNeil-Lehrer Television News Hour at 11 am daily except Sunday, and the CBS Evening News at 1.30 pm. American films are occasionally screened in the evenings. The library is open

Sunday to Thursday from 10 am to 4 pm (until 8 pm on Monday and Wednesday); anyone temporarily visiting Alexandria is free to browse around (☎ 482-4117).

Film & Photography Photo shops are dotted along Sharia Saad Zaghloul. For passport photos, there's a booth in Masr station.

Medical Services There's no shortage of pharmacies in Alexandria, especially along Sharia Saad Zaghloul. The one opposite Ramla station, next to the Baskin Robbins ice-cream shop, is open until midnight.

Hospitals in Alexandria include:

University Hospital, Chatby (☎ 482-2929)
Al-Moassa Hospital, Tariq al-Hurriya, Al-Hadara (☎ 421-2885)
El Seginy Hospital, 10 Sharia Bilous, Ibrahimiya (☎ 597-0671)

Emergency If you have a medical emergency, telephone the special 'urgent help' number, ☎ 123. Other emergency services are as follows:

ambulance ☎ 492-5810
fire brigade ☎ 180
police (police secours) ☎ 122
tourist police ☎ 809611 (central) or 547-3814 (Montazah)

Ancient Alexandria

There is little left of ancient Alexandria – the modern metropolis is built over or among the ruins of the great classical city. A few archaeological sites, often discovered accidentally, have been excavated and preserved, but for the most part only an odd column or two or a gateway marks the location of legendary Ptolemaic or Roman edifices.

Much of the romance of Alexandria lies in the past, not the present, and it's often a case of simply using your imagination. If you stand at the intersection of Sharia an-Nabi Daniel and Tariq al-Hurriya, for instance, you are also at the crossroads of the ancient city, then acclaimed as one of the most glorious places in the world. In those days, Tariq al-Hurriya was known as the Canopic Way, and it extended from the city's Gate of the

Sun in the east to the Gate of the Moon in the west. According to a 5th century bishop, 'a range of columns went from one end of it to the other'.

Just south of this intersection, on Sharia an-Nabi Daniel, you will find what is believed to be the site of the renowned Mouseion and library, where the greatest philosophers, writers and scientists of ancient times gathered to exchange ideas.

Nearby is the modern, fairly uninteresting Mosque of an-Nabi Daniel, built on what is believed by some to be the site of Alexander the Great's tomb. Rumour has it that the great Macedonian still lies wrapped in gold in his glass coffin, somewhere in the unexplored cellars below.

Graeco-Roman Museum

The 21 rooms of this excellent museum (☎ 483-6434) contain about 40,000 valuable relics dating from as early as the 3rd century BC. The museum's own guidebook gives little indication of where to find anything other than the rooms and some numbered exhibits. The collection includes a splendid black granite sculpture of Apis (the sacred bull revered by Egyptians), many statues of Serapis (the fusion of Apis and Osiris, the god of the underworld and lord of the dead), and busts and statues of various Greeks and Romans. There are also mummies, sarcophagi, pottery, tiny terracotta figures, bas reliefs, jewellery, coins and tapestries.

The museum is at 5 Sharia al-Mathaf ar-Romani, just north-west of Tariq al-Hurriya and seven blocks from Sharia an-Nabi Daniel. It's open from 9 am to 4 pm daily, except on Friday, when it closes at 11.30 am for two hours. Admission costs E£8 (E£4 for students); the camera/video fee is E£10/150.

Roman Amphitheatre

The 13 white marble terraces of the only Roman theatre in Egypt were discovered quite recently, when the foundations for a new apartment building were being dug. The terraces, arranged in a semicircle around the arena, are excellently preserved.

The area under excavation has now shifted

to the north of the theatre, where a Polish team is still working. The theatre is on Sharia Yousef, east of Sharia an-Nabi Daniel. It's open daily from 9 am to 4 pm. Admission costs E£6, or E£3 for students, as well as E£150 to take a video.

Pompey's Pillar & the Serapeum

This massive yet unimpressive 25m-high pink granite column, which the Crusaders mistakenly credited to Pompey, rises out of the disappointing remains of the far more splendid and acclaimed Serapeum, which is in an archaeological park south-west of the city centre, near the Mahmudiya Canal. What was once an acropolis, topped by the Temple of Serapis and surrounded by subsidiary shrines and buildings, including Cleopatra's library, now merely features excavated subterranean galleries, the ruins of the Temple of Isis, a few sphinxes, a Nilometer and Pompey's Pillar.

The pillar, which has a circumference of nine metres, was erected in around 297 AD amidst the Serapeum complex for Diocletian, not Pompey. During the final assault on the so-called pagan intellectuals of Alexandria in about 391 AD, the Christians destroyed the Serapeum and library, leaving only the pillar.

The site is open from 9 am to 4 pm. Admission costs E£6, or E£3 for students. There is no fee for using your camera.

To get there, take yellow tram No 16 from Midan Saad Zaghloul for 10 pt. It stops right by the entrance. You can also get a local service taxi (minivan) from opposite Masr railway station for 15 pt.

Catacombs of Kom ash-Shuqqafa

These catacombs, the largest known Roman burial site in Egypt, were discovered accidentally in 1900 when a donkey cart fell through a part of the roof. They consist of three tiers of tombs and chambers cut into the rock to a depth of about 35m. Constructed in the 2nd century AD, probably as a family crypt, they were later expanded to hold more than 300 corpses. There is even a banquet hall where grieving relatives paid their last

Fort Qait Bey was built in medieval times using the debris and foundations of the legendary Pharos lighthouse, one of the Seven Wonders of the Ancient World.

respects with a funeral feast. In another hall, named after the emperor Caracalla, the bones of young men were found. According to the story, they ended up down here after being killed by an irate Caracalla in 215 AD for having insulted him.

The eerie nature of the catacombs is accentuated by the weird blend of Egyptian and Roman features in the sculptures and reliefs. The catacombs have been excavated, but the bottom level is usually flooded and inaccessible.

Kom ash-Shuqqafa (Hill of Potsherds) is about five to 10 minutes walk south of Pompey's Pillar. Follow the wall to the right after you leave the Serapeum and follow the street straight on. The entrance to the catacombs is on the left. They are open from 9 am to 4 pm. Admission costs E£12, or E£6 for students, plus E£10 for taking photographs.

Fort Qait Bey

This 15th century medieval fort guards the entrance to the Eastern Harbour. It is built on the foundations of the Pharos lighthouse (see the boxed story on the lighthouse), one of the ancient Seven Wonders of the World. In about 1480, the Mamluk sultan Qait Bey fortified the peninsula, using the foundations and debris of the lighthouse to build his fort, incorporating a castle and mosque within the walls. Mohammed Ali modernised the fort's defences in the 19th century, but the minaret and castle were severely damaged by a British bombardment in 1882.

Early this decade, Egypt's Supreme Council of Antiquities (SCA) commissioned the dumping of concrete blocks at the entrance of the Eastern Harbour in order to create a breakwater to protect the fort. Unfortunately, the blocks were dumped in an area known to contain many submerged antiquities. The public outcry which followed was strong enough to convince the SCA to commission a survey of the area and, by late 1995, more than 35 objects had been raised from the sea including a headless statue, believed to be that of Ptolemy, and granite blocks thought to come from the lighthouse. The SCA is now investigating new ways to protect the fort once the breakwater is dismantled.

The three floors of the fort house a small naval museum. Although little progress seems to have been made in the past few years, the stated objective is to create a full museum of naval history. At the moment, there are various displays including Ottoman weaponry and bits and pieces recovered from Napoleon's unhappy fleet, savaged by Nelson on 1 and 2 August 1798. Having debarked his army in Egypt at Abu Qir, east of Alexandria, Napoleon left behind him a fleet of 17 ships with 1116 cannons to assure supplies while he marched on Cairo.

The fleet lined up two km off the coast, all guns pointed seaward, so Nelson, with fewer ships and inferior fire power, sneaked in-between the French and the coast and sent much of the French fleet, including the flagship *Orient*, to the bottom. Among the debris of this disaster on display is a collection of French republican coins.

The fort is open from 9 am to 4 pm. Admission is E£6 (E£3 for students), plus an extra E£10 to get into the naval museum. It costs an extra E£10 to take photographs

---

Pharos Lighthouse

Alexandria's original sentinel was built during the reign of Ptolemy Philadelphus around 280 BC, on what was then Pharos Island A causeway, formed when silt blocked the channel between the island and the mainland, now connects the island with the mainland and divides the harbour in two. The lighthouse stood about 150m high. It had a square lower storey with 300 rooms, a double spiral staircase leading up through the octagonal 2nd storey, and a circular 3rd storey leading to the lantern room, topped by a statue of Poseidon.

It is not known exactly what reflected the firelight out to sea to guide and warn approaching ships, but writings of the time suggest it was a mysterious mirror or a lens through which the Pharos keeper could detect ships not seen by the naked eye. If the scientists of ancient Alexandria had discovered the lens, its secret was lost when the two upper storeys were wrecked. Legend has it that the Byzantine emperor could not attack Alexandria because of the lighthouse, so he instructed his agents in the city to spread rumours that it was built on top of the treasure of Alexander the Great. Before the Alexandrians could do anything to stop him, the Egyptian caliph had demolished the top half of the lighthouse, sending the mechanism into the sea.

Several Muslim leaders attempted its restoration, but the lighthouse was eventually completely destroyed by an earthquake in the 14th century, and left in ruins. ∎

inside the museum, or E£20 to use a video camera. The views of the city from the fort are superb.

To get to the fort and the nearby aquarium, take yellow tram No 15 from Midan Ramla or any of about six buses going to Ras at-Tin.

Aquarium & Marine Life Museum

Also known as the National Institute of Oceanography, this aquarium is housed in the wing of the fort you meet before getting to the main entrance. The ticket office is in a poorly marked office across the road. It has a variety of stuffed and lacquered fish, a whale skeleton, sponges and coral. All this for E£1, and it's open from 9 am to 2 pm.

Ras at-Tin Palace

The palace buildings, built by Mohammed Ali on the western side of the peninsula, are closed to the public, but the surrounding gardens are open – for an entrance fee of 25 pt. King Farouk owned the palace until his abdication in 1952. The 300 rooms have been kept as they were in the '50s, and are used for state guests and other VIPs.

Necropolis of Al-Anfushi

Follow the tram tracks past the entrance to the Ras at-Tin Gardens and the terminus and on the right you'll reach this necropolis, which dates from as far back as 250 BC. Two of the five tombs here were discovered in 1901; the other three 20 years later. The two main tombs contain some much faded wall decoration, supposedly imitating marble, and the remains of someone's skull lurk in one of the vaults. They are not as interesting as the catacombs of Kom ash-Suqqafa. The tombs are open from 9 am to 4 pm and entry costs E£12 or half for students plus E£5/50 for a camera/video.

Mosque of Abu al-Abbas Mursi

Dominating the main square on Sharia Tatwig, about one km south of the fort, is a modern but impressive example of Islamic architecture. The original mosque on the site was built by Algerians in 1767 over the tomb of a 13th century Muslim saint. The present structure was erected in 1943 when the largely decayed original was demolished. Yellow tram No 15 from Ramla tram station stops in front of the mosque.

Synagogue

Built over a century ago, this last vestige of what was once a thriving Jewish community now serves only about 50 elderly people, mainly women. Before the wars with Israel there were about 15,000 Alexandrian Jews, who could trace their ancestry back to the founding of the city by Alexander the Great. The synagogue, a fabulous Italian-built structure with pink marble pillars, is at 69 Sharia an-Nabi Daniel. It's generally closed to tourists though you may be able to have a look around if you ask.

Cavafy Museum

The museum dedicated to the great Alexandrian poet Constantine Cavafy is housed in the apartment where Cavafy spent the most productive and last years of his life, from 1908 until his death in 1933. Two of the six rooms have been arranged to give an idea of what the place was like while he lived and worked there. The others are being used for research. The building is at 4 Sharia Sharm el-Sheikh, a narrow street one block east of the intersection of Sharia Sultan Hussein and Sharia an-Nabi Daniel. It's supposed to be open daily (except Monday) from 10 am to 3 pm, and from 6 to 8 pm on Thursday and Sunday, however, it's frequently closed during these hours. Admission is free.

Museum of Fine Arts

A limited but interesting collection of modern Egyptian art, and Alexandria's public library, are housed in this museum, also known as the Hussein Sobhy Museum of Fine Arts, at 18 Sharia Menasha, east of Masr station and south of the tracks.

It's open from 8 am to 2 pm, except Friday. Admission is free. Yellow tram No 14 will take you part of the way from Midan Ramla.

The museum also organises a biennial of arts from countries around the Mediterranean Sea.

Zoo

The Alexandria zoo is on a small hill surrounded by the Nouzha and Antoniadis gardens. It's small in comparison to Cairo zoo but still has its share of animals living in atrocious conditions – the big cats, elephants, hyenas and bears fare particularly badly. It's about 40 minutes walk from Midan Saad Zaghloul, or you can take bus No 303 or minibus 703 from Midan Orabi, or a taxi for E£2. Admission to the zoo is 10 pt, the Nouzha Gardens 15 pt and to the Antoniadis Gardens 50 pt. All are open from 9 am to 4 pm.

Montazah Palace

Montazah Palace, at the eastern end of Sharia al-Geish, was built by Khedive Abbas II. It was the summer residence of the royal family before the 1952 Revolution and King Farouk's abdication (these days it's used as a summer residence of the president). The adjacent Salamlek Hotel (now closed), also built by Abbas II, was designed in the style of a chalet to please his Austrian mistress.

The magnificent gardens and groves and the semiprivate beach (E£5 to use it) make this an ideal place to spend a relaxing day, although the palace is open only to the big nobs of the government. The grounds, which once featured a menagerie of lions, tigers and bears, include the rather tasteless but high-class Palestine Hotel, which is a little west of the Salamlek.

Admission to the palace grounds costs E£2 (E£3 on public holidays). The palace gets very crowded on Fridays.

Getting There & Away Bus No 260 from Midan Orabi passes the gardens on its way to Abu Qir, as does bus No 250 from Masr station. Minibus Nos 735 and 728 go to Montazah from Ras at-Tin and Masr station respectively. Minibus Nos 220 and 736 (from Midan Orabi) pass by on their way to Mamoura. You can also reach Montazah on the local train from Masr or Sidi Gaber stations on the way to Abu Qir.

Royal Jewellery Museum

This museum is at 27 Sharia Ahmed Yehia Pacha, Zizinia (or Zezeniya), next to the governor's residence, and is one of Alexandria's prize attractions. Formerly one of King Farouk's palaces, it now houses a stunning collection of jewels from the time of Mohammed Ali's early 19th century rule in Egypt until Farouk's abdication, including diamond-encrusted garden tools, jewelled watches with hand-painted miniature portraits, necklaces and a diamond-studded chess set. Check out the sumptuous bathrooms, which have been cordoned off. The not entirely tasteful tile work is as interesting as the jewels – so this is how guests of the king carried out their ablutions!

The museum is open from 9 am to 4 pm (closed for two hours on Friday from 11.30 am). Admission is E£10, or E£5 pt for students.

To get there take blue tram No 2 from Ramla tram station and get off at Qasr el-Safa, or any bus on the Corniche going towards Montazah, and get off at Zizinia.

Necropolises

If you haven't had enough of tombs, there are two more sets of them. The necropolis at **Chatby** (next to the youth hostel) is considered to be the oldest found in Alexandria. It was discovered in 1904. Further east, on Sharia Maskar Romani opposite American Express, is the **Mustafa Kamal** necropolis. Two of the four tombs are interesting for the Doric columns at their centre. Both tombs are open from 9 am to 4 pm. Entry is E£6 for the former and E£12 for the latter; half for students. The guardians of these places may want some baksheesh.

Getting There & Away Bus No 218 will drop you near the Chatby necropolis. To get to the Mustafa Kamal necropolis, take tram No 1 or No 2 to Mustafa Kamal as-Sughayya and walk east a couple of blocks to Sharia Maskar Romani. Turn left here (towards the sea) and walk a couple more blocks. The necropolis is on the left.

Beaches

There are several public or semipublic beaches along Alexandria's waterfront, but most of the ones between the Eastern Harbour and Montazah are usually crowded and grubby. These include **Sidi Gaber**, **Mandarra** (which is not recommended) and **Montazah**. At most beaches you can rent chairs and umbrellas for about E£2 per day. At Montazah, you must pay E£8 to go onto the beach; umbrellas cost E£11 a day and a cabana costs E£200.

Mamoura Beach, about one km east of Montazah Palace, is one of the best; it even has a few small waves rolling in and is the only beach where women are likely to feel comfortable stripping down to a one-piece swimsuit. The local authorities are trying to keep this beach suburb exclusive by charging everyone who enters the Mamoura area a fee of E£1.30; it's payable at the toll booth as you drive in off Sharia Abu Qir.

However, the beaches at **Agami** and **Hannoville**, about 17 km west of central Alexandria, are even better as they are cleaner and less crowded. There is nothing terribly attractive, though, about the backdrop of semi-high-rise apartment blocks. Nor is the ride out, past steel and cement works, uplifting.

You can get to Mamoura Beach on minibus Nos 735 and 736 (50 pt) or bus Nos 220 and 221 (35 pt), which run along the Corniche.

From Masr station, minibus No 755 goes to Bitash (Agami) and minibus No 765 heads to Agami Zahra (Hannoville).

From Midan Saad Zaghloul, minibus Nos 750 and 760 service Hannoville.

From Midan Orabi, you can take bus Nos 450 and 460 to Agami.

Canopus

On Mamoura Bay, near Abu Qir, is the site of ancient Canopus, famous in Greek legends long before the founding of Alexandria. The settlement, at the end of a limestone ridge extending from the Western Desert, overlooked the Canopic mouth of the Nile (which has long since dried up), and was for a time a noted religious centre. In 450 BC, Herodotus claimed to have seen a temple to Hercules on the site, and was informed that Paris and Helen had sought refuge at Canopus during their escape to Troy. Another Greek legend claims that the district was named after a pilot of Menelaus' fleet who died there by the Nile on the Greeks' return journey from the Trojan War. Egyptian mythology, however, claims that Canopus was a god whose body was an earthenware jar! From this, early archaeologists coined the term 'Canopic jar' for the vessels used to store the viscera of mummies.

Abu Qir

This coastal town, 24 km east of central Alexandria, is historically important for two major 18th century battles between the French and English. During the Battle of the Nile in 1798, Admiral Nelson surprised and destroyed the French fleet in the bay at Abu Qir. Although Napoleon still controlled Egypt, his contact with France by sea was effectively severed. The British landed 15,000 Turkish soldiers at Abu Qir in 1799, but the French force of 10,000 men, mostly cavalry led personally by Napoleon, forced the Turks back into the sea, drowning at least 5000 of them.

It is best to go to Abu Qir during the week to avoid the crowds of Alexandrians who flock there on the weekends. If you're into seafood, this is definitely the place to go (see the Alexandria Places to Eat section).

There are plenty of buses from central Alexandria to Abu Qir every day (for example bus Nos 260 and 261 or minibus No 729 from Midan Orabi), or you can catch a service taxi for 50 pt from in front of Masr station.

Diving

It's possible to learn scuba diving at Alexandria, however, there's not much to see here compared with the Red Sea, and prices for open-water certification courses are roughly the same as you'd pay in Hurghada or the Sinai. If you're interested, contact Montazah

Water Sports (☎ 547-6637) on the waterfront at Montazah.

Language Courses & Work

Many people coming to Egypt looking for work or wanting to study Arabic simply overlook Alexandria as a possibility. The opportunities are not as abundant as Cairo, but TEFLA qualified teachers (see Teaching English under Work in the Facts for the Visitor chapter), if interested, should call in at the British Council to check out the demand.

Most of the cultural centres also run courses in Arabic.

Places to Stay

The summer months of June to September are the high season in Alexandria, and many places increase their prices during this time. August is particularly busy, so you may have difficulty finding a hotel room even at some of the bottom-end places.

Places to Stay – bottom end

Unless stated otherwise, the prices below include taxes and breakfast.

Hostels The *Youth Hostel* (☎ 597-4559), at 13 Sharia Port Said, costs E£6.10 for members in dorms (eight beds) or E£10 to E£15 in one of the new double rooms. Non-members pay E£4 extra and breakfast is an additional E£2. The place is acceptable, but not outstanding. To get there, take any blue tram from Ramla station and get off at the Chatby Casino, in front of the College of St Mark. Cross to the waterfront side of the college and walk back west a short way along Sharia Port Said. Alternatively catch bus No 218. It's open from 8 am to 11 pm.

Hotels – East of Midan Saad Zaghloul
Right on the Corniche is a series of waterfront pensions worth investigating, but only if you're really strapped for money. Standing on the Corniche facing the Darwish restaurant, you'll see signs for the Bahrein Modern, Philip House and Bahrein pensions; the staff at all three speak Arabic only. The

entrance to the *Bahrein Modern* is on the left side of the building, past a little shop. The pension is on the 3rd floor above a doctor's surgery and has doubles, triples and quads for E£10. This must be one of the cheapest deals in town but, be warned, the rooms are pretty grotty, the sheets are rarely changed and there's no elevator (or breakfast).

On the right side of the same building (next to the Denis Restaurant) is the 2nd floor *Philip House*. At the time of writing this place was closed but according to locals it was still operating. On the floor above is the *Bahrein*, a hovel asking E£25 for dingy doubles.

There are two hotels on Sharia Amine Fekry which offer very good value if you've got a few extra pounds to spare. The *Hotel Ailema* (☎ 483-2916) is at No 21 (7th floor), and prices its rooms according to sea views, whether or not there are bathrooms in the rooms and so on. Singles range from E£21 to E£34, and doubles between E£30 and E£47. The better rooms have enclosed balconies with commanding views of the Eastern Harbour and are clean, spacious and comfortable, if not overly furnished. The staff are amiable.

The *Seastar Hotel* (☎ 483-1787; fax 483-2388) just up the road at No 24, is almost a lower mid-range place, and is clean and very comfortable (though some of the single rooms are a bit cramped). Singles/doubles with bath cost E£45/50, or E£27/35 without.

Hotels – West of Midan Saad Zaghloul
The streets due west of the midan are full of cheap hotels and pensions. First up is the *Hotel Acropole* (☎ 805980), 4th floor, 1 Sharia Gamal ad-Din Yassin. It's centrally located but is not as hot a deal as it once was. The noise from the bus station and trams below can detract from the good Mediterranean views from the more expensive rooms. The staff (and the elevator) are pretty blasé, some of the beds are not all that comfortable, and none of the rooms have bathrooms. The shared bathrooms are kept clean, but hot water seems erratic at best. It costs between E£15 and E£20 for a single, depending on

the location of the room. Doubles range from E£25 to E£30, and there are a couple of triples.

Across the street is the 5th floor *Hotel Triomphe* (☎ 807585), or *Nasr* in Arabic, which means the same thing. The rooms are scruffy, and some have sagging beds but, at E£8/12 for a single/double, they aren't too bad. Breakfast is E£2.50 and there supposedly is hot water but don't count on it. Some of the rooms have sea glimpses.

A few doors down from the Triomphe, on Sharia Gamal ad-Din Yassin, is a building with four pensions. It's worth checking them all out – after all, there's not very far to walk between them! On the 5th floor is the *New Hotel Welcome House* (☎ 806402) whose keen new owners offer spacious rooms for E£6 per person.

The other three pensions are all on the 4th floor. The *Hotel Gamil* (☎ 815458) has seven rooms, but compare them as they're not the same. The better rooms are clean and comfortable and the shared bathroom is spotless. It's a family-run pension, and Mustafa Gamil, the present manager, may be willing to drop his price a little. Singles/ doubles are E£17/20 and breakfast is E£2 extra.

The *Hotel Normandie* (☎ 806830) is across the hall from Hotel Gamil; some rooms have good views of the harbour. Most of the pension is furnished with French antiques, a reminder of the French lady who owned this place until her death. Rooms cost E£16.50/20; breakfast is not available.

Adjacent to Hotel Gamil is the *Mekka* (☎ 808940) which charges E£20 for a room with three beds; there's no concession for single travellers. The shared baths are clean and the rooms have small balconies.

One block west of these pensions is the *Hotel Union* (☎ 807312). The hotel, on the 5th floor, is well maintained and great value. Some rooms have TVs, sparkling tiled bathrooms, balconies and fantastic harbour views. Singles/doubles without bath cost E£26/32, or E£36/46 with bath. Breakfast is E£5 extra. It's costs more than other bottom-end places, but if you want some comfort, it's definitely worth the extra money.

The 1st floor *Hotel Fouad* (☎ 808308) is three blocks west of the Hotel Union. It's a small place (often full) and is run by the friendly Tareq. The atmosphere is homely and double rooms cost E£20.

Down on Midan Orabi, the *Holiday Hotel* (☎ 803517; fax 801559) is well managed and popular with trans-African travellers on overland trucks. Singles/doubles with private bathroom cost E£37/53, or E£31/41 without. Breakfast is not included. Some rooms have good views of the square and Mediterranean. The staff are helpful and the place has had some good reports from travellers.

There are also a couple of places south of Midan Saad Zaghloul which are worth investigating. The *New Capry Hotel* (☎ 809310), on the 8th floor in the same building as the tourist office has singles/doubles for E£28/42 without bath; E£39/46 with bath. The views from some rooms are almost vertiginous, but you are high enough to avoid much of the noise from Midan Saad Zaghloul below.

The *Hotel Leroy* (☎ 482-9224) is more or less opposite the passport office, on the top floor of an office building at 25 Sharia Talaat Harb. Most of the rooms have balconies, but you may find the sheets haven't been changed since the previous occupants left. Singles/doubles/triples range in price from E£22/30/40 to E£25/35/46, depending on their position and whether or not they have balconies. You get a panoramic look over the city, but not much in the line of sea views. There's hot water in one of the shared showers. Take the marked lift to the left of the main lift, or you'll have trouble getting into the hotel.

In the same building (but best entered from Sharia Sisostris) is the 6th floor *Pension Wiener Heim* (☎ 483-5933). Run by an elderly eccentric couple, it has enormous rooms with an assortment of old furniture for E£10 per person. The spacious bathrooms have cold showers and huge round windows – the latter are the only reminders of the building's Art-Deco era. Breakfast is not provided.

Hotels – Around Masr Station The *Hotel Piccadilly* (☎ 493-4802) is on the 6th floor, 11 Tariq al-Hurriya, three blocks north of Masr station. Rooms cost from E£10 to E£14 for a single or E£12 to E£17 for a large double with bath; some rooms have balconies. It's sort of a last resort, because no-one has ever recommended it.

One block behind the telephone office on Midan al-Gomhurriya is the *El Rouda Hotel* (☎ 492-0518) on Sharia Morsy Badr. The rooms all have fans and range from E£17/28 for a single/double without private shower, to E£22/34 with shower. Few foreigners ever stay here but if you need to be close to Masr railway station and don't mind a bit of street noise it's ideal.

Places to Stay – middle
The *Semiramis Hotel* (☎ 482-6837/7837) is a tourist-class hotel on the Corniche that really should be downgraded. Walking down corridors with disgusting carpet and paint-splotched walls into tatty rooms is a little depressing. The rooms have TVs and if you get a corner one, the views from the balcony are as good as you'll get. The prices (including breakfast and taxes) are ridiculous at E£52/71 for a street view, or E£64/92 facing the sea.

Also very central is the *Metropole Hotel* (☎ 482-1465; fax 482-2040), 52 Sharia Saad Zaghloul, which has some class and some faded reminders of another age. The well-maintained rooms have sea views. There is a cosy little bar downstairs. Singles/doubles cost about E£76/106.

There is a string of two and three star hotels stretching along the waterfront between the Eastern Harbour and Montazah. They are quite a long way from the main transport hub and the centre of the town, but mostly well situated to benefit from views of the Mediterranean.

One of the first up and quite expensive is the three star *San Giovanni Hotel* (☎ 546-7774; fax 546-4408) at 205 Sharia al-Geish, jutting out over the sea at Stanley Bay. The setting is superb and you can hear the waves crashing as you fall asleep. Singles/doubles/

triples are US$62/81/97 including breakfast and tax.

At Glym Beach, the *Hotel New Swiss Cottage* (☎ 587-5863), at 346 Sharia al-Geish, has rooms at prices starting from E£68/83 including breakfast.

The *Salamlek Hotel*, in the grounds of Montazah Palace, once served as the guest palace for King Farouk's visitors but at the time of writing was closed for renovations. It's due to reopen in late 1996.

The *Mamoura Palace Hotel* (☎ 547-3450; fax 547-3383) is the only hotel at Mamoura Beach. It's one block back from the beach and overlooks a pleasant garden. Single rooms cost US$43 to US$60 and doubles range between E£54 and E£75, excluding breakfast and taxes. In summer, rooms are let on a half-board basis only.

If you happen to be staying around for a while, you can rent flats at Mamoura and along the Corniche – ask at Misr Travel at Mamoura.

Heading away from the city, the *Agami Palace Hotel* (☎ 433-0230), Agami Beach, 17 km west of Alexandria, is well situated on the beach, although there's not much besides the beach in terms of attractions in the area. Singles/doubles are E£84/118.

The *Hannoville Hotel* (☎ 430-3138), Hannoville Beach, is a little further west of the Agami Palace Hotel, and somewhat better. Singles/doubles are overpriced at E£155/200 before taxes.

Places to Stay – top end
The *Cecil Hotel* (☎ 483-7173; fax 483-6401), overlooking Midan Saad Zaghloul, is a grand and elegant place and something of an institution in Alexandria. Its history is one of romance and intrigue. Its guests over the years have included Somerset Maugham, Lawrence Durrell and Winston Churchill, and during WWII it was the headquarters of the British Secret Service. These days, rooms start at US$114/140.

The *Helnan Palestine Hotel* (☎ 547-3500; fax 547-3378) is a five star hotel in the Montazah Palace complex. Singles/doubles are US$105/130 including tax, but prices are

US$50 higher from 1 June to mid-October. The buffet breakfast is E£25. You can use the beach for E£15/25 in winter/summer, or rent a cabin for the day for between E£100 and E£200.

The five star *Sheraton* (☎ 548-0550; fax 540-1331), across the street from the Montazah Palace grounds, is situated so that most of the rooms have decent views of the Mediterranean. The rooms, restaurants and facilities are of a quality that you would expect from most Sheraton hotels, though the building itself is quite ordinary. Singles/doubles start at US$117/145 not including 22% tax. The pool is for guests only.

There are a few other four star hotels dotted along this end of the Alexandria seaside.

Places to Eat

Sharia Safia Zaghloul is Alexandria's main dining hub with everything from first-class restaurants to fast-food outlets. At the Ramla station end of the street, close to the waterfront, there are a number of cafes, juice stands, shawarma stands and bakeries.

Breakfast If you're content with a croissant and a cup of coffee (or hot chocolate) for breakfast, there are a few great places to try. The *Brazilian Coffee Store*, on Sharia Saad Zaghloul, was established in 1929 and is about the oldest coffee shop in the city; there's another branch on Sharia Salah Salem. The *Sofianopoulo Coffee Shop*, near the telephone office at the western end of Sharia Saad Zaghloul, is just as aromatic, but larger and more modern.

For a cheese roll, washed down with a tub of yoghurt laced with honey, go to the 24 hour milk shop on Sharia al-Kineesa al-Kobtiyya (Coptic Church St), off Sharia an-Nabi Daniel.

Restaurants – Along Sharia Safia Zaghloul Moving up the street from Ramla station area you come to *Al-Ekhlass* (☎ 482-4434) at No 49 which serves very good but pricey Egyptian food. Kebab and kofta cost about E£15. There's a variety of meat dishes

with Oriental rice and salad for E£20. The *Papillon* cafe, part of the same establishment, serves good food for about half the price, but has a minimum charge of E£4.

Just across the road is a teahouse filled with men playing dominoes and an adjoining eatery, where you can get a pretty decent hamburger imitation for E£1.50.

Next is *Lourantos* (☎ 483-3576), 44 Sharia Safia Zaghloul, which serves kofta, roast beef, kibda (liver) and chicken sandwiches.

Elite (☎ 482-3592), at 43 Sharia Safia Zaghloul, near the Cinema Metro, is one of Alexandria's institutions. Its Greek owner, Madame Christina, spends most of her evenings in the bar here talking with the many journalists, artists, actors and singers who frequent her establishment – over the years she has seen the likes of Edith Piaf and other such notables breezing through. The walls are decorated with prints by Chagall, Picasso and Toulouse-Lautrec and originals by famous Egyptian artists such as Seif Wanly and Ahmed Moustafa. The place is generally buzzing even when other places around town seem dead. The usual menu is quite long, but unfortunately the waiters prefer to give travellers the shorter, more expensive one. Look for the full menu on the wall. Pizza, moussaka (sometimes) and espresso is available, or you can just sit down for a beer (E£5.30 including complementary pastry nibblies). Prices range from E£6 to about E£15 for simpler main meals.

Across the road from Elite is the *Santa Lucia* (☎ 482-0372), at 40 Sharia Safia Zaghloul, one of Alexandria's best restaurants. In fact, you can see the Grand Collar award it won in 1980 in Madrid declaring it 'one of the best in the world'. A full seafood meal with homemade tarama salata, calamari and side salad will cost you about E£40 – it ain't cheap, but they know how to cook fish.

Next to the Santa Lucia is *Cafeteria Asteria* (☎ 482-2293) which serves good light meals. Small tasty pizzas cost from E£8, sandwiches are about E£1.60, and salads are about E£1.20. Ice cream, espresso and beer are also available.

Restaurants – City Centre The *Fuul Mohammed Ahmed*, 317 Sharia Shakor, is one block south of Sharia Saad Zaghloul and one street east of Sharia an-Nabi Daniel; the sign is in Arabic. It is, without doubt, the best place in town for a cheap, simple meal of fuul or ta'amiyya, plus all the usual accompaniments. There's also a popular takeaway section.

There are a number of interesting places around Ramla station. The *Taverna*, near the station, serves a variety of meat and fish dishes for around E£20. The salad bar is pretty good – for E£5.25 you can have as much as you want of 20 different salads and dips. The milkshakes aren't bad at all. Downstairs is a takeaway pizza and shawarma stand.

Just up from it is a terrific ice-cream parlour called *Sultana*. More expensive ice creams are available from Baskin Robbins just along the street or, for cheapies, join the crowds in front of the circular snack bar at Ramla station.

Restaurant Denis (☎ 483-0457), 1 Sharia Ibn Basaam, three blocks east of Ramla station, serves fresh seafood by weight. A kg of fish like snapper or calamari costs E£27/23 respectively. A kg of shrimps (prawns to some) is E£75. There's not much else on the menu, but the rice is good and the beers (E£6) are cold. The fish is OK, and for people on a budget but willing to splash out a little for a decent seafood meal, this is a more realistic alternative than some of the other, better known fish restaurants.

On the waterfront are a couple of mediocre restaurants: the *Darwish*, where a main meal costs an average E£17 and a kg of fish E£42; the *Omar el-Khayyam*; and the *Moustafa Darwish*. These places are OK for a drink, but you can get the same food cheaper and better elsewhere.

A number of eateries are situated either on Tariq al-Hurriya or in the alleys coming off it. *La Pizzeria* (☎ 486-4470), 14 Tariq al-Hurriya, has pizza and other cheap dishes. It's easy to miss. In a nearby side street is *Chez Gaby au Ritrovo*, a fairly up-market French restaurant. Next door is the *Café Royal*. It's open for lunch from 1 to 3 pm and again from 8 pm to 12.30 am.

The *Tandoor* at 25 Tariq al-Hurriya has pizzas for E£8 to E£10 (despite the name, there's no Indian cuisine in sight) and a pleasant terrace in the laneway out the back.

Down towards Midan Orabi, *Hassan Bleik*, at 18 Sharia Saad Zaghloul next to the Sofianopoulo Coffee Shop, serves excellent Lebanese food in a small restaurant nestled behind a patisserie. Mezzes go for around E£1.80 to E£3, sanbousak (puff pastry with meat/cheese/spinach) for E£2.50 and fish meals are E£15. It's open from noon to 6 pm only.

Heading west around the bay you'll come to the *Tikka Grill* (☎ 805114), on the waterfront near the Mosque of Abu al-Abbas Mursi. It has great views and mains for around E£15. You can pile your plate up with extras from the salad bar for E£4.

Restaurants – Elsewhere in Alexandria
The restaurant in the *San Giovanni Hotel* is one of the best eating places in Alexandria. The food is very good (especially the shrimp and rice dish), and the soft lighting and view of the beach extremely pleasant, but don't bother coming if money is a problem. A main meal costs E£30, soup E£7. It's open from 1.30 to 4 pm and 8.30 pm to midnight. There's also a 24 hour coffee shop.

Abu Qir Coffeeshop, in the Landmark Hotel, one block back from San Stefano Beach at Midan San Stefano, serves ravioli, seafood, chicken and various other dishes. It's open 24 hours a day. In the same hotel is *Ras el-Teen Restaurant*, which has international food at fair prices. A plate of hoummos, tahina, baba ghanoug, olives and pickles is a particularly cheap favourite.

The *New China Restaurant* (☎ 548-0996), on the 4th floor of the Hotel Corail, 802 Sharia al-Geish, Mandarra Bay (near Montazah Palace), has splendid views of the Mediterranean.

The *Zephyrion* (☎ 560-1319) in Abu Qir is reputedly one of the best restaurants in Egypt. Its location alone warrants that honour. Zephyrion is Greek for 'breeze of the sea', and this restaurant, on a magnificent terrace overlooking the ocean with waves breaking below, certainly has that.

West of the city, on the way to Agami Beach, is the *Seagull Restaurant* (☎ 445-5575), reputedly one of the best seafood restaurants in the Alexandria area. To get there, take the Agami bus and get off at the Al-Max bus stop. The restaurant is in a huge, castle-like building overlooking the waterfront.

Cafes Alexandria boasts a cafe scene that you won't find anywhere else in Egypt. Left over from the 1920s when the city was frequented by artists and writers like EM Forster and Lawrence Durrell, these nostalgic cafes are wonderful places to have a cup of tea and a cake, and take in the street life.

The *Trianon Café*, under the Metropole Hotel, is the most chic of the bunch. Most of the ice creams and desserts cost E£4 to E£7, and it reputedly makes the best om ali (cornflour pudding with nuts and cream) in Egypt. There is a E£4 cover charge and 17% in taxes thrown in.

Turn right off Sharia Safia Zaghloul to find *Pastroudis Café* (☎ 492 9609) at 39 Tariq al-Hurriya. This place features in Durrell's *The Alexandria Quartet*, and is still a fine place to watch the passing parade while drinking Turkish coffee or fresh lemonade at the tables on the footpath. The cakes are superb. The minimum charge is E£5.

The *Vinous* teahouse, just down the road from Pastroudis on Tariq al-Hurriya, is for Art Deco lovers. The tea and cakes are nothing special, but the decor makes a visit worthwhile. It's very popular with canoodling Egyptian couples, and charges E£1.50 for a cake.

Though part of the city's cafe history, the *Athineos Café*, opposite Ramla station, these days lacks opulence and character. *Patisserie Délices*, just down the road from the Trianon Café, is much the same.

Fast Food There are several *Wimpy*, *Kentucky Fried Chicken*, *Chicken Tikka* and *Pizza Hut* outlets scattered around Alexan-dria. A combination of three of these is located in the gardens of the Montazah Palace, and another cluster is at Mamoura. There's another Wimpy in Rushdy, and a Kentucky Fried Chicken in Sharia al-Kineesa al-Kobtiyya and another next to the waterfront Tikka Grill restaurant.

Entertainment

The notice board at the Elite restaurant will keep you up to date with the live music and theatre scenes. In summer, theatre groups often perform in the gardens at Montazah Palace.

Note that there's not much happening along the Eastern Harbour beyond the Darwish restaurant. The activity starts up again as you head east around Chatby Beach. In summer, the whole waterfront comes to life. All the cafes are overflowing, and the string of music venues on the water are jumping. These are not discos though, but good clean family fun, with lots of Egyptian music, people (usually men) getting up and dancing, and general gaiety.

If you don't have anything better to do with your money, there is a casino in the Hotel Cecil.

Cinemas There are several good cinemas in Alexandria that show English-language films and charge E£6 to E£15 admission, depending on where you sit. The best of them are the *Amir* on Tariq al-Hurriya and the nearby *Metro* on Sharia Safia Zaghloul. Check with the tourist office for details of cinemas and films.

For one week every September, Alexandria hosts an International Film Festival of uncensored films from at least 26 countries. The tourist office should have the details.

Nightclubs Most of Alexandria's major hotels have nightclubs and discos, and live music is a feature of the many clubs along the Corniche. The most popular include the *Crazy Horse*, above Athineos Café, which starts at 11 pm, features a belly dancer, and costs E£50 including a meal. You should not expect too much from these places – this is

Top: The pristine sand and inviting waters of the Mediterranean make the beaches around Marsa Matruh among the most picturesque in Egypt.
Left: An old, shaky minaret at the Oracle of Amun, Siwa
Right: Taking a dip in Cleopatra's Bath, Siwa.

TONY WHEELER

LEANNE LOGAN

CHRIS BARTON

Although Alexandria thrives on the romantic reputation of its past, it is a city with much more to offer: colourful fishing boats moored at one of the city's piers (top); the heart of the waterfront city, Midan Saad Zaghloul (middle); the reliefs of the eerie catacombs of Kom ash-Shuqqafa, with their strange blend of Egyptian and Roman features (bottom).

not London or New York, and half the time they're all but empty.

Some of the restaurants also have discos and nightclubs during the summer, such as the *Santa Lucia* and *Lourantos*.

Pubs & Bars If you want a drink in a tucked-away bar with low lights and decent pub music, head straight for the tiny *Spitfire Bar*, off Sharia Saad Zaghloul near the telephone office, where cold Stellas (E£5) and Heineken (E£12) are served with complimentary peanuts (closed Sunday). Closing time is midnight, but there are plenty of good local bars in the vicinity to hunt out afterwards. For example, you could try the big *National Grand*, diagonally opposite the GPO, which is open until 1 am, or the intimate little Art-Nouveau leftover, the *Cap d'Or Bar*, at 4 Sharia Adib just round the corner from the Hassan Bleik restaurant. Last drinkers are tipped out at 3 am.

Many of the waterfront restaurants and cafes from Midan Orabi all the way down to Montazah have beer available if you drink *inside*.

Getting There & Away

Air There are direct international flights from Alexandria to Athens (Olympic Airways) and Frankfurt (Lufthansa), and to Saudi Arabia and Dubai (EgyptAir). Some airline offices in Alexandria include:

Air France
    22 Sharia Salah Salem (☎ 802086)
EgyptAir
    19 Midan Saad Zaghloul (☎ 482-5071)
Gulf Air
    33 Sharia Safia Zaghloul (☎ 482-5211)
KLM
    6 Tariq al-Hurriya (☎ 482-8547)
Lufthansa
    6 Sharia Talaat Harb (☎ 483-7031)
Olympic Airways
    19 Midan Saad Zaghloul (☎ 482-1014)

Air travel to Alexandria from within Egypt is expensive; the one-way fare for the 40 minute flight from Cairo is E£214. Unless you are in a tremendous hurry, it is best to get to and from Alexandria by bus, taxi or train. And in fact, by the time you take getting to and from airports into account, you're not likely to save any time whatsoever.

Bus There are three places to get buses from, so it can get a little confusing. The West Delta Bus Company runs buses from Midan Saad Zaghloul (usually referred to as Ramla) near the Cecil Hotel, Sidi Gaber railway station and from opposite the Roman Theatre in front of Masr railway station *(mahattat Masr)*. Superjet runs its luxury buses from Midan Saad Zaghloul only.

Superjet buses leave for Cairo and Cairo airport every half hour from 5.30 am to 9.30 pm. The trip to Cairo (2½ hours) costs E£19 to E£21. The trip to Cairo airport is E£24 before 4.30 pm and E£30 after. It also has a 'VIP' service at 8 and 10 am and 4 pm to Cairo for E£28, and to the airport for E£32.

There is a daily (summer only) Superjet service to Marsa Matruh (E£22) at 7.15 am and 4 and 8 pm. There are also services to Port Said (E£28, four hours) at 6.30 am, to Hurghada (E£60, seven hours) at 8 pm and Sharm el-Sheikh (E£71) at 6.30 pm. All these buses have air-con, video, on-board toilets and a snack service.

Next to Superjet is the West Delta Bus Company stand. You can buy tickets for same-day travel to Cairo and Marsa Matruh here, but if you want to book a place for later on, or for services leaving from other stations, go to the office around the corner from the New Imperial restaurant. The two windows on the right are for Cairo; the others for other destinations.

West Delta's comfy buses to Cairo and on to Cairo airport run every hour from 5.30 am to 10 pm from Midan Saad Zaghloul and cost E£15 and E£20 respectively. They take the Desert Highway and the trip to Cairo centre takes about 2¾ hours. From Cairo airport, they start from a stand in front of the old terminal.

In summer, three West Delta buses leave here for Marsa Matruh (E£17, four hours) at 7 and 9 am and 3 pm.

In front of Masr station, the blue and white buses of the West Delta Bus Company depart for a variety of destinations. These tend to be the no-frills buses, and many of them start in Sidi Gaber, so there may be some excitement in getting on and finding a seat. If you want to be sure, book ahead at Midan Saad Zaghloul.

Buses to Cairo on the Delta Highway leave hourly from Sidi Gaber from 7 am to 6 pm and cost E£8 to E£10, depending on whether or not there is any so-called air-conditioning. Notice this is a lot cheaper than the luxury buses, but they also take longer.

Buses to Sallum (the Libyan border) leave at 10 am (air-con) and noon. They cost E£16 and stop at Marsa Matruh.

There is a direct bus to Siwa (E£13.50) via Marsa Matruh at 10 am. It arrives in Marsa Matruh at around 3 pm and in Siwa at about 7 or 8 pm. On Saturday, Monday and Wednesday only there is a second bus to Siwa for E£20. It has air-con and departs at noon from Masr station, arriving in Siwa by 9 pm.

Most of these buses stop in El Alamein, and will stop at Sidi Abdel Rahman if you want to get off there (that will cost about E£6). Alternatively, slower and cheaper buses to El Alamein (E£4) leave every two hours from Masr station.

There is a bus to Sohag (E£24) via Al-Minya (E£15) and Asyut (E£20) at 6 pm. A bus to Tanta costs E£3.50.

The West Delta Bus Company has four buses to Port Said from its Sidi Gaber lot. They leave at 6, 8 and noon and 4.30 pm. The first and last of these cost E£20, the other two E£15. To Suez (E£13) there are buses at 9 and 11 am.

You can also book trips via Nuweiba and Aqaba (Jordan) through to destinations as far flung as Amman, Damascus, Saudi Arabia, Kuwait and Bahrain. Generally it is cheaper to do these trips in stages, paying for each leg locally as you go.

Libya West Delta and Superjet both run buses to Benghazi and Tripoli in Libya from Midan Saad Zaghloul. The West Delta bus leaves at 1 pm, costs E£75 and terminates 17 hours later in Benghazi from where you can get another bus on to Tripoli.

Superjet's bus leaves at 11 am, and costs E£90 to Benghazi and E£195 for the 32 hour trip to Tripoli.

Train Alexandria's main train terminal is Masr station. First and 2nd class air-con tickets must be bought from the ticket office next to the tourist information booth. Third-class and 2nd class ordinary tickets are purchased from the front hall.

Cairo-bound trains leave from here at least hourly, from about 5 am to 10 pm (there's also one at 3.25 am), stopping at Sidi Gaber station, Damanhur, Tanta and Benha (and often elsewhere as well). The longest trip can take five hours; the shortest about two hours. The direct trains to Cairo, some of which are Turbos, leave at 7 and 8 am and 2, 3, 6, 7 and 10.10 pm. They cost E£22/17. The 10.10 pm train (No 934) goes on to Luxor.

The so-called 'French-line' trains to Cairo (E£20/12) stop in Damanhur, Tanta (E£9/6 in 1st/2nd class) and Benha, leaving at 6, 8.15, 10, 11 am and 1, 3.30, 5, 7.30, 8 and 9.30 pm; the 11 am and 7.30 pm services stop in Tanta only.

Two trains a day leave Alexandria for Marsa Matruh (about six hours). You must check whether these trains leave from Masr station or from Moharram Bey. To get to the latter, you can take the No 14 tram from Midan Ramla or Masr station. The 6.45 am train costs E£17 in 2nd class (air-con); the 11.20 am train is not air-conditioned and costs E£8.10/3.60 in 2nd/3rd class. The bus service on this route is faster and more comfortable.

As with all trains in Egypt, check for the latest schedules and fares before making your travel arrangements.

Service Taxi The service-taxi depot is a sprawling mess opposite Masr station. Trying to find your way to the right taxi (many of them are microbuses) can be a headache, although there is vague order. The fares are between E£8 and E£10 to Cairo or

Marsa Matruh, depending on whom you talk to.

To more local destinations, some sample fares are: Zagazig E£8; Tanta E£5; Mansura E£8; Abu Qir 50 pt; and Amariyya al-Gadeeda (for Abu Mina) E£2.25.

Service taxis to Rosetta (Rashid) leave from Midan Tahrir; the fare is E£4.

Car See the Getting Around section in the Cairo chapter for addresses of car rental companies operating in Alexandria.

Boat At the time of writing, there was only one passenger boat, the MS *Dahab*, linking several Mediterranean ports with Alexandria. Run by Misr Shipping Company, it mainly goes to Beirut (Lebanon), Lattakia (Syria) and Antalya (Turkey). It leaves Alexandria on a Sunday and returns the following Saturday. However, in summer the route changes slightly, going via Lattakia, Beirut, Limassol (Cyprus), Antalya and Rhodes (Greece), before returning to Alexandria. You can interrupt your trip at any of the stops concerned and rejoin the ship within three months, providing a berth is available. You have to notify them of your intention to do this when you buy the ticket.

Round-trip tickets cost E£750/1000 in winter/summer for Pullman seats; meals are not included. Cabins with one/two beds cost E£3500/2000 per person, and with three/four beds E£1700/1500 per person including meals. A one-way ticket (in Pullman class) from Alexandria to Beirut costs E£380; to Lattakia it costs E£340/380 in winter/summer.

If you're taking a car or motorcycle it will cost more – you'll be looking at about an extra US$200/75 respectively; bicycles are free.

Note that various embarkation and landing dues may not be included in the ticket, however, the E£21 embarkation fee payable in Alexandria is included.

The company's shipping agent in Alexandria is Menatours (☎ 808407; fax 482-5827) on Midan Saad Zaghloul. It will be able to provide you with more information and up-to-date schedules.

Roughly once every 25 days there is a boat to Libya run by the General National Maritime Transport Company of Libya, but it has no fixed schedule and offers 1st class tickets only. The trip to Benghazi takes one day and costs E£1061; to Tripoli it's three days and E£1116. Again, information can be obtained from Menatours.

At various times, other shipping companies run ferries between Alexandria and various ports around the Mediterranean; ask at the tourist office.

Yacht Yachts can anchor near Fort Qait Bey at the Yacht Club (☎ 802759; fax 818190). There are various fees involved in staying here, including E£100 per day for the jetty, E£30 in administrative costs, E£10 for six hours water supply plus the same again for electricity, E£6 for a quarantine certificate, and E£3 for the permission from the coast guard. Departing yachties must pay E£2 per person to the coast guard plus a E£26 harbour departure fee. The club has a notice board and various facilities including a good restaurant.

Getting Around

The Airport The airport (☎ 424-0526) is south-west of the city centre. To get there, you can take bus No 203 from Ramla station or No 703 from Midan Orabi. A taxi should cost about E£10, but don't be surprised to be hit for E£20.

Bus & Minibus Most of Alexandria's local buses leave from Ramla station, which is actually on Midan Saad Zaghloul (the tram station is a little further east), but some leave from Midan Orabi, Ras at-Tin and from Masr railway station. Services operate from 5.30 am to 1 am the next morning. Single trips around Alexandria cost 10 to 25 pt, and 50 pt out to the beaches of Agami and Hanno-ville.

Train The slow 3rd class train from Masr station to Abu Qir stops, among other places, at Sidi Gaber, Montazah and Mamoura. The fare is 40 pt.

Tram You can get to most places around central Alexandria by tram. Ramla station is the main tram station. Lime-yellow coloured trams go west from Ramla station: No 14 goes to Masr railway station and Moharram Bey, No 15 goes to the Mosque of Abu al-Abbas Mursi and Fort Qait Bey, and No 16 goes past Pompey's Pillar to Karmous terminal. Blue trams go east from Ramla: No 2 goes about two-thirds of the way to Montazah via Zizinia, Nos 3 and 7 to Sidi Gaber North, Nos 4 and 6 to Sidi Gaber South, and Nos 5 and 8 to San Stefano.

Another No 6 tram goes from Ras at-Tin to Moharram Bey.

Some trams have two or three carriages, in which case one of them is reserved for women. It causes considerable amusement when an unsuspecting foreigner gets in the wrong carriage! The standard fare is 10 pt.

Taxi You can expect to pay for taxis in Alexandria what you would pay in Cairo. A short trip, say from Midan Saad Zaghloul to Masr station, will cost E£1, while between E£3 and E£4 is reasonable for a trip to the eastern beaches.

Around Alexandria

ABU MINA
St Mina is said to have fallen victim to anti-Christian feeling in the Roman Empire of the early 4th century. Born in West Africa, he did a stint in the Roman army before deserting and finally being tortured and beheaded for his faith. He was buried at a place near the present site of Abu Mina, which eventually became a place of pilgrimage. Churches and even a basilica were built, all subsequently destroyed. In the 14th century, a Mamluk army supposedly rediscovered the site and the bones of St Mina, which could not be burned (proving to the Mamluks that they belonged to a saint).

A German team has been working on Abu Mina since 1969 (excavations have uncovered the early medieval Church of the Martyr, where St Mina's remains are believed to be buried), and although the site is not officially open to visitors, it may be possible to look over it with a monk from the nearby modern monastery. The monastery (or *deir*) itself, built in 1976 and still being added to, is of little interest.

You can get a service taxi to the monastery from in front of Masr station in Alexandria. Ask around for something going past Deir Mar Mina and you'll soon be shuffled into a service taxi heading to one of the new towns springing up off the Desert Highway between Cairo and Alexandria (E£2.50). If you have your own car, head for Amariyya al-Gadeeda (also known as Burg al-Arab al-Gadeeda). From there, it's about 12 km west to the monastery. You may also be able to get on a private bus organised from St Mark's Cathedral in Alexandria – inquire at the cathedral bookshop. The main entrance to the cathedral is a block west of Sharia an-Nabi Daniel on Sharia al-Kineesa al-Kobtiyya (Coptic Church St).

ROSETTA (RASHID)
The ancient city of Rosetta, also known by its newer name of Rashid, is 65 km east of Alexandria, where the western (Rosetta) branch of the Nile empties into the Mediterranean. Founded in the 9th century, Rosetta is most famous for the Rosetta stone (see the Rosetta Stone boxed story, following).

Rosetta became one of the most important ports in Egypt when Alexandria declined between the 8th and 19th centuries. It reached its height in the 17th and 18th centuries, but as modern Alexandria began to develop, Rosetta became a backwater.

Rosetta has a certain charm, although its beautiful palm groves tend to shelter a city besmirched with garbage and manure. The main attractions are its fine old Ottoman-era buildings with colourful facades and superbly intricate *mashrabiyyah* screens. The best of these include Bait Qili, which houses a small museum, Al-Amaciali and the

Inscribed with Egyptian hieroglyphs, demotic Egyptian and Greek, the Rosetta stone provided the key to the interpretation of Egyptian hieroglyphs.

The Rosetta Stone

Now housed in the British Museum, the Rosetta stone is an inscribed stone that was unearthed by Napoleon's soldiers in 1799 near the town of Rosetta. The stone is part of a large black stele dating from the reign of Ptolemy V (about 196 BC). The inscriptions were supposedly written by the priests of Memphis in commemoration of Ptolemy's accession to the throne and are represented in three languages: Egyptian hieroglyphs, demotic Egyptian (a cursive form of hieroglyphs) and Greek.

In 1801 the Rosetta stone was conceded to the British and transported to the British Museum. Various attempts were made to decode the hieroglyphs. Englishman Thomas Young established the direction in which the hieroglyphs should be read, and deciphered that the hieroglyphs enclosed within oval rings (cartouches) were the names of royalty.

However, it was Jean François Champollion who, in 1821, began to formulate the translation of Egyptian hieroglyphs based on the study of the Rosetta stone. By 1823 he had established a complete list of signs with their Greek equivalents and published *Précis du Système Hièroglyphique*. Champollion was the first Egyptologist to perceive that signs could be alphabetic, syllabic or determinative, and also established that the hieroglyphs inscribed on the Rosetta stone were actually a translation from the Greek, and not the other way around. His obsessive work not only solved the mystery of the Pharaonic script but also contributed significantly to a modern understanding of ancient Egypt. ■

House of Ali al-Fatairi (the latter has been turned into an office and it's not possible to visit). The Mosque of Zaghloul, at the bottom of the main street, was founded in 1600 AD, and the Mosque of Mohammed al-Abbas, near the Nile, was built in 1809.

Getting There & Away

Although buses and trains operate between Alexandria and Rosetta, the easiest way to get there and away is by hire car or service taxi. The latter should cost about E£4.

West Delta runs about 10 buses a day to Rosetta (E£1.50, one hour). They leave from in front of Masr railway station in Alexandria.

You can catch a train from Sidi Gaber station in Alexandria to Mamoura, just east of Montazah Palace, and then another train from there to Rosetta.

The Mediterranean Coast

The 105 km stretch of coastline between El Alamein and Alexandria is slated for massive tourist development, and you can see the results already. Sprawling, generally ugly 'tourist villages' are spreading along the coast like a lava flow, covering everything in a layer of concrete. Places such as the Maraqiyyah and Marabella tourist villages, the Atic and Aida Beach hotels and, close to El Alamein, the Seagull Marina are generally aimed at Egyptian tourists and more often than not involve long-term lets. The water out here is magnificent, but these resorts are generally not. The number of projects under way or planned seems infinite.

Permits Travel into the interior from the Mediterranean coast is limited to certain routes. If you have plans to take a 4WD off the beaten track, say towards the Qattara Depression, or anywhere beyond about a 40 km radius around Siwa Oasis (except on the Marsa Matruh and Bahariyya roads), you'll need to arrange special permits with the Ministry of the Interior.

EL ALAMEIN

The small coastal village of El Alamein, 105 km west of Alexandria, is most famous as the scene of a decisive Allied victory over the Axis powers during WWII.

Today, El Alamein (the name literally means 'two flags', but according to locals refers more to its position between two places whose names began with 'Alam') is a busy construction area. An oil pipeline and new port facilities for shipping Egypt's oil are being built, and there are plans for a canal across the Qattara Depression from the Nile. The canal project is designed to open up new areas of arable land for Egypt's expanding population, but is being delayed by the many WWII minefields in the Western Desert. These unexploded mines are also a hazard to wandering travellers, so stick to the beaten tracks.

The town's two hotels, museum, Commonwealth cemetery and so on are actually along a side road that leaves the main highway at the Greek War Memorial and rejoins it again after passing right through the town. Should you need to make a phone call while you're here, there's a phone office a little way beyond the museum.

Though it's possible to stay overnight, many people visit El Alamein as a day trip from Alexandria as the town's accommodation options are basic in the extreme and, as one traveller put it, 'there's not much here to detain even the most dedicated military historian for more than a few hours'.

The War Museum

On the western side of town, the War Museum has been brushed up and made more presentable, and contains a good col-

> ### Battle of El Alamein
> The massive battle of El Alamein, between the Allied tank divisions under the command of Field Marshal Montgomery and the German-Italian armoured force of Field Marshal Rommel's Afrika Korps, altered the course of the war in North Africa.
>
> In June 1942, Rommel, nicknamed the Desert Fox, launched an offensive from Tobruk in Libya in an attempt to push his troops and 500 tanks all the way through the Allied lines to Alexandria and the Suez Canal. It was not the first attempt in what had been two years of seesaw battles, but this time the Axis forces were confident of a breakthrough. The Allies, however, thwarted their advance with a line of defence stretching southward from El Alamein to the Qattara Depression. On 23 October 1942, Montgomery's 8th army swooped down from Alexandria with a thousand tanks, and within two weeks routed the German and Italian forces, driving Rommel and what was left of his Afrika Korps back to Tunis.
>
> More than 80,000 soldiers were killed or wounded at El Alamein and the subsequent battles for control of North Africa. The thousands of graves in the three massive war cemeteries in the vicinity of the town, the area's main tourist attractions, are a bleak and moving reminder of the war. ∎

lection of uniforms, memorabilia and pictorial material relating to the Battle of El Alamein and the North African campaigns in general. There is a huge diorama display which, in conjunction with a short tape, lights up to show the main paths of advance and retreat until the Axis forces surrendered to the Allies in Tunis in 1943. Maps and explanations of various phases in the campaign in Arabic, English, German and Italian complement the exhibits, as does a 30 minute Italian-made documentary on the battle that you can view at the end of your visit. Outside the museum stands a collection of tanks, artillery and hardware from the fields of battle.

The museum is open from 8 am to 6 pm and admission is E£5 (E£2.50 for students). Photography inside costs E£5 extra. There's a pleasant cafeteria here but it only stocks chips, soft drinks and biscuits.

Commonwealth War Cemetery

The cemetery, on the eastern side of town, is a haunting place where more than 7000 tombstones cover a slope overlooking the desert battlefield of El Alamein. Soldiers from the UK, Australia, New Zealand, France, Greece, South Africa, east and west Africa, Malaysia and India who fought for the Allied cause lie here. The cemetery is maintained by the War Graves Commission, and admission is free. Outside is a small separate memorial to the Australian contingent, and a little further east is a Greek war memorial.

German & Italian War Memorials

Seven km west of El Alamein, on a bluff overlooking the sea is what looks like a hermetically sealed sandstone fortress. Inside this silent but unmistakable reminder of war lie the tombs of German servicemen and, in the centre, a memorial obelisk.

Four km further on is the Italian memorial with, as its focal point, a tall, slender tower. Before reaching the German memorial, you may notice on the left side of the road what seems a little like a glorified milestone. On it is inscribed 'We were short on luck, not on bravery' in Italian (*Mancò la fortuna, non il valore*).

Places to Stay & Eat

The *Al Amana Hotel*, almost opposite the museum, has simple double rooms that are nothing special, but they are a damn sight better than rooms in the rest house down the road. For E£15 you'll get a room without bath, or for E£20 one with a bath (though running water can be problematic). It also has a small cafeteria where you can get chicken and rice meals, omelettes and fuul as well as drinks and biscuits.

The *El Alamein Rest House* (☎ 430-2785) was once *the* place to stay but it's now extremely dilapidated – water, electricity and food are all in doubtful supply and the rooms are coated in dust. Should you choose to overnight here and can talk the manager into letting you stay, rooms cost E£10.

The three star *Hotel Atic* (☎ 950717), 15 km east of El Alamein, has singles/doubles from US$50/90, plus taxes. It's really part of the chain of so-called beach resorts stretching between El Alamein and Alexandria.

It may be possible to camp on the beaches, but you'll have to hunt around for the police and attempt to get a permit (*tasreeh*).

Getting There & Away

Bus West Delta buses leave for Marsa Matruh and destinations beyond at regular intervals from the bus station in front of Masr station in Alexandria. It can take two hours to get to El Alamein on one of these buses as they stop frequently en route. The cost is E£4. You'll be dropped on the main road about 200m down the hill from the museum. Faster air-con buses from Midan Saad Zaghloul to Marsa Matruh will drop you at El Alamein but, if you take one of these, you'll have to pay the full Marsa Matruh fare (E£17). Note that the summertime luxury bus services to Marsa Matruh generally do *not* stop at El Alamein. See the Alexandria Getting There & Away section for more details. You can also get a West Delta or Superjet bus to Marsa Matruh from Cairo – it also stops at El Alamein. See Cairo Getting There & Away.

There is no reason for not doing the same from the opposite direction. Any ordinary bus from Marsa Matruh to Cairo or Alexandria should generally be able to drop you at El Alamein on the way. The trip will take about 2½ hours.

Train The train to Marsa Matruh calls at El Alamein, but it takes ages and the station is out in the desert well south of the town.

Service Taxi Service taxis leave from the lot in front of Masr station in Alexandria and cost about E£6. More often than not they are of the microbus variety. It is pretty easy to pick up one of these from El Alamein to get back to Alexandria or to head further west to Sidi Abdel Rahman. Otherwise traffic is fairly regular, but remember to bring water with you, as the heat can be blistering.

SIDI ABDEL RAHMAN

The fine, white sandy beach and the sparkling turquoise of the Mediterranean make
this stunning place, 23 km west of El
Alamein, a real coastal beauty spot, and with
the exception of one fairly unobtrusive resort
(and another going up nearby), there is, as
yet, nothing much around to spoil it.

Bedouins occasionally congregate in a
small village about three km in from the
beach. They belong to the Awlad Ali tribe,
who came into the region several hundred
years ago from Libyan Cyrenaica and
subdued the smaller local tribes of the
Morabiteen. There are now five main tribes
subdivided into clans, each of which has
several thousand members. The Egyptian
government has been attempting to settle
these nomads, so nowadays most of the Bedouins have forsaken their tents and herd their
sheep and goats from the immobility of gov-
ernment-built stone and concrete houses.

The spectacular beach, Bedouin village,
and the expensive hotel are about all there is
to Sidi Abdel Rahman.

Places to Stay & Eat

The *El Alamein Hotel* (☎ 492-1228), a semi-
deluxe place right on the beach, has single/
double rooms for E£200/305 with full board
in the low season. There are also various
villas and more expensive suites. The hotel
has a restaurant, cafe and nightclub.

About three km further west there is
another turn-off, this time to Hanna Beach
(Shaata al-Hanna). At the height of summer
you may find a few tents set up here for
passers-by but don't count on it. You may
well be able to camp further along the beach,
but again, technically at least, you'll need a
permit.

Apart from the expensive restaurant at the
El Alamein Hotel, there is a small roadside
place where you can get a few basic snacks
just west of the turn-off for Hanna Beach.

Getting There & Away

The same buses that can drop you at El
Alamein en route to or from Marsa Matruh
can also drop you here. They generally stop
for a break just after the Hanna Beach turn-
off. There are service taxis operating
between El Alamein and Sidi Abdel Rahman
and to places further west, but nothing much
happens after early afternoon.

RAS AL-HIKMA

About 48 km short of Marsa Matruh, this is
little more than another small Bedouin
village with some attractive beaches. There
is supposedly an official camping site here.
Ordinary buses between Alexandria and
Marsa Matruh can let you off here, or you
can pick up the occasional service taxi to
Marsa Matruh.

MARSA MATRUH

The large waterfront town of Marsa Matruh,
built around a charming bay of clear Mediterranean waters and clean white sandy
beaches, is a popular summer destination
with Egyptians, as yet not overly infected by
the plague of resorts and beach flats spreading west from Alexandria. The water is
beautiful, especially on the beaches outside
town, but the town itself, with a population
of about 80,000, is a bit on the grotty side.

There is a strong military presence in the
area, as Libya is only 226 km away. Improving relations between the two countries does
not seem to have induced the government to
lower the army's profile here. At the time of
writing, traffic in both directions was heavy,
so there should be no reason for not going
there. Keep your ear to the ground though –
relations between the two have been known
to take sudden turns for the worse with little
prior warning, and a few times they have
seemed on the brink of fighting. If things
look bad, it may be better to stay away.

Orientation

There are really only two streets in Marsa
Matruh that you need to know: the Corniche
(or Sharia al-Corniche), which runs all the
way around the waterfront, and Sharia
Iskendariyya, which runs perpendicular to
the Corniche, towards the hill behind the
town.

The more expensive hotels are along the

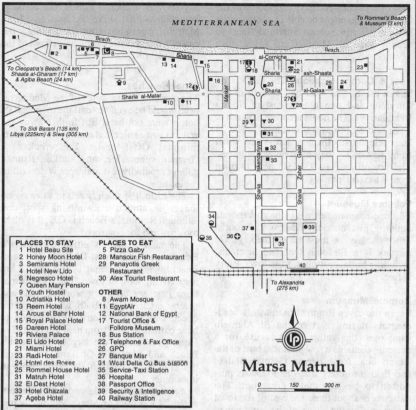

Marsa Matruh

0   150   300 m

PLACES TO STAY
1 Hotel Beau Site
2 Honey Moon Hotel
3 Semiramis Hotel
4 Hotel New Lido
6 Negresco Hotel
7 Queen Mary Pension
9 Youth Hostel
10 Adriatika Hotel
13 Reem Hotel
14 Arous el Bahr Hotel
15 Royal Palace Hotel
16 Dareen Hotel
19 Riviera Palace
20 El Lido Hotel
22 Miami Hotel
23 Radi Hotel
24 Hotel des Roses
25 Rommel House Hotel
31 Matruh Hotel
32 El Dest Hotel
33 Hotel Ghazala
37 Ageba Hotel

PLACES TO EAT
5 Pizza Gaby
28 Mansour Fish Restaurant
29 Panayotis Greek
   Restaurant
30 Alex Tourist Restaurant

OTHER
8 Awam Mosque
11 EgyptAir
12 National Bank of Egypt
17 Tourist Office &
   Folklore Museum
18 Bus Station
22 Telephone & Fax Office
26 GPO
27 Banque Misr
34 West Delta Co Bus Station
35 Service-Taxi Station
36 Hospital
38 Passport Office
39 Security & Intelligence
40 Railway Station

Corniche. Others are dotted around the town, mostly not too far from Sharia Iskendariyya. The bulk of the restaurants and shops are on or around Sharia Iskendariyya. You'll find a market stretching south from the Corniche, a few blocks west of Sharia Iskendariyya.

Information

Registration & Visas The passport office (☎ 934424) is just off Sharia Iskendariyya, a couple of blocks north of the railway station. It's open daily from 8.30 am to 2 pm and 6 to 9 am in summer; 5 to 8 pm in winter. If you're coming in from Libya, you can regis-

ter here. You can also get visa extensions and re-entry visas.

Tourist Office The tourist office (☎ 931841) is on the ground floor of the governorate building one block west of Sharia Iskendariyya on the corner of the Corniche. It is open daily from 8.30 am to 6 pm (until 9 pm in summer). The tourist police are next door.

Money There are two banks in Marsa Matruh. You can change cash and cheques at the National Bank of Egypt, a few blocks west of Sharia Iskendariyya and south of the Corniche. You *might* be able to convince the Banque Misr branch on Sharia al-Galaa to accept Visa or MasterCard for a cash advance.

Post & Communications

The GPO is on Sharia ash-Shaata, one block south of the Corniche and two blocks east of Sharia Iskendariyya. The hours are from 8.30 am to 3 pm (closed Friday and Saturday). The 24 hour telephone office is across the street from the GPO – they have no card phones. The fax office (fax 931331) here is open from 8 am to 1 pm.

Folklore Museum

This one-room museum is in the governorate building, just round the side from the tourist office (where you must ask for the key). On display is a Bedouin tent and artefacts, including bridal costumes, from Siwa. Entry is free.

Rommel Museum

Set in the caves Rommel used as his headquarters during part of the El Alamein campaign, this rather poor excuse for a museum contains a few photos, a bust of the Desert Fox, some ageing German, Italian and British military maps and what is purported to be Rommel's greatcoat. The museum is about three km east of the town centre, out by the beach of the same name. The turn-off to the museum and beach is signposted. The museum is open from 9.30 am to 4 pm in summer only and costs 50 pt. You can arrange to see it in winter through the tourist office or the staff at the governorate building.

Rommel's Beach

This beach, a little east of the museum, is supposedly where Rommel took time off from his tanks and troops to have his daily swim. It's popular with holidaying Egyptians in summer, and women will feel uncomfortable bathing here. You can hire paddle boards for E£3 an hour.

To get here you can walk around the little

bay (or hire a bike or *careta*, the donkey-drawn carts that serve as taxis in Marsa Matruh), or get a boat from the landing at the end of a road off the Corniche in front of the Radi Hotel (50 pt).

Other Beaches

The stunning azure water of the Mediterranean would be even better if the town and its hotels were not here. But further away the water is just as nice and man's infringements minimal. Offshore lies the wreck of a German submarine, and sunken Roman galleys reputedly rest in deeper waters off to the east.

The **Lido**, the main beach in town, is no longer an attractive swimming spot, and although Rommel's Beach is OK, it is often too crowded for comfort.

The next choice is either **Cleopatra's Beach** or **Shaata al-Gharam** (Lovers' Beach), which are about 14 km and 17 km respectively west of town. The rock formations here are certainly worth a look and nearby is Cleopatra's Bath, where the great queen and Marc Antony are supposed to have bathed. A boat from near the Beau Site Hotel goes across the bay to Cleopatra's Beach and Shaata al-Gharam. Like most things in Marsa Matruh, the boats only run in summer.

Agiba means 'miracle' and **Agiba Beach**, about 24 km west of Marsa Matruh, is just that. It is a small but spectacular beach, accessible only by a path leading down from the clifftop. There is a cafe (open in summer only) nearby where you can get light refreshments, and the hassle potential for women who actually want to strip down to a swimsuit is considerably lower than elsewhere.

Places to Stay

Accommodation prices vary greatly from winter to summer, and substantial discounts are sometimes available until early June. As the research for this book was done in winter, you'll have to expect summer prices to be anywhere from 20 to 50% higher. Some places are closed in winter.

Places to Stay – bottom end

Camping It's best to inform the folks at the tourist office if you plan to camp out along the beach or at Rommel's Beach.

Hostels The *Youth Hostel* (☎ 932331), a couple of blocks south of the Awam Mosque, is OK. Members pay E£5.10 for a comfortable enough bunk bed in a cramped room of six or eight. There seems to be no problem if nonmembers stay. The toilets are fairly clean.

Hotels A popular backpackers' stop is the *Ghazala Hotel* (☎ 933519) just off Sharia Iskendariyya; the entry is sandwiched between some shops and is easily overlooked. The charge is E£7.50 per person for a basic but clean bed. Most rooms have balconies (but no view to speak of) and the shared toilet/shower combinations are clean, if lacking in hot water.

Queen Mary is a four storey pension (there's no sign or telephone) one block back from the water next to the Awam Mosque. In winter, it has double rooms with private bathrooms for E£15 and larger doubles with refrigerator and big balcony for E£20. Prices are five times higher in summer. It's open all year and, out of the high season, is a great budget option providing you don't mind walking into town for food or supplies, and the fact that a mosque lurks directly across the road.

The *Hotel des Roses* is another cheap place, but it hardly ever seems to be open.

The *Matruh Hotel* (☎ 933300), also known as the *Hamada Hotel*, is on Sharia Iskendariyya. At E£6 (winter) or E£20 (summer) for a double (no singles) and with no hot water, it's not a particularly good deal.

A similar place, with doubles for E£12, is the *El Dest Hotel*, around the corner from the Hotel Ghazala.

The *Ageba Hotel* up near the railway station has OK rooms with tiny toilet/shower combinations for E£10 per person.

There are a few other cheap and nasty places around town, some near the main bus station.

Places to Stay – middle & top end

Town Centre Near the road to Sallum and Siwa, the *Dareen Hotel* (☎ 935607) has reasonably comfortable rooms with bath and breakfast for E£26/40 (E£10 more in summer). The owners seem willing to bring the price down a bit, but hot water seems an empty promise. Some may also find the hotel's proximity to the nearby mosque a drawback.

East of Sharia Iskendariyya there are three places to consider, although none can be said to be the pick of the crop. The *Radi Hotel* (☎ 934827; fax 934828) is just off the Corniche, however, there's no beach in this area. It offers doubles without breakfast for E£100. Some of the rooms have TV, and all are fully carpeted and have a bathroom and fan, but even so they're way overpriced. Were it not for the hot water, it would only be a slightly better version of the Dareen.

Two blocks away is the *Rommel House Hotel* (☎ 935466) which is open all year. Rooms with bath, TV, refrigerator and breakfast cost E£83/107. Although in a slightly higher league than the Radi, this place is really overpriced.

In front of the telephone office is the *Miami Hotel* (☎ 934810). This 200 room three star hotel charges E£120/140 (winter) or E£136/184 (summer) for singles/doubles and is open all year.

The *El Lido Hotel* (☎ 932249; fax 932248), on the corner of Sharia Iskendariyya and Sharia al-Galaa, has singles/doubles for E£30/40 with breakfast, or E£25/30 without. In summer, prices are about E£15 to E£20 more expensive. For that you'll get a poky room with TV, phone and bath.

Just across Sharia Iskendariyya is the better value *Riviera Palace* (☎ 933045; fax 930004). You get better and bigger rooms with partial views of the bay. In winter they cost E£36/55 without breakfast; in summer you must take the room plus half-board which comes to E£75/132. This is one of the better hotels in this price range.

The *Adriatika Hotel* (☎ 935195), a little way down the road from the EgyptAir office,

THE MEDITERRANEAN COAS

has acceptable singles/doubles for E£28/40 including breakfast. It's set back from the road, so it's not too noisy. The restaurant serves chicken (E£12) and beer.

Along the Corniche There is a string of places on the waterfront heading west of Sharia Iskendariyya. However, most of them are closed in winter.

The first of them, the 10 storey, 126 room *Royal Palace Hotel* (☎ 934295), has reasonable rooms with bath, TV and phone for E£26/37 (winter) and E£37/48 (summer). The price includes breakfast and most rooms have balconies looking straight out onto the sea. It's closed for part of the winter.

Next up is the popular *Arous el Bahr Hotel* (☎ 934419). It has slightly grubbier rooms than the Royal Palace, but otherwise is much of a muchness. Singles/doubles cost E£35/52, and breakfast is E£8. It has a restaurant but no bar.

The *Reem Hotel* (☎ 933605), right on the beach, has clean rooms with balcony for E£36/48 without breakfast. Its restaurant is open in summer only.

The three star *Negresco Hotel* (☎ 934492; fax 933960) has spotless rooms, but at E£130/260 in the high season, is a bit on the expensive side. In winter it's reasonable at E£30/40.

The one star *Hotel New Lido* (☎ 932248) is a bit of an odd animal. It rents out what it likes to call flats for between E£40 and E£50. You get two beds, a bathroom, a kitchen area and some very large cockroaches. It's closed in winter.

After the *Semiramis* and *Honey Moon* hotels, both of which are closed in winter, you arrive at the *Hotel Beau Site* (☎ 934012; fax 933319). The 'luxury' rooms on the beach cost E£177/220 in winter and E£193/240 in summer, not including 19% taxes. The rooms come with breakfast and all the mod cons, without exceeding its three star status. In summer it's mandatory to take full-board, which bumps the price up by another E£80. There are tiny rooms available above the disco with great balconies but little else for E£85/100.

Places to Eat
The *Panayotis Greek Restaurant* is on Sharia Iskendariyya. Except for a short interval while Allied and Axis forces waltzed back and forward across North Africa during WWII, the restaurant has been going since 1922, when the first of the Panayotis family came over from Agios Nikolaos in Crete. The restaurant serves a decent plate of fish for E£18 and calamari for E£15. You can also get a Stella beer here. In fact, from 11 to 11.30 pm, it seems to serve as the town's takeaway liquor store – you can get beer or the ouzo-style firewater, zibiba.

Across the road is the *Alex Tourist Restaurant*, where you can also drink a Stella, but not take it away. It serves kebabs, kofta and the like, but stops serving food at about 10.30 pm.

Next door is a small pizza place with a shawarma takeaway stand. The pizzas are OK, and cost E£10 with the lot, but if you really want pizza, there is better (see the following entry on Pizza Gaby). Next to this is an unassuming little fuul place. A filling meal of fuul, ta'amiyya, tahina, salad and bread costs just E£1.70.

There are a couple of good teahouses around here for a tea and shisha.

A few blocks east of Sharia Iskendariyya is the *Mansour Fish Restaurant*.

For excellent pizza (summer only), head down to the Corniche. Just after the Negresco Hotel you'll find *Pizza Gaby*, where most of the pizzas cost around E£10. There is no beer however.

The *Beau Site Restaurant* in the hotel of the same name is fairly good, but beware of the prices.

Entertainment
A couple of hotels put on discos during the summer. Don't expect too much, but if you're desperate for mirror balls, try the *Hotel Beau Site* or *Disco 54* in the Radi Hotel.

Getting There & Away
Air Although you can get an EgyptAir flight between Cairo and Marsa Matruh on Sunday,

Tuesday and Thursday for E£344 one way, buses and service taxis are much cheaper and easier ways to make the trip. The EgyptAir office is on the roundabout by the road to Siwa and Sallum.

Bus For details on buses from Cairo or Alexandria to Marsa Matruh, see the Getting There & Away sections in those cities.

Matruh has two bus stations – one near the tourist office and the main station up near the railway line.

Superjet buses to Alexandria (E£22, summer only) leave at 8 am, noon, 3 and 5 pm. Also in summer only, Superjet has three buses to Cairo (E£35) at 8 and 11 am and 3.30 pm. These buses depart from the station near the tourist office.

West Delta operates luxury buses throughout the year to Alexandria (E£17, four hours) at 9 am and 3 pm. It also has deluxe buses to Cairo (five hours) leaving at 2.30 pm (E£30) throughout the year, as well as at 8.30 am and 3.30 and 5 pm in summer only (these buses cost E£35). These luxury buses all leave from outside the tourist office.

From the main bus station, there is a daily bus (without air-con) to Cairo (E£18) that departs at 7.30 am.

At least nine buses make the run to Alexandria, and cost from E£9 to E£11. Some of these are en route from Siwa or Sallum.

Buses for Siwa leave daily at 7.30 am (E£7) and 3.30 (E£10) and on Saturday, Monday and Wednesday at 5.30 pm (E£10). It takes about five hours to cover the 300 km.

Buses for Sallum (stopping at Sidi Barani on the way) leave at 7 am, 3.30 and 5 pm and cost between E£4 and E£5 to Sidi Barani and E£7 to E£8 to Sallum. The trip to Sallum (218 km) takes about 3½ hours, or more depending on stops and breakdowns.

As usual, all these times and fares are subject to change so check to be sure of current schedules.

Train This is the hard way to go overland between Alexandria and Marsa Matruh. Two trains a day leave for Alexandria, at 4 and 9.20 pm. Second class air-con costs E£17,

and ordinary 2nd/3rd class tickets are E£6.40/2.80. It takes anywhere from six to seven hours.

Service Taxi The service-taxi lot in Marsa Matruh is across from the bus station. Service taxis to Siwa cost E£10, if there are enough people going. Other fares include: to Sidi Barani (E£6), Sallum (E£10) and Alexandria (E£8).

Hitching It shouldn't be too difficult to get a lift from Alexandria or Sallum to Marsa Matruh, or vice versa, but remember that the area is hot, dry, and sparsely populated. Take plenty of water and be careful about sun exposure. As you are usually expected to pay for rides, it's unlikely to work out more cheaply than simply getting a bus or service taxi.

Getting Around
Caretas, or donkey carts, are the most common form of transport around the streets of Marsa Matruh. Some are like little covered wagons with colourful canvas awnings. A ride across town should cost no more than E£1. From the centre to Rommel's Museum is E£1.50.

Private taxis or pick-ups can be hired for the day, but you must negotiate and bargain aggressively, especially in the summer.

In summer there are supposedly regular buses to Cleopatra's, and Agiba beaches. Failing this, you can get a pick-up to Agiba from in front of the Ramses Hotel for E£2 a person.

Bicycles can be rented next to the Riviera Palace Hotel for E£7 per day. They can also be rented from a place opposite the Radi Hotel for E£2 an hour or so from a couple of spots along the Corniche.

SIDI BARANI
About 135 km west of Marsa Matruh on the way to Libya is this small but busy Bedouin town. There's very little of interest here, although the cool waters of the Mediterranean are temptingly close. It's a bit of a food and petrol way-station for traffic coming in

THE MEDITERRANEAN COAST

from Libya, but that's about it. There's a small hotel and a few places to eat. Buses between Marsa Matruh and Sallum stop here. The fare to Sallum is E£1.75; to Marsa Matruh from E£4 to E£5, depending on the bus and the time of day. Service taxis also pass through.

SALLUM

Nestled at the foot of Gebel as-Sallum on the gulf of the same name, this friendly Bedouin frontier town is 79 km west of Sidi Barani. Since a ban on international flights to and from Libya was imposed in 1992 (following Libya's refusal to hand over two suspects accused of bombing a Pan Am flight over Lockerbie in 1988), Sallum has become a crucial transit point to and from Libya. It also became the site of a huge refugee camp in late 1995 following Libya's expulsion of 30,000 Palestinians and thousands of Egyptian and Sudanese workers.

The dearth of western travellers coming through here means there is little sign of the hassling so common elsewhere in the country. There is a post office here and a branch of the National Bank of Egypt.

As usual, the water is crystal clear, but in town the rubbish on the beach detracts from it. Head east for a while and you can pick yourself out some secluded stretch of beach, but ask first if the spot you've chosen is OK. Some parts of the beach are government property. And remember that being on the beach without a permit after about 5 pm can get you into strife.

On the eastern entrance to the town is a WWII Commonwealth War Cemetery, a somewhat more modest version of the El Alamein cemetery.

Places to Stay & Eat

The *Hotel al-Ahram* is probably the best place to stay. It costs E£10/15 for basic rooms. When there is water, it's cold. There are a couple of *lokandas* (another name for a basic, cheap place to doss) with their names in Arabic only.

At the border, 12 km further on, is the *Hotel at-Ta'un* (name in Arabic only). There are one or two modest fuul stands around, but ask first how much the food costs. One place seems to consider E£8 reasonable for two plates of salad, a plate of fuul mixed with tinned meat and a couple of drinks!

Getting There & Away

There are buses and the odd service taxi from Alexandria and Marsa Matruh; see the relevant Getting There & Away sections.

From Sallum, buses for Marsa Matruh (E£7 and E£8, 3½ hours) depart three times a day; some of these go on to Alexandria (E£16). A service taxi to Marsa Matruh will cost about E£10. The train from Marsa Matruh is apparently reserved for military purposes alone, at least for now.

Libya The border crossing point of Amsaad, just north of the Halfaya Pass, is 12 km west of Sallum. Service taxis run up the mountain between the town and the Egyptian side of the crossing for E£2 to E£3. Once through passport control and customs on both sides (you walk through), you can get a Libyan service taxi on to Al-Burdi for about LD1. From there you can get buses on to Tobruk and Benghazi. There is some talk of establishing a rail link between Egypt and Libya, but that may well be pie in the sky. Note that, at the time of writing, it was not possible to get a Libyan visa on the border.

The Suez Canal & the Red Sea Coast

The Suez Canal, one of the greatest feats of modern engineering, links the Mediterranean with the northern end of the Red Sea.

Among the area's many highlights are the ancient monasteries of St Anthony and St Paul. The Red Sea is renowned for its spectacular marine life, and a visit to this region offers the chance to sample some of the best snorkelling and diving you'll find anywhere in the world.

The Suez Canal

The Suez Canal represents the culmination of centuries of effort to enhance trade and expand the empires of Egypt by connecting the Red Sea and the Mediterranean Sea. Although the modern canal was by no means the first project of its kind, it was the only one to bypass the Nile as a means of connecting the two seas, and excavate across the Isthmus of Suez to provide a major shipping route between Europe and Asia.

HISTORY
Earliest Attempts
The first recorded canal was begun by Pharaoh Necho, between 610 and 595 BC, and stretched from the Nile Delta town of Bubastis, near present-day Zagazig, to the Red Sea via the Bitter Lakes. Despite his oracle's prophecy that the canal would be of more use to invading barbarians than to the Egyptians, Necho persevered until, having caused the death of, it is said, more than 100,000 workers, he was forced to abandon the project.

His canal was completed about a century later under Darius, one of Egypt's Persian rulers, and was maintained by the Ptolemies. Cleopatra, in a bid to save what was left of her fleet after the Egyptian defeat at Actium (off the west coast of Greece), attempted to sail up the canal to the Red Sea, failing only because of the low flood level of the Nile that year.

The canal was improved by the Romans under Trajan, but over the next several centuries it was either neglected and left to silt up, or dredged by various rulers for limited use, depending on the available resources.

In 649 AD it was restored by Amr, the Arab conqueror of Egypt, to facilitate the export of corn to Arabia. Twenty years later it was filled in by another caliph, to stop the supply of grain to Mecca and Medina, so he could starve the people against whom he was waging war.

The Suez Canal Company
Following the French invasion in 1798, the importance of some sort of sea route south to Asia was again recognised. For the first time the digging of a canal directly from the Mediterranean to the Red Sea, across the comparatively narrow Isthmus of Suez, was considered. The idea was abandoned, however, because Napoleon's engineers mistakenly calculated that there was a 10m difference between the two sea levels.

British reports corrected that mistake several years later, but it was the French consul to Egypt, Ferdinand de Lesseps, who pursued the Suez canal idea through to its conclusion.

In 1854 de Lesseps presented his proposal to the Egyptian khedive (ruler) Said Pasha, who authorised him to excavate the canal. Although de Lesseps had financial backing from private investors, the project was initially hindered by the British and French governments. Finally, in 1855, the scheme was approved and the Suez Canal Company, headed by de Lesseps, was formed and began issuing shares to raise the necessary revenue. Said Pasha granted the company a 99 year concession to operate the canal, with the Egyptian government to receive 15% of the annual profits.

Construction began in 1859, but it was not

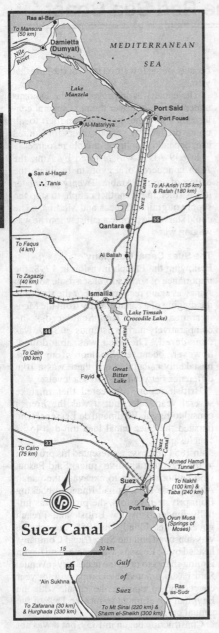

THE RED SEA COAST

Suez Canal

0   15   30 km

an easy project. At one stage, following an outbreak of cholera, all de Lesseps' workers ran away. There was also the major problem of fresh water, or rather the lack of it. Until the company built a canal to service the construction works, 3000 camels were used to carry fresh water from the Nile.

In 1863, Said was succeeded as khedive by Pasha Ismail, who quickened the pace of construction because the American Civil War had disrupted the world cotton markets. There was increased demand for Egyptian cotton and the completion of the canal would facilitate its export.

The canal was completed amidst much fanfare and celebration in 1869. It had cost the lives of thousands of labourers and incurred several million pounds of unanticipated debt to European finance houses, a large part of which was due to the extravagant festivities Ismail had planned for the opening of the canal.

In his desire to establish Egypt as a major world power, Ismail sought to impress the kings, queens and various potentates of Europe with a four day party to mark the completion of the new sea route between Europe and Asia.

Suez Canal Inauguration (1869)

The inauguration ceremony on 16 November 1869 was a grand affair. When two small fleets, one originating in Port Said and the other in Suez, met at the new town of Ismailia, the Suez Canal was declared open and Africa was officially severed from Asia.

In Cairo, Ismail built the Opera House and Pyramids Rd, the road from the city to Giza. The latter was constructed so that his most important guest, the French empress Eugénie, could travel to the Great Pyramids of Giza in her carriage. In Ismailia he built a new palace for the occasion, and all along the canal various special events were held. In Port Said, fireworks, feasts and the official opening ball for 6000 guests were just the start of weeks of lavish hospitality offered to the visiting dignitaries.

The celebration and resulting debts nearly finished Pasha Ismail. By 1875 he had to sell almost half his shares in the Suez Canal Company to the British government. This appeased the creditors but ushered in a period of British control over Egypt which lasted until Nasser overthrew King Farouk in the 1952 Revolution.

Nationalisation & Wars
In 1956 Nasser nationalised the Suez Canal to raise money for the construction of the High Dam near Aswan. The USA, UK and France had withdrawn financial backing for the project because of Nasser's willingness to deal with both the Soviet countries and the west.

By halting the flow of revenue from the canal to French, British and other foreign shareholders, Nasser was also making a statement about western control in the affairs of Egypt. His move precipitated an invasion of the canal area by France, the UK and Israel; but with world opinion against them and no support from the UN, they were forced to withdraw.

After the Six Day War in 1967 – when Israel returned to the area after Egypt tried to block the Straits of Tiran, the former's only outlet to the Red Sea – the canal was closed for about eight years.

The Israelis entrenched themselves along the eastern bank of the canal by building a line of fortifications called the Bar Lev Line. In 1973 Egypt tried, but failed, to take Sinai and the Suez Canal back from Israel by blasting the Bar Lev Line with water cannons. By this time the canal was full of sunken ships and sea traffic remained paralysed until 1975, when Sadat reopened the canal.

The Canal Today
Following the 1978 Camp David Agreement and the 1979 peace treaty signed between Egypt and Israel, the Suez Canal has been filled with a constant flow of maritime traffic. It is 163 km long but is still not wide enough to accommodate modern ships sailing in opposite directions. There are plans to widen the canal but, for now, ships can pass at four points – Port Said, Al-Ballah, Lake Timsah and the Great Bitter Lake. With a depth of 19m, the canal is deep enough for most ships other than supertankers.

The canal is a prime source of hard currency for Egypt's beleaguered economy. Each ship that passes through the canal is charged a fee based on its size and weight. With an average fee of about US$70,000, the canal usually raises revenue in the vicinity of US$2 billion every year. More than 50 ships make the 15 hour journey each day; the canal's daily capacity is 75 ships.

Canal enthusiasts may be interested in the free booklet handed out at the Port Said tourist office. It gives details on the number of vessels passing through each month, their tonnage, and the canal's influence on world trade.

PORT SAID
The main attraction of Port Said, and the reason for its establishment on the Mediterranean, is the Suez Canal. Its status as a duty-free port also makes it the most flourishing of the canal cities. Along some of Port Said's original city streets are some fine old buildings with wooden balconies. This turn-of-the-century architecture, some in a pretty sad state, seems to contain all the convoluted history of this international port town in its fibre, and is well worth a wander around.

The spectacle of the huge ships and tankers lining up to pass through the northern entrance of the canal is also something to be seen.

Egyptians think of Port Said as a summer resort, and hundreds of beach bungalows line the Mediterranean coast along the city's northern edge. However, unlike Alexandria, Port Said has not yet been overrun by throngs of Egyptians seeking sun, sand and sea.

History
Port Said was founded in 1859 by its namesake, the khedive Said Pasha, when excavation for the Suez Canal began. Much of the city is an island, created by filling in part of Lake Manzela, to the west, with sand from the canal site. The city continued to grow until 1956, when much of it was bombed during the Suez Crisis. It suffered

THE RED SEA COAST

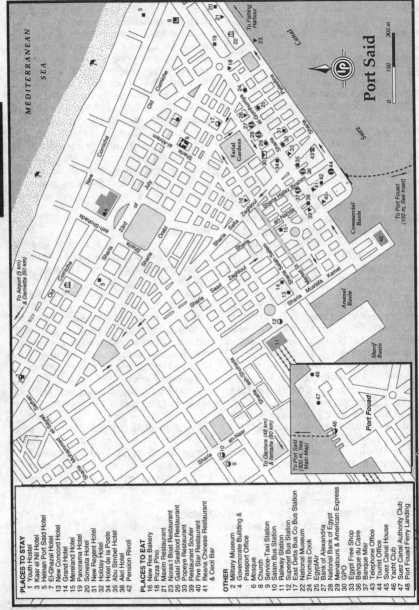

MEDITERRANEAN SEA

To Fishing Harbour

Port Said

To Port Fouad (100 m, See Inset)

To Airport (5 km) & Damietta (80 km)

To Qantara (48 km) & Ismailia (80 km)

To Port Said (300 m, See Main Map)

Port Fouad

PLACES TO STAY
1   Youth Hostel
3   Kasr el Nil Hotel
5   Helnan Port Said Hotel
7   El-Ghazal Hotel
13 New Concord Hotel
14 Grand Hotel
15 Mereland Hotel
19 Panorama Hotel
20 Sonesta Hotel
31 New Regent Hotel
32 Holiday Hotel
34 Hotel de la Poste
35 Abu Simbel Hotel
38 Akri Hotel
42 Pension Rivoli

PLACES TO EAT
16 New Rex Bakery
18 Pizza Pino
21 Maxim Restaurant
23 Noras I Boat Restaurant
26 Galal Seafood Restaurant
33 Popeye Restaurant
39 Restaurant Soufer
40 Five Star Restaurant
41 Reana Chinese Restaurant
    & Cecil Bar

OTHER
2   Military Museum
4   Governorate Building &
    Passport Office
6   Mosque
8   Church
9   Service-Taxi Station
10 Salam Bus Station
11 Railway Station
12 Superjet Bus Station
17 East Delta Bus Co Bus Station
22 National Museum
24 Thomas Cook
25 EgyptAir
27 Bank of Alexandria
28 National Bank of Egypt
29 Menatours & American Express
30 GPO
33 Egypt Free Shop
36 Banque du Caire
37 Banque Misr
43 Telephone Office
44 Tourist Office
45 Suez Canal House
46 Yacht Club
47 Suez Canal Authority Club
48 Port Fouad Ferry Landing

again during the 1967 and 1973 wars with Israel. Damage can still be seen but most of the city, which these days is home to about 400,000 people, has been rebuilt.

Orientation

Port Said is connected to the mainland by a bridge to the south and a causeway to the west. There is also a ferry across Lake Manzela to Al-Matariyya, and another between Port Said and its sister town, Port Fouad, on the other side of the canal.

Most of the banks and important services are either on Sharia Palestine, which runs along the canal, or on Sharia al-Gomhurriya, which runs parallel to Sharia Palestine, a couple of blocks in.

Information

Registration & Visas If you need to register your arrival in Egypt or get a visa extension, the passport office is in the governorate building (in the left wing on the 4th floor; window seven) and is open from 8 am to 2 pm; closed Friday.

Customs Port Said was declared a duty-free port in 1976, so everyone must pass through customs when entering and leaving the city. Be sure to have your passport with you, and if you are given the choice of declaring cameras, lenses, radios, cassette players and the like on entering, do so. It has not been known to happen often, but if you get unlucky, bored customs officials might slap on some tax if they think you bought any dutiable items in Port Said. If you do want to buy anything, check in the shop whether or not duty must be paid on a particular item – some, including a few electrical items, can be taken out without problems. Varying rates of tax apply to others.

Tourist Office The tourist office (☎ 223868), at 43 Sharia Palestine, has maps and some information about the Suez Canal and the port. The office is open from 9 am to 1.30 pm and 3 to 8 pm Saturday to Thursday, closed on Friday. There's also a branch office at the railway station.

Money There is a branch of Banque Misr on Sharia al-Gomhurriya, but this branch accepts cash only. You can use Visa or MasterCard for cash advances. Diagonally opposite is the Banque du Caire (cash only). About midway along Sharia al-Gomhurriya are branches of the Bank of Alexandria and the National Bank of Egypt. The latter seems to be the least complicated bank to change travellers' cheques.

There are also numerous moneychangers – try along Sharia Hafez Ibrahim. They usually deal in cash only but might be worth a try, as their rates are sometimes marginally better than in the banks.

Thomas Cook (☎ 227559; fax 236111), at 43 Sharia al-Gomhurriya, is open daily from 9 am to 6 pm. In the same street, in the Menatours office, is an agent of American Express (☎ 336888). It's open from 10 am to 3 pm but does not have foreign exchange facilities.

Post & Communications The GPO is opposite the Farial Gardens, one block from Sharia al-Gomhurriya, and is open from 9 am to 5 pm, Sunday to Thursday.

The telephone and telegraph office is on Sharia Palestine, two blocks north of the tourist office. There's another one behind the Governorate building. Both are open 24 hours daily.

You can have mail forwarded to the American Express office.

Suez Canal House

If you've ever seen a picture of Port Said, it was probably of the striking green domes of Suez Canal House. One of the best views of the Suez Canal used to be from this white-columned building south of the ferry terminal and tourist office, which was built in time for the inauguration of the canal in 1869. It is off limits to visitors, although you might try to talk your way past the guards and go up to the central dome.

Town Centre

For many, Port Said is a boring stop on a trip through Egypt, and few bother with it at all.

The five storey buildings with their wooden balconies and high verandahs in grand turn-of-the-century style are, however, one of those little surprise packets that should be fascinating for anyone with an interest in architecture and/or the life of late 19th century colonial centres.

You can turn up some odd remnants as you wander around: the old 'Postes françaises'; a sign for shipchandlers to the pre-Soviet 'volunteer Russian fleet', another for the Bible Society and other odds and ends. Perhaps the oddest is the Italian consulate building, erected in the 1930s and adorned with a piece of engraved propaganda to the Fascist dictator Benito Mussolini: 'Rome – once again at the heart of an Empire'. On the canal near the new Sonesta Hotel is a huge stone block which held a statue of de Lesseps until it was torn down after the 1952 Revolution. The block overlooks a busy harbour filled with small fishing boats.

Like all important port and commercial centres, this place must have had all sorts of characters from every corner of the globe wandering around. Much of the grandeur of the centre is unfortunately being sacrificed to modern ugly buildings, and little is being done to preserve the old ones. But the place still has character and a hum of activity, partly attributable to its status as a free port.

Port Fouad

This is really a suburb of civil servants, across the canal from Port Said. It was founded in 1925. The yacht club in Port Fouad is the place to go to find a passage or work on a vessel plying the canal, as the captains are sometimes looking for crew members. Free ferries from Port Said to Port Fouad offer a great view of the canal, and leave about every 10 minutes from a terminal near the tourist office.

Although not as interesting as canal-side central Port Said, a short visit and stroll around the streets near the quay repays the effort. Sprawling residences with lush gardens and sloping tiled roofs are a refreshing sight after the standard Middle Eastern poured-concrete boxes – and a reminder of the west's one-time presence here. Whoever inherited the houses does not seem to have the resources or desire to maintain them – they could do with a dusting off.

National Museum

Opened in 1987 at the top end of Sharia Palestine, this museum houses a varied collection representative of most periods in Egyptian history. The ground floor is dedicated to prehistory and the Pharaonic period. You can see statuary, utensils, pottery and a couple of mummies and colourful sarcophagi.

The 1st floor contains a modest display of Islamic and Coptic exhibits, including textiles, manuscripts and coins. There is also a room full of memorabilia of the family of Mohammed Ali's successors, who saw through the construction of the canal.

The museum is open daily from 9 am to 4 pm (but closed between 11 am and 1 pm on Friday), and admission costs E£6 (E£3 for students). Since tourists don't exactly flock to Port Said, you'll probably have the place to yourself. There's not a bad view of the canal from the 1st floor.

Military Museum

This small museum on Sharia 23rd of July has some interesting relics from the 1956 Anglo-French war and the 1967 and 1973 wars with Israel. There are captured US tanks with Stars of David painted on them, a couple of unexploded bombs and various other unpleasant reminders of recent wars, as well as a small display of ancient Pharaonic and Islamic conflicts. The museum is open daily from 9 am (8 am in summer) to 2 pm; 10 am to 1.30 pm on Friday.

Farial Gardens

If you get tired of watching ships cruise in and out of the canal, the Farial Gardens offer a pleasant refuge for a stroll or a picnic. They're in the centre of town next to the bus station.

Swimming

West of the Helnan Port Said Hotel, most of

the shelly beaches are open to the public. They're not the greatest beaches in the world, and women will probably feel very uncomfortable about peeling down to a swimsuit (leave the bikini at home). If that doesn't appeal, for a E£25 minimum charge you can use the Helnan's pool facilities. The pool at the Sonesta Hotel is out of the range of most people – you must pay for a 'day use' room (US$50) to get anywhere near the pool.

Canal Cruise

The *Noras I* boat restaurant (☎ 326804), docked at the top of the canal, offers a 1¼ hour tour of the canal for E£10, including a soft drink. It departs daily at 3 and 9 pm. You can also have a decent seafood meal on board for between E£25 and E£45.

Al-Matariyya Ferry

For E£2, you can chug west across shallow lakes and lagoons to the Delta town of Al-Matariyya, and perhaps watch as becalmed feluccas are taken in tow on the way. There's nothing to do at Al-Matariyya but wait for the return boat. To get to the ferry, you must first go to Station Lench, about 15 minutes away by taxi towards Damietta (Dumyat).

Places to Stay – bottom end

Hostels The *Youth Hostel* (☎ 228702) on Sharia 23rd of July, near the stadium, is the cheapest place to stay in Port Said. It costs E£3.25 with membership card and E£1 more without. It has basic bunk beds, with 20 beds per room. It's OK, but in a highly inconvenient location.

Hotels The area around the canal is crawling with little dives, not all of which seem to be operating. The *Pension Rivoli*, in a lane off Sharia al-Gomhurriya, charges E£5 a night for a bed – don't expect much for your money.

Two hotels offer better deals in town. The Greek-owned *Akri Hotel* (☎ 221013), at 24 Sharia al-Gomhurriya, has clean singles/doubles for about E£15/21, or E£20/25 with bath. The rooms have balconies, a bit of charm and are nicely furnished. Breakfast is

not included. The *El-Ghazal Hotel* (☎ 223586), at 42 Sharia 23rd of July, has ordinary rooms for E£11.50/16.50 including breakfast and private shower, but tends to fill up in summer.

Two blocks north-west from the Akri is the *Mereland Hotel* (☎ 227020) on a lane between Sharia Saad Zafhloul and Sharia an-Nahda, which offers big clean rooms with decent communal bathrooms for E£15/19, or E£20/25 with private bath. Breakfast is extra.

Out by the Military Museum, the *Kasr el Nil Hotel* has rooms for E£20, but they don't seem keen on foreigners – it's a bit of a dump anyway.

The *Grand Hotel* (☎ 329730), down near the Port Authority on Sharia Salah Salem, has cramped but clean rooms, some with TV, for E£22/27. The rooms have baths and fans, and the price includes breakfast.

Places to Stay – middle

The *Hotel de la Poste* (☎ 224048), at 42 Sharia al-Gomhurriya, has a fading elegance which the management has attempted to salvage through careful renovation. Singles/doubles on the street side with bath and balconies cost E£33/40 without breakfast. Rooms off the street cost E£22/27. Some rooms have a TV and refrigerator. There's a restaurant, bar and patisserie downstairs.

The *Abu Simbel Hotel* (☎ 221150; fax 224511) on the 3rd floor of 15 Sharia al-Gomhurriya is old and dusty but still manages to be full in summer. All rooms have shower, toilet, TV, fan and refrigerator. At E£22/£32 for a single/double, including breakfast, it's slightly overpriced.

The *New Regent Hotel* (☎ 235000; fax 224891), in a lane just off Sharia al-Gomhurriya, has decent, modern rooms for E£88/118 and a restaurant.

The three star *New Concord Hotel* (☎ 235341; fax 235930), a block along from the Grand, has totally characterless rooms with wall-to-wall carpet, bath, fan and TV. Some of the rooms on the higher floors have reasonable views of the canal. At E£94/122 with breakfast, it's way over the top.

Places to stay – top end

Edging into the top bracket is the *Holiday Hotel* (☎ & fax 220710) on Sharia al-Gomhurriya opposite the Hotel de la Poste. It has singles/doubles for E£130/160, including taxes and breakfast.

The modern three star *Panorama Hotel* (☎ 325101; fax 325103) on Sharia al-Gomhurriya has rooms with air-con, private bath and TV for E£130/170. Its position directly opposite a mosque may be a drawback for some.

The *Helnan Port Said Hotel* (☎ 320890; fax 323762), on the beach front, gets a five star rating from the tourist office, mostly because of the views. Singles are US$110 and doubles US$147; prices include taxes and breakfast. There's a restaurant, bar and several shops.

In direct competition to the Helnan is the relatively new *Sonesta Hotel* (☎ 325511; fax 324825) at the northern end of the canal. Prices (including tax) for rooms facing the city are US$124/148, or US$148/178 overlooking the canal. The building itself is nothing special but it does have excellent views of the canal and boasts two restaurants, a bar, and a swimming pool.

Places to Eat

Not surprisingly, there are plenty of seafood restaurants in Port Said. One of the cheapest is *Galal*, on the corner of Sharia al-Gomhurriya and Sharia Gaberti. A plate of calamari will set you back E£12 – but it's worth it. Fish dishes start at around E£14. It has a few tables outside and a takeaway stand selling shawarma and a range of Greek mezzes such as dolmades (stuffed vine leaves). Beer can only be drunk with a meal if you dine inside.

At the front of the *Hotel de la Poste* there's a bar, cafe and a restaurant. The latter has cheap hamburgers, sandwiches, salads and what is called pizza. The terrace here is a popular retreat for coffee and cake, or for a refreshing lime juice.

Across the road is *Popeye*, which is an OK place to sit on the footpath and watch the town bustle around you. The food is nothing special, but the banana splits are enormous. A similar place is the *Five Star Restaurant* opposite Akri Hotel.

Round the corner from the Akri is the very cheap and very good *Restaurant Soufer*. This rustic place is owned by an affable man who makes arguably the best hoummos in Egypt. He also has seafood displayed on ice at the front of the restaurant.

If you want pizza, you could try the flashy *Pizza Pino* on Sharia al-Gomhurriya, or the new branch of *Pizza Inn* situated inside the Panorama Hotel.

For Chinese or Korean food, there's *Reana*, also on Sharia al-Gomhurriya. It's above the Cecil bar and has a wide range of dishes including seafood mains from E£15 to E£35 as well as a few offerings for vegetarians. The portions are generous and you can drink a beer with your meal. *Cecil* is one of the few bars in town where you come close to sitting on the sidewalk terrace; it's open until quite late.

For something of a splurge try *Maxim*, on the 1st floor of the shopping centre next to the Sonesta Hotel, where a full fish dinner will set you back around E£25. Dishes such as fried squid or pasta, however, are considerably cheaper.

If it's an unobstructed view of the ships entering the canal that you're after, head over to the *Suez Canal Authority Club* on the waterfront in Port Fouad. At lunchtime only, you can dine on chicken or meat with rice and salad for E£7 (plus a E£3 entry ticket) on the club's breezy terrace. The club is immediately to your left once you get off the ferry; the entrance is opposite the tennis courts. Another option here is the *Yacht Club*, just up the road, which has a pleasant grassy garden. However, meals here may need to be ordered in advance.

In the streets about three blocks north of Sharia al-Gomhurriya there's a lively fruit and vegetable market, as well as the popular *New Rex* bakery at the western end of the market street.

Things to Buy

Almost anything can be bought in Port Said, from the latest western fashions to Sony Walkman personal stereos, VCRs and alcohol, at duty-free prices. The best deals can be found along Sharia al-Gomhurriya, which is one of the main shopping streets. This whole business is designed mostly for people passing through on vessels headed down the canal. If you're interested in buying anything and heading out again overland, check with the store owners what you'll be liable for in duty. You may be able to get away with small items, as customs checks of foreigners seem fairly lax. There's an Egypt Free Shop on Sharia al-Gomhurriya.

Getting There & Away

You must go through a customs check before leaving Port Said. The train and bus stations all have customs halls.

Air EgyptAir (☎ 222871) has an office at 39 Sharia al-Gomhurriya. However, in October 1995, all EgyptAir flights to/from Port Said were cancelled due to lack of passengers – it's not known if or when they'll resume. The airport is about five km from town en route to Damietta.

Bus There are three bus terminals. The Superjet buses to Cairo (E£15, three hours) leave 11 times a day from in front of the railway station. They also have a bus to Alexandria (E£28, four hours) at 3.30 pm. Bookings are advisable –for this you'll need to go to the Superjet office.

The East Delta Bus Co runs buses to destinations outside the Delta (and Tanta in the Delta for some reason) from its terminal near the Farial Gardens (also known as the 'Lux terminal'). Remember to get there early because you must first pass through customs.

Buses to Cairo leave from here every hour from 6 am to 6 pm. Fares range from E£10 for the ordinary no-frills bus to E£16 for this company's luxury bus, with air-con, loud video, toilet and expensive snacks. Those in-between (E£11/14/15) have varying combinations of some of these added extras. The luxury buses don't make stops, usually shaving about a half hour off the three to 3½ hour ride.

There are four buses via Damietta to Alexandria (E£15 to E£20), at 7 and 10 am, and 1.30 and 4.30 pm.

Buses to Ismailia (E£5) depart hourly between 6 am and 6 pm. To Suez (E£9, 2¼ hours) there are departures at 6 and 10 am, and 1 and 4 pm. For Al-Arish, you must first go to Ismailia or Qantara, and take a bus or service taxi from there.

There are seven buses a day to Tanta (E£10, 3½ hours) in the eastern Delta.

The other terminal, known as Salam station, is on Sharia an-Nasr, north-west from the railway station. It predominantly covers destinations within the Delta (except Tanta). Every hour on the half hour, a bus also goes south to Qantara (E£2.25).

To the Delta town of Damietta (E£2.75, 50 minutes) there are hourly departures – get there early or you'll stand most of the way. There are also buses to Mansura (E£4), Zagazig (E£5.50) and Benha (E£6.50) in the Delta.

Train There are four trains to Cairo (four hours). This is the slowest, but can also be the cheapest, way to get there. There are no 1st class services. The 2nd class air-con fare is E£14. The 2nd class ordinary is E£5.50 and 3rd class costs E£3. The train stops in Ismailia.

There are five other trains to Ismailia only. Tickets costs E£6/2.30/1. You can take the Cairo train to Zagazig too – tickets cost E£10/4.20/2.

Two trains make the long loop via Ismailia and Zagazig to Alexandria. Tickets costs E£28/8.50/4.

Service Taxi Service taxis leave from a mucky lot behind the Salam bus station, and there doesn't appear to be a lot happening in the afternoon. The Cairo fare, for once, is cheaper than that of the buses – E£8. Others include: Alexandria (E£11), Ismailia (E£3.50), Suez (E£6), Qantara (E£2.50) and Zagazig (E£6).

Boat The only ship sailing between Port Said and Limassol (Cyprus) is the MV *Atalante*. It's a 'five star super deluxe' vessel and is pricey – one-way tickets cost E£1200 for a single cabin, or E£806/625 per person in a double/triple cabin including all taxes, food and transfers. It operates from about mid-March until mid-November, leaving Port Said every Tuesday at 4 pm. The voyage takes about 12 hours. Tickets should be booked two days before departure – you can do this at Menatours (☎ 225742) on Sharia al-Gomhurriya. You could also inquire at their offices in Alexandria or at Menatours in Cairo.

From Limassol you can connect with vessels heading on to Haifa (Israel) or to several Greek islands – but that's the expensive way to get around.

Unless you are a merchant sailor, getting a passage on a merchant vessel going through the canal is nearly impossible. However, you may be able to get a passage or work on a private yacht from Port Fouad.

Getting Around

The best and most enjoyable way to tour Port Said, especially around sunset, is by *hantour*, or horse-drawn carriage. The carriage and driver can be hired for about E£10 per hour. Otherwise there are plenty of blue and white taxis.

QANTARA

The only reason to visit the town of Qantara, 50 km south of Port Said, is to cross to the east side of the canal and leave again as quickly as possible. Two ferries make the crossing – the free passenger ferry is virtually opposite the town while the vehicle ferry crosses further to the south. Be prepared to join a stampede of people, chickens, donkeys and bicycles for a space on the passenger ferry. It can be fun if your sense of humour is still intact after trying to talk a donkey out of your seat. Service taxis leave from the east bank – you'll be looking at E£5 to Al-Arish.

Most of Qantara was destroyed during the 1973 war with Israel and the town's buildings are still pocked with bullet holes.

ISMAILIA

Ismailia was founded by and named after Pasha Ismail, the khedive of Egypt during the construction of the Suez Canal in the 1860s. Ferdinand de Lesseps, the director of the Suez Canal Company, lived in the city until the canal was completed.

As in Port Said, a stroll around the elegant colonial streets of Ismailia can be an unexpected pleasure. Obviously we're not talking about great monuments, but it's interesting how this canal city grew in the image of the British and French masters pulling the strings in Egypt in the 19th and first half of this century.

A few areas around Ismailia are fed by springs, and many crops, including tomatoes, mangos and strawberries, are cultivated in this green belt.

Orientation

Ismailia is perhaps the most picturesque of the new canal towns, yet it has been quickly developing, or rather devolving, into an urban mess. The city of about 300,000 people is divided in two by the railway line, which marks a boundary between well-tended streets on one side and a veritable disaster area on the other.

The streets and squares on the eastern side of the rail tracks are lined with trees and dotted with malls and parks. The Sweetwater Canal, named for its freshwater connection with the Nile, weaves through this half of Ismailia, around lush thickets of trees to Lake Timsah, or Crocodile Lake, which is the smallest of the Bitter Lakes.

Just on the other side of the tracks you'll find the main bus and service-taxi stations – a microcosm of the surrounding neighbourhood, which features muddy, potholed streets, horn-honking maniacs and smoking piles of garbage.

In so far as Ismailia can be said to have a main street, it's probably Sharia Sultan Hussein, which runs between the railway line north of the railway station and the Sweetwater Canal. The central square, Midan al-Gomhurriya, is a quiet affair, and in fact the whole eastern part of town is rather

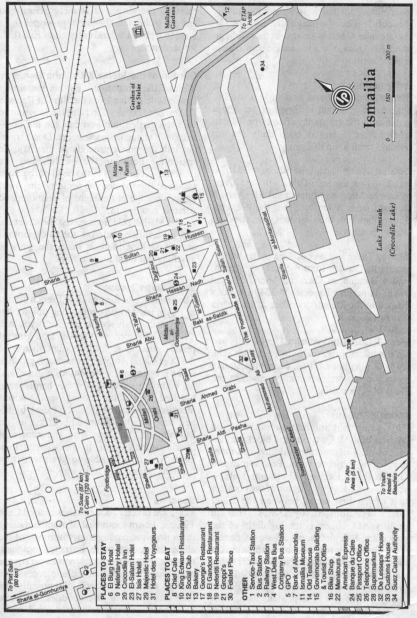

THE RED SEA COAST

Ismailia

Lake Timsah
(Crocodile Lake)

Mallaha Gardens

Garden of
the Stelae

To ETAP
Hotel

To Port Said
(80 km)

To Suez (87 km)
& Cairo (120 km)

To Abu
Atwa (5 km)

To Youth
Hostel &
Beaches

Sharia al-Gomhurriya

PLACES TO STAY
6 El Burg Hotel
9 Nefertary Hotel
20 Crocodile Inn
23 El-Salam Hotel
27 Isis Hotel
29 Majestic Hotel
31 Hotel des Voyageurs

PLACES TO EAT
8 Chief Cafe
10 King Edward Restaurant
12 Social Club
13 Bakery
17 George's Restaurant
18 El Gandool Restaurant
19 Nefertiti Restaurant
21 Gropp's
30 Felafel Place

OTHER
1 Service-Taxi Station
2 Bus Station
3 Railway Station
4 West Delta Bus
   Company Bus Station
5 GPO
7 Bank of Alexandria
11 Ismailia Museum
14 Old Teahouse
15 Governorate Building
   & Tourist Office
16 Bike Shop
22 Menatours &
   American Express
24 Banque du Caire
25 Passport Office
26 Telephone Office
28 Supermarket
32 De Lesseps' House
33 Customs House
34 Suez Canal Authority

exceptional in that it is all comparatively peaceful. The thoroughfare beside the Sweetwater Canal is known as the Mohammed Ali Quay, the Promenade and Sharia Salah Salem.

Information
Registration & Visas Should you need to register your arrival in Egypt or get a visa extension, the passport office is on Midan al-Gomhurriya and is open daily (except Friday) from 8 am to 2 pm.

Tourist Office The tourist office (☎ 321074, ext 284) is at the end of a hall, in the Governorate building on Mohammed Ali Quay. It is open from 8 am to 2 pm daily except Friday but has little besides the standard glossy brochures.

Money There's a Bank of Alexandria branch across the square from the railway station, and a Banque du Caire on Sharia Hassan Nadh. American Express (☎ 324361) has a branch in the Menatours office at 12 Sharia Sultan Hussein.

Post & Communications The GPO is just up the tracks from the railway station. The 24 hour telephone office, across the square from the station, is virtually opposite the Bank of Alexandria.

Ismailia Museum
This small but interesting museum on Mohammed Ali Quay, several blocks northeast of the Governorate building, has more than 4000 objects from Pharaonic and Graeco-Roman times. There are statues, scarabs and stelae, and details of the completion of the first canal, between the Bitter Lakes and Bubastis, by Darius. The 4th century AD mosaic is the highlight of the collection. It depicts some classic characters from Greek storytelling and mythology. On the top, Phaedra is sending a love letter to her son, Hippolyte – he ended up in a bad way, his father setting Poseidon on to him. Below, Dionysus, the god of wine, tags along on a chariot driven by Eros. The bottom section

recounts the virtues of Heracles, demi-god and son of Jupiter. The museum is open from 9 am to 4 pm daily, and entry costs E£6 (half for students).

Garden of the Stelae & Mallaha Gardens
West of the museum is a garden containing a poor little sphinx from the time of Ramses II. You need permission from the museum to visit the garden, but you can see the unremarkable statue from the street. Don't try to get into the pretty grounds of the majestic residence between the garden and the museum – it belongs to the head of the Suez Canal Authority, and the security chaps get rather on edge at the sight of unauthorised persons strolling in.

The Mallaha Gardens across the street are OK for a quick cycle but the thick lantana and dense pine thickets make the gardens anything but ideal for strolling.

De Lesseps' House
The residence of the one-time French consul to Egypt used to be open to the public, but now you can only see the interior if you're a VIP of some sort, as it serves as a kind of private guesthouse for important visitors of the Suez Canal Authority. Inside the grounds is his private carriage encased in glass, and his bedroom looks as if it has hardly been touched. Old photos, books and various utensils are scattered around the desk by his bed and on the floor. The house is on Mohammed Ali Quay near the corner of Sharia Ahmed Orabi. If you want to look inside you may be able to get permission from the Suez Canal Authority.

Beaches
There are several good beaches around Lake Timsah, 12 km south-east of town, but using them involves paying to get into one of the clubs that dot the shore. Entrance fees vary, as some include a buffet lunch as part of the admission price, but all include access to a private swimming beach. Supposedly the lake was once full of crocodiles, but there have been no sightings for a good many

centuries and certainly no record of any swimming tourists being mistaken for lunch.

According to the locals, the best beach is **Le Jardin des Enfants**, which is two km north-east of the ETAP Hotel. It belongs to the Suez Canal Authority, but is open to the public for a E£5 entrance fee. Follow the main road past the ETAP, and just before the Suez Canal ferry landing you'll find the club.

For other beaches, head south along the canal past the turn-off down to the Customs House and follow the road around the lake towards the Youth Hostel. There are a few beaches out here, just walk in and ask how much they want.

Abu Atwa

There is supposedly a **war museum** in this village, about five km south-east of Ismailia. The museum consists of a small crumbling memorial, five captured Israeli tanks in various stages of decay and displays about the tank battle during the 1973 October War. If you have a bicycle, it's not an unpleasant ride out through some citrus groves to the village, but otherwise there's really nothing here. Follow the road on either side of the canal for a couple of km and then follow the signs leading you over a bridge to the left and on to Abu Atwa. Just keep following the main road until it hits a road in a deformed T-junction – the museum is a little way off to the left.

Places to Stay – bottom end

Camping There is no official camping ground in the Ismailia area; however, it is possible to camp on the beach around Lake Timsah. You should notify the tourist office if you intend to do so.

Hostels The relatively new, high-rise *Youth Hostel* (☎ 322850), out on a beach around Lake Timsah, has rooms with two/four/six beds for E£18/15/8 including breakfast. The rooms are clean and comfortable and have lockers and views over the lake. The white-tiled toilets and showers blind you with their cleanliness. They don't seem too concerned

about whether or not you have a membership card.

Hotels The *Hotel des Voyageurs*, on Sharia Ahmed Orabi, a short way in from the railway station, is a big, derelict place that offers basic but acceptable lodgings for E£10/16 for singles/doubles. Bathrooms are outside. The *Atlanta*, across the road, is grotty and not recommended. The *Majestic* (☎ 223607), a block south, charges E£5 per person.

The *Isis Hotel* (☎ 227821) on Midan Orabi, opposite the railway station, is about the best deal in town. Its clean and comfortable rooms with bath and fan cost E£18/25, or E£10/15 without bath. Breakfast is an extra E£3.

The *El Burg Hotel* (☎ 326327) on the other side of the square, has rooms with bath, air-con and TV for E£30/50/75 a single/double/triple. Breakfast is E£5 extra. It's OK, but the colourful exterior is simply a facade for drab, overpriced rooms.

The *Nefertary Hotel* (☎ 322822), 41 Sharia Sultan Hussein, is similar to the Isis. Singles/doubles with bath and air-con cost E£30/32. Breakfast is E£3, and they also have a small bar with dim red lights.

Places to Stay – middle & top end

The *El-Salam Hotel* (☎ 324401), on Sharia al-Geish, has clean double rooms with baths and breakfast for E£50, or E£66 with air-con. A lone guests pays the same price. Some rooms have a TV.

The five storey *Crocodile Inn* (☎ 331555; fax 331666), on the corner of Sharia Saad Zaghloul and Sharia Sultan Hussein, has a lounge and restaurant as well as a 24 hour coffee shop and bar. The old, somewhat musty singles/doubles cost E£45/61 with breakfast. There are also newly renovated rooms for E£91/130 but they're hardly worth the extra money.

The *ETAP* (☎ 338040; fax 338043), right on the lake at Gezirat al-Fursan, has all the amenities of an expensive hotel. Singles/doubles start at US$97/150. For around E£20 you can use their swimming poo~~~

beach, but on Friday you have to pay for the buffet as well – E£47 all up.

Places to Eat

There are some cheap eateries in the mall near George's and the Nefertiti restaurants. The *El Gandool*, which is in among them, would like to sell you a kg of mixed meats for E£35, but you can settle for a plate of spaghetti for a couple of pounds instead.

George's and the *Nefertiti*, both on Sharia Sultan Hussein, serve fish and meat dishes. The fish at the Greek-run George's is particularly good, the atmosphere is intimate and there's a lovely old bar that has been enticing drinkers for over 40 years. Nefertiti is cheaper, with meals ranging from E£10 to E£15, but the decor is bland. Both are open until 10 pm.

A more expensive restaurant is the *King Edward* (☎ 325451) at 171 Sharia at-Tahrir. They have meat and fish dishes, all for around E£15 to E£20, as well as pizzas from E£6. The chicken curry is quite good and makes a nice change from the usual fare. Beers are not available.

Round the corner from the Hotel des Voyageurs is an excellent little ta'amiyya (felafel) place where you can dine in or takeaway.

The tiny *Chief Cafe*, Sharia al-Hurriya, specialises in an unusual combination of kushari, cakes and chocolates. All are very good and the kushari is cheap. There are tables on the sidewalk only.

Groppi's is just across the street from the Nefertiti. It's a smaller version of the Cairo Groppi's, but with just as good a selection of pastries and ice cream.

The *Social Club* is a garden cafeteria in Mallaha Gardens, run by the Ismailia Governorate, where you can get drinks (nonalcoholic) and snacks.

Some of the middle-range hotels have restaurants too, and the El Burg has a fairly gloomy *tearoom*.

For do-it-yourself supplies, try the well-stocked supermarket round the corner from the Isis Hotel, or the bakery near the end of the pedestrian mall. A block from the latter

is an old *teahouse* with a great atmosphere. There are juice stalls at the bus station.

Getting There & Away

Bus Buses to Cairo (2½ hours) leave from two stations. On Midan Orabi, the West Delta Bus Co has frequent departures; tickets cost E£5. At 7 am and 2.30 pm buses leave for Alexandria (E£12).

Buses for Cairo also leave from the East Delta Bus Co station on Sharia al-Gomhurriya, on the other side of the railway line, with the same frequency and at the same price.

Port Said buses leave the East Delta Bus Co station every 30 to 45 minutes, and cost E£5. There is a bus every 15 to 20 minutes to Suez for E£4.50.

To Sinai, there is a bus every hour or so to Al-Arish (three hours) from 7 am to 7 pm. It usually costs E£7, but prices may fluctuate for through buses from Cairo. At 8 am and noon there are buses to Sharm el-Sheikh (E£15).

Train There are about 10 trains from Cairo via Zagazig to Ismailia. Tickets cost E£8/4.20/1.80 for 2nd class air-con, 2nd class ordinary and 3rd class and the trip can easily take three hours. To Port Said, there are 10 trains per day; the trip takes 1½ hours and costs E£6/2.30/1. Trains to Alexandria (five hours) leave at 8.30 am and 7.50 am and cost E£15/6.70/3.

There are at least nine trains to Suez; tickets cost E£2/1 in 2nd/3rd class. It's a painfully slow way to go, and the station in Suez is well out of town.

Service Taxi Service taxis depart from the lot across the road from the East Delta Bus Co terminal. Destinations include Suez (E£3), Port Said (E£3.50), Zagazig (E£3), Mansura (E£5.50), Cairo (E£5) and Al-Arish (E£6).

Getting Around

Ismailia's parks and tree-lined streets are good bike-riding territory. There are a few bike shops on the side streets off Mohammed

Ali Quay – just ask around for the best deal. The one behind the El Gandool Restaurant wants about E£3 a day. There are always plenty of orange and white taxis shuttling around.

SUEZ

Suez is a city going through a metamorphosis. It was all but destroyed during the 1967 and 1973 wars with Israel, although there is little obvious evidence of the devastation today. The revamped main streets, however, are mostly a facade hiding a sordid mess of back-street slums. A memorial on Sharia al-Galaa commemorates the wars.

Suez sprawls around the shores of the gulf where the Red Sea meets the southern entrance of the Suez Canal. There is nothing much to do there except take in the best view of the ships passing in or out of the canal, and there's little in the way of tourist facilities. Suez is basically just a transit point, not only for the great tankers, cargo vessels and private yachts en route to or from the Mediterranean, but for travellers and the Muslim faithful as well. Suez is one of the departure points for the haj, or pilgrimage to Mecca; most other people just pass through on their way to Sinai or the Red Sea beaches.

Information

Registration & Visas If Suez is your point of entry into Egypt and you want to get registered here, or if you want to extend your visa, the passport office is on Sharia al-Hurriya.

Tourist Office The staff at the tourist office (☎ 221141) in Port Tawfiq are keen to provide information about the city, canal and surrounding sites, their enthusiasm limited only by the lack of things to see and do. The office is open daily from 8 am to 6 pm; Friday until 2 pm.

Foreign Consulates The Saudi Arabian consulate (☎ 222461) in Port Tawfiq (around the corner from the tourist office), is open from 9 am to 3 pm; closed Friday. There are separate sections for work and haj visas.

Tourism seems to fall between the two stools. Getting any sort of visa here can take up to one month – you'll need to show an air ticket plus a letter from your embassy. Visitors visas are E£184; transit visas (if you're en route to Port Sudan in Sudan) cost E£46.

Money Most of the main banks have branches in Suez (some are indicated on the map); there are also a few moneychangers around Suez itself and down in Port Tawfiq. Again, the Menatours office houses a branch of American Express (☎ 220269) at 3 Sharia al-Marwa next to the tourist office.

Post & Communications The GPO is on Sharia Hoda Shaarawi. There is another small post office in Port Tawfiq, next to the tourist office. The telephone office is on the corner of Sharia Shohada and Sharia Saad Zaghloul.

Places to Stay – bottom end

During the month of the haj, the bottom-end places tend to fill up with passengers travelling to and from Saudi Arabia by sea.

Hostels The *Youth Hostel* (☎ 221945) is on the main road heading west out of Suez. It's cheap (E£5 with membership card and E£6 without), grungy and a long way from anything.

Hotels If you have a hankering to stay in Port Tawfiq, the cheapest place there seems to be the *Arafat Hotel* (☎ 228896), in a street of the same name. Singles/doubles cost E£15/20 (E£5 more with bath). There's no breakfast and really no good reason to stay here.

In the centre of town, there's a handful of cheapies clustered around Sharia at-Tahrir (known locally as Sharia el-Nemsa) and Sharia Talaat Harb. One of the cheapest is the *Haramein Hotel* (☎ 320051) near the end of Sharia at-Tahrir. The outside of the hotel looks much better than the dingy rooms inside, but at E£5/6 for a single/double rog without fan it's quite popular. ...all the

THE RED SEA COAST

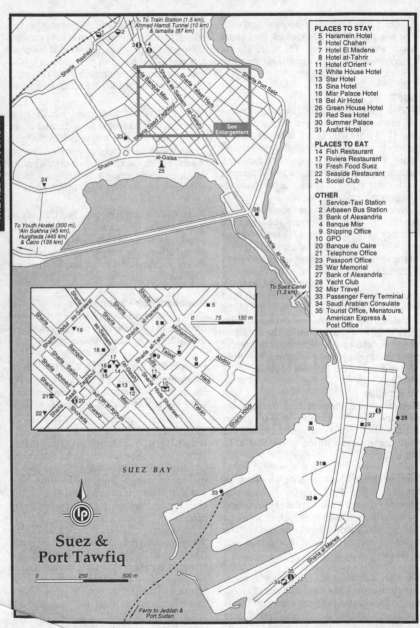

PLACES TO STAY
5 Haramein Hotel
6 Hotel Chahen
7 Hotel El Madena
8 Hotel at-Tahrir
11 Hotel d'Orient
12 White House Hotel
13 Star Hotel
15 Sina Hotel
16 Misr Palace Hotel
18 Bel Air Hotel
26 Green House Hotel
29 Red Sea Hotel
30 Summer Palace
31 Arafat Hotel

PLACES TO EAT
14 Fish Restaurant
17 Riviera Restaurant
19 Fresh Food Suez
22 Seaside Restaurant
24 Social Club

OTHER
1 Service-Taxi Station
2 Arbaeen Bus Station
3 Bank of Alexandria
4 Banque Misr
9 Shipping Office
10 GPO
20 Banque du Caire
21 Telephone Office
23 Passport Office
25 War Memorial
27 Bank of Alexandria
28 Yacht Club
32 Misr Travel
33 Passenger Ferry Terminal
34 Saudi Arabian Consulate
35 Tourist Office, Menatours, American Express & Post Office

To Train Station (1.5 km), Ahmed Hamdi Tunnel (10 km) & Ismailia (87 km)

Sharia Rashed

Sharia Banque Misr

Sharia Saad Zaghloul

Sharia as-Salaam (al-Geish)

Sharia Talaat Harb

Sharia Port Said

See Enlargement

al-Galaa

Sharia

Sharia al-Geish

To Youth Hostel (300 m), 'Ain Sukhna (45 km), Hurghada (445 km) & Cairo (135 km)

To Suez Canal (1.3 km)

SUEZ BAY

Sharia Abdul as-Scarawat
Sharia as-Salaam
Sharia Banque
Sharia Salah
Sharia Ahmed
Sharia Saad Zaghloul
Sharia al-Hareem
Sharia at-Tahrir
Sharia (al-Geish)
Mohammed
Talaat
Adli
Sharia Hoda Shaarawi
Sharia SacrDin al-Ayyoub
Shawei
Shohada
Abdou
Harb
Yakan
Sharia Khidr

0   75   150 m

Suez & Port Tawfiq

0   250   500 m

Sharia al-Marwa

To Suez Canal

35

34

Ferry to Jeddah & Port Sudan

impecunious. The communal facilities are passable.

In much the same league is the overpriced *Hotel at-Tahrir*, just down the road and signposted in Arabic only, and the *Hotel Chahen*, on Sharia Talaat Harb, where rooms cost E£4/8.

Marginally better is the *Hotel El Madena* (☎ 224056), also on Sharia Talaat Harb, which charges E£7/12 for singles/doubles. Up another rung on the ladder is the *Hotel d'Orient* on Sharia Hoda Shaarawi, which has basic abodes for E£10/12. There's a billiard hall next door.

Across Sharia as-Salaam is another couple of places which tend to be much better than those already mentioned.

The *Star Hotel* (☎ 228737) in Sharia Banque Misr has quite decent rooms with fans for E£9/12, or E£12/15 with bath. There is no breakfast. The shared facilities are very clean.

Further along the street, at No 21, is the *Sina Hotel* (☎ 220394), which has singles/doubles/triples for E£12.30/20.50/30, not including breakfast. It also has air-con doubles/triples for E£25/35. It's a little better than the Star and is often full. Breakfast is E£3 extra.

Places to Stay – middle

The *Misr Palace Hotel* (☎ 223031), 2 Sharia Saad Zaghloul, has 101 beds in single and double rooms of varying prices, standards and degrees of cleanliness. Singles/doubles with bath, air-con and breakfast start at E£20/35. It's good for the money without being spectacular.

The *White House Hotel* (☎ 227599; fax 223330), 322 Sharia as-Salaam, is a clean, respectable and popular place, although a bit worn around the edges. Singles/doubles with showers are E£35/45; breakfast is included in the price.

The *Bel Air Hotel* (☎ 223211; fax 225781) on Sharia Saad Zaghloul, opposite the Misr Palace, has clean, quiet, fully carpeted rooms with phone, TV, air-con and bath for E£42/62 with breakfast. The hotel is a bit run-down and the rooms slightly overpriced but, if you

can extract a 10% discount from them, it's one of the better deals.

Places to Stay – top end

The *Green House Hotel* (☎ 223337; fax 223330) is a relatively new joint on Sharia Port Said, on the way out of Suez to Port Tawfiq. The lobby area really is a sickly green colour. The hotel has a 24 hour restaurant, pool (E£3 for nonguests), bar and branch of the Banque du Caire. Comfortable rooms with bath, air-con, TV, refrigerator and balconies with a view of the canal cost US$41/52.

One thing the *Summer Palace* (☎ 224475; fax 321944) is not, is a palace. Ordinary rooms, at US$43/57 including taxes and breakfast, are ridiculously expensive. You're paying for the Gulf views and the seawater pools, which you can use for E£7 if you're not a hotel guest. It has an ordinary restaurant (open 24 hours) and a tranquil waterfront bar where you can get a reasonably priced Stella until 11 pm.

The *Red Sea Hotel* (☎ 223334; fax 227761), 13 Sharia Riad, Port Tawfiq, is Suez' premier establishment. Its 81 rooms have TV, bath, phone, and air-con, and are comfortable and clean. Singles/doubles cost US$41/52, including breakfast and taxes. It has a 6th floor restaurant with a great panoramic view of the canal. Meals cost between E£15 and E£20.

Places to Eat

For the cheap old favourites like ta'amiyya and shawarma, a wander around the streets bounded by Sharia Talaat Harb, Sharia Abdul as-Sarawat, Sharia Banque Misr and Sharia Khidr will soon reveal what you're after. There are also a few juice stands and plenty of cafes and teahouses. The spotlessly clean *Fresh Food Suez* snack bar on Sharia Abdul as-Sarawat sells hamburgers for E£1.

The *Fish Restaurant*, between the White House and Bel Air hotels, is exactly what it calls itself. They sell the day's catch by weight and grill it. A big meal will cost around E£20, but sometimes they overcook it a bit. It's open until 2 am.

A few metres further towards the Bel Air are a couple of other places. The one that has the sweets counter inside (called the *Riviera* in Arabic) serves a variety of big meat and seafood dishes and generous soups. A meal too big for most shouldn't cost much more than about E£10. It has a quite pleasant terrace area out the back as well as a formal dining room with five fake stained-glass windows.

The restaurant in the *White House Hotel* offers a wide range of meat and fish dishes for about E£11, and soups and salad for E£1.50 to E£3. Other gems listed on the menu include 'pile shrimps' 'poiled crops' and 'gateou kake'! It has beers for E£6.

On Sharia Saad Zaghloul, not far from the telephone office, is the 24 hour *Seaside*. Half a chicken costs E£10, a plate of spaghetti is E£2 and a meal of shrimps (prawns to some) E£30. Beer is not served. Attached to it is a popular kebab bar.

The *Social Club*, on the Corniche, is a huge round air-con restaurant serving fish meals for E£22. It has hazy views of the Gulf of Suez and the surrounding mountains and is open from 10 am to 8 pm but, except for functions, is often empty and there's no beer.

All of the top-end hotels also have restaurants.

For a late afternoon soft drink, you could join the locals at the string of little drink kiosks, all with outdoor chairs and tables and loud music, along Sharia al-Galaa near the war memorial.

There is a series of cafes down in Port Tawfiq, if you happen to stumble off a boat from Saudi Arabia or Sudan and want to sit down for a breather.

Getting There & Away

Bus All buses to Cairo, Ismailia, the Red Sea beaches and Sinai leave from Arbaeen bus station on Sharia al-Faarz, not far from the centre of town.

Buses to Cairo (E£5, 1½ to two hours) leave every half an hour from 6 am to 8 pm. Buses to Ismailia (E£4.50, one hour) depart every 15 to 20 minutes. There are three buses

directly to Port Said (E£9, 2¼ hours) at 7 and 9 am and 3.30 pm, and buses to Alexandria (E£13) at 9 and 11 am.

Buses to 'Ain Sukhna (E£3) depart at 6 and 10 am, and 2 pm. There are six services a day to Zafarana (E£6) and Hurghada (E£17, five hours), leaving at 6, 7, 8 and 9 am and 5 and 6 pm; they should be booked well ahead at the Arbaeen bus station. Most of these go on to Qena (E£22 to E£38, nine to 10 hours) via Port Safaga.

At 10.30 am there is a bus all the way to Aswan (E£26, 15 hours) via Luxor (E£24, 10 hours). At 6 pm, there is another bus to Luxor (E£31). Book ahead.

If you want to go to Al-Arish, it's best to go to Ismailia and catch another bus from there. Alternatively, you can catch the bus for Nakhl (pronounced Nekhl) at 3 pm, which costs E£8, and try to make a connection from there. However, very few vehicles use the road between Nakhl and Al-Arish, so there's a good chance you'll be waiting a long time for a ride. The same bus goes on to Taba (E£30, five hours) and Nuweiba (E£25, six hours). This bus is then said to head on to Sharm el-Sheikh (that would really be the long way!).

Two buses that do go to Sharm el-Sheikh (E£20, 5½ hours) the more direct route down the Gulf of Suez leave at 11 am and 3 pm. They go on to Dahab (E£22, 6½ hours) and to Nuweiba (E£20). There is a bus for St Catherine's (E£17, five hours) via Wadi Feran at 11 am.

Minibuses sometimes run to destinations in Sinai too – you'll be looking at about E£20 a head to St Catherine's, E£25 to Sharm el-Sheikh or Nuweiba, and E£30 to Dahab. Ask around at the bus station.

Buses to Oyun Musa (one hour), Ras as-Sudr (E£6, 1¼ hours), Hammam Fara'un (1¾ hours) and El-Tor (four hours) leave at odd intervals during the day. The 11 am and 3 pm services mentioned to Sharm el-Sheikh, and the 11 am bus to St Catherine's, can let you off at these places along the way.

Departure times are always subject to change, so remember to check them in advance with the staff at the bus station.

The art of Mahmoud Eed features unbaked clay figurines set in scenes of traditional village life. These magical creations are on display in the Oasis Heritage Museum. Bahariyya Oasis.

CHRIS BARTON

CHRIS BARTON

Top: Hidden within the barren cliffs of the Eastern Desert, the Coptic Christian Monastery of St Anthony is one of Egypt's oldest, and represents the beginning of the Christian monastic tradition.

Bottom: Fishermen repair their nets, Suez.

Train Only a masochist would want to travel to or from Suez by train. The station is two km west of the Arbaeen bus station. From it depart six Cairo-bound trains that take 2¼ hours and only make it as far as 'Ain Shams. The fare is E£2.60/1.05 in 2nd/3rd class.

To Ismailia (2½ hours) there are nine very slow trains; 2nd/3rd class tickets cost E£2/1.

If you want to do this, a microbus from near Arbaeen will take you along the main road and next to the railway line out to the station for 25 pt.

Service Taxi Service taxis depart from near the bus station to many of the destinations serviced by buses and trains, except in Sinai, where no structured service-taxi system exists (which partly explains why getting a taxi there is so outrageously expensive).

Destinations include Cairo (E£5), Ismailia (E£3), Port Said (E£6) and Hurghada (E£20, 3½ to four hours). The one exception in Sinai is El-Tor. The trip there costs E£10.

With a group of seven people you can hire a 'special' taxi to get you to St Catherine's (E£175), 'Ain Sukhna (E£100/150 one way/return), or to the Red Sea monasteries and back for E£350.

Boat It is possible to travel by boat between Suez, Jeddah (Saudi Arabia) and Port Sudan (Sudan), though very few travellers take on this arduous method of getting to Sudan.

The Suez-Jeddah leg of the trip takes about three days; the Jeddah-Port Sudan section is another 24 hours. On top of that, it's not unknown for the ship to dock for three days at Jeddah before continuing to Port Sudan – if you have a transit visa for Saudi Arabia, you will not be allowed off the ship during that time.

At the time of writing, the *Zahrat Salim* was sailing every five days to Jeddah only. Those heading to Sudan must travel on either the *El-Mahoursa* or *El-Rede*, one of which departs from Suez every Sunday at about noon. These departures are, of course, subject to change, so check in advance.

There are four classes of fare to Jeddah: E£300 in 1st class; E£250 in 2nd class; E£170 in Pullman and E£145 in deck class. To Port Sudan, tickets cost E£405 in 1st class, E£377 in 2nd and E£270 in deck class. Food on both legs of the trip is extra.

You can book tickets to Jeddah at Misr Travel (☎ 223949) in Port Tawfiq. Port Sudan tickets are available only from the shipping office on Sharia at-Tahrir in the town centre.

Apparently it's impossible to get a ticket during the haj. You won't be sold a ticket if you don't already have the necessary visas, which, considering the difficulty of getting them, is quite sensible.

Getting Around

There are regular microbus services along Sharia as-Salaam from the Arbaeen bus station to Port Tawfiq. They stop to pick you up or drop you off wherever you want along the route and cost 25 pt.

The Red Sea Coast

Egypt's Red Sea coast stretches for more than 800 km from Suez in the north to the village of Bir Shalatayn near the disputed border with Sudan. Famed for its brilliant turquoise waters, splendid coral and exotic creatures of the deep, the Red Sea attracts more than 200,000 tourists annually. It's Egypt's most rapidly developing area, with more hotels and resorts constructed here in the last few years than anywhere else in the country.

Unfortunately, much of the development during the freewheeling boom of the last decade has gone unchecked, resulting in massive environmental damage. An estimated 60 to 80% of the coral reefs around the coast's premier resort town, Hurghada, have been damaged due to illegal landfilling by developers and irresponsible use of the reef by tourist operators. In places the coast has simply eroded away due to developers building solid concrete jetties which have altered the natural shorelines. The many recently enacted laws have now

Red Sea Coast

THE RED SEA COAST

of these practises illegal, there appears to be little to contain the speculative boom on the area's future as a major source of tourist growth. Even towns south of Hurghada, including the far-from-beautiful Port Safaga and Al-Quseir, are showing signs of going the same way.

Warning

There is a heavy military presence along much of the coast, and some is said to be mined. Most of the beaches are OK, but if you have any doubts, it might be worth checking with local authorities. Be prudent about where you aim your cameras, too.

'AIN SUKHNA

'Ain Sukhna, which simply means 'hot spring', is the site of springs originating from within Gebel Ataka, the highest mountain on the Red Sea coast. There's not much to 'Ain Sukhna, but it is quite an attractive bit of coast. The road squeezes along between the water and the hills that slope almost down to the relatively clean beach. The place is 45 km south of Suez, and is a popular resort with Egyptians. It's possible to visit 'Ain Sukhna on a day trip from the canal city.

There are three buses a day from Suez and the trip costs E£3. However, there's little in the way of refreshments, so, unless you bring some food with you, you'll have to dine at the hotels.

If you want to stay longer there is the *'Ain Sukhna Village Hotel* (☎ 773939; fax 775226), which has 80 double rooms for E£140, and cabins for E£80 (breakfast is not included). The more expensive *Mena Oasis* (☎ 222525) is 15 km further south. Rooms here cost E£115/175, or there are chalets for E£95/150. The price includes compulsory half board. At least one other resort is under construction.

ZAFARANA

This town, 62 km south of 'Ain Sukhna and 150 km east of Beni Suef on the Nile, is little more than a way-station for visits to the isolated Coptic monasteries of St Anthony and St Paul in the mountains overlooking the

Gulf of Suez. Should you want to stay overnight, there is the *Sahara Inn Motel*.

Buses running between Suez and Hurghada will drop you at Zafarana. There's also one bus a day from Beni Suef.

MONASTERIES OF ST ANTHONY & ST PAUL

The Coptic Christian monasteries of St Anthony and St Paul are Egypt's oldest monasteries. As the crow flies, they are only about 35 km apart, but thanks to the cliffs and plateau of Gebel al-Galala al-Qibliya (which rises to between 900 and 1300m) they're around 82 km apart by road.

It is possible to hike between the two monasteries along a so-called trail across the top of the plateau. However, this area is commonly known as 'devil's country' and hiking this uncharitable land is only for the fit and experienced. A wrong turn could see you over a cliff or lost without water. Those who have made the hike recommend starting from St Paul's; ideally, you should reach St Anthony's in two days.

Information

The monasteries are open for day trips between 9 am and 5 pm. It's possible to stay overnight, but if you plan to stay at St Paul's you'll need permission from its residence in Cairo. Even if you plan to stay at St Anthony's, it's probably best to phone the residence first rather than just turn up. St Paul's monastery residence (☎ 590-0218) and that of St Anthony's (☎ 590-6025) are both around St Mark's Cathedral off Sharia al-Galaa in central Cairo. The monks won't accept visitors during Lent.

Monastery of St Anthony

Hidden away in the barren cliffs of the Eastern Desert, the fortified religious community of St Anthony's represented the beginning of the Christian monastic tradition. Built in the 4th century AD by the disciples of St Anthony, the walled village at the foot of Gebel al-Galala al-Qibliya is the largest of the Coptic monasteries.

This founding monastic order sprang up around the son of a merchant who had given up his worldly possessions to devote his life to God. Anthony actually retreated into the desert, in about 294 AD, to escape the disciples he had attracted to his hermit's cave by the Nile. While his followers adopted an austere communal life at the foot of the mountain, Anthony took himself off to a cave, high above the developing monastery village, where he lived to the ripe old age of 105.

Despite its isolation, the monastery suffered Bedouin raids in the 8th and 9th centuries, attacks from irate Muslims in the 11th century and a 15th century revolt by bloodthirsty servants that resulted in the massacre of the monks.

Following the example set by St Anthony, St Paul and their followers 16 centuries ago, the 25 monks and five novices who live at St Anthony's today have dedicated their lives to poverty, chastity, obedience and prayer.

St Anthony's has several churches, chapels, dormitories, a guesthouse, bakery, vegetable garden and a spring. The oldest part of the monastery is the **Church of St Anthony**, built over the saint's tomb.

If you're hiking in from the main road make sure you're properly equipped, especially with water, as it's a long, hot and dry walk. If you do get this far you should also hike up to the **Cave of St Anthony**, which is north-east of the monastery. The medieval graffiti on the walls is fascinating and there is a breathtaking view of the hills and valley below.

Monastery of St Paul

The most fascinating part of this large complex, in the cliffs of Gebel al-Galala al-Qibliya, is the **Church of St Paul**, cluttered with altars, candles, ostrich eggs (the symbol of the Resurrection) and colourful murals. It was built in and around the cave where Paul lived for nearly 90 years, during the 4th century, after founding the monastery as a show of devotion to St Anthony. The **fortress**, above the church, was where the monks retreated during Bedouin raids. and a

Visitors are more than welco

couple of the monks, who speak excellent English, give guided tours. St Paul's has two guesthouses, one inside the monastery for men and one outside for women. Food and lodging are provided free of charge, so don't abuse the monks' hospitality.

Getting There & Away

Buses running between Suez and Hurghada will take you to Zafarana. Direct access to the monasteries is limited to private vehicles and tour buses from Cairo or Hurghada. The easiest way is to join one of the tours from Hurghada. A few of the hotels occasionally organise such trips, or you can ask at Misr Travel. Otherwise, it's you, your feet and, if you get really lucky, your thumb.

St Anthony's is 45 km inland from the Red Sea. To get there you follow the road which runs between Zafarana and Beni Suef. The turn-off to the monastery is about 35 km from Zafarana and from there it's around a 10 km walk south through the desert to St Anthony's.

To get to St Paul's you can take one of the buses that run between Suez and Hurghada and get off after Zafarana at the turn-off to the monastery, which is south of the Zafarana lighthouse. Buses between Qena, north of Luxor on the Nile, and Suez go via Port Safaga and Hurghada and can also drop you at the turn-off. It's then a 13 km hike along the badly surfaced road through the desert.

Another alternative is to get a group together and hire a taxi from Suez or Hurghada to the monasteries. Beni Suef is also a departure point for the 150 km trek across the desert to the monasteries. A bus supposedly runs between Hurghada and Beni Suef via Zafarana, so you might be able to get it to stop at the turn-off to either monastery on the way. Otherwise you'd be better off with your own transport to make this journey. It might be difficult to hire a service taxi in Beni Suef for the whole trip.

RAS GHARIB

This oil workers' town, 160 km north of Hurghada, is not worth stopping for. Unfortunately, some service-taxi drivers seem to

think it makes the perfect rest stop on the way to or from Hurghada.

HURGHADA (AL-GHARDAKA)

Little more than a decade ago Hurghada had two hotels separated by nothing more than virgin beach. A one-time isolated and modest fishing village, it's now home to some 35,000 people and packed with close to 100 resorts and hotels catering to sun seekers and diving enthusiasts the world over. But while the crystal-clear waters and fascinating reefs have made Hurghada, or Al-Ghardaka as the Egyptians call it, Egypt's most popular resort town, if you're not into beaches, diving or snorkelling then this ever-developing resort town has little to offer.

Much of the town is marred by chunks of concrete, iron rods and empty oil drums – the results of the ongoing construction boom. Every spare bit of dirt or sand in the town is being turned into a building site. For 20 km or more to the south, a dense band of concrete in the form of four and five star resorts threatens the kind of disaster so often repeated on the more glamorous shores of Europe.

One of the few positive observations that can be made about all this is that most of the building has been low-level due to local laws preventing high-rises. However, even this is starting to change, and as the amount of available waterfront land dries up, buildings are now spreading up instead of out. Another positive aspect is the work being carried out by the Hurghada Environmental Protection and Conservation Association (HEPCA), a relatively new conservation group set up to address many of the local environmental problems.

Hurghada's peak tourist season is from November to February. At this time it feels as if half of Europe – well, all the Germans, Dutch, Belgians, Russians and eastern Europeans at any rate – have flown in on all-inclusive package holidays.

Orientation

The main town area, where virtually all the budget accommodation is located and most

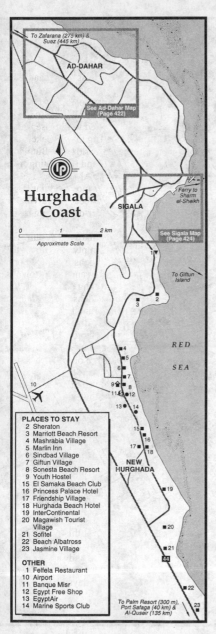

Hurghada Coast

0   1   2 km

Approximate Scale

To Zafarana (275 km) &
Suez (445 km)

AD-DAHAR

See Ad-Dahar Map
(Page 422)

SIGALA

Ferry to
Sharm
el-Sheikh

See Sigala Map
(Page 424)

To Giffun
Island

RED

SEA

NEW
HURGHADA

To Palm Resort (300 m),
Port Safaga (40 km) &
Al-Quseir (135 km)

PLACES TO STAY
2 Sheraton
3 Marriott Beach Resort
4 Mashrabia Village
5 Marlin Inn
6 Sindbad Village
7 Giftun Village
8 Sonesta Beach Resort
9 Youth Hostel
15 El Samaka Beach Club
16 Princess Palace Hotel
17 Friendship Village
18 Hurghada Beach Hotel
19 InterContinental
20 Magawish Tourist
   Village
21 Sofitel
22 Beach Albatross
23 Jasmine Village

OTHER
1 Felfela Restaurant
10 Airport
11 Banque Misr
12 Egypt Free Shop
13 EgyptAir
14 Marine Sports Club

of the locals live, is at the northern end of the stretch of resorts that makes up the whole area. It is called Ad-Dahar, and sits at the base of Gebel el-Afish which effectively blocks any views or breeze from the sea. The main road through Ad-Dahar is Sharia an-Nasr – the highway linking Hurghada to Port Safaga and Suez.

A few km down the coast is Sigala. There are some more hotels here and a couple of decent restaurants, but apart from its proximity to the port, from where the ferry to Sharm el-Sheikh leaves, it has little to attract people.

South of Sigala, a road winds down along the coast through the 'resort strip'. At the five star 'tourist village' of Magawish, about 15 km south of Ad-Dahar, the road meets another a few km inland to head down past the newer resorts and the incomplete shells of future pleasure domes on the way to Port Safaga.

Maps Those with their own boat will no doubt find the Admiralty chart (No 62188) entitled 'Approaches to Al-Ghardaka' useful in avoiding the many reefs.

Information
Registration & Visas You can register your arrival in Egypt or obtain visa extensions and re-entry visas at the passports section in the Passports & Immigration office (☎ 546727), at the northern end of Ad-Dahar on Sharia an-Nasr. It's open daily except Friday from 8 am to 2 pm.

Tourist Office Hurghada's tourist office (☎ 546513), just off Sharia an-Nasr beside the Ritz Hotel, is open daily except Friday from 8.30 am to 3 pm. There's also a tiny branch office behind Fishers Restaurant near the port in Sigala but it's rarely, if ever, open.

Money In Ad-Dahar, branches of Banque Misr, the National Bank of Egypt and the Bank of Alexandria are dotted along Sharia an-Nasr. The first two give cash advances on Visa or MasterCard. They are generally open seven days a week for exchange purposes from 9 am to 1 pm and 6 to 9 pm.

THE RED SEA COAST

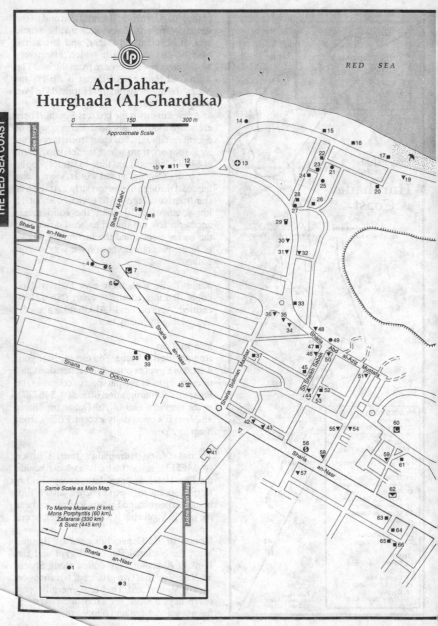

Ad-Dahar, Hurghada (Al-Ghardaka)

RED SEA

See Inset

0   150   300 m
Approximate Scale

Sharia al-Bahr

Sharia an-Nasr

Sharia an-Nasr

Sharia 6th of October

Sharia Soliman Mazhar

Sharia Shiekh Sabak

Sharia Abd al-Aziz Mustafa

Sharia an-Nasr

Joins Main Map

Same Scale as Main Map

To Marine Museum (5 km),
Mons Porphyritis (60 km),
Zafarana (330 km)
& Suez (445 km)

Sharia   an-Nasr

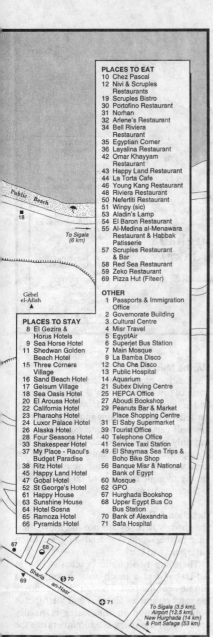

PLACES TO EAT
10 Chez Pascal
12 Nivi & Scruples
    Restaurants
19 Scruples Bistro
30 Portofino Restaurant
31 Norhan
32 Arlene's Restaurant
34 Bell Riviera
    Restaurant
35 Egyptian Corner
36 Layalina Restaurant
42 Omar Khayyam
    Restaurant
43 Happy Land Restaurant
44 La Torta Cafe
46 Young Kang Restaurant
48 Riviera Restaurant
50 Nefertiti Restaurant
52 Winpy (sic)
53 Aladin's Lamp
54 El Baron Restaurant
55 Al-Medina al-Menawara
    Restaurant & Habbak
    Patisserie
57 Scruples Restaurant
    & Bar
58 Red Sea Restaurant
59 Zeko Restaurant
69 Pizza Hut (Fiteer)

OTHER
1   Passports & Immigration
    Office
2   Governorate Building
3   Cultural Centre
4   Misr Travel
5   EgyptAir
6   Superjet Bus Station
7   Main Mosque
9   La Bamba Disco
12 Cha Cha Disco
13 Public Hospital
14 Aquarium
21 Subex Diving Centre
25 HEPCA Office
27 Aboudi Bookshop
29 Peanuts Bar & Market
    Place Shopping Centre
31 El Saby Supermarket
39 Tourist Office
40 Telephone Office
41 Service Taxi Station
49 El Shaymaa Sea Trips &
    Boho Bike Shop
56 Banque Misr & National
    Bank of Egypt
60 Mosque
62 GPO
67 Hurghada Bookshop
68 Upper Egypt Bus Co
    Bus Station
70 Bank of Alexandria
71 Safa Hospital

PLACES TO STAY
8   El Gezira &
    Horus Hotels
5   Sea Horse Hotel
11 Shedwan Golden
    Beach Hotel
15 Three Corners
    Village
16 Sand Beach Hotel
17 Geisum Village
18 Sea Oasis Hotel
20 El Arousa Hotel
22 California Hotel
23 Pharaohs Hotel
24 Luxor Palace Hotel
26 Alaska Hotel
28 Four Seasons Hotel
33 Shakespear Hotel
37 My Place - Raoul's
    Budget Paradise
38 Ritz Hotel
45 Happy Land Hotel
47 Gobal Hotel
52 St George's Hotel
61 Happy House
63 Sunshine House
64 Hotel Sosna
65 Ramoza Hotel
66 Pyramids Hotel

In Sigala, you'll find a new office of Thomas Cook (☎ 443338) on Sharia Sheraton; it is open daily from 9 am to 2 pm and 6 to 9 pm.

On the resort strip, the only bank is the new branch of Banque Misr, just south of the old youth hostel. Most of the resorts have a branch of the National Bank of Egypt.

Post & Communications The GPO is on Sharia an-Nasr, towards the southern end of Ad-Dahar. The 24 hour telephone office is further along the same road. Opposite is a fax booth (fax 544581) open daily except Friday from 8 am to 2 pm and 8 to 10 pm.

Travel Agencies Misr Travel (☎ 546600) has an office in Ad-Dahar near the main mosque in addition to a branch office (☎ 442130) in the shopping centre on Sharia Sheraton in Sigala. For details on the trips they offer, see the following Organised Tours section.

The Thomas Cook office in Sigala can organise general travel arrangements.

Bookshops The new Aboudi Bookshop, opposite the Market Place shopping centre in Ad-Dahar, is the best place in town for foreign and Egyptian literature, maps, guidebooks, foreign newspapers and postcards. It sells a small range of French and German books too, and is open daily from 10 am to midnight. Otherwise, the Hurghada Bookshop, near the bus station, has overpriced second-hand material in various languages. A lot of it is pulp novels.

Medical Services & Emergency There are two hospitals in Ad-Dahar: the private Safa hospital is near the Upper Egypt Bus Co bus station while the public hospital (☎ 546740) is at the other end of town near Shedwan Golden Beach Hotel.

Emergency telephone numbers include: ambulance (☎ 546490), police (☎ 546723) and tourist police (☎ 546765).

Warning Despite being Egypt's premier resort, Hurghada is still a tradition...own

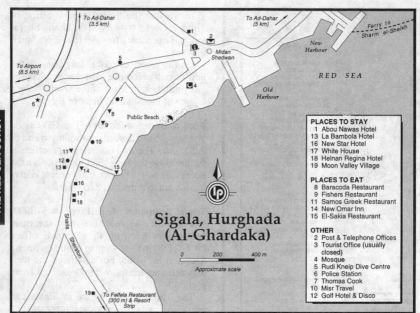

PLACES TO STAY
1 Abou Nawas Hotel
13 La Bambola Hotel
16 New Star Hotel
17 White House
18 Helnan Regina Hotel
19 Moon Valley Village

PLACES TO EAT
8 Baracoda Restaurant
9 Fishers Restaurant
11 Samos Greek Restaurant
14 New Omar Inn
15 El-Sakia Restaurant

OTHER
2 Post & Telephone Offices
3 Tourist Office (usually closed)
4 Mosque
5 Rudi Kneip Dive Centre
6 Police Station
7 Thomas Cook
10 Misr Travel
12 Golf Hotel & Disco

and local sensibilities must be considered when you move away from the beach area. In recent years an alarming number of tourists have taken to wandering around the market quarter in Ad-Dahar in shorts and skimpy tops, and the trend seems to be growing. Flaunting local customs like this is a sure-fire way of creating the type of tension that lead to a German tourist being shot dead in the bazaar in 1994.

Aquarium
If you've ended up in Hurghada and don't want to put your head under the water, you can still get an idea of some of the life teeming in the waters of the Red Sea by paying a visit to the Aquarium, just north of the public hospital in Ad-Dahar. They have quite a good selection of fish and various other odd-looking creatures. It's open from 9 am to 10 pm and costs E£5 (no student discount); permission to use cameras/videos costs E£10 extra.

Marine Museum
The marine biology station, about five km north of town, has a pretty decrepit museum and a mini-aquarium. If you like dusty stuffed dugongs, dolphins and turtles, maybe this will captivate your interest, though it's certainly not worth the E£4 admission fee. It's open daily from 8 am to 8 pm. To get there you can pick up a microbus from near the big mosque heading out on the highway to Suez for 50 pt.

Beaches & Pools
Hurghada's beaches are not the most stunning in the world – indeed they are often quite bare and stark.

There are two public beaches – one in **Ad-Dahar** and a much smaller version in **Sigala** near the port. Though clean enough, the sand resembles fine dirt and the rubbish bobbing around in the water is hardly appetising for a swim. No foreigners use the little known beach at Sigala (in part due to

Rescuing the Red Sea

Conservationists estimate 350 boats each week ply back and forth between Hurghada and the many reefs situated within an hour of the town. Combined, they ferry at least 2500 visitors to diving and snorkelling sites. Up until recently, there was nothing to stop skippers on these boats from anchoring to the coral, or snorkellers and divers breaking off a colourful chunk to take home. But thanks largely to the efforts of the Hurghada Environmental Protection and Conservation Association, better known as HEPCA, the Red Sea's reefs are at last being protected.

Set up in 1992 by 15 of the town's larger and more reputable dive companies, HEPCA's programme to conserve the Red Sea's coral reefs is manifold. Public awareness campaigns are underway, direct community action has been taken, and the Egyptian government has been lobbied to introduce appropriate laws. As a result, the area has become part of the protected Elba region which encompasses much of the coastline and offshore islands further south. Eventually, the whole coast will be known as the Red Sea Islands Protected Area.

More than 60 mooring buoys have been installed at the more popular dive sites around Hurghada, enabling boat captains to drop anchor on a buoy rather than on the coral itself. Under new laws, all tourist boats must now be licensed and, as of 1996, two marine rangers were to be employed to police the seas. Captains found mooring to the reef rather than to the buoys will be prosecuted.

A 'reef conservation tax' of E£1 has been introduced and is payable by anyone using the reefs for diving, snorkelling or any other boating activity. It's a symbolic amount, designed to create public awareness more than to raise funds (though HEPCA certainly won't refuse donations of any kind). According to HEPCA organiser, Philip Jones, the idea is simply to make visitors aware that the coral reefs and offshore islands are now protected areas. This means, among many other things, that it is illegal for snorkelling guides to present their guests with chunks of coral – a practice much flaunted in the past because of the good baksheesh from tourists. Fish feeding, collecting marine life, fishing, standing on the reef, littering, anchoring and spearfishing are also banned. ■

its position next to a mosque which makes stripping down to anything more daring than long trousers and a T-shirt unsuitable). Women are also likely to feel uncomfortable sunbathing or swimming in Ad-Dahar as men often congregate along the beach wall to sit and stare. Admission to either costs E£1.

Your only other option close to town is to pay to use one of the beaches at the resorts, or head to the small beach at El-Sakia Restaurant in Sigala where there's a minimum charge of E£5 (including a drink). Unfortunately, being so close to the port, the water here is still pretty dirty.

You may be able to sneak onto one of the paying beaches at the resorts if you act confidently enough; otherwise you'll be looking at fees of up to E£40. The Three Corners Village and the Sheraton both charge E£10 for access to their beach and pool; the Helnan Regina in Sigala wants E£15 for the privilege and the Shedwan charges E£40 (which includes lunch).

Snorkelling

Although there is some easily accessible coral at the beach south of the Sheraton, the best reefs are offshore and the only way to see them is to take a boat and make a snorkelling or diving excursion of at least one day.

For years, **Giftun Island** has been one of the most popular sites. The average day trip to Giftun, including transport to and from the harbour, two stops on a reef, snorkelling gear and lunch on the boat or the island, range from E£25 to E£40. Overnight trips are also possible, however, you'll need to carefully choose the captain and crew. Groups of women alone may face unwanted advances or worse from their male 'guides', and the occasional tales about beach parties getting out of hand sound far from pleasant. Other trips for longer periods to more distant islands can also be arranged.

You will find no shortage of places offering these kinds of trips. The best advice is to shop around a little and see where you can get a deal that suits you. Simply relying on your hotel (and many of the smaller hotels work hard to get you to join the trips for which they are getting commission) may not be the best way to do things. Several people have complained of not getting everything they thought they would. Eliminating at least one intermediary might reduce the risk of disappointment. Some of the more reputable dive clubs also take snorkellers out and, by going with one of them, you're almost assured of reef protection practices being put into action.

Take your passport with you on any boat excursions; you may have to show it at the port.

Remember when swimming and snorkelling to use sun screen. It is probably a good idea for most people to wear a T-shirt while in the water. Also note that coral is very sharp and can easily cut your feet to pieces – if you don't step on it, you shouldn't have any worries. And, lastly, don't disturb the reef and remember some creatures are best avoided. (See the Flora & Fauna and Ecology & Environment sections in the Facts about the Country chapter for information on marine hazards and reef protection.)

Diving

Dive clubs, like resorts, have mushroomed in Hurghada in the last decade and there are now more than 50 clubs operating. Between them, they offer the whole range of diving options, from one-off introductory dives to the most advanced certificates.

To get a rough idea of prices, see Diving in the Activities section of the Facts for the Visitor chapter. For information about choosing a dive club, see the boxed story Choosing a Dive Club.

Dive Sites The reefs close to Hurghada have been all but trashed in the past few years and experienced divers these days look for sites further afield, often sailing at least two hours from Hurghada. Some simply opt for dive clubs further down the coast. However, with HEPCA's determination to protect the reefs and as the reefs themselves regrow, the situation around Hurghada will undoubtedly improve.

Choosing a Dive Club

Choosing one from the throng of dive clubs in Hurghada may appear daunting, but making a conscious decision about who takes you onto the reef is an important factor in keeping the Red Sea's reefs alive – not to mention yourself. Blind faith in your hotel's choice of dive club is not a good idea, nor is simply choosing the cheapest.

Many of the companies which have sprung up in recent years are simply out to make a fast buck, and they care little about conserving the reef, or the diver's safety. Some of these backyard outfits even don't have the minimum of safety equipment – such as a dive boat fitted with a VHF radio and oxygen for handling decompression accidents – and they employ dive instructors with very little experience. They're also accused of giving insufficient supervision to inexperienced divers, which in the past has led to fatalities.

In response to this situation (not to mention to the avalanche of bad publicity in the European media about diving in Hurghada), seven of the reputable clubs joined forces in mid-1995 to form the Hurghada Quality Dive Club (HQDC). Member clubs will display the HQDC logo – a diver's 'OK' symbol (the thumb and second finger joined to make a circle). The HQDC's primary aim is to improve the quality of diving operations in Hurghada. Members of the club must meet certain criteria, including offering quality equipment, dive boats fitted with at least the minimum safety equipment, and qualified and highly experienced instructors. In addition, dive clubs must also belong to the Hurghada Environmental Protection and Conservation Association (HEPCA).

Even if you choose not to dive with a HQDC member (these clubs tend to be among the more expensive ones), it's imperative for the protection of the reef that the club you go with is affiliated with HEPCA. At the time of writing, there were 14 HEPCA members, including the excellent Swiss outfit, Subex (☎ 547593; fax 547471). For a list of current members, drop into the HEPCA office one block south of Subex. ■

In response to demand, more and more companies are now offering 'liveaboards' – dive safaris, usually of several days to a week, which take in distant sites ranging from the relatively close **Shedwan Island** to the distant shores of the **Brother** or **Rocky islands.** One of the best companies for these safaris is Rudi Kneip (☎ 442960) in Sigala.

Diving Emergency Centre There is a decompression chamber operated by Dr Hussain Mahmoud Nassef (☎ 442625) at Magawish Tourist Village. It is an old unit that, at the time of writing, was still operating. In the event that it is out of action, divers have to be transferred to the relatively new chamber in Sharm el-Sheikh.

Other Water Sports
Plenty of the bigger resorts cater for most tastes in water sports. Windsurfing at the Three Corners Village resort, for instance, costs E£30 an hour or E£90 a day with all equipment. If you have your own (!) they can store it for you. Paragliding and waterskiing are also available at some resorts.

Horse & Camel Rides
These animals can be rented for ridiculously inflated prices from a stall next to the Friendship Village on the resort strip.

Organised Tours
The range of possible organised excursions from Hurghada is all-encompassing. Most of the bigger hotels, some small tour agents on Sharia Abd al-Aziz Mustafa and Misr Travel all organise some or all of the following, many of them aimed at people flying in directly on charters and not planning on travelling through the country. For those with a lot of stamina, the more ambitious tours include a whirlwind one day tour to Cairo for E£174 (leaving at 3 am and returning at 10 pm) or a slightly more leisurely two day tour for E£350. A one day jaunt to Luxor costs E£250.

More feasible are some of the desert jeep safaris, which tend to include visits to at least one of two sites of Roman settlements and quarries, Mons Porphyritis and Mons Claudianus. These trips cost about E£120. A full-day excursion to the monasteries of St Paul and St Anthony costs about E£150. A half-day desert safari including a one hour camel trek is E£60; an evening excursion into the desert including a sunset drive, camel ride and BBQ dinner costs E£75.

A minimum number of people is needed for most of these trips, so it's best to inquire several days in advance.

Water Excursions The *Sindbad Submarine* is one way to plumb the depths and stay bone dry. This yellow submarine can carry 46 people to a depth of 22m. It costs US$25 a head for the 'two hour' trip, however, an hour of that is spent on a boat travelling between Sindbad Village resort and the site where the submarine is moored. For more information, contact Sindbad Village (☎ 443261).

Alternatively there's the *Aquascope*, a new contraption that looks like it escaped from a 1970s science fiction movie. It floats and has a submerged bubble-shaped cabin from where a maximum of 10 people can view the underwater world. An hour in this thing costs US$35. For more details call (☎ 542849), or inquire at the Marine Sports Club on the resort strip.

If glass-bottom boats are your thing, many of the hotels can organise jaunts at about E£15 to E£20 an hour.

Places to Stay – bottom end
Most of the hotels in this range are either in Ad-Dahar town centre or north of the centre, built around the base of Gebel el-Afish and relatively close to the sea.

Camping There is a *National Youth Camp* about five km north of town, but they say you need to book ahead in Cairo – by the looks of the place, you really wouldn't want to.

Hostels Hurghada's little old *Youth Hostel* (☎ 442432) is on the resort strip, opposite the Sonesta Beach Resort. It was to stay open until about the end of 1996, when a big new purpose-built hostel with 300 beds was due to open about five km north of Ad-Dahar, past the Marine Museum. Both locations are inconvenient for the town centre. The old hostel offers quite reasonable bunk-bed rooms and the location is fine if you just want to hang out on resort beaches. It costs E£8 a night (E£9 for nonmembers) and E£3 extra for breakfast. The new place will have dorms, double rooms and quads and should be open 24 hours.

Hotels – Ad-Dahar centre The *Sunshine House* on Sharia an-Nasr opposite the post office used to be a good bottom-end place, however, it seems to have gone downhill a bit in recent times. Many travellers have reported that the staff tend to be very pushy when it comes to snorkelling trips and buying ferry tickets and that the rooms are not all that secure and the location is noisy. The rooms have flyscreens, rugs and powerful overhead fans. The bathrooms are clean and even hot water is available 24 hours. There's a common room and a kitchen with a refrigerator available for guests. It is E£5 per person.

Happy House, on the main square by the mosque in the centre of Ad-Dahar, is a humble pension that was run, until his recent death, by the well known Captain Mohammed. It's now maintained by his son, and has two double rooms with kitchen and refrigerator. It is a clean basic place to stay for E£7 per person.

Near the main Coptic church is another cheap place with a homy atmosphere called *My Place – Raoul's Budget Paradise*. Paradise is overstating it, but it's not a bad deal at E£5 a head. Breakfast is an extra E£2.

The *St George's Hotel*, just by the Aladin's Lamp Restaurant in the centre of Ad-Dahar, has exceedingly average rooms without bath or breakfast for E£15/20. With bath they cost E£18/25.

The *Shakespear Hotel* (☎ 446256), at the top end of Sharia Abd al-Aziz Mustafa, has some very spacious, comfortable doubles with communal baths for about E£22 – ask to see a few rooms to compare, because some are much better than others. All rooms have

fans. Those with private facilities cost E£6 more. Breakfast is not available but you can easily pop across the road to the Bell Riviera for its E£3 breakfast.

There are a couple of places in this same upper end of the budget bracket nearby on Sharia Sheikh Sebak. The *Gobal Hotel* (☎ 546623) has singles/doubles with breakfast, and sometimes with private bath, for E£15/25. All the rooms have fans and the bathrooms are clean with plenty of hot water. The *Happy Land Hotel* (☎ 547373) has OK rooms without/with bath for E£18/26 a double; breakfast not included.

Back down near the Sunshine House are two dark, uninviting and overpriced places. The *Ramoza Hotel* (☎ 546608) has singles without/with bath for E£20/25; doubles are E£25/30 and triples E£30/35. The *Pyramids Hotel* (☎ 546625) next door is marginally better for about the same price.

On the other side of the road is the *Hotel Sosna* (☎ 546647), which is better than the last two but still a bit over the top. It has rooms that are clean, relatively new and cost E£20/30, or E£25/35 with bath.

Hotels – Seaside Ad-Dahar There's quite a family of little hotels in the dirt lanes between the Market Place shopping centre and the sea. Though relatively close to the water, very few rooms in these places have sea views.

One of the best for the price in this area is the *California Hotel* (☎ 549101). Recently enlarged and renovated, it now sports exotic murals and new beds, and has rooms with private bath and balcony on the new 2nd floor. The older rooms with shared bathrooms cost E£10/15 including breakfast, the new rooms are a bit more.

Nearby and also recommended is the *Luxor Palace Hotel* (☎ 549260). It's small and relatively quiet, and has singles/doubles for E£10/20 with breakfast. The communal bathrooms are a bit cramped but they're clean. The same people own the *Four Seasons* (☎ 549260) next door, however, it's a bit more upmarket and has rooms with private bathroom only. They're good value at E£15/25 without air-con but with fan, balcony and breakfast. Air-con rooms cost a little more.

The *Alaska* (☎ 548413), on the slope up behind the Aboudi Bookshop, charges E£8.50 per person plus E£2 for breakfast and is a good, comfortable place to stay.

Close to the public beach (but without sea views) is the *Sea Oasis Hotel* (☎ 548338; fax 547360). It's popular with backpackers, and has large doubles for E£20/30 with communal/private bathrooms. There's no discount for solo travellers. Breakfast is included.

The *Pharaohs Hotel* (☎ 547577), near the Luxor Palace, is rapidly hurtling out of the budget end. If you like big rooms, this may be your place, but at E£30/45 for a basic single/double with balcony but shared bathroom, you'll certainly be paying for that space and it's without doubt overpriced. Breakfast is included.

Hotels – Sigala Should you want to be close to the port, try the *Abou Nawas Hotel* (☎ 442830) behind the post and telephone office in Sigala. It has big, clean rooms with fan and communal bathrooms for E£14/25, but it's a tad overpriced and usually pretty empty. There's a pleasant street-front terrace where you can get a beer.

Places to Stay – middle
Ad-Dahar The *Ritz Hotel* (☎ 547031) is about the only mid-range option in Ad-Dahar centre. It's a laid-back place with singles/doubles for E£40/50. There's a restaurant and bar, and you get free access to the beach at either the Shedwan Golden Beach Hotel or Three Corners Village.

Up the slope is the *El Arousa Hotel* (☎ 548434; fax 549190), one of the best places in this range. It's only a few years old and has immaculate air-con rooms (with bath towels twisted into imaginative duck formations!) all with private bath, TV, phone and balconies with sea views for E£80/140 with obligatory half board. It has a billiard table, an indoor pool (E£10 fee for nonguests) and a poolside bar, and guests have free access to the beach at Geisum Village across the road.

Bookings are recommended as it's popular with divers.

The *Geisum Village* (☎ 546692; fax 547995) is the cheapest of the three places here which are right on the beach. It charges E£100/169 for singles/doubles on a half-board basis.

There's a trio of places just off Sharia Al-Bahr north of the main mosque. The *Sea Horse Hotel* (☎ & fax 548704) is an old but quite OK three star place that, as with many of its ilk, caters mainly to tour groups. Most rooms have air-con, TV, phone, wall-to-wall carpet and their own bath. The views from some are good. In the high season (winter), rooms costs E£98/110 with breakfast, but come down about E£25 in summer.

Adjacent to the Sea Horse and also one of the older establishments in this bracket is the *El Geziza Hotel* (☎ 547785; fax 548708). If you don't mind taking half board (obligatory) it's quite a good deal, with single/double/triple rooms going for E£68/88/114. All rooms have air-con, telephone, carpet and private bathroom. A few rooms also have TV. The same company owns the Sand Beach Hotel, so you can use their beach and pool for free.

Next door to the El Gezira is the spanking new, six storey *Horus Hotel* (☎ 549801; fax 549801). It was one of the first hotels in Ad-Dahar to climb above three levels, and is a bit of a blot on the horizon. It's popular with Belgian tourists and has tacky rooms with air-con, TV and refrigerator for £E100/135 including breakfast.

Sigala Most of the mid-range places here are set back about 250m from the water on Sharia Sheraton. The *White House* (☎ 443699; fax 442085) is the best value in this area and is popular with Russian tour groups. It's relatively new and has singles/doubles/triples at the back for E£39/59/74, or streetfront rooms at E£51/71/86. All rooms have air-con and breakfast is included. Guests get free access to the beach at Giftun Village on the resort strip.

Just down the road, the *New Star Hotel* (☎ 442588) has rooms with air-con for

E£40/60/100 including breakfast. The rooms are OK and cost slightly less if you opt for a fan instead of air-con, but the hotel in general is old and unappealing.

La Bambola (☎ 442013), a three star place across the road, has singles/doubles for E£73/106 with breakfast. It's a bit overpriced really, and in any case is often full with Czech, Polish and Russian groups. They have a disco (no minimum charge), as does the *Golf Hotel* next door.

The *Moon Valley Village* (☎ 442811), on Sharia Sheraton at the start of the resort strip, has the best location of any of the mid-range places in Sigala. It has 30 rooms costing E£90/130 and a good aspect over the Red Sea. They have a private chunk of beach directly across the road.

Places to Stay – top end

With the exception of Cairo, Hurghada has the greatest concentration of four and five star hotels and resorts in all of Egypt. Almost all of these places are on the resort strip which starts just south of Sigala and stretches for 20-odd km down the coast. Several of the older places (and newer ones like the Hilton) are also dotted along the coast between Ad-Dahar and Sigala.

The hotels in this category, as in fact many of the middle ones already mentioned, cater mainly, if not almost exclusively, to groups, who get discounts just for being part of the organised tourism game. Travel agencies in Europe and Cairo offer reductions on these places if you book in advance. In Cairo many of the agencies along Sharia Talaat Harb and Midan Tahrir have signs in their front windows advertising special deals for these resorts.

Ad-Dahar There is a handful of three star places on the waterfront here. The cheapest for individual travellers is the *Three Corners Village* (☎ 447816; fax 447514), which has 132 rooms, most with sea views. There's a very good windsurfing centre and a pool. Single/double rooms are US$40/70 with half board. The nearby Chez Pascal restaurant and Cha Cha Disco are part of the same

group, as are the new Market Place shopping centre and the massive Empire Hotel (due to open in late 1996) behind it.

Next to it is the *Sand Beach Hotel* (☎ 547821; fax 547822), an impersonal place with rooms for US$60/100 on a half-board basis.

The *Shedwan Golden Beach Hotel* (☎ 547007; fax 548045) has air-con rooms with tiled floors and private bathrooms for US$55/95 including breakfast and taxes.

Resort Strip For the time being, the southernmost place on the strip is the *Palm Resort*, followed closely by the *Jasmine Village* (☎ 442442; fax 442441), which has 434 bungalow-style air-con rooms and caters mostly to German groups. As with most of the other complexes, it has a full water-sports centre, which includes diving and windsurfing facilities. Singles/doubles start at US$46/54. It is in fact only a three star place.

One km further north is the five star *Beach Albatross* (☎ 442571; fax 442570). This place boasts 500 rooms – the greatest number in all Hurghada – and is capable of sleeping more than 700 people. Should you want to be one of the throng, rooms start at US$106/132.

Next up are a couple of four star places including the new *Sofitel* (☎ 442261; fax 442260) with rooms from US$55/65, and then the *Magawish Tourist Village* (☎ 442620; fax 442759). Singles/doubles here start at US$60/75. It's operated by Misr Travel, so you can get more information, particularly on possible discounts, from them.

Until recently, a few km of blessed emptiness separated Magawish from the next place but it has since been consumed by the five star *InterContinental* (☎ 443911; fax 443910) which boasts the strip's only casino.

Next up is the relatively low-grade *Hurghada Beach Hotel* (☎ & fax 443710), also known as Hor Palace Village. It charges US$49/76 for half board. From here until you exit Hurghada on the north side, it is practically wall-to-wall hotels and resorts. Even the vacant land across the four-lane highway from the beach is now under construction as resorts, unable to expand up or out, spread across the road.

Next door is the *Princess Palace Hotel* (☎ 443100; fax 443109), which has a variety of rates for its 300 rooms depending on whether you stay in the main 'palace' or the 'club'. Prices start at US$42/48 per person with half board in the club/palace. Cheaper rooms are available in its *Friendship Village* across the road.

The *El Samaka Beach Club* (☎ 443014; fax 442227) is yet another three star group tourism place, again with a heavy German emphasis and a new offshoot across the road. It has a windsurfing and diving centre. Singles/doubles start at US$35/60.

The relatively new four star *Sonesta Beach Resort* (☎ 443660; fax 443665) has rooms for US$80/100.

The old *Giftun Village* (☎ 442665; fax 442666) has 380 bright whitewashed rooms with polished floors and air-con for US$39/61 on a half-board basis. There's also a diving and windsurfing centre known as the Barakuda International Aquanautic Club.

Sindbad Village (☎ 443261), which operates the yellow submarine, is next up, followed by the new *Marlin Inn* and the *Mashrabia Village*. Round the corner from here rises the new *Marriott Beach Resort* (☎ 443950; fax 443970). This peach-coloured, seven storey place is the tallest resort in Hurghada and has rooms from US$120/150.

Round the headland, about five km south of Ad-Dahar, is the four star *Sheraton* (☎ 442000; fax 443333). Built in 1973, it was the first resort to be built on the strip and has a circular design that is definitely out of fashion for the 90s. That being the case, it's still a damn sight more intimate than the Marriott's modern monstrosity next door. Rooms cost US$132/176 including taxes.

Sigala The new, four star *Helnan Regina* (☎ 442275; fax 442276), on the southern edge of Sigala, is a palatial place with rooms from US$71/86 including taxes. The beach here is certainly nothing to rave about.

Places to Eat

The beginning of April to mid-October is lobster spawning season and, during this period, it is illegal to catch lobsters. Even so, you may see some unscrupulous restaurants offering them at this time.

Ad-Dahar Centre The *El Baron* is a cheap and cheerful little eatery in the thick of things in Ad-Dahar. A satisfying meal of chicken, fasooliyya, rice and salad will cost you about E£4.

Opposite the Baron is a more pretentious and expensive cheapie, if there is such a thing, called the *Al-Medina al-Menawara*, and next to it the *Habbak* patisserie. A couple of doors further down from the Baron towards Sharia an-Nasr is a nameless chicken macaroni place.

There are a few cheap eating places opposite the Happy House Hotel, including one called *Zeko* which, like many others, specialises in grilled chicken. You'll also find a couple of teahouses around here.

A block north-west of the Baron and in a side lane to the right is the *Aladin's Lamp*, where a small plate of calamari costs E£5.50 and chicken E£8. It's a cosy, casual little niche to crawl into away from the bustle outside, and staff can arrange for beers (E£5).

One block away on Sharia Sheikh Sabak is *La Torta*. This pristine little cafe is quite unlike anything else in Ad-Dahar and serves a smorgasbord of pastries and cakes.

If it's far eastern cooking you're after, head for *Young Kang*, also on Sharia Sheikh Sabak. The food here, although not the cheapest around, is very good. Fried rice is E£10 and sweet & sour chicken costs E£17.

There are quite a few options along Sharia Abd al-Aziz Mustafa including, at the southern end, a new *Winpy* (sic), notable only for its misspelt sign.

One of the most popular places on this street, especially among backpackers, is the *Bell Riviera* (not to be confused with its more expensive sister restaurant, *Riviera*, across the road). It has an excellent lentil soup for E£1.50, spaghetti for E£2.50, pizzas for between E£5 and E£10 and calamari for E£9. You can also get breakfast for E£3.

Another option for breakfast is the *Egyptian Corner* next door, a tiny little place with a very limited menu.

Still on Sharia Abd al-Aziz Mustafa, the *Nefertiti* restaurant serves up calamari for E£13, some casserole dishes that aren't bad at all and a limited variety of seafood. The 'milkshakes', at E£4 a pop, are not much good.

If you're hankering for a fiteer, you could do worse than try the unassuming little *Pizza Hut* place across the road from the bus station, where a decent-sized fiteer costs E£5 to E£7.

The tiny *Omar Khayyam* on Sharia an-Nasr has fried fish for E£8 and Stella beers for E£4 (or E£5 if you want them cold!).

Just south of the Omar Khayyam is the *Happy Land*, which tends to concentrate on seafood. Lobster costs E£90 a kg, if you can eat that much (smaller serves are available).

Still on Sharia an-Nasr, across the road from the National Bank of Egypt, is *Scruples*, a 'pub and steak house' which has two other outlets around Ad-Dahar. It's a rather formal air-con place with a dark upstairs bar that tends to entice cuddling Egyptian couples only.

In the same league but infinitely more inviting is the *Red Sea Restaurant* in a street off Sharia an-Nasr. It's popular with package tourists wanting a night away from their resorts and the rooftop terrace gets quite crowded in the evenings. It's a good place for a drink though meals are a bit overpriced.

Seaside Ad-Dahar The road running from the Shakespear Hotel right around to the Shedwan Golden Beach Hotel is lined with shops and restaurants.

One of the first up is *Norhan*, an unpretentious little diner with a few terrace tables and a limited menu. Mains such as shepherd's pie or chicken range from E£5 to E£9 and come with a complimentary soft drink (no beer is served). The pizzas start at E£6 and are cheap enough though a bit doughy. The El Saby Supermarket next door is well stocked.

Across the road is *Arlene's*, one of the more well-established eateries in Hurghada. It serves everything from fish to steak, lousy Egyptian fare and hamburgers. Main courses cost around E£15 to E£20. This is one of the few places in Egypt you'll find nachos. Beers cost E£6.

A little further along is *Portofino*, a supposedly Italian place with quite pricey food. They serve Stella in nice mugs and the service is excellent.

The *Nivi* Restaurant is one of several mid to upper-range places close to the waterfront. It has pizzas of a sort for around E£15, seafood and grills, and everything is translated in Russian.

A bit further down the road from Nivi is the Belgian-owned *Chez Pascal*. Some travellers have reported being disappointed with the food here and, unfortunately for beer connoisseurs, they don't stock any of Belgium's excellent brews (though a couple of German ones are on tap).

Next door to Nivi is one of the mushrooming branches of *Scruples*, serving beer, pizza and pasta, but it's more expensive than the beach-front *Scruples Bistro* up the road where you can get a generous tahina salad with fresh rolls for E£2.50, garlic potatoes for E£1.50 and sandwiches for E£7; a beer here costs E£5.

Sigala There are several fairly nondescript cheapies in Sigala, but a couple of places are worth singling out. The *El-Sakia* restaurant is right down on the water's edge and has a wonderful view of the fishing boats in the old port. The food, a mixture of seafood and Egyptian cuisine, is good but a little expensive, with mains averaging E£20. If nothing else, it's a pleasant place to sit outside and enjoy a beer (E£6).

You'll know you've reached the turn-off for El-Sakia when you see the *New Omar Inn* and, opposite, *Samos* Greek restaurant, both on Sharia Sheraton. The latter has a versatile menu and moderate prices.

For really cheap fare you could try the kushari and ta'amiyya places just up from Samos or, better still, *Baracoda* (sic) near

Thomas Cook. This tiny place has just five tables and as many items on its menu. The pizzas, at E£4, are certainly passable.

Resort Strip A couple of km along the road, past the Moon Valley Village, is the best located *Felfela* restaurant in the country. Sitting on a rise and gentle bend in the coastline, it is a splendid place for a modestly priced meal – which is the standard fare served up by this growing chain (see Cairo Places to Eat for more on the original restaurant and its offshoots).

The resorts all have restaurants catering to most tastes, but are generally suitably expensive and sometimes quite uninspiring.

Entertainment
Most of the bigger hotels offer some sort of spectacle – usually a Russian or African show – as well as belly-dancing performances in their discos. The *Cha Cha Disco* next to the Nivi restaurant in Ad-Dahar has a happy hour between 10 and 11 pm. Admission is free for women but E£50 for men, including unlimited drinks. The *La Bamba Disco*, just down the road at the Sea Horse Hotel, is one of the *in* places and has a E£35 minimum charge. For this kind of nightlife you virtually have no choice but to go to the big hotels.

Those into gambling the night away can head to the *casino* at the InterContinental Hotel on the resort strip. Admission is free but you might be asked to show your passport. Smart casual dress is the required attire, and only foreign currencies are accepted.

If it's just a beer or two you're after, there are a few restaurants around Ad-Dahar where you can drink without having to eat. *Layalina*, near the Bell Riviera restaurant, is one such place. Its terrace is pleasant for an evening tipple and the cheap beers come with complimentary peanuts. Most of the other restaurants serving beers have been mentioned in the previous Places to Eat section.

Alternatively, head straight to the new *Peanuts Bar* in the Market Place complex in Ad-Dahar. Open 24 hours, this place is the haunt of dive instructors and has pricey Stellas for E£7.75 plus on-tap German beers for E£10. Those with the munchies can stuff themselves on an unlimited supply of unshelled peanuts.

Things to Buy
With the influx of Russian and eastern European tourists to Hurghada in the past few years, the trade in marine curios has taken off. There's an alarming number of stalls and shops in Ad-Dahar selling everything from stuffed sharks to lamps made out of triggerfish! Clams, starfish, pufferfish and seashells are, however, the most common victims of this illegal racket.

At the time of writing, the police had started raiding these stalls and many had been shut down. However, if demand warrants it, they'll probably spring up again in the back alleys around the market area. Refusing to buy such hideous objets d'art will at least help to break this trade.

Naf Naf and Benetton have outlets in the Giftun Village arcade. Those wanting tax-free goods can go to either the Egypt Free Shop branch opposite EgyptAir on the resort strip or to the one at the airport.

Getting There & Away
Air There are two EgyptAir offices in Hurghada. The office (☎ 546788) next to the main mosque in Ad-Dahar is also a travel agent for tours within Egypt, while the office (☎ 443592) on the resort strip near the Sonesta Beach Resort is for air tickets only. There are daily flights between Hurghada and Cairo (E£391 one way) plus two flights per week to Sharm el-Sheikh (E£286), Luxor (E£163) and Aswan (E£323, via Luxor).

There are charter flights from various European cities to Hurghada throughout the winter. If you want to head directly to Europe, it is a good idea to check around to see what charters are available for the one-way flight.

Bus Two bus companies operate services from Hurghada.

Superjet has its office (☎ 546768) and

terminal near the main mosque in Ad-Dahar. It has three buses a day to Cairo (six hours) – the buses at noon and 2.30 pm cost E£40 while the 5 pm service is E£45. To Alexandria (E£60, seven hours) there's a daily bus at 2.30 pm. There may also be services to Qena.

The Upper Egypt Bus Co operates from the main bus station at the southern end of Ad-Dahar. It runs buses almost hourly to Cairo (six hours) from 6 am to midnight. They cost E£25 to E£40, depending on onboard services. A couple of these set down in Suez as well, but some bypass it.

There are other buses bound only for Suez (E£17, five hours) leaving at 7, 9.30, 10 and 10.30 am and 1 and 3 pm.

About 10 buses a day go to Qena (three hours), starting at 6 am and finishing at 11 pm. The rides cost E£8, except for the last one, which is a few pounds more.

Buses to Luxor (five hours) leave at 6 am, noon and 4 pm and cost E£8. The 11 pm one is a deluxe service and costs E£31.

The 3.30 pm service to Aswan (which one would have thought would stop in Luxor but, according to the staff at the ticket office, doesn't) costs E£27 and takes about seven hours. The 11 pm bus to Qena and Luxor goes on to Aswan for E£35.

There is a bus to Al-Quseir that goes on to Marsa Alam and Bir Shalatayn at 7 am. The fare to Al-Quseir is E£7.

There are also occasional services to Beni Suef, Al-Minya (E£24), Sohag and Asyut (E£16), and more regular ones to Qift and Qus.

This timetable should be checked with the staff at the bus station, as changes are more than likely. It may be an idea to book ahead on the longer-distance rides such as Luxor and Cairo.

Service Taxi The service-taxi station is near the telephone office in Ad-Dahar. Taxis go to Cairo for E£30 a head (a trip of about six hours) – you'll save about E£5 by getting a service taxi as far as Suez and getting another one from there to Cairo for E£5. Others go to Suez (E£20, 3½ to four hours), Qena

(E£10), Al-Quseir (E£10) and Port Safaga (E£5). They don't go to Luxor or Aswan – although of course you could always try to bargain one into going. If successful, you may have to pay a E£10 fee for a mysterious 'ticket' at a police checkpoint before crossing the mountains. This is a so-called security measure.

Boat At the time of writing, only one vessel was plying the waters from Hurghada to Sharm el-Sheikh, departing Sunday, Tuesday and Thursday from Hurghada. There supposedly exists a hovercraft, but it never seems to be in action. Rumours also had it that a second boat may be operating from about mid-1996, in which case there would be almost daily voyages. The folks at El Shaymaa Sea Trips (see below) should be able to fill you in on the current situation.

With the existing vessel, it takes seven hours to cover the 144 km. As the boat is relatively small, it can be an irksome ride if the Red Sea is heaving at all. Lie down or look up, and try to ignore the people being sick around you. The service is cancelled when waves east of Shedwan Island are above three metres; this usually happens between November and January only. On a more positive note, it's not uncommon to see flying fish or to have dolphins racing beside the boat as you near Ras Mohammed.

Although it's possible to get a ticket at the port on the morning, it's safer to book ahead. You can do this at El Shaymaa Sea Trips (☎ 546901) on Sharia Abd al-Aziz Mustafa, Ad-Dahar. The cost is E£100 one way (though some travellers have reported bargaining it down to E£95) and the boat departs from the port in Sigala sometime between 9 and 10 am; you should be there at least half an hour beforehand.

Arriving in Sharm el-Sheikh, passengers are met by an open-sided bus, known as a *tof-tof*, which, after waiting for everyone to pile on, promptly drops you 100m away at an immigration hall. After being herded (with luggage) through x-ray machines, you'll be loaded back on the bus and driven to either the bus station in Sharm el Sheikh

(1.5 km away) or onto Na'ama Bay. The price is E£2 irrespective of where you get off and if you don't have the correct fare you can kiss your change goodbye. All in all this is one of Sinai's biggest rip-offs. It may be possible to avoid all this nonsense by just walking straight out of the port once you disembark and simply hitching into town.

Getting Around

The Airport A taxi fare from the airport, which is close to the resort strip, to downtown Ad-Dahar is E£10.

Microbus In the mornings, microbuses full of day labourers go from anywhere along Sharia an-Nasr almost all the way to the Palm Resort for about E£1. Throughout the day, microbuses regularly run from central Ad-Dahar at least as far south as the InterContinental for E£1. This appears to be the terminus. Short rides around Ad-Dahar cost 25 pt.

Taxi Taxis from central Ad-Dahar will take you as far south as the Sheraton for about E£10 (or more if there are plenty of tourists around). Taxi drivers here are, appropriately enough, a school of sharks.

Bicycle Bicycles can be rented in town from Boho, next to El Shaymaa Sea Trips on Sharia Abd al-Aziz Mustafa, for E£1/10 per hour/day. Be warned – strong headwinds can make cycling very hard going.

Hitching It's possible to hitch around town or out to the beaches, but the locals seem accustomed to receiving payment from travellers.

AROUND HURGHADA
Mons Porphyritis
About 40 km into the desert, along a side track off the main coast road 20 km north of Hurghada, lie ancient porphyry quarries worked by the Romans. The precious white and purple crystalline stone was mined for use in sarcophagi, columns and other decorative work. The quarries were under the

direct control of the imperial family in Rome, which had encampments, workshops and even temples built for the workers and engineers here. Evidence, albeit not much of it standing, of this quarry town can still be seen. Tours out of Hurghada increasingly make the trip. If you want to do it yourself, make sure you have a guide or driver who knows the way. Taxi drivers eager to make a pound have been known to volunteer for the job without really knowing what they are doing. This is unpleasant territory to get stuck in without adequate water.

Sharm an-Naga
About halfway down to Port Safaga, this is a fairly low-key beach resort used mainly by divers, though those with their own tent can also camp. Day trippers wanting to use the beach (there's some good snorkelling here) must pay E£10. Misr Travel in Hurghada often runs snorkelling excursions to this spot.

PORT SAFAGA
Port Safaga (often referred to simply as Safaga) is 53 km south of Hurghada and is first and foremost a port for the export of phosphates from local mines (and from the mines at Abu Tartur hundreds of km away in the New Valley). During the haj, plenty of pilgrims embark here on their voyage to Mecca.

It is hardly an attractive place to hang about and there's not much in the way of accommodation for budget travellers, though there are some expensive resorts north of town where you can organise diving courses. The plague of construction around Hurghada is thus repeated on a smaller scale here.

Orientation & Information
Sharia al-Gomhurriya, the main road on the waterfront, has most of the services you might need. The bus station is near the southern end of town. Heading north there is a motley collection of small, cheap eateries and tacky souvenir stalls, and beyond them the post office. About two km north of the

bus station is the service-taxi station. Next to it is the main telephone and telex office. Alongside the telephone office are branches of Banque Misr and the Banque du Caire. Further north, next to the Maka Hotel, is the Bank of Alexandria. You can catch a microbus up and down Sharia al-Gomhurriya for 25 pt; when heading south many of these vehicles will drop you about 400m north of the bus station. Many microbuses also shuttle back and forth between the town and the northern resorts.

Things to See & Do

There's not really much in either category, although some of the beaches are good for **swimming** and **snorkelling**. Check at the bigger hotels for some of the better possibilities.

About 40 km along the Qena road, a track breaks off north towards **Mons Claudianus,** a one-time Roman fortress complex for the protection of nearby quarries. You really need a guide for this trip, but the bigger hotels may organise excursions there. There are remains of a Roman road, columns and other evidence of the quarries and Roman military presence.

Places to Stay & Eat

The only budget option is the *Maka Hotel* (☎ 451866) at the northern end of town near the turn-off to Qena. It's a rip-off at E£20 for a very ordinary double with fan and private bathroom. There is no concession for single travellers.

A few hundred metres further north is the *Cleopatra Hotel* (☎ 451544). It's much better, but costs E£43/55 for singles/doubles with bathroom; breakfast is E£7 extra.

About 200m up from the Cleopatra, on the northern edge of town, is the new *Hotel Marina* (☎ 451133; fax 452670). Single/ double rooms with air-con start at US$32/50, including breakfast, or there are tent-shaped cabanas – hot little sweat boxes which are not air-conditioned – for US$19/40. It's one of the more ugly new resorts.

Heading north out of town there are at least six resorts: the *Menaville* and *Lotus Bay*

are on the main road while the *Sun Beach Camp*, *Shams Paradise*, *Holiday Inn* and *Shams Safaga* are all on a side road leading around a bay. The Lotus Bay (☎ 451040) is the cheapest of the lot, charging US$40/48 for singles/doubles; at the other end of the scale is the Holiday Inn (☎ 451145) charging US$78/89 for singles/doubles.

As already noted, there is a whole string of cheap eats heading north from the bus station along Sharia al-Gomhurriya. Otherwise, you could try the small *pizzeria* attached to the Cleopatra Hotel (which, incidentally, also has a bar) or the expensive resort restaurants.

Getting There & Away

Bus There are buses going all over the place, many of them originating elsewhere. There are five buses a day to Cairo (E£25 to E£40). The same buses stop in Suez for E£35. There are seven buses to Hurghada, costing from E£2.50 to E£5. Buses leave at 5 am and 2 pm to Al-Quseir (E£8). To Marsa Alam and Bir Shalatayn there's a bus on Tuesday, Thursday and Sunday at about noon. If you're heading that far south you'd probably be quicker to hitch. More or less regular services to Qena cost between E£5 and E£10. To Luxor (E£17) and on to Aswan (E£30) there are one or two buses per day.

Service Taxi The taxis basically do three routes. Hurghada takes about 40 minutes and costs E£5. The trip to Al-Quseir (try early in the morning) costs E£3.50, and to Qena E£8. Be prepared to haggle as the asking prices are ludicrous.

Boat The only passenger boats from Port Safaga are those going to Duba and Jeddah in Saudi Arabia. To Duba there's a daily boat which costs E£150 to E£170 in 1st class, E£120 in 2nd class and E£100 in deck class. It takes about seven hours. To Jeddah there are two boats a week; the voyage takes 30 hours and costs roughly double the fare to Duba. Apparently, during the haj, a hydrofoil also operates to Jeddah.

EL-HAMARAWEIN

You'll see this phosphate processing centre 65 km south of Port Safaga long before you reach it. With prevailing northerly winds, the coastline for several km south of El-Hamarawein is obscured in a pall of dust from the phosphates being loaded onto ships.

There is absolutely no reason to stop, unless you're booked into the *Daly Dive Resort* (☎ 432039; fax 432038) on the northern edge of the community. It has easy access to some great, unspoilt dive sites and is popular with groups from Europe. Independent travellers are welcome to stay if there's room – you'll be looking at US$38/56 for a night's accommodation and half board.

AL-QUSEIR

The medieval port town of Al-Quseir (population 4000) is 85 km south of Port Safaga and about 160 km east of Qift on the Nile. Until the 10th century it was one of the most important exit points for pilgrims travelling to Mecca and was also a thriving centre of trade and export between the Nile Valley and the Red Sea and beyond. After centuries of neglect, the Ottomans cranked it up again for a while, but the opening of the Suez Canal in 1869 put an end to all that. These days, it's the next link in the chain for developers looking to exploit the Red Sea coastline and, like Port Safaga and Hurghada before it, the big hotel chains have already discovered Al-Quseir.

Orientation & Information

A branch of the National Bank of Egypt is just north-west of the main roundabout on the way into town from Port Safaga. The 24 hour telephone office is right on the roundabout, while the post office is off to the east, down towards the waterfront.

Things to See & Do

The 16th century **fort** and small **souq** are worth checking out, and there's excellent **snorkelling** at various beaches to the north and south of town.

One that is often recommended is **Kilo Ashara**, a small beach 10 km south of town.

You can't really miss it, as it's one of the few obvious places for a swim on your way out of town – one of the many Red Sea coast military installations is up on the bluff at the southern end. If you talk to the locals, they'll recommend other beaches as well, most of them seemingly placed at suspiciously convenient-sounding 10 km intervals.

Places to Stay

The obvious choice for those travelling on a tight budget is the *Sea Princess Hotel* (☎ 430044), just south of the bus station. Small cabin-like singles/doubles with fan

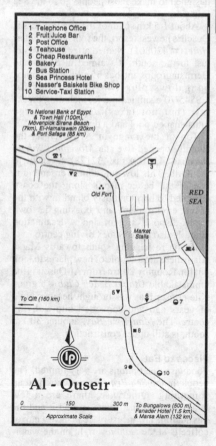

1 Telephone Office
2 Fruit Juice Bar
3 Post Office
4 Teahouse
5 Cheap Restaurants
6 Bakery
7 Bus Station
8 Sea Princess Hotel
9 Nasser's Baiskels Bike Shop
10 Service-Taxi Station

To National Bank of Egypt
& Town Hall (100m),
Mövenpick Sirena Beach
(7km), El-Hamarawein (20km)
& Port Safaga (85 km)

Old Fort

RED SEA

Market Stalls

To Qift (160 km)

Al - Quseir

0   150   300 m
Approximate Scale

To Bungalows (500 m),
Fanader Hotel (1.5 km)
& Marsa Alam (132 km)

cost E£12/20 plus taxes. Breakfast is a couple of pounds extra. They have a few masks and snorkels to rent. The toilet/shower combinations can be a bit smelly, but hot water is reliable.

Further south, right on the beach (don't get too excited, it's not at its best here) are some bungalows run by the local town hall. They're not bad at E£20 a head with your own bath and cooker. The pain is you have to head to the northern end of town to look for someone at the town hall who can give you the appropriate pieces of paper before you can actually move in – perfectly designed to make most people go to the Sea Princess.

About 1.5 km south of the Sea Princess is Quseir's newest resort, the four star *Fanader Hotel* (☎ 430861). Named after a rocky islet just to the south, it's aimed at Swiss and German groups and has 55 adjoining domed bungalows plus two large villas for US$45/70 a single/double, including breakfast (but not taxes). There's a large lotus-shaped pool and a dive centre.

Top of the range in Al-Quseir is the recently opened five star *Mövenpick Sirena Beach* (☎ 432100; fax 432128), seven km to the north. This low-set, domed ensemble is one of the better resorts along the coast, designed to harmoniously blend in with the desert environment and boasting its own waste disposal system and a desalination plant. It also has a Subex diving centre.

If you're heading south towards Marsa Alam there are a couple of new places to look out for. Roughly 20 km from Al-Quseir is the unmistakable *Utopia Beach Club* – a green Nile cruiser that was brought here a couple of years ago and converted into a diving centre. The *Mangrove Bay*, another 30 km south, is still under construction.

Places to Eat

Foodwise, the options are very limited. The people in the *Sea Princess* can cook you up something. Otherwise, there are a few ta'amiyya and fish joints around it and the bus station. The nicest place to have a cup of coffee is at the *teahouse* right on the water-front. At the *Fanader Hotel*, the buffet dinner costs E£60 and is open to nonguests – if you are walking there, it's quicker to follow the beach round rather than hiking along the road.

Getting There & Away

Bus There is a bus all the way to Cairo (E£42, 11 hours) via Port Safaga, Hurghada and Suez which leaves at 5 am. There may also be another one or two cheaper services to Cairo. The bus south to Marsa Alam (E£5) and beyond leaves Tuesday, Thursday and Sunday at 1.30 pm. There are two connections for the trip to Qena (E£6.50, four hours) via Qift. The first leaves at 7 am and the second at 12.30 pm.

Service Taxi The service-taxi station is at the southern end of town. Taxis leave when full, which doesn't always happen all that quickly, and there's very little activity in the afternoon. The officially prescribed fares are: Cairo E£30; Suez E£25; Hurghada E£10; Port Safaga E£3.50; Qena E£8; Qift E£7; and Luxor E£10.

Getting Around

Nasser's Baiskels has a few old bicycles for rent. He wants E£5 for the day, but this can probably be bargained down. His workshop is virtually opposite the service-taxi station (and about 100m from the Sea Princess Hotel) near the southern exit of town.

AROUND AL-QUSEIR

One could just as easily say 'around Qena', for about halfway along the road connecting the two towns is an interesting but rarely visited collection of **Pharaonic graffiti**. The wayward chisellings of Wadi Hammamet were first extensively examined by the Russian Egyptologist Vladimir Golenischeff late last century. The high, smooth walls of the wadi have made it an ideal resting place for travellers through the ages, and indeed there is graffiti from post-Pharaonic times as well, right down to Egypt's 20th century King Farouk. The road runs on an ancient trade path, and remains of old wells and other evidence of the trail's long history can also be seen. You could get the early bus from Al-Quseir or Qena (one leaves each at 7 am) to drop you at Wadi Hammamet, and try to get a lift on the next one either way about four or five hours later, or simply hitch.

MARSA ALAM

Marsa Alam is a fishing village 132 km south of Al-Quseir. A road also connects the village with Edfu, 230 km across the desert to the west. Phosphate mining is the big thing in this part of the country, and an exploration company is looking for new sources of mineral wealth in the area. The village is basically a T-junction of the road from Edfu with the coast road. South of the junction is the bulk of the village with a small, incongruous-looking shopping arcade (which has a pharmacy), a school and a telephone office, from where you can sometimes call overseas.

The main thing to do here is have a snorkel or dive. As a military pass (issued from Cairo) is required for travel south of Marsa Alam, you may not be able to use what is apparently a particularly good snorkelling beach seven km south of the town. Luckily, there is another beach the same distance to the north.

About 145 km south-west into the desert is the **Tomb of Sayyid ash-Shadhili**, a 13th century sheikh who is revered by many as one of the more important Sufi leaders. His tomb was restored under the orders of King Farouk in 1947 but, without a guide or a good map, is nearly impossible to find.

Warning

Remember, much of this southern coastal area is mined and in some cases there is not even barbed wire to warn you. Don't go wandering onto beaches without checking with the locals first.

Places to Stay

The Pharaoh's Gold Mining company's rest house *(istiraha)* is the only place to stay in town but is often fully occupied by employees. At E£10 per person for a spartan room,

you get the use of a kitchen, fridge and lounge room, and have your own porch. There's no sign on this place – just look for the cluster of three houses – one blue trimmed, one green and one brown – on the northern edge of town about 700m from the Edfu turn-off.

The only alternative, apart from simply pitching a tent somewhere on the beach, is the *Beach Safari Camp* (☎ 364-7970) about seven km north of the town. Draped around two azure bays connected by a path around a small headland, the camp has five semi-permanent 'tents' each with two double rooms, as well as four four-person tents, and a communal shower block with very limited water. At E£35 per night with breakfast (white cheese, an omelette and bread) or E£65 for half board (the meals are OK but not extravagant), the prices are a bit over the top. However, for those in search of peace and solitude it's rather an idyllic setting, and if you've got your own tent you can pitch it here for about E£5. From the beach, a sandy passage leads into deeper water, making an ideal entry point for snorkellers and divers. The camp rents out snorkelling gear and has a modest diving club with all the necessary equipment.

If you do stay here, don't walk along the beach north of the main headland – it's definitely mined.

The only way to get to Beach Safari, other than waiting for one of the infrequent buses between Marsa Alam and Al-Quseir, is to hitch. It's not too difficult and you'll see the camp about 200m off the road. Depending on the time of the day, you may also be able to get a ride with the camp's pick-up which usually drops into their office at the shopping arcade (about 200m south of the road junction) in Marsa Alam.

Places to Eat

There are a couple of *cafes* at the junction where you can occasionally get some dubious-looking ta'amiyya, as well as a pair of grocery stores with scant supplies. The only other option is the *Kavaterya* (read 'cafeteria') next to the service station. The young owner is very friendly but the choice of food is limited to stale sandwiches, packet soups and frozen hamburgers. There's a *bakery* next door.

Getting There & Away

The bus across the desert to Marsa Alam departs from Aswan at 6.15 am, passes through Edfu between 8 and 8.30 am and arrives in Marsa Alam about three hours later. It goes on to Bir Shalatayn but, at the time of writing, it was unlikely you'd get past the military checkpoint south of Marsa Alam. The bus going back to Aswan (E£10.50) via Edfu (E£7) leaves from the cafes at the junction at about 7 am.

On Monday, Wednesday and Saturday there's an 8 am bus to Al-Quseir (E£5, 1½ hours) from where there are more frequent connections further north. A bus coming down the other way leaves Port Safaga at noon and Al-Quseir at 1.30 pm on Tuesday, Thursday and Sunday.

BERENICE

The military centre and small port of Berenice, 150 km south of Marsa Alam, was founded in 275 BC by Ptolemy II Euergetes I and was an important trading post until the 5th century AD. Near the town, the ruins of the **Temple of Seramis** can be seen. The US Navy occasionally brings its aircraft carriers here. Apparently, this is one of the staging areas for the US Rapid Deployment Forces. As a military permit is required for land travel south of Marsa Alam, it may not be possible to get this far south down the coast.

BIR SHALATAYN

This tiny village 90 km south of Berenice marks the administrative boundary between Egypt and Sudan, although Egypt at least considers the political boundary to be another 175 km south-east, beyond the town of Halaib, once an important Red Sea port but long fallen into obscurity.

Some of the best dive sites in the Red Sea are located in this area and dive companies from further north are increasingly organising boat safaris to the region. Divers are about the only civilians who make it this far south these days as all the necessary permits are either arranged well in advance, or hastily put together thanks to a bit of baksheesh by the various dive clubs.

There were rumours that a new resort catering exclusively to divers was to open here in mid-1996. It can only be hoped this virgin area escapes the destruction that took place around Hurghada.

Sinai

Sinai, a region of awesome and incredible beauty, has been a place of refuge, conflict and curiosity for thousands of years. Wedged between Africa and Asia, its northern coast is bordered by the Mediterranean Sea, and its southern peninsula by the Red Sea gulfs of Aqaba and Suez. Row upon row of barren, jagged, red-brown mountains fill the southern interior, surrounded by relentlessly dry, yet colourful, desert plains. From the palm-lined coast, dunes and swamps of the north to the white-sand beaches and superb coral reefs of the Red Sea, Sinai is full of contrasts.

In Pharaonic times, the quarries of Sinai provided enormous quantities of turquoise, gold and copper. The great strategic importance of the 'Land of Turquoise' also made it the goal of empire builders and the setting for countless wars.

Sinai is a land of miracles and holy places. Elijah, Jacob and Abraham, the prophets of Judaism, Christianity and Islam, wandered through its hills and deserts. It was here that God is said to have first spoken to Moses from a burning bush and, later, delivered the Israelites from the Egyptian army with the celebrated parting of the Red Sea.

And Moses stretched out his hand over the sea; and the Lord caused the sea to go back...And the children of Israel went into the midst of the sea upon the dry ground: and the waters were a wall unto them on their right hand, and on their left. And the Egyptians pursued...and the Lord overthrew the Egyptians in the midst of the sea. And the waters returned and covered the chariots, and the horsemen, and all the host of Pharaoh that came into the sea after them; there remained not so much as one of them...Thus the Lord saved Israel that day out of the hand of the Egyptians; and Israel saw the Egyptians dead upon the sea shore. (Exodus 14: 21-30)

Sinai is the 'great and terrible wilderness' of the Bible, across which the Israelites journeyed in search of the Promised Land, and it was from the summit of Mt Sinai that God delivered his Ten Commandments to Moses:

Tell the children of Israel; Ye have seen what I did unto the Egyptians...If ye will obey my voice and keep my covenant, then ye shall be a peculiar treasure unto me above all people: for all the earth is mine. And ye shall be unto me a kingdom of priests, and a holy nation.

And Mount Sinai was altogether in smoke, because the Lord descended upon it in fire; and the whole mount quaked greatly...And the Lord came down upon Mount Sinai...and called Moses up to the top of the mount...And God spoke all these words, saying, I am the Lord thy God, which have brought thee out of the land of Egypt, out of the house of bondage. Thou shalt have no other gods before me... (Exodus 19:4-20:3)

History

In the 16th century BC, the soldiers of the Egyptian army, under Pharaoh Tuthmosis III, were far more fortunate than their biblical ancestors – they successfully crossed the Red Sea and Sinai to conquer Palestine and Syria. Alexander the Great marched across Sinai to conquer Egypt in 332 BC and, in 48 BC, just east of present-day Port Said, the opposing armies of Cleopatra and Ptolemy, her brother, battled for the Egyptian throne. Throughout Sinai, holy places mark the spots where Mary, Joseph and Jesus supposedly rested during their flight into Sinai to escape King Herod.

The Arab general Amr led his forces through Sinai in 639 AD to conquer Egypt and bring Islam to Africa. In 1160, Salah ad-Din (known to the West as Saladin) built a fortress at Qalat al-Gindi, to protect Muslim pilgrims and to guard Egypt against the invading Crusaders. In the 16th century, the Ottomans crossed Sinai to make Egypt part of their empire.

The Ottomans' power struggle with the French under Napoleon and with the British under Allenby continued to see the passage of armies back and forth across Sinai, right up to the beginning of this century. The international border of Sinai, from Rafah to Eilat, was actually drawn up by the British, prior to WWI, to keep the Germans and

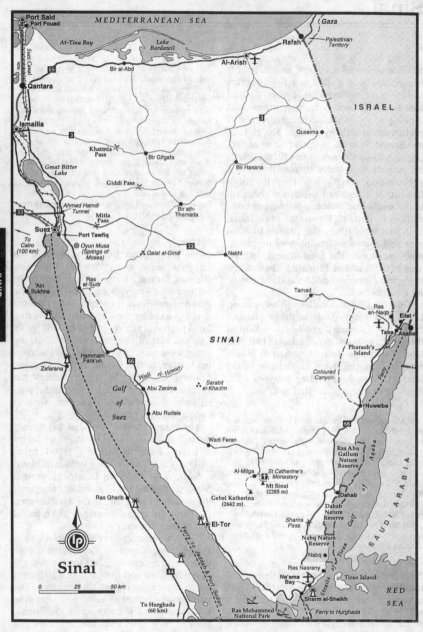

MEDITERRANEAN SEA

Port Said
Port Fouad

At-Tina Bay

Lake
Bardawil

Gaza

Rafah

Palestinian
Territory

Al-Arish

55

Bir al-Abd

Qantara

ISRAEL

Ismailia

3

Khatmia
Pass

Bir Gifgafa

Quseima

Great Bitter
Lake

Giddi Pass

Bir Hasana

Ahmed Hamdi
Tunnel

Mitla
Pass

Bir ath-
Thamada

33

Suez
Port Tawfiq

To
Cairo
(100 km)

Oyun Musa
(Springs of
Moses)

Qalat al-Gindi

33

Nakhl

'Ain
Sukhna

Ras
al-Sudr

SINAI

Tamad

Ras
an-Naqb

Eilat
Taba Aqaba

Hammam
Fara'un

Wadi el-Homur

Sarabit
el-Khadim

Pharaoh's
Island

Zafarana

Gulf
of
Suez

66

Abu Zenima

Coloured
Canyon

Abu Rudeis

Nuweiba

Wadi Feran

66

Ras Abu
Gallum
Nature
Reserve

Ras Gharib

Al-Milga

St Catherine's
Monastery
Mt Sinai
(2285 m)

Gebel Katherina
(2642 m)

Dahab

Dahab
Nature
Reserve

Gulf
of
Aqaba

SAUDI ARABIA

El-Tor

Sharira
Pass

Nabq Nature
Reserve

Nabq

Sinai

0   25   50 km

Ras Nasrany

Na'ama
Bay

Tiran Island

Straits of Tiran

Sharm el-Sheikh

RED
SEA

To Hurghada
(60 km)

Ras Mohammed
National Park

Ferry to Hurghada

44

Ferry to Jeddah & Port Sudan

SINAI

Turks away from the Suez Canal. In 1948, 1956 and from 1967 to 1979 the battle for Sinai was fought between Egypt and Israel.

Israel briefly took Sinai in its 1948 War of Independence, but was pressured by the UK into returning it to the Egyptians. In 1956, Israel, with the support of the UK and France, took control of the canal and Sinai. Although Israel held the region for four months, a lack of US and UN support forced its return to Egypt.

In 1967, Egypt's President Nasser closed the strategic Straits of Tiran, a narrow passage situated at the southern tip of Sinai, blocking Israel's access to the sea. The Israelis again captured Sinai, and kept it by building a series of fortifications along the eastern bank of the Suez Canal. Sinai remained impregnable until 1973, when the Egyptians, under President Sadat, used their 'secret weapon', water cannons, to blast the sand-dune barriers of the so-called Bar Lev Line.

Within two weeks, the Israelis had mustered their forces for a counterattack. Crossing the Suez Canal, they encircled the 30,000 strong Egyptian Third Army, took the city of Suez and came within striking distance of Cairo. Peace negotiations began at the now-famous Km 101, culminating in President Sadat's historic visit to Jerusalem, the Camp David Agreement and, in March 1979, the signing of a peace treaty by Begin (prime minister of Israel) and Sadat in Washington DC.

In accordance with the treaty, Israel withdrew from most of Sinai by 1982. A UN Multinational Force & Observers group, the MFO, was established to ensure adherence to the treaty by both Egypt and Israel. Most of the MFO was stationed at Na'ama Bay and Al-Arish but, these days, there is only a token force still stationed in Na'ama Bay.

In recent years Sinai has become the focus of development and 'reconstruction' in much the same way as the New Valley did during the 1970s and 1980s (when landless fellahin from an overcrowded Nile Valley were encouraged to move to the desert oases). The government is building a new pipeline to bring freshwater from the Suez Canal to various areas targeted for resettlement. Roads are being paved and desalination plants are being installed in coastal towns. By offering these incentives the government is hoping to attract an estimated three million newcomers. Tourism, too, has made great inroads in the last 15 or so years, especially around the south-east. The Bedouins, now a minority in their native land, have little means to resist all this change.

Geology

Some of Egypt's most striking geological features appear in Sinai. Sandstone and granitic mountains are cut by deep wadis and coral reefs embrace the peninsula. Here, some 70 million years ago, the African and Arabian continental plates began to move apart, creating the rather shallow (95m deep) Gulf of Suez and the much deeper (1800m) Gulf of Aqaba. The Gulf of Aqaba, which varies from 14 to 25 km in width, is actually part of a rift (a crack in the earth's top layer) which extends for some 6000 km from the Dead Sea in Israel through the Red Sea, Ethiopia and Kenya down to Mozambique in southern Africa.

Climate

It gets hot in Sinai, so remember to carry water always, use copious amounts of sun screen, wear sensible clothes to avoid sunburn (wearing a T-shirt while snorkelling is advisable), and use a hat or scarf. While summer temperatures can climb to 50°C (120°F), it gets very cold at night and the mountains can be freezing even during the day; come prepared with warm clothing. Camping out in winter definitely requires a sleeping bag – it has been known to snow on Mt Sinai!

Occasionally some of the coast is whipped by strong winds causing sand storms – they usually only last a few hours. Even on normal days, there are often strong northerly winds blowing along the Gulf of Aqaba coast. See the table in the Climate section of the Facts for the Visitor chapter for further details.

Balancing Sinai's Ecosystem

Although much of Sinai is hot dry desert, it is not devoid of life. A very delicate ecosystem is in place, however, it's under direct threat from the onslaught of tourism.

Sinai is a unique land of craggy mountains sliced by dry, gravel wadis in which the odd acacia tree or clump of gnarled tamarisk manages to survive. On the edge of all this are the coastal dunes where a variety of plants tenuously hold onto life in loose, sandy soil. Once every few decades, when storm clouds gather over the mountains and dump colossal amounts of water on this parched landscape, the whole scene is transformed into a sea of greenery. Seeds that have lain dormant in the soil for years suddenly burst into life. For Sinai's wildlife, such as the gazelle and rock hyrax (as well as for the goats herded by local Bedouins), these rare occasions are times of plenty.

Up until relatively recently, the only people to wander through this region were Bedouins on camel; nowadays, groups of tourists looking for outback adventure and pristine spots are ploughing their way through in 4WD vehicles and 'quads' (four wheeled motorcycles) which churn up the soil, uproot plants and create erosion. Aware of the danger this poses to Sinai's ecosystem, the authorities have banned vehicles from going off-road in certain areas, such as Ras Mohammed National Park and in the protected areas of Nabq and Ras Abu Gallum. But banning something and actually enforcing it in areas as vast as these are two different things. Rangers do patrol Ras Mohammed, however, it's largely up to tourists themselves to follow the rules. So try not to be persuaded by over-eager guides wanting to show you something that's off the beaten track. If you really want to explore the region in depth, do it in the age old fashion – go by foot or hire a camel.

A much more obvious impact of tourism is rubbish. Egypt is not exactly garbage free but modern litter is most evident and a sad sight in Sinai. It's a combination of attitude and environment. The Bedouins were used to moving on and leaving their debris behind them. No matter, it was all biodegradable and if it took a little longer to rot away in the dry desert environment that was no problem – after all there weren't many people in Sinai to see it. Now there are a lot more people and their modern plastic garbage doesn't decay at all. The whole of Sinai is becoming covered in a scattering of plastic bags and some places are real horror stories. Moses would have no trouble at all finding his way to the top of Mt Sinai today – he could just follow the empty plastic mineral water bottles and used toilet paper. It's a pity he didn't bring down one more commandment – Thou Shalt Not Litter.

On the bright side, isolated efforts are being made to resist the tide of junk. Annual clean-up days are organised in Sharm el-Sheikh, and the popular budget travellers' haunt at Dahab has also somewhat cleaned up its act. It's still far from perfect, but any sign of improvement is welcome. Treat Sinai, above and below the sea, with care and do what you can to preserve the natural beauty of this very special place. ■

Ecology & Environment

Conservationists and environmentalists are concerned that extensive tourism and related development, especially along the south-east coast, will upset the delicate coastal and marine ecosystems. From Ras Mohammed, Egypt's first national park, to the protected areas of Nabq and Ras Abu Gallum, south and north of Dahab, the effects of tourism on the environment are obvious.

On a single day in 1995, volunteers in Sharm el-Sheikh collected almost a tonne of garbage from beaches near local dive sites. What's more, they did the same the year before. Why ruin a beautiful place by leaving garbage in the water, on the beach or in the mountains? Carry out all rubbish with you, and dispose of it thoughtfully.

Assist in the protection of Sinai's unique marine life by minimising your disturbance. When diving or snorkelling, do not touch the coral and plants, nor turn over rocks.

When exploring on land, stick to the beaten tracks – for your own protection (some of the region is mined) and for the sake of the environment.

Information

Visas If you're entering Egypt by way of Sinai from Israel, you will need an Egyptian visa. This can only be obtained before you get to the border. On arrival in Egypt, you must register with the police within seven days.

If you intend only to visit the eastern Sinai coast from Taba down to Sharm el-Sheikh,

The Bedouins

The nomadic lifestyle of the 14 Bedouin tribes of Sinai is rapidly changing as the 20th century encroaches on the age-old customs of these desert people. Once, they moved on, with their black goatskin tents, camels and goats, whenever the wells, wadis or other desert watercourses ran dry. Their tradition of hospitality used to be one of the major attractions for many of the travellers who visited the region. Now, as tourism and hotel projects continue to spring up along Sinai coasts, contact with Bedouins who don't work with tourists is becoming increasingly rare.

Not that the Bedouins are uniformly pleased by the developments. In many cases they have been pushed to the fringes of the profit-making by Egyptians, who have come into Sinai from elsewhere. In a place like Dahab, they generally find themselves shunted aside and left to pick up the crumbs through driving taxis and organising camel treks, although a few of the camps are still Bedouin-run.

Most of their ancestors came from the Arabian peninsula, however, the Bedouins' laws, customs and religion (which blends Islam and pagan beliefs), as well as their resilience and amazing hospitality, were born of their lifestyle in Sinai – the isolation, the harsh, dry climate and the need to keep moving on in search of water.

The wealth of a Bedouin is still measured in camels and children, but

Sinai's Bedouins can often still be identified by their traditional dress of loose, layered robes and head cloth. Tourism, however, has proved a major threat to their traditional nomadic lifestyle.

western technology is making its presence felt. While you may see the traditional Bedouin goatskin tents and camels in Sinai, there are also pick-up trucks and settlements of crude cement huts, or palm-frond shacks, with corrugated roofs and TV antennae.

Ever since the reign of Mohammed Ali, early in the 19th century, governments have been trying to settle the Bedouin tribes. Like the Israelis before them, the Egyptians have built schools, medical clinics and social centres for the Bedouins. They have also placed hundreds of 200l barrels of water strategically, at points where they wish to create stable settlements. Many of Sinai's 50,000 Bedouins now harvest dates, cultivate grain, grow vegetables and cater to the tourists. ■

you can get a 14 day pass on the border. See the Getting There & Away chapter and the Taba section for more information on crossing from Israel into Egypt.

Visa extensions are available only from the office in El-Tor.

Money Changing money in Sinai is not a problem. The banks and hotels in Sharm el-Sheikh, Na'ama Bay, Dahab, Nuweiba, Taba, St Catherine's Monastery and Al-Arish will change travellers' cheques and occasionally accept credit cards, but otherwise you may have to try to change cash privately.

Costs Many visitors to Sinai coming across from Israel, are pleasantly surprised by the apparent cheapness of the place. Those coming the other way, from somewhere in Egypt, are usually taken aback by how expensive it is. There is virtually no budget accommodation in the Sharm el-Sheikh and Na'ama Bay area. The backpacker havens in Dahab and Nuweiba, where you can stay in basic huts for as little as E£5, are the exception to this rule.

Groceries, meals and drinks are more expensive here than elsewhere in Egypt. Drinks such as tea, coffee or soft drinks all tend to be E£1 or more, and where but here would anyone consider asking E£2 to E£3 for ta'amiyya?

Sinai buses are the most expensive in the country (and the only ones with separate, higher fares for tourists), and service taxis are worse still. Travellers on a budget who intend to eat in the cafes two or three times a day should count on average daily costs of E£50, although you can bring it down considerably by cooking your own food and getting lucky when hitching.

Warning Despite what local tour operators may tell you, some areas of Sinai still contain land mines leftover from the wars with Israel. Be very wary about going off the beaten track as, unlike in areas along the Mediterranean and Red Sea coasts where danger spots are often fenced off or signposted, here there are no warnings.

Water Sports
For general information about diving and snorkelling, see the Activities section in the Facts for the Visitor chapter. Individual dive clubs are detailed in the relevant town sections of this chapter.

For information about some of the weird, wonderful or potentially dangerous creatures that you may meet while in the water, refer to Flora & Fauna in the Facts about the Country chapter. Information on ways to help protect the marine environment are detailed in the Ecology & Environment section in the Facts about the Country chapter.

Getting Around
The few paved roads through the desert and hills link only the permanent settlements,

and transport is not as regular as elsewhere in Egypt. You can get to most places you'd be likely to want to reach by bus, but in many cases there are only a couple of connections a day, sometimes only one. Service taxis, in the organised sense of the word, do not exist. As drivers in Suez will tell you, beyond the coast route to El-Tor, you can only get hold of a service taxi by bargaining and paying far more than would be the case over similar distances elsewhere in Egypt. The reason is simple: there are not enough locals around in need of a fully built up transport system.

If you are driving yourself, you must stick to the main roads, as foreigners are forbidden to leave them.

OYUN MUSA
Oyun Musa, or the 'springs of Moses', is said to be the place where Moses, on discovering that the water there was too bitter to drink, took the advice of God and threw a special tree into the springs, miraculously sweetening the water.

Seven of the 12 original springs still exist and, around them, a small settlement has grown up. The palm trees are a bit unusual, as most have had their crowns blown off in various Sinai wars and still haven't quite returned to their previous state.

Oyun Musa is about 25 km south of the Ahmed Hamdi Tunnel, which goes under the Suez Canal near Suez. Completed in 1982, the 1.6 km long tunnel is named after a martyr of the 1973 war and is now open 24 hours. Camping at Oyun Musa is possible but, as the spring water is too brackish, there is no drinkable water – and there's no sign of the special tree that Moses used.

Getting There & Away
The buses from Cairo (six a day) and from Suez (leaving at 11 am and 3 pm) to Sharm el-Sheikh and St Catherine's Monastery pass through Oyun Musa.

RAS AL-SUDR
Ras al-Sudr, or Sudr, is about 60 km south of the Ahmed Hamdi Tunnel. The town developed around one of the country's biggest oil

refineries, yet for some strange reason the Egyptians decided to build a tourist resort here, which has been followed by a couple of others.

Places to Stay & Eat

About 10 km north of Sudr, there's a cluster of resorts in the middle of nowhere. Coming from Suez the first place you'll come to is *El-Marosa*. Following this is *Mesalla* (☎ 678411) and then the *Banana Beach Village* (☎ 247-5258). The trio's prices range between E£32 and E£45 for a single room and E£40 to E£60 for a double.

In the town itself, the *Sudr Beach Inn* (☎ 770752) has hotel rooms and self-contained villas, near the refinery and on the beach, from E£56/70 per night.

The *Daghash Land Village* (☎ 777049), on the highway 10 km south of Sudr, is the cheapest place in this whole unlikely resort area, charging E£16/23 for colourful cabanas right on the beach.

Further south still, about 38 km from Sudr, is the three star *Moon Beach Resort* (☎ 291-5023) which offers concrete, beach-front bungalows at US$30/40.

The Helnan hotels chain is also building a resort along this stretch of coastline.

Getting There & Away

All buses from Cairo and Suez to Sharm el-Sheikh and St Catherine's Monastery pass through Sudr; the ones from Suez leave at 11 am and 3 pm. The trip takes 1¼ hours going either way.

QALAT AL-GINDI & NAKHL

Eighty km south-east of the Ahmed Hamdi Tunnel is Qalat al-Gindi, which features the 800 year-old Fortress of Salah ad-Din. In the 12th century AD, Muslims from Africa and the Mediterranean streamed across Sinai on their way to Mecca. As the three caravan routes they followed all converged at Qalat al-Gindi, Salah ad-Din built a fortress here to protect the pilgrims making their haj. He also planned to use the fort, which is still largely intact, as a base from which to launch attacks on the Crusaders, who had advanced as far as Jerusalem. As it turned out, Salah ad-Din managed to evict the Crusaders from the Holy City even before the completion of his fortress.

Qalat al-Gindi is definitely off the beaten track and it is rarely visited. From the coast, you must turn off at Ras al-Sudr. There is no public transport, so you must either have your own vehicle or hire a taxi.

Continuing north from Qalat al-Gindi for about 20 km you'll get to the turn-off for Nakhl, another 60 km east. This little one horse community sits almost smack in the centre of the Sinai peninsula and is surrounded by a vast wilderness. It boasts a population of about 60 people, and has a hotel (of sorts) for the odd traveller who passes this way, a petrol station, supermarket and bakery.

HAMMAM FARA'UN

Hammam Fara'un, or 'the Pharaoh's bath', is about 50 km south of Ras al-Sudr. The Egyptians who travel here to relax in the hot springs and streams and lie on the beautiful, isolated beach rave about the place.

Getting There & Away

Sinai buses from Cairo and Suez or going the other way can drop you off at the turn-off to Hammam Fara'un and the beach is not too far from the main road. The time to Suez is about 1¾ hours.

FROM ABU ZENIMA TO EL-TOR

Several of Egypt's development schemes in Sinai are being implemented along this 90 km stretch of coastline beside the Gulf of Suez. Most of the projects relate to the off-shore oil fields; consequently, the area is marred by jumbled masses of pipes, derricks and machinery.

The community of **Abu Zenima**, about six km south of the turn-off to Wadi el-Homur and the old turquoise mines of Sarabit el-Khadim, is little more than a way-station for passing buses. There's a manganese processing plant here where local manganese is upgraded with stuff from South Africa. Most buses stop at a rest house on the highway

SINAI

where you can get shish kebabs and drinks. The only other diner en route to El-Tor is the new Manta rest house at the turn-off to St Catherine's Monastery; petrol is sold there too.

El-Tor, also known as **Tur Sinai**, is the administrative capital of the South Sinai Governorate. It's something of a boom town, with a broad, clean central avenue bordered by new apartment buildings. If you do decide to stay here, there are a couple of hotels in town, such as the *Tur Sinai Hotel* (☎ 770059) at the bus station or the *Lido Hotel* (☎ 771780) down on the waterfront, as well as some impressive coral and sea life to observe close to shore. There are also several banks, and this is the nearest place for visa extensions to the resorts of Sharm el-Sheikh and beyond – go to the town's Mogamma, the main administrative building on the main road in the centre of town.

RAS MOHAMMED NATIONAL PARK

Ras Mohammed is Egypt's first national park. It occupies Sinai's most southern point and was declared a National Marine Park in 1988, though its boundaries were pushed up close to the town of Sharm el-Sheikh the following year. The actual headland of Ras Mohammed is about 30 km short of Sharm el-Sheikh, on the road from El-Tor.

At the time of its declaration, the park was the subject of much controversy, but it appears the project is meeting with some success. Hotels cannot develop the area, and only 12 per cent of the park is accessible to visitors. In addition, a ceiling has been applied to the number of boats allowed into the area with divers. However, despite these limitations, Ras Mohammed is the catch cry of nearly every tourist operator in Sharm el-Sheikh and nearby Na'ama Bay, and the park is inundated with visitors each year.

There are two entries to the park – one to the north-west and the other in the north-east corner closer to Sharm el-Sheikh. The park's salmon-toned, fish-shaped visitors' centre and restaurant are also in the north-east in an area known as Marsa Ghoslane. Videos are shown here, and you may be able to pick up an interesting booklet highlighting the park's fauna. Camping permits (E£5 per person per night) are also available from the centre but camping is allowed only in designated areas. Vehicles are permitted to enter (US$5 per person), but access is restricted to certain parts of the park and, for conservation reasons, it's forbidden to leave the official tracks.

If you are going to camp, respect the environment you're in and clean up after yourselves. Don't enter areas you know to be off limits. To get around you really need your own vehicle, or you can join one of the many day tours by jeep or bus from Sharm el-Sheikh and Na'ama Bay. Divers are often brought in by boat instead.

Take your passport with you to Ras Mohammed. Visitors to Sinai who are on Sinai-only permits supposedly cannot go to Ras Mohammed, which is beyond the Sharm el-Sheikh boundary of the permit, but should not have any problem on boat dive trips. Check with the dive clubs if you have any doubts. See the Snorkelling and Diving sections in Sharm el-Sheikh & Na'ama Bay for details on these activities within Ras Mohammed itself.

SHARM EL-SHEIKH & NA'AMA BAY

The southern coast of the Gulf of Aqaba, between Tiran Island in the straits and Ras Mohammed at the tip of Sinai, features some of the world's most brilliant and amazing underwater scenery. The crystal-clear water, the rare and lovely reefs and the incredible variety of exotic fish darting in and out of the colourful coral have made this a snorkelling and scuba-diving paradise, attracting a growing number of divers from all over the globe.

If you've never explored the living treasures of the deep, this is the place to do it. The reefs are easily accessible and you'll find all the necessary diving equipment, as well as accommodation, restaurants, bars and public services, around Na'ama Bay and in nearby Sharm el-Sheikh – which is commonly known as Sharm.

Na'ama Bay is a resort that has grown

Bedouin woman at a street market in Al-Arish, wearing the traditional black dress and head cover. Married women wear a red veil, as pictured, while single women wear blue. Veils are often decorated with coins or shells and cross-stitch embroidery.

GEERT COLE

GEOFF STRINGER

KRISTIE BURNS

LEANNE LOGAN

Top Left: Bedouin camp, Sinai.
Top Right: Greek Orthodox chapel at the summit of Mt Sinai.
Bottom Left: Bedouin women trade silver, textiles and jewellery at the souq in Al-Arish.
Bottom Right: Typical camp-style accommodation in Dahab on the Gulf of Aqaba.

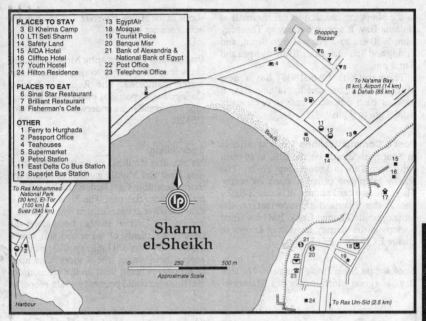

PLACES TO STAY
3 El Kheima Camp
10 LTI Seti Sharm
14 Safety Land
15 AIDA Hotel
16 Clifftop Hotel
17 Youth Hostel
24 Hilton Residence

PLACES TO EAT
6 Sinai Star Restaurant
7 Brilliant Restaurant
8 Fisherman's Cafe

OTHER
1 Ferry to Hurghada
2 Passport Office
4 Teahouses
5 Supermarket
9 Petrol Station
11 East Delta Co Bus Station
12 Superjet Bus Station

13 EgyptAir
18 Mosque
19 Tourist Police
20 Banque Misr
21 Bank of Alexandria & National Bank of Egypt
22 Post Office
23 Telephone Office

Shopping Bazaar

To Na'ama Bay (6 km), Airport (14 km) & Dahab (85 km)

To Ras Mohammed National Park (30 km), El-Tor (100 km) & Suez (340 km)

Sharm el-Sheikh

0   250   500 m
Approximate Scale

Beach

Harbour

To Ras Um-Sid (2.5 km)

SINAI

from virtually nothing since the early 1980s, while Sharm el-Sheikh, initially developed by the Israelis during their occupation of the peninsula, is a long-standing settlement. Both are heading in the direction of Hurghada – becoming an unending building site, spreading the blight of hotels up and down a once untouched coastline. Despite all this construction, there's not much on hand for budget travellers – the cheapest place is the Youth Hostel in Sharm el-Sheikh, at E£14 per person. There are more accommodation possibilities in Na'ama Bay, as well as the bulk of the dive clubs.

Sharm el-Sheikh is six km short of Na'ama Bay and is where the coast road south from Suez and Cairo turns the corner to run north up to the Israeli border.

Information
Registration If you intend to travel beyond Sinai coast between Taba and Sharm el-Sheikh while in Egypt, you'll need to register

with the police within seven days (you also need to have entered with a visa). You can do this at the passport office in Sharm el-Sheikh. It's to the left of the harbour entrance and is open daily except Friday from 9.30 am to 2 pm. The process takes a couple of minutes. Hotels will also do it for you, but charge up to E£5.

Visa extensions are available only at the office in El-Tor.

Tourist Police There is no tourist office. The tourist police office is up on the hill in Sharm el-Sheikh. They also have a booth next to the Marina Sharm Hotel in Na'ama Bay.

Money Banque Misr, the Bank of Alexandria and the National Bank of Egypt all have branches in Sharm el-Sheikh (on the hill) and in Na'ama Bay. Banque Misr handles MasterCard and the Bank of Alexandria handles Visa. American Express operates through the Egyptian American Bank (EAB) in the shopping bazaar just off the mall at Na'ama Bay. It's open Sunday to Thursday from 8.30 am to 2 pm and 6 to 9 pm, and Friday and Saturday from 10 am to 1 pm and 6 to 9 pm.

Thomas Cook (☎ 601808) has a new office on the main road in Na'ama Bay. It handles cash advances and is open daily from 9 am to 9 pm.

Post & Communications The post office is in Sharm el-Sheikh on the hill. It is open daily from 8 am to 3 pm, except Friday. The nearby telephone office is open 24 hours. There are two card phones in Na'ama Bay – one at the Shamandura supermarket, the other opposite Thomas Cook. But be warned – shops in the vicinity have been known to charge E£30 for a E£15 card.

Bookshops Sinai Book Centre in Na'ama Bay has a good selection of books. The book-

shops in the Hilton Fayrouz and Mövenpick hotels are not bad too.

Underwater Photography Most of the dive clubs rent out cameras to snap some underwater memories. The Red Sea Diving College has a specialist underwater photography shop and rents underwater cameras for US$20.

Snorkelling
Na'ama Bay itself has no reefs, but the stunning Near and Middle gardens and the even more incredible Far Garden can be reached by foot from the bay. The Near Garden is near the point at the northern end of the bay, and the Far Garden another hour along the coast. Take plenty of water and sun screen with you. How much longer you'll be able to access these places free is moot, as a huge new resort is being built on the promontory and this area could become private property.

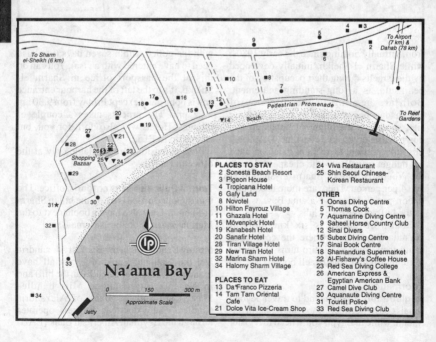

PLACES TO STAY
2 Sonesta Beach Resort
3 Pigeon House
4 Tropicana Hotel
6 Gafy Land
8 Novotel
10 Hilton Fayrouz Village
11 Ghazala Hotel
16 Mövenpick Hotel
19 Kanabesh Hotel
20 Sanafir Hotel
28 Tiran Village Hotel
29 New Tiran Hotel
32 Marina Sharm Hotel
34 Halomy Sharm Village

PLACES TO EAT
13 Da'Franco Pizzeria
14 Tam Tam Oriental Cafe
21 Dolce Vita Ice-Cream Shop

24 Viva Restaurant
25 Shin Seoul Chinese-Korean Restaurant

OTHER
1 Oonas Diving Centre
5 Thomas Cook
7 Aquamarine Diving Centre
9 Saheel Horse Country Club
12 Sinai Divers
15 Subex Diving Centre
17 Sinai Book Centre
18 Shamandura Supermarket
22 Al-Fishawy's Coffee House
23 Red Sea Diving College
26 American Express & Egyptian American Bank
27 Camel Dive Club
30 Aquanaute Diving Centre
31 Tourist Police
33 Red Sea Diving Club

Na'ama Bay

Another excellent spot for snorkelling is Ras um Sid near the lighthouse at Sharm el-Sheikh. A new resort has taken over part of the beach, where you can rent umbrellas and deck chairs for E£5 per day, but the area near the lighthouse is open to the public. For more details on this and other possible snorkelling spots see the following section on Dive Sites.

It's possible to get to some of the more distant sites by joining a dive boat – inquire at some of the dive clubs in town. You'll be looking at anywhere between US$20 to US$45 for a day trip. Many of the clubs also do snorkelling trips to Ras Mohammed for about US$50, however, the deep drop-offs there are not ideal for snorkelling, and the cross currents (formed by the collision of the two gulfs) can be strong.

Most of the dive clubs rent masks, snorkels and flippers, usually for around E£6-10 per set for a full day.

Diving
The trips to the Straits of Tiran, Ras Mohammed or the wrecks to the west are usually a little more expensive than dives at closer sites. Discounts are available on five day and 10 day packages and can bring the daily diving cost down. To get an idea of prices for dive courses see Diving in the Activities section of the Facts for the Visitor chapter.

The following goes for diving anywhere, but particularly for Ras Mohammed: ecologists fear the number of divers visiting this area will bring permanent damage to the coral and marine life. Try to enjoy it without touching or taking away anything and don't feed the fish.

Dive Sites The following is a list of some of the dive sites from around Tiran Island (north of Na'ama Bay) stretching down past Sharm el-Sheikh and Ras Mohammed to the wreck of the *Thistlegorm* in the Gulf of Suez.

Small & Large Lagoons – Off the north-west tip of Tiran Island, featuring a shallow reef and the wreck of the *Sangria*. The currents are strong here, and there is a mooring so that boats don't

have to drop anchor onto the reef. The Large Lagoon, just below it, has reef and sand fish.

Jackson Reef – Midway between Tiran Island and the mainland, home to sharks and large pelagic fish. There is a 70m drop-off, but be warned, this is not for beginners – the currents are dangerous.

Gordon Reef – Close to Ras Nasrany and a popular site with experienced divers. There are sharks and open-water fish here and a wreck on the reef. Thomas and Woodhouse reefs also have some good diving.

Ras Nasrany – There are two sites worth noting here, The Light and The Point. There are 40m drop-offs and heaps of reef and pelagic fish.

Shark Bay – For details on this site see the Shark Bay section, later in this chapter.

The Tower – South of Na'ama Bay, this is a remarkable wall dropping 60m into the depths just off shore.

Amphoras – Also known as the Mercury site. A Turkish galleon lies at the bottom of the sea here. Evidence of its cargo of mercury can be seen in among the coral. Other dives between here and Ras Um Sid include Turtle Bay, Paradise and Fiasco.

Ras Um Sid – A prime diving site to a deep, sloping wall, easily accessible near the lighthouse, a 30 minute walk from Sharm el-Sheikh. The beautiful coral garden has lots of colourful fan coral and a great variety of fish. Divers generally use the access path to the left of the lighthouse; snorkellers can follow the path to the right of the lighthouse which leads to a large beach.

Temple – Three large pinnacles rising to the surface from a depth of about 20m, just around the point.

Ras Mohammed – Without doubt, one of the best diving sites in the world. In an attempt to protect the National Marine Park, the number of boats that can bring in divers is subject to limits. You'll have to organise dives here through the dive clubs. There are 20 dive sites within the park, including Shark Observatory, Sting Ray Alley and Eel Garden – descriptive names! There's a shipwreck (at 10 to 15m) which scattered hundreds of toilet bowls on the bottom, and off to the south-west is the wreck of the *Dunraven*, a British vessel which went down (and turned over) in 1876 on a voyage from Bombay to Newcastle in England. Many dive clubs combine diving this wreck with that of the *Thistlegorm*.

Thistlegorm – Sinai's most prized wreck. It was a British war ship which sunk with a full consignment of war supplies – including tanks, jeeps and guns – after being bombed during WWII. Rediscovered in 1993, lying at a depth of 17 to 35m to the north-west of Ras Mohammed, it is currently *the* wreck to explore in the Red Sea (though it has already been stripped of much of its wartime memorabilia). It's best dived on an overnight trip,

SINAI

as it takes 3½ hours each way from Sharm el-Sheikh by boat. It is often too rough to dive here.

Carnatic – This boat went down in 1879 and, with its rotting wooden beams, it's now almost a reef in itself. It's a popular site among divers, along with the nearby wrecks of two Greek cargo ships, the *Giannus D* and the *Chrisoula K*, which both sunk in the early 1980s. The three are about 45 minutes by boat from the point of Ras Mohammed.

Dive Clubs There are more than two dozen dive centres around here, most of them in Na'ama Bay. All offer trips and equipment, but it pays to shop around, especially in the low season when some of the clubs offer cut-price deals. Another low-season advantage (the blistering summer months) is the chance of getting closer attention – it is not unknown for instructors to take classes of one!

For a few tips in choosing a good club, see Diving in the Activities section in the Facts for the Visitor chapter. Also, make sure you know where they are going to take you. There's little point in saving a few dollars if you're going to less interesting sites than those offered by competitors.

Some of the better clubs in Na'ama Bay include:

Aquamarine Diving Centre (☎ 600276; fax 600176) Based at the Novotel. It is a popular, reputable club offering a wide variety of diving possibilities and runs courses through the Red Sea Diving College.

Aquanaute (☎ 600187; fax 600619) This Belgian outfit has a good reputation. It is located in what used to be the White House Restaurant (where the Egyptian leader Anwar Sadat and his Israeli opposite number, Menachem Begin, met while the Israeli air force bombed an Iraqi nuclear power plant – an embarrassment to Sadat).

Camel Dive Club (☎ 600700; fax 600601) Next door to the Tiran Village Hotel.

Oonas Diving Centre (☎ 600581) At the northern end of the bay. This is a popular cheery centre and, for those following a course, it offers relatively cheap accommodation – air-con rooms cost US$32/56 including breakfast.

Red Sea Diving Club (☎ 600342) Near the jetty. It is run by the brothers Drs Wael and Hussam Nasef. It sometimes has quite cheap deals.

Red Sea Diving College (☎ 600313; fax 600312) Operates in conjunction with Scuba Pro International, which provides one of the world's best diving curricula. It runs courses only and also has reasonably cheap accommodation for course-members – B&B in an air-con dorm (eight beds) for U\$10 per night.

Sinai Divers (☎ 600150) Located in the Ghazala Hotel. It offers 20% discounts to members of the Cairo Divers Group.

Subex (☎ 600100) Swiss-based dive club at the Mövenpick Hotel with years of experience in the Red Sea.

Diving Emergency Centre A modern decompression chamber, built largely with US-government aid money, went into operation in 1993 a little way past the ferry harbour in Sharm el-Sheikh on the road to El-Tor. It's part of the Hyperbaric Medical Centre (☎ 600922) run by Dr Adel Taher, and has a capacity of six people.

Other Water Sports

Most of the big hotels also offer above-water sports, including sailing lessons (E£35 per hour), windsurfing (E£40 per hour), parasailing (E£120 per hour), pedalos (E£20 per hour), glass-bottom boats (E£30 per hour), banana boats (E£25 for 15 minutes) and the like.

The use of a hotel swimming pool costs about E£30 per person, per day. All of the beach space at Na'ama Bay has been taken up by hotels – the last stretch of public beach disappeared with the opening of the new Marriott Hotel. Not all the hotels take much notice of nonguests using their beach, but many do, so if you're unable to blend in with the crowd you'll have to pay. It's illegal to swim off Na'ama Bay after 11 pm.

Camel Rides

Camel rides to 'traditional Bedouin villages' for 'traditional Bedouin meals' are staged for about US$35 to US$40. If you want to experience the desert from the back of a camel and in the company of the Bedouins, it's better negotiating treks with the Bedouins direct at one of the tourist spots further north, such as Dahab.

Horse Riding

There are a couple of 'farms' around where

you can hire a horse. At the Saheel Horse Country Club (☎ 600197/8), across the road from the Hilton Fayrouz Village in Na'ama Bay, a morning or sunset ride for one/two/three hours costs US$25/35/45. A full-day 'trek' costs US$75, and an overnight trip costs US$125. Lessons cost US$10 an hour – all pretty pricey stuff.

Organised Tours

Most bigger hotels and agencies like Top Team (☎ 600961), in the shopping bazaar at Na'ama Bay, are organising a growing range of things to do out of the water. Jeep or bus trips to St Catherine's Monastery, or such desert sights as the Coloured Canyon (see the Nuweiba section, later in this chapter) are available for about US$45 to US$50.

For those only visiting Sinai, quick excursions are also organised to Cairo.

Places to Stay – bottom end

Sharm el-Sheikh The cheapest place to stay in an area geared to tourists with comparatively fat wallets is the *Youth Hostel* (☎ 600317), which is up on the hill. A bed in a fairly standard eight bed dorm costs E£14 (E£16 for nonmembers) with breakfast. It's open from 7 to 9 am and 2 to 11 pm, and they don't seem overly fussed about membership cards. It's a good place to stay if you want to spend your days snorkelling off the beach at Ras Um Sid (see Dive Sites, earlier in this chapter, for details). Lunch (E£8) and dinner (E£14) are available.

Safety Land (☎ 600359; fax 600458), almost opposite the bus station, has beds in a big military tent for E£22, or there are hot cement bungalows with fans at E£39/60 for singles/doubles. Both these options have communal showers. A few single/double/triple rooms with air-con and private bathroom cost E£81/100/144, or E£49/75/98 without bathroom. Prices include a standard breakfast. They have a bit of beach to themselves, although there's no snorkelling to speak of.

The *El Kheima Camp* (☎ 600167; fax 600166), the first place you pass on your way from the port, has bamboo-style bungalows

at E£35/55 and rooms for E£65/90/110, including breakfast. It's not bad, but a little inconveniently located.

Na'ama Bay The *Pigeon House* (☎ 600996; fax 600965), on the northern edge of town, has 37 basic huts (or bungalows, depending on what you want to call these bamboo structures) with fans for E£38/56. Quite small rooms are not such hot value, although clean and comfortable, at E£65/85/105. Prices include breakfast and the communal facilities are clean. This place is often fully booked. There's also a bar selling Stella for E£7.50.

The *Red Sea Diving College* offers cheap accommodation but only for people taking diving courses with the college.

Places to Stay – middle

Sharm el-Sheikh The *Clifftop Hotel* (☎ 600251), part of the Helnan group of hotels, has pleasant singles/doubles/ triples with TV, air-con, fridge, phone and bathroom for US$43/56/67 including breakfast.

Na'ama Bay The best place in this range is the *Sanafir* (☎ 600197; fax 600196). It has two classes of rooms and three seasonal rates. You'll be looking at US$45/56/63 for a 'superior' air-con single/double/triple room in the low season, and US$64/82/93 in the high season. 'Standard' rooms (which have private toilet but communal showers) are roughly US$15 less. The prices include breakfast but not tax. It's the Moorish-style brainchild of the dashing Adly al-Mestekawi, who is a combination of Indiana Jones and Omar Sharif. Once in a while, he rides his horse through the arched hotel entrance and into the central courtyard cafe, bar and restaurant area. Rooms have white-washed walls, domed ceilings, and beds raised two or three steps above the floor. The shared showers for the cheaper rooms are very clean. Guests receive a free pass to use the beach at Aquanaute dive club.

The *Tropicana Hotel* (☎ 600649; 600644) is a new place on the western side of the highway. It can only be described as a cheap imitation of Sanafir (though the rooms are more expensive!). Rooms with air-con, TV, phone and breakfast cost US$51/65/78. The hotel does not have access to a beach but there is a small pool from where you get good views of the mountains.

Virtually across the road, and with its own patch of beach, is *Gafy Land* (☎ 600211; fax 600210) which offers modern rooms with low ceilings, TV, air-con, phone, minibar and a big bath for US$55/72 plus taxes.

Places to Stay – top end

There's an enormous new resort under construction on Na'ama Bay's northern promontory, and a new five star hotel, *Coral Bay*, has opened two km north of Na'ama Bay, just before Shark Bay. In Na'ama Bay itself, the new *Marriott Hotel* opened on the bay's last patch of beach-front land in 1996. Several new Egyptian-owned resorts started up in 1994/95 – such as the *Cataract*, *Kahramana* and the *Falcon Aldair* – but none of them offer anything remarkable. Unless stated otherwise, prices for the following places do not include taxes or breakfast.

Sharm el-Sheikh Some of the top-end options include:

AIDA Hotel (☎ 600719; fax 600722), which is a new place with a commanding position on the hill. Double-storey rooms, all with air-con and satellite TV, are built around a large swimming pool. One of the unique facilities of this place is the 10 lane bowling alley. Prices start at US$120 for a double.

Hilton Residence (☎ 600266; fax 600269) on the clifftop which has even better views over the Red Sea and doubles for US$147.

LTI Seti Sharm (☎ 600870; fax 600147), a relatively new waterfront hotel with 230 air-conditioned rooms of a fairly nondescript nature. The rooms are reasonably priced at US$90/135 including half-board.

Na'ama Bay There are a number of top-end options in Na'ama Bay:

Ghazala Hotel (☎ 600150; fax 600155) is a medium-size complex offering rooms and cool bungalows with carpeting and polished wood-slat walls. Singles/doubles/triples cost US$90/126/135, including breakfast and all taxes.

Halomy Sharm Village (☎ 600681; fax 600134) on the headland offers sweeping views of the Red Sea and 'chalets' in various categories. The cheapest are US$90/115.

Hilton Fayrouz Village (☎ 600136; fax 601040) in the heart of Na'ama Bay is a sprawling 'village' of deluxe air-conditioned bungalows. It has almost everything you'd expect of a Hilton hotel, including high prices – singles/doubles are US$144/172. Larger suites are even more expensive.

Kanabesh Hotel (☎ 600184; fax 600185) has relatively modest rooms for US$91/115. For an extra US$12 per person, you can get half board.

Marina Sharm Hotel (☎ 600170; fax 600171) dominates the southern end of Na'ama Bay and was the Israeli hotel which pioneered Na'ama Bay as a resort. Rooms cost US$99/130.

M"venpick Hotel (☎ 600100/5; fax 600111) is the biggest and perhaps most awful addition to the Na'ama Bay waterfront. This five star place has three zones – the Villa Area (facing the promenade), the Front Area (between the Villa Area and the road) and the so-called Sports Area (spilling into the desert across the highway). Singles/doubles/triples in the 'cheap' sports area start at US$126/163/193 (summer) and US$147/187/221 (winter), including taxes and buffet breakfast. Rooms in the other sections are more expensive still.

New Tiran Hotel (☎ 600225; fax 600220) is one of the cheaper top-enders. The hotel's angular, rabbit-warren design is unattractive, but the rooms are fine for US$73/96 including breakfast.

Novotel (☎ 600178; fax 600177), still known by its old name of Hotel Aquamarine, has singles/doubles/triples for US$120/162/190.

Sonesta Beach Resort (☎ 600725; fax 600733) is one of the newer five star places, boasting five restaurants, four bars and three pools (one heated). Rooms start from US$143/175/195.

Tiran Village (☎ 600221; fax 600220), a block back from the promenade, is a three star hotel offering rooms on a half-board basis for US$66/93/120.

Places to Eat

Sharm el-Sheikh There are a couple of small restaurants/cafes in the shopping bazaar behind the bus station. The *Sinai Star* serves some excellent fish meals for about E£12 a person.

The nearby *Brilliant Restaurant* offers a range of traditional Egyptian food at reasonable prices. A plate of kofta with salad should cost about E£12. They also have sweets. The

Fisherman's Cafe serves chicken or fish with generous portions of rice, salad, tahina and bread for E£11. Beers are a pricey E£9.

The *Aftet el-Mesk* and *El Ghazal*, also in this area, are popular teahouses.

If you're into dining under the stars while the waves wash gently up onto the beach, head to *Safety Land*. There's no formal restaurant here, but meals (fish or calamari for E£24) and snacks (omelettes and salad) can be arranged, and you can dine within metres of the water. Beers are a very reasonable E£6.

Self-caterers will find a well-stocked supermarket in the bazaar, as well as a wholesale beer shop – talking the manager into selling a bottle or two (rather than the customary crate) is not too difficult.

If you're down at Ras Um Sid beach you might like to pop into the *Dar um el Sid* restaurant at the base of the lighthouse. It's an open-air Bedouin-style restaurant with sunken alcoves and inflated prices, but the view of the sea is marvellous and you can get a cold Stella (E£10).

Na'ama Bay There are a lot of places to eat here, but don't expect to dine cheaply (by the standards of the rest of the country anyway). The *Tam Tam Oriental Cafe* is one of the cheapest restaurants in Na'ama Bay and is deservedly popular. Jutting out onto the beach, it's a laid-back place where you can delve into a range of Egyptian fare including mezzes for E£1.75 (cold) or E£2.75 (hot) a bowl, fuul or felafel for E£3.75, sambousek (pastry stuffed with meat), kushari E£5 and roast pigeon E£13. Finish up with an om ali for E£4.50, or wash it all down with a Stella (E£7.50). Even shishas are on the menu – E£1.50 for normal or E£2 for apple-flavoured tobacco.

Viva on the promenade is popular with divers and instructors. The food is reasonable.

There are a couple of Chinese-Korean restaurants – the *Shin Seoul* in the mall and another in the Sanafir Hotel.

The hotels have a wide range of restaurants, offering everything from seafood to Thai dishes. None of these places suits a budget traveller's pocket, but what does around here? *Da Franco Pizzeria* on the promenade in front of the Ghazala Hotel has pizzas starting from E£15 and is very popular.

Dolce Vita, at the end of the mall, has great ice cream, but at E£2.50 a scoop, it's an expensive treat.

If it's just a cup of tea or coffee you're after, *Al-Fishawy's* in the mall is a poor imitation of its Cairo namesake.

Entertainment
There are bars and dance establishments in many of the hotels, including the *Cactus Disco* in the Mövenpick complex, another disco in the *Hilton Fayrouz Village* and the *New Bar* in the Kanabesh Hotel. The popular rooftop bar at the *Sanafir Hotel* has a minimum charge of E£10 (beers here cost E£6). The Tropicana Hotel's *Hot Shot Pub* rolls on until 3am.

The Mövenpick's Casino Royale is the only place in town where visitors (no Egyptians allowed) can gamble away their foreign bucks (no Egyptian pounds thank you).

Getting There & Away
Air EgyptAir has a new office in Sharm el-Sheikh at the start of the road to Na'ama Bay. It flies daily to Cairo (E£412) and twice a week to Hurghada (E£286) and Luxor (E£412).

Air Sinai flies from Cairo to Sharm el-Sheikh twice a week in the winter only. The one way/return fare is E£445/890, and these flights proceed to Tel Aviv.

Charter flights from various European cities run virtually all year round.

Bus & Minibus The bus station is in Sharm el-Sheikh; buses heading on to Dahab and beyond occasionally stop on the highway in Na'ama Bay but don't count on it. Likewise, if you're catching a bus in the direction of Suez or Cairo, it's advisable to go to the bus station in Sharm el-Sheikh, as assurances about the buses stopping at Na'ama Bay 'about an hour before leaving Sharm el-

Sheikh' seem vague at best. Seats to Cairo can and should be booked ahead.

Minibuses also cover the route between Sharm el-Sheikh and Suez and Cairo, as well as north to Dahab, but they're not all that common or frequent – ask around at the bus station.

For details on buses from Cairo, see the Getting There & Away section in the Cairo chapter.

From Sharm el-Sheikh, the cheapest East Delta Co direct services to Cairo (seven hours) run at 7, 8, 10 am and 1 pm and cost E£26. The 4 pm bus is E£30; the 11.30 pm is E£40 and the one at midnight E£50.

Superjet has a bus to Cairo (E£50) leaving at 11 pm from its terminus next to East Delta Co; the service from Cairo to Sharm el-Sheikh departs at the same time. There's also a bus to Alexandria (E£71).

It is cheaper to get a bus to Suez and then another bus or service taxi from there to Cairo (the same is also true in reverse). Buses to Suez (E£20, 5½ hours) depart at 7.30, 9 and 10.30 am.

Six buses go to Dahab (1½ hours). The 7.30 am, and 10.30 and 11.30 pm buses cost E£8; the 9 am and 3 and 5 pm services cost E£7. The same 9 am and 5 pm buses go on to Nuweiba (E£10); the 9 am bus then continues all the way to Taba (E£15). The 7.30 am bus goes on to St Catherine's Monastery (E£15).

Boat Barring breakdowns and other problems, there is a ferry between Sharm el-Sheikh and Hurghada on Monday, Wednesday and Saturday, leaving the harbour at 9 or 10 am. However, as of 1996, there may be a new boat which will increase the service to six days a week. Tickets can be booked through most hotels or at Thomas Cook in Na'ama Bay. For details on the voyage see the Hurghada Getting There & Away section.

Getting Around
The Airport The airport is about eight km north of Na'ama Bay at Ras Nasrany. A taxi will cost about E£15 from Na'ama Bay.

Bus An open-sided public bus, known as a *tof-tof*, runs every 40 minutes or so until about 11 pm between Sharm el-Sheikh and Na'ama Bay. It costs 50 pt for locals and E£1 for tourists. You can also get Toyota pick-ups for the same price, although they are less rigid about extracting the tourist rate. Other than that, it is quite possible to hitch, as there is a fair amount of traffic on the roads. The usual warnings about hitching apply.

A private bus runs between the two Hilton hotels too.

Passengers arriving by ferry from Hurghada are also met by a tof-tof but the ride into Sharm el-Sheikh is a real rip-off at E£2.

Car Many of the big name car rental companies have offices in Na'ama Bay, usually in one of the bigger hotels. Avis (☎ 600979) is in the Sonesta Beach Resort, Hertz (☎ 600459) at the Mövenpick Hotel and Europcar (☎ 600686) in the Hilton Fayrouz Village. The Sanafir Hotel rents 4WD jeeps for US$80 a day while Fox Safari (☎ 601074 ext 510), also in Na'ama Bay, has them for US$120 including a driver.

Bicycle Normal and cross-country bicycles are for hire from stands along the promenade in Na'ama Bay for E£5 a day.

Boat Many dive clubs operating out of Na'ama Bay actually anchor their boats overnight at Sharm el-Sheikh and bring them back to Na'ama Bay again early each morning. It's possible to hitch a ride either way on one of these vessels – ask around at the harbour in Sharm el-Sheikh at about 6.30 am or, going in the reverse direction, in Na'ama Bay from around 4 pm.

SHARK BAY
Also known as Shark's Bay or Beit al-Irsh, this low-key resort camp is about five km north of Na'ama Bay (about 2 km down a track off the main road). Located on a pebbly beach from where you can walk in to some quite good snorkelling, it is particularly popular with Germans and Israelis, most of

whom dive a nearby 15 to 20m-deep canyon with the Embarak dive club there. Unfortunately, the solitary bliss of this place has been spoilt a bit thanks to the new Coral Bay Hotel being built right on the doorstep.

The only way in and out is to hitch or bargain with taxi drivers. Trying to get there in the dead of night may well entail walking the whole way.

Places to Stay & Eat
The two star *Shark's Bay Camp* (☎ 600941; fax 600943) has clean and comfortable huts for E£40/55. Or you can pitch a tent on the beach or just sleep in the open for E£15. Put off by this price, some people have managed to camp free, just south of the beach and camp area without any hassles. However, that may not be an option once the Coral Bay Hotel opens its doors. The camp has clean toilets and showers with hot water. Meals are available for E£21.

DAHAB
The village beach resort of Dahab is 85 km north of Sharm el-Sheikh on the Gulf of Aqaba. Dahab means 'gold' in Arabic, and the Bedouins named the beach after its glimmering sands, which resemble gold dust.

There are two parts to Dahab – in the new part, referred to by the locals rather euphemistically as 'Dahab City', are some of the more expensive hotels, bus station, post and phone offices and bank. The other part, called Assalah, was a Bedouin village, about 2½ km north of town. It now has more low-budget travellers and Egyptian entrepreneurs than Bedouins in residence and is made up of a higgledy-piggledy stretch of 'camps' and laid-back restaurants in among the palm trees, as well as a busy little bazaar.

Accommodation virtually on the beach can cost as little as E£6 a night. The camps are spreading around the coast and a couple have put second and third storeys on – a most unwelcome development. Small hotels offering air-con rooms have also sprung up in the last year or two.

Dahab, like other places further up the coast, gets very crowded on Israeli holidays.

It can also be very windy, making it cooler than Sharm el-Sheikh but also pretty cold in winter.

While many travellers love lazing around here for a few days (or a few weeks in some cases), Dahab is certainly not everyone's cup of tea. As Jodi Hayes and Jeremy Kull, two travellers from Canada, put it: 'We stepped out the cab to be bombarded by tie-dyes, bikini babes, Arnold Schwarzenegger lookalikes and the smell of pot everywhere...had we wanted to be in Daytona Beach we would have saved the US$1000 to fly to Egypt and driven to Florida.'

Orientation & Information
The tourist police office is near the Novotel's Holiday Village in Dahab City. It is possible to register your arrival in Egypt in Dahab.

Just next to the Dolphin camp is an excavation site of Islamic and Coptic ruins. Just what the small site was is still unclear, but it is an intriguing diversion to think of this small town thriving in centuries gone by.

Money There is a branch of the National Bank of Egypt at the Novotel Holiday Village (open from 9.30 am to 12.30 pm and 6.30 to 8.30 pm) and another near the bus station. A rather dubious looking Banque 'de' Caire has been set up at the entrance to Sabry Palace Camp in Assalah. It's open daily from 9 am to 2 pm and 5 to 10 pm.

Post & Communications The post and telephone offices are opposite the bus station in Dahab City. The latter is open 24 hours every day and has a card phone. There are also two card phones in Assalah – one at the Oxford supermarket and the other at the papyrus shop in the heart of the bazaar; both sell phone cards. To save going to the post office, you can also drop letters into the airmail postal box (supposedly emptied every day at 10 am) outside the Ghazala supermarket in Assalah but you'll need to have brought stamps with you.

Warning
Tap water in Dahab is not drinkable (plenty

SINAI

SINAI

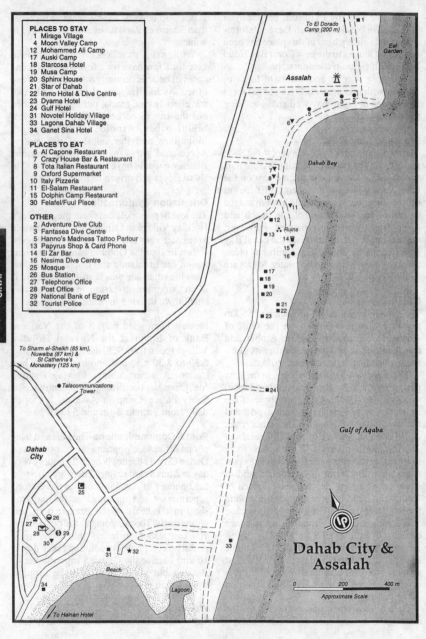

PLACES TO STAY
1. Mirage Village
4. Moon Valley Camp
12. Mohammed Ali Camp
17. Auski Camp
18. Starcosa Hotel
19. Musa Camp
20. Sphinx House
21. Star of Dahab
22. Inmo Hotel & Dive Centre
23. Dyarna Hotel
24. Gulf Hotel
31. Novotel Holiday Village
33. Lagona Dahab Village
34. Ganet Sina Hotel

PLACES TO EAT
6. Al Capone Restaurant
7. Crazy House Bar & Restaurant
8. Tota Italian Restaurant
9. Oxford Supermarket
10. Italy Pizzeria
11. El-Salam Restaurant
15. Dolphin Camp Restaurant
30. Felafel/Fuul Place

OTHER
2. Adventure Dive Club
3. Fantasea Dive Centre
5. Hanno's Madness Tattoo Parlour
13. Papyrus Shop & Card Phone
14. El Zar Bar
16. Nesima Dive Centre
25. Mosque
26. Bus Station
27. Telephone Office
28. Post Office
29. National Bank of Egypt
32. Tourist Police

To El Dorado
Camp (200 m)

Eel
Garden

Assalah

Dahab Bay

To Sharm el-Sheikh (85 km),
Nuweiba (87 km) &
St Catherine's
Monastery (125 km)

Telecommunications
Tower

Dahab
City

Gulf of Aqaba

Ruins

Beach

Lagoon

To Helnan Hotel

Dahab City &
Assalah

0   200   400 m

Approximate Scale

of shops sell bottled water). Also, please respect local sensitivities and refrain from sunbathing topless.

Drugs Nothing anyone can say or write will stop people from buying and using marijuana in Dahab. It's freely available (about E£20 for a 'cup' – a small Arabic coffee cup full) and in wide use. It appears other drugs, including acid, are in limited circulation, brought in from Israel.

If you are going to indulge, at least try to be discreet. Although there is not a huge police presence, penalties for drug offences are high in Egypt, and people have been arrested here. Dealing and smuggling attract sentences of 25 years' jail or death by hanging. The first execution for such an offence took place in 1989. The rules apply equally to foreigners, and although simple possession of marijuana attracts lower penalties, there is nothing funny about Egyptian jails, even for a day.

Diving

After lounging around, diving is the most popular activity in Dahab. Dive boats do not go out from Dahab as the sea here is often too choppy. It's probably a good thing anyway, as there are no mooring facilities along this stretch of coast.

Dahab's various dive clubs all offer a full range of diving possibilities, however, you should choose your club carefully as some do not have good reputations for following safety standards. For an indication of prices, look under Diving in the Activities section of the Facts for the Visitor chapter.

Something unique to dive clubs in Dahab are camel/diving safaris. Most of the clubs offer these trips and they're a wonderful way to explore both above and below the sea. The safaris tend to range from one to three days – a typical day trip involves a couple of hours on camel-back plus two dives and lunch.

Diving sites Some of the best sites, from north to south, include:

Bells – A cliff dive only for the relatively experienced.

The Blue Hole – An 80m-deep pool in the reef, only a few metres out from shore. This infamous deep dive has claimed the lives of many divers in recent years due to nitrogen narcosis or improper use of equipment (which isn't difficult at such a depth). It can't be stressed enough that it is only for very experienced divers, and even they should be wary. There is nothing to see down there and, according to some dive club managers, it's way overrated.

The Bridge – This dip in the reef close to the Blue Hole attracts much more marine life than the hole itself, and is close enough to the surface to be viewed by snorkellers.

The Canyon – A popular shore dive but, to an inexperienced diver, it will seem somewhat harrowing at first. From the shore, you snorkel along the reef before diving, past a wall of coral, to the edge of the Canyon. It is dark, narrow and seems capable of swallowing you. Other sights in the vicinity include Canyon's Table, Abu Talha and Abu Helal.

Eel Garden – About 15 minutes walk north of the lighthouse area in Assalah, this is a popular snorkelling spot which is also good for learner divers. The maximum depth is 17m and there's a sandy bottom.

Oasis – A secluded spot excellent for a variety of marine life, eight km south of Dahab City. Nearby are the Three Pools.

The Islands – A collection of coral pinnacles about 18 km south of Dahab.

Dive Clubs The number of dive clubs in Dahab is on the increase. There are now seven centres, some of the better including:

Inmo (☎ 640370; fax 640372) Run by Mohammed & Ingrid El-Kabany. It was one of the first dive clubs to start operating in Dahab. It's situated between the Gulf Hotel and the southernmost camps along the beach, and follows strict safety procedures. They have an attractive domed complex, with hotel accommodation and restaurant, and offer the full range of diving services. Their three day camel/diving safari goes to virgin dive sites south of Dahab and costs US$115 a day.

Nesima Dive Centre (☎ 640320; fax 640321) A reputable club which should have its own accommodation by the end of 1996. It is next to the Dolphin camp in Assalah.

Fantasea Dive Centre (☎ & fax 640043) Owned by Chris Harding and Mohammed Rafaie, an Australian/Egyptian couple who recently set up on the northern end of Assalah. At the time of writing, the club was building accommodation for its divers. They do a one day camel/diving safari for E£80.

SINAI

Other Water Sports

Many snorkellers head for Eel Garden, just north of the village. You can hire snorkelling gear from places along the restaurant strip for about E£5 a day, as well as pedalos (E£20 an hour) and kayaks (E£10 an hour). There's a windsurfing school at the Novotel Holiday Village – the bay there is excellent for it.

Jet skis can be hired for E£50/60 for one/two people for 15 minutes. The drone from these noisy beasts is in flagrant opposition to the tranquillity of Dahab and, with any luck, they'll be banned here as they have been in Hurghada.

There's no 'beach' to speak of in Assalah itself, instead the rocky coastline leads straight out onto the reef. For the golden sands, after which Dahab was named, you must go down to the bay at the Novotel Holiday Village.

Camel Treks

Many of the local Bedouins organise camel trips to the interior of Sinai. In the morning, camel drivers and their camels congregate along the waterfront in the village. Register with the police before beginning the trek, and don't pay the camel driver until you return to the village. Prices for a one day trip start at E£50. As all drivers seem to have agreed among themselves on this price, bargaining will probably get you nowhere. The price includes food.

Jeep Treks

Jeep trips to the Coloured Canyon (see the Nuweiba section for details) and Ras Abu Gallum are among the treks organised from the Holiday Village. You can also negotiate similar trips in Assalah.

Hanno's Madness, a tattoo and body piercing parlour in the hub of Assalah, has diversified its offerings and also runs jeep excursions. Itineraries are pretty much custom-designed but, as an example of prices, you'll be looking at E£10 per person (with a minimum of four people) for a morning of snorkelling at the Blue Hole or E£30 to E£40 for an evening trip into the mountains with dinner at a Bedouin camp.

Horse Riding

It is also possible to hire horses. Ask around or look for the Moses Stables. From the Novotel Holiday Village you can ride around the lagoon on horseback for E£30.

Places to Stay – bottom end

Most, if not all, low-budget travellers head straight for the Bedouin village. There is a plethora of so-called camps, which are basically compounds with simple stone, cement or reed rooms (huts may be a better description) of two or three mattresses and communal bathroom facilities. The camps south of the Nesima dive club tend to be the best as they are sheltered from the wind, have more space and some even have attractive waterfront areas shaded by groves of palms.

Many of the camps have started to introduce proper rooms with private bathrooms. These are considerably more expensive than the huts, although prices are negotiable.

There are a few things to keep in mind when hunting for a good place. Remember that concrete huts with iron roofs are hotter than those made of reeds, but the latter may be less secure; ask for a padlock. Check that there's electricity and running water – some places have hot water – as well as decent mattresses, fly screens and fans. The following options are listed from north to south:

El Dorado Camp is about 20 minutes walk from the bazaar area, up towards the Eel Garden. It has nine reed huts for E£8 per person and three basic cement rooms with toilet and shower for E£20 per person. It's right on the waterfront but is very exposed (don't be surprised if it gets washed away in a king tide).

Mirage Village (☎ 640341), on the waterfront just north of the lighthouse area, is a new place owned and run by a young Bedouin. It's very friendly, clean and secure. There are two types of rooms – large rooms with mattresses on the ground where you can stay for E£10 per person, or proper single/double rooms for E£33/54 without shower; E£50/68 with. Triples/quads without shower cost E£61/68. All the rooms have fly screens, a fan and a cupboard. Meals and beers (expensive) are available.

The *Moon Valley Camp* in the thick of things along the restaurant strip has an enthusiastic new owner who asks E£10 per person in a hot box or in one of the new hexagonal reed huts; both have fans.

Mohammed Ali in the centre of Assalah is the largest and longest running of the camps. However, the staff are indifferent and the tap water in the larger rooms with private baths was positively poisonous when we visited.

Auski Camp, next to Starcosa Hotel, is run by the amiable Nasser, who charges E£5 per person in either a small or large room. The big rooms have private baths and are excellent value but they'll probably jump up in price once this camp is better established. There's hot water but unfortunately no beach.

Musa Camp has double rooms with shower, toilet and mosquito nets for E£30 as well as cheaper huts. The gravelly beach is shaded by a lush palm grove and is very inviting.

Star of Dahab, next to Inmo, has a bit of class and is appropriately named. They charge E£10 per person (negotiable) whether you stay in one of the small, apricot-toned rooms or in a beehive-shaped reed hut (which have candles only) near the water. The communal bathrooms are clean and there's hot water plus a small laundry. The restaurant here is OK though nothing to rave about. Those with a tent can camp on the gravelly waterfront area for E£5 per person, although there's room for two small tents only and there's no shade.

Places to Stay – middle

Heading south from Assalah, the new *Starcosa Hotel* (☎ & fax 640366) is a comfortable place to stay offering single/double rooms with fans, private bathroom and hot water for E£50/70, including breakfast.

The nearby *Sphinx House* (☎ 640032) charges E£40 for a room with fan, fly screens, breakfast and communal bath, or E£80 with private bath and E£120 with air-con. The rooms are big, there's a restaurant and billiard room and beers are available.

The *Gulf Hotel* (☎ 640147; fax 640460), south of Assalah, is an old and pretty bleak place with double rooms with fan ranging from E£28 to E£40, depending on size. Breakfast is included. There's no concession for single occupancy. The cheapest of these is camp style but with comfortable beds and fan. Beers are available.

Places to Stay – top end

At the lower end of this bracket is the *Ganet*

Sina (☎ 640440; fax 640441) on the bay in Dahab City. Popular with groups from Cairo, it has singles/doubles without breakfast for E£135/170 plus taxes. The small, chalet-style rooms are comfortable, but really overpriced and the grounds have sparse vegetation. All in all it's pretty unenticing.

The 42 room *Dyarna Hotel* (☎ 640120; fax 640122) is at the southern end of Assalah. Its name means 'home' in Arabic but, unfortunately, it's nothing special though the staff are very friendly. There's a pool, two restaurants and a disco. Rooms are E£90/110/150, or E£160 for a double with air-con. It's certainly better than the Ganet Sina.

The nearby *Inmo* (☎ 640370; fax 640372) caters mainly to people on diving packages from Europe, especially Germany, although they do take in stray travellers if there's room. They have two types of rooms and different rates for divers and nondivers. Singles/doubles/triples/quads with private bathrooms are E£118/155/187/216 for divers, or about E£15 more for nondivers. The smaller 'backpacker' rooms go for E£54/74 a single/double for divers, or E£59/81 for nondivers. The colourful rooms have fans, domed ceilings and attractive furnishings. There are a few mountain bikes for guests to use.

The spanking new *Lagona Dahab Village* (☎ 640352; fax 640351) is plump in the middle of nowhere on the beach between Dahab City and Assalah. The domed-shaped rooms cost E£101/149/185 for a single/double/triple, including breakfast and taxes, and are comfortable enough but the whole place has the air of a big, highly structured resort. There's a restaurant where alcohol is not served. The dive club here caters primarily to package holiday-makers.

Despite its prime location on a quiet bay, the old *Novotel Holiday Village* (☎ & fax 640301) is an unattractive place. Rooms in various categories range from US$45 to US$85 (singles) and US$65 to US$105 (doubles). They also have well-kept two bed bungalows for E£20 per person. Outsiders can use the beach for E£25. There is also a dive club.

SINAI

Places to Eat

There is a string of places to eat at along the waterfront in Assalah. They serve breakfast, lunch and dinner and most seem to have identical menus hanging up out the front – a meal will generally cost you between E£6 and E£15. It's best not to turn up with a raging hunger as service can be slow. Generally, people hang out in these places, occasionally summoning the strength of mind and soul to flop into the sparkling waters of the Gulf of Aqaba for a while and then emerge to collapse back into a state of idyllic inertia and order a tea or cola.

For those sick of the usual Egyptian fare, especially at breakfast, the sweet pancakes with fruit and ice cream will be a treat. The *El-Salam* seems particularly good for these.

Tota, a ship-shaped place in the heart of Assalah, has the best Italian kitchen on the strip. It serves excellent soup complete with garlic bread for E£4, large doughy pizzas (which are a bit light on toppings) for E£9, as well as a range of other dishes and morish chocolate cake (E£3.50).

Next door, the two storey *Italy Pizzeria* does arguably better pizzas. If you prefer a thin crust, this is your place.

Few people seem to stay at the *Dolphin Camp* but the food here is good, the servings generous and it's one of the few camps where you can drink a beer with your meal.

A few of the restaurants, including *Al Capone* and *Crazy House*, serve fish meals, displaying their catch out the front and selling by weight.

For something a bit more classy, though still reasonably priced, try the restaurant at the Nesima dive club.

If it's just a plain old ta'amiyya that you're craving, try the stall behind the Fantasea dive club or, in Dahab City, the small felafel/fuul place in the shopping centre next to the bank.

Entertainment

Alcohol was banned in the cafes and restaurants in Assalah for several years, however, it's slowly creeping back in and there are now a couple of places where you can get a drink.

If it's beer, wine or billiard tables you're after, try the *Crazy House*. The *El Zar Bar*, next to the Dolphin Camp, has cold Stellas at normal prices and generally loud rock music.

The *Shipwreck Bar* at Nesima dive club is very popular with divers and others; in summer you can drink on the rooftop terrace and they may have a happy hour from 8 to 9 pm.

Otherwise your only options are the *Black Prince* disco (E£5 entry) in the Gulf Hotel which, during the time of prohibition, was *the* night-hangout place, or the Dyarna Hotel's rustic *Savana Disco* which gets going from 9 pm and is free.

Getting There & Away

Bus The bus station is in Dahab City. The most regular connection is to Sharm el-Sheikh (E£8, 1½ hours), with six or seven buses running between the two, most of them on part of other longer runs. Departure times are posted at the bus station. There are buses to Nuweiba (E£6) at 10.30 am and 6.30 and 10.30 pm. The 10.30 am service goes on to Taba (E£10). The 9.30 am bus to St Catherine's (E£10) takes two to three hours. Buses to Cairo (nine hours) leave at 8 am (E£45), 11 am (E£42) and 9.30 pm (E£50). Buses for Suez (E£22, 6½ hours) depart at 8.15 am and 10 am.

Service Taxi As a rule, service taxis are much more expensive than buses – they know you're only using them because the bus doesn't suit and the hitching possibilities are limited. They have a captive market. Although a trip to, say, St Catherine's can cost as little as E£10 a person, it will often cost closer to E£20. A whole taxi (with a maximum of seven passengers) to Nuweiba or Sharm el-Sheikh costs about E£50 to E£60, to Taba it's about E£15 per person. Part of the reason for the high fares is that few locals do such trips, so pricing has not been regulated at a level that Egyptians would be able to afford.

Getting Around

Pick-ups usually meet incoming buses and will shuttle you to the Bedouin village for about E£1.

NUWEIBA

The beach and port town of Nuweiba is 87 km north of Dahab. During the Israeli occupation, it was also the site of a major *moshav* (farming settlement), which has now been converted into a residence for Egyptian government officials.

Nuweiba is certainly not the most attractive of Sinai beach resorts; the area has become something of a major port, with a continual flow of people and vehicle traffic on and off the ferry between Nuweiba and Aqaba. However, the mountain scenery is beautiful and the coral reefs, for which Nuweiba is renowned, are spectacular. On top of that, you may even be able to swim with a dolphin.

Orientation

Nuweiba is divided into three parts. To the south is the port with a large bus station, banks, a couple of fairly awful hotels and the new Hilton. Eight km further north is Nuweiba 'City', a small though spread-out settlement with a variety of accommodation options, one of the area's two dive centres, a bazaar with tourist shops and several cheap places to eat. North of here, a 15 minute walk along the beach is Tarabin. Draped along the northern end of Nuweiba's calm bay, this once tranquil beach-side oasis is rapidly turning into a party and pick-up place, especially during Israeli holidays. While it offers a wide beach, tepid waters and cheap beachfront accommodation, it is less popular among international travellers than Dahab and has a distinctly artificial air.

Information

The post office and the telephone office (open 24 hours) are near the hospital in Nuweiba City. There's another post office at the port, as well as branches of the National Bank of Egypt and Banque Misr (neither will handle Jordanian dinars), a Misr Travel

The Dolphin of Nuweiba

A couple of years ago, a young Bedouin man from Mizela, a tiny village about one km south of Nuweiba port, noticed a lone dolphin frequenting the bay over which his village looks. He started to befriend her, swimming out into the turquoise water and diving to her depths. After a while he gave her a name – Holeen – and took to calling her as he splashed the water's surface; Holeen responded by turning up and taking Abdel for a swim. In the months and years that have followed, the two have become 'an item'.

This incredible bonding between a human and a wild marine mammal has, of course, attracted plenty of onlookers and eager participants, and visitors are now swamping Abdel's village in the hope of swimming with Holeen. The village elders charge visitors E£6 to go for a swim and E£5 to rent a mask and snorkel. They are also attempting, with little success, to regulate the number of people swimming at any one time.

If you do take the plunge, remember to take off any jewellery or sharp items before entering the water and try to be content with viewing rather than chasing and grabbing at Holeen. One flick of her tail is enough to propel her away from unwanted suitors, but if the attention becomes too much this graceful creature of the deep is just as likely to go back from where she came. ■

office and an Egypt Free (duty free) shop. The tourist police are located near the Helnan Nuweiba Hotel in Nuweiba City, and a branch of the National Bank of Egypt is inside the Helnan. The latter is open Saturday to Thursday from 9.30 am to noon and 6.30 to 9 pm; Friday from 9 to 11 am.

Warning Topless sunbathing is gaining ground among visitors to Nuweiba, especially Israelis staying in Tarabin. You should think twice before taking part in what is little more than a strip show for the local men.

Coloured Canyon

The Coloured Canyon, that lies between St Catherine's and Nuweiba, derives its name from the layers of bright, multicoloured stones that resemble paintings on the

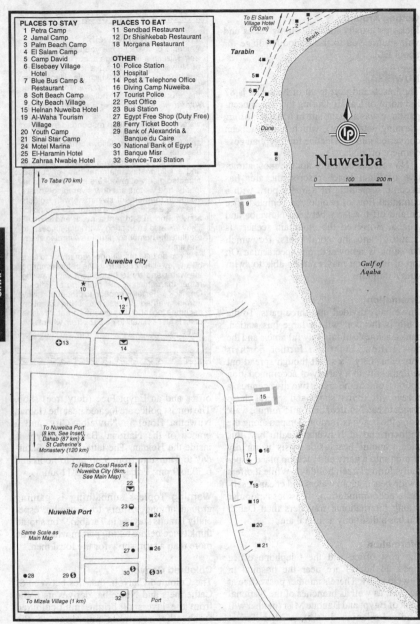

PLACES TO STAY
1 Petra Camp
2 Jamal Camp
3 Palm Beach Camp
4 El Salam Camp
5 Camp David
6 Elsebaey Village Hotel
7 Blue Bus Camp & Restaurant
8 Soft Beach Camp
9 City Beach Village
15 Helnan Nuweiba Hotel
19 Al-Waha Tourism Village
20 Youth Camp
21 Sinai Star Camp
24 Motel Marina
25 El-Haramin Hotel
26 Zahraa Nwabie Hotel

PLACES TO EAT
11 Sendbad Restaurant
12 Dr Shishkebab Restaurant
18 Morgana Restaurant

OTHER
10 Police Station
13 Hospital
14 Post & Telephone Office
16 Diving Camp Nuweiba
17 Tourist Police
22 Post Office
23 Bus Station
27 Egypt Free Shop (Duty Free)
28 Ferry Ticket Booth
29 Bank of Alexandria & Banque du Caire
30 National Bank of Egypt
31 Banque Misr
32 Service-Taxi Station

To El Salam Village Hotel (700 m)

Tarabin

Beach

Dune

Nuweiba

0   100   200 m

Gulf of Aqaba

To Taba (70 km)

Nuweiba City

SINAI

To Nuweiba Port
(8 km, See Inset),
Dahab (87 km) &
St Catherine's
Monastery (120 km)

Beach

To Hilton Coral Resort &
Nuweiba City (8km,
See Main Map)

Nuweiba Port

Same Scale as
Main Map

To Mizela Village (1 km)

Port

canyon's very steep, narrow walls. Total silence (the canyon is sheltered from the wind) adds to the eeriness. The canyon is sometimes known as the Blue Valley because a Swiss man painted the whole valley blue about 10 years ago. Most tourists visiting this area do so with a group from Nuweiba or Dahab. A permit from the tourist police may be needed – check before you set off. The canyon is about five km from the main road; vehicles can drive to within 100m of it.

Water Sports

Once again, underwater delights are the feature attraction and scuba diving and snorkelling the prime activities.

The Diving Camp Nuweiba (☎ 500402), run by Hartmut Janssen and Sylvia May, is in the Helnan Nuweiba Hotel camping area. It offers the usual courses but is considerably more expensive than dive clubs in Dahab or Na'ama Bay. CMAS certificate courses for beginners cost US$330; the manual, log books and certificate are US$25 extra. The centre also hires out pedal boats and jet skis (though they're talking about doing away with the latter).

The only other dive club in the vicinity is Aquasport at the new Hilton. It offers PADI open-water courses for US$280 plus US$80 for all the extras. Windsurf boards can also be hired from here.

Those into kayaks should ask at the Al-Waha Tourism Village.

Camel & Jeep Treks

Check with the reception desk of the Helnan Nuweiba Hotel about camel or jeep trips into the mountains. Trips by jeep to the Khudra Oasis, 'Ain Mahmed and 'Ain Furtaga can last for three days or so, or longer on camel. The trip to the Coloured Canyon can be done in a day. They charge about E£80 a day including food. Half-day excursions without food cost E£30. Take plenty of water as it gets very hot in these regions.

Other camel trips can be arranged by talking to the Bedouins in Nuweiba or Tarabin. Trips generally cost from E£40 to

E£50 a day, though the asking price will be higher.

Places to Stay

Nuweiba Port There are only three hotels close to the port, all of which are fairly unimpressive. A fourth hotel, the Baracuda, collapsed during an earthquake in late 1995.

The *Zahraa Nwabie* is the worst and they have the cheek to ask for E£25/36 for a single/double. Avoid this place. Across the road is the *El-Haramin*, which is slightly cheaper and marginally better, however, they're very reluctant to take in solo women.

Across the road is the new *Motel Marina*, the best of the trio. Small doubles with shower and air-con are E£30; larger quads cost E£70. It has a quite pleasant shaded terrace.

The only other option in the vicinity is the new four star *Hilton Coral Resort* (☎ 520320; fax 520327), on the beach-front just north of the port. Singles/doubles start from US$98/112.

Nuweiba City There are a couple of simple camps with a few huts along the beach south of the Al-Waha Tourism Village (see the following section on Camps), including the overpriced *Sinai Star* and the relaxing *Duna*.

With your own tent, you can camp at the Morgana Restaurant for E£3 but there's precious little shade; passing overland trucks usually base themselves here. The Helnan Nuweiba Hotel and City Beach Village (see below) also take campers.

The *Helnan Nuweiba Hotel* (☎ 500401; fax 500407) caters mainly to package tourists. Formerly known as the Holiday Village (and still largely referred to as such), it has single/double rooms with breakfast from US$65/85 plus taxes. Next door, in its *Holiday Camp*, there are cheaper cabins for E£40/50/60 a single/double/triple; breakfast is E£8.50 extra. Camping costs E£10 and is a bit of a rip-off, however simply using their beach for the day would cost the same anyway. Women should be aware that the shower block here is large and somewhat

SINAI

isolated and it's not unknown for local men to sneak in for a perve.

Further down the road is the *Al-Waha Tourism Village* (☎ & fax 500420/1), which has 16 large tents at E£15/18/24 for one/two/three people or stuffy pastel-toned bungalows (no fan) for E£25/35/45. They also have quite pleasant air-con rooms with bathrooms at E£74/98/125. Breakfast is not included in these prices. The restaurant here is ordinary but there's an attractive beachside bar (E£7 for a Stella).

The *Youth Camp* next door is for Egyptians only.

The *City Beach Village*, halfway between Nuweiba City and Tarabin, is one of the best options if you just want to sit all day on a tranquil beach. You can pitch a tent for E£5, camp out in one of their reed huts for E£10 per person or go for a clean, comfortable single/double room for E£35/55, in which case breakfast is included. The restaurant has a limited range of food, including breakfast (from E£5 to E£8) and fish and steak meals (about E£15); beers are E£7.

Tarabin As Tarabin develops along Dahab lines, the choice of accommodation is becoming wider. You can get a mattress in a bamboo or concrete hut at one of the camps for E£5, and there are a couple of hotels.

Camps Judge for yourself which camps have the more solid huts – the differences are not too great. Most of these places have cafes selling food and drinks. Sudanese run a few of them, inducing their own special laid-back touch. From north to south, the camps include:

Petra Camp Sitting in its own small palm grove, it is arguably Tarabin's most pleasant camp. Double huts cost E£15.

Jamal A big place popular with young Israelis; all the signs are in Hebrew. Double rooms with bath but without air-con cost E£40, or E£60 with air-con. Huts for two people are E£20; some rooms are located on the roof.

Palm Beach Tidy and boasting a large relaxation area, draped with vines and shaded by palms.

El Salam It has more sterile surroundings, loud music and aggressive people.

Camp David Rooms with three beds, private bathroom, fan and small concrete terrace cost E£50; reed huts are E£10 per person.

Blue Bus One of Tarabin's original establishments, this is more a place to eat than a camp. However, it does have three doorless huts (E£5) with rickety reed recliners.

Soft Beach A new camp just south of the sand dune, run by Sudanese. They charge E£14 for two in small huts.

Hotels The *Elsebaey Village* (☎ 500373), a spanking new hotel in the heart of Tarabin, has 15 tiled rooms with fan, cupboard, and a double bed, plus communal bathroom facilities, for E£40 per room. A rooftop bar, restaurant and rooms with private baths are in the throws of construction.

The *El Salam Village* (☎ 500440) is a spacious place occupying the point at the northern end of Nuweiba bay. However, the setting is austere and inconvenient to anything but the sea. Many Israelis stay here but, at E£68/101 for air-con singles/doubles (with breakfast, TV and refrigerator) or E£51/68 for hot, horrible prefab bungalows, it's overpriced.

Places to Eat

If you're staying at either the port or Tarabin, dining options are limited mainly to the hotels and camps. At the port, you'll also find a gang of cheap eateries about 150m off to your left (with your back to the port entrance). In Tarabin there's a supermarket in front of Elsebaey Village selling lots of junk food.

The choice of eateries in Nuweiba City is significantly better; in fact, the open-air bazaar here has some of the best budget diners found in all of Sinai. The immensely popular *Dr Shishkebab* offers a generous spread of ta'amiyya, salad, fried eggplant, hoummos and bread for E£5, or a half chicken with salad, chips and bread at E£12. The unmistakable 'doctor' is a white-turbaned, big, cheerful man wandering from table to table, attentively waiting on all those who eat here.

Another superb place in the bazaar is the new *Sendbad*. Its portions are even bigger and cheaper than at Dr Shishkebab, and the owner is just as genial.

At the Helnan Holiday Camp's *beachside bar* you can get chicken/fish meals for E£15/20, as well as cheaper snacks and Stella.

The next door *Morgana* has moderately priced meals such as fish, chips and salad for E£20, or calamari for E£24. A cold Stella costs E£6 (E£7 if you don't eat there).

Getting There & Away

Bus Getting a bus out of Nuweiba can be a bit confusing, especially if you're staying in nearby Tarabin. Buses going to or from Taba pass down the highway and turn at the hospital to do a circuit by the Helnan Holiday Camp and Dr Shishkebab, before heading out again and proceeding on their way. They usually also call in at the port, stopping at either the bus station or in front of the Motel Marina just opposite. You can presumably pick the buses up at any of these places (you can certainly get off). However, if possible, check the routing for your specific bus with the locals as the pick-up points have been known to change and not all the buses call into the port.

Buses to Cairo and other destinations generally meet incoming ferries. The bus from Taba to Cairo (E£40) via St Catherine's (E£10) stops at the hospital at around 11 am (sometimes earlier). There's another bus to Cairo at 3 pm which costs E£55. Buses to Sharm el-Sheikh (E£10) via Dahab (E£6) leave at 6.30 am and 4 pm; to Taba at 6 am (E£8) and at noon (E£6); and to Suez at 6 am (E£20, six hours via Nakhl).

Service Taxi There is a big service-taxi station by the port, and for once in Sinai there are flat rates commensurate with what Egyptians might be prepared to pay. The fare to Suez is E£30 a person and E£35 to Midan Ulali in Cairo.

As Tarabin's popularity has grown, service taxis here take people directly out on the road north to Israel or south to Dahab, St Catherine's or Sharm el-Sheikh.

Car Rental vehicles are available from Europcar at the Hilton Coral Resort.

Boat For information about ferries and speedboats to Aqaba in Jordan, see the Sea section in the Getting There & Away chapter.

Getting Around

A tof-tof (open-sided bus) shuttles between the port, Nuweiba City and Tarabin from about 6 am to 6 pm. It costs 75 pt and will stop anywhere. At the time of writing it was off the road following an accident, but it should be operating again by now.

In Tarabin, service taxis ask an outrageous E£5 to E£10 for the few kms between Tarabin and Nuweiba City, and E£15 to the port. The only other option here for getting to one of the bus stops in Nuweiba City is to walk the two km.

NUWEIBA TO TABA

Along the coastline north of Nuweiba, especially near Taba, are some large, expensive 'tourist villages', in various stages of completion. Although most of them have been designed with at least some modesty (no skyscrapers here), they mar the wild beauty of this desert coast, as indeed will the plane and bus loads of package tourists they are hoping to attract.

Beaches

There are still some desolate beaches backed by stunning blue waters and pockets of fringing reefs to be found along this stretch of road. The only way to get to them is by service taxi, hitching or bus (but you'll probably have to pay the full Nuweiba to Taba fare).

Seven km north of Nuweiba is *Maagana*, where a row of huts, in honeycomb formation, is stretched out along a lovely bay. On the road a little further north is a place for snacks and drinks.

Another seven km on is *Barracuda Village* which has a series of waterfront stone huts (and a big ugly resort going up nearby). Three km further is the quite isolated *Bawaki* where you can walk virtually from your beach-front hut straight into some great snorkelling sites.

Basata (☎ 500481 or ☎ 350-1829 in Cairo) is about 23 km north of Nuweiba. Basata, which means 'simplicity' in Arabic, is a simple, clean and carefree travellers' settlement with a common kitchen hut, its own bakery and a camping ground. Its bamboo huts cost E£18 per person. If you want to sleep on the beach it is E£10, and to use the beach there is a E£4 day charge. A set dinner costs between E£12 and E£18 depending on whether it's vegetarian or with fish. It's advisable to book ahead; it can get quite crowded with groups.

Further north of Basata are the *Club Aqua Sun* and *Sally Land Holiday Village*, both close to some good beaches and reef.

The Fjord

This small protected bay is a popular sun-bathing spot only about 15 km short of Taba. Up on the rise to the north is the small, clean *Salima Cafeteria* (☎ 530130), run by the amiable Mohammed Magdi. It has six basic rooms where you can stay for E£35/50; meals cost E£7/16/20 for breakfast/lunch/dinner. Book ahead if you want to stay overnight as it's very popular with Israelis.

Pharaoh's Island

Only seven km short of Taba, Pharaoh's Island (Geziret Fara'un) lies about 250m off the Egyptian coast. The islet is dominated by the much restored Castle of Salah ad-Din, a fortress actually built by the Crusaders in 1115, but captured and expanded by Salah ad-Din in 1170 as a bulwark against feared Crusader penetration south from Palestine. At the height of Crusader successes, it was feared they might attempt to head for the holy cities of Mecca and Medina. Some of the modern restoration is painfully obvious (concrete was not a prime building material in Salah ad-Din's time), but the island is a pleasant place for a half-day trip. The limpid aqua waters are extremely inviting, and a lot

of Israeli pleasure boats carrying divers cruise down here from nearby Eilat. From the island you can see the Taba Hilton and the port city of Aqaba in Jordan.

Pharaoh's Island is open from 9 am to 5 pm and entry costs E£8 (E£4 for students), but the boat ride there and back is an outlandish E£10.50. Tickets for the boat are available in the cafeteria by the hotel (see Places to Stay & Eat, following), and those for the island on landing.

The *Salah el Din Village* (☎ 530340) has 120 low-key rooms, where singles/doubles cost E£47/58. All rooms have air-con and bathrooms and there's a restaurant. Dinner is sometimes accompanied by a floor show. There is also a fairly pricey cafe on the island.

TABA

Until 1989, a few hundred metres of beach, a luxury hotel and a coffee shop at Taba, a place on the Israel-Egypt border, was a minor point of contention between the two countries. After several years of squabbling and formal arbitration, the land was returned to Egypt. Since 1982, when the rest of Sinai was returned by Israel, Taba has served as a busy border crossing. The border is open 24 hours a day, except from Friday to Saturday night, the Jewish Sabbath.

There is a small post and telephone office in the 'town', along with a hospital, bakery and an EgyptAir office (often closed). You can change money at booths of Banque du Caire (unreliable opening hours) and Banque Misr (open 24 hours), both 100m before the border, or at the Taba Hilton Hotel. Their rates vary only slightly.

Places to Stay & Eat

The 11 storey *Taba Hilton* (☎ 530300) has rooms for US$154/199, including taxes, and a diving centre.

The *Panorama Restaurant*, opposite the bus station, seems to have been abandoned by all and sundry, probably because it charges E£3 for a cola. Slightly cheaper but pretty unwelcoming is the *cafeteria* at the bus station where you'll need to bargain for a meal of fish, rice and salad (E£12) as well as for a coffee or water.

Getting There & Away

Israel The No 15 bus runs between Eilat and the border from 7 am and costs 4 NIS. Alternatively, you can catch a taxi for about 20 NIS. Leaving Israel, you must pay an exit fee of 50 NIS at the border and then pass through immigration. Leaving Egypt there is no fee.

On the Egyptian side, you first reach immigration. You can ask for a 14 day pass to Sinai here, or have your standard visa stamped (see Visas & Documents in the Facts for the Visitor chapter and also Israel & the Palestinian Territories in the Getting There & Away chapter for more details). Remember that you must register with the police within seven days if you have a standard tourist visa. You then pass through customs and have a one km walk past the Taba Hilton (change here if you have no Egyptian money) to the border tax collection point (E£17) and then the bus and taxi stand.

Air Air Sinai runs twice a week (winter only) flights from Cairo to Ras an-Naqb airport, 38 km away from Taba, for E£430.

Bus East Delta Bus Co runs several buses from Taba. The 10 am bus goes to Nuweiba (E£8), St Catherine's Monastery (E£20) and on to Cairo (E£50). Another bus to Cairo (E£65) leaves at 2 pm but goes via Nakhl. Other buses leave at 9 am and 3 pm for Sharm el-Sheikh (E£15), stopping at Nuweiba (E£6) and Dahab (E£10). To Nuweiba only there's another bus at 2 pm. To Suez (E£30; five hours via Nakhl) there's one at 7 am.

Getting Around

Service Taxi A taxi (up to seven people) to Nuweiba costs E£175 and E£300 to Sharm el-Sheikh. You may also find a minibus or two which will take you to Dahab for about E£15 per person. Your bargaining power increases if the bus is not too far off.

Car The only rental-car option here is Europcar (☎ 379222; fax 379660) at the Hilton.

ST CATHERINE'S MONASTERY

Twenty-two Greek Orthodox monks live in this ancient monastery at the foot of Mt Sinai. The monastic order was founded in the 4th century AD by the Byzantine empress Helena, who had a small chapel built beside what was believed to be the burning bush from which God spoke to Moses.

The chapel is dedicated to St Catherine, the legendary martyr of Alexandria, who was tortured on a spiked wheel and then beheaded for her Christianity. Her body was supposedly transported by angels to Gebel Katherina, the highest mountain in Egypt, which is about six km south of Mt Sinai. There, the body was 'found', about 300 years later, by monks from the monastery.

In the 6th century, Emperor Justinian ordered the building of a fortress, with a basilica and a monastery, as well as the original chapel, to serve as a secure home for the monks of St Catherine's and as a refuge for the Christians of southern Sinai.

Despite the isolated setting, the monastery and Mt Sinai attract a great many tourists and pilgrims, and the place can be choked with tour buses and people, especially in the mornings. When you visit, remember that this is still a functioning monastery, not just a museum piece. The only parts of the monastery to which members of the public are admitted are the chapel and a rather macabre room full of the bones of deceased monks; you are also permitted to view part of a splendid collection of icons and jewelled crosses. St Catherine's monastery is open to visitors daily except on Friday, Sunday and holidays from 9 am to noon.

Orientation & Information

The monastery is about 3.5 km from the village of Al-Milga or two km from the large roundabout on the road between the two. At Al-Milga there is a bank, telephone office (open 24 hours), police station (where you can register your arrival in Egypt – it's up on the hill about 200m past the petrol station),

SINAI

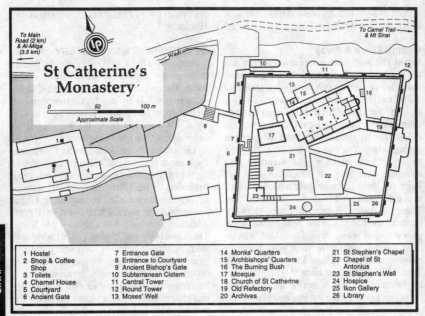

To Main Road (2 km) & Al-Milga (3.5 km)

To Camel Trail & Mt Sinai

Wadi

St Catherine's Monastery

0   50   100 m

Approximate Scale

1 Hostel	7 Entrance Gate	14 Monks' Quarters	21 St Stephen's Chapel
2 Shop & Coffee Shop	8 Entrance to Courtyard	15 Archbishops' Quarters	22 Chapel of St Antonius
3 Toilets	9 Ancient Bishop's Gate	16 The Burning Bush	23 St Stephen's Well
4 Charnel House	10 Subterranean Cistern	17 Mosque	24 Hospice
5 Courtyard	11 Central Tower	18 Church of St Catherine	25 Ikon Gallery
6 Ancient Gate	12 Round Tower	19 Old Refectory	26 Library
	13 Moses' Well	20 Archives	

tourist police office (next to the mosque), a couple of hotels and a variety of shops and cafes. The Banque Misr will change cash or travellers' cheques, and may accept Visa and MasterCard for a cash advance. It's open from 9 am to 2 pm and 6 to 9 pm.

Mt Sinai

Although some archaeologists and historians dispute Mt Sinai's biblical claim to fame, it is revered by Christians, Muslims and Jews, all of whom believe that God delivered his Ten Commandments to Moses from its summit.

At a height of 2285m, Mt Sinai (Gebel Musa is the local name) towers over St Catherine's Monastery. It is easy to climb and there are two well-defined routes to the summit – the camel trail and the Steps of Repentance. Mt Sinai is not, however, the mountain directly up the valley behind the monastery – that one is far lower! From the

top you can look across to the even higher summit of Gebel Katherina.

The camel trail is the easier route and this climb takes about two hours. Along the way, you'll probably be greeted by Bedouin camel 'cowboys' anxious to put you in the saddle, although they can take you only as far as the final steps leading to the summit. Usually, there are at least four or five tea and Coca-Cola stands on the trail, catering to those in need of a caffeine fix. At the stand where the camel trail meets the steps, a full breakfast is sometimes available.

The alternative path to the summit, the taxing 3000 Steps of Repentance, was laid by one monk as a form of penance. If you want to try both routes, it's best to take the path on the way up and the steps on the way back down, particularly if you want a great view of the monastery.

During the summer, you should avoid the heat by beginning your hike at 2 or 3 am. This way, you'll also see the sunrise. The trail can be a bit difficult in parts, so a torch (flash-light) is essential.

If you plan to spend the night on the summit, make sure you have plenty of food and water. As it gets cold and windy there, even in summer, you will also need warm clothes and a sleeping bag (there is no space to pitch a tent). Sometimes you can rent a blanket for a pound or two. As late as mid-May, be prepared to share the summit with hordes of tourists, some bearing ghetto-blasters, others carrying Bibles and hymn books. With the music and singing, and people nudging each other for a space on the holy mountain, don't expect to get much sleep, especially in the wee small hours before sunrise.

Just below the summit, along the Steps of Repentance, the small plateau known as Elijah's Hollow is dominated by a 500 year-old cypress tree, marking the spot where the prophet Elijah heard the voice of God. On the summit itself is a Greek Orthodox chapel containing beautiful paintings and orna-ments, and a small mosque. Unfortunately, they'll probably be locked. The summit also offers spectacular views of the surrounding bare, jagged mountains and plunging valleys where, throughout the day, the rocks and cliffs change colour as if they were stone chameleons.

Places to Stay

St Catherine's Monastery runs a *hostel* which is open every day. Although the recep-tion is open all day, check-in is only between 8 am and 1 pm, and 4 and 10 pm. The hostel offers single-sex dormitories (seven beds) which cost E£35 per person, and rooms with three beds and private bathroom for E£40 a head. The facilities are basic but clean. Breakfast costs E£4, lunch or dinner is E£8. You can partake of a meal as well as leave baggage in one of the rooms while you hike up Mt Sinai. This service will cost you about E£2 in baksheesh.

Blending in wonderfully with the sur-rounding landscape, right by the roundabout

In spite of its isolated but dramatic location at the foot of Mt Sinai, thousands of tourists and pil-grims flock to St Catherine's Monastery each year.

two km west of the monastery, is the pricey *St Catherine's Tourist Village* (☎ 470333; fax 470323) where singles/ doubles/triples cost US$114/135/168 including breakfast and dinner. The air-con rooms, all with TV and bathroom, have views of the distant monastery.

Up the hill beside the Tourist Village is the somewhat grubby *Al-Fairoz Hotel* (☎ 470446) with a variety of somewhat overpriced options. Self-contained rooms cost E£60/70/80, dormitory beds are E£15 and a mattress in a big tent or out in the open costs E£8. With your own bedroll, you can sleep outdoors for E£5.

Off to your right about 200m before you reach the mosque in Al-Milga, on the hill opposite Al-Fairoz, is the new three star *Daniela Village* (☎ 470279). It has a collection of low-set, stone bungalows with comfortable enough rooms for US$45/60/70; there's a restaurant and bar.

About six km on the Nuweiba road is *Morgenland Village* (☎ 470331) where single/double rooms cost US$55/74, including dinner and breakfast. Four km further on, at the turn-off to Dahab, is the very basic *Green Lodge Camping* (☎ 470314) with restaurant. Another 10 km on, five km down the Dahab turn-off and next to the airport, is the *El Salam Hotel* (☎ 470409).

Places to Eat

In Al-Milga there's a bakery opposite the mosque and a couple of well-stocked supermarkets in the shopping arcade. Just behind the bakery are a few small restaurants, the most reasonable of which is *Look Here* – try its chicken broth. Just by the bus stop the *Catrien Rest House* (no accommodation though) is open for lunch only and serves a filling chicken, rice and vegetable meal.

Across the square, near the bank, is the *Restaurant for Friends*. The new *Panorama Restaurant*, on the main road just down from the post office, has the most extensive budget menu in town. Pizzas cost between E£5 and E£18 and there are sandwiches, pancakes, burgers, salads and soups. A cup of tea or coffee is an outrageous E£3.

The modern *Al Monagah* cafeteria right by the roundabout principally caters to tour bus groups.

Getting There & Away

Bus You can ask the driver to drop you off at the roundabout, which is closer to the monastery. Buses leave from the square in Al-Milga. Sometime between noon and 1 pm, a bus leaves for Sharm el-Sheikh (E£15) via Dahab (E£10). The bus for Suez (E£17, five hours) leaves at 6 am, which is much better value than the direct Cairo bus, as you can get a bus or service taxi from Suez to Cairo for about E£5. At 10 am there's a bus to Cairo (E£40) en route from Taba. A bus to Taba (E£20) via Nuweiba (E£10) departs at 3.30 pm, but it sometimes goes to Nuweiba only.

Service Taxi Service taxis travel in and out of the village irregularly and infrequently. If you're lucky, you might be able to find a taxi driver who is willing to take you all the way to Cairo. If so, the trip could cost about E£300 for the taxi (up to a maximum of seven people). A similar taxi to Suez will cost about E£175, after intense bargaining. At the monastery taxis often wait for people coming down from Mt Sinai in the early afternoon. Count on between E£10 and E£20 per person to Dahab or Nuweiba.

WADI FERAN

This lush date-palm oasis, a Bedouin outpost between the west coast of Sinai and St Catherine's Monastery, lays amidst rough, barren desert and harsh, rocky hills. There is a convent on the western edge of Wadi Feran, but you need permission from St Catherine's Monastery if you want to visit it.

AL-ARISH

Much of the north coast of Sinai, from Port Fouad most of the way to Al-Arish, is dominated by the swampy lagoon of Lake Bardawil, separated from the Mediterranean by a limestone ridge and making the area hardly attractive for swimming. The road follows what must be one of the oldest march routes throughout history, used by the Pharaohs to penetrate into what is now Israel, Jordan and on to Syria, and by the Persians, Greeks, Crusaders, Arab Muslims and many others coming the other way.

Al-Arish, beyond Lake Bardawil, is the capital of North Sinai Governorate and has a population of about 40,000. Its greatest asset, a palm-fringed beach, is becoming increasingly fragmented by expanding construction along the coast. The place, at present, is not heavily visited by either Egyptians or foreign tourists, except in the height of summer.

Orientation & Information

The main coastal road, Sharia Fouad Zekry, forms a T-junction with Sharia 23rd of July, which runs a couple of km south (changing name to Sharia Tahrir on the way) to the bus and service-taxi stations.

Tourist Office The tourist office is on Sharia Fouad Zekry, just down from Sinai Beach Hotel. Opening hours are unclear – it never seems to be open.

Money The National Bank of Egypt, on Sharia Tahrir, is open Sunday to Thursday

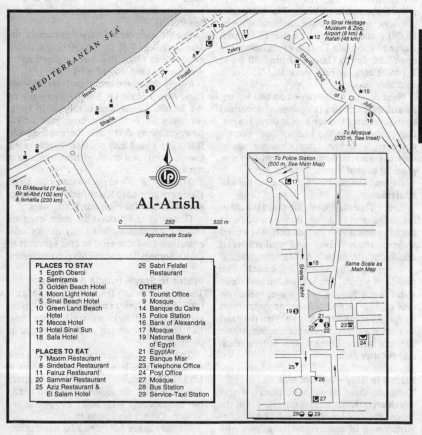

SINAI

Al-Arish

0   250   500 m

Approximate Scale

To El-Masa'id (7 km),
Bir al-Abd (102 km)
& Ismailia (230 km)

MEDITERRANEAN SEA

Beach

Sharia

Fouad

Zekry

Sharia 23rd of July

To Sinai Heritage
Museum & Zoo,
Airport (8 km) &
Rafah (48 km)

To Mosque
(300 m, See Inset)

To Police Station
(500 m, See Main Map)

Same Scale as
Main Map

Sharia Tahrir

PLACES TO STAY
1 Egoth Oberoi
2 Semiramis
3 Golden Beach Hotel
4 Moon Light Hotel
5 Sinai Beach Hotel
10 Green Land Beach Hotel
12 Mecca Hotel
13 Hotel Sinai Sun
18 Safa Hotel

PLACES TO EAT
7 Maxim Restaurant
8 Sindebad Restaurant
11 Fairuz Restaurant
20 Sammar Restaurant
25 Aziz Restaurant & El Salam Hotel

26 Sabri Felafel Restaurant

OTHER
6 Tourist Office
9 Mosque
14 Banque du Caire
15 Police Station
16 Bank of Alexandria
17 Mosque
19 National Bank of Egypt
21 EgyptAir
22 Banque Misr
23 Telephone Office
24 Post Office
27 Mosque
28 Bus Station
29 Service-Taxi Station

from 9 am to 2.30 pm. Nearby, a street back from Sharia Tahrir, is Banque Misr. The Bank of Alexandria and Banque du Caire both have branches on Sharia 23rd of July.

Post & Communications The post office, open from 8.30 am to 2.30 pm except on Friday, is a block east of Banque Misr. The 24 hour telephone office is round the corner from the post office.

Things to See & Do
The **Sinai Heritage Museum**, on the coastal road to Rafah on the outskirts of town, was established several years ago to inform people about life in Sinai. The museum's displays include Bedouin handicrafts, tools, clothing and traditional medicines, supplemented by the odd English explanation. It's open Saturday to Thursday from 9.30 am to 2 pm. Entry is E£1 plus E£5/25 for a camera/video.

Next door is a miserable **zoo** and among its unhappy inmates is a range of nocturnal desert creatures that are kept in barred cages, unprotected from the blazing sun. There's not even a darkened anti-chamber where they can secrete themselves. This is a disgrace to animal lovers.

Beyond the bus station are the remains of a **fortress**.

Every Thursday, when the **souq** is held in the oldest part of town, Bedouins come in from the desert with their camels. The veiled women trade silver and embroidered dresses, while the men sell camel saddles.

The main attraction is the **beach**. The parade of palms, fine white sand and clean water (even the odd small wave) make this one of the nicer Mediterranean spots in Egypt. As is unfortunately so often the case, women may feel somewhat uncomfortable swimming here. There is supposedly a beach curfew after dark.

Places to Stay – bottom end
There are three cheap, basic places to stay which are OK for budget travellers. On the beach, the *Golden Beach Hotel* has a conglomeration of drab cement bungalows with up to three beds at E£15 per bungalow. They also have cold showers; breakfast is not included. Just up the road and marginally better is the *Moon Light Hotel*, which has singles/doubles at E£10/20 including breakfast. Finally, *Safa Hotel*, on Sharia Tahrir, is a noisy place on the 2nd floor and has doubles with private bath (cold) for E£10 a person, or E£5 without bath. Solo women would be ill advised to stay here.

Better is the *El Salam Hotel* (☎ 331219), above the Aziz Restaurant on Midan al-Baladiyya. Rooms with two or three beds cost E£12.50 per bed. Ask for a room at the back if you're not into street noise. This place's main advantage is being close to the bus station.

Behind the New Golden Beach is the *Mecca Hotel* (☎ & fax 344909), a friendly, good, clean place that has singles/doubles with fan and hot water for E£30/40.

Surely one of the better deals is the *Green Land Beach Hotel* (☎ 340601), virtually on the beach. Clean and comfortable triple rooms with bathroom cost just E£15, however many occupants there are. Breakfast is extra (and may not be available in the low season), and most of the rooms have terraces.

You may be able to pitch a tent at the *Youth Camp* on the road to Rafah, although it seems to be reserved for Egyptian youngsters.

Dotted in and around the palm trees are *chalets*, which are often fairly mucky self-contained flats that tend to cost upwards of E£40. Some belong to the Maxim restaurant.

Places to Stay – middle & top end
The popular beach-front restaurant, *Maxim* (☎ 340850), has expanded to now offer rooms and chalets as well. They cost E£40/60/80 in winter, and double that in summer.

The *Hotel Sinai Sun* (☎ 341855) is a reasonable middle-level place, with rooms at US$21/25 (summer) or E£14/18 (winter). The price does not include breakfast (E£5), but rooms come with bath, TV, phone and air-con. Dinner here costs E£25.

Slightly better but quite a bit more pricey

is the *Sinai Beach Hotel* (☎ 341713). Some of the rooms, which cost E£115/130 without breakfast, have balconies looking across to the sea. There's also a restaurant and a coffee shop.

Further to the south-west are Al-Arish's two luxury establishments. The *Semiramis* (☎ 344166; fax 344168) has rooms away from the beach for US$60/76 (summer) and US$40/50 (winter). Suites facing the beach cost more. The pool costs E£10 for non-guests.

Rooms at the *Egoth Oberoi* (☎ 351321; fax 352352) cost US$94/119; continental breakfast is E£12, while a buffet breakfast is E£24. Those not staying at the hotel can use the pool for E£25.

About 10 km west of the Egoth Oberoi, the developers are at work, with two sprawling tourist villages under construction.

Places to Eat

There's not a huge range of places to get a meal in Al-Arish. About as good as you'll find in the budget range is *Aziz Restaurant* on Sharia Tahrir. It has good meals of fuul and ta'amiyya as well as grilled chicken, kofta, rice and spaghetti, and are also open for breakfast.

Sabri, opposite Aziz in the back corner of a little square, makes the best felafel.

At the *Sammar Restaurant* (signposted in Arabic) on Sharia Tahrir you can get kebab and kofta.

At the junction of Sharia Fouad Zekry and Sharia 23rd of July is the *Fairuz Restaurant*. It serves kofta, kebab, fish and chicken in reasonably generous portions, although it's closed in winter.

Further west along Sharia Fouad Zekry is the *Sindebad*, a fuul and ta'amiyya place.

Right on the beach, among the palms, is the classier *Maxim*, which specialises in fish dishes costing about E£20 to E£35. The food is good, but it's open in summer only.

Getting There & Away

Air EgyptAir (☎ 342450) has two flights a week between Cairo and Al-Arish. The one

way fare is E£328. The airport is eight km from town.

Bus For details on buses from Cairo, see the Getting There & Away section in the Cairo chapter. Buses for Cairo (five hours) leave Al-Arish at 7 am (E£25) and 4 pm (E£35).

There is a bus via Qantara (E£5) to Ismailia (E£7, three hours) every hour until 3pm. The 7 am and 3 pm Ismailia buses go on to Mansura (E£11), and the 7, 7.45 and 9 am and 3 pm buses go to Zagazig (E£9). For Suez, you have to go to Ismailia and take another bus from there. A bus to Tanta (E£14) leaves at 8.30 am.

At 7.15 and 10.30 am there's a bus to Rafah, which can drop you about a km short of the border at the T-junction where the bus turns left to Rafah. They cost E£1.

Service Taxi A cheaper alternative to the expensive Sinai buses to Cairo is a service taxi, which costs about E£12 per person. Service taxis to Qantara cost E£5, E£6 to Ismailia, and to the border (or vice versa) they like to charge anything from E£5 to E£7.

Getting Around

There is a pretty regular stream of buses, microbuses and service taxis – huge US limousines dating back to the 1960s at least – running between the bus station and the satellite residential area of El-Masa'id to the south-west. Microbuses shuttle between the bus station and the beach for 25 pt.

RAFAH

This coastal town, 48 km north of Al-Arish, marks the border with the Gaza Strip, and Israel. Although town fathers apparently feel the warm Mediterranean location could make it an ideal resort, it has no hotels (there are some *chalets*). The nearest cheap hotel is in Sheikh Zuweid, 17 km short of Rafah.

The border crossing is actually three to four km from the town.

A new road linking Rafah directly with Taba on the Gulf of Aqaba may open up new options for travelling around Sinai however, as of late 1995, this road was still being used by the military only.

Getting There & Away

If you plan to cross into Egypt via Rafah, there is only the one Egged bus (No 362) from Tel Aviv to Rafah via Ashkelon. It departs Tel Aviv daily at 9.00 am and costs 27 NIS. Going the other way, it leaves at 3 pm. There are no other connections from Ashkelon and nothing from Jerusalem. Otherwise you will have to take a *sherut* (an Israeli service taxi) to Rafah (Rafiah to Palestinians and Israelis).

The border is open 24 hours daily, and security is heavy. The bulk of the people coming through are Palestinians or tourists on through buses to and from Cairo.

There is a hefty US$30 (or shekel equivalent) exit tax. Once through formalities on the Israel side, people are loaded on to a shuttle bus to cover the few hundred metres of trenches, barbed wire and man traps that

separate the two countries. (The bus costs E£5 from the Egyptian side, 10 NIS from the Israeli side.)

On entering Egypt you pay a tax of E£7 (payable in pounds; a few bank booths, located nearby, exchange money) and then proceed through immigration and customs. You need to have a visa, which you can obtain at the Egyptian embassy in Tel Aviv or the consulate in Eilat.

Going the other way, there is an Egyptian exit tax of E£17, but no Israeli entry fee.

Once through Egyptian customs, there is a service-taxi stand a few hundred metres down the road. The trip to Cairo should be E£20; it's sometimes a long wait before a taxi is full. To Al-Arish the fare is E£5.

For information on buses from Cairo to Rafah, see the Getting There & Away section in the Cairo chapter.

A couple of local buses run between Rafah town (three km from the border) and Al-Arish for E£1.

Health Appendix

Travel Health

Staying healthy while on the road depends on your predeparture preparations, your day-to-day health care and how you handle any medical problem or emergency that does develop. Recommendations for predeparture planning and day-to-day health care, as well as information on potential dangers are covered here. However, with a little luck, some basic precautions and adequate information few travellers experience more than upset stomachs.

Travel Health Guides

There are a number of books on travel health:

Staying Healthy in Asia, Africa & Latin America, Dirk Schroeder, Moon Publications, 1994. Probably the best all-round guide to carry, as it's compact but very detailed and well organised.

Travellers' Health, Dr Richard Dawood, Oxford University Press, 1995. Comprehensive, easy to read, authoritative and also highly recommended, although it's rather large to lug around.

Where There is No Doctor, David Werner, Macmillan, 1994. A very detailed guide intended for someone, like a Peace Corps worker, going to work in an developing country, rather than for the average traveller.

Travel with Children, Maureen Wheeler, Lonely Planet Publications, 1995. Includes basic advice on travel health for younger children.

Predeparture Planning

Health Insurance A travel insurance policy to cover theft, loss and medical problems is a wise idea. There are a wide variety of policies and your travel agent will have recommendations. The international student travel policies handled by STA Travel or other student travel organisations are usually good value. Some policies offer lower and higher medical-expense options but the higher one is chiefly for countries like the USA which have extremely high medical costs. Check the small print:

- Some policies specifically exclude 'dangerous activities' which can include scuba diving, motorcycling, even trekking. If such activities are on your agenda you don't want that sort of policy. A locally acquired motorcycle licence may not be valid under your policy.
- You may prefer a policy which pays doctors or hospitals directly rather than you having to pay on the spot and claim later. If you have to claim later make sure you keep all documentation. Some policies ask you to call back (reverse charges) to a centre in your home country where an immediate assessment of your problem is made.
- Check if the policy covers ambulances or an emergency flight home. If you have to stretch out you will need two seats and somebody has to pay for them!

Medical Kit A compact, straightforward medical kit is a wise thing to carry. A kit should include:

- Aspirin or paracetamol (acetaminophen in the US) – for pain or fever.
- Antihistamine (such as Benadryl) – useful as a decongestant for colds and allergies, to ease the itch from insect bites or stings, and to help prevent motion sickness. There are several antihistamines on the market, all with different pros and cons (for example a tendency to cause drowsiness), so it's worth discussing your requirements with a pharmacist or doctor. Antihistamines may cause sedation and interact with alcohol so care should be taken when using them.
- Antibiotics – useful if you're travelling well off the beaten track, but they must be prescribed and you should carry the prescription with you.
- Loperamide (for example, Imodium) or Lomotil for diarrhoea; prochlorperazine (for example, Stemetil) or metaclopramide (for example, Maxalon) for nausea and vomiting. Antidiarrhoea medication should not be given to children under the age of 12.
- Rehydration mixture – for treatment of severe diarrhoea. This is particularly important if travelling with children, but is recommended for everyone.
- Antiseptic such as Betadine, which comes as impregnated swabs or ointment, and an antibiotic powder or similar 'dry' spray – for cuts and grazes.
- Calamine lotion – to ease irritation from bites or stings.
- Bandages and Band-Aids – for minor injuries.
- Scissors, tweezers and a thermometer (note that mercury thermometers are prohibited by airlines).

HEALTH

- Insect repellent, sun block, suntan lotion, chap stick and water purification tablets.
- A couple of syringes, in case you need injections in a country with medical hygiene problems. Ask your doctor for a note explaining why they have been prescribed.

Ideally, antibiotics should be administered only under medical supervision and should never be taken indiscriminately. Take only the recommended dose at the prescribed intervals and continue using the antibiotic for the prescribed period, even if the illness seems to be cured earlier. Some individuals are allergic to commonly prescribed antibiotics such as penicillin or sulpha drugs. It would be sensible to always carry this information when travelling. Antibiotics are quite specific to the infections they can treat. Stop immediately if there are any serious reactions and don't use the antibiotic at all if you are unsure that you have the correct one.

Medicines are widely available over the counter in Egypt; prescriptions are often not needed. If the medicine is produced locally, it will be much cheaper than in the west. However, be careful if buying drugs in Egypt, particularly where the expiry date may have passed or correct storage conditions may not have been followed. Bogus drugs are common and it's possible that drugs which are no longer recommended, or have even been banned, in the west are still being dispensed in many Third World countries.

In many countries it may be a good idea to leave unwanted medicines, syringes etc with a local clinic, rather than carry them home.

Health Preparations Make sure you're healthy before you start travelling. If you are embarking on a long trip make sure your teeth are OK; there are lots of places where a visit to the dentist would be the last thing you'd want. If you have an emergency, however, there are English-speaking dentists in most of Egypt's cities and towns. In Cairo, consult your embassy.

If you wear glasses take a spare pair and your prescription. Losing your glasses can be a real problem, although in Egypt's major cities you can get new spectacles made up quickly, cheaply and competently.

If you require a particular medication take an adequate supply, as it may not be available locally. Take the prescription or, better still, part of the packaging showing the generic rather than the brand name (which may not be locally available), as it will make getting replacements easier. It's a wise idea to have a legible prescription with you to show you legally use the medication – it's surprising how often over-the-counter drugs from one place are illegal without a prescription or even banned in another. However, this rarely poses a problem in Egypt.

Immunisations Vaccinations provide protection against diseases you might meet along the way. For some countries no immunisations are necessary, but the further off the beaten track you go the more necessary it is to take precautions. For travel to Egypt, the vaccinations listed below should all be considered.

It is important to understand the distinction between vaccines recommended for travel in certain areas and those required by law. Essentially the number of vaccines subject to international health regulations has been dramatically reduced over the last 10 years. Currently yellow fever is the only vaccine subject to international health regulations. Vaccination as an entry requirement is usually only enforced when coming from an infected area.

Occasionally travellers face bureaucratic problems regarding cholera vaccine even though all countries have dropped it as a health requirement for travel. Under some situations it may be wise to have the vaccine despite its poor protection, for example, for those travelling across Africa to Egypt.

On the other hand a number of vaccines are recommended for travel in certain areas. These may not be required by law but are recommended for your own personal protection.

All vaccinations should be recorded on an

International Health Certificate, which is available from your physician or government health department.

Plan ahead for getting your vaccinations: some of them require an initial shot followed by a booster, while some vaccinations should not be given together. It is recommended you seek medical advice at least six weeks prior to travel.

Most travellers from western countries will have been immunised against various diseases during childhood but your doctor may still recommend booster shots against measles or polio, diseases still prevalent in many other countries. The period of protection offered by vaccinations differs widely and some are contraindicated if you are pregnant.

Vaccinations to consider include:

Smallpox Smallpox has now been wiped out worldwide, so immunisation is no longer necessary.

Cholera Not required by law but occasionally travellers face bureaucratic problems on some border crossings. Protection is poor and it lasts only six months. It is contraindicated in pregnancy.

Tetanus & Diphtheria Boosters are necessary every 10 years and protection is highly recommended.

Polio A booster of either the oral or injected vaccine is required every 10 years to maintain our immunity from childhood vaccination. Polio is a very serious, easily transmitted disease which is still prevalent in many Middle Eastern countries.

Typhoid Available either as an injection or oral capsules. Protection lasts from one to five years depending on the vaccine and is useful if you are travelling for long periods in rural, tropical areas. You may get some side effects such as pain at the injection site, fever, headache and a general unwell feeling. A new single-dose injectable vaccine, which appears to have few side effects, is now available but is more expensive. Side effects are unusual with the oral form but occasionally an individual will have stomach cramps.

Hepatitis A The most common travel-acquired illness which can be prevented by vaccination. Protection can be provided in two ways–either with the antibody gamma globulin or with a new vaccine called Havrix.

Havrix provides long term immunity (possibly more than 10 years) after an initial course of two injections and a booster at one year. It may be more expensive than gamma globulin but certainly has many advantages, including length of protection and ease of administration. It is important to know that being a vaccine it will take about three weeks to provide satisfactory protection–hence the need for careful planning prior to travel.

Gamma globulin is not a vaccination but a ready-made antibody which has proven very successful in reducing the chances of hepatitis infection. As it may interfere with the development of immunity, it should not be given until at least 10 days after administration of the last vaccine needed; it should also be given as close as possible to departure because it is at its most effective in the first few weeks after administration and the effectiveness tapers off gradually between three and six months.

Hepatitis B Travellers at risk of contact (see Infectious Diseases, later) are strongly advised to be vaccinated, especially if they are children or will have close contact with children. The vaccination course comprises three injections given over a six month period then boosters every three to five years. The initial course of injections can be given over as short a period as 28 days then boosted after 12 months if more rapid protection is required.

Yellow Fever Protection lasts 10 years and is recommended where the disease is endemic, chiefly in Africa and South America. It is not required for Egypt, but is necessary for many other African countries. You usually have to go to a special yellow-fever vaccination centre. Vaccination is contraindicated during pregnancy but if you must travel to a high-risk area it is probably advisable to have the vaccination anyway.

Meningococcal Meningitis Vaccination is recommended for those planning to stay for three months or more in Egypt, or for one month or more in the south, near Sudan. It is also required of all haj pilgrims entering Saudi Arabia. A single injection will give good protection against the A, C, W and Y groups of the bacteria for at least a year. The vaccine is not, however, recommended for children under two years because they do not develop satisfactory immunity from it.

If you are travelling through Africa from Egypt you can get vaccinations for yellow fever and cholera in Cairo at the government Public Health Unit, at the back of the lobby of the Continental Hotel on Midan Opera. Make sure you take a sterilised syringe with you; these are available at pharmacies.

Basic Rules

Care in what you eat and drink is the most important health rule; stomach upsets are the most likely travel health problem (between 30 and 50% of travellers in a two week stay experience this) but the majority of these upsets will be relatively minor. Don't become paranoid; trying the local food is part of the experience of travel, after all.

Water Tap water in Cairo is generally safe to drink, but elsewhere in Egypt bottled water is recommended. Cairo's tap water is so heavily chlorinated that most microbes and other little beasties are annihilated. Unfortunately, the excessive chlorination can sometimes be hard on your stomach. If the tap water makes you feel sick try the bottled water. Make sure that the bottles have been properly sealed, as there used to be a scam of refilling them with tap water. Only use water from containers with a serrated seal – not tops or corks. Take care with fruit juice, particularly if water may have been added. Milk should be treated with suspicion, as it is often unpasteurised. Boiled milk is fine if it is kept hygienically and yoghurt is always good. Tea or coffee should also be OK, since the water should have been boiled.

In the countryside the water is not so safe. If you don't know for certain that the water is safe always assume the worst.

Water Purification The simplest way of purifying water is to boil it thoroughly. Vigorously boiling for five minutes should be satisfactory. Simple filtering will not remove all dangerous organisms, so if you cannot boil water it should be treated chemically. Chlorine tablets (Puritabs, Steritabs or other brand names) will kill many but not all pathogens. They will not kill giardia and amoebic cysts. Iodine is very effective in purifying water and is available in tablet form (such as Potable Aqua), but follow the directions carefully and remember that too much iodine can be harmful.

If you can't find tablets, tincture of iodine (2%) or iodine crystals can be used. Four drops of tincture of iodine per litre or quart of clear water is the recommended dosage; the treated water should be left to stand for 20 to 30 minutes before drinking. Iodine crystals can also be used to purify water but this is a more complicated process, as you have to first prepare a saturated iodine solution. Iodine loses its effectiveness if exposed to air or damp, so keep it in a tightly sealed container. Flavoured powder will disguise the taste of treated water and is a good idea if you are travelling with children.

Food There are also a few common-sense precautions to take with food in Egypt. Salads and fruit should be washed with purified water or peeled where possible. Egyptians sometimes fertilise their fields with human excrement and this waste has a way of sticking to the produce. The food isn't always well washed before it reaches your plate. If you can't wash or peel it, don't eat it. On the other hand, many travellers have eaten salads regularly in Egypt with few ill effects. If you think that you are particularly susceptible to stomach troubles, then you should avoid salads.

Most processed and packaged ice cream is safe but beware of ice cream that has melted and been refrozen. Thoroughly cooked food is safest but not if it has been left to cool or if it has been reheated. Shellfish such as mussels, oysters and clams should be avoided as well as undercooked meat, particularly in the form of mince. Steaming does not make shellfish safe for eating.

If a place looks clean and well run and if the vendor also looks clean and healthy, then the food is probably safe. In general, places that are packed with travellers or locals will be fine, while empty restaurants are questionable. The food in busy restaurants is cooked and eaten quite quickly with little standing around and is probably not reheated.

Nutrition If your food is poor or limited in availability, if you're travelling hard and fast and therefore missing meals, or if you simply lose your appetite, you can soon start to lose weight and place your health at risk.

Make sure your diet is well balanced. Eggs, tofu, beans, lentils and nuts are all safe ways to get protein. Fruit you can peel (such as bananas, oranges or mandarins) is always safe and a good source of vitamins. Try to eat plenty of grains (rice) and bread. Remember that although food is generally safer if it is cooked well, overcooked food loses much of its nutritional value. If your diet isn't well balanced or if your food intake is insufficient, it's a good idea to take vitamin and iron pills.

In hot climates make sure you drink enough – don't rely on feeling thirsty to indicate when you should drink. Not needing to urinate or very dark yellow urine is a danger sign. Always carry a water bottle with you on long trips. Excessive sweating can lead to loss of salt and therefore muscle cramping and, in some countries, adding salt to food can help. However, this should not be necessary in Egypt where salt is used liberally in cooking.

Everyday Health Normal body temperature is 98.6°F or 37°C; more than 2°C (4°F) higher indicates a 'high' fever. The normal adult pulse rate is 60 to 100 per minute (children 80 to 100, babies 100 to 140). You should know how to take a temperature and a pulse rate. As a general rule the pulse increases about 20 beats per minute for each °C (or 2°F) rise in fever.

Respiration (breathing) rate is also an indicator of illness. Count the number of breaths per minute: between 12 and 20 is normal for adults and older children (up to 30 for younger children, 40 for babies). People with a high fever or serious respiratory illness (like pneumonia) breathe more quickly than normal. More than 40 shallow breaths a minute usually means pneumonia.

In western countries with safe water and excellent human waste disposal systems we often take good health for granted. In years gone by, when public health facilities were not as good as they are today, certain rules attached to eating and drinking were observed, for example, washing your hands before a meal. It is important for people travelling in areas of Egypt with poor sanitation to be aware of this and adjust their own personal hygiene habits.

You can avoid insect bites by covering bare skin when insects are around, by screening windows or beds and by using insect repellents. Seek local advice: if you're told the water is unsafe due to jellyfish, crocodiles or bilharzia, don't go in. In situations where there is no information, discretion is the better part of valour.

Medical Problems & Treatment

Potential medical problems can be broken down into several areas. Firstly there are the problems caused by extremes of temperature, altitude or motion. Then there are diseases and illnesses caused through poor environmental sanitation, insect bites or stings, and animal or human contact. Simple cuts, bites and scratches can also cause problems.

Self-diagnosis and treatment can be risky, so wherever possible seek qualified help. Although we do give drug dosages in this section, they are for emergency use only. Medical advice should be sought where possible before administering any drugs.

An embassy or consulate can usually recommend a good place to go for such advice. So can five star hotels, although they often recommend doctors with five star prices. (This is when that medical insurance really comes in handy!)

Hospitals There are hospitals throughout Egypt; for hospital addresses, refer to Medical Services in the Information section of cities and major towns. Most of the doctors are well trained and often have to deal with a greater variety of diseases and ailments than their western counterparts. On the other hand, most medical facilities are *not* well equipped and, consequently, it is not unusual for diagnoses to be inaccurate. If you need an operation, don't have it here. London or other European cities are only a few hours away by plane.

Some hospitals require you to pay a deposit of about E£500 if you are admitted; check with the hospital when you get there.

HEALTH

Climatic & Geographical Considerations
Sunburn In the tropics, the desert or at high altitude you can get sunburnt surprisingly quickly, even through cloud. Use a sun screen and take extra care to cover areas which don't normally see sun – for example, your feet. A hat provides added protection, and you should also use zinc cream or some other barrier cream for your nose and lips. Calamine lotion is good for mild sunburn.

Prickly Heat Prickly heat is an itchy rash caused by excessive perspiration trapped under the skin. It usually strikes people who have just arrived in a hot climate and whose pores have not yet opened sufficiently to cope with greater sweating. Keeping cool but bathing often, using a mild talcum powder or even resorting to air-con may help until you acclimatise.

Heat Exhaustion Dehydration or salt deficiency can cause heat exhaustion. Take time to acclimatise to high temperatures and make sure you get sufficient liquids. Wear loose clothing and a broad-brimmed hat. Do not do anything too physically demanding.

Salt deficiency is characterised by fatigue, lethargy, headaches, giddiness and muscle cramps and in this case salt tablets may help. Vomiting or diarrhoea can deplete your liquid and salt levels. Anhydrotic heat exhaustion, caused by an inability to sweat, is quite rare. Unlike the other forms of heat exhaustion it is likely to strike people who have been in a hot climate for some time, rather than newcomers.

Heat Stroke This serious, sometimes fatal, condition can occur if the body's heat-regulating mechanism breaks down and the body temperature rises to dangerous levels. Long, continuous periods of exposure to high temperatures can leave you vulnerable to heat stroke. Avoid excessive alcohol or strenuous activity when you first arrive in a hot climate.

The symptoms are feeling unwell, not sweating very much, if at all, and a high body temperature (39 to 41°C). Where sweating has ceased the skin becomes flushed and red.

Severe, throbbing headaches and lack of coordination will also occur, and the sufferer may be confused or aggressive. Eventually the victim will become delirious or convulse. Hospitalisation is essential, but meanwhile get victims out of the sun, remove their clothing, cover them with a wet sheet or towel and then fan continually.

Fungal Infections Fungal infections, which occur with greater frequency in hot weather, are most likely to occur on the scalp, between the toes or fingers (athlete's foot), in the groin (jock itch or crotch rot) and on the body (ringworm). You get ringworm (which is a fungal infection, not a worm) from infected animals or by walking on damp areas, like shower floors.

To prevent fungal infections wear loose, comfortable clothes, avoid artificial fibres, wash frequently and dry carefully. If you do get an infection, wash the infected area daily with a disinfectant or medicated soap and water, and rinse and dry well. Apply an anti-fungal powder like the widely available Tinaderm. Try to expose the infected area to air or sunlight as much as possible and wash all towels and underwear in hot water as well as changing them often.

Motion Sickness Eating lightly before and during a trip will reduce the chances of motion sickness. If you are prone to motion sickness try to find a place that minimises disturbance – near the wing on aircraft, close to midships on boats, near the centre on buses. Fresh air usually helps; reading and cigarette smoke don't. Commercial motion-sickness preparations, which can cause drowsiness, have to be taken before the trip commences; when you're feeling sick it's too late. Ginger and peppermint sweets are available in capsule form.

Jet Lag Jet lag is experienced when a person travels by air across more than three time zones (each time zone usually represents a one hour time difference). It occurs because many of the functions of the human body (such as temperature, pulse rate and emptying of the bladder and bowels) are regulated by internal 24 hour cycles called circadian rhythms. When we travel long distances rapidly, our bodies take time to adjust to the 'new time' of our destination, and we may experience fatigue, disorientation, insomnia, anxiety, impaired concentration and loss of appetite. These effects will usually be gone within three days of arrival, but there are ways of minimising the impact of jet lag:

* Rest for a couple of days prior to departure; try to avoid late nights and last-minute dashes for travellers' cheques, passport etc.
* Try to select flight schedules that minimise sleep deprivation; arriving late in the day means you can go to sleep soon after you arrive. For very long flights, try to organise a stopover.
* Avoid excessive eating (which bloats the stomach) and alcohol (which causes dehydration) during the flight. Instead, drink plenty of non-carbonated, non-alcoholic drinks such as fruit juice or water.
* Avoid smoking, as this reduces the amount of oxygen in the aeroplane cabin even further and causes greater fatigue.
* Make yourself comfortable by wearing loose-fitting clothes and perhaps bringing an eye mask and ear plugs to help you sleep.

Infectious Diseases

Diarrhoea A change of water, food or climate can all cause the runs; diarrhoea caused by contaminated food or water is more serious. Despite all your precautions you may still have a mild bout of travellers' diarrhoea, known locally as Pharaoh's Revenge, but a few rushed toilet trips with no other symptoms is not indicative of a serious problem. Moderate diarrhoea, involving half-a-dozen loose movements in a day, is more of a nuisance.

Dehydration is the main danger with any diarrhoea, particularly for children for whom dehydration can occur quite quickly. Fluid replacement remains the mainstay of management. Weak black tea with a little sugar, soda water, or soft drinks allowed to go flat and diluted 50% with water are all good. With severe diarrhoea a rehydrating solution is necessary to replace minerals and salts. Commercially available ORS (oral rehydration salts) are very useful; add the contents of one sachet to a litre of boiled or bottled water. In an emergency you can make up a solution of eight teaspoons of sugar to a litre of boiled water and provide salted cracker biscuits at the same time. Stick to a bland diet as you recover.

Lomotil or Imodium can be used to bring relief from the symptoms, although they do not actually cure the problem. Only use these drugs if absolutely necessary – for example, if you *must* travel. For children under 12 years Lomotil and Imodium are not recommended. Under all circumstances fluid replacement is the most important thing to remember. Do not use these drugs if the person has a high fever or is severely dehydrated.

In certain situations antibiotics may be indicated:

* Watery diarrhoea with blood and mucous. (Gut-paralysing drugs like Imodium or Lomotil should be avoided in this situation.)
* Watery diarrhoea with fever and lethargy.
* Persistent diarrhoea for more than five days.
* Severe diarrhoea, if it is logistically difficult to stay in one place.

The recommended drugs (adults only) would be either norfloxacin 400 mg twice daily for three days or ciprofloxacin 500 mg twice daily for three days.

The drug bismuth subsalicylate has also been used successfully. It is not available in Australia. The dosage for adults is two tablets or 30 ml, and for children it is one tablet or 10 ml. This dose can be repeated every 30 minutes to one hour, with no more than eight doses in a 24 hour period.

The drug of choice for children would be co-trimoxazole (Bactrim, Septrin, Resprim) with dosage dependent on weight. A three day course is also given.

Ampicillin has been recommended in the past and may still be an alternative.

Giardiasis The parasite causing this intestinal disorder is present in contaminated water. The symptoms are stomach cramps, nausea, a bloated stomach, watery, foul-smelling diarrhoea and frequent gas. Giardiasis can appear several weeks after you have been exposed to the parasite. The symptoms may disappear for a few days and then return; this can go on for several weeks. Tinidazole, known as Fasigyn, or metronidazole (Flagyl) are the recommended drugs for treatment. Either can be used in a single treatment dose. Antibiotics are of no use.

Dysentery This serious illness is caused by contaminated food or water and is characterised by severe diarrhoea, often with blood or mucus in the stool. There are two kinds of dysentery. Bacillary dysentery is characterised by a high fever and rapid onset; headache, vomiting and stomach pains are also symptoms. It generally does not last longer than a week, but it is highly contagious.

Amoebic dysentery is often more gradual in the onset of symptoms, with cramping abdominal pain and vomiting less likely; fever may not be present. It is not a self-limiting disease: it will persist until treated and can recur and cause long-term health problems.

A stool test is necessary to diagnose which kind of dysentery you have, so you should seek medical help urgently. In case of an emergency the drugs norfloxacin or ciprofloxacin can be used as presumptive treatment for bacillary dysentery, and metronidazole (Flagyl) for amoebic dysentery.

For bacillary dysentery, norfloxacin 400 mg twice daily for seven days or ciprofloxacin 500 mg twice daily for seven days are the recommended dosages. If you're unable to find either of these drugs then a useful alternative is co-trimoxazole 160/800 mg (Bactrim, Septrin, Resprim) twice daily for seven days. This is a sulpha drug and must not be used by people with a known sulpha allergy. In the case of children the drug co-trimoxazole is a reasonable first-line treatment.

For amoebic dysentery, the recommended adult dosage of metronidazole (Flagyl) is one 750 to 800 mg capsule three times daily for five days. Children aged between eight and 12 years should have half the adult dose;

the dosage for younger children is one third of the adult dose. An alternative to Flagyl is Fasigyn, taken as a two gram daily dose for three days. Alcohol must be avoided during treatment and for 48 hours afterwards.

Cholera Cholera vaccination is not very effective. The bacteria responsible for this disease are waterborne, so attention to the rules of eating and drinking should protect the traveller.

Outbreaks of cholera are generally widely reported, so you can avoid such problem areas. The disease is characterised by a sudden onset of acute diarrhoea with 'rice water' stools, vomiting, muscular cramps, and extreme weakness. You need medical help – but treat for dehydration, which can be extreme, and if there is an appreciable delay in getting to hospital then begin taking tetracycline. The adult dose is 250 mg four times daily. It is not recommended for children aged eight years or under nor for pregnant women. An alternative drug is Ampicillin. Remember that while antibiotics might kill the bacteria, it is a toxin produced by the bacteria which causes the massive fluid loss. Fluid replacement is by far the most important aspect of treatment.

Viral Gastroenteritis This is caused not by bacteria but, as the name suggests, by a virus. It is characterised by stomach cramps, diarrhoea, and sometimes by vomiting and/or a slight fever. All you can do is rest and drink lots of fluids.

Hepatitis Hepatitis is a general term for inflammation of the liver. There are many causes of this condition: drugs, alcohol and infections are but a few.

The discovery of new strains has led to a virtual alphabet soup, with hepatitis A, B, C, D, E and a rumoured G. These letters identify specific agents that cause viral hepatitis. Viral hepatitis is an infection of the liver, which can lead to jaundice (yellow skin), fever, lethargy and digestive problems. It can have no symptoms at all, with the infected person not knowing that they have the disease. Travellers shouldn't be too paranoid about this apparent proliferation of hepatitis strains; hep C, D, E and G are fairly rare (so far) and following the same precautions as for A and B should be all that's necessary to avoid them.

Viral hepatitis can be divided into two groups on the basis of how it is spread. The first route of transmission is via contaminated food and water, and the second route is via blood and bodily fluids.

The following types of hepatitis are spread by contaminated food and water:

Hepatitis A This is a common disease in Egypt. Most people in countries where Hepatitis A is common are infected as children; they often don't develop symptoms, but do develop life-long immunity. The disease poses a real threat to the traveller, as people are unlikely to have been exposed to hepatitis A in Western countries.

The symptoms are fever, chills, headache, fatigue, feelings of weakness and aches and pains, followed by loss of appetite, nausea, vomiting, abdominal pain, dark urine, light coloured faeces, jaundiced skin and the whites of the eyes may turn yellow. In some cases you may feel unwell, tired, have no appetite, experience aches and pains and be jaundiced. You should seek medical advice, but in general there is not much you can do apart from resting, drinking lots of fluids, eating lightly and avoiding fatty foods. People who have had hepatitis must forego alcohol for six months after the illness, as hepatitis attacks the liver and it needs that amount of time to recover.

The routes of transmission are via contaminated water, shellfish contaminated by sewerage, or foodstuffs sold by food handlers with poor standards of hygiene. Taking care with what you eat and drink can therefore go a long way towards preventing this disease. But this is a very infectious virus, so if there is any risk of exposure, additional cover is highly recommended. This cover comes in two forms: gamma globulin and Havrix. Gamma globulin is an injection where you are given the antibodies for hepatitis A, which provide immunity for a limited time. Havrix is a vaccine, where you develop your own antibodies, which gives lasting immunity. (See the earlier Immunisations section for more information.)

Hepatitis E This is a very recently discovered virus, of which little is yet known. It appears to be rather common in some African and Middle Eastern countries, generally causing mild hepatitis, although it can be very serious in pregnant women.

Care with water supplies is the only current prevention, as there are no specific vaccines for this type of hepatitis. At present it doesn't appear to be too great a risk for travellers.

The following strains are spread by contact with blood and bodily fluids:

Hepatitis B This is also a very common disease, with almost 300 million chronic carriers in the world. Hepatitis B, which used to be called serum hepatitis, is spread through contact with infected blood, blood products or bodily fluids, for example through sexual contact, unsterilised needles and blood transfusions or via small breaks in the skin. Other risk situations include having a shave or tattoo in a local shop, or having your body pierced.

The symptoms of type B are much the same as type A except that they are more severe and may lead to irreparable liver damage or even liver cancer. Although there is no treatment for hepatitis B, a cheap and effective vaccine is available; the only problem is that for long-lasting cover you need a six month course. The immunisation schedule requires two injections at least a month apart followed by a third dose five months after the second. Persons who should receive a hepatitis B vaccination include anyone who anticipates contact with blood or other bodily secretions, either as a healthcare worker or through sexual contact with the local population, particularly those who intend to stay in the country for a long period of time.

Hepatitis C This is another recently defined virus. It is a concern because it seems to lead to liver disease more rapidly than hepatitis B. The virus is spread by contact with blood – usually via contaminated transfusions or shared needles. Avoiding these is the only means of prevention, as there is no available vaccine.

Hepatitis D Often referred to as the 'Delta' virus, this infection only occurs in chronic carriers of hepatitis B. It is transmitted by blood and bodily fluids. Again there is no vaccine for this virus, so avoidance is the best prevention. The risk to travellers is certainly limited.

Typhoid Typhoid fever is another gut infection that travels the faecal-oral route – that is, via contaminated water and food. Vaccination against typhoid is not totally effective and it is one of the most dangerous infections, so medical help must be sought.

In its early stages typhoid resembles many other illnesses: sufferers may feel like they have a bad cold or flu on the way, as early symptoms are a headache, a sore throat, and a fever which rises a little each day until it is around 40°C or more. The victim's pulse is often slow relative to the degree of fever present and gets slower as the fever rises – unlike a normal fever where the pulse increases. There may also be vomiting, diarrhoea or constipation.

In the second week the high fever and slow pulse continue and a few pink spots may appear on the body; trembling, delirium, weakness, weight loss and dehydration are other symptoms. If there are no further complications, the fever and other symptoms will slowly diminish during the third week. However, you must get medical help before this, firstly because pneumonia (acute infection of the lungs) or peritonitis (perforated bowel) are common complications and secondly, because typhoid is very infectious.

The fever should be treated by keeping the victim cool and dehydration should also be watched for.

The drug of choice is ciprofloxacin at a dose of one gram daily for 14 days. It is quite expensive and may not be available. The alternative, chloramphenicol, has been the mainstay of treatment for many years. In many countries it is still the recommended antibiotic but there are fewer side affects with Ampicillin. The adult dosage is two 250-mg capsules, four times a day. Children aged between eight and 12 years should have half the adult dose; younger children should have one third of the adult dose.

People who are allergic to penicillin should not be given Ampicillin.

Worms These parasites are most common in rural, tropical areas and a stool test when you return home is not a bad idea. They can be present on unwashed vegetables or in undercooked meat and you can pick them up through your skin by walking in bare feet. Infestations may not show up for some time, and although they are generally not serious, if left untreated they can cause severe health problems. A stool test is necessary to pinpoint the problem and medication is often available over the counter.

Tetanus This potentially fatal disease is found in undeveloped tropical areas. It is difficult to treat but is preventable with immunisation. Tetanus occurs when a wound becomes infected by a germ which lives in soil the faeces horses and other animals, so clean all cuts, punctures or animal bites. Tetanus is also known as lockjaw, and the first symptom may be discomfort in swallowing, or stiffening of the jaw and neck; this is followed by painful convulsions of the jaw and whole body.

Rabies Rabies is a fatal viral infection found in many countries. It is caused by a bite or scratch from an infected animal. Dogs are noted carriers, as are monkeys and cats. Any bite, scratch or even lick from a warm-blooded, furry animal should be cleaned immediately and thoroughly. Scrub with soap and running water, and then clean with an alcohol or iodine solution. If there is any possibility that the animal is infected medical help should be sought immediately to prevent the onset of symptoms and death. In a person who has not been immunised against rabies this involves having five injections of vaccine and one of immunoglobulin over 28 days starting as soon as possible after the exposure. Even if the animal is not rabid, all bites should be treated seriously as they can become infected or can result in tetanus.

A rabies vaccination is now available and should be considered if you are in a high-risk category – for example, if you intend to explore caves (bat bites can be dangerous) or work with animals.

Meningococcal Meningitis This is a bacterial infection of the lining of the brain. It is endemic along the Nile.

The disease is spread by close contact with people who carry it in their throats and noses, who spread it through coughs and sneezes and may not be aware that they are carriers.

This very serious disease attacks the brain and can be fatal. A scattered, blotchy rash, fever, severe headache, sensitivity to light and neck stiffness which prevents forward bending of the head are the first symptoms. Death can occur within a few hours, so immediate treatment is crucial.

Treatment is large doses of penicillin given intravenously, or, if that is not possible, intramuscularly (that is, in the buttocks). Vaccination offers good protection for over a year, but you should also check for reports of current epidemics.

Tuberculosis (TB) There is a worldwide resurgence of Tuberculosis. It is a bacterial infection which is usually transmitted from person to person by coughing but may be transmitted through consumption of unpasteurised milk. Milk that has been boiled is safe to drink, and the souring of milk to make yoghurt or cheese also kills the bacilli. Typically many months of contact with the infected person are required before the disease is passed on. The usual site of the

disease is the lungs, although other organs may be involved. Most infected people never develop symptoms. In those who do, especially infants, symptoms may arise within weeks of the infection occurring and may be severe. In most, however, the disease lies dormant for many years until, for some reason, the infected person becomes physically run down. Symptoms include fever, weight loss, night sweats and coughing.

Bilharzia Bilharzia is carried in water by minute worms. The larvae infect certain varieties of freshwater snails found in rivers, streams, lakes and particularly behind dams. The worms multiply and are eventually discharged into the water surrounding the snails.

They attach themselves to your intestines or bladder, where they produce large numbers of eggs. The worm enters through the skin, and the first symptom may be a tingling and sometimes a light rash around the area where it entered. Weeks later, when the worm is busy producing eggs, a high fever may develop. A general feeling of being unwell may be the first symptom; once the disease is established abdominal pain and blood in the urine are other signs. The infection often causes no symptoms until the disease is well established (several months to years after exposure) and damage to internal organs irreversible.

Bilharzia is prevalent in Egypt. The Nile and the Nile Delta are infested with the parasite – do not drink, wash, paddle or even stand in water that may be infested, and do *not* swim in the Nile! If you must do so in the middle, where the risk of being infected is much lower than along the banks. If you do get wet, dry off quickly and dry your clothes as well. Seek medical attention if you have been exposed to the disease – even if you don't have symptoms – and tell the doctor your suspicions, as bilharzia in the early stages can be confused with malaria or typhoid. If you cannot get medical help immediately, praziquantel (Biltricide) is the recommended treatment. The recommended dosage is 40 mg/kg in divided doses over one day. Niridazole is an alternative drug.

Diphtheria Diphtheria can be a skin infection or a more dangerous throat infection. It is spread by contaminated dust contacting the skin or by the inhalation of infected cough or sneeze droplets. Frequent washing and keeping the skin dry will help prevent skin infection. A vaccination is available to prevent the throat infection.

Sexually Transmitted Diseases Sexual contact with an infected sexual partner spreads these diseases. While abstinence is the only 100% preventative, using condoms is also effective. Gonorrhoea, herpes and syphilis are the most common of these diseases; sores, blisters or rashes around the genitals, discharges or pain when urinating are common symptoms. Syphilis symptoms eventually disappear completely but the disease continues and can cause severe problems in later years. The treatment of gonorrhoea and syphilis is by antibiotics.

There are numerous other sexually transmitted diseases, for most of which effective treatment is available. However, there is no cure for herpes and there is also currently no cure for AIDS.

HIV/AIDS HIV, the Human Immunodeficiency Virus, may develop into AIDS, Acquired Immune Deficiency Syndrome. HIV is a major problem in many countries. While the reported cases in Egypt are relatively few, their numbers probably belie the real statistics as there is little public awareness of the problem. This is compounded by the fact that extramarital affairs, prostitution and homosexual relationships, though taboo, are all part of life in Egypt.

Any exposure to blood, blood products or bodily fluids may put the individual at risk. In many countries in Africa and the Middle East transmission is predominantly through heterosexual sexual activity. This is quite different from industrialised countries where transmission is mostly through contact between homosexual or bisexual males, or via contaminated needles shared by IV drug users. Apart from abstinence, the most effective preventative is always to practise safe sex using condoms. It is impossible to detect the HIV-positive status of an otherwise healthy-looking person without a blood test.

HIV/AIDS can also be spread through infected blood transfusions; some countries cannot afford to screen blood for transfusions, however, Egypt supposedly does screen. It can also be spread by dirty needles – vaccinations, acupuncture, tattooing and ear or nose piercing can potentially be as dangerous as intravenous drug use if the equipment is not clean. If you do need an injection, ask to see the syringe unwrapped in front of you, or better still, take a needle and syringe pack with you overseas – it is a cheap insurance package against infection with HIV.

Fear of HIV infection should never preclude treatment for serious medical conditions. Although there may be a risk of infection, it is very small indeed.

Insect-Borne Diseases

Insect-borne diseases such as malaria, dengue fever, typhus, filariasis and West Nile fever all occur along the Nile. The risk of contracting these diseases are low unless travelling off the beaten track. However, it would be wise to avoid insect bites.

Malaria This serious disease is spread by mosquito bites. Symptoms include headache, fever, chills and sweating which may subside and recur. Without treatment malaria can develop more serious, potentially fatal effects. Malaria risk exists from June to October in the Al-Faiyum area. Those intending to travel to this region are advised to consider taking malarial prophylactics. Antimalarial drugs do not prevent you from being infected but kill the parasites during a stage in their development.

There are a number of different types of malaria. The type that is of most concern is falciparum malaria, responsible for the very serious cerebral malaria. Falciparum is the predominant form in Egypt. Contrary to popular belief cerebral malaria is not a new strain.

Expert advice should be sought, as there are many factors to consider when deciding on the type of antimalarial medication, including the area to be visited, the risk of exposure to malaria-carrying mosquitoes, your current medical condition, and your age and pregnancy status. It is also important to discuss the side-effect profile of the medication, so you can work out some level of risk versus benefit ratio. Be sure of the correct dosage of the medication prescribed to you. Some people have inadvertently taken weekly medication (chloroquine) on a daily basis, with disastrous effects. While discussing dosages for prevention of malaria, it is often advisable to include the dosages required for treatment, especially if your trip is through a high-risk area that would isolate you from medical care.

The main messages are:

Primary prevention must always be in the form of mosquito-avoidance measures. The mosquitoes that transmit malaria bite from dusk to dawn and during this period travellers are advised to:
- wear light coloured clothing
- wear long pants and long sleeved shirts
- use mosquito repellents containing the compound DEET on exposed areas (overuse of DEET may be harmful, especially to children, but its use is considered preferable to being bitten by disease-transmitting mosquitoes)
- avoid highly scented perfumes or aftershave
- use a mosquito net – it may be worth taking your own

While no antimalarial is 100% effective, taking the most appropriate drug significantly reduces the risk of contracting the disease.

No one should ever die from malaria. It can be diagnosed by a simple blood test. Symptoms range from fever, chills and sweating, headache and abdominal pains to a vague feeling of ill-health, so seek examination immediately if there is any suggestion of malaria.

Contrary to popular belief, once a traveller contracts malaria he/she does not have it for life. The species of the parasite may lie dormant in the liver but they can also be eradicated using a specific medication.

Malaria is curable, as long as the traveller seeks medical help when symptoms occur.

Dengue Fever There is no prophylactic available for this mosquito-spread disease; the main preventative measure is to avoid mosquito bites. A sudden onset of fever, headaches and severe joint and muscle pains are the first signs before a rash starts on the trunk of the body and spreads to the limbs and face. After a further few days, the fever will subside and recovery will begin. Serious complications are not common but full recovery can take up to a month or more.

West Nile Fever This is a dengue fever-like virus, transmitted by mosquitoes.

Filariasis This is a mosquito-transmitted parasitic infection which is found in many parts of Africa, including Egypt. There is a range of possible manifestations of the infection, depending on which filarial parasite species has caused the infection. These include fever, pain and swelling of the lymph glands; inflammation of lymph drainage areas; swelling of a limb or the scrotum; skin rashes and blindness. Treatment is available to eliminate the parasites from the body, but some of the damage they cause may not be reversible. Medical advice should be obtained promptly if the infection is suspected.

Typhus Typhus is spread by ticks, mites or lice. It begins with fever, chills, headache and muscle pains followed a few days later by a body rash. There is often a large painful sore at the site of the bite and nearby lymph nodes are swollen and painful. Treatment is with tetracycline, or chloramphenicol under medical supervision.

Tick typhus is spread by ticks. Trekkers may be at risk from cattle or wild-animal ticks. Scrub typhus is spread by mites that feed on infected rodents, but this strain of typhus exists mainly in Asia and the Pacific Islands. Seek local advice on areas where ticks pose a danger and always check your skin carefully for ticks after walking in a

HEALTH

danger area. A strong insect repellent can help, and serious walkers in tick areas should consider having their boots and trousers impregnated with benzyl benzoate and dibutylphthalate.

Cuts, Bites & Stings

Cuts & Scratches Skin punctures can easily become infected in hot climates and may be difficult to heal. Treat any cut with an antiseptic such as povidone-iodine. Where possible avoid bandages and Band-Aids, which can keep wounds wet. Coral cuts are notoriously slow to heal, as the coral injects a weak venom into the wound. You can avoid coral cuts by not walking on reefs or touching corals – both activities are harmful to the corals anyway. Should you get a cut, clean it thoroughly with sodium peroxide, if available.

Bites & Stings Bee and wasp stings are usually painful rather than dangerous. Calamine lotion or Stingose spray will give relief and ice packs will reduce the pain and swelling. There are some spiders with dangerous bites but antivenenes are usually available. Scorpion stings are notoriously painful; scorpions often shelter in shoes or clothing.

There are various fish and other sea creatures which can sting or bite dangerously or which are dangerous to eat. Again, local advice is the best suggestion.

Snakes To minimise your chances of being bitten always wear boots, socks and long trousers when walking through undergrowth or desert environments where snakes may be present. Don't put your hands into holes and crevices, and be careful when collecting firewood.

Snake bites do not cause instantaneous death and antivenenes are usually available. Keep the victim calm and still, wrap the bitten limb tightly, as you would for a sprained ankle, and then attach a splint to immobilise it. Then seek medical help, if possible with the dead snake for identification. Don't attempt to catch the snake if there is even a remote possibility of being bitten

again. Tourniquets and sucking out the poison are now comprehensively discredited.

Jellyfish Local advice is the best way of avoiding contact with these sea creatures which have stinging tentacles. Dousing in vinegar will de-activate any stingers which have not 'fired'. Calamine lotion, antihistamines and analgesics may reduce the reaction and relieve the pain.

Bedbugs & Lice Bedbugs live in various places, but particularly in dirty mattresses and bedding. Spots of blood on bedclothes or on the wall around the bed can be read as a suggestion to find another hotel. Bedbugs leave itchy bites in neat rows. Calamine lotion may help.

All lice cause itching and discomfort. They make themselves at home in your hair (head lice), your clothing (body lice) or in your pubic hair (crabs). You catch lice through direct contact with infected people or by sharing combs, clothing and the like. Powder or shampoo treatment will kill the lice and infected clothing should then be washed in very hot water.

Women's Health

Gynaecological Problems Poor diet, lowered resistance due to the use of antibiotics for stomach upsets and even the use of contraceptive pills can lead to vaginal infections when travelling in hot climates. Keeping the genital area clean, and wearing skirts or loose-fitting trousers and cotton underwear will help to prevent infections.

Yeast infections, characterised by a rash, itch and discharge, can be treated with a vinegar or lemon-juice douche, or with yoghurt. Nystatin suppositories are the usual medical prescription. Trichomoniasis and gardnerella are more serious infections; symptoms are a smelly discharge and sometimes a burning sensation when urinating. Male sexual partners must also be treated, and if a vinegar-water douche is not effective medical attention should be sought. Metronidazole (Flagyl) is the prescribed drug.

Pregnancy Most miscarriages occur during the first three months of pregnancy, so this is the most risky time to travel as far as your own health is concerned. Miscarriage is not uncommon, and can occasionally lead to severe bleeding. The last three months of pregnancy should also be spent within reasonable distance of good medical care. A baby born as early as 24 weeks stands a chance of survival, but only in a good modern hospital.

Pregnant women should avoid all unnecessary medication, but vaccinations and malarial prophylactics should still be taken where possible. Additional care should be taken to prevent illness and particular attention should be paid to diet and nutrition. Alcohol and nicotine, for example, should be avoided.

Women travellers often find that their periods become irregular or even cease while they're on the road. Remember that a missed period in these circumstances doesn't necessarily indicate pregnancy. There are health posts or Family Planning clinics in Egypt, where you can seek advice and have a urine test to determine whether or not you are pregnant.

Glossary

abd – son, servant
abu – father, saint
ahwa – coffee
'ain – well, spring

bab – stone gate built in medieval times
bahr – river
baladi – local, rural
bayt – house
bir – spring, well
birket – lake
Book of the Dead – ancient theological compositions, or hymns, that were the subject of most of the colourful paintings and reliefs on tomb walls. Extracts from these so-called books were believed to assist the deceased person safely into the afterlife via the Kingdom of the Dead. The texts were sometimes also painted on a roll of papyrus and buried with the dead.
burg – tower

caliph – Islamic ruler; also spelt khalif
Canopic jars – pottery jars which held the embalmed internal organs and viscera (liver, stomach, lungs, intestines) of the mummified Pharaoh. They were placed in the burial chamber near the sarcophagus.
capitals – in Pharaonic and Graeco-Roman architecture the top, or capital, of a column was decorated with plant forms, such as the papyrus, palm or lotus, or other motifs, like the human face and cow's ears of the goddess Hathor
caravanserai – large inn enclosing a courtyard, providing accommodation for caravans
careta – donkey cart
cartouche – oblong figure enclosing the hieroglyphs of royal or divine names
cenotaph – symbolic tomb, temple or place of cult worship that was additional to the Pharaoh's actual burial place

darb – track, street
deir – monastery, convent

electrum – alloy of gold and silver used for jewellery, ornaments and decorating buildings
emir – Islamic ruler, military commander or governor

false door – fake, seemingly half-open ka door in a tomb wall which enabled the Pharaoh's spirit, or life force, to come and go at will
fellahin – the peasant farmers or agricultural workers who make up the majority of Egypt's population. Fellahin literally means ploughman or tiller of the soil.

gaffir – caretaker, guard
galabiyya – full-length robe worn by men
gebel – mountain or mountain range
geziret – island
ghard – desert sand dune
girish – piastre
guinay – pound

haj – pilgrimage to Mecca. All Muslims should make the journey at least once in their lifetime.
hamman – bathhouse
hantour – horse-drawn carriage
haramlik – women's quarters
haret – small lane, alley
Heb-Sed Festival – five day celebration of royal rejuvenation, held after 30 years of a Pharaoh's reign and then every three years thereafter
Heb-Sed Race – traditional re-enactment, during the Heb-Sed Festival, of a Pharaoh's coronation. The king sat first on the throne of Upper Egypt and then on the throne of Lower Egypt to symbolise the unification of the country and the renewal of his reign.
hieroglyphs – ancient Egyptian form of writing, which used pictures and symbols to represent objects, words or sounds
hypostyle hall – hall in which the roof is supported by columns

iconostasis – screen with doors and icons set in tiers, used in eastern Christian churches

imam – a man schooled in Islam and who often doubles as the muezzin

ithyphallic – denoting the erect phallus of a Pharaoh or god (usually used in reference to the god Min); a sign of fertility

iwan – vaulted hall, opening into a central court, in the madrassa of a mosque

ka – spirit, or 'double', of a living person which gained its own identity with the death of that person. The survival of the ka, however, required the continued existence of the body, hence mummification. The ka was also the vital force emanating from a god and transferred through the Pharaoh to his people.

khamsin – hot wind from the Western Desert

khedive – Egyptian viceroy under Ottoman suzerainty (1867-1914)

kineesa – church

kiosk – open-sided pavilion

kuttab – Qur'anic school for boys

lotus – white waterlily regarded as sacred by the ancient Egyptians, who likened their land to the lotus – the Nile Delta was the flower, Al-Faiyum the bud, and the Nile and its valley the stem. The lotus was specifically identified with Upper Egypt.

madrassa – theological college that is part of a noncongregational mosque

mammisi – birth house. In these small chapels or temples, erected in the vicinity of a main temple, the rituals of the divine birth of the living king were performed. All Pharaohs were believed to be incarnations of the falcon-god Horus.

mashrabiyyah – ornate carved wooden panel or screen; a feature of Islamic architecture

mastaba – Arabic word for 'bench'; a mud-brick structure above tombs from which the pyramids were developed

midan – town or city square

mihrab – niche in the wall of a mosque that indicates the direction of Mecca

minbar – pulpit in a mosque

misr – another name for Egypt and Cairo; also written as Masr

mortuary complex – a Pharaoh's last resting place. It usually comprised: a pyramid which was the king's tomb and the repository for all his household goods, clothes and treasure; a funerary temple on the east side of the pyramid which served as a cult temple for worship of the dead Pharaoh; pits for the solar barques; a valley temple on the banks of the Nile, where the mummification process was carried out; and a massive causeway from the river to the pyramid.

moulid – festival celebrating the birthday of a local saint or holy person

muezzin – mosque official who calls the faithful to prayer five times a day from the minaret

mugzzabin – Sufi followers who participate in zikrs in order to achieve unity with Allah

natron – whitish mineral of hydrated sodium carbonate that occurs in saline deposits and salt lakes and acts as a natural preservative. It was used in ancient Egypt to pack and dry the body during mummification.

Nilometer – pit descending into the Nile containing a central column marked with graduations. The marks were used to measure and record the level of the river, especially during the inundation.

nome – administrative division or province of ancient Egypt, introduced during the Old Kingdom era. There were 22 nomes in Upper Egypt and 20 in Lower Egypt.

obelisk – monolithic stone pillar, with square sides tapering to a pyramidal, often guilded, top; used as a monument in ancient Egypt. Obelisks were usually carved from pink granite and set up in pairs at the entrance to a tomb or temple. A single obelisk was sometimes the object of cult worship.

Opet Festival – celebration held in Luxor (Thebes) during the Nile inundation season, when statues of the Theban triad – Amun, Mut and Khons – would be transported by

river from Karnak Temple to Luxor Temple
to join in the festivities

papyrus – plant identified with Lower
Egypt; writing material made from the pith
of this plant; a document written on such
paper

porphyry – from Greek *porphyros* (purple);
a reddish-purple rock highly resistant to
erosion. Many sarcophagi were made from
this rock.

pylon – monumental gateway at the entrance
to a temple

pyramid texts – paintings and reliefs on the
walls of the internal rooms and burial
chamber of pyramids and often on the sarcophagus itself. The texts recorded the
Pharaoh's burial ceremonies, associated
temple rituals, the hymns vital to his passage
into the afterlife and, sometimes, major
events in his life.

qasr – castle

ramadan – ninth month of the lunar Islamic
calendar during which Muslims fast from
sunrise to sunset

ras – headland

sabil – covered public drinking fountain

sarcophagus – huge stone or marble coffin
used to encase other wooden coffins and the
mummy of the Pharaoh or queen

scarab – dung beetle regarded as sacred in
ancient Egypt and represented on amulets or
in hieroglyphs as a symbol of the sun-god Ra

selamlik – men's quarters

serapeum – network of subterranean galleries constructed as tombs for the mummified
sacred Apis bulls; the most important temple
of the Graeco-Egyptian god Serapis

serdab – hidden cellar in a tomb, or a stone
room in front of some pyramids, containing
a coffin with a life-size, lifelike, painted

statue of the dead king. Serdabs were
designed so that the Pharaoh's ka could communicate with the outside world.

sharia – Arabic for road or way

shari'a – Islamic law, the body of doctrine
that regulates the lives of Muslims

sharm – bay

shay – tea

shisha – waterpipe

solar barque – wooden boat placed in or
around the Pharaoh's tomb. It was the symbolic vessel of transport for his journey over
the sea of death to the Kingdom of the Dead
to be judged before Osiris, and for his final
passage to the eternal afterlife.

souq – market

speos – rock-cut tomb or chapel

stele (pl: stelae) – stone or wooden commemorative slab or column decorated with
inscriptions or figures

sufi – follower of any of the Islamic mystical
orders which emphasise dancing, chanting
and trances in order to attain unity with God

ulama – group of Muslim scholars or religious leaders; a member of this group

uraeus – rearing cobra with inflated hood,
associated with the goddess Renenutet. This
was the most characteristic symbol of Egyptian royalty and was worn on the Pharaoh's
forehead or crown. The sacred fire-spitting
serpent was an agent of destruction and protector of the king.

wadi – desert watercourse, dry except in the
rainy season

wahah – oasis

wakala – inn for travelling merchants. It was
built around a courtyard, with living quarters
above the warehouses and stables.

zikr – long sessions of dancing, chanting and
swaying usually carried out by Sufi mugzzabin to achieve oneness with God

Index

MAPS

Abydos 259
Al-Arish 473
Al-Minya 244
Al-Quseir 437
Alexandria 366-7
  Around Midan Saad Zaghloul
  371
  Central Alexandria 369
Around Cairo 219
Aswan 320
  Central Aswan 321
Aswan Dams 335
Asyut 252

Bahariyya Oasis 355
  Bawiti 356
Beni Suef 241

Cairo
  Central Cairo 142-3
  Doqqi 155
  Egyptian Museum 150-1
  Garden City 146
  Greater Cairo 138-9
  Heliopolis 158
  Islamic Cairo 160
  Islamic Cairo (Citadel Area) 162
  Khan al Khalili 170
  Mohandiseen & Agouza 156
  Mosque of Al-Hakim 174
  Old Cairo 178
  Ramses Station Area 210
  Zamalek 154
Dahab City & Assalah 458
Dakhla Oasis 347
  Mut 348
Deir al-Bahri 289

Dendara 263

Edfu & Temple of Horus 314
Egypt 12
  Highlights 10
  Regional Key Map 8
Esna 311

Farafra Oasis 352
  Qasr al-Farafra 353

Giza 181
  Great Pyramids of Giza 182

Hermopolis, Tuna al-Gebel &
  Tell al-Amarna 248
Hurghada Coast 421
  Ad-Dahar, Hurghada 422-3
  Sigala; Hurghada 424

Ismailia 409

Kharga Oasis 343
  Al Kharga 344

Luxor 268-9
  Around Luxor 266
  Karnak: Temple of Amun 274
  Luxor: the West Bank 279
  Luxor Temple 272

Marsa Matruh 393
Medinet al-Faiyum 229
Medinat Habu 298
Mediterranean Coast 365

Na'ama Bay 450
Nile Valley, The 240

Nuweiba 464

Port Said 402

Qena 261

Ramesseum, The 295
Red Sea Coast 418

Saqqara 220
  North Saqqara 222
Sharm el-Sheikh 449
Sinai 442
Siwa Oasis 358
  Siwa 359
Sohag 256
Southern Upper Egypt 312
St Catherine's Monastery 470
Suez & Port Tawfiq 414
Suez Canal 400

Temple of Horus 314
Temple of Kom Ombo 318
Temple of Philae 335
Tomb of Amenophis II 285
Tomb of Amunherkhepshep 297
Tomb of Horemheb 287
Tomb of Khaemhet 293
Tomb of Nakht 57
Tomb of Nefertari 296
Tomb of Ramose 292
Tomb of Tutankhamun 288
Tomb of Tuthmosis III 284
Tomb of Tuthmosis IV 285

Valley of the Kings 282

Western Oases, The 342

BOXED STORIES

Air Travel Glossary 116-17
Al-Hakim 175
Ancient Egyptian Cosmogonies
  159
Ancient Rites at Edfu 315
Balancing Sinai's Ecosystem
  444
Battle of El Alamein 390
Bedouins 445
Choosing a Dive Club 426

Code of Ethics for Reef
  Protection 27
Cult of Isis 336
Cult of Osiris 260
Dolphin of Nuweiba 463
EgyptAir Domestic Flights 126
Exhibit Highlights 150-2
Great Pyramids of Giza 184, **182**
Hatshepsut 290
Hazards of Night Driving 129

High Dam 338
In Search of that Special
  Souvenir 109
Islamic Holidays 96
Mahfouz Naguib – Cairo's
  Dickens & Nobel Laureate 36
Migratory Birds Under Threat 26
Moulid Celebrations 40
On the Road During Ramadan
  96

Papyrus 28
Pharos Lighthouse 375
Preparation for Life Eternal 14
Rescuing the Red Sea 425
Rosetta Stone 389
Safety Tips for Women
  Travellers 92
Sayyidna Al-Hussein 171

Shagarat Ad-Durr 163
Siwan Crafts 363
Telephone Codes 83
Things Change 113
Tips on Tipping: Mastering the
  Payment of Baksheesh 81
Tomb of Alexander the
  Great? 360

Tomb of the Sons of
  Ramses II 288
Travelling by Freighter 122
Troubles in the Nile Valley 245
Understanding Body
  Language 38

TEXT

Map references are in **bold** type.

Abbasids 17
Abu Mina 388
Abu Qir 378
Abu Shuruf 361
Abu Simbel 339-41
Abu Sir 225
Abu Zenima 447
Abydos 258-60, **259**
accommodation 101-3
  hostel card 74
Achmin 257
Ad-Dahar, see Hurghada
Ad-Din, Salah 18, 136, 441
afterlife 14
Agami Beach 378
Agiba Beach 394
Agouza 157, **156**
'ain As-Siliin 231
'ain Bishawi 353
'ain Qurayshat 361
'ain Safi 361
'ain Sukhna 418
air travel 113-19
  airports & airlines 113-14
  buying tickets 114-15
  departure tax 124
  special needs 115
  terminology 116-17
  to/from Egypt 115-19
  within Egypt 126
Aker 61
Akhenaten 15
Al-Arish 472-5, **473**
Al-Azhar Mosque 18
Al-Aziz 18
Al-Balyana 258-61
Al-Burg 239
Al-Faiyum 29
Al-Faiyum Oasis 228-33
Al-Hakim 18, 175
Al-Kab 313
Al-Kharga 343-6, **344**
Al-Minya 243-6, **244**
Al-Muizz 18
Al-Muzawaka Tombs 350

Al-Qahira 136
Al-Qasr 349
Al-Quseir 437-8, **437**
Al-Qusiya 251-2
alcohol 39
Alexander the Great 16, 359,
  360, 365
Alexandria 365-89, **366-7, 369,**
  371
  activities 378-9
  entertainment 384-5
  getting around 387-8
  getting there & away 385-7
  history 365-8
  information 370-3
  museums & galleries 373, 376-7
  orientation 368-70
  places to eat 382-4
  places to stay 379-82
  things to see 373-8
Ali, Mohammed 20, 367
Amenemhet 13
Amenophis II 15
Amenophis III 15
Amenophis IV 15
Amr 399, 441
Amun 62
antiquities permit 75
Anubis 62
Apis 62
Apophis 62
Arab Conquest, The 17-19
Arab League 21
Arabic 42
  Egyptian Colloquial Arabic 42
architecture 50-60
  columns 52-3
  cult temples 58-60
  early buildings 50-1
  funerary architecture 54-8
  Islamic 36-7
  mastabas 54-5
  pyramids 55-6
  rock-cut tombs 57-8
  temple architecture 50-60
Armant 310
arts 33-7

tomb art 34, 61-7
Assasif Tombs 291
Aswan 319-34, **320, 321**
  activities 326
  entertainment 331
  felucca rides 326, 332-3, 334
  getting around 334
  getting there & away 331-4
  history 319
  information 322
  orientation 320-2
  places to eat 330-1
  places to stay 327-30
  things to see 322-6
Aswan Dam 334-5, **335**
Asyut 252-4, **252**
Asyut Barrage 253
Aten 62
Atum 63
Ayyubids 19, 136
Az-Zahir 19
Az-Zeitun 361

Bahariyya 357
Bahariyya Oasis 354-7, **355**
baksheesh 81
Balat 349
ballooning 299
Baltim 239
Bar Lev Line 401, 443
bargaining 81, 109
Baris 347
bars 108
Bashandi 349-50
Bastet 63
Bawiti 354-7, **356**
Bedouins 33, 352, 361, 443-4
belly-dancing 35
Beni Hasan 246-7
Beni Suef 241-2, **241**
Bent Pyramid 227
Berbers 33, 359
Berenice 440
Bes 63
bicycles, see cycling
Bilad ar-Rum 361
Bir al-Gebel 350

Bir al-Ghaba 355
Bir al-Mattar 355
Bir Shalatayn 440
birds, see fauna 29
Birket Qarun 231
Birqash Camel Market 233-4
Black Mountain 355
boat travel 131-2
    departure taxes 124
    felucca 131
    ferry 131
    freighter 122
    to/from Egypt 122
    yacht 131-2
books 85-8, see also literature
    food 88
    guidebooks 85-6
    history & politics 86-7
    language 88
    Lonely Planet 85
    people, culture & society 87-8
    travel 85-6
    wildlife 88
border crossings 120
British Occupation 20-1
Bubastis 237
burial rituals 14
bus travel
    departure taxes 124
    to/from Egypt 121-2, 124
    within Egypt 127, 132
business hours 96
Buto 238
Byzantine Rule 17

Caesar, Julius 16
Cairo 18, 135-217, **138-9, 142-3,**
    146, 210, 219
    activities 187-9
    Agouza 157, **156**
    airport 113
    churches & monasteries 178-9
    Citadel, The 164-5
    City of the Dead 174-6
    cultural centres 147
    Doqqi 157, **155**
    Egyptian Museum 149-52,
    150-1
    entertainment 203-6
    getting around 212-17
    getting there & away 206-12
    Gezira 153-6, 157
    Giza 180-7
    Great Pyramids of Giza 13,
    181-6, **182**
    hammams 167, 172, 173, 188
    Heliopolis 157-9, **158**
    history 135-6
    information 137-49

Islamic Cairo 159-76, **162, 160**
    Khan al-Khalili 169-71, **170**
    medical services 148-9
    metro 132
    Mohandiseen **156**
    Monastery of St George 178
    mosques & mausoleums 161-76
    museums & galleries 149-57,
        168, 176, 178, 183
    Nilometer 177
    Old Cairo 177-80, **178**
    orientation 136-7
    places to eat 196-203
    places to stay 189-95
    registration 137
    shopping 171, 186-7, 206
    souqs 171
    Sphinx, The 185
    things to see & do 149-87
    tourist offices 140
    tours 189
    walking tours 161-76
    Zamalek 153-7, **154**
    zoo 186-7
camel caravans 357
camel markets 130, 233-4
camel rides
    Bahariyya 357
    Dahab 460
    Dakhla Oasis 349
    Hurghada (Al-Ghardaka) 427
    Luxor 299
    Na'ama Bay 452
    Nuweiba 465
camel travel 130-1
Camp David Agreement 401
camping 101
Canopic Way 373
Canopus 378
car travel 119-21, 129-30
    4WD 130
    Automobile & Touring Club of
        Egypt 120
    border crossings 120
    hazards 129
    insurance 120
    licence 120
    permits 119
    rental 130
    road rules 129-30
Careta 133
carpets 110
casinos 108
Catacombs of Kom
    ash-Shuqqafa 374-5
Cenotaph Temple of Seti I 259
Chatby Necropolis 377
Cheops 13
Chephren 13

children, travel with 93-4
Christianity 17, 366
Christians 42
churches 178-9
cinema 35, 108
Citadel, The, see Cairo
City of the Dead, see Cairo
Civil War 13
Cleopatra 16, 366
Cleopatra's Bath 361
Cleopatra's Beach 394
climate 24-5
coffee houses 108
Colossi of Memnon 15, 298-9
Coloured Canyon 463-5
conduct, see cultural
    considerations
consulates, see embassies
Coptic Christianity 17, 41-2,
    177, 234
Coptic Language 41
Cosmogonies 159
costs, see money
courses 99-100, 379
    American University 99-100
    Egyptian Universities 100
    language 99, 187-8
Crusaders 18
cult temples 58-60
cultural considerations 39
    attitudes to women 91-2
    body language 38
    dress 39, 93
culture 37-9
currency, see money
customs 78
    duty-free 78
cycling 120, 130
    Aswan 334
    Luxor 309

Dahab 30, 457-63, **458**
Dahshur 227
Dairut 250
Dakhla Oasis 347-52, **347**
Damietta 238
dance 34-5
dangers, see safety
Daraw 319
Darius 399
De Lesseps, Ferdinand 399
Deir Abu Makar (Makarios) 235
Deir al-Abyad 256
Deir al-Adhra 242
Deir al-Ahmar 256
Deir al-Anba Bishoi 235
Deir al-Bahri 289, **289**
Deir al-Baramus 235
Deir al-Haqqar 350

Deir al-Medina 294
Deir al-Muharraq 251
Deir as-Suriani 235
Dendara 262-3, **263**
departure taxes 124
disabled travellers 93-4
discos 108
diving & snorkelling 97-9
  Alexandria 378
  Cairo 188
  camel/diving safaris 98
  clubs & courses 98
  costs 98
  Dahab 459
  Gulf of Aqaba 448
  Hurghada (Al-Ghardaka) 426
  marine hazards 98-9
  Na'ama Bay 450
  Nuweiba 465
  Port Safaga 436
  Ras Mohammed 97
  Ras um Sid 451
  Red Sea Coast 98
  Sharm el-Sheikh 450-2
  Sinai Peninsula 97
  tours 125
donkey rides 131, 299
Doqqi 157, **155**
dress 93
drinks 106-7
  teahouses 108
drugs 94-5
Dumyat, *see* Damietta
duty-free 78

economy 31-2
Edfu 313-6, **314**
education 33
Egyptian Museum 149-52, **150-1**
El Alamein 390-1
El-Hamarawein 437
El-Tor 448
electricity 90
Elephantine Island 319, 323
embassies 75-8
entertainment 107-8
  gay bars 93
environmental considerations
  25-7
  air pollution 25
  Egyptian Environmental Affairs
    Agency (EEAA) 25
  endangered species 25
  landfilling 25
  protected zones 26
  Red Sea 425
  reef destruction 25
  reef protection 27
  responsible tourism 26-7

rubbish 27, 444
  Sinai 444
  water pollution 25
Esna 311-3, **311**

Fantasy Island 361
Farafra 352
Farafra Oasis 352-4, **352**
Fareed al-Atrash 35
Farouk, King 21
Fatimids 18, 135
fauna 28-30
  bird watching 29
  birds 29
  mammals 28-9
  marine life 29-30
fax services 84
felucca rides 131
  Aswan 326, 332-4
  Cairo 188
  Luxor 299, 308-9
ferry travel 131
festivals
  International Rowing Festival
    300
  Moulid of Abou El-Haggag 300
  Opet Festival 300
  Siwan Festival 362
fezzes 110
Fjord, The 468
flora 28
food 103-6
Fort Qait Bey 375-6
Frazer Tombs 242-3
French Occupation 19
Fuad I 20

Gama'a al-Islamiyya 23
Gamal Abdel Nasser 21
Gamasa 239
Gate of the Moon 373
Gate of the Sun 373
Gawhar 18
gay travellers 93
Geb 63
Gebel al-Mawta 360-1
Gebel at-Teir 242-3
Gebel Ataka 418
Gebel Dakrur 361
Gebel Katherina 469
Gebel Musa, *see* Mt Sinai
geography 24
Gezira 153-7
Geziret Al-Moz 253
Geziret Fara'un 468
Giza 180-7, **181**
  Sound & Light Show 185-8
gods & goddesses 61-7
government 30-1

Great Pyramid of Cheops 183
Great Pyramids of Giza 13,
  181-6, **182**
Great Temple of Ramses II 339
Greek Rule 16-7
Gulf of Aqaba 448
Gulf War 23

Hammam Fara'un 447
hammams 166-7, 172-3, 188
handicrafts 108-10, 186, 363
  Siwan crafts 363
Hannoville Beach 378
Hantour 133
Hapy 63
Hathor 63
Hatshepsut 15, 290
health 477-91
  Cairo hospitals 148
  cuts, bites & stings 490
  immunisations 478-9
  infectious diseases 483-8
  insect-borne diseases 488-90
  insurance 74, 477
  international health card 75
  medical kit 477
  medical problems & treatment
    481
  medical services 148-9
  predeparture planning 477-9
  vaccinations 478-9
  water 480
  women's health 490-1
Heb-Sed Race 221
Heliopolis 157-9, **158**
Helwan 227-8
Heracleopolis 13
Hermopolis 247-8, **248**
High Dam 337-8
history 11-24
  Abbasids 17
  Arab Conquest, The 17-19
  Arab League 21
  Arab Republic of Egypt 21
  Ayyubids 19, 136
  British Occupation 20-1
  Byzantine Rule 17
  Camp David Agreement 22
  Christianity 17, 366
  Civil War 13
  Crusaders 18
  Fatimids 18, 135
  French Occupation 19
  Gama'a al-Islamiyya 23
  Greek Rule 16-7
  Hittites 16
  Hyksos 13
  Mamluks, the 17-9, 136
  Middle Kingdom 13

New Kingdom 13, 267
Nonaligned Movement 21
October War 21-2
Old Kingdom 11
Omayyads 17
Peace with Israel 22
Pharaonic Times 11-16
Post-Revolution Egypt 21
Ptolemaic Dynasty 16
Revolution of 1952 21, 367
Roman Rule 16, 17
Seljuks 18
Six Day War 21-22, 401
Suez Crisis 21
Turkish Rule 19-20
United Arab Republic (UAR) 21
WWI 20, 136
WWII 20, 136, 367, 390
hitching 130
Hittites 16
holidays 96
horse riding
  Cairo 188
  Dahab 460
  Hurghada (Al-Ghardaka) 427
  Na'ama Bay 452
Horus 63
hospitals 148, 373
hostel card 74
hostels 102
hotels 102-3
Hurghada (Al-Ghardaka)
  420-35, **421**, **422-3, 424**
  entertainment 433
  getting around 435
  getting there & away 433-5
  information 421-4
  orientation 420-1
  places to eat 431-3
  places to stay 427-31
  shopping 433
  things to see 424-5
  tours 427
Hyksos 13

Ibn Tulun 18
Imhotep 11
insurance 74
International Rowing Festival 300
Isis 64, 336
Islam 17, 39-41
Islamic architecture 36-7
Islamic Jihad 23
Ismailia 408-13, **409**
itineraries, suggested 69-70

jewellery 109
Judaism 42
Justinian, Emperor 469

Karanis 230
Karnak 14, 273-78, **274**
Kharga Oasis 343-6, **343**
Kharmisah 361
Khepri 64
Khnum 64
Khons 64
Kitchener's Island 324-5
Kolthum, Om 34-5
Kom al-Ahmar 313
Kom Ombo 316-9, **318**

Lake Mariyut 368
Lake Nasser 337
Lake Qarun 29
land mines 24, 94
language 42-8, 99
  Arabic 42
  Arabic Language Institute 99
  body language 38
  British Council 99
  Coptic 41
  courses 99-100, 187-8
  Egyptian Colloquial Arabic
  (ECA) 42
  International Language
  Institute 99
  Modern Standard Arabic
  (MSA) 42
laundry 91
legal matters 95
lesbian travellers 93
Lldo 394
literature 35-6, *see also* books
Luxor 266-310, **266, 268-9, 279**
  activities 299-300
  entertainment 307
  getting around 309-10
  getting there & away 307-9
  history 267
  information 267-70
  orientation 267
  places to eat 306-7
  places to stay 300-6
  shopping 307
  things to see 270-99
  tours 300
Luxor Temple 15, 271-3, **272**

Maat 64
magazines 88
Mahmudiya Canal 368
Mallawi 247
Mamluks 17-19, 136
Mamoura Beach 378
Mandarra Beach 378
Mansura 238
maps 68-9
marine life, *see* fauna

Marsa Alam 439-40
Marsa Matruh 392-7, **393**
Mastaba of Ti 224
Mastabas 54-5
Mastabat Al-Faraun 225
Mausoleum of the Aga Khan 325
medical issues, *see* health
Medinet al-Faiyum 228-33, **229**
Medinat Habu 297-8, **298**
Mediterranean Coast 389-98, **365**
Memphis 13, 159, 218-20
Menes 11, 218
Mentuhotep 13
Mentuhotep II 13
Meretseger 65
Min 65
Modern Standard Arabic (MSA)
  42
monasteries 178-9
  Deir Abu Makar
  (Makarios) 235
  Deir al-Abyad 256
  Deir al-Adhra 242
  Deir al-Ahmar 256
  Deir al-Anba Bishoi 235
  Deir al-Baramus 235
  Deir al-Medina 295
  Deir al-Muharraq 251
  Deir as-Suriani 235
  Monastery of St Anthony 419
  Monastery of St George 178
  Monastery of St Jeremiah 223
  Monastery of St Paul 419-20
  Monastery of St Simeon 325
  Red Monastery 256-7
  St Catherine's Monastery 469
  White Monastery 256
money 78-82
  bargaining 81-2
  costs 78-9
  credit cards 80
  exchange rates 80
  security 79
  tipping 81
Mons Claudianus 436
Mons Porphyritis 435
Montazah Beach 378
Montu 65
Mortuary Temple of Ramses III
  297
motorcycle travel 129-30
Moulid 40
Moulid of Abou el-Haggag 300
Mouseion 373
Mt Sinai 470-1
Mubarak, Hosni 22-4, 30
mummification 14, 225, 234
music 34, 111
Muslims 367

Mustafa Kamal Necropolis 377
Mut 65, 347-52, **348**
Mycerinus 13

Na'ama Bay 448-56, **450**
Nabq 30
Naguib, Mahfouz 35-6
Nakhl 447
Napoleon 19, 367
Nasser, Gamal Abdel 21, 338, 401, 443
national parks & protected areas 30
    Dahab 30
    Nabq 30
    Ras Abu Gallum 30, 446
    Ras Mohammed National Park 446, 448-9
    Zaranik Reserve 29, 30
Naucratis 238
Necho 399
Necropolis of Al-Anfushi 376
Necropolis of Al-Bagawat 345
Nefertiti 15
Neith 65
Nekhbet 65
Nekheb 313
Nephthys 65
newspapers 88-9
nightclubs 108
Nile Barrages 236
Nile Delta 236-9
Nile River 11, 24, 236, 240, 338
    Cruises 124-5, 133
Nile Valley 240-341, **240**
Nilometer 177
Nubians 33
Nun 66
Nut 66
Nuweiba 463-7, **464**

Octavian 17
October War 21-2
Omayyads 17
on-line services 88-9
Opet Festival 300
Osiris 66, 260
Oyun Musa 446

painting 33-4
papyrus 28, 109
Pasha Ismail 20
perfumes 111
Persian tombs 223
Pharaoh's Island 468
Pharaonic religion 42
Pharaonic times 11-16
Pharos Island 368, 375
Pharos Lighthouse 366, 375

Philae 336
Philosophers' Circle 223-4
photography 89-90
    cultural considerations 90
    film & equipment 89
    hints 90
    underwater photography 450
politics, see government
Pompey's Pillar 374
population 32
Port Fouad 404
Port Safaga 435-6
Port Said 401-8, **402**
Port Tawfiq **414**
postal services 82-3
Ptah 66
Ptolemaic Dynasty 16, 366
Ptolemy I 16
Ptolemy XIII 16
Ptolemy XIV 16
public holidays, see holidays
pyramids 14, 55-6
    Abu Sir 225
    Bent Pyramid 227
    Great Pyramid of Cheops 183
    Great Pyramids of Giza 13, 181-6, **182**
    Pyramid of Al-Lahun 230
    Pyramid of Amenemhet III 230
    Pyramid of Chephren 183-4
    Pyramid of Djedkare 226
    Pyramid of Meidum 12-3, 233
    Pyramid of Mycerinus 184
    Pyramid of Neferirkare 225
    Pyramid of Nyuserre 225
    Pyramid of Pepi II 226
    Pyramid of Sahu Ra 225
    Pyramid of Sekhemket 223
    Pyramid of Unas 222
    Red Pyramid, Dahshur 13
    Southern Pyramids 225-6
    Step Pyramid 11, 221-2

Qalamun 350
Qalat al-Gindi 447
Qalaun 19
Qanater 236
Qantara 408
Qara 361
Qasr al-Farafra 352-4, **353**
Qasr ad-Dush 346
Qasr Qarun 231
Qena 261-4, **261**
Qift 264
Qus 265

Ra 66
radio 89-90
Rafah 475-6

Ramadan 96, 97
Ramesseum, The, 294, **295**
Ramses I 16
Ramses II 16
Ramses III 16
Ras Abu Gallum 30, 444
Ras al-Bar 238-9
Ras al-Hikma 392
Ras al-Sudr 446-7
Ras Gharib 420
Ras Mohammed 448
Ras Mohammed National Park 444, 448-9
Rashid, see Rosetta
Red Monastery 256-7
Red Sea 425
Red Sea Coast 417-40, **418**
registration 73
religion 39-42, see also individual entries
Renenutet 67
rituals 61
Roda Island 176-7
Rommel 390
Rommel's Beach 394
Rosetta (Rashid) 388-9
Rosetta Stone 389

Sadat, Anwar 21
Sadd Al-Ali 337
safaris 125
safety 94-5
    drugs 95
    land mines 24, 94
    marine hazards 99
    pollution 95
    sectarian violence 245, 250
    smoking 95
    terrorism 94-5
    theft 95
    women travellers 92
Sais 237
Saladin, see Ad-Din, Salah
Sallum 398
Saqqara 220-7, **220, 222**
    Step Pyramid 221-2
Sea of Sand 361
Sehel Island 334
Sekhmet 67
Seljuks 18
Selket 67
senior travellers 93
Sesostris 13
Seth 67
Shaabi 34
Shaata al-Gharam 394
Shagarat ad-Durr 19, 163
Shali 360
Shark Bay 456-7

Sharm an-Naga 435
Sharm el-Sheikh 448-56, **449**
shopping 108-12, *see also*
    handicrafts
Shu 67
Sidi Abdel Rahman 392
Sidi Barani 397-8
Sidi Gaber 378
Silsileh 316
Sinai 441-76, **442**
Siwa 357-64, **359**
    crafts 363
    cultural considerations 358
    getting around 364
Siwa Oasis 357-64, **358**
Siwan Festival 362
Sneferu 11
snorkelling, *see* diving &
    snorkelling
Sobek 67
Sohag 255-8, **256**
souqs 171
Southern Pyramids 225-6
Sphinx, The 185
spices 111
sport 108
St Catherine's Monastery 469,
    470
St Makarios 234
Step Pyramid 221-2
student cards 74-5
Suez 413-17, **414**
Suez Canal 32, 399-417, **400**
Suez Crisis 21
Sultan Hassan 19
Sunt 319
swimming
    Aswan 326
    Cairo 188
    Luxor 299-300
    Port Safaga 436
    Port Said 404

Taba 468
Tanis 237
Tanta 237
Taweret 67
taxi travel 128-9, 132
teahouses 108
Tefnut 67
telegraph services 84
telephone services 83-4
    area codes 83
Tell al-Amarna 249-50, **248**
Temple of Al-Ghueita 345
Temple of Amun 360, **274**
Temple of An-Nadura 345
Temple of As-Sayyan 345
Temple of Beit Al-Wali 339

Temple of Hathor 339
Temple of Hatshepsut 289
Temple of Heqaib 324
Temple of Hibis 345
Temple of Horus 315-6, **314**
Temple of Kalabsha 338
Temple of Kertassi 339
Temple of Khnum 312, 324
Temple of Kom Ombo 317, **318**
Temple of Nekhbet 313
Temple of Osiris 258
Temple of Philae 335-7, **335**
Temple of Ramses II 259-60
Temple of Satis 324
Temple of Seti I 281
Temples of Karnak 273-8, **274**
terrorism 94
Thebes 13, 266-7
theft 95
Thoth 67
time 91
tipping, *see* money
toilets 91
Tomb of Ahmose 250
Tomb of Akhti-Hotep &
    Ptah-Hotep 223
Tomb of Amenemhet 246
Tomb of Amenophis II 285-6,
    285
Tomb of Amunherkhepshep 297,
    297
Tomb of Aneuka 296
Tomb of Ay 250, 284
Tomb of Baqet 246
Tomb of Heqaib 326
Tomb of Horemheb 286-7,
    287
Tomb of Huya 250
Tomb of Khaemhet 292-3, **293**
Tomb of Khenthawes 185
Tomb of Kheti 246
Tomb of Khnumhotep 246
Tomb of Mahu 250
Tomb of Merirye 250
Tomb of Merneptah 283
Tomb of Mery-Re II 250
Tomb of Monthu-Hir-Khopshef
    284
Tomb of Nefertari 296-7, **296**
Tomb of Panehse 250
Tomb of Peshedu 296
Tomb of Petosiris 248
Tomb of Prince Sarenput I 326
Tomb of Prince Sarenput II 326
Tomb of Ptahshepses 225
Tomb of Queen
    Tawsert/Sethnakt 283
Tomb of Ramose 292-3, **292**
Tomb of Ramses I 283

Tomb of Ramses II 283
Tomb of Ramses III 283
Tomb of Ramses IV 282
Tomb of Ramses IX 283
Tomb of Ramses VI 283
Tomb of Saptah 286
Tomb of Sayyid Ash-Shadhili
    439
Tomb of Sennedjem 295
Tomb of Seti I 284
Tomb of Seti II 283
Tomb of Tutankhamun 286-9,
    288
Tomb of Tuthmosis III 284-5,
    284
Tomb of Tuthmosis IV 285, **285**
Tombs of Khonsu, Userhet &
    Benia 291
Tombs of Mekhu & Sabni 326
Tombs of Menna & Nakht 292
Tombs of Mir 251
Tombs of Nefer-Ronpet,
    Dhutmosi & Nefer-Sekheru
    293-4
Tombs of Sennofer & Rekhmire
    293
Tombs of Teti, Mereruka &
    Ankhma-Hor 224-5
Tombs of the Nobles 291,
    325-6
tourist offices 71-2
tours 124-5, 133-4, 188-9, 300,
    427
    diving 125
    jeep treks 460
    Nile cruises 124-5, 133
    package tours 124-5
    safaris 125
    walking tours 161-76
train travel
    classes 128
    Metro 132
    reservations 128
    wagons-lits 128
    within Egypt 127-8
tram travel 132
travellers' cheques 79
Tuna al-Gebel 247-9, **248**
Tur Sinai 448
Tutankhamun 16, *see also* Tomb
    of Tutankhamun
Tuthmosis I 15
Tuthmosis III 15, 441
Tuthmosis IV 15
TV 35, 89-90

UAR, *see* United Arab Republic
Unfinished Obelisks 323
United Arab Republic (UAR) 21

Valley of the Kings 57, 281-94, **282**
Valley of the Queens 296-7
video 90
visas 72-5

Wadi Feran 472
Wadi Natrun 234-6
wagons-lits, *see* train travel
water 480

weights & measures 91
White Desert 353-4, 356
White Monastery 256
wildlife, *see* fauna
women travellers 39, 92-3
    attitudes to women 92-3
    harassment 93
    safety 92
    women's health 490-1
women, Egyptian 92

work 100-1, 379
    English 100

yachting 131-2

Zafarana 418-9
Zagazig 236-7
Zamalek 153-7, **154**
Zaranik Reserve 29, 30
Zoser 11

THANKS
From Leanne & Geert

To Richard Hoath from the American University in Cairo (AUC) we owe a special thanks – not just for the time and information you gave us but also for your devotion to Egypt's wildlife. Your wholehearted attempt to get Stella Birdie back into the air after she fell prey to the nets on the Mediterranean coast was nothing short of wondrous. Thanks, too, to your AUC students for supplementing her diet of flies and bugs. Although she wasn't destined to return to her flock, your dedication was admirable.

In the same league is Philip Jones of the Hurghada Environmental Protection and Conservation Association (HEPCA). Thanks, Philip, for your unflagging commitment to protecting the Red Sea.

We'd also like to thank the following tourist office staff for their keen support: Nazmi Amin Farad (Egyptian Tourist Authority, Cairo), Hussein Abdel Hafez (Asyut), Hakeem Hussein & Farag Goma'a (Aswan), Omar Ahmed (Mut, Dakhla), Mahdi Hweity (Siwa), Salwa Abuzeid & Ms Nariman (Alexandria), Maurice Raouf Iskander (Al-Minya), and Nabil Hanzal (Medinet al-Faiyum).

Others in Egypt that we'd like to thank include: Mohammed Shafek (Al-Qasr, Dakhla Oasis) for guiding us through his village and showing us true Egyptian hospitality; Osama Haroun Emam (Cairo) for the best salads we had in Egypt; the owner of the Soufer Restaurant (Port Said) for setting free the turtle; Mohammed Raafat and family, Summer, Ahmed and Shinea (Farafra Oasis), for boiling the billy in the White Desert; Yahia (Bawiti, Bahariyya Oasis) for tea, talk and time; Samilia El Nasr (Sohag); and Patricia Steelman (AUC Library, Cairo).

To fellow LP author, Andrew Humphreys, thanks for taking time out to share information and a beer. To Michelle Glynn, our sincere appreciation for writing the Tomb & Temple Architecture section in Pharaonic Egypt, and to Christine Niven our thanks for writing the section on Gods & Goddesses in Tomb & Temple Art. And to all the others in LP's Melbourne office who also worked on this book, a big *shukran*.

On the home front, we'd like to thank Narelle & Keith Werder, David & Maureen Logan and Ray Hartley for supplying equipment when it was most needed; Richard Owen for giving us a home base; Robin, Peter & Dylan Osborne for keeping an eye on things; and lastly, to Bluey & Sixy, for amusing the kids along the way.

From the Publisher

Thanks to the many travellers who wrote in with helpful hints, useful advice, and interesting and funny stories.

Jacqui Abonyi, Pierre Antoine, Thomas Arbs, Lode Baptist, Geary Bartmess, RN Barton, Louise Bater, Anita Batistic, John S Bell, Paul Berry, F & C Beudeker-Prochaska, GM Bilgig, Dominic Booth, Fraser Borwick, Pierre-Antoine Briandet, Gerard Brockhoff, Julie Burnett, Delia Burrage, Philip Camilleri, Michael Camron, Feli Carmen, Geoff Carver, Supriya Chawla, Matt Christiansen, Catherine Clark, Bart Coghill, Susan Colley, Sarah Constence, Jane Cudmore, Susan Deconti, Roland Degoux, M Cristina della Marra, Mieke Denys, Judith De Wevek, James Dickson, G Digweed, R Dosanjh, John Downing, Audrey Duffy, Pat Easton, Greg Eastwood, Angharad Evans, Anita Falk, Bob Foo, Mary Fox, Miss J Gage, Judy & Rick Galliner, Ms AJ Garrett, Udo Gergaut, John Gilroy, Kate Goldberg, Steven Gregory, Andrew Griffin, Marleen Haenfjans, Seffi Hanegbi, J Harris, Mandy Harris, Sue Haskins, Bakre Hassan, Lone Hellehoj, Mark Higgins, Karen Hillick, Jim Hitch, Clark Holloway, Melanie Holton, James Hopper, Philip Housiaux, James Howlett, Sharon Ichikawa, Bernard Idowu, Anne Ingram, Nick Jacobs, Steen B Jensen, Chee Charng Jing, Dr Alan Kaye, M & D Lambert, Ernie & Kathy Landolt, Paul Lau, Luc Lauwers, Steven-Andrew Lee, Darren Lee, Rosalind Lester, Angela Lloyd, L N MacKenzie, Peter Mackie, Harriett O Mahony, Julie Main, Catherine Maingaud, Michel Malfliet, Herman Felix Mann, Clare Mason, Bernhard Matz, Barrie McCormick, James McKeague, Chelsea McKinny, Jo Measure, Simon Messing, David Montgomery, Robyn Moore, Timothy Nagy, Simon Neal, Eric Neighbour, Paul D Nelson, Michael S Newman, Conny Olde Olthof, Valerie Oppel, Charles Owen, J Oxley, Tina Pachero, Mathew Palmer, Dana Petric, P Phillips, Paul Phillips, Shirley Porsche, Tay Potier, Sarah Raine, Andy Rees, Simon Reid, Vincent Roger-Machart, Therisa Rogers, Peter Roll, Boaz Rottem, Saleh S Sabh, Sally Salter, Matthias Schluter, Dr EM Scrimgeour, MJR Sedgwick, Jan Skaarup, BJ Skane, Mrs LE Smee,

504 Thanks

Robert Snyder, Carole Spiers, Damien Spry, Tomasz
Stafiej, Allison Stanfield, Diane Stash, Dr Thomas
Straub, William Suter, Paula Swancoat, Amanda
Talbot, Cathy Temple-Brown, Lee Thienny, Greg
Thomas, Ernest Thompson, Sarah Thurston, Kevin
Turley, Vincent Vermeire, Kees van Boven, Andrea &

Kevin Wall, Martin Wallace, Joanna Warr, Ruth
Webb, Yvonne Weber, Barry Wellman, Erik Wilde,
Dean Wilkinson, Toni Wills, A Woodford, Patrick
Wullaert, Marjorie & Eduardo Xavier, Sukyung Yoon
and Carl Zaissen.

Update – March 1997

VISAS
Visas are also available at Luxor airport for E£10, which is cheaper than E£15 at Egypt's London Embassy.

GETTING THERE & AWAY
Air
There is a popular and cheap overnight flight between Cairo and Budapest with Malev, the Hungarian Airline. In October 1996, an Apex return ticket cost about US$240 in Budapest.

Land
Your Own Transport The Egyptian Ministry of Finance has now decreased the amount of taxes and simplified the procedures concerning the regulations governing the temporary transit of vehicles and yachts in Egypt.

Vehicles accompanied by their owners can stay for a maximum period of six months. A short stay of up to one month incurs a E£100 fee, three months costs anywhere between E£250 to E£1000, depending on the engine's size.

Yachts are allowed to stay for up to 12 months. The fee for each of the two first four month periods is E£3000 and for the last four month period the fee rises to E£4000.

GETTING AROUND
The Cairo airport duty-free shop accepts only US dollars and doesn't take credit cards.

LUXOR
The bus station has moved next to the service-taxi station, about one block inland from the Luxor Museum.

Hurghada
There seems to be no ferry on Wednesday and Friday as stated in the guide.

William Gets

Dear traveller
Prices go up, good places go bad, bad places go bankrupt...and every guidebook is inevitably outdated in places. Fortunately, many travellers write to us about their experiences, telling us when things have changed. If we reprint a book between editions, we try to include the best of this information in an Update section. We also make travellers' tips immediately available on our award-winning World Wide Web Internet site (http://www.lonelyplanet.com) and in a free quarterly newsletter, *Planet Talk*.

Although much of this information has not been verified by our own first-hand research, we believe it can be very useful. We cannot vouch for its accuracy, however, so bear in mind that it could be wrong.

We really enjoy hearing from people out on the road, and apart from guaranteeing that others will benefit from your good and bad experiences, we're prepared to bribe you with an offer of a free book for sending us substantial useful information.

I hope you do find this book useful – and that you let us know when it isn't. Thank you to everyone who has written.

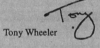

Tony Wheeler

INTERNET INFO
For the latest travel information, check out the Lonely Planet web site:

http://www.lonelyplanet.com

This award-winning site contains updates, recent travellers' letters and a useful travellers' bulletin board.

ACKNOWLEDGMENTS
The information in this Update was compiled by Richard Nebesky from various sources, including reports from the following travellers: Laura Coggins, William Gets, Eddie O'Grady, Louise Smith and Zoltán Ungvari.

LONELY PLANET JOURNEYS

JOURNEYS is a unique collection of travel writing – published by the company that understands travel better than anyone else. It is a series for anyone who has ever experienced – or dreamed of – the magical moment when they encountered a strange culture or saw a place for the first time. They are tales to read while you're planning a trip, while you're on the road or while you're in an armchair, in front of a fire.

JOURNEYS books catch the spirit of a place, illuminate a culture, recount a crazy adventure, or introduce a fascinating way of life. They always entertain, and always enrich the experience of travel.

THE GATES OF DAMASCUS
Lieve Joris
Translated by Sam Garrett

This best-selling book is a beautifully drawn portrait of day-to-day life in modern Syria. Through her intimate contact with local people, Lieve Joris draws us into the fascinating world that lies behind the gates of Damascus. Hala's husband is a political prisoner, jailed for his opposition to the Assad regime; through the author's friendship with Hala we see how Syrian politics impacts on the lives of ordinary people.

Lieve Joris, who was born in Belgium, is one of Europe's leading travel writers. In addition to an award-winning book on Hungary, she has published widely acclaimed accounts of her journeys to the Middle East and Africa. *The Gates of Damascus* is her fifth book.

'Expands the boundaries of travel writing' – Times Literary Supplement

---

KINGDOM OF THE FILM STARS
Journey into Jordan
Annie Caulfield

Kingdom of the Film Stars is a travel book and a love story. With honesty and humour, Annie Caulfield writes of travelling in Jordan and falling in love with a Bedouin. Her book offers fascinating insights into the country – from the traditional tent life of nomadic tribes to the first woman MP's battle with fundamentalist colleagues. *Kingdom of the Film Stars* unpicks some of the tight-woven Western myths about the Arab world, presenting cultural and political issues within the intimate framework of a compelling love story.

Annie Caulfield, who was born in Ireland and currently lives in London, is an award-winning playwright and journalist. She has travelled widely in the Middle East.

'Annie Caulfield is a remarkable traveller. Her story is fresh, courageous, moving, witty and sexy!' – Dawn French

LONELY PLANET TRAVEL ATLASES

Lonely Planet has long been famous for the number and quality of its guidebook maps. Now we've gone one step further and in conjunction with Steinhart Katzir Publishers produced a handy companion series: Lonely Planet travel atlases – maps of a country produced in book form.

Unlike other maps, which look good but lead travellers astray, our travel atlases have been researched on the road by Lonely Planet's experienced team of writers. All details are carefully checked to ensure the atlas corresponds with the equivalent Lonely Planet guidebook.

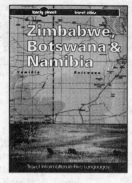

The handy atlas format means no holes, wrinkles, torn sections or constant folding and unfolding. These atlases can survive long periods on the road, unlike cumbersome fold-out maps. The comprehensive index ensures easy reference.

- full-colour throughout
- maps researched and checked by Lonely Planet authors
- place names correspond with Lonely Planet guidebooks
  – no confusing spelling differences
- legend and travelling information in English, French, German, Japanese and Spanish
- size: 230 x 160 mm

Available now:
Chile & Easter Island • Egypt • India & Bangladesh • Israel & the Palestinian Territories •Jordan, Syria & Lebanon • Kenya • Laos • Portugal • South Africa, Lesotho & Swaziland • Thailand • Vietnam • Zimbabwe, Botswana & Namibia

---

LONELY PLANET TV SERIES & VIDEOS

Lonely Planet travel guides have been brought to life on television screens around the world. Like our guides, the programmes are based on the joy of independent travel, and look honestly at some of the most exciting, picturesque and frustrating places in the world. Each show is presented by one of three travellers from Australia, England or the USA and combines an innovative mixture of video, Super-8 film, atmospheric soundscapes and original music.

Videos of each episode – containing additional footage not shown on television – are available from good book and video shops, but the availability of individual videos varies with regional screening schedules.

Video destinations include: Alaska • American Rockies • Australia – The South-East • Baja California & the Copper Canyon • Brazil • Central Asia • Chile & Easter Island • Corsica, Sicily & Sardinia – The Mediterranean Islands • East Africa (Tanzania & Zanzibar) • Ecuador & the Galapagos Islands • Greenland & Iceland • Indonesia • Israel & the Sinai Desert • Jamaica • Japan • La Ruta Maya • Morocco • New York • North India • Pacific Islands (Fiji, Solomon Islands & Vanuatu) • South India • South West China • Turkey • Vietnam • West Africa • Zimbabwe, Botswana & Namibia

The Lonely Planet TV series is produced by:
Pilot Productions
Duke of Sussex Studios
44 Uxbridge St
London W8 7TG UK

Lonely Planet videos are distributed by:
IVN Communications Inc
2246 Camino Ramon
California 94583, USA

107 Power Road, Chiswick
London W4 5PL UK

Music from the TV series is available on CD & cassette.
For video availability and ordering information contact your nearest Lonely Planet office.

PLANET TALK

Lonely Planet's FREE quarterly newsletter

We love hearing from you and think you'd like to hear from us.

When...is the right time to see reindeer in Finland?
Where...can you hear the best palm-wine music in Ghana?
How...do you get from Asunción to Areguá by steam train?
What...is the best way to see India?

For the answer to these and many other questions read PLANET TALK.

Every issue is packed with up-to-date travel news and advice including:

- a letter from Lonely Planet co-founders Tony and Maureen Wheeler
- go behind the scenes on the road with a Lonely Planet author
- feature article on an important and topical travel issue
- a selection of recent letters from travellers
- details on forthcoming Lonely Planet promotions
- complete list of Lonely Planet products

To join our mailing list contact any Lonely Planet office.

Also available: Lonely Planet T-shirts. 100% heavyweight cotton.

LONELY PLANET ONLINE

Get the latest travel information before you leave or while you're on the road

Whether you've just begun planning your next trip, or you're chasing down specific info on currency regulations or visa requirements, check out Lonely Planet Online for up-to-the minute travel information.

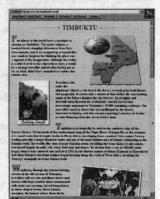

As well as travel profiles of your favourite destinations (including maps and photos), you'll find current reports from our researchers and other travellers, updates on health and visas, travel advisories, and discussion of the ecological and political issues you need to be aware of as you travel.

There's also an online travellers' forum where you can share your experience of life on the road, meet travel companions and ask other travellers for their recommendations and advice. We also have plenty of links to other online sites useful to independent travellers.

And of course we have a complete and up-to-date list of all Lonely Planet travel products including guides, phrasebooks, atlases, Journeys and videos and a simple online ordering facility if you can't find the book you want elsewhere.

www.lonelyplanet.com
or
AOL keyword: lp

LONELY PLANET PRODUCTS

Lonely Planet is known worldwide for publishing practical, reliable and no-nonsense travel information in our guides and on our web site. The Lonely Planet list covers just about every accessible part of the world. Currently there are eight series: *travel guides, shoestring guides, walking guides, city guides, phrasebooks, audio packs, travel atlases* and *Journeys* – a unique collection of travel writing.

EUROPE

Amsterdam • Austria • Baltic States & Kaliningrad • Baltic States phrasebook • Britain • Central Europe on a shoestring • Central Europe phrasebook • Czech & Slovak Republics • Denmark • Dublin • Eastern Europe on a shoestring • Eastern Europe phrasebook • Finland • France • Greece • Greek phrasebook • Hungary • Iceland, Greenland & the Faroe Islands • Ireland • Italy • Mediterranean Europe on a shoestring • Mediterranean Europe phrasebook • Paris • Poland • Portugal • Portugal travel atlas • Prague • Russia, Ukraine & Belarus • Russian phrasebook • Scandinavian & Baltic Europe on a shoestring • Scandinavian Europe phrasebook • Slovenia • Spain • St Petersburg • Switzerland • Trekking in Greece • Trekking in Spain • Ukrainian phrasebook • Vienna • Walking in Britain • Walking in Switzerland • Western Europe on a shoestring • Western Europe phrasebook

NORTH AMERICA

Alaska • Backpacking in Alaska • Baja California • California & Nevada • Canada • Florida • Hawaii • Honolulu • Los Angeles • Mexico • Miami • New England • New Orleans • New York, New Jersey & Pennsylvania • Pacific Northwest USA • Rocky Mountain States • San Francisco • Southwest USA • USA phrasebook • Washington, DC & the Capital Region

CENTRAL AMERICA & THE CARIBBEAN

Bermuda • Central America on a shoestring • Costa Rica • Cuba • Eastern Caribbean • Guatemala, Belize & Yucatán: La Ruta Maya • Jamaica

SOUTH AMERICA

Argentina, Uruguay & Paraguay • Bolivia • Brazil • Brazilian phrasebook • Buenos Aires • Chile & Easter Island • Chile & Easter Island travel atlas • Colombia • Ecuador & the Galápagos Islands • Latin American Spanish phrasebook • Peru • Quechua phrasebook • Rio de Janeiro • South America on a shoestring • Trekking in the Patagonian Andes • Venezuela

Travel Literature: Full Circle: A South American Journey

ANTARCTICA

Antarctica

ISLANDS OF THE INDIAN OCEAN

Madagascar & Comoros • Maldives & Islands of the East Indian Ocean • Mauritius, Réunion & Seychelles

AFRICA

Arabic (Moroccan) phrasebook • Africa on a shoestring • Cape Town • Central Africa • East Africa • Egypt • Egypt travel atlas • Ethiopian (Amharic) phrasebook • Kenya • Kenya travel atlas • Morocco • North Africa • South Africa, Lesotho & Swaziland • South Africa, Lesotho & Swaziland travel atlas • Swahili phrasebook • Trekking in East Africa • West Africa • Zimbabwe, Botswana & Namibia • Zimbabwe, Botswana & Namibia travel atlas

Travel Literature: The Rainbird: A Central African Journey • Songs to an African Sunset: A Zimbabwean Story